Handbook of Research on Investigations in Artificial Life Research and Development

Maki Habib
The American University in Cairo, Egypt

A volume in the Advances in Computational
Intelligence and Robotics (ACIR) Book Series

Published in the United States of America by
  IGI Global
  Engineering Science Reference (an imprint of IGI Global)
  701 E. Chocolate Avenue
  Hershey PA, USA 17033
  Tel: 717-533-8845
  Fax: 717-533-8661
  E-mail: cust@igi-global.com
  Web site: http://www.igi-global.com

Library of Congress Cataloging-in-Publication Data

Names: Habib, Maki K., 1955- editor.
Title: Handbook of research on investigations in artificial life research and
  development / Maki Habib, editor.
Description: Hershey, PA : Engineering Science Reference, [2018] | Includes
  bibliographical references.
Identifiers: LCCN 2017043497| ISBN 9781522553960 (hardcover) | ISBN
  9781522553977 (eISBN)
Subjects: LCSH: Intelligent personal assistants (Computer software) |
  Automatic machinery. | Artificial intelligence. | Artificial life.
Classification: LCC QA76.76.I58 H333 2018 | DDC 006.3--dc23 LC record available at https://lccn.loc.gov/2017043497

This book is published in the IGI Global book series Advances in Computational Intelligence and Robotics (ACIR) (ISSN:
2327-0411; eISSN: 2327-042X)

British Cataloguing in Publication Data
A Cataloguing in Publication record for this book is available from the British Library.

The views expressed in this book are those of the authors, but not necessarily of the publisher.

For electronic access to this publication, please contact: eresources@igi-global.com.

Advances in Computational Intelligence and Robotics (ACIR) Book Series

Ivan Giannoccaro
University of Salento, Italy

ISSN:2327-0411
EISSN:2327-042X

MISSION

While intelligence is traditionally a term applied to humans and human cognition, technology has progressed in such a way to allow for the development of intelligent systems able to simulate many human traits. With this new era of simulated and artificial intelligence, much research is needed in order to continue to advance the field and also to evaluate the ethical and societal concerns of the existence of artificial life and machine learning.

The **Advances in Computational Intelligence and Robotics (ACIR) Book Series** encourages scholarly discourse on all topics pertaining to evolutionary computing, artificial life, computational intelligence, machine learning, and robotics. ACIR presents the latest research being conducted on diverse topics in intelligence technologies with the goal of advancing knowledge and applications in this rapidly evolving field.

COVERAGE

- Computational Logic
- Heuristics
- Pattern Recognition
- Synthetic Emotions
- Cognitive Informatics
- Natural Language Processing
- Brain Simulation
- Intelligent control
- Machine Learning
- Artificial life

IGI Global is currently accepting manuscripts for publication within this series. To submit a proposal for a volume in this series, please contact our Acquisition Editors at Acquisitions@igi-global.com or visit: http://www.igi-global.com/publish/.

Titles in this Series

For a list of additional titles in this series, please visit: www.igi-global.com/book-series

701 East Chocolate Avenue, Hershey, PA 17033, USA
Tel: 717-533-8845 x100 • Fax: 717-533-8661
E-Mail: cust@igi-global.com • www.igi-global.com

List of Contributors

Table of Contents

Detailed Table of Contents

Chapter 1

Ericka Janet Rechy-Ramirez, Universidad Veracruzana, Mexico
Huosheng Hu, University of Essex, UK

A bio-signal-based human machine interface is proposed for hands-free control of a wheelchair. An Emotiv EPOC sensor is used to detect facial expressions and head movements of users. Nine facial expressions and up-down head movements can be chosen to form five commands: move-forward and backward, turn-left and right, and stop. Four uni-modal modes, three bi-modal modes, and three fuzzy bi-modal modes are created to control a wheelchair. Fuzzy modes use the users' strength in making the head movement and facial expression to adjust the wheelchair speed via a fuzzy logic system. Two subjects tested the ten modes with several command configurations. Means, minimum, and maximum values of the traveling times achieved by each subject in each mode were collected. Results showed that both subjects achieved the lowest mean, minimum and maximum traveling times using fuzzy modes. Statistical tests showed that there were significant differences between traveling times of fuzzy modes of subject B and traveling times of bi-modal modes and those of the respective fuzzy modes of both subjects.

Chapter 2

Axel Steinhage, Future-Shape GmbH, Germany
Christl Lauterbach, Future-Shape GmbH, Germany
Axel Techmer, Future-Shape GmbH, Germany
Raoul Hoffmann, Future-Shape GmbH, Germany
Miguel Sousa, Future-Shape GmbH, Germany

The following chapter describes new functions and applications that the authors have developed for the capacitive sensor system SensFloor® during the last five years. Some of these features have already found their way into the market while others are still in the research phase. From the first large-scale installations in 2012 up to now, the focus was put on applications for healthcare and ambient assisted living (AAL). However, as will be described later in this chapter, the authors have realized projects in many other domains as well, such as medical assessments, retail, security, and multimedia. The chapter starts out with a description of the underlying technology. After that, examples of the various domains of application are presented. The authors conclude with a summary and future research plans.

Chapter 3

Jia Wang, University of Greenwich, UK
Rui Li, University at Albany (SUNY), USA & Sichuan Fine Arts Institute, China

This chapter assesses underlying spatial relations for pedestrian wayfinding by examining navigational directions given in both forms of sketch maps and verbal descriptions. An experiment was conducted to investigate characteristics of navigational directions provided by participants in the form of sketch maps and verbal descriptions. The authors were specifically interested in the landmarks and spatial relationships such as route topology, linear order relation, and relative orientation extracted from the navigational directions. A new ontological approach to sketch and verbal interpretations was adopted for spatial analysis. The results pointed to the advantage of including sketch components into pedestrian navigation systems over solely turn-by-turn instructions. In addition, the results showed the differences between visual and verbal directions, which suggest the necessity of having different levels of directions for giving specific types of navigational instructions.

Chapter 4

Kevin Warwick, Coventry University, UK

In this chapter, the author describes his personal experience in experimenting as a cyborg (part biology/ part technology) by having technology implanted in his body, which he lived with over a period. A look is also taken at the author's experiments into creating cyborgs by growing biological brains which are subsequently given a robot body. The experiments are dealt with in separate sections. In each case the nature of the experiment is briefly described along with the results obtained and this is followed by an indication of the experience, including personal feelings and emotions felt in and around the time of the experiments and subsequently as a result of the experiments. Although the subject can be treated scientifically from an external perspective, it is really through individual, personal experience that a true reflection can be gained on what might be possible in the future.

Chapter 5

Konstantinos Domdouzis, Sheffield Hallam University, UK

The complexity of crisis-related situations requires the use of advanced technological infrastructures. In order to develop such infrastructures, specific architectures need to be applied such as the service-oriented architectures (SOAs). The purpose of this chapter is to indicate how SOAs can be used in modern crisis management systems, such as the ATHENA system. The chapter underlines the need for a detailed study of specific biological systems, such as the human brain's hippocampus which follows the current, intense attempts of improvement of the current artificial-intelligence-based systems and the development of a new area in artificial intelligence. A number of conclusions are drawn on how biologically inspired systems can benefit the development of service-oriented architectures.

A skyline query retrieves all objects in a dataset that are not dominated by other objects according to some given criteria. There exist many skyline algorithms which can be classified into generic, index-based, and lattice-based algorithms. This chapter takes a tour through lattice-based skyline algorithms. It summarizes the basic concepts and properties, presents high-performance parallel approaches, shows how one overcomes the low-cardinality restriction of lattice structures, and finally presents an application on data streams for real-time skyline computation. Experimental results on synthetic and real datasets show that lattice-based algorithms outperform state-of-the-art skyline techniques, and additionally have a linear runtime complexity.

Chapter 7

Trial-and-error methods in foundries to determine optimum molding sand properties consume more time and result in reduced productivity, high rejection, and cost. Hence, current research is focused towards development and application of modelling and optimization tools. In foundry, there is requirement of mound properties with conflicting nature (that is, minimize: gas evolution and collapsibility; maximize: compression strength, mound hardness, and permeability) and determining best combination among them is often a difficult task. Optimization of resin-bonded molding sand system is discussed in this book chapter. Six different case studies are considered by assigning different combination of weight fractions for multiple objective functions and corresponding desirability (Do) values are determined for DFA, GA, PSO, and MOPSO-CD. The obtained highest desirability value is considered as the optimum solution. Better performance of non-traditional tools might be due to parallel computing approach. GA and PSO have yielded almost similar results, whereas MOPSO-CD produced better results.

Chapter 8

Intrusion detection system plays an important role in network security. However, network intrusion detection (NID) suffers from several problems, such as false positives, operational issues in high dimensional data, and the difficulty of detecting unknown threats. Most of the problems with intrusion detection are caused by improper implementation of the network intrusion detection system (NIDS). Over the past few years, computational intelligence (CI) has become an effective area in extending research capabilities. Thus, NIDS based upon CI is currently attracting considerable interest from the research community. The scope of this review will encompass the concept of NID and presents the core methods of CI, including support vector machine, hidden naïve Bayes, particle swarm optimization, genetic algorithm, and fuzzy logic. The findings of this review should provide useful insights into the application of different CI methods for NIDS over the literature, allowing to clearly define existing research challenges and progress, and to highlight promising new research directions.

Chapter 9
Performance Comparison of PSO and Hybrid PSO-GA in Hiding Fuzzy Sensitive Association
Rules 175

Sathiyapriya Krishnamoorthy, PSG College of Technology, India
Sudha Sadasivam G., PSG College of Technology, India
Rajalakshmi M., Coimbatore Institute of Technology, India

Explosion of data analysis techniques facilitate organizations to publish microdata about individuals. While the released data sets provide valuable information to researchers, it is possible to infer sensitive information from the published non-sensitive data using association rule mining. An association rule is characterized as sensitive if its confidence is above disclosure threshold. These sensitive rules should be made uninteresting before releasing the dataset publicly. This is done by modifying the data that support the sensitive rules, so that the confidence of these sensitive rules is reduced below disclosure threshold. The main goal of the proposed system is to hide a set of sensitive association rules by perturbing the quantitative data that contains sensitive knowledge using PSO and hybrid PSO-GA with minimum side effects like lost rules, ghost rules. The performance of PSO and Hybrid PSO-GA approach in effectively hiding fuzzy association rule is also compared. Experimental results demonstrate that hybrid approach is efficient in terms of lost rules, number of modifications, hiding failure.

Chapter 10
Modeling Fish Population Dynamics for Sustainability and Resilience.. 199

Nayem Rahman, Portland State University, USA
Mahmud Ullah, University of Dhaka, Bangladesh

Conservation of any living creature is very vital to maintain the balance of ecosystem. Fish is one of the most regularly consumed living creatures, and hence its conservation is essential for sustainable fish population to help maintain a balanced ecosystem. It is possible to keep a sustainable fish population only if a balance between consumption and growth of fish population can be ensured. Developing a model on fish population dynamics is needed to achieve this objective. In this chapter, the authors present a system dynamics model. This model will provide the scientific tools for determining fish population, its growth, and harvesting. The model's sensitivity to changes in key parameters and initial values resulting from the changes in basic scenarios and boundary conditions was tested several times. Model results show that fish birth, growth, stocks, and catch can be controlled timely and effectively in different real-world changing conditions to maintain a sustainable fish population.

Chapter 11
Search for an Optimal Solution to Vague Traffic Problems Using the PSK Method.......................... 219

P. Senthil Kumar, Jamal Mohamed College (Autonomous), India

There are several algorithms, in literature, for obtaining the fuzzy optimal solution of fuzzy transportation problems (FTPs). To the best of the author's knowledge, in the history of mathematics, no one has been able to solve transportation problem (TP) under four different uncertain environment using single method in the past years. So, in this chapter, the author tried to categories the TP under four different environments and formulates the problem and utilizes the crisp numbers, triangular fuzzy numbers (TFNs), and trapezoidal fuzzy numbers (TrFNs) to solve the TP. A new method, namely, PSK (P. Senthil Kumar) method for finding a fuzzy optimal solution to fuzzy transportation problem (FTP) is proposed. Practical usefulness of the PSK method over other existing methods is demonstrated with four different numerical examples. To illustrate the PSK method different types of FTP is solved by using the PSK method and the obtained results are discussed.

 Manuel Kolp, Université catholique de Louvain, Belgium
 Yves Wautelet, KU Leuven, Belgium
 Samedi Heng, Université catholique de Lovuain, Belgium

Multi-agent systems (MAS) architectures are popular for building open, distributed, and evolving software required by today's business IT applications such as e-business systems, web services, or enterprise knowledge bases. Since the fundamental concepts of MAS are social and intentional rather than object, functional, or implementation-oriented, the design of MAS architectures can be eased by using social patterns. They are detailed agent-oriented design idioms to describe MAS architectures as composed of autonomous agents that interact and coordinate to achieve their intentions like actors in human organizations. This chapter presents social patterns and focuses on a framework aimed to gain insight into these patterns. The framework can be integrated into agent-oriented software engineering methodologies used to build MAS. The authors consider the broker social pattern to illustrate the framework. The mapping from system architectural design (through organizational architectural styles), to system detailed design (through social patterns), is overviewed with a data integration case study.

 Yves Wautelet, KU Leuven, Belgium
 Christophe Schinckus, Royal Melbourne Institute of Technology, Australia
 Manuel Kolp, Université catholique de Lovuain, Belgium

Information systems are deeply linked to human activities. Unfortunately, development methodologies have been traditionally inspired by programming concepts and not by organizational and human ones. This leads to ontological and semantic gaps between the systems and their environments. The adoption of agent orientation and multi-agent systems (MAS) helps to reduce these gaps by offering modeling tools based on organizational concepts (actors, agents, goals, objectives, responsibilities, social dependencies, etc.) as fundamentals to conceive systems through all the development process. Moreover, software development is becoming increasingly complex. Stakeholders' expectations are growing higher while the development agendas have to be as short as possible. Project managers, business analysts, and software developers need adequate processes and models to specify the organizational context, capture requirements, and build efficient and flexible systems.

Chapter 14

Mahua Bose, University of Kalyani, India
Kalyani Mali, University of Kalyani, India

In recent years, several methods for forecasting fuzzy time series have been presented in different areas, such as stock price, student enrollments, climatology, production sector, etc. Choice of data partitioning technique is a central factor and it highly influences the forecast accuracy. In all existing works on fuzzy time series model, cluster with highest membership is used to form fuzzy logical relationships. But the position of the element within the cluster is not considered. The present study incorporates the idea of fuzzy discretization and shadowed set theory in defining intervals and uses the positional information of elements within a cluster in selection of rules for decision making. The objective of this work is to show the effect of the elements, lying outside the core area on forecast. Performance of the presented model is evaluated on standard datasets.

Chapter 15

Palash Dutta, Dibrugarh University, India

It is always utmost essential to accumulate knowledge on the nature of each and every accessible data, information, and model parameters in risk assessment. It is noticed that more often model parameters, data, information are fouled with uncertainty due to lack of precision, deficiency in data, diminutive sample sizes. In such environments, fuzzy set theory or Dempster-Shafer theory (DST) can be explored to represent this type of uncertainty. Most frequently, both types of uncertainty representation theories coexist in human health risk assessment and need to merge within the same framework. For this purpose, this chapter presents two algorithms to combine Dempster-Shafer structure (DSS) with generalized/ normal fuzzy focal elements, generalized/normal fuzzy numbers within the same framework. Computer codes are generated using Matlab M-files. Finally, human health risk assessment is carried out under this setting and it is observed that the results are obtained in the form of fuzzy numbers (normal/generalized) at different fractiles.

Chapter 16

V. Vaidehi, VIT University, India
Ravi Pathak, Striim Inc., India
Renta Chintala Bhargavi, VIT University Chennai, India
Kirupa Ganapathy, Saveetha University, India
C. Sweetlin Hemalatha, VIT University, India
A. Annis Fathima, VIT University, India
P. T. V. Bhuvaneswari, Madras Institute of Technology, India & Anna University, India
Sibi Chakkaravarthy S., Madras Institute of Technology, India & Anna University, India
Xavier Fernando, Ryerson University, Canada

Advances in information and communication technology (ICT) have paved way for improved healthcare and facilitates remote health monitoring. Geriatric remote health monitoring system (GRHMS) uses

WBAN (wireless body area network) which provides flexibility and mobility for the patients. GRHMS uses complex event processing (CEP) to detect the abnormality in patient's health condition, formulate contexts based on spatiotemporal relations between vital parameters, learn rules dynamically, and generate alerts in real time. Even though CEP is powerful in detecting abnormal events, its capability is limited due to uncertain incoming events, static rule base, and scalability problem. To address the above challenges, this chapter proposes an enhanced CEP (eCEP) which encompasses augmented CEP (a-CEP), a statistical event refinement model to minimize the error due to uncertainty, dynamic CEP (DCEP) to add and delete rules dynamically into the rule base and scalable CEP (SCEP) to address scalability problem. Experimental results show that the proposed framework has better accuracy in decision making.

Chapter 17

Anissa Benlarabi, Mohamed V University, Morocco
Amal Khtira, Mohammed V University, Morocco
Bouchra El Asri, Mohamed V University, Morocco

Software product line engineering is a development paradigm based on reuse. It builds a common platform from which a set of applications can be derived. Despite its advantage of enhancing time to market and costs, it presents some complications. Among them, the complexity of its evolution because all the components are shared between the derived products. For this reason, the change impact analysis and the evolution understanding in software product lines require greater focus than in single software. In this chapter, the authors present CASPL platform for co-evolution analysis in software product lines. The platform uses evolutionary trees that are mainly used in biology to analyze the co-evolution between applications. The major goal is to enhance the change understanding and to compare the history of changes in the applications of the family, at the aim of correcting divergences between them.

Chapter 18

Banage T. G. S. Kumara, Sabaragamuwa University of Sri Lanka, Sri Lanka
Incheon Paik, University of Aizu, Japan
Koswatte R. C. Koswatte, Sri Lanka Institute of Information Technology, Sri Lanka

With the large number of web services now available via the internet, service discovery, recommendation, and selection have become a challenging and time-consuming task. Organizing services into similar clusters is a very efficient approach. A principal issue for clustering is computing the semantic similarity. Current approaches use methods such as keyword, information retrieval, or ontology-based methods. These approaches have problems that include discovering semantic characteristics, loss of semantic information, and a shortage of high-quality ontologies. Thus, the authors present a method that first adopts ontology learning to generate ontologies via the hidden semantic patterns existing within complex terms. Then, they propose service recommendation and selection approaches based on proposed clustering approach. Experimental results show that the term-similarity approach outperforms comparable existing clustering approaches. Further, empirical study of the prototyping recommendation and selection approaches have proved the effectiveness of proposed approaches.

Chapter 19

U. K. Sridevi, Sri Krishna College of Engineering and Technology, India

P. Shanthi, Sri Krishna College of Engineering and Technology, India

N. Nagaveni, Coimbatore Institute of Technology, India

Searching of relevant documents from the web has become more challenging due to the rapid growth in information. Although there is enormous amount of information available online, most of the documents are uncategorized. It is a time-consuming task for the users to browse through a large number of documents and search for information about the specific topics. The automatic clustering from these documents could be important and has great potential to improve the efficiency of information seeking behaviors. To address this issue, the authors propose a deep ontology-based approach to document clustering. The obtained results are encouraging and in implementation annotation rules are used. The work compared the information extraction capabilities of annotated framework of using ontology and without using ontology. The increase in F-measure is achieved when ontology as the distance measure. The improvement of 11% is achieved by ontology in comparison with keyword search.

Preface

INTRODUCTION

The evolution of nature and biological systems is helping to create new reality with great potential to resolve many research and development challenges. Hence, there is a need to study and examine nature, its models, elements, processes, systems, structures, mechanisms, etc. to take inspiration from, or emulate, nature's best biological ideas and products in order to solve modern science and engineering problems.

Artificial Life is featured as an emerging, interdisciplinary and unifying field of research to study phenomena or abilities of living systems in nature including human and analyze research findings to integrate effectively scientific information for the purpose to develop life like artificial systems and machines that exhibit the autonomous behavioral and characteristics of natural living systems. These systems are normally based on computer simulations and hardware designs of state-of-the-art technologies that span brain and cognitive sciences, the origin of life and living systems, self-assembly and development of evolutionary and ecological dynamics, animal and machine behaviors including robots, social organization, and cultural evolution to improve and comprehend real-world problems.

ORGANIZATION OF THE BOOK

This handbook includes 19 chapters that contribute with the state-of-art and up-to-date knowledge on research advancement in the field of Artificial Life research and development. The chapters provide theoretical knowledge, practices, algorithms, technological evolution and new findings. Furthermore, the handbook helps to prepare engineers and scientists who are looking to develop innovative, challenging, intelligent, bioinspired systems and value added ideas for autonomous and smart interdisciplinary software, hardware and systems to meet today's and future most pressing challenges.

Chapter 1: An Electric Wheelchair Controlled by Head Movements and Facial Expressions

A bio-signal based human machine interface is proposed for hands-free control of a wheelchair. An Emotiv EPOC sensor is used to detect facial expressions and head movements of users. Nine facial expressions and up-down head movements can be chosen to form five commands: move-forward and backward, turn-left and right, and stop. Four unimodal modes, three bi-modal modes and three fuzzy bi-modal modes are created to control a wheelchair. Fuzzy modes use the users' strength in making the head movement and facial expression to adjust the wheelchair speed via a fuzzy logic system. The developed system was tested and evaluated.

Chapter 2: Innovative Features and Applications Provided by a Large-Area Sensor Floor

This chapter describes new functions, features and applications of the developed capacitive sensor system SensFloor®. The chapter focuses on applications for health care and Ambient Assisted Living (AAL). In addition, the chapter presents applications in other domains as well, such as medical assessments, retail, security and multimedia.

Chapter 3: Reassessing Underlying Spatial Relations in Pedestrian Navigation – A Comparison Between Sketch Maps and Verbal Descriptions

The chapter assesses underlying spatial relations for pedestrian wayfinding by examining and experimenting navigational directions given in both forms of sketch maps and verbal descriptions. The authors were specifically interested in the landmarks and spatial relationships such as route topology, linear order relation and relative orientation extracted from the navigational directions. A new ontological approach to sketch and verbal interpretations was adopted for spatial analysis.

Chapter 4: What Is It Like to Be a Cyborg?

This chapter describes the personal experience of the author experimenting a Cyborg (part biology/part technology) by having technology implanted in his body, which he lived with over a period of time. A look is also taken at the author's experiments into creating Cyborgs by growing biological brains which are subsequently given a robot body. In each case the nature of the experiment is briefly described along with the results obtained and this is followed by an indication of the experience, including personal feelings and emotions felt in and around the time of the experiments and subsequently as a result of the experiments.

Chapter 5: Artificial-Intelligence-Based Service-Oriented Architectures (SOAs) for Crisis Management

This chapter deals with the complexity of crisis-related situations that requires the use of advanced technological infrastructures. In order to develop such infrastructures, specific architectures need to be applied such as the Service-Oriented Architectures (SOAs). The purpose of this chapter is to indicate how SOAs can be used in modern Crisis Management systems, such as the ATHENA system. It also underlines the need for a detailed study of specific biological systems, such as the human brain's hippocampus which follows the current, intense attempts of improvement of the current Artificial Intelligence-based systems and the development of a new area in Artificial Intelligence.

Chapter 6: A Tour of Lattice-Based Skyline Algorithms

There exist many Skyline algorithms which can be classified into generic, index-based, and lattice-based algorithms. The work in this chapter takes a tour through lattice-based Skyline algorithms summarizing its basic concepts and properties, presents high-performance parallel approaches. In addition, it introduces how to overcome the low-cardinality restriction of lattice structures. Experimental results on synthetic and real datasets show that lattice-based algorithms outperform state-of-the-art Skyline techniques.

Chapter 7: Swarm Optimization Application to Molding Sand System in Foundries

In this chapter optimization of resin-bonded molding sand system is discussed. Six different case studies are considered by assigning different combination of weight fractions for multiple objective functions and corresponding desirability (Do) values are determined for DFA, GA, PSO and MOPSO-CD. The highest desirability value is considered as the optimum solution.

Chapter 8: Application of Computational Intelligence in Network Intrusion Detection – A Review

Network Intrusion detection (NID) suffers from several problems, such as false positives, operational issues in high dimensional data, and the difficulty of detecting unknown threats. Most of the problems with intrusion detection are caused by improper implementation of the network intrusion detection system (NIDS). The scope of this chapter encompasses the concept of NID and presents the core methods that use computational intelligence and cover Support vector machine, Hidden Naïve Bayes, Particle Swarm Optimization, Genetic Algorithm and Fuzzy logic techniques. The findings of this study highlight current research challenges and progress with focus on the promising new research directions.

Chapter 9: Performance Comparison of PSO and Hybrid PSO-GA in Hiding Fuzzy Sensitive Association Rules

It is possible to infer sensitive information from the published non sensitive data using association rule mining. An association rule is characterized as sensitive if its confidence is above disclosure threshold. This chapter proposes a system with aim to hide a set of sensitive association rules by perturbing the quantitative data that contains sensitive knowledge using PSO and Hybrid PSO-GA with minimum side effects like lost rules, ghost rules. The performance of PSO and Hybrid PSO-GA approach in effectively hiding Fuzzy association rule is also compared.

Chapter 10: Modeling Fish Population Dynamics for Sustainability and Resilience

Conservation of any living creature is very vital to maintain the balance of ecosystem. Fish is one of the most regularly consumed living creatures, and hence its conservation is essential for sustainable fish population to help maintain a balanced ecosystem. Developing a model on fish population dynamics is needed to achieve this objective. This chapter presents a system dynamics model that provides the scientific tools for determining fish population, its growth, and harvesting. The model's sensitivity to changes in key parameters and initial values resulting from the changes in basic scenarios and boundary conditions were tested under different real-world changing conditions to maintain a sustainable fish population.

Chapter 11: Search for an Optimal Solution to Vague Traffic Problems Using the PSK Method

This chapter tries to categorize the transportation problem (TP) under four different environments and formulates the problem and utilizes the crisp numbers, triangular fuzzy numbers (TFNs) and trapezoidal fuzzy numbers (TrFNs) to solve the TP. A new method, namely, PSK (P. Senthil Kumar) method for finding a fuzzy optimal solution to fuzzy transportation problem (FTP) is proposed I this chapter. Practical usefulness of the PSK method over other existing methods is demonstrated and discussed.

Chapter 12: Design Patterns for Social Intelligent Agent Architectures Implementation

Multi-Agent Systems (MAS) architectures are popular for building open, distributed, and evolving software required by today's business IT applications such as eBusiness systems, web services or enterprise knowledge bases. Since the fundamental concepts of MAS are social and intentional rather than object, functional, or implementation-oriented, the design of MAS architectures can be eased by using social patterns. This chapter presents social patterns and focuses on a framework aimed to gain insight into these patterns.

Chapter 13: Agent-Based Software Engineering, Paradigm Shift, or Research Program Evolution

Information systems are deeply linked to human activities. Unfortunately, development methodologies have been traditionally inspired by programming concepts and not by organizational and human ones. This leads to ontological and semantic gaps between the systems and their environments. This chapter presents the adoption of agent orientation and Multi-Agent Systems (MAS) to reduce these gaps by offering modeling tools based on organizational concepts (actors, agents, goals, objectives, responsibilities, social dependencies, etc.) as fundamentals to conceive systems through all the development process.

Chapter 14: Application of Fuzzy Sets and Shadowed Sets in Predicting Time Series Data

In all existing works on fuzzy time series model, cluster with highest membership is used to form fuzzy logical relationships. However, the position of the element within the cluster is not considered. This chapter incorporates the idea of fuzzy discretization and shadowed set theory in defining intervals and uses the positional information of elements within a cluster in selection of rules for decision making. The objective is to show the effect of the elements, lying outside the core area on forecast.

Chapter 15: Fuzzy-DSS Human Health Risk Assessment Under Uncertain Environment

It is noticed that often model parameters, data, information are fouled with uncertainty due to lack of precision, deficiency in data, diminutive sample sizes, etc. In such environments, fuzzy set theory or Dempster-Shafer theory (DST) can be explored to represent this type of uncertainty. This chapter presents two algorithms to combine Dempster-Shafer structure (DSS) with generalized/normal fuzzy focal elements, generalized/normal fuzzy numbers within the same framework. Finally, human health risk assessment is carried out under these setting.

Chapter 16: Enhanced Complex Event Processing Framework for Geriatric Remote Healthcare

Geriatric Remote Health Monitoring System (GRHMS) uses WBAN (Wireless Body Area Network) which provides flexibility and mobility for the patients. GRHMS uses Complex Event Processing (CEP) to detect the abnormality in patient's health condition, formulate contexts based on spatiotemporal relations between vital parameters, learn rules dynamically and generate alerts in real time. Though, CEP is powerful in detecting abnormal events, its capability is limited due to uncertain incoming events, static rule base and scalability problem. Hence, this chapter addresses these challenges and proposes an enhanced CEP (eCEP) which encompasses augmented CEP (a-CEP), a statistical event refinement model to minimize the error due to uncertainty, Dynamic CEP (DCEP) to add and delete rules dynamically into the rule base and Scalable CEP (SCEP) to address scalability problem. Experimental results show that the proposed framework has better accuracy in decision making.

Chapter 17: CASPL – A Coevolution Analysis Platform for Software Product Lines

It is important to recognize that the change impact analysis and the evolution understanding in software product lines require greater focus than in single software. This chapter presents CASPL platform for co-evolution analysis in software product lines. The platform uses evolutionary trees that are mainly used in biology to analyze the co-evolution between applications. The major goal is to enhance the change understanding and to compare the history of changes in the applications of the family, at the aim of correcting divergences between them.

Chapter 18: Hybrid Term-Similarity-Based Clustering Approach and Its Applications

This chapter presents a method that first adopts ontology learning to generate ontologies via the hidden semantic patterns existing within complex terms. Then, it proposes service recommendation and selection approaches based on the proposed clustering approach. Experimental results show that developed term-similarity approach outperforms comparable existing clustering approaches. Further, empirical study of the prototyping recommendation and selection approaches have proved the effectiveness of proposed novel two approaches.

Chapter 19: Deep Model Framework for Ontology-Based Document Clustering

Although there is enormous amount of information available online, most of the documents are uncategorized. It is time consuming task for the users to browse through a large number of documents and search for information about specific topics. The ability of automatic clustering from uncategorized documents is important and has great potential to improve the efficiency of information seeking behaviors. To address this issue this chapter proposes a deep ontology based approach to document clustering. The obtained results are used to implement annotation rules and the information extraction capabilities of annotated framework are compared with and without using ontology.

Maki K. Habib
The American University in Cairo, Egypt

Chapter 1
An Electric Wheelchair Controlled by Head Movements and Facial Expressions:
Uni-Modal, Bi-Modal, and Fuzzy Bi-Modal Modes

Ericka Janet Rechy-Ramirez
Universidad Veracruzana, Mexico

Huosheng Hu
University of Essex, UK

ABSTRACT

A bio-signal-based human machine interface is proposed for hands-free control of a wheelchair. An Emotiv EPOC sensor is used to detect facial expressions and head movements of users. Nine facial expressions and up-down head movements can be chosen to form five commands: move-forward and backward, turn-left and right, and stop. Four uni-modal modes, three bi-modal modes, and three fuzzy bi-modal modes are created to control a wheelchair. Fuzzy modes use the users' strength in making the head movement and facial expression to adjust the wheelchair speed via a fuzzy logic system. Two subjects tested the ten modes with several command configurations. Means, minimum, and maximum values of the traveling times achieved by each subject in each mode were collected. Results showed that both subjects achieved the lowest mean, minimum and maximum traveling times using fuzzy modes. Statistical tests showed that there were significant differences between traveling times of fuzzy modes of subject B and traveling times of bi-modal modes and those of the respective fuzzy modes of both subjects.

DOI: 10.4018/978-1-5225-5396-0.ch001

INTRODUCTION

The current electric powered wheelchairs (EPWs) are mostly joystick-driven. Consequently, disabled people whose autonomies are seriously affected by spinal cord injuries, tetraplegia or amputation, as well as the elderly people with limited mobility, might not be able to use these EPWs. Up to now, several human machine interfaces (HMIs) have been developed for hands-free control of a wheelchair in order to assist the disabled and elderly people. Electromyography (EMG), Electroencephalography (EEG), and Electrooculography (EOG) signals as well as vision techniques have been used for identifying facial expressions, thoughts, eye-gaze, head, hand and shoulder movements from users to operate a wheelchair.

Human Wheelchair Interfaces Based on Head Movements

In terms of head movements, vision techniques have been employed to detect head movements to control a wheelchair. For instance, the direction of the head has been used to provide commands to a wheelchair (Adachi et al., 1998). Specifically, the authors used a camera in front of the user to track ten features-points around the eyes, nose and mouth; therefore, the direction of the head is identified. Another study (Christensen & Garcia, 2005) used forward-backward head movements to move forward and backward the wheelchair, and turn left-right head movements to turn the wheelchair. An infrared sensor placed behind the user's head was employed to detect these head movements. Likewise, Jia et al. (2007) developed a visual HMI to detect head movements for giving the commands to the wheelchair. In this research, the nose position on user's face is utilized for head motion detection. Conversely, the gyroscope of an Emotiv EPOC sensor was used to detect up, down, left and right head movements in order to control a wheelchair (Rechy-Ramirez & Hu, 2012).

Human Wheelchair Interfaces Based on Facial Expressions

Electromyography (EMG) signals –muscular activity- are widely used to obtain facial expressions for hands-free control of a wheelchair. A finite state machine has been employed to command the wheelchair through one facial expression (Felzer & Freisleben, 2002). In this research, the user performs a facial expression (i.e. raising the eyebrow) until the desired command is reached instead of employing one expression per control command. Furthermore, three types of facial expressions have been employed to control a wheelchair: winking with the right eye (to turn to the right), winking with the left eye (to turn to the left) and biting (to go forward and stop) (Tamura et al., 2010). Another study (Firoozabadi, Oskoei & Hu, 2008) has used four facial expressions to operate a wheelchair: smiling (to go forward), tensing the eyebrows and pulling them up (to go backward), retracting and pulling the right lip corners upward (to turn right), and retracting and pulling the left lip corners upward (to turn left). To stop the wheelchair, users should relax facial muscles. Moreover, an incremental online learning algorithm in real-time has been employed to process EMG signals from facial movements for adaptive control of a wheelchair (Xu et al., 2013).

Human Wheelchair Interfaces Based on Eye-Gaze

Electrooculography signal (EOG), vision techniques and infrared photo sensors have been used for detecting users' eye gaze, which is utilized to control a wheelchair. For example, Crisman et al. (1991) employed timed eyewinks, i.e. short and long closings from one or both eyelids for operating a wheelchair. The detection of the timed eyewinks was performed through two pairs of infrared photo sensors attached to the earpieces of a normal pair of eyeglass frames. Conversely, various studies (Barea et al., 2000; Barea et al., 2003; Kuo et al. 2009) have used EOG signal (i.e. using electrodes placed on the outer side of the eyes) to detect eye-gaze, which is employed to control the wheelchair. Mishra et al. (2017) proposed a HMI based on measurement of EOG using fractal electrode without any conductive gel. Consequently, eye movements (up, down, left, and right) were used to control the wheelchair. Another study (Bartolein et al., 2008) used an eye-tracking device called SensoMotoric Instruments GmbH to control a wheelchair via the user's eye gaze behavior. On the other hand, Gajwani and Chhabria (2010) used eye tracking and eye blinking obtained by a camera mounted on a cap to control a wheelchair. Moreover, another study created an eye-gaze tracker -glasses frame- to operate the wheelchair (Nguyen and Jo, 2012). This tracker used an infrared camera with two LEDs and a 3D orientation sensor to detect the user's eye gaze.

Human Wheelchair Interfaces Based on Thoughts

Despite the slow response of Electroencephalography signal (EEG) for giving commands to a wheelchair, several brain-computer interfaces (BCIs) controlled through EEG signal have been implemented. In this context, studies (Rebsamen et al., 2007; He et al. 2017) have used P300 event-related potential to control a wheelchair in a predefined map with desired destinations. According to Thulasidas et al. (2006), a P300 signal "is created in the central sites of EEG measurements when an infrequent and anticipated event occurs. P300 is the signature of the user's brain registering the event, and typically occurs around 300 ms after the infrequent event takes place." Generally, in these BCIs, users focus their attention on a specific button to execute a command or to select a destination. Similarly, another study (Palankar et al., 2008) used a mounted robotic arm to control a wheelchair in a simulated environment. The robotic arm is operated via a P300 BCI, in which the user is able to control the motion of the arm and chair by focusing attention on a specific character on the screen. Zhang et al. (2016) proposed a BCI, in which the user can choose a destination from a map and stop the wheelchair employing motor imagery or P300. Once the destination is selected, the navigation system controls the wheelchair until the destination. Another study (Cao et al., 2014) implemented a hybrid BCI to control the direction (go forward, turn left and right) and speed (drive at an uniform velocity, accelerate, decelerate) of a real wheelchair. This BCI combines motor imagery based bio-signals and steady-state visual evoked potentials.

Multi-Modal Human Wheelchair Interfaces

Other approaches have integrated different modalities to control a wheelchair. For example, a HMI based on vision (Bergasa et al., 2000) has integrated head movements, lip hiding and eye winking to operate a wheelchair. A 2D-face tracker and a fuzzy detector were employed to detect these human movements. Another HMI based on vision controlled a wheelchair via face inclination and two mouth shapes performed by the user (Ju et al., 2009). Conversely, other HMI (Law et al., 2002) used three Ag/AgCl electrodes attached to a cap to detect three types of facial motions to control a wheelchair: (i) looking to the left (for turning left), (ii) looking to the right (for turning right), and (iii) tighten the jaw (for going forward). When the wheelchair is moving (turning or going forward), the user can stop the wheelchair by performing a jaw motion.

Moreover, EMG and EOG signals have been employed to identify eyebrow tension and lateral eyes movements, respectively (Tsui et al., 2007). These facial expressions were used to execute the commands on the wheelchair. Both signals were obtained via a CyberLink sensor (a headband with three sensors). Likewise, Wei and Hu (2010) integrated EMG signal and facial images to identify eye winking and jaw clenching. These movements were used to provide control commands to a wheelchair. Another HMI (Taher et al., 2015) integrated EEG signal and eye tracking to control a simulated wheelchair. Vision techniques were used to detect the eye tracking through a camera, whereas facial expressions (left eye-gaze and right eye-gaze, raise furrow and smirk left) were obtained via the 'expressiv® suite' of Emotiv EPOC. Similarly, Wang et al. (2014a) combined EEG and EOG signals. In this HMI, motor imagery was used to move forward and backward (motion state) and turn a wheelchair, and P300 potentials were employed to accelerate and decelerate the wheelchair's speed. Additionally, EOG (eye blinking three times consecutively) was used to stop and wait for a request of a motion state. On the other hand, Herweg et al. (2016) integrated EEG signal and tactile stimulators to control a virtual wheelchair through P300 signal. These tactile stimulators were placed on legs, abdomen and back of the users in order to stimulate their left and right thighs above the knee, abdomen and lower neck. Another HMI (Wang et al., 2014b) has used EEG signal and speech. Specifically, EEG signal was analyzed to move a wheelchair through P300 potentials and turn a wheelchair through left and right hand motor imagery, whereas the stop command was executed through speech.

Other Methods

Other studies (Han et al., 2003; Moon et al., 2005) have used shoulder movements detected through EMG signal in order to control a wheelchair. Likewise, Thorp et al. (2016) controlled a wheelchair using shoulder movements; however, two inertial measurement units (IMUs) placed on the shoulder were employed to detect the movements instead of EMG electrodes.

On the other hand, Kaiser et al. (2016) have employed EMG signal to detect four hand and finger movements (wrist extension, wrist flexion, thumb movement, and finger movement except thumb), which were used for stopping, moving forward, and turning left and right a wheelchair. Conversely, Yokota et al. (2009) employed the upper body motion of the user to control a wheelchair, i.e. users operate the wheelchair by leaning their bodies to the desired direction (forward, backward, left or right). The user's motion was detected via a BPMS (Body Pressure Measurement System), a pressure sensor, and an inclinometer attached to the user.

Nevertheless, some disabled people might not be able to move their hands, shoulders and bodies; therefore, alternative ways are required. In this context, a HMI (Huo & Ghovanloo, 2009) has proposed to use tongue movements to operate a wheelchair, in which the movement data were obtained from a magnetic tracer on the tongue. Although, this HMI was flexible in its configuration for giving the commands, it was invasive for long-term usage because the user should receive a tongue piercing embedded with the magnetic tracer.

Due to technological advances, there is an EEG sensor in the market able to provide potential applications in hands-free HMIs called Emotiv EPOC. This sensor provides a three-axis gyroscope to detect head movements and three suites: 'cognitiv® suite' to detect thoughts, 'expressiv® suite' to detect facial expressions and 'affectiv® suite' to detect emotions. Until now, Emotiv has applications in different areas (Rechy-Ramirez et al., 2017), e.g. assistive technology, education and training, robot control, smart home environments, virtual tours, emotion recognition and driver fatigue recognition.

Contribution of this Research

Although some advanced HMIs have been developed for hands-free control of a wheelchair, they might not be user-friendly and robust. Looking at the HMIs based on vision, a main shortcoming is that their performances are vulnerable to environmental illumination, brightness, camera position and background of the image; thus, these HMIs might not be used in environments with poor illumination. Regarding the HMIs using eye-gaze for giving commands, a main drawback is that users might feel dizzy while controlling the wheelchair due to the movement of the eye's pupil. Moreover, most of the existing HMIs have fixed configurations. As a result, users might not select the command configuration according to their needs and preferences. The contributions in this chapter are as follows:

- A fuzzy logic system is proposed to adjust the wheelchair speed according to the strength applied by the user during the performance of the facial expression or head movement.
- Flexible control modes based on head movements and facial expressions are proposed to operate hands-free a wheelchair in environments with good or poor illumination. Therefore, users might choose: the way of giving commands, and the facial expressions to be employed according to their needs.
- It is empirically proved that the Emotiv sensor has a reliable response to stimuli provided by users (either head movements or facial expressions) in situations, which fast actions are required to achieve tasks properly. Hence, the Emotiv sensor might be used for implementing hands-free control applications to assist disabled and elderly people in their daily lives.

OVERVIEW OF THE PROPOSED HMI

In this chapter, ten control modes are proposed in our HMI to provide flexibility on the wheelchair operation. Three of them only employ facial expressions to give commands, and one mode only uses head movements. These four modes are called uni-modal. On the other hand, three modes (bi-modal modes) employ both head movements and facial expressions to control the wheelchair. Finally, a fuzzy logic system to adjust the move-forward wheelchair speed is implemented on these three bi-modal modes (fuzzy bi-modal modes).

As shown in Figure 1, the Emotiv EPOC is used to detect facial expressions and head movements to generate the ten control modes. The reasons for the selection of the Emotiv sensor to implement the control modes are: i) it is easy to wear, ii) it can recognize different facial expressions and head movements for a flexible control, and iii) its response to the head movements and facial expressions performed by users is fast and accurate.

Apparatus

The Emotiv EPOC Headset

It can measure EEG activities from 14 saline electrodes (plus CMS/DRL references, P3/P4 locations). These electrodes are arranged according to the 10/20 system, and their locations are AF3, F7, F3, FC5, T7, P7, O1, O2, P8, T8, FC6, F4, F8 and AF4 (https://www.emotiv.com/comparison/, retrieved on 14

Figure 1. Architecture of the proposed HMI

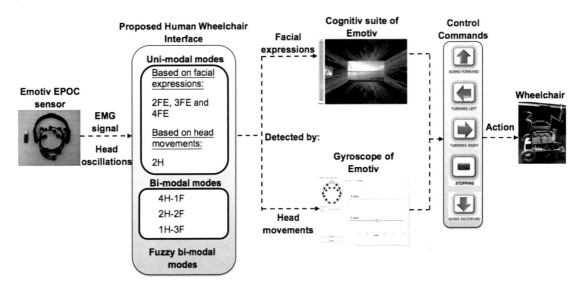

September 2017). The Emotiv Software Development Kit (SDK) for research includes an API to develop applications using the three emotiv suites: 'cognitiv®', 'expressiv®' and 'affectiv®' suites. Each suite has different functions as follows:

- The 'cognitiv® suite' recognizes 14 conscious thoughts of the user (i.e. 'neutral', 'right', 'left', 'push', 'pull', 'lift', 'drop', 'rotate left', 'rotate right', 'rotate clockwise', 'rotate anti-clockwise', 'rotate forwards', 'rotate reverse' and 'disappear'); but only a maximum of 4 actions can be used apart from the neutral action in each session.
- The 'expressiv® suite' recognizes facial expressions (i.e. 'blink', 'right wink', 'left wink', 'look right/left', 'raise brow', 'furrow brow', 'smile', 'clench', 'right smirk', 'left smirk' and 'laugh').
- The 'affectiv® suite' recognizes emotional states of the user, including engagement, boredom, frustration, meditation, instantaneous excitement and long-term excitement.

According to (Emotiv SDK, 2010), "the EmoEngine communicates with the Emotiv headset, receives preprocessed EEG and gyroscope data, manages user-specific or application specific settings, performs post-processing, and translates the Emotiv detection results into an easy-to-use structure called an EmoState. An EmoState is an opaque data structure that contains the current state of the Emotiv detections, which, in turn, reflects the user's facial, emotional and cognitive state." Apart from the suites, the Emotiv EPOC sensor has a gyroscope with three axes, 'X', 'Y', and 'Z' through which the EmoEngine of the Emotiv gives the position data of the user's head. This research is focused on using the X-axis that provides data of horizontal head movements and Y-axis that gives data of vertical head movements.

The Wheelchair

The wheelchair employed in this research is equipped with an embedded PC with the following features:

- Processor: Intel Atom CPD 525, 1.80 GHz;
- Installed memory (RAM): 4.00 GB;
- Operating system: Windows 7;
- Installed software: Microsoft Visual Studio 2010 and
- Emotiv research edition SDK 1.0.0.4.

The detailed description of the hardware structure of the wheelchair system can be found in (Jia et al., 2007).

Methodology

Notations and Definitions

Definition 1

The facial expressions trained by users involve the following movements:

1. FOREHEAD:
    a. FB (furrow brows). Users furrow their brows without closing eyes;
    b. RB (raise brows). Users raise their brows;
2. EYES:
    a. BEC (both eyes closed). Users close both eyes and take one deep breath;
    b. LEC (left eye closed). Users close the left eye only;
    c. REC (right eye closed). Users close the right eye only;
3. MOUTH:
    a. S (smile). Users perform a big smile;
    b. PJ (pulling the jaw). Users pull and exert force on their jaw muscles.
    c. SMIRK EXPRESSIONS:
        i. LS (left smirk). Users pull the left side of the lip to the left.
        ii. RS (right smirk). Users pull the right side of the lip to the right.

Definition 2

States = {stop, forward, left, right, ready, backward} are the actions that users can execute on the wheelchair:

1. **Stop:** For stopping the wheelchair;
2. **Forward:** For moving forward the wheelchair;
3. **Left:** For turning to the left the wheelchair;
4. **Right:** For turning to the right the wheelchair;
5. **Ready:** For indicating that the user can give a new command;
6. **Backward:** For moving backward the wheelchair.

Definition 3

The control modes implemented on our HMI are:

1. **2FE:** Uses two facial expressions;
2. **3FE:** Uses three facial expressions;
3. **4FE:** Uses four facial expressions;
4. **2H:** Uses up and down head movements;
5. **4H-1F:** Uses four head movements (up, left, right, and down) and one facial expression;
6. **2H-2F:** Uses two head movements (up and down) and two facial expressions;
7. **1H-3F:** Uses one head movement (either up or down) and three facial expressions.
8. **Fuzzy Bi-Modal Modes:** 4H-1F, 2H-2F and 1H-3F using a fuzzy logic system to adjust the move-forward wheelchair speed.

Definition 4

In order to have an optimal response from the facial expressions, these expressions were selected based on the following rules:

*   **Rule 1:** Facial expressions must be different.
*   **Rule 2:** Only one FOREHEAD expression must be used on a control mode.
*   **Rule 3:** SMIRK expressions cannot be selected on a mode, if a 'smile (S)' has been selected, and vice versa.

The rules 2 and 3 were considered because these expressions are likely to have false detections between them.

Uni-Modal Control Modes

Using Facial Expressions

From preliminary experiments, it was noticed that the classifier of the 'cognitiv® suite' was unable to detect thoughts. Nevertheless, in this research it was used to detect facial expressions without a delay. The 'cognitiv® suite' is more accurate to detect facial expressions than the 'expressiv® suite'. Thresholds have been used to detect the facial expressions employed to activate the required commands. Moreover, the control modes offer flexibility in the selection of the facial expressions to give the commands, if the 'cognitiv® suite' is used. Consequently, users might train their preferred expressions. To provide comfort in all control modes, users might perform the facial expression for approximately 2 seconds in order to issue the command. Then, users might return to a 'normal pose' (neutral gesture) for giving the next command. As a result, users do not have to maintain the facial expression while the control command is being executed.

*   2FE (*expression1*, *expression2*): Using Two Facial Expressions

As can be seen from Figure 2a, each facial expression in this mode is associated with two commands. One facial expression triggers the 'going forward' and 'turning left' commands (expression1), whereas the other facial expression (expression2) issues 'turning right' and 'stopping' commands. Therefore, a double performance of the facial expression is required to execute 'turning left' and 'stopping' commands.

Figure 2. State machines: 2FE, 3FE and 4FE

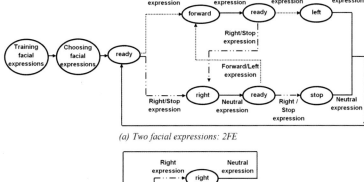

(a) Two facial expressions: 2FE

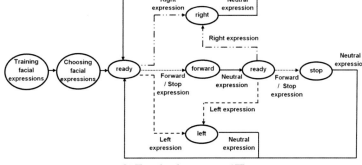

(b) Three facial expressions: 3FE

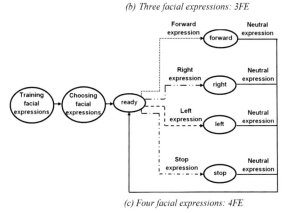

(c) Four facial expressions: 4FE

- 3FE (*expression1*, *expression2*, *expression3*): Using Three Facial Expressions

In this mode, only one facial expression (expression1) issues two commands: 'going forward' and 'stopping' (Figure 2b). Therefore, 'expression1' has to be performed twice in order to trigger the 'stopping' command. In contrast, 'expression2' and 'expression3' execute one command only: 'turning left' and 'turning right', respectively.

- 4FE (*expression1*, *expression2*, *expression3*, *expression4*): Using Four Facial Expressions

This mode employs the maximum of facial expressions allowed by the 'cognitiv® suite' of the Emotiv sensor (Figure 2c). Each facial expression is associated with just one command. 'expression1' issues the 'going forward' command, 'expression2' executes 'turning left' command, 'expression3' triggers 'turning right' command, and 'expression4' stops the wheelchair.

- The Training Process of Facial Expressions

The 'cognitiv® suite' has been employed to train the facial expressions that will be used to give the commands. This suite has 14 actions, but only a maximum of 4 actions apart from 'neutral state' can be used per session that the user opens. When a user is training a 'cognitiv® action' (e.g. 'right', 'left', 'push'), a cube presented in its GUI (Graphical User Interface) will move according to the trained action. Each 'cognitiv® action' has an associated facial expression, e.g. the 'right-cognitiv action' corresponds to 'right smirk'. It is important to remark that in order to train the facial expressions, the Emotiv's electrodes must be deployed. Consequently, the electrodes have to be wetted with saline solution.

The procedure to train the facial expressions using the 'cognitiv® suite' is as follows:

1. First, the user has to train a 'neutral state' (normal pose). The neutral action can be trained via two modalities: one modality lasts 8 seconds and the other one lasts 30 seconds. During the training process of this action, the user has to keep a normal pose without doing any facial expression, so that action data can be recorded through the 'cognitiv® suite'. This action needs more training than the other ones in order to avoid false-triggered expressions. For our experiments, the subjects trained the 'neutral state' 10 times using the '8 seconds modality' and 3 times using the '30 seconds modality'.
2. Then, the user has to train each facial expression during which the pose has to be kept for 8 seconds. Each facial expression has to be trained in the same way for several times until the action is performed easily and reliably. One way to check whether the user is performing the same expression is to examine the skill rating of the training in the suite's GUI; it should be increasing every time. Before training a facial expression in the 'cognitiv® suite', its sensitivity of the action should be set as 'high'. In this way, the user can normally achieve a training rate of 80% or more after 6 trials. For our experiments, all the subjects trained the expressions in 6 trials.
3. Finally, if necessary, users can adjust their facial expressions by decreasing the sensitivity of each action associated to each expression in the 'cognitiv® suite'. In our experiments, the sensitivities of all the expressions trained by both subjects were decreased in three units below 'high sensitivity'; that is between medium and high sensitivities.

Using Head Movements

Although the Emotiv sensor provides a gyroscope with three axes, only the Y-axis was used in this mode to provide commands through vertical head movements. A positive value of the Y-axis represents an 'up movement' and a negative value represents a 'down movement'. Moreover, users are not required to maintain the head movements in this mode in order to keep running the command.

- 2H (*movement1, movement2*): Using Two Head Movements

This mode uses two head movements (up and down) to operate the wheelchair as follows:

1. *movement1* has associated two actions: (i) to display the sequences of the control commands through a rotation technique; (ii) to execute the command displayed in the GUI of our HMI.
2. *movement2* is employed to stop the wheelchair at any time.

Each command is displayed for one second in the GUI and will be repeated in a rotation technique until the user executes one of them. The user can execute the control command shown in the GUI by performing the head movement (movement1) for displaying/executing commands again. The user can stop the wheelchair at any time by performing the head movement for stopping (movement2). The deployment sequence of the commands is shown in Figure 3. The algorithm of this mode is presented in Figure 4.

Bimodal Modes: Using Head Movements and Facial Expressions

In these modes, facial expressions and head movements are integrated in order to provide the commands to the wheelchair. In other words, the 'cognitiv® suite' and gyroscope detections are used to form the modes.

4H-1F (Expression1): Using Four Head Movements and One Facial Expression

In this mode, an 'up' head movement (identified through the Y-axis of the gyroscope) and two horizontal head movements (identified through the X-axis of the gyroscope) are used to indicate the desired command to be executed. Once, the command is indicated, the facial expression (expression1) is employed to confirm the execution of the command. Only the 'down' head movement does not need a confirmation. This head movement executes immediately the stopping command. The three head movements specify intentions to execute different commands as follows:

Figure 3. Deployment sequences of the commands: 2HM

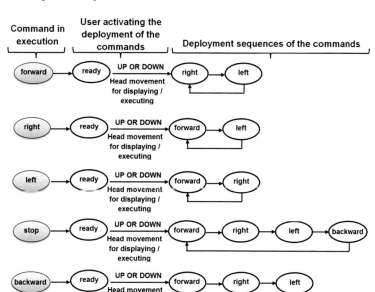

Figure 4. Algorithm: 2HM

```
1: Inputs:
          H1 = head movement for displaying/executing the commands.
          H2 = head movement for stopping the wheelchair
2: Start at stopping state
3: do
4: if H1 is performed then
5:       do
6:               Display the sequence of the commands according to the
                 command in execution
7:               if H1 is performed then
8:                       executes the command shown in the graphical
                         user interface of the mode at that moment
9:               end if
10:              if H2 is performed then
11:                      stops the wheelchair
12:              end if
13:      while H1 or H2 have not been executed
14: end if
15: while the mode is being executed
```

1. **Up Movement:** A going forward command is desirable to be executed.
2. **Left Movement:** A turning left command is desirable to be executed
3. **Right Movement:** A turning right command is desirable to be executed.

2H-2F (Expression1, Expression2): Using Two Head Movements and Two Facial Expressions

As shown in figure 5a, this mode works in the following manner:

1. *'expression1'* and *'expression2'* are used to execute 'turning right' and 'turning left' commands, respectively;
2. One head movement (up or down) is used to trigger the 'going forward' command;
3. The remaining head movement is employed to stop the wheelchair.

1H-3F (Expression1, Expression2, Expression3): Using One Head Movement and Three Facial Expressions

As shown in Figure 5b, each facial expression has associated one command in this mode:

1. *'expression1'* issues the 'going forward' command, *'expression2'* executes 'turning right' command, and *'expression3'* triggers 'turning left' command.
2. The 'stopping command' is executed via one head movement depending on which movement is chosen for the user to do it ('up' or 'down' head movement).

In these bi-modal modes, the user has to be at the 'stopping command' and performs again the head movement associated to it for executing the 'going backward' command.

Figure 5. Bi-modal modes: 2H-2F and 1H-3F

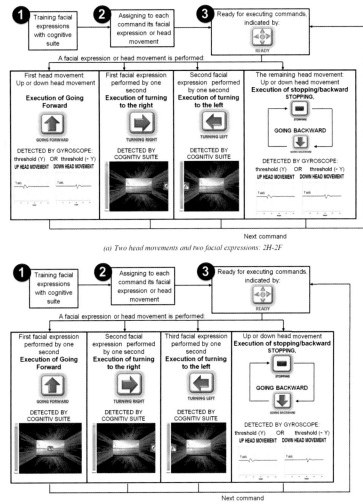

Fuzzy Bi-Modal Modes

Figure 6 shows a simple fuzzy logic system (FLS) implemented on the bi-modal modes in order to use different speeds on the wheelchair. This FLS operates as follows:

1. Crisp values are obtained from either the power provided by the 'cognitiv® suite' (facial expression) or the Y-axis of the gyroscope (head movement).
2. The crisp value is translated into input-linguistic-values through the fuzzy-input-sets (Fuzzification).
3. The rules are evaluated to determine the output-linguistic-values, i.e. normal, fast and very fast speeds (Fuzzy inference).
4. The output-linguistic-values (normal, fast and very fast speeds) are translated into a crisp value, i.e. a specific speed value (Defuzzification).
5. Finally, the crisp value is applied as the wheelchair speed.

Figure 6. Overview of the fuzzy logic system

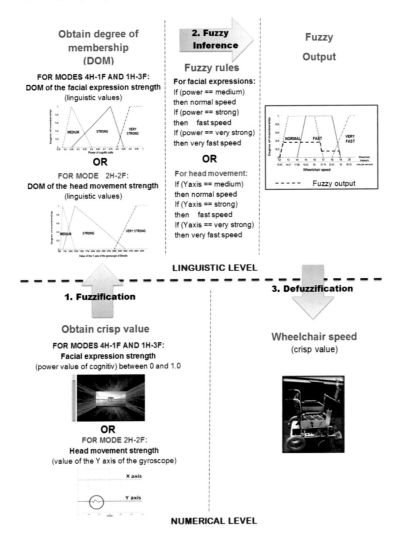

Fuzzification

The wheelchair speed is calculated based on the users' strength in making the facial expression or head movement. In terms of 'Emotiv sensor', either the Y-axis value of the gyroscope (head movement) or the power value provided by the 'cognitiv® suite' (facial expression) is examined to activate the proper command.

In this context, fuzzy-input-sets are defined for head movements (Y-axis value of the gyroscope) and facial expressions (cognitiv® power-value). The cognitiv® power-value ranges from 0 to 1. Based on previous experiences, it was noticed that a facial expression is created reliably if the cognitiv® power is greater than 0.37. Consequently, the facial expressions may be classified as 'MEDIUM', 'STRONG' and 'VERY STRONG' depending on the strength of the users' muscles involved in making the expression. A triangular function is used for mapping the crisp values of the cognitiv® power into the fuzzy-input-sets of 'MEDIUM', 'STRONG' and 'VERY STRONG' expressions (see Figure 7).

Figure 7. Fuzzy-Input-sets of facial expressions

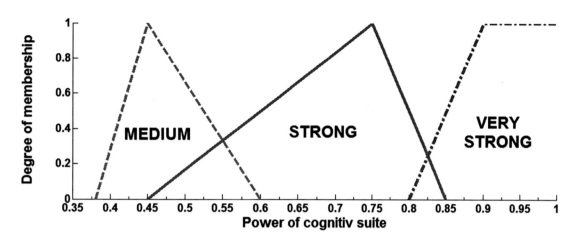

Regarding the head movements, based on previous experiments, the 'up' head movement is more suitable than the 'down' head movement to execute the 'going-forward' command on the 2H-2F-mode. Therefore, only this movement has been considered to adjust the wheelchair speed with fuzzy logic. Although the head movement varies according to each size of the user's head, it was concluded from previous experiments that a value greater than 540 of the Y-axis might correspond to a valid head movement. A triangular membership function is used to implement the fuzzy-input-sets for the head movement (see Figure 8).

For this preliminary fuzzy logic system, only the speed for 'moving the wheelchair forward' is adjusted based on users' strength in creating a facial expression or a head movement. Three membership-output-sets for this speed ('NORMAL', 'FAST' and 'VERY FAST') are defined using trapezoidal membership functions (see Figure 9).

Figure 8. Fuzzy-Input-sets of up head movement

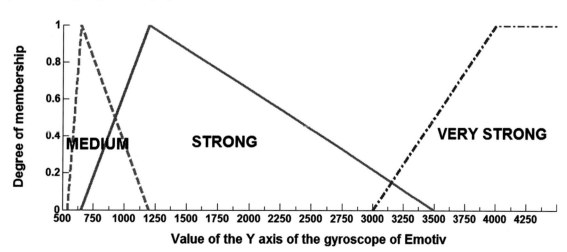

Figure 9. Fuzzy-output-sets for forward speed expressed in wheelchair measure (wm) and centimeters per second

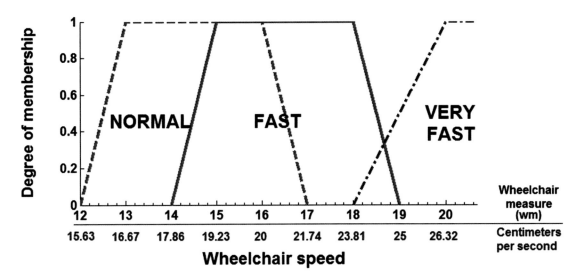

Fuzzy Inference

There are fuzzy-input-sets for facial expressions and head movements, depending on the fuzzy bi-modal mode that is being used for controlling the wheelchair. The rules to determine the forward speed in 4H-1F and 1H-3F modes are the followings:

- **Rule 1:** If (facial expression == 'medium') then normal speed
- **Rule 2:** If (facial expression == 'strong') then fast speed
- **Rule 3:** If (facial expression == 'very strong') then very fast speed

On the other hand, the rules to obtain the speed for moving the wheelchair forward in 2H-2F are the followings:

- **Rule 1:** If (up-movement == 'medium') then normal speed
- **Rule 2:** If (up-movement == 'strong') then fast speed
- **Rule 3:** If (up-movement == 'very strong') then very fast speed

Defuzzification

The 'center of maximum' is used for mapping the fuzzy value into a crisp value.

$$z^* = \frac{\sum x_n \mu_n}{\sum \mu_n} \tag{1}$$

where Σ denotes an algebraic sum; x_n is the mean of the numerical values corresponding to the degree of membership at which the wheelchair-speed membership function (n) is scaled, and μn is the degree of membership at which the wheelchair-speed membership function (n) is scaled.

EVALUATION

Participants

Two healthy subjects (A and B) have controlled the wheelchair using the control modes with different command configurations. To choose the facial expressions for controlling the wheelchair, users deployed the 'cognitiv® suite' of Emotiv. In order to identify the most comfortable expressions for users, the expressions were tested to execute commands on the wheelchair without moving it. Both subjects identified various facial expressions to be used in the control modes. Table 1 provides the configurations tested by both subjects per each mode. Due to time availability of Subject B, he only used one configuration per mode.

Regarding the subjects' experiences in controlling wheelchairs with these types of modes, Subject A –a female in her early 30's- has experience in using these control modes due to her participation in the project. Conversely, subject B – a male in his early 30's- has no experience with these control modes. For this reason, prior to the experiments reported in this chapter, he followed the route once (an informal trial) per each control mode.

Experiment

It is important to remark that with the aim of evaluating how fast the responses of the control modes are during the operation of the wheelchair; none of them dealt with obstacle avoidance. Consequently, the control of the wheelchair only relies on the way of giving the commands in each mode.

All control modes were tested in an indoor environment. Five experiments were performed per each control mode. In each experiment, the subject has to follow the route shown in Figure 10 without hitting obstacles. Each subject did a round of five trials per day. The order in which the control modes were tested is indicated in Table 1.

RESULTS

Standard deviations (std), means, minimum (min) and maximum (max) values of the traveling times of each control mode (uni-modal, bi-modal and fuzzy modes) per each subject were calculated. Regarding the uni-modal modes (see Tables 2-3), the lowest traveling-time means were reported by 2H <down,up> mode in the case of subject A (138.4 s) and by 2FE <RB, S> mode in the case of subject B (153.4 s). Additionally, subjects A and B reported the lowest minimum values among the uni-modal modes using 3FE <FB, LS, RS> (121 s) and 2H <down, up> (135 s), respectively. Conversely, 3FE <REC, BEC, RB> (215 s) and 2H <down, up> (192 s) were reported by subjects A and B as the modes with the highest maximum values among the uni-modal modes, as well as the modes with the highest standard deviations.

Table 1. Control modes and configurations tested by subjects A and B

Subject A			Subject B		
Control Mode	**Configuration**	**Testing Order**	**Control Mode**	**Configuration**	**Testing Order**
2FE	<LS, RS>	1st	2FE		20th
	<RS, BEC>	2nd			
3FE	<FB, LS, RS>	3rd	3FE		21th
	<REC, BEC, RB>	4th			
	<S, BEC, RB>	5th			
4FE	<RB, LS, RS, PJ>	6th			
2H	<Up, Down>	7th	2H	<Up, Down>	22th
	<Down, Up>	8th		<Down, Up>	23th
4H-1F	<FB>	9th	4H-1F	<S>	24th
	<LS>	10th			
	<RS>	11th			
	<S>	12th			
2H-2F	<LS, RS>	13th	2H-2F	<RB, S>	25th
	<S, FB>	14th			
	<LS, FB>	15th			
1H-3F	<FB, LS, RS>	16th	1H-3F	<RB, S, LEC>	26th
Fuzzy 4H-1F	<S>	17th	Fuzzy 4H-1F	<S>	27th
Fuzzy 2H-2F	<LS, RS>	18th	Fuzzy 2H-2F	<S, RB>	28th
Fuzzy 1H-3F	<FB, LS, RS>	19th	Fuzzy 1H-3F	<LEC, S, RB>	29th

Considering bi-modal modes (Tables 4-5), 4H-1F reported the highest standard deviations and maximum values of the traveling times in subject A (expression = <FB>, std = 22.338 s, max = 205 s) and subject B (expression = <S>, std = 39.506 s, max = 240 s). Moreover, subjects A and B obtained the lowest means through 1H-3F (147.6 s) and 2H-2F (154.8 s), respectively. Conversely, the lowest minimum values of the traveling times were acquired via 2H-2F <S, FB> (136 s) by subject A and 1H-3F (142 s) by subject B.

In terms of fuzzy bi-modal modes (see Table 6), subject A obtained the lowest minimum value of the traveling times (105 s) and the highest values for standard deviation (12.309 s) and maximum traveling time (134 s) using 2H-2F. Similarly, subject B achieved the highest standard deviation (9.975 s) and lowest values for mean (112 s) and minimum traveling time (101 s) employing the 2H-2F. On the other hand, 4H-1F reported the lowest mean (119.8 s) in the case of subject A and the highest maximum value of the traveling times (136 s) in the case of Subject B.

Statistical analysis was performed to conduct a comparison between the traveling times obtained in each control mode. First, a Shapiro-Wilk test was applied to the traveling times of each control mode in order to assess the normality of their samples. As can be seen from Table 7, only the 3FE <FB, LS, RS> mode employed by Subject A does not follow a normal distribution.

Figure 10. The route to follow in the experiments is indicated in dotted line

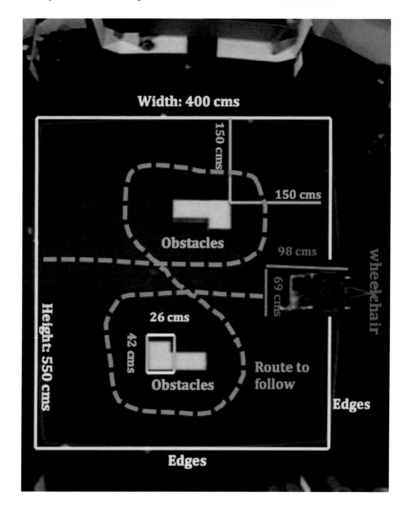

Table 2. Standard deviations, means, minimum and maximum values of the traveling times obtained by subject A using uni-modal modes with different configurations: Traveling times are expressed in seconds. Note: reference values are in italics.

	Uni-Modal Control Modes							
	Facial Expressions						Head Movements 2H	
	2FE		3FE			4FE		
	LS, RS	RS, BEC	FB, LS, RS	REC, BEC, RB	S, BEC, RB	RB, LS, RS, PJ	Up, Down	Down, Up
Standard deviation	8.8	16.2	16.1	*28.4*	23.3	16.8	25.4	4.9
Mean	157.4	159.2	149.6	185	178.6	185.8	156	*138.4*
Minimum value	152	145	*121*	145	150	168	135	133
Maximum value	168	187	159	*215*	213	205	200	146

Table 3. Standard deviations, means, minimum and maximum values of the traveling times obtained by subject B using uni-modal modes. Traveling times are expressed in seconds. Note: reference values are in italics.

	Uni-Modal Control Modes			
	Facial Expressions		Head Movements 2H	
	2FE	3FE		
	RB, S	RB, S, LEC	Up, Down	Down, Up
Standard deviation	8.4	9.5	6.2	*22.7*
Mean	*153.4*	167.6	154	160.2
Minimum value	140	155	144	*135*
Maximum value	162	180	159	*192*

Table 4. Standard deviations, means, minimum and maximum values of the traveling times obtained by subject A using bi-modal modes with different configurations: Traveling times are expressed in seconds. Note: reference values are in italics.

	Bi-Modal Control Modes							
	4H-1F				2H-2F			1H-3F
	FB	LS	RS	S	LS, RS	S, FB	LS, FB	FB, LS, RS
Standard deviation	*22.338*	8.961	9.094	5.45	10.2	9.2	3.5	3.5
Mean	170	154.60	166.20	148.80	156.8	151.2	148.4	*147.6*
Minimum value	150	147	155	143	142	*136*	145	144
Maximum value	*205*	168	175	156	165	159	154	152

Table 5. Standard deviations, means, minimum and maximum values of the traveling times obtained by subject B using bi-modal modes: Traveling times are expressed in seconds. Note: reference values are in italics.

	Bi-Modal Control Modes		
	4H-1F	2H-2F	1H-3F
	S	RB, S	RB, S, LEC
Standard deviation	*39.506*	9.2	14.6
Mean	182.20	*154.8*	159.2
Minimum value	152	145	*142*
Maximum value	*240*	166	180

Table 6. Standard deviations, means, medians, minimum and maximum values of the traveling times obtained by subjects A and B using fuzzy bi-modal modes: Traveling times are expressed in seconds. Note: reference values are in italics.

	Fuzzy bi-modal modes					
	Subject A			Subject B		
	4H-1F	2H-2F	1H-3F	4H-1F	2H-2F	1H-3F
	RS	LS, RS	FB, LS, RS	S	S, RB	LEC, S, RB
Standard deviation	7.981	*12.309*	4.879	8.044	*9.975*	3.347
Mean	*119.80*	122	120.6	125.20	*112*	122.20
Minimum value	113	*105*	115	117	*101*	117
Maximum value	133	*134*	128	*136*	128	125

Several comparisons between control modes used by each subject were performed based on the following cases:

- **Case 1:** This comparison includes the different configurations of a control mode employed by a subject. This case applies especially to subject A that used several configurations per control mode (e.g. 2FE mode with two configurations: <LS,RS>, <RS, BEC>).
- **Case 2:** This comparison includes control modes using only facial expressions by a subject (e.g. a comparison between 2FE, 3FE, and 4FE with every configuration employed by subject A).
- **Case 3:** This comparison includes bi-modal modes performed by a subject (e.g. 4H-1F, 2H-2F, and 1H-3F modes used by subject B).
- **Case 4:** This comparison includes fuzzy bi-modal modes employed by a subject.
- **Case 5:** This comparison includes a bi-modal mode with its corresponding fuzzy bi-modal mode used by a subject (e.g. 1H-3F bimodal mode and fuzzy 1H-3F bimodal mode employed by subject A).

Moreover, in order to assess the feasibility of using ANOVA test, Bartlett's test was applied to determine the homogeneity of variances of the comparison cases (see Table 8). Depending on the number of groups included in a comparison, the normality of the samples, and the homogeneity of variances; a two-tailed t-test (Table 9), one-tailed ANOVA (Table 10) or a Kruskal-Wallis test (Table 11) were employed to compare the traveling times obtained in the control modes. Additionally, a Tukey's Honestly Significant Difference (HSD) was applied as a post-hoc test when the ANOVA test found significant differences between the modes. It can be seen from Tables 9-11 that there were no significant differences in comparison cases: 1, 2 and 3. On the other hand, a one-tailed ANOVA at $\alpha = 0.05$ (Table 10) revealed that there were significant differences between the traveling times of fuzzy bi-modal modes used by subject B (comparison-case 4: F (2,12) = 4.095, HSD = 10.537, p-value = 0.04409). Furthermore, it can be seen from Tables 9 and 10 that all the possible scenarios for the comparison-case 5 reported significant differences based on t-test and ANOVA results. According to the post-hoc HSD (Table 10), the largest difference of the traveling times (HSD = 21.758) corresponded to subject A in the comparison between the traveling times of 4H-1F and those of its fuzzy version (comparison-case 5).

Table 7. Shapiro-Wilk statistics of control modes operated by subjects A and B at α = 0.05 and critical value of W = 0.77510; Note: control modes not following a normal distribution are in italics.

Subject A			Subject B		
Control Mode	**Statistic**	**p-value**	**Control Mode**	**Statistic**	**p-value**
2FE <LS,RS>	0.93308	0.61756	2FE <RB, S>	0.92642	0.57216
2FE <RS, BEC>	0.80553	0.08984			
3FE *<FB, LS, RS>*	*0.67129*	*0.00468*	3FE <RB, S, LEC>	0.99704	0.99759
3FE <REC, BEC, RB>	0.91696	0.51052			
3FE <S, BEC, RB>	0.96729	0.85763			
4FE <RB, LS, RS, PJ>	0.87944	0.30681			
2H <up, down>	0.78767	0.06406	2H <up, down>	0.84652	0.18378
2H <down, up>	0.94928	0.73207	2H <down, up>	0.95572	0.77792
4H-1F <FB>	0.87809	0.30078	4H-1F <S>	0.80837	0.09466
4H-1F <LS>	0.88433	0.32942			
4H-1F <RS>	0.86474	0.24577			
4H-1F <S>	0.94065	0.77510			
2H-2F <LS, RS>	0.82405	0.12543	2H-2F <RB, S>	0.90134	0.41734
2H-2F <S, FB>	0.86477	0.24590			
2H-2F <LS, FB>	0.91398	0.49192			
1H-3F <FB, LS, RS>	0.89392	0.37722	1H-3F <RB, S, LEC>	0.97096	0.88140
Fuzzy 4H-1F	0.85280	0.20355	Fuzzy 4H-1F	0.93125	0.60496
Fuzzy 2H-2F	0.92055	0.53354	Fuzzy 2H-2F	0.92161	0.54038
Fuzzy 1H-3F	0.96922	0.87027	Fuzzy 1H-3F	0.88103	0.31404

After finishing all the experiments, both subjects were asked about their top three preferred and most comfortable modes. Both subjects agreed that in first place is fuzzy bi-modal 2H-2F, followed by fuzzy bi-modal 1H-3F, and then 2H mode. In the case of subject A, she mentioned that the <LS, RS> facial expressions were the most comfortable ones for the 2H-2F mode. Both subjects agreed that the <up, down> configuration was the most comfortable for the 2H mode. It is important to remark that both subjects in each experiment of each control mode were able to complete the route indicated in Figure 10 without colliding with the obstacles.

Table 8. Bartlett's Test at α = 0.05 of comparison cases between control modes;Note: comparison cases having unequal variances are in italics.

	Comparison Case	Control Modes	p-Value
Subject A	*1*	*Between 4H-1F configurations*	*0.046*
	1	Between 2H-2F configurations	0.156
	3	*Between bi-modal modes*	*0.00717*
	4	Between fuzzy bi-modal modes	0.242
	5	Between 4H-1F and fuzzy 4H-1F	0.055
	5	Between 2H-2F and fuzzy 2H-2F	0.193
Subject B	*3*	*Between bi-modal modes*	*0.022*
	4	Between fuzzy bi-modal modes	0.16

Table 9. Two-tailed t-test at α = 0.05; Note: Significant t-test values and t(4) = 2.776 are in italics.

	Comparison Case	Control Modes	T-Test Value	p-Value
Subject A	1	Between 2FE configurations	-0.27373	0.79784
	1	Between 2H configurations	1.50996	0.20556
	5	*Between 1H-3F and fuzzy 1H-3F*	*11.40958*	*0.00033*
Subject B	2	Between facial modes	-1.90027	0.13019
	1	Between 2H configurations	-0.65594	0.54767
	5	*Between 4H-1F and fuzzy 4H-1F*	*3.48703*	*0.02519*
	5	*Between 2H-2F and fuzzy 2H-2F*	*8.57029*	*0.00101*
	5	*Between 1H-3F and fuzzy 1H-3F*	*4.6213*	*0.00987*

Table 10. One-tailed ANOVA at α = 0.05; Note: HSD stands for Tukey's Honestly Significant Difference, which is a post-hoc test. This value is given when the null hypothesis is rejected, i.e. when there are significant differences between the control modes. Significant values are in italics.

	Comparison Case	Control Modes	Critical F	F Value	p-Value
Subject A	1	Between 2H-2F configurations	3.885	F(2, 12) = 1.347	0.29663
	4	Between fuzzy bi-modal modes	3.885	F(2,12) = 0.078	0.92559
	5	*Between 4H-1F and fuzzy 4H-1F*	*2.866*	*F(4,20) = 3.068* *HSD = 21.758*	*0.000021*
	5	*Between 2H-2F and fuzzy 2H-2F*	*3.239*	*F(3,16) = 13.468* *HSD = 15,377*	*0.000120*
Subject B	*4*	*Between fuzzy bi-modal modes*	*3.885*	*F(2,12) = 4.095* *HSD = 10.537*	*0.04409*

Table 11. Kruskal-Wallis at α = 0.05; This test was employed due to a non-normality from 3FE <FB, LS, RS> mode used by subject A, and unequal variances between bi-modal modes of both subjects and 4H-1F configurations of subject A.

	Comparison Case	Control Modes	p-Value
Subject A	1	Between 3FE configurations	0.114178
	1	Between 4H-1F configurations	0.196857
	2	Between facial modes	0.055606
	3	Between bi-modal modes	0.204421
Subject B	3	Between bi-modal modes	0.376734

Figure 11. Trajectories of the best times per uni-modal and bi-modal modalities and fuzzy bi-modal modes: subject A

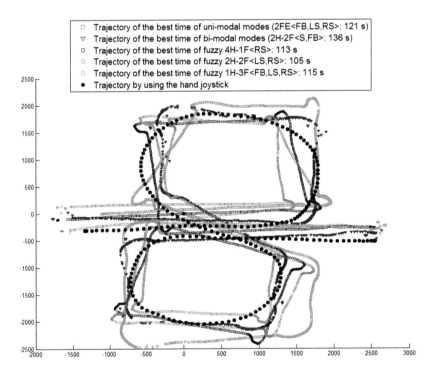

Trajectories of the routes per each experiment were recorded. A Vicon system was used to track five markers attached to the wheelchair in order to detect the wheelchair position. Figure 11 shows the trajectories of the uni-modal mode and the bi-modal mode with the lowest traveling times, as well as, the trajectories of each fuzzy bi-modal mode with the lowest traveling times executed by subject A. Likewise, Figure 12 presents those trajectories with the lowest traveling times executed by subject B. Moreover, both figures illustrate a trajectory done by each subject using the joystick as a reference. Considering the joystick trajectory as the ground-truth reference, it can be seen from Figure 11 that subject A produced the most mismatched trajectory using the uni-modal mode. On the other hand, it can be noticed from Figure 12 that it is difficult to identify the most mismatched trajectory produced by subject B.

Figure 12. Trajectories of the best times per uni-modal and bi-modal modalities and fuzzy bi-modal modes: subject B

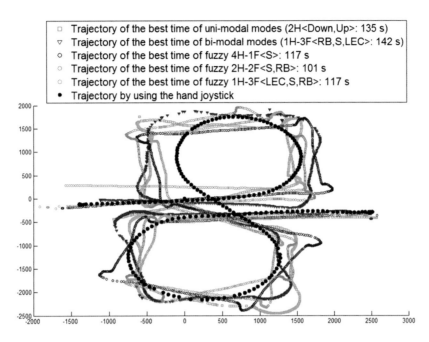

DISCUSSION

The proposed control modes represent alternative control methods for the hands-free operation of a wheelchair; however, there are some associated limitations. The main limitation of the 2FE and 3FE modes is that some expressions have associated two control commands; consequently, the execution of some commands (i.e. turning left and stopping) is slow. Likewise, the 2H mode might have a slow command execution due to a rotation technique employed for displaying the commands. In contrast to uni-modal modes that have a slow response, the bi-modal modes offer a reliable alternative for hands-free control of a wheelchair, due to their fast execution of commands. Furthermore, these modes provide flexibility in choosing the facial expressions involved in the configuration; therefore, users can select their most comfortable expressions. Additionally, the fuzzy bi-modal modes allow modifying the wheelchair speed based on the strength that a user employs in making the head movement and the facial expression.

In terms of training, it can be seen that the 2H mode is straightforward to use, because there is no need to train the head movements. Consequently, this mode can be used without deploying the Emotiv's electrodes. On the other hand, the remaining modes need to train the facial expressions through the 'cognitiv® suite' of Emotiv; therefore, the Emotiv's electrodes have to be wetted with saline solution. As a consequence, the modes using a facial expression take more time to start operating the wheelchair than the 2H mode. Furthermore, after performing experiments, this study has found that training two facial expressions is relatively easy, whereas the training of three expressions is considered to require a medium effort from users. Nevertheless, training four facial expressions is challenging.

Regarding the selection of the Emotiv EPOC sensor, the results of this investigation show that this sensor represents a reliable option for detecting several facial expressions and head movements from users. Moreover, its 'cognitiv®️ suite' can offer fast and accurate facial expression detections.

Though this study only provides five experiments per each control mode with two healthy subjects, it represents a reliable starting point to evaluate the use of these control modes for hands-free control of a wheelchair.

FUTURE RESEARCH DIRECTIONS

Our future work will be focused on deploying different fuzzy logic systems to adjust wheelchair speeds. Moreover, more participants will assess our control modes. On the other hand, the fusion of facial expressions and head movements through neural networks and fuzzy logic systems will be explored in order to improve the recognition of facial expressions and head movements used to execute the commands.

CONCLUSION

In this chapter, it was proposed a bio-signal based HMI able to provide ten different control modes with different configurations to operate a wheelchair via head movements and facial expressions. After performing experiments with two subjects, it is clear that the bi-modal modes and fuzzy modes provide i) flexibility in the facial expressions used for giving the commands, and ii) a fast execution of all the commands.

With the aim of offering comfort to users, the proposed HMI does not require users to keep the facial expression or head movement during the execution of commands. Moreover, statistical analysis revealed that there were significant differences between the traveling times achieved by bi-modal modes and those obtained by the corresponding fuzzy modes. In fact, both subjects achieved the lowest mean, minimum and maximum values of the traveling times using the fuzzy bi-modal modes.

In conclusion, the bi-modal modes and their corresponding fuzzy modes could be reliable for controlling a wheelchair. Furthermore, the Emotiv sensor is a feasible option for implementing hands-free applications to assist the disabled and elderly people.

REFERENCES

Adachi, Y., Kuno, Y., Shimada, N., & Shirai, Y. (1998). Intelligent wheelchair using visual information on human faces. In *Intelligent Robots and Systems, Proceedings: IEEE/RSJ International Conference* (vol. 1, pp. 354–359). IEEE.

Barea, R., Boquete, L., Bergasa, L. M., López, E., & Mazo, M. (2003). Electrooculography guidance of a wheelchair using eye movement's codification. *The International Journal of Robotics Research*, 22(7-8), 641–652. doi:10.1177/02783649030227012

Barea, R., Boquete, L., Mazo, M., López, E., & Bergasa, L. M. (2000). EOG guidance of a wheelchair using neural networks. In *Proceedings of the 15th International Conference on Pattern Recognition* (*vol. 4*, pp. 668–671). Academic Press. 10.1109/ICPR.2000.903006

Bartolein, C., Wagner, A., Jipp, M., & Badreddin, E. (2008). Easing wheelchair control by gaze-based estimation of intended motion. In *Proceedings of the International Federation of Automatic Control World Congress* (*vol. 17*, pp. 9162–9167). Academic Press. 10.3182/20080706-5-KR-1001.01549

Bergasa, L. M., Mazo, M., Gardel, A., Barea, R., & Boquete, L. (2000). Commands generation by face movements applied to the guidance of a wheelchair for handicapped people. In *Proceedings of the 15th International Conference on Pattern Recognition* (*vol. 4*, pp. 660–663). Academic Press. 10.1109/ICPR.2000.903004

Cao, L., Li, J., Ji, H., & Jiang, C. (2014). A hybrid brain computer interface system based on the neurophysiological protocol and brain-actuated switch for wheelchair control. *Journal of Neuroscience Methods*, *229*, 33–43. doi:10.1016/j.jneumeth.2014.03.011 PMID:24713576

Christensen, H. V., & Garcia, J. C. (2005). Infrared non-contact head sensor for control of wheelchair movements. In A. Pruski & H. Knops (Eds.), *Assistive technology: from virtuality to reality* (pp. 336–340). IOS Press.

Crisman, E. E., Loomis, A., Shaw, R., & Laszewski, Z. (1991). Using the eye wink control interface to control a powered wheelchair. In *Engineering in Medicine and Biology Society: Proceedings of the Annual International Conference of the IEEE* (vol. 13, pp.1821–1822). IEEE.

Emotiv SDK. (2010. *Software Development Kit User manual for release 1.0.0.4.* Author.

Felzer, T., & Freisleben, B. (2002). HaWCoS: the hands-free wheelchair control system. In *Proceedings of the fifth international ACM conference on assistive technologies* (pp. 127–134). ACM. 10.1145/638249.638273

Firoozabadi, S. M. P., Oskoei, M. A., & Hu, H. (2008). A human-computer Interface based on forehead multi-channel bio-signals to control a virtual wheelchair. In *Proceedings of the 14th Iranian Conference on Biomedical Engineering* (pp. 272–277). Academic Press.

Gajwani, P. S., & Chhabria, S. A. (2010). Eye motion tracking for wheelchair control. *International Journal of Information Technology*, *2*(2), 185–187.

Han, J. S., Zenn Bien, Z., Kim, D. J., & Lee, H. E., & Kim. J.S. (2003). Human machine interface for wheelchair control with EMG and its evaluation. In *Engineering in Medicine and Biology Society: Proceedings of the 25th Annual International Conference of the IEEE* (*vol. 2*, pp.1602–1605). IEEE.

He, S., Zhang, R., Wang, Q., Chen, Y., Yang, T., Feng, Z., & Li, Y. (2017). A P300-Based Threshold-Free Brain Switch and Its Application in Wheelchair Control. *IEEE Transactions on Neural Systems and Rehabilitation Engineering*, *25*(6), 715–725. doi:10.1109/TNSRE.2016.2591012 PMID:27416603

Herweg, A., Gutzeit, J., Kleih, S., & Kübler, A. (2016). Wheelchair control by elderly participants in a virtual environment with a brain-computer interface (BCI) and tactile stimulation. *Biological Psychology*, *121*(Pt A), 117-124.

Huo, X., & Ghovanloo, M. (2009). Using unconstrained tongue motion as an alternative control mechanism for wheeled mobility. *IEEE Transactions on Biomedical Engineering*, *56*(6), 1719–1726. doi:10.1109/TBME.2009.2018632 PMID:19362901

Jia, P., Hu, H., Lu, T., & Yuan, K. (2007). Head gesture recognition for hands-free control of an intelligent wheelchair. *Industrial Robot: An International Journal*, *34*(1), 60–68. doi:10.1108/01439910710718469

Ju, J. S., Shin, Y., & Kim, E. Y. (2009). Intelligent wheelchair interface using face and mouth recognition. In *Proceedings of the 14th international conference on Intelligent user interfaces* (pp. 307–314). Academic Press.

Kaiser, M. S., Chowdhury, Z. I., Al Mamun, S., Hussain, A., & Mahmud, M. (2016). A neuro-fuzzy control system based on feature extraction of surface electromyogram signal for solar-powered wheelchair. *Cognitive Computation*, *8*(5), 946–954. doi:10.100712559-016-9398-4

Kuo, C. H., Chan, Y. C., Chou, H. C., & Siao, J. W. (2009). Eyeglasses based electro-oculography human-wheelchair interface. In *Systems* (pp. 4746–4751). Man and Cybernetics.

Law, C. K. H., Leung, M. Y. Y., Xu, Y., & Tso, S. K. (2002). A cap as interface for wheelchair control. In Intelligent Robots and Systems (vol. 2, pp. 1439–1444). Academic Press.

Mishra, S., Norton, J. J., Lee, Y., Lee, D. S., Agee, N., Chen, Y., ... Yeo, W. H. (2017). Soft, conformal bioelectronics for a wireless human-wheelchair interface. *Biosensors & Bioelectronics*, *91*, 796–803. doi:10.1016/j.bios.2017.01.044 PMID:28152485

Moon, I., Lee, M., Chu, J., & Mun, M. (2005). Wearable EMG-based HCI for electric-powered wheelchair users with motor disabilities. In *Proceedings of the IEEE International Conference on Robotics and Automation* (pp. 2649–2654). IEEE.

Nguyen, Q. X., & Jo, S. (2012). Electric wheelchair control using head pose free eye-gaze tracker. *Electronics Letters*, *48*(13), 750–752. doi:10.1049/el.2012.1530

Palankar, M., De Laurentis, K. J., Alqasemi, R., Veras, E., Dubey, R., Arbel, Y., & Donchin, E. (2008). Control of a 9-DoF wheelchair-mounted robotic arm system using a P300 brain computer interface: Initial experiments. In Robotics and Biomimetics (pp. 348–353). Academic Press.

Rebsamen, B., Burdet, E., Guan, C., Teo, C. L., Zeng, Q., Ang, M., & Laugier, C. (2007). Controlling a wheelchair using a BCI with low information transfer rate. In Rehabilitation Robotics (pp. 1003–1008). Academic Press.

Rechy-Ramirez, E. J., Hu, H., & McDonald-Maier, K. (2012). Head movements based control of an intelligent wheelchair in an indoor environment. In *Proceedings of IEEE International Conference on Robotics and Biomimetics (ROBIO)* (pp. 1464-1469). IEEE. 10.1109/ROBIO.2012.6491175

Rechy-Ramirez, E. J., Marin-Hernandez, A., & Rios-Figueroa, H. V. (2017). Impact of commercial sensors in human computer interaction: a review. Journal of Ambient Intelligent Human Computing. doi:10.100712652-017-0568-3

Taher, F. B., Amor, N. B., & Jallouli, M. (2015). A multimodal wheelchair control system based on EEG signals and Eye tracking fusion. In *Innovations in Intelligent SysTems and Applications (INISTA), 2015 International Symposium on* (pp. 1-8). Academic Press.

Tamura, H., Manabe, T., Goto, T., Yamashita, Y., & Tanno, K. (2010). A study of the electric wheelchair hands-free safety control system using the surface-electromygram of facial muscles. *Intelligent Robotics and Applications LNCS*, *6425*, 97–104. doi:10.1007/978-3-642-16587-0_10

Thorp, E. B., Abdollahi, F., Chen, D., Farshchiansadegh, A., Lee, M. H., Pedersen, J. P., ... Mussa-Ivaldi, F. A. (2016). Upper body-based power wheelchair control interface for individuals with tetraplegia. *IEEE Transactions on Neural Systems and Rehabilitation Engineering*, *24*(2), 249–260. doi:10.1109/TNSRE.2015.2439240 PMID:26054071

Thulasidas, M., Guan, C., & Wu, J. (2006). Robust classification of EEG signal for brain-computer interface. *IEEE Transactions on Neural Systems and Rehabilitation Engineering*, *14*(1), 24–29. doi:10.1109/TNSRE.2005.862695 PMID:16562628

Tsui, C. S. L., Jia, P., Gan, J. Q., Hu, H., & Yuan, K. (2007). EMG-based hands-free wheelchair control with EOG attention shift detection. In *IEEE International Conference on Robotics and Biomimetics* (pp. 1266–1271). IEEE.

Wang, H., Li, Y., Long, J., Yu, T., & Gu, Z. (2014a). An asynchronous wheelchair control by hybrid EEG–EOG brain–computer interface. *Cognitive Neurodynamics*, *8*(5), 399–409. doi:10.100711571-014-9296-y PMID:25206933

Wang, H. T., Li, Y. Q., & Yu, T. Y. (2014b). Coordinated control of an intelligent wheelchair based on a brain-computer interface and speech recognition. *Journal of Zhejiang University-SCIENCE C*, *15*(10), 832–838. doi:10.1631/jzus.C1400150

Wei, L., & Hu, H. (2010). EMG and visual based HMI for hands-free control of an intelligent wheelchair. In *8th World Congress on Intelligent Control and Automation* (pp. 1027–1032). Academic Press. 10.1109/WCICA.2010.5554766

Xu, X. D., Zhang, Y., Luo, Y., & Chen, D. Y. (2013). Robust Bio-Signal based Control of an Intelligent Wheelchair. *Robotics*, *2*(4), 187–197. doi:10.3390/robotics2040187

Yokota, S., Hashimoto, H., Ohyama, Y., & She, J. H. (2009). Electric wheelchair controlled by human body motion interface. *IEEJ Transactions on Electronics Information Systems*, *129*(10), 1874–1880.

Zhang, R., Li, Y., Yan, Y., Zhang, H., Wu, S., Yu, T., & Gu, Z. (2016). Control of a Wheelchair in an Indoor Environment Based on a Brain–Computer Interface and Automated Navigation. *IEEE Transactions on Neural Systems and Rehabilitation Engineering*, *24*(1), 128–139. doi:10.1109/TNSRE.2015.2439298 PMID:26054072

ADDITIONAL READING

Kulkarni, A. D. (2001). *Computer vision and fuzzy-neural systems*. Upper Saddle River, NJ, USA: Prentice Hall PTR.

Liarokapis, F., Debattista, K., Vourvopoulos, A., Petridis, P., & Ene, A. (2014). Comparing interaction techniques for serious games through brain–computer interfaces: A user perception evaluation study. *Entertainment Computing*, *5*(4), 391–399. doi:10.1016/j.entcom.2014.10.004

Mendel, J. M. (1995). Fuzzy logic systems for engineering: A tutorial. *Proceedings of the IEEE*, *83*(3), 345–377. doi:10.1109/5.364485

Ross, T. J. (2009). *Fuzzy logic with engineering applications*. Chichester, West Sussex, UK: John Wiley & Sons.

Sörnmo, L., & Laguna, P. (2005). *Bioelectrical signal processing in cardiac and neurological applications*. Elsevier Academic Press.

Wu, Y., Zhang, B., Lu, J., & Du, K. L. (2011). Fuzzy Logic and Neuro-fuzzy Systems: A Systematic Introduction. *International Journal of Artificial Intelligence and Expert Systems*, *2*(2), 47–80.

Zadeh, L. A. (1999). Fuzzy sets as a basis for a theory of possibility. *Fuzzy Sets and Systems*, *100*, 9–34. doi:10.1016/S0165-0114(99)80004-9

KEY TERMS AND DEFINITIONS

Bi-Modal: In this chapter, this term is used to indicate that control modes use two modalities for issuing commands to the wheelchair: head movements and facial expressions.

Cognitiv® Suite of Emotiv: It is a suite provided by the Emotiv EPOC sensor. This suite recognized 14 thoughts: neutral, right, left, push, pull, lift, drop, rotate-left, rotate-right, rotate-clockwise, rotate-anticlockwise, rotate-forwards, rotate-reverse, and disappear.

Emotiv EPOC: A sensor that measures EEG activity from 14 saline electrodes. The Emotiv EPOC has one gyroscope and three suites: affectiv, expressiv, and cognitiv.

Expressiv® Suite of Emotiv: It is a suite provided by the Emotiv EPOC sensor. This suite detects facial expressions from the user (i.e., blink, right-wink, left-wink, look right/left, raise-brow, furrow-brow, smile, clench, right-smirk, left-smirk, and laugh).

Fuzzy Logic: Lotfi Zadeh introduced fuzzy logic in 1965. This technique is used to cope with data uncertainty. It involves a fuzzification process, fuzzy inference, and defuzzification process.

Human-Machine Interface: It is an interface, which provides a friendly, intuitive and transparent interaction between the human and the control system of any device.

Uni-Modal: In this chapter, this term is used to indicate that control modes use one modality for issuing commands to the wheelchair: either head movements or facial expressions.

Chapter 2

Innovative Features and Applications Provided by a Large-Area Sensor Floor

Axel Steinhage
Future-Shape GmbH, Germany

Christl Lauterbach
Future-Shape GmbH, Germany

Axel Techmer
Future-Shape GmbH, Germany

Raoul Hoffmann
Future-Shape GmbH, Germany

Miguel Sousa
Future-Shape GmbH, Germany

ABSTRACT

The following chapter describes new functions and applications that the authors have developed for the capacitive sensor system SensFloor® during the last five years. Some of these features have already found their way into the market while others are still in the research phase. From the first large-scale installations in 2012 up to now, the focus was put on applications for healthcare and ambient assisted living (AAL). However, as will be described later in this chapter, the authors have realized projects in many other domains as well, such as medical assessments, retail, security, and multimedia. The chapter starts out with a description of the underlying technology. After that, examples of the various domains of application are presented. The authors conclude with a summary and future research plans.

DOI: 10.4018/978-1-5225-5396-0.ch002

INTRODUCTION: A SENSOR SYSTEM BASED ON A LARGE-AREA CAPACITIVE FLOOR

SensFloor® is a large-area capacitive sensor floor, installable beneath all kind of flooring – invisible and discreet. Persons walking across the floor trigger signals, which are sent wirelessly to a transceiver. This system can calculate the number of persons on the floor, their direction and speed as well as detect falls. Several standard-interfaces are available for client-specific data analysis infrastructure. This sensor floor offers a variety of applications in health care, Ambient Assisted Living, home automation, security and multimedia. (Steinhage & Lauterbach, 2011). Although the result of these functions is obvious to the user, the sensor system itself remains invisible and does not interfere with the material or design of the floor covering in any way. In this respect, the technology presented here is an example of a new class of systems summarized under the expression *Ambient Assisted Living* (AAL). As this expression indicates, these systems' main purpose is to provide a wide range of Smart Home comfort functions, as well as to assist handicapped people within their daily life (Lauterbach, Steinhage & Techmer, 2013; Lauterbach & Steinhage, 2012). An example is the recognition of falls and the following automatic activation of an alarm call. Depending on the installation site (nursing home, hospital, senior residence, private home) and the existing infrastructure, these alarms are either transmitted to the nurses' ward and/or to their wireless phones, to care service providers or to the mobile phones of relatives or neighbours.

However, fall detection is just one of many possible functions in this domain. Based on the high spatial and temporal resolution of the sensor floor, the number and exact location of all people in the room can be recorded together with the velocity and direction of their movements. These data can be used to enhance peoples' comfort and safety e.g. by automatically adapting heating, air condition and lighting to the presence and whereabouts of people. Experts can detect changes in the health status of a person by comparing typical movement patterns over a long period. On a short time scale, automatically recording, visualizing and analysing the gait patterns of patients can increase the accuracy and objectivity of physiological assessments of the health status.

Standard technologies for movement recognition and emergency detection are based on conventional infrared-, ultrasonic- or radar motion sensors. The acquisition of peoples' exact location and movement tracking requires more advanced systems usually based on camera image processing or wireless identification tags. In addition to the technical problems brought about by varying lighting conditions, blind spots caused by furniture in the room and the still unsolved computational task of robustly detecting arbitrarily dressed persons in a video image, cameras installed in every room may interfere with the inhabitant's desire for privacy. The latter does also hold for wireless identification tags as they allow for a labelled behavioural protocol of individuals. In addition, systems like these are not ambient as they require a visible installation.

In particular, in the case of elderly or handicapped persons knowing their current location or behavioural status is crucial. Many wearable sensor systems have been developed for this purpose already. There exist alarm buttons, for instance, which can be pressed in emergencies. This requires, however, that the person is conscious and still able to press the button. Automatic sensors, such as accelerometers, can detect specific situations like a fall, for instance. These entire wearable sensors require, however, that the users carry them at all times, even in the bathroom. This may become cumbersome for the user and in addition, other people might directly associate these devices with disabilities of their carriers. The adequate operation, charging and maintenance of these devices often overburdens the growing group of patients that suffer from diseases like dementia.

SensFloor® relies on a much more direct way of detection: a grid of sensors underneath the flooring detects local capacitive changes in the environment brought about by humans walking or standing on the floor. By design, this method does not allow for an identification of individuals. However, the persons' location is acquired very accurately based on the spatial resolution of the sensor grid. By collecting and processing the sensor patterns over time, it is possible to assign movement trajectories to the persons, which allows for a variety of applications.

The capacitive measurement principle detects humidity and conductive materials. It has unique advantages compared to conventional pressure sensors, which, for instance, are used in fall detection mats or several other smart floor projects (Richardson, Paradiso, Leydon & Fernstrom, 2004; UKARI, 2013; Tarkett's *Floor in Motion*). By design, pressure sensors require a mechanical deformation such that only those falls can be detected that go along with some mechanical impact. A large portion of falls occurs without such an impact, e.g. when persons glide from the bed or toilet seat (see Eto, F., 2001; and references therein). Just like with wearable fall detection devices based on acceleration sensors (e.g. Wu, Zhao, Zhao, & Zhong, 2015) those type of falls are hard to detect by mechanical sensors. The capacitive flooring provides proximity sensing. Therefore, no pressure is necessary and instead of detecting the impact, SensFloor® recognises the result of the fall, i.e. the person lying on the floor. The capacitive sensing principle allows for the installation beneath not only flexible flooring, as it is the case in pressure-sensitive systems, but beneath all kind of flooring like fibreboards, parquet, laminate, or tiles. This results in a high mechanical stability, which is crucial for health care environments, where heavy beds are standing on the floor. However, the system is not restricted to the floor alone: it dissolves seamlessly into any large surfaces such as glass panels and walls, providing them with interactive functionality.

SYSTEM DESCRIPTION

The SensFloor® system consists of a textile-based sensor underlay with integrated capacitive sensor plates, power supply lines and radio modules (Lauterbach, Steinhage, Techmer, Jakob, Nowakowski & Pessenhofer, 2010; Lauterbach & Steinhage, 2009). The electronics modules measure the capacitance of the triangular sensor plates continuously. Whenever a person is standing on or walking across the floor, a sequence of location- and time-specific sensor events is generated (Lauterbach, Steinhage & Techmer, 2012). This information is transmitted wirelessly to a transceiver.

Based on data processing and pattern recognition, the position and movement direction of people is reconstructed. This allows for countless applications in the domains of security, healthcare, comfort, energy saving, entertainment, robotics and market research.

Figure 1 shows a schematic of the SensFloor® system. The textile underlay contains a grid of triangular shaped sensor plates. Eight triangles together with an electronics module in the centre form a sensor panel. Depending on the application, either the panels have a size of 50cm x 50cm or 50cm x 100cm (see Figure 1). This leads to a spatial sensor density of 32 or 16 plates per square meter. The sensor resolution of 16 plates per square meter is sufficient for human movement tracking, activity monitoring or fall detection in smart home or health care scenarios. When a body part comes into a range of about 10cm above a sensor plate, the electrical capacitance of that plate is slightly increased. This change in capacitance can be detected by the electronics module by means of a specific software that runs on the microcontroller of the module. A body lying on the floor activates a large area of adjoining sensor areas

Figure 1. Schematic of the SensFloor® system: The sensor underlay (left) contains radio modules (small brown squares) that measure the capacitance of the triangular sensor fields (grey). People walking across the floor trigger sensor signals, which are send wirelessly to the transceiver. The analyzed signals are further transmitted via standard interfaces to building automation systems, displays or indoor call systems.

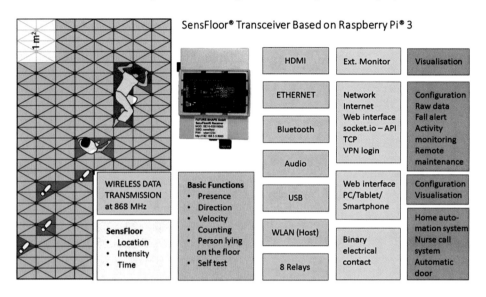

and therefore generates a characteristic sensor pattern with high capacitance values due to the small distance between body and sensor plates.

The SensFloor® underlay is produced using a roll-to-roll process as shown in Figure 2. For the textile underlay, a conductive fleece is used, which is laminated on a non-conductive fleece. This textile composite is structured by removing the conductive fleece within all areas intended to be electrically isolating. As a result, the textile represents a large-area, single-layer circuit board with power supply lines and sensor areas. In Figure 2, the variant with 16 sensor plates is shown. An example with 32 sensor plates is displayed in Figure 4. However, as the sensor pattern is structured by a computer controlled cutting plotter, alternative patterns can be easily realized.

For redundancy, the modules are connected to two supply and ground lines at opposite sides. A single connection to a 9-12 Volts switched power adapter at one corner or edge of the underlay is sufficient for powering all radio modules in the reel. For forming large sensor areas, the reels are installed side by side and their power supply lines care connected by means of conductive adhesive tape.

The radio modules broadcast sensor events together with a unique address that identifies the module and the sensor plate(s). Based on this information, the exact location of the event can be identified. The standard transmission frequency for Europe is 868.3 MHz but an adaptation to 920 MHz is possible. Flexibility is granted due to a unified and self-containing SensFloor® message format: in every message the origin and meaning of the message is unambiguously encoded in addition to a payload data packet. This allows any recipient to decide whether the message is for him, where it comes from and what to do with it.

Compared with other implementations of capacitive sensor flooring, where the sensor data is transmitted over wires woven into the textile underlay (Li, 1998), or from the sensor fields to the electronics in the floor's skirting (e.g. Lowe, 2013), the wireless transmission makes the realization of additional

Figure 2. Roll-to-roll production of the textile-based sensor underlay in a width of 1.50 meters, with integrated radio modules: In this case, the resolution of the sensor areas is 16 per square meter.

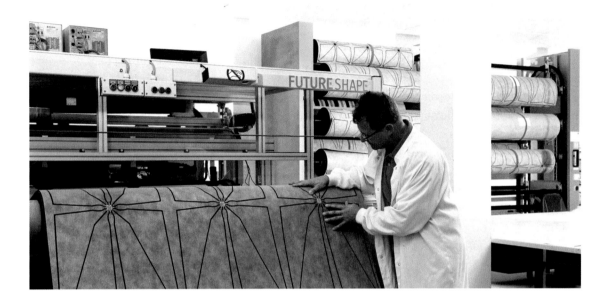

applications very easy: once the SensFloor® underlay is installed. The messages are received and interpreted by any wireless device that works on the same frequency. However, a proprietary protocol is used and the messages can be encrypted such that only authorized transceivers can decrypt them.

In the standard configuration, wireless messages are generated only when there is activity within the room. However, due to the high spatial density of the sensor plates in the underlay, a large number of messages is generated when many people walk across the floor. Although every single message is very short and the wireless bandwidth is high, it is, in principle, possible that some messages are lost due to collisions on the wireless channel. However, all applications of the SensFloor® system are based on evaluating whole populations of sensor events rather than single signals. Therefore, missing some events does not impair the overall function of the system and loosing messages is explicitly allowed. As the sender usually does not wait for an acknowledgement from the receiver, there is no protocol overhead and virtually no delay between the detection and the reception of a sensor signal. However, it is possible to define critical messages, such as a fall alarm, for instance, which require an acknowledgement by the receiver.

If required, bidirectional data transmission can be used to read the status of the floor modules (self-test), to reconfigure their transmission characteristics or to request the temperature of the modules, which is determined by the built-in temperature sensor on each module. With the latter, a temperature map of the entire floor is obtained. This can be used for maintenance and control of floor heating, as SensFloor® is compatible with these systems as well.

Many parameters of the modules, such as the detection sensitivity or the recalibration interval can be changed wirelessly even after installation under the flooring. In addition, a *bootloader* was added to the firmware of the modules allowing for an over-the-air update of the complete firmware without physical contact.

In a range of about 20 meters, the broadcasted messages are received by one or more radio transceivers that are mounted on the DIN rail in the electrical installation box of the apartment (see Figure 1 middle). This device is based on the widely known Raspberry Pi® embedded computer, which the authors equipped with an expansion board that contains the radio receiver and eight potential-free relays. By means of a web-server software on an SD-memory card in the Raspberry Pi®, the customer can configure the relays according to the functions, locations and devices that should be used (see Figure 1). As an example, stepping into the area besides the bed operates a relay that switches an orientation light at night.

By connecting the receiver to a local or cloud-based server through a secured VPN line, alarms and other information with relevance for the health status can be transmitted to authorized subscribers such as care services, relatives or medical experts.

By means of the potential-free relays, the basic functionality of SensFloor® can easily be integrated into any building automation infrastructure as the relays act like simple switches or pushbuttons. Higher-level functions are realized by using the standard interfaces of the Raspberry Pi®, such as LAN or WLAN (see Figure 1). Raw and pre-processed sensor data is accessible through a programming interface (API) which provides information such as number, location, direction and velocity of moving persons as well as events such as a fall.

In the following, the authors show a couple of application scenarios in detail.

Figure 3. Web-application to configure the functions on the SensFloor®: Through a simple click-and-point interface, the installer of the SensFloor® maps the ground plan of the sensitive floor (left) and associates locations such as rooms or the bedside area to functions such as presence- or fall-detection. The functions' status are associated to the state of the receiver's relays (right) by which appliances such as lamps, alarm devices or any other home-automation equipment are controlled. A live view of the activity and the events on the floor is also displayed in real time (left).

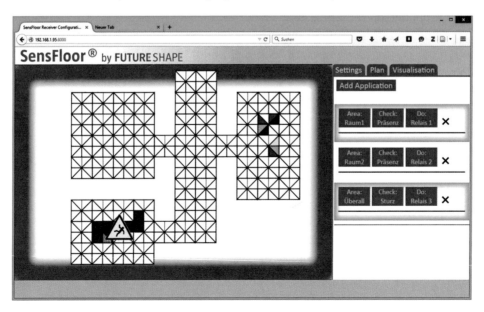

Figure 4. High resolution SensFloor underneath laminate (design floor panels): As the capacitive measurement principle is not dependent on pressure, even stone tiles as floor covering are possible. In the picture, the power supply connections made of conductive stripes are visible.

APPLICATIONS OF SENSFLOOR®

As mentioned already, one of the intrinsic characteristics of SensFloor® is the fact that the technology remains invisible to the user whereas the function is apparent. From the user's perspective, SensFloor® functions can be classified into several categories, such as Ambient Assisted Living, health care, medical assessments, safety and security, retail, research and multimedia. In the following, implementation examples for each of these domains are presented.

Ambient Assisted Living: SensFloor® in a Senior Residence

In 2015 VITAD'ORO in Bad Griesbach, Bavaria, Germany, presented a new individual concept of personal comfort and safety for a long and independent life at home. Within this project, accessible living concepts and communal facilities guarantee a high standard of living up to a ripe old age. The integrated clubhouse of this residence is the central service centre. It offers not only regular events for the residents, but also various leisure, sport, cultural, and service packages as well as individual ranges of care and service. In this application, the SensFloor® system provides a wide range of functions, which are individually adapted to the residents (Steinhage et al., 2014; Lauterbach et al., 2014).

Figure 5 shows the floorplan of the sample house with the SensFloor installation. The basic functions of the system combined with building automation and intrusion alarm are depicted in the floor plan: (1) fall detection, (2) control of the orientation light, (3) activity monitoring, (4) presence-controlled lighting, (5) localization of intruders, (6) leak-water detection. Available individually configurable add-on modules are (7) remote maintenance, (8) automatic doors, (9) presence-controlled energy saving, (10) prevention of the dementia patients' tendency to run away. Integrated into a KNX building automation system, detected events will trigger alarms indoor or be transferred to the central clubhouse of the residence. The general idea is to provide comfort functions to elderly residents while they are still able to lead an independent life. Once personal care is necessary, the associated assistive care functions are activated on the push of a button.

Figure 5. SensFloor functions in the individual house of a senior residence: AAL applications can be added to the comfort and security functions if needed.

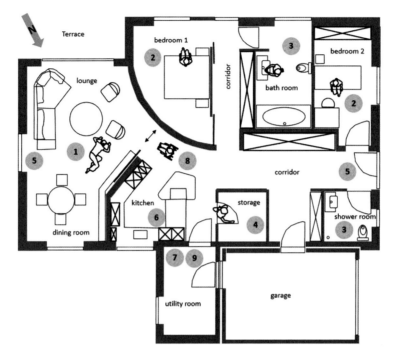

Professional Care: SensFloor® in a Nursing Home

Depending on the severity of their condition, patients suffering from dementia or prone to falling make great demands on their caretakers. The latter not only have to care and provide for their patients but frequently are required to pay an extra amount of attention e.g. if their charges have an increased need to move or are prone to falling or hurting themselves. For this reason, the operator of a new care home build 2012 in Pfaffenhoffen (France) made effective fall detection and prevention a special priority. The goal was not only to relieve carers but at the same time to allow residents a high degree of safety and freedom. Special attention was given to patients suffering from Alzheimer. They are not kept from wandering, but can move safely within their part of the building. The sensor floor was installed in all 70 rooms and bathrooms for fall detection and orientation light control. As soon as a fall is detected an alarm is triggered and the nurse is able to react immediately, avoiding that the person is lying helplessly on the floor for a longer time.

After this first large scale installation of SensFloor in 2012 which put the focus on fall prevention and –detection, many higher level functions have been realized based on the high spatial resolution of the sensor data. Monitoring the activity of persons, i.e. detecting and recording the number, exact location, movement and walking speed of people allows for completely new applications.

As described earlier, the SensFloor® receivers in the patients' rooms do not only control the orientation light and send alarms to the nurse call system by means of their built-in relays but can also deliver activity data via LAN to a central touch screen terminal in the ward. The status and recent events are displayed for all connected rooms on an intuitive web interface, which is again controlled by a Raspberry

Figure 6. SensFloor in a nursing home in France before (left) and after (right) installation: The implemented functions are orientation light (for fall prevention) and fall detection through the Ackermann nurse call system.

Figure 7. Ward terminal with touch screen interface to display current and recent events in the rooms equipped with SensFloor

Pi® computer. The user can touch the symbol of an individual room and obtain the current activity on the sensor floor. This way, a fall alarm can quickly be verified from the ward (Figure 7).

Further, the movement trajectories for selectable periods within the room during the last 24 to 48 hours are displayed when the corresponding room is selected (figure 8). As wandering movements especially during the night provide valuable information for carers concerning changes in the health status of patients, this information can help to optimize medication and individual therapy. All of the applications run in authorized and registered mobile web browsers as well such that doctors and care personnel can discuss the contents of the displays together with the patients in their room. This system is installed, for instance, in the senior residence *Am Schlossanger* in Hoehenkirchen, Germany, where ten apartments

Figure 8. Movement activity in the patient's room aggregated over several periods during the night; In this case, the frequent visits of the bathroom indicates nocturia, which can be medicated.

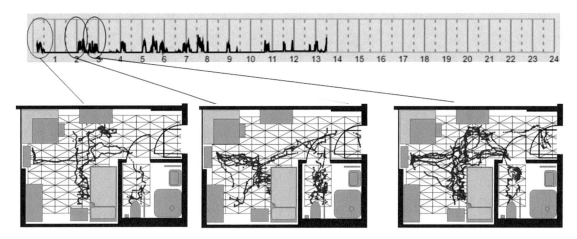

are equipped with SensFloor®. The work is supported by the EU Horizon 2020 project UNCAP (n.d.), which makes use of solutions and technologies developed in previous research projects to realize an open, scalable and privacy-savvy ICT infrastructure designed to help aging people live independently while maintaining and improving their lifestyle. As a part of this project, the potential of SensFloor® in reducing the number of falls is being investigated.

Medical Assessments: SensFloor® for Gait Analysis

The sensitive floor is also applied to support medical assessments (Hoffmann et al., 2016) and to quantify the success of rehabilitation measures. Figure 9 shows an installation at the emergency ward of the Klinikum Frankfurt/Oder, Germany. In this case, a 6m by 1m high-resolution underlay is used to record gait patterns of patients in order to obtain an initial assessment of their physical ability. Visual inspection of a patient's gait is a well-known part of a neurological assessment as the symmetry, speed, uniformity and peculiarity of the steps provide valuable information about a person's health status to an expert (Brach et al., 2005; Verghese et al., 2009; Hausdorf et al., 2001). With the help of SensFloor®, these parameters are recorded during a patient's walk along the corridor automatically.

Unlike other devices, which are pressure sensitive and must be placed on top of the floor covering (e.g. Strideway™ or GAITRite®), the SensFloor® system is invisible and the floor's visual and haptic characteristic remains natural and unchanged. This makes the patients walk in their natural way without changing their steps according to a special and uncommon flooring.

Figure 10 shows some examples of typical gait patterns together with an indication of known diseases of the test persons. The blue line is the trajectory of the person's centre of mass which is calculated from the capacitance values that are produced by the steps (coloured circles). As the analysis and visualization of the gait pattern is realized as local web application running on a Raspberry Pi® computer, the doctor can either display the result on the provided touch screen terminal or on his own mobile device that is connected via Wi-Fi to the Raspberry Pi®. The patterns can be printed and stored so that parameters of the same patient can be compared before and after a rehabilitation program.

Figure 9. A 6 by 1 meter high-resolution installation of SensFloor® in a corridor of the emergency ward of the Klinikum Frankfurt/Oder, Germany (left) serves for the initial gait pattern assessment of patients. After reinstallation of the floor covering, the corridor looks like before and is used in an ordinary way (right). During gait analysis in this normal environment, patients show their individual natural walking behavior.

Research: SensFloor® in Living Labs

In various living labs, researchers develop AAL applications based on SensFloor® data. Here, the transparent programming interface (API) facilitates the integration of high-precision location- and movement data provided by the sensitive floor into research platforms with various other sensor modalities. In the German government funded project CogAge (BMBF FKZ 16SV7311), for instance, the behaviour of a person living in an apartment equipped with SensFloor and other sensor systems is adaptively analysed in order to predict changes in the health status from changes in the inhabitant's daily routines. Unlike camera systems or RFID tags, the sensitive floor respects the privacy of the user as no pictures or personal data are recorded.

In other research projects, interactive applications, so called *serious games*, are developed which aim at training mental and physical abilities of elderly persons in an entertaining and unobtrusive way (e.g. project SolSEns (2017) at IMT Atlantique in Brest, France). In some of these applications, an area equipped with SensFloor acts like a giant touchpad that is operated by walking between locations or along trajectories indicated on a screen. In the same way as with the gait analysis described before, performance parameters recorded during the sessions provide quantitative information about the success of rehabilitation and training measures.

Applications Beyond AAL and Health Care: SensFloor®
for Counting and Customer Flow Measurement

Apart from AAL, health care and medical applications, SensFloor® delivers valuable data for counting and tracking people to control heating, air-condition and illumination for energy saving and in retail to

Figure 10. Examples of real gait patterns of patients suffering from the indicated diseases: The blue line is the trajectory of the person's center of mass calculated based on the SensFloor® activity signals that are produced by the steps (colored circles). The medical expert can detect and compare asymmetries (second panel), lacking uniformity (first and fourth panel), peculiarities, and very low velocity (third panel) based on the images obtained during an initial assessment and after rehabilitation.

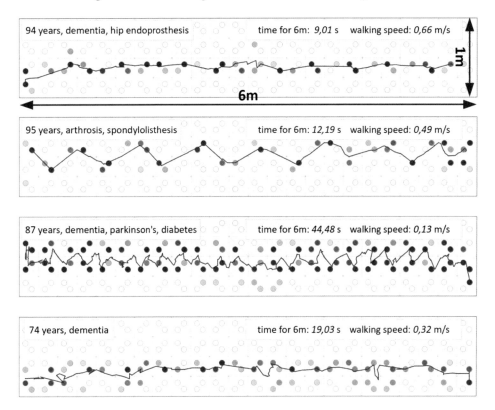

analyse customer flows. Figure 12 shows the interface for this purpose. On a touch screen terminal the user can select an origin and a destination within a ground plan and the recorded trajectories of people having walked along these pathways within a certain period are displayed. By means of this information, conclusions about the attractiveness of regions can be drawn as well as hints on how to improve ergonomics and safety of passages on mass events or on how to make facility management more efficient (Steinhage & Lauterbach, 2008). The data is obtained and analysed without interfering with people's privacy, as the floor, by design, cannot determine the identity of people.

By making these anonymous data available to authorized users over a cloud-based platform, SensFloor® becomes an IoT (Internet of Things) system. Such systems are typically embedded in the environment and continuously provide sensor data about parameters of their surroundings. A local or cloud-based server can aggregate and analyse customer flow data from many different locations such as points of sales in a shopping mall, or different entries and exists at a large public event.

When doorways are equipped with SensFloor®, another application provides additional comfort: using a piece of SensFloor® to control an automatic door can contribute to energy saving: opening the door only for a robot, a wheelchair or a walking person whose movement trajectory indicates the intention to pass the door prevents its unintended opening. This puts the SensFloor® system in contrast to

Figure 11. Living lab at the Institut méditeranéen des métiers de la longévité (I2ML) in Nîmes, France equipped with 50 m² of SensFloor. Data from the floor is integrated with data from other sensor systems to analyze the behavior of test persons and to improve assistive technology for daily life. (Image: Fondation Partenariale I2ML)

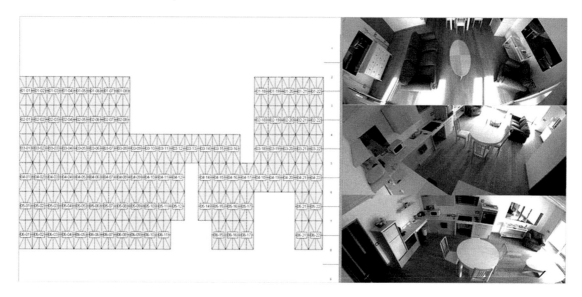

movement detectors that react already whenever someone just enters the range of the detector without intending to pass the doorway.

Applications Beyond AAL and Health Care: SensFloor® for Entertainment

Some of the first customers of the system came from the domain of trade fairs and entertainment. Here, SensFloor® equips an installation with interactivity: the visitors control illumination and multimedia as they move through the site (see e.g. the project *Breaking the Surface*, by Vasnjik, 2014).

Figure 13 shows some examples from this domain. The advantage of separating the sensor data acquisition from the data analysis becomes obvious: without changing the sensor underlay a variety of different applications runs simultaneously or one after the other on the same surface.

CONCLUSION AND OUTLOOK

The authors have presented SensFloor® as an example of intelligent systems, which are integrated invisibly into our environment. The capacitive proximity measurement technology transforms the floor into a large sensor surface and makes use of the fact that people spend most of their waking lives in direct contact with the floor. This way, the behaviour of the user generates a continuous stream of sensor data from which the behavioural state is reconstructed. As the sensor is unobtrusively embedded in the surrounding, this behavioural state is not influenced by the presence of the sensor system itself. This unique feature is supported even more by the fact that the sensor does not impose any specific characteristics on the workspace: any conventional floor covering can be used, the receivers can be hidden anywhere in the

Figure 12. Touch interface for displaying visitor flows: The top panel shows the number and trajectories of all persons who walked in an area between four locations A,B,C and D within a 48 hour period (top panel). Selecting by touch a time interval and a sequence (here from B to A), only those pathways are displayed (red lines in bottom panel).

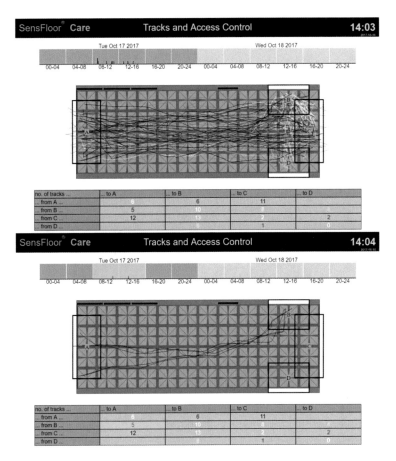

room and no data-cables have to be installed. Flexibility is also in the functions and thus in the various domains of application, some of which have been presented within this chapter. As demonstrated, some applications offer enhanced functionality compared to already existing technology such as the intelligent intrusion alarm or the efficient control of automatic doors, for instance. In particular, the AAL- and health care applications allow for completely new functions such as the long-term activity monitoring or gait analysis using the sensor floor.

Regarding the recent advances in the domains of *Internet of Things*, *Quantified Self*, *Deep Learning* and *Artificial Intelligence*, the SensFloor® system provides ideal characteristics as a source of large amounts of data that are directly associated with our daily living. This topic is addressed in the aforementioned research project CogAge, where the detection of deviations from a previously learned behavioural profile serves as indicator for a changing health status of elderly people. In the future, this principle will be generalized to analyse and predict behaviour of groups of people. In retail applications, for instance, it will not only be possible to quantify the attractiveness of points of sales in real time but to detect preferred pathways over longer periods.

Figure 13. Multimedia, games, arts and advertising campaigns based on SensFloor®: Sensor areas are shaped like piano keys and a wireless receiver generates MIDI signals for a synthesizer (upper left). Circle-shaped sensor fields serve as input for the jump-and-run game "Hopathon" during an entertainment event in Abu Dhabi (upper right image: 3Monkeys company). In Oslo, the Scandinavian Design Group and the company Lundin realized an interactive arts installation where objects lower from the ceiling depending on visitors' locations detected by SensFloor® (lower left image: The Scandinavian Design Group). During an advertising campaign for the company Netflix, visitors of the shopping mall Les 4 Temps in Paris activated videos by stepping on a staircase equipped with SensFloor® (lower right image: companies Biborg and Clear Channel).

Further, the analysis of walking patterns will be refined in order to extract additional parameters that are characteristic for the health status of persons. As the number and size of data sets increase, methods of deep learning will be applied to investigate whether there are hidden correlations between walking patterns and parameters other than health status, e.g. age or gender.

On the technical side, the processes of installation, mapping and remote maintenance of SensFloor® will become more facile. For example, a new mapping procedure is currently being developed which allows the installer to photograph QR-codes of the IDs of sensor patches by means of a smartphone right after installation. From these IDs, the mapping of sensor addresses to real world coordinates is automatically generated.

As conclusion, the authors believe that the future will provide many more innovative applications of the SensFloor® system in research and technology.

REFERENCES

Brach, J. S., Berlin, J. E., VanSwearingen, J. M., Newman, A. B., & Studenski, S. A. (2005). Too much or too little step width variability is associated with a fall history in older persons who walk at or near normal gait speed. *Journal of Neuroengineering and Rehabilitation, 2*(1), 1. doi:10.1186/1743-0003-2-21 PMID:16042812

CogAge project. (n.d.). *German government-funded project 2015-2018.* Retrieved from https://www. technik-zum-menschen-bringen.de/projekte/cogage

Eto, F. (2001). Causes of Falls in the Elderly. *Japan Medical Association Journal: JMAJ, 44*(7), 299–305.

GAITRite® gait analysis mat. (n.d.). Retrieved from http://www.gaitrite.com

Hausdorff, J. M., Rios, D. A., & Edelberg, H. K. (2001). Gait variability and fall risk in community-living older adults: A 1-year prospective study. *Archives of Physical Medicine and Rehabilitation, 82*(8), 1050–1056. doi:10.1053/apmr.2001.24893 PMID:11494184

Hoffmann, R., Lauterbach, C., Techmer, A., Conradt, J., & Steinhage, A. (2016). Recognising gait patterns of people in risk of falling with a multi-layer perceptron. In *Information Technologies in Medicine* (pp. 87–97). Springer. doi:10.1007/978-3-319-39904-1_8

Lauterbach, C., Glaser, R., Savio, D., Schnell, M., Weber, W., Kornely, S., & Stöhr, A. (2005). A self-organizing and fault-tolerant wired peer-to-peer sensor network for textile applications. In *Engineering self-organizing applications* (pp. 256-266). Springer-Verlag Berlin Heidelberg.

Lauterbach, C., & Steinhage, A. (2009). Large-area smart textiles. In Technical Textiles 4/09. IBP International Business Press Publisher.

Lauterbach, C., & Steinhage, A. (2012). A large-area sensor system for Ambient Assisted Living. *Toward Optimal Healing Environments: Proc. of Symposium on Assistive Systems for Social, Personal, and Health Interaction 2010/2011*, 59-63.

Lauterbach, C., Steinhage, A., & Techmer, A. (2012). *Large-area wireless sensor system based on smart textiles. In Proc. of the 9th International Multi-Conference on Systems, Signals & Devices, SSD'12.* Chemnitz, Germany: IEEE publications.

Lauterbach, C., Steinhage, A., & Techmer, A. (2013). A large-area sensor system underneath the floor for Ambient Assisted Living applications. In Pervasive and Mobile Sensing and Computing for Healthcare (pp. 69-87). Springer Verlag. doi:10.1007/978-3-642-32538-0_3

Lauterbach, C., Steinhage, A., & Techmer, A. (2014). Ambient Assisted Living Concept Based on a Sensitive Floor. *Proc. of the 9th IEEE Int. Symposium on Medical Measurements and Applications MeMeA.*

Lauterbach, C., Steinhage, A., Techmer, A., Jakob, M. M., Nowakowski, C., & Pessenhofer, W. (2010). Large-area smart textiles. Word Journal of Engineering, 7(2), 266-271.

Li, S. (1998). Hayashi, a.robot navigation in outdoor environments by using GPS information and panoramic views. *Proc. of International Conference on Intelligent Robots and Systems, 1*, 570-575.

LoweC. (2013). Retrieved from http://telecareaware.com/smart-flooring-that-can-simplify-alerting/

Richardson, R., Paradiso, J., Leydon, K., & Fernstrom, M. (2004). Z-tiles: Building blocks for modular pressure-sensing. *Proc of Conf. on Human Factors in Computing Systems Chi04*, 1529-1532.

SolSEns. (2017). *Sol Sensitif pour Analyse Cognitive et Actimétrique*. Brest, France: IMT Atlantique.

Steinhage, A., & Lauterbach, C. (2011). SensFloor® and NaviFloor®: Large-area sensor systems beneath Your Feet. In Ambient Intelligence and Smart Environments, Trends and Perspectives. IGI Global.

Steinhage, A., & Lauterbach, C. (2008). Monitoring movement behaviour by means of a large-area proximity sensor array in the floor. *Proc. of the 2nd Workshop on Behaviour Monitoring and Interpretation (BMI 2008). 31st German Conference on Artificial Intelligence (KI2008)*, 15-27.

Steinhage, A., Lauterbach, C., Schmitmeier, H., & Plischke, H. (2014). Erste Seniorenresidenz mit ganzheitlichem AAL Konzept. *Proc. of the 7. Deutscher AAL-Kongress 2014*. Retrieved from http://www.tekscan.com

Tarkett Floor in Motion. (2018). Retrieved from http://www.floorinmotion.com/en

UKARI project. (2013). Retrieved from http://open-ukari.nict.go.jp/Ukari-Project-e.html

UNCAP. (n.d.). *EU Horizon 2020 project 2014-2017*. Retrieved from http://www.uncap.eu/

Vasnjik, F. (2014). *Breaking the Surface – Responsive 'ocean' of acrylic actuators*. Retrieved from http://www.creativeapplications.net/openframeworks/breaking-the-surface/

Verghese, J., Holtzer, R., Lipton, R. B., & Wang, C. (2009). Quantitative gait markers and incident fall risk in older adults. *The Journals of Gerontology. Series A, Biological Sciences and Medical Sciences*, 64(8), 896–901. doi:10.1093/gerona/glp033 PMID:19349593

Wu, F., Zhao, H., Zhao, Y., & Zhong, H. (2015). Development of a Wearable-Sensor-Based Fall Detection System. *Int. Journal of Telemedicine and Applications*.

KEY TERMS AND DEFINITIONS

Ambient Assisted Living (AAL): Research field for evaluating technology and services to allow elderly or people in need of care to stay longer in their private homes instead of moving to nursing homes.

Capacitive Sensor: Sensor that measures an electrical property of matter even from a distance. Certain materials like metals, water, or body parts have a high capacitance.

Fall Detection: Recognizing a fall from characteristic sensor information.

Gait Pattern: Visual representation of a sequence of steps of a person.

Internet of Things (IoT): Aim to connect distributed objects with the internet in order to collect or access information about the local environment of these objects.

Living Lab: Apartment equipped with sensors that serves as test environment for investigating the interaction between people and technology in realistic living situations.

Medical Assessment: Observation of the physical or behavioral characteristics of a person in order to classify the health status.

Movement Trajectory: Graphical representation of the walking path of people.

Pressure Sensor: Device that measures a mechanical indentation caused by force or weight.

Proximity Sensing: Measuring properties of objects from a distance.

Redundancy: The fact that instances of important data elements or physical objects exist multiple times such that the loss of one element does not impair the overall function.

Textile Underlay: Polyester fleece with built-in electronics modules for capacitance sensing underneath the floor covering.

Wireless Transmission: Cables are not required for exchanging sensor and configuration data.

Chapter 3

Reassessing Underlying Spatial Relations in Pedestrian Navigation:
A Comparison Between Sketch Maps and Verbal Descriptions

Jia Wang
University of Greenwich, UK

Rui Li
University at Albany (SUNY), USA & Sichuan Fine Arts Institute, China

ABSTRACT

This chapter assesses underlying spatial relations for pedestrian wayfinding by examining navigational directions given in both forms of sketch maps and verbal descriptions. An experiment was conducted to investigate characteristics of navigational directions provided by participants in the form of sketch maps and verbal descriptions. The authors were specifically interested in the landmarks and spatial relationships such as route topology, linear order relation, and relative orientation extracted from the navigational directions. A new ontological approach to sketch and verbal interpretations was adopted for spatial analysis. The results pointed to the advantage of including sketch components into pedestrian navigation systems over solely turn-by-turn instructions. In addition, the results showed the differences between visual and verbal directions, which suggest the necessity of having different levels of directions for giving specific types of navigational instructions.

DOI: 10.4018/978-1-5225-5396-0.ch003

INTRODUCTION

Spatial knowledge is important for pedestrian navigation and has strong correlation to wayfinding success in an urban environment. Better spatial knowledge contributes to improved understanding of a walking environment, which consequently increases travel confidence and potentially allows more active walking (Wang & Worboys, 2016). As Dalton (2003) suggested, if a person has a good knowledge of a space, he or she can presumably find his or her way with fewer errors and better configurational knowledge of distance and direction; he or she can also take shortcuts because the person knows which direction to go at a decision point.

Nowadays, most pedestrians rely heavily on navigation devices for wayfinding. Existing pedestrian navigation systems focus mostly on the instructions given in the form of turn-by-turn fashion. These navigation systems can lead users to efficiently reach destinations without getting lost (most of the time), but their increased use also has a negative impact on spatial knowledge acquisition. Lynch (1960, p. 3) suggested that wayfinding requires "a consistent use and organization of definite sensory cues from the external environment". By doing that, wayfinders gradually build the mental images of their traveled spaces. Existing studies suggest that the reliance on the existing navigation systems may detach people from surroundings, which could degrade their mental representations because of lacking active navigation.

This study investigates the spatial knowledge externalized in both sketch maps and verbal directions using newly developed methodology after our previous collaborative effort (Wang & Li, 2013). In the current study, we empirically assess pedestrian navigational instructions given in the visual form of sketch maps and in the verbal forms of directions from two aspects: landmarks and their spatial relations including topology, distance and orientation through a new means of sketch and verbal interpretation. The purpose is to demonstrate the advantage and reliability of adding sketch components for navigation over sole sequence-based verbal descriptions. Based on the authors' previous collaboration (Wang & Li, 2013), this study furthers the understanding of how sketch maps reflect pedestrians' route and survey knowledge, as well as provides the implications to the design of maps for navigation. Furthermore, the study points out the characteristics of spatial information embedded in both visual and verbal forms and their differences due to levels of details (Brunyé, Taylor & Worboys, 2007). Consequently, our investigation continues on spatial relations to facilitate orientation during wayfinding.

The rest of the paper is structured as follows. First, we introduce the background and related work that shed light on the current study followed by the design and procedure of our experiment. The method of sketch and verbal interpretation is introduced afterwards. Finally, we present the results of the comparison of sketch maps and verbal descriptions, before concluding with a discussion and future work.

BACKGROUND

We review related work in three aspects: sequenced-based (or turn-by-turn) navigational directions and spatial knowledge acquisition, sketch maps and cognitive maps, and existing approaches to sketch interpretation and representation.

Giving Directions

Almost all directions given by existing pedestrian navigation systems are sequence-based, which facilitate the ease of navigation but greatly degrade a person's development of their spatial knowledge. The problem is that when a pedestrian follows a specific route guidance, the configurational understanding of his/her walking environment is not acquired. For example, empirical investigations suggest that directions generated by navigation devices hinter users from learning their immediate surroundings and impact their acquisition of spatial knowledge at the configurational level (Parush, Ahuvia, & Erev, 2007). The lack of configurational knowledge can cause disorientation when a navigation device does not work (Krüger, Aslan, & Zimmer, 2004). Such impact is also suggested in other studies (see Bertel *et al.*, 2017; Ishikawa *et al.*, 2008; Wang & Worboys 2016; Willis *et al.*, 2009).

Sketch Maps and Cognitive Maps

Cognitive maps are mental models that encompass internal processes enabling people to acquire and operate spatial information about the world (Downs & Stea, 1973). Different from traditional cartographic maps that are developed through a data-driven approach through which a large amount of data is represented for various purposes. Cognitive maps, however, are developed by humans through their cognitive and perceptual sensors. Cognitive maps are developed from coarse, fragmented, and distorted spatial knowledge and refine over time (Klippel *et al.*, 2005). Sketch maps have been used as externalizations of cognitive maps to study how people internally represent their local cities (e.g., Lynch, 1960). Kim and Penn (2004) stated that sketches provided useful data such as the mix point, line and areal features including the order of cues along routes or the order of segments and turns along routes. Recent studies (Schwering *et al.*, 2014; Wang & Schwering, 2015) on the alignment of sketch and conventional metric maps demonstrated the feasibility of using sketch maps as a reliable source to visualize survey knowledge of a local urban environment. Wang and Li (2013) suggested that navigational instructions given in the form of sketch maps contain fewer errors in giving initial walking directions and convey more global orientation information compared with turn-by-turn verbal descriptions.

Sketch Interpretation and Representation

The way humans perceive space, in the process of developing cognitive maps, is different from the way space is measured for traditional map production. Tversky (2005) outlined the differences. According to her, space is primary in traditional maps and the geometry of features is measured and located in the space; for humans, spatial objects are primary and they have spatial relations to each other with respect to certain reference frames. Therefore, a map metaphor such as a sketch map of an internal cognitive representation of space is misleading in some ways (Kuipers, 1978; Taylor & Tversky, 1992). Sketch maps are often schematized, simplified, categorical, and consisting of numerous distortion errors (Montello, 2005; Tversky, 2003, 2005). Since people do not perceive absolute locations and quantitative relations but rather relative locations and qualitative relations (Kuipers, 1978; Lynch, 1960; Montello, 2001), sketch maps are qualitative other than quantitative in nature. Thus, interpretation and representation of sketch maps should be qualitative as well.

One of the early and notable work of sketch representation, *spatial-query-by-sketch*, from Egenhofer (1997), was founded on a mathematical model of spatial relations and their relaxations. Egenhofer suggested a sketch representation by using five types of spatial relations, which were the coarse topological relations based on the 9-intersection model, the detailed topological relations and their refinements, and the coarse and detailed projection-based cardinal directional relations. Inspired by this approach, researchers developed a qualitative framework of detecting, extracting and representing relevant sketch aspects (Chipofya *et al.*, 2015; Sahib *et al.*, 2017; Schwering *et al.*, 2014).

Wang and Worboys (2017) recently develop a well-defined hierarchical structure to which sketch map entities handled during interpretation can be assigned at different ontological levels. This ontological contribution helps to establish a common sketch interpretation by linking distinctive sketch entities from the lowest material levels to the highest real-world representational level.

METHODS

In this section, we introduce the design and procedure of our experiment as well as the methodology adopted for the interpretation of sketch maps and verbal descriptions.

Experiment

Participants familiar with the study area were asked to give directions for new visitors to reach a destination. The design of this experiment was to simulate the daily situation of getting from one place to the other.

Materials

One of the authors' uptown campus located in Albany, New York was selected as the study area. This campus hosts the majority of student classes and activities. Another reason to choose the uptown campus was because its environment and structure were so symmetrical that new members of the campus community often get disoriented or lost very easily. The uptown campus is located between two almost paralleled streets, Washington Ave. and Western Ave. However, almost all local bus lines operate through Washington Ave. next to a big open plaza called Collins Circle. In this case, most students who utilize bus to get to the uptown campus would need to reach their destinations on foot through the symmetrical environment. The study area is at the environmental scale according to the relative scale of space (Montello, 1993). This indicates that the spatial knowledge of this area could not be acquired at a given vantage point at a given time. Instead, a person has to utilize locomotion and cognitive maps to develop his or her spatial knowledge.

We designed the tasks in this experiment to resemble the experiences one can have on campus involving pedestrian wayfinding. Specific tasks include giving directions in two different formats: one in the form of sketch maps drawn on blank papers and one in the form of verbal descriptions typed on a portable computer. Participants were asked to give directions from the bus stop to the physical education (PE) building. Both locations were of particular familiarity to students as they utilize them on a daily basis. The participants were asked to use any spatial entities or information available to help a person who is visiting the campus for the first time. As shown in Figure 1 (left), the symbols indicate the bus stop, the PE building, as well as other important academic buildings on the uptown campus where the experiment took place.

Participants

So far, a total number of six participants (2 males and 4 female students) were recruited in this experiment. They were recruited through on-campus flyer. Only students who indicated that they were familiar with the campus were allowed to participate. Each participant received eight dollars as reimbursement.

Procedure

All experiments were carried out on a one-on-one basis in the author's laboratory. The experimenter introduced the purpose of the experiment to the participants at the beginning of this experiment. After giving content, the experimenter started the tasks of the experiment. Each participant was asked to assume that one friend, who was a new visitor to the uptown campus, needed directions for walking from the bus stop to the PE building to visit him/her. Participants were told to first give directions in the format of sketch maps and verbal descriptions afterwards. When a participant completed a sketch map on a blank piece of paper, he/she was then directed to type his/her verbal description on a computer. Each participant was then further directed to fill in their personal information such as age, sex, and major. Each participant completed the experiment within 30 minutes.

Figure 1. Area of uptown campus selected for the experiment: On the left, the line starts from the bus stop (triangle) and goes to the P.E. building (star). On the right, one participant drew the route from the bus stop to the P.E. Building with labeled university buildings.

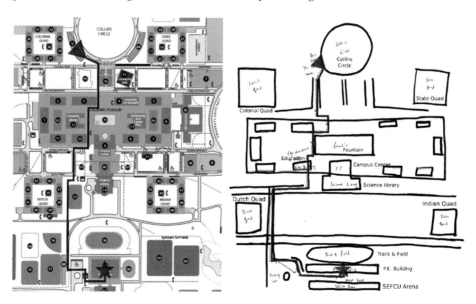

Sketch Map Interpretation

The hierarchical structure and formal representation spaces (Figure 2) proposed by Wang and Worboys (2017) were adapted for sketch map interpretation in our study. The bottom-level textual and graphic primitives (letters and arcs) support the sketch image and real-world representations at higher levels. The middle level of sketch image representation addresses only the visual features without making use of any context about the depicted reality. A sketch map at this level is interpreted as a collection of user-drawn objects that are similar to glyphs defined in CogSketch (Forbus *et al.*, 2011). The top level of real-world representation deals with real-world objects drawn as sketch entities using domain-specific knowledge. We interpret and represent our sketch maps only at the top level because the entities (spatial object and spatial relationships) at this level reflect participants' spatial knowledge acquired from navigation. A generic ontological view of the formal real-world representation at the top level is shown in Figure 3.

*Spatial object*s are defined as a collection of sequential objects such as walking routes and non-sequential objects such as individual buildings, traffic signs, and districts. Spatial objects represent either artificial or natural entities in reality, which are the cognitive reference points (Tversky, 2000) externalized on sketch maps due to perceptual salience, functional significance and their relevance to sketching tasks (Wang, 2014).

Figure 2. Structure and categorization of sketch interpretation and representation proposed by Wang and Worboys (2017)

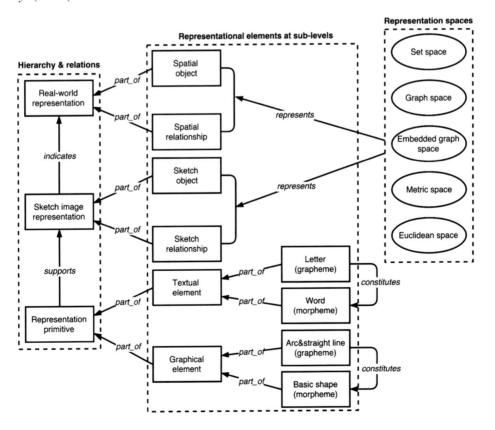

Spatial relationships are pair-wise relationships calculated between spatial objects using the five representation spaces shown in Figure 2. These spaces are chosen because they provide a tiered formal representation of sketch maps based on standard mathematical structures. The set-, graph-, embedded graph-, and metric- based spaces provide underling structures for the Euclidean space. The set space allows identification and classification of spatial objects. In the abstract graph space, we can represent how spatial objects are connected to each other using nodes (as spatial objects) and edges (as connections). When the abstract graph space is embedded in a 2-dimensional Euclidean space, the concept of 'face' becomes available so we can represent topological relations such as *intersection* and *insideness* between spatial objects. In the metric space, the concepts of 'distance' and 'face' are both available. Distance is necessary for defining positional relations such as *at*, *adjacent*, and *far away* between spatial objects. When a direction is given, linear order relations among spatial objects can also be reasoned based on positional relations. Euclidean space is a highly organized space. It brings richer geometries and well-defined relationships (topology, distance and orientation) that can act upon point-, line- and area- based spatial objects.

We discuss the calculi used to compute spatial relations in detail as follows.

Route Topology

Route topology refers to both connectivity and orientation of route segments and can be computed in the embedded planar graph space. Route segments extracted from sketch maps are oriented and thus they can be considered as dipoles (Schlieder, 1995). A *dipole* is an oriented line segment and determined by a start and an end point. The orientation of a dipole is pointed from its start point to its end point. A dipole defined by a start point A and an end point B is written as $\vec{d}_{AB}$.

Figure 3. A generic ontological view of the top level formal real-world representation (Wang & Worboys 2017): IAO is the information artefact ontology proposed by Smith et al. (2013).

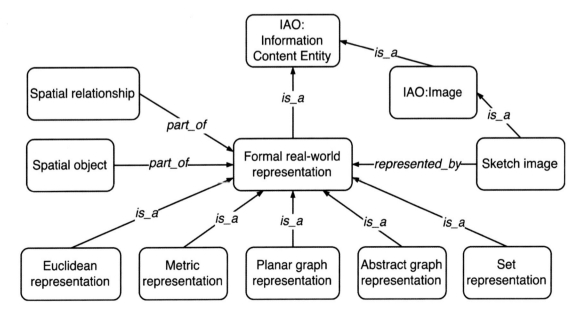

Similar to our previous work (Wang & Li, 2013), we used the coarse-grained Dipole Relation Algebra (DRA$_c$) proposed by Dylla and Moratz (2005) to analyze route topology. DRA$_c$ represents how two dipoles $\overrightarrow{d}_{AB}$ and $\overrightarrow{d}_{CD}$ are connected with the restriction that no three disjointed points are collinear. So, the base relations of DRA$_c$ between the start and end point of one dipole and the other are only the possible combinations of *right*, *left*, *start* and *end*. When DRA$_c$ was applied to sketch map interpretation, $\overrightarrow{d}_{AB}$ and $\overrightarrow{d}_{CD}$ were defined by two route segments with walking direction indicating their orientation. DRA$_c$ was calculated individually for each sketch map because routes drawn by different participants were varied.

Linear Order Relation

In the metric space, Allen's (1983) Interval Algebra (IA) is applied to represent and reason order relations based on distance. IA was proposed for describing the mereotopological relation between two intervals. These two intervals are defined by a start and an end point on a unidirectional time line, e.g., a time interval A is represented as a tuple of A$_s$ as its start point and A$_e$ as its end point. There are in total 13 base relations (before, before inverse, meets, meets inverse, overlaps, overlaps inverse, starts, starts inverse, during, during inverse, finishes, finishes inverse, equals) derived from comparing the start and end point of pair-wise intervals. Table 1 gives examples and definitions of the seven non-inverse relations of IA calculus.

A route in a sketch map is projected as an axis and spatial objects along the route are projected as intervals to the axis. Figure 4 shows how IA calculus can be applied to sketches: each areal spatial object A, B and C is first represented by a minimum bounding box and then projected to the route to form an interval. The linear order relations of the three objects along the route is *C o B o A*.

Table 1. Example and definition of IA.

Relation	Description	Example	Definition
b	A before B	AAA BBB	$A_e < B_s$
m	A meets B	AAA BBB	$A_e = B_s$
o	A overlaps B	AAA BBB	$A_s < B_s < A_e \wedge A_e < B_e$
d	A during B	AAA BBBBBB	$A_s > B_s \wedge A_e < B_e$
s	A starts B	AAA BBBBBB	$A_s = B_s \wedge A_e < B_e$
f	A finishes B	AAA BBBBBB	$A_s > B_s \wedge A_e = B_e$
eq	A equals B	AAA BBB	$A_s = B_s \wedge A_e = B_e$

Figure 4. The IA calculus is used to represent the linear order of three spatial objects along a route on a sketch map.

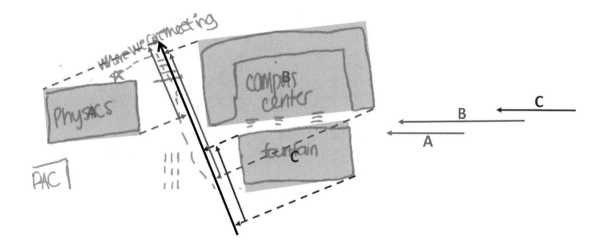

Orientation Relation

We calculated the relative orientation of landmarks with respect to adjacent route segments in the Euclidean space. *Landmarks* are non-path-like atomic elements in sketch maps. Different from Lynch who defined landmarks as point features (Lynch, 1960), we allow landmarks to be point or areal features depending on how landmarks are drawn and which method is used for representation.

The representation of orientation relation consists of six binary relations (Sahib *et al.*, 2015): *left_of*, *right_of*, *crosses*, *crossed_by*, *front_of*, and *back_of* based on the Left-Right (LR) calculus defined for point-based objects by Scivos and Nebel (2004). Figure 5 shows an example of the orientation relations computed from one of our sketch maps. Four buildings PE (physical education), CC (campus center), PA (performing art) and LC (lecture center) are adjacent to the reference route segment AB, and their orientation relations with respect to AB using LR are shown in Figure 5 (right). A polygon-shaped building is said to be *left_of* a route segment when all the vertices in that polygon are on the left side of the route segment. The *right_of* relation is the inverse relation of *left_of*. Definitions and rules of all the other relation types and the means of computing adjacency can be found in the paper from Sahib *et al.* (2015).

Verbal Description Interpretation

Besides the investigation on sketch maps, the authors are also interested in identifying spatial information included in the verbal descriptions indicating orientation with respect to other spatial objects or a person's location to support spatial orientation. For example, provided directions by participants include information to orient a person instead of simply giving turn-by-turn instructions:

You will see to your front, Dutch Quad, to your left the Campus Center, and to your right the left entrance to the campus. Walk towards Dutch Quad, but do not enter the building. You will take a left after you

Figure 5. Schematic view of the modified LR calculus of extended objects (right) applied to a sketch map (left)

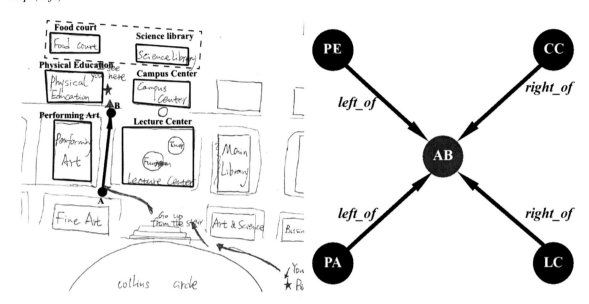

are near Dutch Quad, you will see a construction site to your left. Walk between Dutch Quad and the construction site.

Different from sketch maps which provide spatial relationships among spatial entities at a configuration level, verbal descriptions embed an egocentric perspective that spatial relationships are established between a person and surrounding entities to support spatial orientation. Therefore, we are also interested in investigating this aspect in verbal descriptions. A classification scheme has been proposed by Anacta and colleagues (Anacta *et al.*, 2016). In this study, the authors adopt this framework to categorize all collected verbal descriptions into meaningful segments with individual actions. The framework was developed based on the skeletal descriptions introduced by Denis (1997) whose method deconstructs verbal descriptions into a set of mega-descriptions consisting individual actions, and then extracts the verbal descriptions to a minimum set of wayfinding instructions. The classification scheme (Anacta *et al.*, 2016) uses the similar approach to develop the mega-descriptions. Instead of producing a minimum set of wayfinding direction, Anacta's framework categorizes individual actions into three major groups: orientation information, action information and commentary. Each group is further divided into subclasses that represent different types of actions involved in wayfinding. In particular, the orientation information group consists of four sub-groups: orientation with global landmark (OGL), orientation with local landmark at a decision point (ODP), orientation with a local landmark along the route (OAR), and orientation without landmark (O). The action information group has six sub-groups: non-turning action with global landmark (NTAGL), non-turning action with local landmark along a route (NTAAR), non-turning action without landmark (NTA), turning action with global landmark (TAGL), turning action with local landmark at a decision point (TADP), turning action without landmark (TA). The commentary group has three sub-categories including describing landmarks (DL), describing environment (DE), and commentary (C).

RESULTS AND DISCUSSION

There are in total six valid sketch maps for analysis. In general, the information density of all the sketch maps is quite low. The average number of spatial objects drawn on the sketch maps is 17 (Min = 11, Max = 26). These hand-draw maps only offer minimal amount of information that is relevant for navigating users from origins to destinations. As expected, the most frequently sketched objects are those located at the decision points such as the turns along the route or the ones close to the origin and the destination. Most spatial objects extracted from sketch maps are artificial such as academic buildings, car parks, fountains and bus stops. Two participants also drew natural objects such as grassland and trees. The result of sketch map interpretation is represented as below, and the comparison with verbal descriptions is demonstrated afterwards. We also discuss in general the spatial orientation represented in verbal description using the classification schema proposed by Anacta *et al.* (2016) at the end of this section.

Route Topology

Two commonly sketched routes connecting the origin at the bus stop next to Collins Circle and the destination at the building of Physical Education were found in our sketch maps. Both routes are mainly formed of pedestrian paths without path names and both routes go cross Academic Podium where most academic buildings are located (Figure 6). All the sketch maps represent route topology accurately (see one example of route topology using DRA_c in Figure 8).

Sketch maps and verbal descriptions show great similarity in representing route topology. The ease and accuracy of conveying connectivity in topology, however, differ in both forms. At first, similar to traditional maps, sketch maps also serve as the cognitive interface between mental representations and external worlds (Barkowsky *et al.*, 2000). Studies have demonstrated the effectiveness of conveying spatial relationship among objects in the environment and facilitation of development of configurational knowledge (MacEachren, 1991). In sketch maps, not only the configuration but also the connectivity among spatial objects is clearly presented and easy to comprehend. In verbal descriptions, the connectivity is clearly presented in a sequential order by mentioning spatial objects in a certain order. Spatial knowledge at the configuration level consisting of all these mentioned spatial objects, however, is difficult to develop as studies show that the development of configurational knowledge is inhibited by following a sequence-based direction (Parush *et al.*, 2007). Since verbal descriptions are always given and perceived in a sequence, a configurational level of spatial knowledge is harder to achieve by a person. Second, compared with traditional maps which require cognitive effects of establishing element-to-element correspondence between objects in maps and entities in the real world (Golledge, 1999; Newcombe & Huttenlocher, 2000), sketch maps which possess similar characteristics of cognitive maps reduce this cognitive load. Therefore, the design of navigational assistance with sketch maps shall address the necessity of establishing the correspondence between map objects and real-world entities in order to facilitate the acquisition of both connectivity and configuration.

Linear Order Relation

Participants showed consistency in representing the linear order of spatial objects along routes, i.e., the spatial objects drawn on papers can also be found in the corresponding verbal descriptions with the same sequential order. In most cases, verbal descriptions contain higher information density by including a

Figure 6. A schematic view of the two commonly sketched routes drawn on the uptown campus map

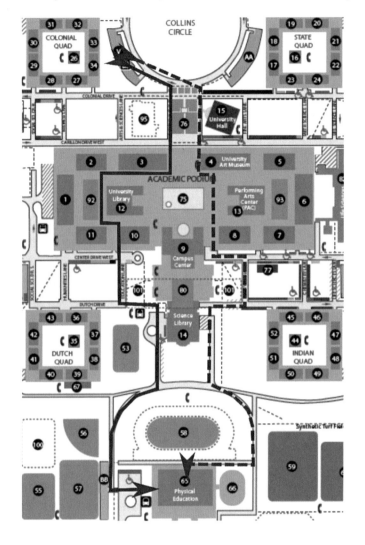

larger number of spatial objects as well as more detailed object descriptions which contain, e.g., material ("glass buildings", "grassy area", "asphalt road"), shape ("rectangular canopy-like area", "double doors") and size ("small stairs", "a flat ground", "large towers", "long staircase"). We also found that verbal descriptions were better at delivering spatial objects along an indoor-outdoor transitional route with height information available. For example, the following verbal description describes a route segment going through the Education building, which is not reflected on the sketch map from the same participant (Figure 7). The lack of route information inside a building may cause difficulty in wayfinding using sketch maps, especially when the building's internal structure is complex.

…Enter the Education building and make right, to a set of double door and a staircase down. Walk down the staircase and make a left towards yet another set of double doors". Walk through it and you'll see the exit of the building…

Figure 7. Route information of going through the Education building (label as 'Edu Building') with 'go downstairs $ out' instruction from a sketch map

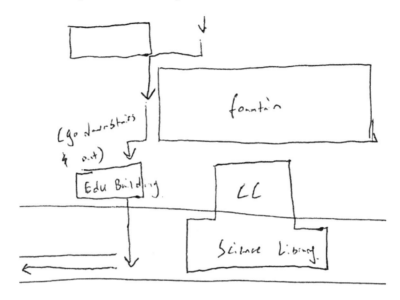

Sketch maps were found better in conveying configurational knowledge in the following aspects that are closely associated with facilitating the awareness of an environment in orienting oneself:

- Intelligently integrate levels of scale that offer more details at important turns and destinations so that sketch map users do not easily get lost
- Contain error indicators, e.g., drawing landmarks a bit further away from the destination, which indicate users that when they are close to those landmarks then they have already passed the destination and should turn back.

Besides, the minimal amount of information from sketch maps is easier to understand than some of the rather confusing and redundant information cluttered with irrelevant details from verbal descriptions.

Orientation Relation

All participants reflected orientation relations of landmarks with respect to route segments accurately except one participant. This participant used a landmark that was not mentioned on the route in the verbal description. The sketched landmark is actually located on the university drive, the only drivable street on campus. This may indicate that the participant's mental map of the campus is heavily influenced by driving experiences instead of walking. Figure 8 illustrates an example of the orientation relation calculated from the sketch map shown in Figure 1 (right).

The comparison between sketch maps and verbal descriptions shows distinct differences in two aspects. At first, the relative orientation in sketch maps is implicit and is decided by the calculus used for sketch interpretation, e.g., the *front_of* relation can be further recognized as *front_left*, *front*, and *front_right* if necessary (Wang & Schwering, 2015). Besides, there are different rules applied to sketch maps to identify the landmarks that are adjacent and along a route and those that are distant from a route

Figure 8. An example of representing orientation relation: the left figure is a schematic view of landmarks along a route interpreted from a sketch map; and the right figure shows both relative orientation relations of landmarks with respect to route segments and route topology calculated using DRA$_c$.

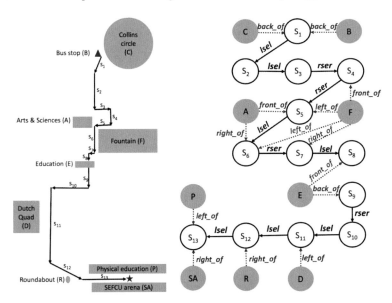

(Sahib *et al.*, 2017). In contrary, the relative orientation is explicitly represented in verbal descriptions such as "you see humanities building on your left-handed side" and "make a left, and you will see a parking lot". The information of spatial disposition (adjacency and along a route) is suggested by the prepositions such as *in front of*, *in back of/behind*, and *right/left of* (Talmy, 1983).

Second, the reference frames used by these two forms are different. In sketch maps, consistent allocentric reference frames can be applied so every landmark with its associated spatial relations are presented at a configurational level. Reasoning orientation relations between distant spatial objects and calculating global orientation relations are feasible in sketch maps. In verbal descriptions, however, an egocentric reference frame is used each time a direction towards a referent landmark is given based on a wayfinder's location and his/her facing direction in the environment. This makes it difficult to reason about the directional relations between spatial objects that are further apart.

We also found mixed use of relative and absolute (cardinal) directions in verbal descriptions, e.g., "when you face to the Collins Circle, and back to the bus station, the building on you right side is Business building. Now you go to north to get that building". The instruction "go to north" can be challenging for wayfinders who do not know where the real North is, and wayfinders may even get confused if the Business building is not to the North of Collins Circle (In reality, the Business building is located southeast to Collins Circle).

Spatial Orientation in Verbal Descriptions

Commonly, the spatial relationships established between a person and his/her surrounding entities in the environment provide essential support for spatial orientation. In the classification framework introduced by Anacta *et al.* (2016), 13 types of actions in verbal descriptions were suggested to have distinctive representation for navigation. In the current study carried out at a smaller environment, the authors identified seven types of wayfinding actions including actions with local landmark (OAR), non-turning action with local landmarks (NTAAR), describing landmark (DL), describing environment (DE), turning action without landmark (TA), turning action with landmark at decision point (TADP), and non-turning actin without landmark (NTA). The count of each type of action is listed in Table 2.

Results showed the majority of descriptions provided in verbal directions are for maintaining spatial orientation by indicating the orientation relations of a person to other spatial objects and are for taking non-turning actions. The turn-by-turn based directions as used in existing pedestrian navigation systems only count for 15.1% of all described actions. Directions that are not common in the existing navigation systems such as orienting with local landmark (OAR) and non-turning action with local landmarks (NTAAR) count for 38.9% and 37.2% of all described actions, respectively. These results also correspond to an earlier study carried out in a different county with irregular street network (Schwering, Li, & Anacta, 2013). While the classification scheme used is slightly different, a major difference is that in the current study no global landmark is used in directions. This is likely due to the much smaller environment (campus) used in this study comparing to the larger environment (city) used in the previous study. In a smaller environment, global landmarks are not often used by participants for spatial orientation. Another reason is possibly because the environment used in our study is structurally regular and symmetrical. The environment used in the previous study (Schwering, Li, & Anacta, 2013), however, is irregular which may be more difficult to orient without the use of global landmarks to initiate orientation for wayfinders.

CONCLUSION AND FUTURE WORK

We assessed pedestrian navigational instructions given in the form of sketch maps and verbal descriptions by using new methods of sketch and verbal interpretations. With regard to route topology, both sketch maps and verbal descriptions are equally functional. Route topology in sketch maps, however, is given in a more concise and straightforward way and thus easier to comprehend. With regard to linear order relation, sketch maps convey the order knowledge with much less complexity while some verbal descriptions are cluttered with irrelevant details and thus difficult for users to memorize and carry out. However, verbal descriptions are better at describing spatial objects along an indoor-outdoor transitional route with height information available, which is difficult to present on a 2-D sketch map. Regarding relative orientation, sketch maps represent it implicitly while verbal descriptions represent it explicitly using mixed forms of reference system (mostly egocentric relative system).

In all, sketch maps collected from our study are more convenient than verbal descriptions for navigation by eliminating extraneous details, simplifying complexity in representing topology and landmark properties, using intelligently mixed levels of scale and containing error indicators. Sketch maps also convey global orientation information that is crucial to develop configurational knowledge of an envi-

Table 2. Specific actions included in given verbal descriptions

OAR	NTAAR	DL	DE	TA	TADP	NTA
44	42	7	3	9	6	2

ronment. The prominence of sketch maps in effectively conveying spatial configuration as well as in facilitating spatial awareness provides insights to improve current turn-by-turn instructions by employing sketch-map-like components. Verbal descriptions seem different from sketch maps in the aspects such as perspective, reference frame, and level of details. The sequence that a person takes to acquire spatial knowledge parallels with the order of wayfinding action that a person takes in order to reach the destination. This is probably the reason that configurational knowledge is less likely to develop after acquiring verbal wayfinding actions. It may be due to the similar structure that verbal descriptions possess higher levels of details than sketch maps. We are interested in investigating if the higher levels of details in verbal descriptions lead to greater cognitive efforts or not. Acknowledge the advantage of sketch maps for providing convenient and configurational knowledge of a space, verbal descriptions may serve a supplementary role of enriching the navigational instructions without impacting cognitive load but increasing efficiency. We will address this aspect thoroughly in our next phase of research.

A continuing trend in studying sketch maps for pedestrian navigation is the diversification of different walking spaces such as indoor space, complex outdoor space, and transitional indoor-outdoor space with different spatial scales (inside a complex building or at city-level). We aim to incorporate more types of space in our future investigation to approach a better understanding of spatial knowledge given in both forms of sketch maps and verbal descriptions.

ACKNOWLEDGMENT

Jia Wang's work was funded by the AGILE ECR Grant and the University of Greenwich's REF Competitive Fund. Rui Li would like to thank the Faculty Research Award Program (FRAP) of State University of New York at Albany for supporting this study. The authors also thank everyone who participated the experiment.

REFERENCES

Allen, J. F. (1983). Maintaining knowledge about temporal intervals. *Communications of the ACM*, *26*(11), 832–843. doi:10.1145/182.358434

Anacta, V. J. A., Schwering, A., Li, R., & Muenzer, S. (2016). Orientation information in wayfinding instructions: Evidences from human verbal and visual instructions. *GeoJournal*, 1–17.

Barkowsky, T., Latecki, L., & Richter, K. (2000). Schematizing maps: Simplification of geographic shape by discrete curve evolution. In C. Freksa, C. Habel, W. Brauer, & K. F. Wender (Eds.), *Spatial Cognition II: Integrating Abstract Theories, Empirical Studies, Formal Methods, and Practical Applications* (Vol. 1849, pp. 41–53). Berlin: Springer. doi:10.1007/3-540-45460-8_4

Bertel, S., Dressel, T., Kohlberg, T., & von Jan, V. (2017). Spatial knowledge acquired from pedestrian urban navigation systems. In *Proceedings of the 19th International Conference on Human-Computer Interaction with Mobile Devices and Services* (p. 32). ACM. 10.1145/3098279.3098543

Brunyé, T. T., Taylor, H. A., & Worboys, M. (2007). Levels of detail in descriptions and depictions of geographic space. *Spatial Cognition and Computation*, *7*(3), 227–266. doi:10.1080/13875860701515472

Chipofya, M., Schwering, A., Schultz, C., Harason, E., & Jan, S. (2015). Left-Right Relations for Qualitative Representation and Alignment of Planar Spatial Networks. In *Proceedings of the Mexican International Conference on Artificial Intelligence* (pp. 435-450). Springer. 10.1007/978-3-319-27101-9_33

Dalton, R. C. (2003). The secret is to follow your nose: Route path selection and angularity. *Environment and Behavior, 35*(1), 107–131. doi:10.1177/0013916502238867

Denis, M. (1997). The description of routes: A cognitive approach to the production of spatial discourse. *Cahiers de Psychologie Cognitive, 16*(4), 409–458.

Downs, R. M., & Stea, D. (1973). Cognitive maps and spatial behavior: Process and products. In R. M. Downs & D. Stea (Eds.), *Image and Environment*. Chicago: Aldine.

Dylla, F., & Moratz, R. (2005). Exploiting qualitative spatial neighborhoods in the situation calculus. *LNAI, 3343*, 304–322.

Egenhofer, M. J. (1997). Query processing in spatial-query-by-sketch. *Journal of Visual Languages and Computing, 8*(4), 403–424. doi:10.1006/jvlc.1997.0054

Forbus, K., Usher, J., Lovett, A., Lockwood, K., & Wetzel, J. (2011). CogSketch: Sketch understanding for cognitive science research and for education. *Topics in Cognitive Science, 3*(4), 648–666. doi:10.1111/j.1756-8765.2011.01149.x PMID:25164503

Golledge, R. G. (1999). Human wayfinding and cognitive maps. In R. G. Golledge (Ed.), *Wayfinding behavior: Cognitive mapping and other spatial processes* (pp. 5–45). The Johns Hopkins University Press.

Ishikawa, T., Fujiwara, H., Imai, O., & Okabe, A. (2008). Wayfinding with a GPS-based mobile navigation system: A comparison with maps and direct experience. *Journal of Environmental Psychology, 28*(1), 74–82. doi:10.1016/j.jenvp.2007.09.002

Kim, Y. O., & Penn, A. (2004). Linking the Spatial Syntax of Cognitive Maps to the Spatial Syntax of the Environment. *Environment and Behavior, 36*(4), 483–504. doi:10.1177/0013916503261384

Klippel, A., Lee, P. U., Fabrikant, S., Montello, D. R., & Bateman, J. (2005). The cognitive conceptual approach as a leitmotif for map design. In *Reasoning with Mental and External Diagrams: Computational Modeling and Spatial Assistance, Proceedings of the AAAI 2005 Spring Symposium* (pp. 21-23). Stanford, CA: AAAI Press.

Krüger, A., Aslan, I., & Zimmer, H. (2004). *The effects of mobile pedestrian navigation systems on the concurrent acquisition of route and survey knowledge. In Mobile Human-Computer Interaction-MobileHCI 2004* (pp. 446–450). Springer. doi:10.1007/978-3-540-28637-0_54

Kuipers, B. (1978). Modeling spatial knowledge. *Cognitive Science, 2*(2), 129–153. doi:10.120715516709cog0202_3

Lynch, K. (1960). *The Image of the City*. Cambridge, MA: MIT Press.

MacEachren, A. M. (1991). The role of maps in spatial knowledge acquisition. *The Cartographic Journal, 28*(2), 152–162. doi:10.1179/caj.1991.28.2.152

Montello, D. R. (1993). Scale and multiple psychologies of space. In A. U. Frank & I. Campari (Eds.), *Spatial information theory: A theoretical basis for GIS* (pp. 312–321). Berlin: Springer-Verlag. doi:10.1007/3-540-57207-4_21

Montello, D. R. (2001). Spatial Cognition. In N. J. Smelser & P. B. Baltes (Eds.), *International Encyclopedia of the Social and Behavioral Science* (pp. 14771–14775). Oxford, UK: Pergamon Press. doi:10.1016/B0-08-043076-7/02492-X

Montello, D. R. (2005). Navigation. In P. Shah & A. Miyake (Eds.), *Cambridge handbook of visuospatial thinking* (pp. 257–294). Cambridge, UK: Cambridge University Press. doi:10.1017/CBO9780511610448.008

Newcombe, N. S., & Huttenlocher, J. (2000). *Making space: The development of spatial representation and reasoning*. Cambridge, MA: MIT Press.

Parush, A., Ahuvia, S., & Erev, I. (2007). Degradation in spatial knowledge acquisition when using automatic navigation systems. In S. Winter (Ed.), COSIT 2007, LNCS 4736 (pp. 238-254). Springer. doi:10.1007/978-3-540-74788-8_15

Sahib, J., Schultz, C., Schwering, A., & Chipofya, M. (2015). Spatial Rules for Capturing Qualitatively Equivalent Configurations in Sketch Maps. *Annals of Computer Science and Information Systems, 7*, 13–20. doi:10.15439/2015F372

Sahib, J., Schwering, A., Schultz, C., & Chipofya, M. C. (2017). Cognitively plausible representations for the alignment of sketch and geo-referenced maps. *Journal of Spatial Information Science, 2017*(14), 31-59.

Schlieder, C. (1995). Reasoning about ordering. *Proceedings of Spatial Information Theory (COSIT '95): A Theoretical Basis for GIS, 988*, 341-349.

Schwering, A., Li, R., & Anacta, V. J. A. (2013). Orientation information in different forms of route instructions. *Short Paper Proceedings of the 16th AGILE Conference on Geographic Information Science*.

Schwering, A., Wang, J., Chipofya, M., Jan, S., Li, R., & Broelemann, K. (2014). SketchMapia: Qualitative representations for the alignment of sketch and metric maps. *Spatial Cognition and Computation, 14*(3), 220–254. doi:10.1080/13875868.2014.917378

Scivos, A., & Nebel, B. (2004). The finest of its class: The natural, point-based ternary calculus LR for qualitative spatial reasoning. *Spatial Cognition IV. Reasoning, Action, Interaction, 3343*, 283–303.

Smith, B., Malytua, T., Rudnick, R., Mandrick, W., Salmen, D., …Parent, K. (2013). IAO-Intel: an ontology of information artifacts in the intelligence domain. In *Proceedings of the 8th Conference on semantic technologies for intelligence, defense, and security*, 12-15 November 2013, Fairfax, VA, USA: CEUR, 33–40.

Talmy, L. (1983). How language structures space. In Spatial Orientation (pp. 225-282). Springer US. doi:10.1007/978-1-4615-9325-6_11

Taylor, H. A., & Tversky, B. (1992). Spatial mental models derived from survey and route descriptions. *Journal of Memory and Language, 31*(2), 261–292. doi:10.1016/0749-596X(92)90014-O

Tversky, B. (2000). Levels and structure of spatial knowledge. *Cognitive mapping: past, present and future*, 24–43.

Tversky, B. (2003). Structure of mental spaces: How people think about space. *Environment and Behavior*, *35*(1), 66–80. doi:10.1177/0013916502238865

Tversky, B. (2005). How to get around by mind and body - Spatial thought, spatial action. In A. Zilhao (Ed.), *Evolution, Rationality and Cognition: A Cognitive Science for the Twenty-first Century* (pp. 135–147). Routledge.

Wang, J. (2014). *Qualitative sketch aspects for sketch map alignment* (PhD thesis). University of Münster.

Wang, J., & Li, R. (2013). An empirical study on pertinent aspects of sketch maps for navigation. *International Journal of Cognitive Informatics and Natural Intelligence*, *7*(4), 26–43. doi:10.4018/ijcini.2013100102

Wang, J., & Schwering, A. (2015). Invariant spatial information in sketch maps—a study of survey sketch maps of urban areas. *Journal of Spatial Information Science*, *2015*(11), 31-52.

Wang, J., & Worboys, M. (2016). Pedestrian navigation aids, spatial knowledge and walkability. In *Short Paper Proceedings of the 9th International Conference on GIScience* (Vol. 1, No. 1). Montreal, Canada: Academic Press. 10.21433/B3114B58K9TP

Wang, J., & Worboys, M. (2017). Ontologies and representation spaces for sketch map interpretation. *International Journal of Geographical Information Science*, 1–25.

Willis, K. S., Hölscher, C., Wilbertz, G., & Li, C. (2009). A comparison of spatial knowledge acquisition with maps and mobile maps. *Computers, Environment and Urban Systems*, *33*(2), 100–110. doi:10.1016/j.compenvurbsys.2009.01.004

Chapter 4
What Is It Like to Be a Cyborg?

Kevin Warwick
Coventry University, UK

ABSTRACT

In this chapter, the author describes his personal experience in experimenting as a cyborg (part biology/part technology) by having technology implanted in his body, which he lived with over a period. A look is also taken at the author's experiments into creating cyborgs by growing biological brains which are subsequently given a robot body. The experiments are dealt with in separate sections. In each case the nature of the experiment is briefly described along with the results obtained and this is followed by an indication of the experience, including personal feelings and emotions felt in and around the time of the experiments and subsequently as a result of the experiments. Although the subject can be treated scientifically from an external perspective, it is really through individual, personal experience that a true reflection can be gained on what might be possible in the future.

INTRODUCTION

The author of this paper has conducted a series of experiments to investigate the merger between humans and technology, essentially creating cyborgs (Warwick, 2013) in doing so. Clearly this raises feelings within the person that are different to those of everyday life. What the author has attempted to do in this chapter is give some indication of what those feelings and emotions amount to.

The first two experiments describe work in which technology was implanted into the author's body, in the second of these the technology was implanted into the author's nervous system. The third experiment was overseen by the author and involved culturing biological brain cells which were then given a robot body with which they could interact with the outside world. So the personal experience was in this case rather one of experiencing first hand what the resultant creature was like.

DOI: 10.4018/978-1-5225-5396-0.ch004

EXPERIMENT 1

On 24 August 1998 the author became the first human to have a Radio Frequency Identification Device (RFID) surgically implanted in his body as a form of identity. The implant was positioned in his upper left arm (see Figure 1). In its simplest form, the device transmits a sequence of pulses by radio which represent a unique number. The number can be pre-programmed to act rather like a PIN number on a credit card. So, with an implant of this type in place, when it is activated, the identity of the person involved can be interrogated by a computer. The device implanted measured 22 mm by 4 mm diameter and it was held in place for the duration of the experiment by a couple of stitches.

An RFID implant of this type does not have its own battery. What it does consist of however is a small antenna and a collection of memory chips enclosed in a glass capsule. The antenna picks up power remotely when passed near to a larger coil of wire which carries an electric current. The power picked up by the antenna in the implant is then employed to transmit by radio the particular signal encoded in the microchip. Because there is no battery, or any moving parts, the implant requires no maintenance, so once it has been implanted it can stay there without problem (see Graafstra, 2007; and Foster & Jaeger, 2007 for more on this).

In the particular experiments we carried out, we had already set up my University building at Reading as an intelligent building. What this means is that at various points in the building different responses could be triggered if and when I was recognized at those points. So the RFID implant allowed me to control lights, open doors and be welcomed "Hello" when entering the front door.

Figure 1. Author being implanted with an RFID by his Doctor, George Boulos

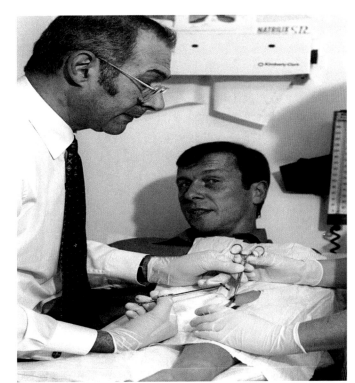

The main reason for selecting my upper left arm for the implant was that, at the time, we were not sure how well it would work. It was reasoned that, if the implant was not working well, possibly due to signal transmission problems, then if it was in my arm it could be waved around until a stronger signal was transmitted. It is interesting however that most present day RFID implants in humans are located in a roughly similar place (the left arm or hand), even though they do not have to be. For example in the James Bond film, *Casino Royale* (the new version), Bond himself has an implant of a not too dissimilar nature in his left arm.

The Experience

Before receiving the implant there were a variety of technical questions such as how to sterilize the implant, whether it would migrate in my body and if it might break. Also, having even minor surgery, when you don't have to for medical purposes was something to be faced. I didn't really worry too much about the possibilities of anything going wrong until maybe the day of the operation. But everything went well and technically it worked pretty much as we had hoped so I was very pleased.

Two things really stick in my mind about the whole experience. One is that it was great fun. Walking around the Department and having doors open for you automatically is fantastic, you actually feel quite powerful. But I never imagined it would receive the sort of media coverage it did at the time. For the next few weeks all I seemed to be doing was media work. Then when the implant was removed a couple of weeks later I felt something was missing, doors didn't open automatically for me any longer. There was certainly a sense of loss for a few days. But it was clear to me from the outset just how beneficial such an implant could be. It is therefore quite a surprise to me that RFID implants have not already been employed more widely especially in the form of extra passport information, where they could be very useful for security purposes. Although in pets they do seem to have filled this role.

After Thoughts

The ongoing consequences of the experiment have been extremely interesting. Although it is generally acknowledged that I was the first to experience such an implant, hardly a year goes by without someone else being credited with being the first in some new related experiment which is generally a copy of what we did in 1998. I suppose the main thing that surprises me with this is that either news reporters do very little or no research before pushing out a story (even omitting a simple Google search) or that they will say anything to make their story a little more important, even if they know certain details to be untrue.

But each year a similar implant, usually much smaller, is being used by a different company to allow its employees to operate photocopiers or gain entry to a building. Each year discussions occur with regard to where and how such an implant could be used, e.g. for passport control. As an example, recently it has been suggested that athletes could have the implant in an attempt to reduce the amount of cheating through drug taking (Stevens, 2017)

EXPERIMENT 2

On 14 March 2002 the author received his second implant. This time it consisted of the first use of the BrainGate microelectrode array (shown in Figure 2) in a human. This event had considerably broader implications than that in the first experiment, extending human capabilities for example. The array was implanted into my median nerve fibers during two hours of neurosurgery at the Radcliffe Infirmary, Oxford, UK, in order to test bidirectional functionality in a series of experiments.

A stimulation current directly into the nervous system allowed information to be received, while control signals were decoded from neural activity in the region of the electrodes. A number of experimental trials were successfully concluded (Warwick et al., 2003; Gasson et al., 2005): In particular:

1. Extra sensory (ultrasonic) input was implemented (see Figure 3), thereby extending my range of sensory perception.
2. Extended control of a robotic hand across the internet was achieved, with feedback from the robotic fingertips being sent back as neural stimulation to give a sense of force being applied to an object (this was achieved between Columbia University, New York, USA and Reading University, England).
3. A primitive form of telegraphic communication directly between the nervous systems of two humans (the author's wife assisted) was performed.
4. A wheelchair was successfully driven around by means of neural signals.
5. The color of jewelry was changed as a result of neural signals – indeed as was the behavior of a collection of small robots. These were set up to either try to collectively chase after another robot aggressively or to try and escape from it as though they were scared – the decision being selected from my nervous system.

In all of the above cases it can be considered that the trial proved useful for purely therapeutic reasons, e.g. the ultrasonic sense could be useful for an individual who is blind or the telegraphic communication could be useful for those with certain forms of Motor Neurone Disease. However each test can also be seen as a potential form of enhancement beyond the human norm for an individual. As with the first

Figure 2. BrainGate implant with 100 electrodes

Figure 3. Author experimenting with ultrasonic sensory input

experiment, I did not need to have the implant for medical purposes to overcome a problem but rather the whole experiment was for scientific exploration and, to an extent at least, to investigate a basis for technological human enhancement.

The Experience

On this occasion there was a four year build up to the surgery which involved several neurosurgeons. The operation itself had to be planned, along with the subsequent experiments. Again, apart from the necessary planning, I didn't worry about the operation itself too much until the night before, but then it was far too late to do anything other than go through with it. There were some harrowing moments however as the different people involved, including the surgeons, expressed their worries about what might happen if something went wrong, such as losing the use of my hand if my nervous system became infected. The main worries I personally had though amounted more to worrying that the whole experiment would not go ahead due to some University insurance issue, ethical refusal or other paperwork problem. But go ahead it did.

During the more than 3 months that the implant was in place it was a tremendously exciting time. A team of 4 researchers and myself were involved on a daily basis in the lab firstly setting up a different experiment and then trying to get results. Sometimes we had problems and it didn't work at first, but we stuck with it and generally got some wonderful results.

As far as being a cyborg is concerned a couple of the experiments immediately spring to mind. Firstly I went to Columbia University in New York and we connected my nervous system, via the internet, to a robot hand in England. I was able to control the robot hand, and feel the force the hand was applying from another continent. When this actually happened it felt incredible, I hadn't really thought about the implications beforehand. You can be extremely powerful as a cyborg with your nervous system extended over the internet. I instantly became conscious of the sheer power offered to individuals with such an implant, particularly in the military domain. What it means is that an individual's brain and body do not have to be in the same place, with a network acting as a nervous system extension.

The second part of the experiment that really blew my mind was when my wife also had electrodes implanted into her nervous system. In the laboratory we sent signals between our nervous systems. Every time she closed her hand, my brain received a pulse. Effectively we were communicating telegraphically from nervous system to nervous system. I realized straight away what this will mean in the future when we have such connections between human brains; it will be a form of telepathy, thought communication (Warwick et al., 2004). It was for me a fantastic experience to be the first to experiment with a new form of communication, to know that when, in the future humans communicate with each other and with technology, by thought signals, so such capabilities will stem back to this particular experiment that was performed.

After Thoughts

I have now had time to reflect on my experience and witness the aftermath of the experiment in which I was the first human to experience the BrainGate microelectrode array implant. In a therapeutic sense the implant has been used in a string of further tests involving paralysed individuals. Although, in each case the person cannot move their arms and hands, due to the paralysis, due to the same implant being placed in their motor cortex, they have been able to control the curser on a computer screen and operate such pieces of technology as a robot hand (Hochberg et al., 2006; Hochberg et al., 2012). The same implant has also been employed to enable a paralysed individual to regain some control over his own arm (Bouton et al., 2016). A 24 year old man who has a C5 paralysis due to a swimming accident received the BrainGate in his motor cortex, this being connected, via a computer, to a sleeve containing muscle stimulating electrodes allowing him to learn to move his wrist and fingers to a limited extent.

What has surprised me greatly though is that there has not yet been any further experimentation with regard to human enhancement as opposed to therapy. Perhaps the ethical issues are a problem for some, but also it might be a big step for a person/researcher to take, receiving an implant, when they are able bodied and do not 'need' the implant. However there is always the possibility that something could go wrong. When you are one of the first people to try an experiment such as this you can have an idea about some of the risks, particularly medical, that could occur, but most of the risks you have very little idea about quite simply because no one has done it before and you have little idea as to how the human body will react to certain new stimuli.

EXPERIMENT 3

Neurons cultured/grown under laboratory conditions on an array of non-invasive electrodes provide an attractive alternative to computer or human control with which to construct a robot controller and to investigate the operation of connected neurons. An experimental control platform, essentially a robot body, can move around within a defined area purely under the control of such a network/brain, and the effects of the brain, controlling the body, can be observed (Warwick et al., 2010).

This research opens up a different approach to the study of the development of the brain itself because of its sensory motor embodiment. This method allows investigations to be carried out into memory formation and reward/punishment scenarios—the elements that underpin the basic functioning of a brain.

In most cases, the growth of networks of brain cells (typically between 100,000 to 150,000) in vitro involves separating neurons obtained from foetal rodent cortical tissue. They are then grown (cultured) in a specialised chamber, where they can be provided with suitable environmental conditions (e.g. kept at an appropriate temperature of 37 degrees centigrade), and fed with a mixture of minerals and nutrients. An array of electrodes embedded in the base of the chamber (a multi-electrode array, MEA) acts as a bidirectional electrical interface to/from the culture. This allows electrical signals to be delivered in order to stimulate the culture and allows for recordings to be made of the outputs from the culture.

The neurons in such cultures spontaneously connect, communicate and develop, giving useful responses within a few weeks and typically continuing to do so for, at present, 3 months. The brain is grown in a glass specimen chamber lined with a flat '8×8' multi-electrode array, which can be used for real-time recordings (see Figure 4). This makes it possible to distinguish the firings of small groups of neurons by monitoring the output signals on the electrodes. A picture of the entire network's global activity can be formed in this way. It is also possible to electrically stimulate the culture via any of the electrodes to induce neural activity. In consequence, the multi-electrode array forms a bidirectional interface with the cultured neurons (Chiappalone, 2007; DeMarse, 2001).

In our experiment the brain was coupled to a physical robot body. Sensory data fed back from the robot was subsequently delivered to the culture, thereby closing the robot-culture loop. In consequence, the

Figure 4. (a) A multi-electrode array (MEA) showing the electrodes, (b)Electrodes in the centre of the MEA seen under an optical microscope, (c) An MEA at ×40 magnification, showing neuronal cells in close proximity to an electrode

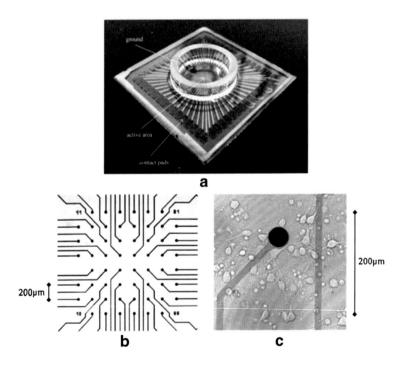

processing of signals can be broken down into two discrete sections, (a) 'culture to robot', in which live neuronal activity is used as the decision-making mechanism for robot control, and (b) 'robot to culture', which involves an input mapping process from the robot sensor to stimulate the culture (Warwick, 2013a).

The actual number of neurons in a brain depends on natural density variations that arise when the culture is seeded in the first place. The electrochemical activity of the culture was sampled, and this was used as input to the robot's wheels. The robot's (ultrasonic) sensor readings were converted into stimulation signals received as input by the culture, thereby closing the loop.

Once the brain had grown on the array for several days, during which time it forms some elementary neural connections, an existing neuronal pathway through the culture was identified by searching for strong relationships between pairs of electrodes. These pairs were defined as those electrode combinations in which neurons close to one electrode responded to stimulation from the other electrode at which the stimulus was applied more than 60% of the time and responded no more than 20% of the time to stimulation on any other electrode. Essentially the pair of electrodes were taking on their roles, one for sensory input and the other for motor output.

In this way, a suitable input/output electrode pair could be chosen in order to provide an initial decision-making pathway for the robot. Essentially the electrodes were polled to see between which electrodes the strongest passageways in the brain had developed. This set up was then employed to control certain aspects of the robot body. For example, if the ultrasonic sensor was active, and we wished the response to cause the robot to turn away from an object that was located ultrasonically (possibly a wall) in order to keep moving (Warwick, 2013a).

For experimental purposes, the intention was for the robot to follow a forward path until it reached a wall, at which point the front sonar value decreased below a certain threshold, triggering a stimulating pulse. If the responding/output electrode registered activity, the robot was required to turn through 90 degrees to avoid the wall, such that it could continue moving forwards. In experiments, the hope was that the robot would turn spontaneously whenever activity was registered on the response electrode.

At first the 'correct' response to a stimulating pulse occurred maybe 20 to 30 percent of the rime, with the robot simply colliding with the corral wall on other occasions. However due to a learning process the success rate improved dramatically over a period of several weeks, even reaching 100 per cent success on some instances. From a neurological perspective, of course, it is however also interesting to speculate why there is activity on the response electrode sometimes when no stimulating pulse has been applied.

As an overall control element for direction and wall avoidance, the cultured brain acted as the sole decision making entity within a feedback loop. Clearly, the neural pathway changes that took place over time in the culture between the stimulating and recording electrodes were an important aspect of the system. From a research point of view, investigations of learning and memory are generally at an early stage. However, the robot can be clearly be seen to improve its performance over time in terms of its wall avoidance ability in the sense that neuronal pathways that bring about a satisfactory action tend to strengthen purely though the process of habitually performing these activities—an example of learning due to habit (Hebb, 1949).

However, the number of variables involved is considerable, and the plasticity process, which occurs over quite a period of time, is (most probably) dependent on such factors as initial seeding and growth near electrodes as well as environmental transients such as temperature and humidity. Learning by reinforcement—rewarding good actions and punishing bad—is a major issue for research in this field (Warwick, 2013b).

The Experience

Rather than an experience as a scientist directly involved themselves in the experiment, as was previously the case, this instance is rather one in which the personal involvement involved experimentation set up, witnessing the results and discussing the follow on.

On many occasions the culture responded as expected, on other occasions it did not, and in some cases it provided a motor signal when it was not expected to do so. But did it 'intentionally' make a different decision to the one we would have expected? We cannot tell, but merely guess. When it comes to robotics, it was shown by the research that a robot can successfully have a biological brain which makes its 'decisions'. The size of such a brain, 100,000–150,000 neurons, is dictated purely by the limitations on the experimentation described. Three-dimensional structures are already being investigated and these permit the creation of cultures of maybe 60 million neurons (Warwick, 2013b).

But seeing the biological brain develop over time was quite an experience. It made one question whether or not such entities should be regarded as living creatures, no matter how small and how limited in their abilities. At the end of the day, if I so desired, as the scientist involved, I could have simply thrown away such a culture. But should I be able to do that, particularly if the brain had many more neurons?

After Thoughts

The potential of such (rat brain robot) systems, including the range of tasks they can deal with, means that the physical body can take on different forms. There is no reason, for example, why the body could not be a two legged, walking robot, with a rotating head and the ability to walk around in a building. It is realistic to assume that such cultures will become larger, potentially growing to sizes of billions of neurons. On top of this, the nature of the neurons may be diversified. At present, rat neurons are generally employed in studies. However, human neurons are also being cultured, thus leading to the possibility of a robot with a human neuron brain. If this brain then consists of billions of neurons, many social and ethical questions will need to be asked (Warwick, 2010), especially regarding the rights of such creatures.

One interesting question is whether or not such a brain is, or could be, conscious. Some (e.g. Searle, 1990) have concluded that consciousness is an emergent property; essentially, it is sufficient to put enough human neurons together with a high degree of connectivity, and consciousness will emerge. In the light of this argument, there is therefore no immediate reason why robots with biological brains composed of sufficient numbers of human neurons should not be conscious. The possibility is real therefore of building a robot with a technological body and a brain that consists of a large number of highly connected human neurons. Should this be perfectly acceptable or should it be regulated? If a robot of this kind, with say 100 billion human neurons (the same roughly as a normal human) decided to commit a crime, then who would be responsible for the consequences, the robot itself?

CONCLUSION

Clearly all of the experiments described involved a sense of the unknown and gave rise to excitement that goes with pure scientific investigation. However they also evoked worries and anguish that the experiment might not go ahead or something might go wrong. At the same time when success was achieved, no matter how slight this might have been, so a sense of elation, a high if you like, was achieved on an unparalleled level.

But in each case there was also an immediate sense of what might be. Each experiment showed that something was possible and led to a certain amount of thinking, particularly after the event, as to what this might lead to. In particular with the entities produced in the third of the experiments, will they be conscious creatures and will they need to be given some sort of rights? Actually witnessing the creatures learning and their brains developing make one think deeply about life and what this involves.

It is one thing to theorize and philosophize about the possibilities with cyborgs but it is quite another to actually carry out practical experimentation in the field. A key point is that before you go ahead you cannot really be sure what exactly is possible and what not. Along the way some things go wrong and you just have to deal with them. Books and academic papers are often no help as their contents, which may appear technically or medically based are in fact merely guesswork or based on speculative tales or even incorrect previous scientific experiments or calculations, simply because the authors knew no better.

ACKNOWLEDGMENT

An initial version of the first two experiments described here appeared in Warwick and Harrison (2014).

REFERENCES

Bouton, C., Shaikhouni, A., Annetta, N., Bockbrader, M., Friedenberg, D., Nielson, D., ... Deogaonkar, M. M. and A. Rezai, "Restoring cortical control of functional movement in a human with quadriplegia. *Nature*. doi:10.1038/nature17435

Chiappalone, M., Vato, A., Berdondini, L., Koudelka-Hep, M., & Martinoia, S. (2007). Network dynamics and synchronous activity in cultured cortical neurons. *International Journal of Neural Systems*, *17*(02), 87–103. doi:10.1142/S0129065707000968 PMID:17565505

DeMarse, T., Wagenaar, D., Blau, A., & Potter, S. (2001). The neutrally controlled animat: Biological brains acting with simulated bodies. *Autonomous Robots*, *11*(3), 305–310. doi:10.1023/A:1012407611130 PMID:18584059

Foster, K., & Jaeger, J. (2007). RFID inside. *IEEE Spectrum*, *44*(3), 24–29. doi:10.1109/MSPEC.2007.323430

Gasson, M., Hutt, B., Goodhew, I., Kyberd, P., & Warwick, K. (2005). Invasive neural prosthesis for neural signal detection and nerve stimulation. *International Journal of Adaptive Control and Signal Processing*, *19*(Issue.5), 365–375.

Graafstra, A. (2007). Hands on. *IEEE Spectrum*, *44*(3), 318–323. doi:10.1109/MSPEC.2007.323420

Hebb, D. (1949). *The organisation of behaviour*. New York: Wiley.

Hochberg, L., Bacher, D., Jarosiewicz, B., Masse, N., Simeral, J., Vogel, J., ... Donoghue, J. (2012). Reach and grasp by people with tetraplegia using a neurally controlled robotic arm. *Nature*, *485*(7398), 372–375. doi:10.1038/nature11076 PMID:22596161

Hochberg, L., Serruya, M., Friehs, G., Mukand, J., Saleh, M., Caplan, A., ... Donoghue, J. (2006). Neuronal ensemble control of prosthetic devices by a human with tetraplegia. *Nature*, *442*(7099), 164–171. doi:10.1038/nature04970 PMID:16838014

Searle, J. (1990). *The mystery of consciousness*. New York: The New York Review of Books.

Stevens, L. (2017). *Sporty cyborgs: Microchips in humans to prevent doping in athletes, suggests Olympians chief*. Retrieved from http://home.bt.com/tech-gadgets/future-tech/microchips-in-humans-to-prevent-doping-11364220161232

Warwick, K. (2010). Implications and consequences of robots with biological brains. *Ethics and Information Technology*, *12*(3), 223–234. doi:10.100710676-010-9218-6

Warwick, K. (2013a). Cyborgs—the neuro-tech version. In E. Katz (Ed.), *Implantable bioelectronics—devices, materials and applications*. New York: Wiley–VCH.

Warwick, K. (2013b). Cyborgs. In *Encyclopaedia of Sciences and Religions* (pp. 570–576). Springer, Netherlands. doi:10.1007/978-1-4020-8265-8_1210

Warwick, K., Gasson, M., Hutt, B., Goodhew, I., Kyberd, P., Andrews, B., ... Shad, A. (2003). The application of implant technology for cybernetic systems. *Archives of Neurology*, *60*(10), pp1369–pp1373. doi:10.1001/archneur.60.10.1369 PMID:14568806

Warwick, K., Gasson, M., Hutt, B., Goodhew, I., Kyberd, P., Schulzrinne, H., & Wu, X. (2004). Thought communication and control: A first step using radiotelegraphy. *IEE Proceedings. Communications*, *151*(3), 185–189. doi:10.1049/ip-com:20040409

Warwick, K., & Harrison, I. (2014). Feelings of a Cyborg. *International Journal of Synthetic Emotions*, *5*(2), 1–6. doi:10.4018/ijse.2014070101

Warwick, K., Xydas, D., Nasuto, S., Becerra, V., Hammond, M., Marshall, S., & Whalley, B. (2010). Controlling a mobile robot with a biological brain. *Defence Science Journal*, *60*(1), 5–14. doi:10.14429/dsj.60.11

Chapter 5
Artificial-Intelligence-Based Service-Oriented Architectures (SOAs) for Crisis Management

Konstantinos Domdouzis
Sheffield Hallam University, UK

ABSTRACT

The complexity of crisis-related situations requires the use of advanced technological infrastructures. In order to develop such infrastructures, specific architectures need to be applied such as the service-oriented architectures (SOAs). The purpose of this chapter is to indicate how SOAs can be used in modern crisis management systems, such as the ATHENA system. The chapter underlines the need for a detailed study of specific biological systems, such as the human brain's hippocampus which follows the current, intense attempts of improvement of the current artificial-intelligence-based systems and the development of a new area in artificial intelligence. A number of conclusions are drawn on how biologically inspired systems can benefit the development of service-oriented architectures.

INTRODUCTION

A large number of crises either in the form of natural disasters or terrorist acts have indicated that there must an organised collaboration of search and rescue services. This collaboration can be realised through the provision of automated ways that will coordinate the work of search and rescue teams. These ways will provide flexibility in the adaptation to the specific conditions and requirements of a crisis. This flexibility is expressed through the efficient use of resources and the clear identification of the different roles that dominate the system (Domdouzis et al., 2016). The necessity of these automated ways can be shown by the fact that natural disasters can cause alterations in the normal functioning of society and these alterations can result to human, economic and environmental effects. These effects require emergency response in order to satisfy critical human needs (IPCC, 2012). There are a number of factors that need to be considered during crises. The first factor is that there must be communication and coordination with community planners and first responders. Also, the concerns of the public during a crisis must be

DOI: 10.4018/978-1-5225-5396-0.ch005

heard while a more comprehensive understanding of the public's values and concerns must be developed. Useful, timely and accurate information must also be provided to the public. Steelman and Caffrey (2013) emphasize the need for pre-crisis communication and preparation so that the citizens will comprehend crisis risks (Steelman & McCaffrey, 2013). Veil et al. (2011) suggest that during a crisis, the public has to know about the risks that they may face. The provision of information to the public will ease uncertainty. Also, there must be comprehension of the public's concerns. Specifically, public opinion must be monitored so that a relationship of credibility and trust to be developed. Crisis communication must be characterised by honesty and openness. Another best practice is the development and maintenance of strong relationships with credible sources. Messages of self-efficacy to the public should also be provided (Veil et al., 2011). The use of new technologies for the monitoring of crises has been studied since the mid-90s. Thomsen (1995) and Heath (1997, 1998) have shown that online databases, web pages and other online tools can help corporations to adjust policies before the occurrence of a crisis. Also, it is evident nowadays that the use of Social Media is necessary and as a result, public participation is considered necessary for the resolution of a crisis (Baron, 2010). A survey that was realised by the American Red Cross revealed that 69% of citizens believe that emergency responders should monitor Social Media in order to arrange the quick transfer of help and 74% of citizens expect search and rescue services to answer social media-based call for help within an hour (Bulldog Reporter, 2010).

Service-oriented architecture (SOA) is an approach that addresses the requirements of distributed computing. Business operations that are realised in a SOA include a number of invocations of different components, often in an event-driven or asynchronous way. The development of a SOA, a highly distributable communications and integration backbone is needed. This is provided by the Enterprise Service Bus (ESB) which is an integration platform which uses Web Services standards in order to support a variety of communications (Papazoglou & Heuvel, 2007). In the case of environmental crises, SOAs enable integration of real-time, heterogeneous geospatial data. Furthermore, they allow geospatial data filtering and the introduction of new services so that natural phenomena can be simulated and decision making mechanisms to be improved (Vescoukis et al., 2012). In a SOA, software resources are packaged as 'services' which are self-contained modules that provide business functionality and they are independent of the state of other services. Services are described in a standard definition language and communicate with each other. SOAs are designed in such a way so that they overcome distributed computing challenges related to transaction management, security policies and application integration. SOAs are focused on developing efficient and effective applications that users can easily interconnect and maintain. SOAs provide flexible architectures that unify business processes through the modularization of large applications into services. A client can access a SOA service in order to create a new business process. SOAs create a collection of services that can communicate with each other using interfaces to pass messages from one service to another or to coordinate an activity between one or more services (Papazoglou & Heuvel, 2007).

Especially in the field of Crisis Management, service-oriented architecture can provide a number of benefits, such as better organisation of the Crisis Management technical platform, better clarification of the roles of the software developers of the platform, the re-usability of the different elements of the platform and the definition of the service inputs and outputs. Also, SOA offers the ability to adapt to business requirements in an agile manner. This agility is shown by the fact that new services can be added and new business requirements can be fulfilled. Furthermore, SOA allows modularization, thus complex problems can be broken into smaller segments (Kawamoto & Lobach, 2007). This is very important for large crises as modularization can allow the better handling of different aspects of a crisis from appropriate teams of experts. The agility offered by SOA is appropriate for the dynamic requirements of crises as it allows the adjustment of the architecture to the needs of the people that have been affected by the crisis. Since there are different types of crises such as terrorist acts, natural disasters, technological crises, population displacements because of wars, armed conflicts, high exposure to diseases, extreme risk and political instability, the need for agility is considered necessary.

INTELLIGENT SERVICE-ORIENTED ARCHITECTURES (SOAs) IN DIFFERENT TYPES OF CRISES

The complexity of software application domains is constantly increasing. Especially for a dynamic field such as crisis management which is characterised by uncertainty, technology needs to find a way to self-adapt to the different conditions. This is considered as the new direction for Artificial Intelligence. Self-adaptive systems are characterised by high-degree of autonomy, therefore it is harder to ensure that they behave as desired (Khakpour et al., 2010).

In the manufacturing industry, there are frequent changing market demands, time-to-market pressure and global competition. Next-generation manufacturing strategies must be developed that will support global competitiveness. Manufacturing systems need to become more strongly time-driven and time-oriented. This requires more adaptability to change. Targets that must be fulfilled in the future by the manufacturing industry include intra-enterprise dynamic integration capabilities, agility through adaptability, fault-tolerant scalability and collaboration among enterprises (Jammes & Smit, 2005). The Service Infrastructure for Real time Embedded Networked Applications (SIRENA) project is an ongoing European R&D project (SIRENA, 2017). The aim of the project is to develop a service-oriented framework for the development of distributed applications in diverse real-time embedded computing environments. SIRENA aims to develop a common communications and control infrastructure among different industrial domains and also domain-specific services for each of the target domain. The SIRENA Project uses Service-oriented Architecture at the lowest level of the device hierarchy and as a result an entire manufacturing installation to be expressed in terms of business processes.

TRIDEC is a system for Collaborative, Complex and Critical Decision-Support in Evolving Crises focuses on real-time intelligent information management in complex, collaborative, critical decision processes related to earth management. The architecture of TRIDEC is based on SOA 2.0, an event-driven extension of Service-Oriented Architecture (SOA) principles. The system analyses real-time data from services (e.g. Sensor Alert Service), business processes or system components (Up2Europe, 2017; Löwe et al., 2013). The SOA 2.0 approach is used for the creation of high-level business events from low-level system events. The creation of events is based on the analysis of real-time data from services (e.g. sensor alert services), business processes or system components (e.g. simulations). This process is facilitated by using data-fusion and pattern-matching techniques (Poslad et al., 2015).

Jadhav and Ade (2014) have proposed a methodology for making medical diagnosis better. The methodology is based on smart pattern matching technique that includes the k-Nearest Neighbour classifier and also integrating the Hopfield Neural Network theory and the Large Memory Storage and Retrieval (LAMSTAR) networks. The system is built on Service-oriented Architecture (SOA) and it has been implemented on a web server that is accessible by anyone including doctors from rural and remote areas (Jadhav & Ade, 2014). A SOA framework for a geriatric telehealth-care system has been presented by Ganapathy et al. (2013). Geriatric patient monitoring includes periodic transmissions of vital information, such as heart rate, ECG and respiration rate. The application server receives sensor data streams and identifies undesirable data patterns. Physicians are immediately alerted when vital signs of patients cross the normal high and low thresholds. There is access, filtering, processing and transfer of health data through the use of services. The proposed SOA framework uses a Service Manager in order to discover the registered users and authenticate them. Service functionalities interface clinical and non-clinical services over the web in order to facilitate personalised healthcare service provision. QoS attributes such as response time and throughput are estimated for the healthcare services (Ganapathy et al., 2013).

The increase of natural disasters has resulted to new research in the development of intelligent Environmental Information Management (EIM) Systems that are capable of collecting, elaborating, and visualising geospatial data (Annoni et al., 2005). In order to efficiently handle and prevent such disasters, scalable and distributed service platforms need to be developed (Maliska et al., 2006). Vescoukis et al. (2012) propose a service-oriented architecture for decision support systems in environmental crisis management (e.g. forest fire crisis management). The proposed architecture is based on the use of SOA principles and addresses interoperability issues in a way that geospatial data of different type and format to be used in the proposed architecture. Additional requirements that are followed are the real-time service delivery, the efficient 3D and contextual representation of the geospatial content, simulation capabilities and data filtering methods for the efficient delivery, handling and presentation of the huge amount of real-time geospatial data. Two different types of geospatial data are supported: the archival and the real-time data. These data are encoded using the specification of the Geospatial Markup Language (GML). Real-time and archival data are published to the Real-Time Middleware using a web service interface. The Real-Time Middleware includes advanced data filtering methods for the pre-processing of the spatial data that are required by the added-value middleware layer. The added-value middleware layer is responsible for the simulation of natural phenomena and the simulation of human behaviour in spatial contexts and thus allows real-time decision making during a natural disaster. The presentation layer collects the geospatial data from the added-value middleware layer and it uses contextual adaptation methods in order for the results to be presented to different types of devices (Vescoukis et al., 2012).

Tapia et al. (2008) describe the Flexible User and Services Oriented Multi-Agent Architecture (FUSION@). The architecture uses intelligent agents as the main elements in supporting a service-oriented approach that distributes the majority of the systems' functionalities into remote and local services and applications. The architecture suggests a new and easier method for developing distributed multi-agent systems where the systems' functionalities are modelled as distributed services which are accessed by agents that act as controllers. FUSION uses a number of applications that use the system functionalities. The core of the architecture is the agents' platform which includes a number of agents with specific characteristics and behaviour. The services consist of the bulk of system functionalities and they are organised as local services, web services or as individual stand-alone services. FUSION uses a communication protocol that allows applications and services to communicate directly with the agents' platform. The protocol is based on the SOAP protocol and it is independent of any programming language (Tapia et al., 2008).

Dang et al. (2008) present a framework of healthcare ontology in order to describe a healthcare network that includes hospital resources, to serve as a knowledge base for healthcare information management systems and to automate personalised healthcare workflows. A workflow includes a number of activities, each of which responsible for realising a service. From a SOA perspective, a workflow is a set of services and a specification for the control and flow of data among these services. The proposed system allows users to manage patients' medical records, to control and monitor the process flow that a patient will go through, to create new processes from a medical service repository and to maintain historical process data for further diagnosis. The workflow management system includes several web applications. There is a BPEL Server deployed on the Oracle application server and a knowledge engine which is used to retrieve business rules from the ontological knowledge base. Healthcare specialists can create medical processes without knowing anything about the IT infrastructure. Specifically, they can choose atomic processes from a service repository and arrange them in sequence or parallel. These atomic processes are stored in a service repository. The pool of available processes is updated based on the hospital status and system performance (Dang et al., 2008).

The Wireless Phone-based Emergency Response (WIPER) system provides emergency planners and responders the capability of detecting possible emergencies and possible crisis decision making options. The system is based on a distributed architecture that uses SOA and web services. WIPER can evaluate potential plans of action using a series of GIS-enabled agent-based simulations that use real-time data from cell phone network providers. WIPER includes three layers: the data source and measurement layer, the detection, simulation and prediction layer and the decision support layer. The Data Source and Management layer handles the acquisition of real-time phone data as the calculation of triangulation information for the calculation of accurate location. The Detection, Simulation and Prediction layer analyses incoming data for possible anomalies and the Decision Support layer presents the information from the other layers to the end-users in terms of summaries of traffic information and real-time maps and simulations (Schoenharl et al., 2006).

The critical infrastructures of a state are highly interconnected through a number of information and communication technologies, called cyber-based systems. These infrastructures include natural gas and petroleum production and distribution, telecommunications, water supply, banking and finance and agriculture. All of the critical infrastructures have a common characteristic – they include elements that interact with each other following a specific learning process. In this case, these infrastructures are called complex adaptive systems (CASs). One effective way to examine CASs is to see them as populations of interacting agents. An agent is characterised by its location, its capabilities and its memory. The entity's location specifies where it is in a physical space while its capabilities define what it can do from that location. The memory of the entity defines the different variables that describe the state of the agent. The agents are interconnected to each other and they function collaboratively in order to produce a set of services (Rinaldi et al., 2001).

Abaas et al. (2014) have reviewed and classified international journal articles and standards in order to identify appropriate methodologies and tools for counter-terrorism. Their review lasted from 2004 till 2013. The selection of the articles and standards was realised based on their applicability. Their review of the literature showed that there is the need for the development of web services that will realise social network analysis and surveillance data sharing. It also showed that there is lack of semantic clustering of relevant information while there is the need for the development of an attribute-based policy model and of a sophisticated objective function that will focus on the terrorists' target valuation and preferences. Intelligence is one of the main resources for anti-terrorism, however each country follows different rules when it comes to reporting terrorist incidents. Many governments lack the electronic intelligence which could help them monitor terrorist incidents. E-information sharing is considered significant in order for the collaboration and coordination between intelligence communities to be successful. Especially this collaboration should be real-time and it should be characterised by information acquisition, emergency responses and crisis expertise (Abaas et al., 2014).

Ying Chen (2005) suggested that the constant evolution of web services and service-oriented architectures has the ability to overcome many technological constraints in the Intelligence Community. The combination of data mining technology and service rating techniques into a SOA-based solving space for the intelligence analysts helped the analysts to explore services produced by other analysts and also compose new ones. Service categorization, discovery and composition has been achieved through data mining. Furthermore, through data mining, hidden data patterns can be extracted from large amounts of data. This extraction is based on specific data mining techniques, such as clustering, association rules and sequential patterns (Ying Chen, 2005).

THE NEW ARTIFICIAL INTELLIGENCE

Artificial Intelligence has been connected to Service-Oriented Architectures (SOAs). The way services are organised and how they communicate can be defined by Artificial Intelligence techniques as they offer adaptation to the constantly changing requirements of a situation. Domdouzis et al. (2016) have suggested that a Service-oriented Architecture can be represented as a set of interfaces and the mechanisms that enable the communication of these interfaces. The architecture includes SOA interfaces, service contracts and the communication mechanism between the service contracts. The role of the service contracts are the initiation of a service by a user. The access of a service contract is realised through an interface. In such an interface, the user can specify the type of data to be transmitted but most importantly access the service contract. The service contract allows the connection of the SOA interface to the communication mechanism that elaborates the transmitted data and passes them to the users (Domdouzis et al., 2016). The comparison of the different definitions for SOA provided by the review of the relevant literature shows that there is lack of definition of how SOA can be adapted to the requirements of different problems and situations. All the SOA definitions that were examined do not provide an accurate image of what SOA is. There is the example of some definitions that present the elements of a SOA but not the exact way these elements communicate with each other. Also, the examined definitions do not provide a description of what exactly a service is and they do not show how its capabilities are achieved. The flow of data from one service to another is not shown (Domdouzis et al., 2016). The review of the literature shows that more adaptive capabilities are required by modern Service-Oriented Architectures. This section shows how these capabilities could be realised through the study of how the human brain operates and of specific modern Artificial Intelligence (Deep Learning) technologies. The human brain is the most adaptive part of the human body and its numerous, unexplored abilities can lead the way to the development of more advanced technologies.

Artificial Intelligence focuses on the efficiency by which the human brain represents and handles information. The human brain is exposed to numerous sensory signals and it is able to capture the critical aspects of these data. One of the challenges that Artificial Intelligence faces is high data dimensionality. Specifically, the learning complexity increases exponentially with linear increase. Recent neuroscience findings have provided with details into the principles that characterise the representation of information in the mammalian brain. One of the key findings is that the neocortex allows the propagation of sensory signals through a complex hierarchy of modules (Lee & Mumford, 2003) that learn to represent observations based on regularities that exhibit (Lee et al., 1998). This led to the development of Deep Machine Learning that focuses on the development of computational models that function in a similar way as the neocortex (Arel et al., 2010).

Figure 1. Service-oriented Architecture (SOA) Definition
(Adapted from Domdouzis et al., 2016)

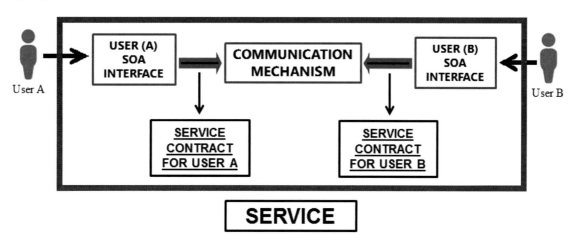

Examples of Deep Learning are the Convolutional Neural Networks (CNNs) and the Deep Belief Networks. Convolutional Neural Networks are a category of Deep Learning which are used in object detection and recognition. The architecture of such networks is suited to object analysis by learning and classifying complex features that represent parts of an object. CNN layers can be thought of as filter banks of complexity that can extract texture features and can be used in texture analysis (Andrearczyk & Whelan, 2016).

Ji et al. (2013) propose the application of CNNs for the extraction of spatial and temporal features from video data for action recognition. These 3D feature extractions acquire motion information from video streams, thus they operate in both the spatial and temporal dimensions. A 3D CNN has been developed based on 3D feature extractors. This architecture produces multiple channels of information from adjacent video frames and performs convolution and subsampling n each channel separately. The 3D convolution is achieved by convolving a 3D kernel to the cube developed by stacking multiple contiguous frames together. In this case, the feature maps are connected to a number of contiguous frames, thus capturing motion information (Ji et al., 2013).

Molchanov et al. (2015a) describe how hand-gesture recognition can be achieved with the use of 3D Convolutional Neural Networks. The examined dataset contains 885 intensity and depth video sequences and 19 different dynamic hand gestures performed by 8 subjects inside a vehicle (Ohn-Bar & Trivedi, 2014). The hand gestures involve hand and/or finger motion. The temporal lengths of the gestures were normalised by first re-sampling each gesture sequence to 32 frames using Nearest-Neighbour Interpolation (NNI) by dropping or repeating frames (Molchanov et al., 2015b). By using the Sobel operator, gradients from the intensity channel were computed. Gradients helped in the improvement of the robustness to the different illumination conditions that characterise the dataset. The suggested convolutional neural network classifier includes two sub-networks: a high-resolution network (HRN) and a low-resolution network (LRN). The process of training a CNN is related to the optimization of the network's parameters in order for the cost function to be minimised. The optimisation was realised via stochastic gradient descent with small parts from the training set. 3D Convolutional Neural Networks are shown to be effective for hand gesture recognition (Molchanov et al., 2015).

A Deep Belief Network is a class of deep neural network that includes multiple layers of hidden units. These units are connected to each other but there are no connections between the units within each layer. DBNs can be considered as very complex non-linear feature extractors in which each layer of the hidden units learn how to represent features that acquire correlations in the original input data. Hinton (2010) describes Deep Belief Networks as probabilistic generative e models that include multiple layers of stochastic latent variables (also called "feature detectors" or "hidden units"). The top two layers have undirected, symmetric connections between them and form an associative memory. The lower layers receive directed connections (top-to-down) from the layer above. DBNs are characterised by two significant, computational capabilities. First, there is an efficient procedure for learning the top-to-down weights that specify how the variables in one layer determine the probabilities of variables in the layer below. Second, after the learning in multiple layers has been concluded, the values of the latent variables in every layer can be inferred by a single, bottom-to-up pass that starts from the bottom layer and uses the weights in the reverse order (Hinton, 2010).

DBNs have been proposed for phone recognition. Mohamed and Deng (2010) suggest a training algorithm for a DBN in which each pair of layers is considered a Restricted Boltzmann Machine (RBN). An RBM is an example of a Markov-Random Field that has one layer of Bernoulli stochastic hidden units and one layer of Bernoulli or Gaussian stochastic visible units. RBMs can be represented as bipartite graphs since all visible units are connected to all hidden units (Mohamed & Deng, 2010).

The hippocampus is a small organ which is located within the brain's medial temporal lobe and it is responsible for the memory and spatial navigation. A damage to the hippocampus can lead to loss of memory and difficulty in developing new memories. For example, in Alzheimer's disease, the hippocampus is one of the first regions of the brain to be affected (Mandal, 2014). Especially for spatial navigation, the way its place cells operate is an example of how brain elaborates information through its own service-oriented architecture. Place cells are pyramidal cells that fire when an animal is in a specific location in its environment (Eichenbaum, 2010). These cells increase their firing rates when the mammal traverses specific regions of its surroundings. Specifically, hippocampal place cells encode spatial information during navigation through the use of rate and temporal codes (Moser et al., 2008; O'Keefe & Burgess, 2005).

The rate codes correspond to an increment in the firing rate at a specific location in a selective manner (O'Keefe & Dostrovksy, 1971). The temporal code includes the timing of spikes in relation to the hippocampal theta rhythm (O'Keefe & Recce, 1993; Buszaki, 2002). Except the elaboration of perpetual information, place cells are directed by self-motion signals. These signals show the location of the mammal in relation to its movements. This process is called 'Path Integration' and it is supported by the so called 'grid cells'. The 'grid cells' are located to the entorhinal cortex and this is main neocortical input to the hippocampus. The 'memory' of a location is maintained even when all orientating cues are removed (Hartley et al., 2014). The anatomy of the hippocampus is such that hippocampal information representations can maintain the topological features of the targets. The hippocampus is characterised by Long-Term Potentiation (LTP) which is a promising memory device (Teyler & DiScenna, 1985). The 2014 Nobel Prize in Physiology or Medicine was awarded to John O'Keefe, May-Britt Moser, and Edvard Moser. O'Keefe contribution is focused on the discovery of the place cells while the Mosers' contribution is focused on the identification of grid cells (Sharlach & Vence, 2014). O'Keefe studied rats by attaching electrodes to the hippocampal region of their brain. O'Keefe showed that certain nerve cells are always active when the rat was at a specific location. By firing in different combinations, the place cells managed to create a spatial map of the rat's surroundings.

Artificial Intelligence systems are characterised by their ability to adapt to the constantly changing conditions. Many real-world applications are characterised by the need of the involved systems to adapt to their requirements through learning and optimization. Optimization characterises machine learning operations while learning and optimization together define adaptation. A very good example of the adaptive capabilities of AI systems is Reinforcement Learning. Reinforcement learning is learning how to map situations to actions. In the standard reinforcement-learning model, an agent is connected to its environment through perception and actions. In mammals, perception of the reality is achieved through a combination of reinforcement learning and sensory processing systems. These systems are expressed through a mass of neural data that indicate parallels between the phasic signals emitted by dopaminergic neurons and temporal difference reinforcement learning algorithms (Mnih et al., 2015). Reinforcement learning agents are distinguished from supervised learning agents in the fact that they do not receive any feedback when they perform poorly (McCallum, 1996). On each step, the agent receives as input the current state of the environment and then it selects a specific action in order to produce an output. The state of the environment changes and this value of this state transition is transferred to the agent through a scalar reinforcement signal (Kaelbling et al., 1996). The elements of reinforcement learning are a policy, a reward function, a value function and a model of the environment. A policy specifies the agent's way of behaving at a specific time. Furthermore, it specifies a set of responses to a number of stimuli. A reward function defines the goal of a reinforcement learning problem. Specifically, it connects each state of the environment to a single number which represents a reward. The objective of the reinforcement learning agent is the maximisation of the total reward. A value function specifies what is good for the agent in the long-term. The value of a state is the total amount of reward an agent can accumulate in the long run starting from that state. The model of the environment simulates the behaviour of the environment. Based on a specific state and action, a model may predict the next state and the next reward (Sutton & Barto, 2014). There is hope that reinforcement learning will be used in a number of real-world situations. It is very probable to see reinforcement learning applied in problems in the field of industrial robotics. Deep reinforcement learning has been used by Google in order for its data centres to become more efficient (Knight, 2017). Deep learning techniques have been used to medical image analysis applications, such as the computerised prognosis of Alzheimer's disease (Suk et al., 2015), organ segmentations (Zhang *et al.*, 2015) and detection (Shin et al., 2013). Deep neural networks are used for predicting pharmacological properties of drugs using transcriptomic data. A pathway activation scoring algorithm applied to a set of data characterised by different concentrations of the drug for different time periods. Figure 2 shows the architecture of the DNN for drug pharmacological properties predictions (Aliper et al., 2016).

APPLICATION OF SOA TO LARGE CRISIS MANAGEMENT: THE ATHENA PLATFORM

The ATHENA Project is a European Union project that with main aim the development of a Crisis Communication Management System that enables the public to communicate through a Social Media-based platform with the emergency search and rescue services. The goal of the ATHENA project is the development of a set of guidelines for the Police, the Law Enforcement Agencies (LEAs) and the first responders for the use of Social Media during large crises. Furthermore, a number of computational tools were developed in order for the crisis decision making realised by the respective authorities to become

Figure 2. Gene expression analysis through a Deep Neural Network
(Adapted from: Aliper et al., 2016)

more efficient. The ATHENA System includes the Crisis Communication & Control Intelligence Dashboard (CCCID), the ATHENA Crisis Mobile and the ATHENA Crisis Information Processing Centre (CIPC). The structure of the ATHENA System is shown in Figure 3.

The ATHENA CCCID communicates with a number of components within the ATHENA System. Some of the components of the CCCID communicate with each other also.

The development of SOAs is based on three stages: Business Process Modelling Notation (BPMN), Business Architecture Modelling (BAM), and System Architecture Modelling (SAM). The Business Process Management Initiative (BPMI) has developed a Business Process Modelling Notation (BPMN). The aim of the development of the BPMN is the creation of business models which will simultaneously handle the complexity which characterises business processes. The BPMN defines a Business Process Diagram (BPD) which includes graphical elements that are used for the modelling of business operations (White, 2004). Business Architecture Modelling (BAM) is used for the identification of the business requirements of the SOA (Elvesæter, 2011). Business architecture is a blueprint of the enterprise that provides an understanding of the organization and aligns strategic objectives and tactical demands (Object Management Group (OMG), 2017). System Architecture Modelling (SIM) is based on the representation of the structure and the behaviour of the system (Domdouzis et al., 2016).

Figure 3. The ATHENA System

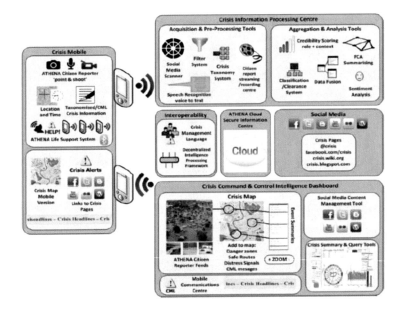

In the case of ATHENA Services, the elements of a service are the service contracts and the mechanism(s) that connects them. Service contracts are the fundamental elements of a service architecture. Service contracts allow the connection between the service consumers and the service producers. In the case of ATHENA, the consumers are the Police, Law Enforcement Agencies (LEAs) and the first responders and the service producers are the citizens. Two interfaces are used for the interaction of the consumers and the producers with their respective service contracts and these interfaces are used to connect the citizens (producers) and the Police, LEAs and first responders (consumers) to the service contract. The service contracts define the bi-directional interaction between the consumers and the producers. Figure 4 shows an example of service for the ATHENA CCCID Citizen Reporter Feeds Service. The mechanism that connects the two service contracts is the core of the service as it needs to adapt to the different requirements of each service contract (Domdouzis et al., 2016).

During large crisis events, the facilitation of information management is achieved through the ATHENA Cloud (A-Cloud) solution. This solution includes two main components: the ATHENA Persistence Cloud (APC) which provides storage capacity based on different combinations of technologies and the ATHENA Logic Cloud (ALC) which provides an abstraction on accessing and handling processes for the data included in the APC. The ALC also allows querying of sensors at runtime, thus it introduces knowledge brokerage among different types of services. The ALC does not store any data, thus it introduces the interoperability for the development of information flows between data producers and

Figure 4. The ATHENA Citizen Reporter Service
(Adapted from Domdouzis et al., 2016)

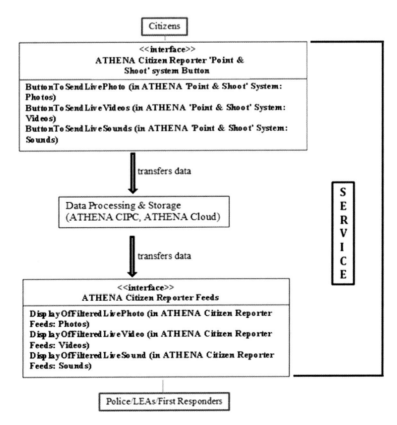

consumers. A DPIF service proxy is a software process that continuously runs on the ALC server and it represents a specific service which is provided either by a domain expert or an automated solution. A DPIF proxy can be considered as a knowledge worker that initiates knowledge brokerage. An expert can communicate with the proxy through an interface while an automated service can be applied within the proxy. Examples of services are data store access mechanisms that allow the manipulation of different types of databases and algorithms that perform data mining and machine learning (de Oude et al., 2017).

Each DPIF proxy that represents a service needs to adopt appropriate standards and transform service outputs to standardized data objects that can be shared with other proxies that represent consumer services. The standards define the semantics in which data are exchanged. A service standard includes a service description, the service invocation data structure and the service response data structure. An important characteristic of DPIF is the ability to adopt and develop new service standards. This is enabled through OntoWizard, a special configuration tool. By using the specific wizard, a service provider can describe the provided service and the required sets of inputs in a standardised way without the need of any technical knowledge of the DPIF technology and service representations. The configuration process generates metadata that are used by the proxy which represents the specific service. That metadata are used for the publication of the service, for the subscription to outputs of other types of services and for the negotiation that filters services. The services can be classified as 'human-based' and 'machine-based'. The process of integrating human-based services into ALC is firstly to find the right service standard through free text. The second step is from the user to select the service standard from the list of service descriptions and this results to an automated generation of metadata that are used by the service proxies in ALC for the purpose of service discovery, filtering and development of information flows. The user can use the OntoWizard in order to specify the context of a specific service. This context describes the parameters under which the specific service can be provided (e.g. Quality of Service, geographical location). The OntoWizard also allows users to specify complementary service types which other types of services that are provided by other proxies. This is again realised through the use of free text descriptions of the service types and the querying of the catalogue of service standards (de Oude et al., 2017).

The current services used in the ATHENA System will be benefited in the future through the advancement of current Artificial Intelligence technologies. A re-definition of Service-oriented Architectures (SOAs) based on the study of the human hippocampus would produce new conclusions on how current SOAs can be re-configured. In this case, new implementations of SOAs could occur in different fields of engineering and science and the complexity of projects such as the ATHENA project could be faced better through a smarter SOA. Specifically, the implementation of smarter SOAs for a project such as ATHENA would provide a new architecture for the system which would be characterised by more reliable outcomes and improvement of the collaboration between the police and the public.

CONCLUSION

Bio-inspired systems have been proven to be the basis of modern technological advancements. The analysis of biological systems can produce useful conclusions on how existing technologies can be reformulated and optimised. In the case of Service-oriented Architectures (SOAs), re-formulation and optimisation are very important as services need to be able to adjust to instantaneous requirements. It is important to comprehend that technology is part of every human activity and all the factors that impact human activities must be considered by technology. The famous MIT Professor Mike Dertouzos once mentioned that technology should become like the oxygen. He predicted that technology will become a necessary part of human life. The way humans interact with technology is described by services. There is the need therefore to integrate the different factors of different type (e.g. social, psychological) on the operation of services. The choice of studying biological systems (e.g. human brain's hippocampus) is based on the fact that biological systems are adjusted to their environments. Hippocampus uses place cells to adjust to different environments and it acts as the human brain's navigation system. These place cells are activated differently depending on spatial and temporal conditions. The adaptability of hippocampus to the changes of the environment is also evident by the fact that the adult hippocampus can produce stem cells during stressful conditions. The complexity of the operations performed by the hippocampus can act as a guide for the development of more advanced services that will represent more accurately reality. For example, spatial navigation is based on a network of closely-interconnected structures that include the hippocampus, the prefrontal cortex and the basal ganglia. The study of these structures would provide details on the processes in learning complex navigational tasks (Hirel et al., 2013). By improving our comprehension of spatial navigation in the mammalian brains, better technologically navigational systems could be developed.

REFERENCES

Abaas, T., Shibghatullah, A. S., Yusof, R., & Alaameri, A. (2014). Importance and Significance of Information Sharing in Terrorism Field. *International Symposium on Research in Innovation and Sustainability (ISoRIS '14)*, 1719-1725.

Aliper, A., Plis, S., Artemov, A., Ulloa, A., Mamoshina, P., & Zhavoronkov, A. (2016). Deep Learning Applications for Predicting Pharmacological Properties of Drugs and Drug Repurposing Using Transcriptomic Data. *Molecular Pharmaceutics*, *13*(7), 2524–2530. doi:10.1021/acs.molpharmaceut.6b00248 PMID:27200455

Andrearczyk, V., & Whelan, P. F. (2016). Using filter banks in Convolutional Neural Networks for texture classification. *Pattern Recognition Letters*, *84*, 63–69. doi:10.1016/j.patrec.2016.08.016

Annoni, A., Bernard, L., Douglas, J., Greenwood, J., Laiz, I., Lloyd, M., ... Usländer, T. (2005). Orchestra: developing a unified open architecture for risk management applications. In *Geo-Information for Disaster Management* (pp. 1–17). Springer. doi:10.1007/3-540-27468-5_1

Arel, I., Rose, D. C., & Karnowski, T. P. (2010). Deep Machine Learning - A New Frontier in Artificial Intelligence Research. *IEEE Computational Intelligence Magazine*, *5*(4), 13–18. doi:10.1109/MCI.2010.938364

Baron, G. (2010). Response suggestions and public participation the new norm in response management. *Crisis Comm*. Retrieved from: http://www.emergencymgmt.com/emergency-blogs/crisis-comm/Response-Suggestions-and-Public-111510.html

Bulldog Reporter. (2010). *Web users increasingly rely on social media to seek help in a disaster: New Red Cross survey shows that 74 percent expect response agencies to answer social media call for help within an hour*. Available at: https://www.bulldogreporter.com/web-users-increasingly-rely-social-media-seek-help-disaster-new-red-cross-survey-sh/

Buzsaki, G. (2002). Theta oscillations in the hippocampus. *Neuron*, *33*(3), 325–340. doi:10.1016/S0896-6273(02)00586-X PMID:11832222

Chen, Y. (2005). Data Mining and Service Rating in Service-Oriented Architectures to Improve Information Sharing. 2005 IEEE Aerospace Conference, 1-11.

Dang, J., Hedayati, A., Hampel, K., & Toklu, C. (2008). An ontological knowledge framework for adaptive medical workflow. *Journal of Biomedical Informatics*, *41*(5), 829–836. doi:10.1016/j.jbi.2008.05.012 PMID:18602872

de Oude, P., Pavlin, G., Quillinan, T., Jeraj, J., & Abouhafc, A. (2017). Cloud-Based Intelligence Aquisition and Processing for Crisis Management. In B. Akhgar, A. Staniforth, & D. Waddington (Eds.), *Application of Social Media in Crisis Management* (pp. 133–153). Springer. doi:10.1007/978-3-319-52419-1_9

Domdouzis, K., Andrews, S., Akhgar, B. (2016). Application of a New Service-Oriented Architecture (SOA) Paradigm on the Design of a Crisis Management Distributed System. *International Journal of Distributed Systems and Technologies*.

Eichenbaum, H. (2010). Hippocampus: Mapping or memory? *Current Biology*, *10*(21), 785–787. doi:10.1016/S0960-9822(00)00763-6 PMID:11084350

Elvesæter, B. (2011). *Service Modelling Service Modelling with SoaML*. Available at: http://www.uio.no/studier/emner/matnat/ifi/INF5120/v11/div/SoaML_Tutorial.pdf

Ganapathy, K., Priya, B., Dhivya, B. P., Prashanth, V., & Vaidehi, V. (2013). SOA Framework for Geriatric Remote Health Care Using Wireless Sensor Network. *Procedia Computer Science*, *19*, 1012–1019. doi:10.1016/j.procs.2013.06.141

Hartley, T., Lever, C., Burgess, N., & O'Keefe, J. (2014). Space in the brain: How the hippocampal formation supports spatial cognition. *Philosophical Transactions of the Royal Society of London. Series B, Biological Sciences*, *369*(1635), 20120510. doi:10.1098/rstb.2012.0510 PMID:24366125

Heath, R. L. (1997). *Strategic Issues Management*. Thousand Oaks, CA: Sage.

Heath, R. L. (1998). New Communication Technologies: An Issues Management Point of View. *Public Relations Review*, *24*(3), 273–288. doi:10.1016/S0363-8111(99)80140-4

Hinton, G. (2010). Deep Belief Nets. Encyclopedia of Machine Learning, 267-269.

Hirel, J., Gaussier, P., Quoy, M., Banquet, J. P., Save, E., & Pucet, B. (2013). The hippocampo-cortical loop: Spatio-temporal learning and goal-oriented planning in navigation. *Neural Networks*, *43*, 8–21. doi:10.1016/j.neunet.2013.01.023 PMID:23500496

IPCC. (2012). Managing the risks of extreme events and disasters to advance climate change adaptation. In *The SREX Report*. Cambridge, UK: Cambridge University Press.

Jammes, F., & Smit, H. (2005). Service-Oriented Paradigms in Industrial Automation. *IEEE Transactions on Industrial Informatics*, *1*(1), 62–70. doi:10.1109/TII.2005.844419

Ji, S., Xu, W., Yang, M., & Yu, K. (2013). 3D Convolutional Neural Networks for Human Action Recognition. *IEEE Transactions on Pattern Analysis and Machine Intelligence*, *35*(1), 221–231. doi:10.1109/TPAMI.2012.59 PMID:22392705

Kaelbling, L. P., Littman, M. L., & Moore, A. W. (1996). Reinforcement Learning: A Survey. *Journal of Artificial Intelligence Research*, *4*, 237–285.

Kawamoto, K., & Lobach, D. F. (2007, March 1). Proposal for Fulfilling Strategic Objectives of the U.S. Roadmap for National Action on Decision Support through a Service-oriented Architecture Leveraging HL7 Services. *Journal of the American Medical Informatics Association*, *14*(2), 146–155. doi:10.1197/jamia.M2298 PMID:17213489

Khakpour, N., Jalili, S., Talcott, C., Sirjani, M., & Mousavi, M. R. (2010). PobSAM: Policy-based managing of actors in self-adaptive systems. *Electronic Notes in Theoretical Computer Science*, *263*, 129–143. doi:10.1016/j.entcs.2010.05.008

Knight, W. (2017). 5 Big Predictions for Artificial Intelligence in 2017. *MIT Technology Review*. Available at: https://www.technologyreview.com/s/603216/5-big-predictions-for-artificial-intelligence-in-2017/

Lee, T., & Mumford, D. (2003). Hierarchical Bayesian inference in the visual cortex. *Journal of the Optical Society of America*, *20*(7), 1434–1448. doi:10.1364/JOSAA.20.001434 PMID:12868647

Leea, T. S., Mumfordb, D., Romeroa, R., & Lammec, A. F. V. (1998). The role of the primary visual cortex in higher level vision. *Vision Research*, *38*(15-16), 2429–2454. doi:10.1016/S0042-6989(97)00464-1 PMID:9798008

Löwe, P., Wächter, J., Hammitzsch, M., Lendholt, M., & Häner, R. (2013). The Evolution of Disaster Early Warning Systems in the TRIDEC Project. *Proceedings of the Twenty-third (2013) International Offshore and Polar Engineering*, 48-52.

Maliska, M., Simo, B., Ciglan, M., Slizik, P., & Hluchy, L. (2006). Lecture Notes in Computer Science: Vol. 3911. *Service oriented architecture for risk assessment of natural disasters*. Berlin: Springer. doi:10.1007/11752578_43

Mandal, A. (2014). *Hippocampus Functions*. News Medical Life Sciences. Available at: https://www.news-medical.net/health/Hippocampus-Functions.aspx

McCallum, A. K. (1996). *Reinforcement Learning with Selective Perception and Hidden State (PhD Thesis)*. Rochester, NY: University of Rochester.

Mnih, V., Kavukcuoglu, K., Silver, D., Rusu, A. A., Veness, J., Bellemare, M. G., ... Hassabis, D. (2015). Human-level control through deep reinforcement learning. *Nature*, *518*(7540), 529–533. doi:10.1038/nature14236 PMID:25719670

Mohamed, A.-r., Yu, D., & Deng, L. (2010). Investigation of Full-Sequence Training of Deep Belief Networks for Speech Recognition. *Interspeech 2010*, 2846-2849.

Molchanov, P., Gupta, S., & Kim, K. (2015a). Hand gesture recognition with 3D convolutional neural networks. *IEEE Conference on Computer Vision and Pattern Recognition Workshops (CVPRW)*. 10.1109/CVPRW.2015.7301342

Molchanov, P., Gupta, S., Kim, K., & Pulli, K. (2015b). Multi-sensor System for Driver's Hand-Gesture Recognition. *11th IEEE International Conference and Workshops on Automatic Face and Gesture Recognition (FG)*, 1.

Moser, E. I., Kropff, E., & Moser, M. B. (2008). Place Cells, Grid Cells, and the Brain's Spatial Representation System. *Annual Review of Neuroscience*, *31*(1), 69–89. doi:10.1146/annurev.neuro.31.061307.090723 PMID:18284371

O'Keefe, J., & Burgess, N. (2005). Dual phase and rate coding in hippocampal place cells: Theoretical significance and relationship to entorhinal grid cells. *Hippocampus*, *15*(7), 853–866. doi:10.1002/hipo.20115 PMID:16145693

O'Keefe, J., & Dostrovsky, J. (1971). The hippocampus as a spatial map. Preliminary evidence from unit activity in the freely-moving rat. *Brain Research*, *34*(1), 171–175. doi:10.1016/0006-8993(71)90358-1 PMID:5124915

O'Keefe, J., & Recce, M. L. (1993). Phase relationship between hippocampal place units and the EEG theta rhythm. *Hippocampus*, *3*(3), 317–330. doi:10.1002/hipo.450030307 PMID:8353611

Object Management Group (OMG). (2017). *Business Architecture Overview*. Available at: http://bawg.omg.org/business_architecture_overview.htm

Ohn-Bar, E., & Trivedi, M. (2014). Hand gesture recognition in real time for automotive interfaces: A multimodal vision-based approach and evaluations. *IEEE Transactions on Intelligent Transportation Systems*, *15*(6), 1–10. doi:10.1109/TITS.2014.2337331

Papazoglou & Heuvel. (2007). Service oriented architectures: approaches, technologies and research issues. *The VLDB Journal - The International Journal on Very Large Data Bases*, *16*(3), 389-415.

Poslad, S., Middleton, S. E., Chaves, F., Tao, R., Necmioglu, O., & Bugel, U. (2015). A Semantic IoT Early Warning System for Natural Environment Crisis Management. *IEEE Transactions on Emerging Topics in Computing*, *3*(2), 246–257. doi:10.1109/TETC.2015.2432742

Rinaldi, S. M., Peerenboom, J. P., & Kelly, T. K. (2001). Identifying, understanding, and analyzing critical infrastructure interdependencies. *IEEE Control Systems*, *21*(6), 11–25. doi:10.1109/37.969131

Schoenharl, T., Bravo, R., & Madey, G. (2006). WIPER: Leveraging the Cell Phone Network for Emergency Response. *International Journal of Intelligent Control and Systems*, *11*(4), 206–216.

Sharlach, M., & Vence, T. (2014). Brain's "Inner GPS" Wins Nobel. *TheScientist*. Available at: http://www.the-scientist.com/?articles.view/articleNo/41155/title/Brain-s--Inner-GPS--Wins-Nobel/

Shin, H.-C., Orton, M. R., Collins, D. J., Doran, S. J., & Leach, M. O. (2013). Stacked Autoencoders for Unsupervised Feature Learning and Multiple Organ Detection in a Pilot Study Using 4D Patient Data. *IEEE Transactions on Pattern Analysis and Machine Intelligence*, *35*(8), 1930–1943. doi:10.1109/TPAMI.2012.277 PMID:23787345

SIRENA. (2017). *Service Infrastructure for Real-time Embedded Networked Applications*. Available at: https://itea3.org/project/sirena.html

Steelman, T. A., & McCaffrey, S. (2013). Best practices in risk and crisis communication: Implications for natural hazards management. *Natural Hazards*, *65*(1), 683–705. doi:10.100711069-012-0386-z

Suk, H.-I., Lee, S.-W., & Shen, D. (2015). Latent Feature Representation with Stacked Auto-Encoder for AD/MCI Diagnosis. *Brain Structure & Function*, *220*(2), 841–859. doi:10.100700429-013-0687-3 PMID:24363140

Sutton, R. S., & Barto, A. G. (1998). *Reinforcement Learning - An Introduction*. Cambridge, MA: The MIT Press.

Tapia, D. I., Rodríguez, S., Bajo, J., & Corchado, J. M. (2008). FUSION@, A SOA-Based Multi-agent Architecture. *International Symposium on Distributed Computing and Artificial Intelligence 2008 (DCAI 2008)*, 99-107.

Teyler, T. J., & DiScenna, P. (1985). The role of hippocampus in memory: A hypothesis. *Neuroscience and Biobehavioral Reviews*, *9*(3), 377–389. doi:10.1016/0149-7634(85)90016-8 PMID:2999655

Thomsen, S. R. (1995). Using Online Databases in Corporate Issues Management. *Public Relations Review*, *21*(2), 103–122. doi:10.1016/0363-8111(95)90002-0

Up2Europe. (2017). *Collaborative, Complex and Critical Decision-Support in Evolving Crises (TRIDEC)*. Available at: https://www.up2europe.eu/european/projects/collaborative-complex-and-critical-decision-support-in-evolving-crises_9985.html

Veil, S. R., Buehner, T., & Palenchar, M. J. (2011). A Work-In-Process Literature Review: Incorporating Social Media in Risk and Crisis Communication. *Journal of Contingencies and Crisis Management*, *19*(2), 110–122. doi:10.1111/j.1468-5973.2011.00639.x

Vescoukis, V., Doulamis, N., & Karagiorgou, S. (2012). A service oriented architecture for decision support systems in environmental crisis management. *Future Generation Computer Systems*, *28*(3), 593–604. doi:10.1016/j.future.2011.03.010

White, S. A. (2004). Introduction to BPMN. *BPTrends*. Available at: http://yoann.nogues.free.fr/IMG/pdf/07-04_WP_Intro_to_BPMN_-_White-2.pdf

Zhang, W., Li, R., Deng, H., Wang, L., Lin, W., Ji, S., & Shen, D. (2015). Deep comvolutional neural networks for multi-modality isointense infant brain image segmentation. *NeuroImage*, *108*, 214–224. doi:10.1016/j.neuroimage.2014.12.061 PMID:25562829

Chapter 6
A Tour of Lattice–Based Skyline Algorithms

Markus Endres
University of Augsburg, Germany

Lena Rudenko
University of Augsburg, Germany

ABSTRACT

A skyline query retrieves all objects in a dataset that are not dominated by other objects according to some given criteria. There exist many skyline algorithms which can be classified into generic, index-based, and lattice-based algorithms. This chapter takes a tour through lattice-based skyline algorithms. It summarizes the basic concepts and properties, presents high-performance parallel approaches, shows how one overcomes the low-cardinality restriction of lattice structures, and finally presents an application on data streams for real-time skyline computation. Experimental results on synthetic and real datasets show that lattice-based algorithms outperform state-of-the-art skyline techniques, and additionally have a linear runtime complexity.

INTRODUCTION

The Skyline operator (Börzsönyi, Kossmann, & Stocker, 2001) has emerged as an important and very popular summarization technique for multi-dimensional datasets. A *Skyline query*, also known as *Pareto preference query*, selects those objects from a dataset D that are not dominated by any others. An object p having d attributes (dimensions) dominates an object q, if p is better than q in at least one dimension and not worse than q in all other dimensions, for a defined comparison function. This dominance criterion defines a partial order and therefore transitivity holds. *The Skyline* is the set of points which are not dominated by any other point of D. Without loss of generality, the Skyline with the *min* function for all attributes is used in this chapter.

The most cited example on Skyline queries is the search for a hotel that is *cheap and close to the beach* (Börzsönyi, Kossmann, & Stocker, 2001). Unfortunately, these two goals are complementary, as the hotels near the beach tend to be more expensive. In Figure 1 each hotel is represented as a point in

DOI: 10.4018/978-1-5225-5396-0.ch006

the two-dimensional space of *price* and *distance* to the beach. Interesting are all hotels that are not worse than any other hotel in both dimensions.

The hotels p_6, p_7, p_8 are dominated by hotel p_3. The hotel p_9 is dominated by p_4, while the hotels p_1, p_2, p_3, p_4, p_5 are not dominated by any other hotels and build the *Skyline*. From the Skyline, one can now make the final decision, thereby weighing the personal preferences for price and distance to the beach.

Algorithms of the *block-nested-loop* class (BNL) (Börzsönyi, Kossmann, & Stocker, 2001) are the most prominent algorithms for computing Skylines. In fact, the basic operation of collecting maxima during a single scan of the input data can be found at the core of several Skyline algorithms, cp. (Godfrey, Shipley, & Gryz, 2007; Chomicki, Ciaccia, & Meneghetti, 2013). There are also algorithms utilizing an index structure to compute the Skyline, e.g., (Tan, Eng, & Ooi, 2001; Papadias, Tao, Fu, & Seeger, 2003; Lee, Zheng, Li, & Lee, 2007; Endres & Weichmann, 2017). However, index-based algorithms are not capable of processing arbitrary data without any preparations.

This chapter takes a tour of *lattice-based Skyline algorithms*, which goes from sequential to parallel approaches to an application in data streams. Lattice Skyline algorithms do *not* depend on tuple comparisons as BNL does, but on the *lattice structure* constructed by a Skyline query over low-cardinality domains. Following (Morse, Patel, & Jagadish, 2007; Chomicki, Ciaccia, & Meneghetti, 2013) many Skyline applications involve domains with small cardinalities – these cardinalities are either inherently small (such as star ratings for hotels), or can naturally be mapped to low-cardinality domains (such as price ranges on hotels). However, since there are still many applications where high-cardinality domains are involved, the *Scalagon* algorithm which overcomes the annoying low-cardinality restriction is also presented.

The remainder of this chapter is organized as follows: Section 2 revisits the concept of Skyline computation. Afterwards the basic sequential lattice-based algorithms *Hexagon* and *LS-B* are discussed in Section 3. Based on this background the high-performance parallel versions of these algorithms, namely *ARL-S* and *HPL-S*, are presented in Section 4. Section 5 describes *Scalagon*, a lattice-based

Figure 1. Skyline example

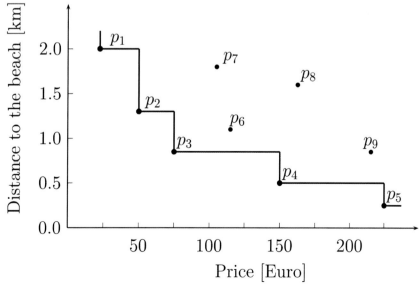

Skyline algorithm for all seasons. The application of lattice-based Skyline algorithms on data streams is depicted in Section 6. Section 7 contains an extensive performance evaluation on synthetic and real datasets. Finally, Section 8 contains concluding remarks.

SKYLINE QUERIES REVISITED

Skyline Queries

The aim of a Skyline query or Pareto preference (Kießling, Endres, & Wenzel, 2011) is to find *the best objects* in a dataset D, denoted by *Sky(D)*. More formally:

Definition 1 (Dominance and Indifference): Assume a set of vectors $D \subseteq \mathbb{R}^d$. Given $p = (p_1, ..., p_n)$, $q = (q_1, ..., q_d) \in D$, p dominates q on D, denoted as $p \prec q$, if the following holds:

$$p \prec q \Leftrightarrow \forall i \in \{1, ..., d\} : p_i \leq q_i \wedge \exists j \in \{1, ..., d\} : p_j < q_j$$

Two objects p and q are called indifferent on D, denoted as $p \sim q$, if and only if $p \not\prec q$ and $q \not\prec p$.

Note that following Definition 1 we consider subsets of $\mathbb{R}^d$ in that we search for Skylines w.r.t. the natural order $\leq$ in each dimension.

Definition 2 (Skyline Sky(D)): The Skyline Sky(D) of D is defined by the maxima in D according to the ordering $\prec$, or explicitly by the set

$$\text{Sky}(D) = \{p \in D \mid \nexists q \in D : q \prec p\}$$

In this sense, the minimal values in each domain are preferred and we write $p \prec q$ if p is better than q.

Skylines are not restricted to numerical domains. For any universe Ω and orderings $\prec_i \in (\Omega \times \Omega)$ ($i \in \{1, ..., d\}$) the Skyline w.r.t. $\prec_i$ can be computed, if there exist scoring functions $g_i : \Omega \to \mathbb{R}$ for all $i \in \{1, ..., d\}$ such that $p <_i q \Leftrightarrow g_i(p) < g_i(q)$. Then the Skyline of a set $M \subseteq \Omega$ w.r.t. $(\prec_i)_{i=1,...d}$ is equivalent to the Skyline of $\{(g(p_1), ..., g(p_d)) \mid p \in M\}$.

Block-Nested-Loop Revisited

Algorithms of the block-nested-loop (BNL) class (Börzsönyi, Kossmann, & Stocker, 2001) are the most well-known methods to evaluate Skylines. BNL-style algorithms linearly scan over the input dataset D. The idea of BNL is to continuously maintain a window (or block) of tuples in main memory containing the maximal elements with respect to the data read so far. When a tuple $p \in D$ is read from the input, p is compared to all tuples of the window and, based on this comparison, p is either eliminated, or placed into the window. Three cases can occur: First, p is dominated by a tuple within the window. In this case, *p* is eliminated and will not be considered in future iterations. Second, *p* dominates one or more tuples in the window. In this case, these tuples are eliminated; that is, these tuples are removed from the window and will not be considered in future iterations while *p* is inserted into the window. And third, *p* is incomparable with all tuples in the window. In this case *p* is inserted into the window. At the end of the algorithm the window contains the maximal elements, i.e., the Skyline.

BNL algorithms work particularly well if the Skyline is small (Godfrey, Shipley, & Gryz, 2007). The average case complexity is of the order $O(n)$, where n counts the number of input tuples. In the worst case, the complexity is $O(n^2)$. The major advantage of a BNL-style algorithm is its simplicity and suitability for computing the maxima of arbitrary partial orders.

Based on this tuple-to-tuple comparison-based approach, several algorithms have been published in the last decade, e.g., SFS (Sort-Filter Skyline) (Chomicki, Godfrey, Gryz, & Liang, 2003) topologically sorts the dataset, whereas LESS (Linear Elimination-Sort for Skyline) (Godfrey, Shipley, & Gryz, 2007) uses dynamic sorting and elimination of tuples from the window. The algorithm sSkyline (Park, Kim, Park, Kim, & Im, 2009) uses a merge method to compute the Skyline, and BSkyTree (Lee, & Hwang, 2010) is based on a balanced pivot point selection. There are other approaches like divide-and-conquer (Börzsönyi, Kossmann, & Stocker, 2001), or parallel variants of the algorithms above, e.g., LazyList BNL (Selke, Lofi, & Balke, 2010), pSkyline (Park, Kim, Park, Kim, & Im, 2009), APSkyline (Liknes, Vlachou, Doulkeridis, & Nørvåg, 2014), and Hybrid (Chester, Sidlauskas, Assent, & Bøgh, 2015), just to name a few.

SEQUENTIAL LATTICE-BASED SKYLINE ALGORITHMS

All algorithms which exploit the lattice structure constructed by a Skyline query are based on the algorithms *Hexagon* (Preisinger & Kießling, 2007; Preisinger, 2009) and *LS-B* (Morse, Patel, & Jagadish, 2007), which follow the same idea: the partial order imposed by a Skyline query / Pareto preference over a low-cardinality domain constitutes a *lattice*. This means if a, $b \in D$, the set *{a,b}* has a least upper bound and a greatest lower bound in D. Visualization of such lattices is often done using *Better-Than-Graphs* (BTG) (Hasse diagrams), graphs in which edges state dominance. The nodes in the BTG represent *equivalence classes*. Each equivalence class contains the objects mapped to the same feature vector. All values in the same class are considered substitutable.

An example of a BTG over a 2-dimensional space is shown in Figure 2a. [2..4] is used to describe a two-dimensional domain where the first attribute A_1 is an element of $\{0,1,2\}$ and attribute A_2 an element of $\{0,1,2,3,4\}$. The arrows show the dominance relationship between elements of the lattice.

The node (0,0) presents the *best node*, i.e., the least upper bound for two arbitrary nodes a and b in the lattice. The node (2, 4) is the *worst node* and serves as the greatest lower bound. The bold numbers next to each node are *unique identifiers* (ID) for each node in the lattice. Nodes having the same level are indifferent. That means for example, that neither the objects in the node (0,4) are better than the objects in (2,2) nor vice versa. They have the same overall *level 4*. A dataset D does not necessarily contain representatives for each lattice node. In Figure 2a the gray nodes are occupied (*non-empty*, marked as *[ne]*) with real elements from the dataset whereas the white nodes have no element (*empty*, marked as *[e]*).

The method to obtain the Skyline can be visualized using the BTG. The elements of the dataset D that compose the Skyline are those in the BTG that have *no path leading to them from another non-empty node in D*. In Figure 2a these are the nodes (0,1) and (2,0). All other nodes have direct or transitive

Figure 2. The Hexagon algorithm revisited

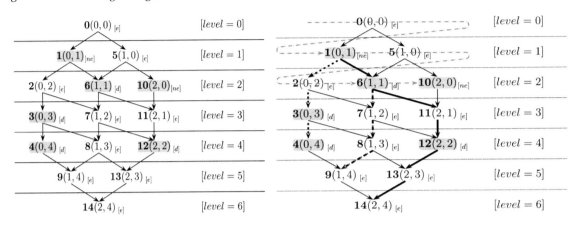

(a) 2d lattice over [2..4]   (b) BFT and DFT in Hexagon

edges from these both nodes, and therefore are *dominated* (dominated nodes are marked with *[d]*). The algorithms in (Preisinger & Kießling, 2007; Morse, Patel, & Jagadish, 2007) exploit these observations and in general consist of three phases:

- **Phase 1:** The *Construction Phase* initializes the data structures. The lattice is represented by an *array* in main memory having the size of the lattice, i.e., the number of nodes. Each position in the array stands for one node ID in the lattice. Initially, all nodes of the lattice are marked as *empty* (**[e]**).
- **Phase 2:** In the *Adding Phase* the algorithm iterates through each element t of the dataset D. For each element t the unique ID and the node of the lattice that corresponds to t is determined. This node is marked *non-empty* (**[ne]**).
- **Phase 3:** *Removal Phase.* After all tuples have been processed, the nodes of the lattice that are marked as *non-empty* and which are not reachable by the transitive dominance relationship from any other *non-empty* node of the lattice represent the Skyline values. Nodes that are *non-empty* but are reachable by the dominance relationship, and hence are not Skyline values, are marked *dominated* (**[d]**) to distinguish them from present Skyline values.

From an algorithmic point of view this is done by a combination of *breadth-first traversal* (BFT) and *depth-first traversal* (DFT). The nodes of the lattice are visited level-by-level in a breadth-first order (the dark gray dashed line in Figure 2b). When an empty node is reached, it is removed from the BFT relation. Each time a *non-empty* and *not dominated* node is found, a DFT is done marking all dominated nodes as *dominated*. For example, the node (0, 1) in Figure 2b is not empty. The DFT walks down to the nodes (1, 1) and (0, 2). Which one will be visited first is controlled by a so-called *edge weight*, cp. (Preisinger and Kießling, 2007). Here, (1,1) will be marked as *dominated* and the DFT will continue with (2,1), etc. (the thick black solid arrows in Figure 2b). If the DFT reaches the bottom node (2,4) (or an already dominated node) it will recursively follow the other edge weights, i.e. the thick black dashed arrows, and afterwards the thick black dotted arrows. After that, the BFT will continue with node (1,0), which will be removed because it is empty. The next non-empty node is (1,1), which is already dominated and therefore continue with (2,0). Since all other nodes are marked as dominated, the algorithm will stop and the non-empty and not dominated nodes (0, 1) and (2, 0) present the Skyline.

The original lattice based algorithms have linear runtime complexity. More precisely, the complexity is $O(dV + dn)$, where d is the dimensionality, n is the number of input tuples, and V is the product of the cardinalities of the d low-cardinality domains from which the attributes are drawn. Since there are V total entries in the lattice, each compared with at most d entries, this step is $O(dV)$. In the original version of Hexagon all entries in the lattice are positioned in an array. Since array accesses are $O(1)$, the pass through the data to mark an entry as *non-empty* is $O(dn)$.

Note that Hexagon and LS-B were developed for Skyline computation over low-cardinality domains. An attribute domain *dom(S)* is said to be low-cardinality if its value is drawn from a set $S = \{s_1, \ldots, s_m\}$, such that the set cardinality m is small. For a low-cardinality domain and $s_i \in \mathbb{R}$ a one-to-one mapping function $f : \mathbb{R} \to \mathbb{N}_0$, $f(s_i) = i - 1$, can be defined to get discrete values as required in all lattice algorithms. Furthermore, the term *node* for $a = (a_1, \ldots a_d) \in \mathbb{N}_0^d$ as an element of the lattice is often used as interchangeable with the term *tuple* $p = (p_1, \ldots, p_d) \in D \subseteq \mathbb{R}^d$, since there is a natural mapping form p to a as described above. Even though many Skyline applications involve domains with small cardinalities (Morse, Patel, & Jagadish, 2007; Chomicki, Ciaccia, & Meneghetti, 2013), this is a strong restriction of the practicability of lattice algorithms. Therefore, the *Scalagon* algorithm is presented in this chapter, which overcomes this restriction. But before that, parallel variants of Hexagon and LS-B are introduced.

PARALLEL LATTICE-BASED SKYLINE ALGORITHMS

For the development of parallel lattice-based Skyline algorithms a *split* approach of the input dataset with a *shared data structure* supporting fine grained locking is combined, cp. (Endres & Kießling, 2014, 2015). The general idea of parallelizing the Hexagon and LS-B algorithms is to parallelize the adding phase (Phase 2) and the removal phase (Phase 3). Phase 1 is not worth to parallelize because of its simple structure and minor time and effort for the initialization. Parallelizing Phase 2 can be done using a simple partitioning approach of the input dataset, whereas for Phase 3 two different approaches can be used: In the first variant, the parallel Phase 3 starts *after* all elements were added to the BTG. This algorithm is called *ARL-Skyline* (Adding-Removal-Lattice-Skyline). The second approach runs the adding and removal simultaneously. This algorithm is called *HPL-Skyline* (High-Parallel-Lattice-Skyline).

The ARL-Skyline Algorithm (ARL-S)

The adding-removal lattice Skyline algorithm (ARL-S) is designed as follows:

- **Phase 1:** Initialize all data structures.
- **Phase 2:** Split the input dataset into c partitions, where c is the number of used threads. For each partition, a worker thread iterates through the partition, determines the *unique identifiers* (IDs) for the elements and marks the corresponding entries in the BTG as *non-empty*.

- **Phase 3:** After adding *all* elements to the BTG a breadth-first walk beginning at the top starts (dashed dark gray line in Figure 3a). For each *non-empty* and *not dominated* node run *tasks* for the depth-first walk with the dominance test. In parallel continue with the breadth-first walk.

For example, if the node (0, 1) is reached in Figure 3a, two further tasks can be started in parallel to run a DFT down to (0,2) and (1,1) (thick black solid arrows). Continue with the BFT and reach the already dominated node (1, 1), afterwards (2, 0). A new DFT task follows the black dashed arrows to mark nodes as dominated. Note that the BFT task might be slower or faster than the DFT from node (0, 1) and therefore the DFT could follow different paths in the depth-first dominance search. The pseudocode for ARL-S reduced to its essence is depicted in Figure 3b; the fork/join task for the DFT can be found in Figure 4b.

The HPL-Skyline Algorithm (HPL-S)

The high-parallel lattice algorithm (HPL-S) combines Phase 2 and 3 of ARL-S to *one* phase and is designed as follows:

- **Phase 1:** Initialize all data structures.
- **Phase 2+3:** Similar to Phase 2 in ARL-S the dataset is split into c partitions, for each partition a worker thread c_i. If one of the worker threads marks a node in the BTG as *non-empty*, it immediately starts a task for the DFT dominance test (if not done yet) and continues with adding elements, cp. Figure 4a. The simplified pseudocode is shown in Figure 4b.

Figure 3. The ARL-Skyline algorithm

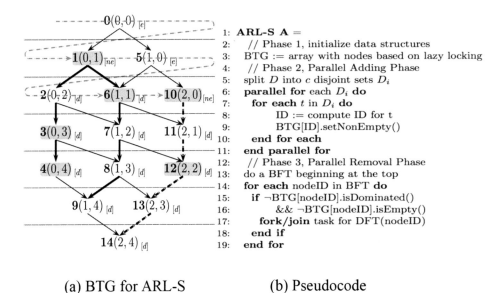

(a) BTG for ARL-S   (b) Pseudocode

Figure 4. The HPL-Skyline algorithm

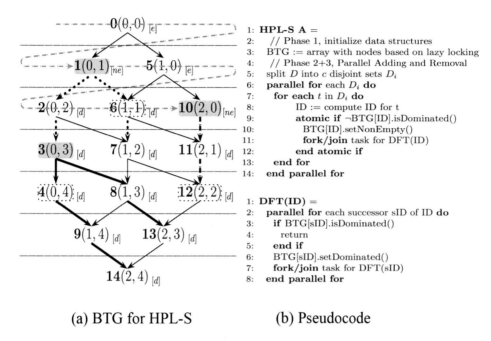

(a) BTG for HPL-S   (b) Pseudocode

For example, thread c_1 adds an element to (0, 3) and immediately starts additional tasks for the DFT (thick black solid arrows). Simultaneously another thread c_2 adds an element to the node (0,1) and starts tasks for the DFT and dominance tests (black dotted arrows). After thread c_1 has finished, it wants to add an element to (1,1). However, since it is already marked as dominated, thread c_1 can continue with adding elements to other nodes in the BTG without performing a DFT dominance test.

After all threads have finished, a breadth-first traversal is done on the remaining nodes (dashed gray line in Figure 4a. Again, the non-empty and not dominated nodes present the Skyline.

The advantage of the HPL-S in comparison to ARL-S is that the DFT search will mark dominated nodes as *dominated* and other parallel running threads do not have to add possible elements to these already dominated nodes. This saves memory and runtime. The ARL-S and HPL-S algorithms with an *array* as BTG representation still have a complexity of *O(dV +dn)*, since they follow the original idea of lattice Skyline algorithms as presented in Section 3, also cp. (Endres & Kießling, 2014, 2015).

THE SCALAGON ALGORITHM

The main disadvantage of current lattice-based Skyline algorithms is their restricted application to low-cardinality domains. First, the BTG must fit into main memory and second the complexity analysis shows that a BTG significantly larger than the number of tuples is slower than BNL-style algorithms. In this section, *Scalagon* (Endres, Roocks, & Kießling, 2015) is introduced, an algorithm which combines the ideas of the lattice approach and a BNL-style algorithm (cp. Section 2.2) to evaluate Skylines on *arbitrary domains.*

The general idea of Scalagon is to scale the original high-cardinality domain of the input data down to a smaller domain and apply a lattice algorithm as pre-filter. Using a lattice Skyline method at first step, there is the advantage of a linear runtime complexity and that the lattice based approach is independent from the data distribution, i.e., whether the data is anti-correlated, correlated, or independent distributed (Endres, Roocks, & Kießling, 2015).

Figure 5 shows the entire filtering process on a weakly anti-correlated dataset, where the size of the scaled domain is $[0..7]^2$. At first, using a lattice based approach called *Hexagon product order* (HPO) (based on the Hexagon algorithm) the maxima on the scaled domain are determined (dark gray tiles) according to the *product order* dominance criteria (a tile is dominated by another tile if it is worse in all components). All objects in the dominated nodes (light gray tiles) are save to be filtered out. The tuples in the dark gray area form a pre-filtered set. On this set a BNL-style algorithm is applied afterwards to finally determine the Skyline.

Note that such a method may be prone to outliers: Adding a single tuple like (10,10) to a scenario as depicted in Figure 5 would introduce a plenty of empty tiles and hence result in a very low number of filtered out tuples (in this case only (10,10) would be filtered out). A simple method to exclude outliers from the scaling and pre-filtering process and adding them directly to the BNL phase solves this problem. For more details see (Endres, Roocks, & Kießling, 2015).

Figure 5. Filtering of Scalagon and Skyline. The light gray squares are dominated during the HPO phase. The dark gray squares contain the pre-filtered set

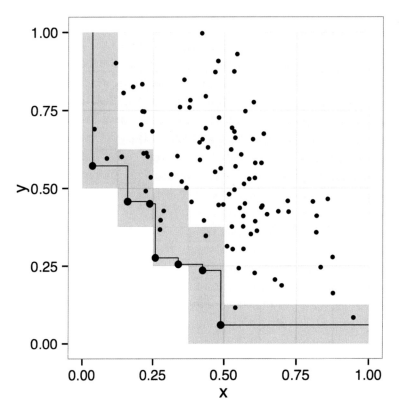

Formal Basics

Let $D \subseteq \mathbb{R}^d$ be a d-dimensional dataset and $n = |D|$ the quantity of the input. Let D_i denote the projection to the i-th component of D, formally

$$D_i := \{x_i \mid (x_1, ..., x_d) \in D\} \ .$$

For the scaling of the input assume scale coefficients $s_1, ..., s_d \in \mathbb{N}_0$ forming the *scale vector* $s = (s_1, ..., s_d)$. The s_i correspond to the cardinality of the scaled domain in the i-th dimension, i.e., the scaled domain is

$$\mathbb{S}(s) = [0..(s_1 - 1)] \times \cdots \times [0..(s_d - 1)]$$

where $[0..(N-1)] := \left\{ 0, 1, ..., \left(N - 1 \right) \right\}$ for $N \in \mathbb{N}_0$. The vectors b_{min} and b_{max} form a bounding box of all tuples which shall be scaled. In the simplest case $b_{min} = (min(D_1), ..., min(D_d))$ and $b_{max} = (max(D_1), ..., max(D_d))$. Tighter limits for outlier detection are discussed in (Endres, Roocks, & Kießling, 2015).

For the following the operators $\{\leq, <\}$ on vectors are defined in the usual way, i.e., $(x_1, ..., x_d) \leq (y_1, ..., y_d) \Leftrightarrow \forall i : x_i \leq y_i$. Formally, the scaling of a tuple $x = (x_1, ..., x_d)$ is realized by the mapping

$$f_{s, b_{min}, b_{max}} : \mathbb{R}^d \to \mathbb{N}_0^d \cup \{out\}$$

$$x \mapsto \begin{cases} (f_1(x_1), ..., f_d(x_d)) & if \ b_{min} \leq x \leq b_{max} \\ out & otherwise \end{cases}$$

where

$$f_i(x_i) := \left\lfloor s_i \cdot \frac{x_i - b_{min,i}}{(b_{max,i} - b_{min,i}) \cdot (1 + \varepsilon)} \right\rfloor$$

Therein $\varepsilon > 0$ is some very small constant, ensuring that the result of the division is strictly smaller than 1. It follows that $0 \leq f_i(x_i) \leq (s_i - 1)$ for all x and thus from the definition of f it follows $f(D) \subseteq S(s) \cup \{out\}$ for any scale vector s.

Scalagon

The Scalagon algorithm can be subdivided in four phases

- **Phase 1:** The Scaling is applied and outliers are isolated.

- **Phase 2:** Hexagon Product Order is executed on the scaled dataset which results in a set of non-dominated tiles.
- **Phase 3:** All the original tuples which correspond to non-dominated tiles in the scaled dataset are picked out.
- **Phase 4:** BNL is applied to the union of these picked tuples and the outliers.

Figure 6 shows the pseudocode of Scalagon.

1. After having determined s, b_{min}, b_{max}, S is defined as

$$S := f_{s,b_{min},b_{max}}(D) \setminus \{\text{out}\}, \quad F_0 := \{x \in D \mid f_{s,b_{min},b_{max}}(x) = \text{out}\}$$

2. Hexagon Product Order is applied to determine the set

$$S_{min} := \{t \in S \mid \nexists u \in S : u < t\}$$

This set is calculated with the HPO algorithm, which works exactly as the standard Hexagon, but the better-than-relation is the *product order* instead of the Pareto order. Note that $<$ on vectors corresponds to the product order, i.e. $x < y \Leftrightarrow \forall i \in [1..d] : x_i \leq y_i$.

Figure 6. The Scalagon algorithm and scaling calculation

Algorithm 1 Scalagon, where f is from Eq. (3)

Input: Skyline order $\prec$, Dataset D, scale vector s, bounds b_{min}, b_{max}
Output: Skyline of D
1: **function** SCALAGON($\prec$,D)
2:     // Scaling
3:     $S \leftarrow f_{s,b_{min},b_{max}}(D)\setminus\{\text{out}\}$
4:     $F_0 \leftarrow \{x \in D \mid f_{...}(x) = \text{out}\}$
5:
6:     // Hexagon product order
7:     $S_{min} \leftarrow$ HPO($<$, S)
8:
9:     // Filter tuples
10:     $F \leftarrow \{x \in D \mid f_{...}(x) \in S_{min}\}$
11:
12:     // BNL
13:     **return** BNL($\prec$, $F \cup F_0$)
14: **end function**

Algorithm 2 Scalagon scaling calculation

Input: D, domain size $(N_i)_{i=1,...,d}$, scale factor α
Output: Scale vector $s = (s_1, ..., s_d)$
1: **function** SCALING($D, (N_i)_{i=1,...,d}, \alpha$)
2:     **for all** $i \in [1..d]$ **do** // Initialization
3:         $s_i \leftarrow \lfloor(|D|/\alpha)^{1/d}\rfloor$
4:     **end for**
5:     $I \leftarrow \emptyset$
6:     // Iterative calculation of the s_i
7:     **while** $\exists i \in ([1..d]\setminus I) : N_i < s_i$ **do**
8:         $I \leftarrow \{i \in [1..d] \mid N_i \leq s_i\}$
9:         **for all** $i \in I$ **do**
10:             $s_i \leftarrow N_i$
11:         **end for**
12:         **for all** $i \in ([1..d]\setminus I)$ **do**
13:             $s_i \leftarrow \lfloor(|D|/(\alpha \cdot \prod_{j\in I} N_j))^{1/(d-|I|)}\rfloor$
14:         **end for**
15:     **end while**
16:     **return** $(s_1, ..., s_d)$
17: **end function**

3. The set of filtered tuples is calculated, containing all tuples from non-dominated tiles (S_{min}) together with the outliers

$$F := \{x \in D \mid f_{s,b_{min},b_{max}}(x) \in S_{min}\} \cup F_0$$

4. Finally, a BNL-style algorithm is applied to find the Skyline within F

$$\mathrm{Sky}(F) := \{t \in F \mid \nexists u \in F : u \prec t\}$$

where $\prec$ is the Pareto order from (1). *Sky(F)* is the output of Scalagon.

Scaling and Complexity

Scalagon heavily depends on the scaling factor. With a fine-grained scaling the filtering efficiency raises, i.e., the number of comparisons in the final BNL phase decreases. At the same time the HPO phase calculating the non-dominated tiles becomes costlier. Hence the decisive criterion is the choice of the scaling coefficients s_i compared to the dataset size $|D|$. To handle this, the *scale factor* α was introduced, which is defined by the ratio of the dataset size $|D|$ and the size of the scaled domain:

$$\alpha = \frac{|D|}{|\mathbb{S}(s)|}$$

This factor allows to continuously change between a BNL-style and a lattice based algorithm. For $\alpha \to 0$ one deals with a lattice based algorithm where $f(x)$ is unique for every tuple $x \in D$. For $\alpha \to \infty$ one retrieves $|S(s)| = 1$, meaning that there is just one equivalence class. Hence there is no filtering and Scalagon acts like a BNL-style algorithm.

Let us now assume that the domain size $(N_1, ..., N_d)$ is given. Typically, N_i is either small (low-cardinality values like hotel ratings, ...) or $N_i = \infty$ (domains like price, ...), meaning that there is a continuous domain. Obviously, it does not make sense to choose a scale vector with $s_i > N_i$. This would introduce just empty tiles in the lattice structure of the HPO-phase. Hence the problem of determining the scaling coefficients for a given α reads as follows:

$$\alpha \approx \frac{|D|}{\prod_{i=1}^{d} s_i} \qquad (S1)$$

$$s_i \leq N_i \ \text{ for all } \ i \in [1..d] \qquad (S2)$$

To solve this problem algorithmically, distinguish the following cases:

1. If the size of the $\prod\limits_{i=1}^{d} N_i$ domain is smaller than $|D|/\alpha$ it does not make any sense to apply Scalagon.

   In this case, Scalagon behaves as a purely lattice based algorithm with some computational overhead. Hence the usual lattice based algorithms should be applied.

2. Otherwise the s_i have to be calculated explicitly to fulfill (S2). To this end, algorithm *Scaling* (Algorithm 2) to determine the s_i is described accordingly.

The idea to iteratively determine the s_i is as follows: First, initialize s_i by

$$s_1 := \ldots := s_d := \left\lceil \left(\frac{|D|}{\alpha}\right)^{1/d} \right\rceil$$

This fulfills (S1). If the domain size $(N_1,\ldots,N_d)$ is sufficiently large (or continuous), (S2) is also fulfilled and we are done. Otherwise for those i where $s_i > N_i$ take the original cardinality $s_i := N_i$. Afterwards the other s_i are recalculated such that (S1) is fulfilled. This step is iterated until a solution for (S1) and (S2) is found.

In the pseudocode of Algorithm 2, $I \subseteq [1..d]$ is used as an index set to mark those s_i which are already set to N_i. The complement is defined as $\bar{I} := [1..d] \setminus I$. To determine the s_i in the iteration step calculate

$$\alpha = \frac{|D|}{|\mathbb{S}(s)|} = \frac{|D|}{\prod\limits_{i=1}^{d} s_i} = \frac{|D|}{\prod\limits_{i \in I} N_i \cdot \prod\limits_{i \in \bar{I}} s_i}$$

Requiring identical s_i values for $i \in \bar{I}$ leads to

$$s_i = \left\lceil \left(\frac{|D|}{\alpha \cdot \prod\limits_{i \in I} N_i} \right)^{1/|\bar{I}|} \right\rceil \text{ for all } i \in \bar{I}$$

This corresponds to line 13 in Algorithm 2.

Note that the while-condition (line 7) together with the assignment to I (line 8) ensures that the set I is strictly growing w.r.t. the inclusion order $\subsetneq$ in every iteration step. As soon as $I = [1..d]$ is reached, one has $\bar{I} = \varnothing$. Thus, the while-condition is trivially false and the algorithm terminates. In the continuous case, there will be a (hyper-)quadratic scaling $s_1 = \ldots = s_d$.

Concerning the complexity of Scalagon, Endres et al. (Endres, Roocks, & Kießling, 2015) have shown that the overall time complexity is

$$C_t(n, s) = O(n^2 + s_1 \cdot \ldots \cdot s_n),$$

whereas the space complexity is

$$C_s(n, s) = O(s_1 \cdot \ldots \cdot s_d + n) \, .$$

Note that in average and realistic cases one has linear costs in the BNL phase (Godfrey, Shipley, & Gryz, 2007) and the actual performance mainly depends on choosing α.

One disadvantage of *Hexagon* (Preisinger & Kießling, 2007) and LS-B (Morse, Patel, & Jagadish, 2007) is that the lattice must fit into main memory. With Scalagon one is now able to scale down the original domain such that the scaled lattice fits into memory, independent from the available memory size.

THE STREAM LATTICE SKYLINE ALGORITHM

Stream data analysis is a high relevant topic in various academic and business fields. Users want to analyze data streams to extract information in order to learn from this ever-growing amount of data. One information filtering approach is Skyline processing on data streams. Therefore, this section shows how to evaluate Skylines on data streams in an efficient manner. Until now, only BNL-style algorithms can be adapted to Skyline evaluation on continuous stream data. The algorithm **SLS** (Stream-Lattice-Skyline) was developed to handle unbounded streams for efficient real-time preference analysis.

The Skyline of a Data Stream

Skyline processing on data streams require efficient evaluation algorithms since a stream is a continuous dataflow and there is no "final" result after some data of the stream is processed. The result must be calculated and adjusted as soon as new data arrive, since new stream objects received later can match the user preferences better than objects already recognized in previously computed (temporary) Skylines.

More detailed: Assume an endless data stream which is divided into a series of (non-overlapping) chunks $c_1, c_2, \ldots$. A BNL-style algorithm would evaluate the Skyline on the first chunk, i.e., $Sky(c_1)$, cp. Eq. 2. Since c_2 could contain better objects w.r.t. the dominance criterion in Eq. 1, one also has to compare the new objects from c_2 to the current Skyline, i.e., compute

$$Sky(Sky(c_1) \cup c_2), \tag{4}$$

and so on. However, this leads to a computational overhead if c_2 is large, which is the usual case. Therefore, this continuous comparing process is the most expensive operation of preference-based stream evaluation.

For more details on how to process data streams with Skyline queries (or the more general *preference* queries) see (Rudenko, Endres, Roocks, & Kießling, 2016; Rudenko & Endres, 2017).

The SLS Algorithm

For real-time Skyline evaluation, the *Stream-Lattice-Skyline algorithm* (SLS) was developed, which avoids the annoying object-to-object comparison of BNL. SLS is based on the lattice algorithms presented in Section 3, can be parallelized as shown in Section 4, adapted to unrestricted domains as in Scalagon, cp. Section 5, and retains a linear runtime complexity.

The SLS approach follows the idea of *Hexagon* and *LS-B*, where some objects are mapped to the lattice w.r.t. some kind of comparison function. As mentioned, data streams are processed in finite chunks, as can be seen in Figure 7.

After constructing the lattice, which only must be done once, all objects of the current chunk (chunk 1) are mapped to the corresponding lattice nodes in a consecutive way, e.g., object *A* is mapped to (2, 0), object *B* to (2, 2), and so on. Assume all gray nodes in Figure 6 are occupied with data from the first chunk.

As in Hexagon run a BFT to find the non-empty nodes (dashed line) and for non-empty nodes start a DFT (bold arrows) to mark all transitive dominated nodes as *dominated*. Afterwards it is possible to present the *temporary Skyline* for the first chunk. Now consider the next chunk (chunk 2). Read all objects form chunk 2, add them to the lattice and perform a BFT and DFT. Again, the remaining nodes (maybe including the objects from the previous computation) contain the temporary best objects. Continue with chunk 3, etc.

In this way, the SLS algorithms consists of the following phases:

- **Phase 1:** The construction phase initializes the data structure.
- **Phase 2:** Adding phase
  - Read the next chunk from the data stream
  - Iterate through the objects of the chunk. Each object will be mapped to one node in the lattice and this node is marked as *non-empty*.
- **Phase 3:** Removal phase: After all objects of the chunk have been processed, start a BFT and DFT to determine a temporary Skyline.
- Since there is a continuous data stream, go to Step 2 and process the next chunk.

Figure 7. Data stream processing with SLS

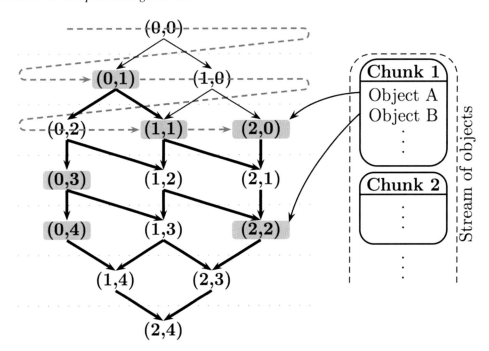

Note that the Skyline computation in Phase 3 can be done after an arbitrary number of processed chunks or after a pre-defined time. Therefore, our algorithm can be used for *real-time* Skyline evaluation. It is also possible to parallelize this approach in the sense of ARL-S and HPL-S as mentioned in Section 4: parallelize the adding of the objects in the chunk, and, after adding an object, directly start a DFT to mark nodes as *dominated*. In this case it is not necessary to "add" objects to the lattice if nodes are already marked as *dominated*.

EXPERIMENTS

This section provides benchmarks on synthetic and real data to reveal the performance of the outlined algorithms. Since this chapter gives an overview on lattice-based Skyline algorithms, only a few characteristics experiments are presented. More comprehensive experiments can be found in (Preisinger & Kießling, 2007; Endres & Kießling, 2014, 2015) and (Endres, Roocks, & Kießling, 2015).

Benchmark Framework

The algorithms used in the benchmarks have been implemented in Java 7.0 using only built-in techniques for locking, compare-and-swap operations, and thread management for the parallel algorithms. The experiments were performed on a single node running Debian Linux 7.1 equipped with two Intel Xeon 2.53 GHz quad-core processors using hyper-threading, that means a total of 16 cores. For the synthetic datasets, the data generator commonly used in Skyline research (Börzsönyi, Kossmann, & Stocker, 2001) was used.

For the experiments on real-world data the well-known *NBA, Household*, and *Zillow* datasets were used. These datasets were crawled from www.nba.com, www.ipums.org, and www.zillow.com. The *NBA* dataset is a small 5-dimensional dataset containing 17264 tuples, where each entry records performance statistics for a NBA player (Chang, Jagadish, Tan, Tung, & Zhang, 2006). *Household* is a larger 6-dimensional dataset having 127931 points and a domain of $[1..10^4]^6$. The *Zillow* dataset contains more than 2M entries about real estates in the United States. Each entry includes *number of bedrooms* and *bathrooms*, *living area* in sqm, and *age* of the building.

Experiments on ARL-S and HPL-S

This section gives an overview of the performance of ARL-S and HPL-S using an array as data structure for the lattice. Using an array means that each index in the array represents a node ID in the lattice. Note that Scalagon is not compared, because ARL-S and HPL-S were designed for low-cardinality domains. Below the results in Figure 8 are discussed in detail.

Figure 8a and 8b show speed-up experiments where independent data, $n = 10^6$ objects, and $d = 3$, 5, 7 dimensions are used. ARL-S and HPL-S were executed using up to 16 threads. The ARL-S algorithm shows a very good speed-up behavior for each dimensionality. Note that the BTG is large enough such that there is no synchronization overhead in the adding or removal phase of the running tasks. The HPL-S algorithm achieves superlinear speed-up until 6 threads, which is the result of a medium BTG size (about 3000 nodes for $d = 7$). In the case of 3 and 5 dimensions the BTG is much smaller, but in these cases, much more synchronization is necessary, because threads may try to lock the same node.

Figure 8. Experimental results for ARL-S and HPL-S

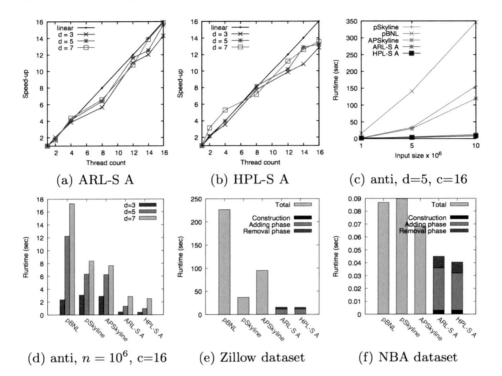

(a) ARL-S A   (b) HPL-S A   (c) anti, d=5, c=16

(d) anti, $n = 10^6$, c=16   (e) Zillow dataset   (f) NBA dataset

Figure 8c shows ARL-S and HPL-S in comparison to the state-of-the-art multicore algorithms *AP-Skyline* (Liknes, Vlachou, Doulkeridis, & Nørvåg, 2014), *pSkyline* (Park, Kim, Park, Kim, & Im, 2009), and the parallel BNL (*pBNL*) (Selke, Lofi, & Balke, 2010) for increasing data size. APSkyline is better than pBNL and pSkyline as mentioned in (Liknes, Vlachou, Doulkeridis, & Nørvåg, 2014). However, the domain derived from [2,3,5,10,100], which is typical for Skyline computation (a few small attributes together with a larger attribute) (Morse, Patel, & Jagadish, 2007), is best suited for lattice-based algorithms, which significantly outperform all others.

Figure 8d shows the obtained results when increasing the number of dimensions: d = 3 ([2,2,100]) to d = 7 ([2,2,2,2,2,2,100]). The number of input tuples (anti) was fixed to n = 10^6 and c = 16. pSkyline and APSkyline are quiet similar for all dimensions, whereas pBNL is better for d = 3. It should be mentioned that the size of the Skyline set normally increases on anti-correlated data with the dimensionality of the dataset (Shang & Kitsuregawa, 2013) (138 Skyline objects for d = 3, 4125 objects for d = 7). This makes Skyline processing for algorithms relying on tuple-to-tuple comparison more demanding. This experiment verifies the advantage of our algorithms based on the lattice structure and not on a tuple comparison, in particular for higher values of dimensionality. Indeed, ARL-S and HPL-S are much better than its tuple comparison competitors.

Figure 8e and Figure 8f show the obtained results for the real-world datasets Zillow and NBA. The parallel BNL algorithm is outperformed in an order of magnitude by all other algorithms. All lattice based algorithms do not rely on any partitioning scheme and are independent from data distribution. Therefore, the best performing algorithms are ARL-S and HPL-S. Thereby the latter one slightly performs better. For all lattice algorithms, the adding phase is the most time-consuming part.

Experiments on Scalagon

This section shows the behavior of Scalagon in selected experiments. More benchmarks can be found in (Endres, Roocks, & Kießling, 2015). Since multicore systems are going mainstream, there is also a parallel variant of Scalagon, namely pScalagon, which follows the idea of the ARL-S algorithm described in Section 4.1. The experiments compare pScalagon to pBNL, pSkyline, and APSkyline. The algorithms HPL-S and ARL-S are skipped, because they cannot be applied on high-cardinality domains.

Endres et al. (Endres, Roocks, & Kießling, 2015) have shown that a scale-factor $\alpha \rightarrow 0$ implies a similar algorithm like Hexagon, as every tuple has its own tile in the scaled setting. Analogously $\alpha \rightarrow \infty$ leads to one tile for all tuples and results in a BNL-style algorithm with some useless computational overhead. It was also shown that $\alpha \in [1,1000]$ is approximately optimal and within this interval the run time is nearly identical. Outside this interval the run time increases and for $\alpha < 0.1$ and $\alpha > 10^5$ the performance of Scalagon tends to be worse than BNL. Hence, α is chosen to be in that range.

- **Figure 9a – Segmented Runtime:** Shows the segmented runtime for pScalagon using different parallel BNL-style algorithms for phase 4. Using $\alpha = 10$, the Hexagon product order (HPO) is a little bit slower than for $\alpha = 100$ because of a larger BTG and a more expensive DFT. For larger α the BNL-style algorithms have to do more work.

- **Figure 9b – Dimensions:** Shows the behavior on different domains $[1..1000]^d$, with $d \in \{3, 5, 7\}$ dimensions, which is a realistic case in Skyline queries. For $d = 3$ all runtimes are quite similar, whereas for higher dimensions pScalagon outperforms its competitors. Note that the size of the Skyline set normally increases with the dimensionality of the dataset on anti-correlated data (Shang & Kitsuregawa, 2013), making Skyline processing for algorithms relying on tuple comparison more demanding. This experiment verifies the advantage of our hybrid algorithm using a data independent lattice approach as pre-filter.

- **Figure 9c – Real-World Data:** Reports the comparison results for real world data. The expectation was that pScalagon is worse than its competitors considering the NBA dataset, because of the hybrid approach which produces some overhead on small datasets. However, for the Household dataset pScalagon outperforms all other algorithms.

- **Figure 9d – Runtime:** Compares pScalagon to the state-of-the-art parallel Skyline algorithms. The domain is $[0..5] \times [0..10^3] \times [0..10^5]$. For the given $\alpha = 50$ this leads to the scaled domain S $= [0..5] \times [0..63] \times [0..63]$ in the case of $n = 10^6$. pScalagon clearly outperforms its competitors, in particular for large datasets.

- **Figure 9e and 9f – Thread Count:** Measured the speed-up on 5 dimensions: $[0..2]^2 \times [0..5] \times [0..10^4]^2$. The observation is that APSkyline and pScalagon have a good speed-up up to 8 threads. From the ninth thread on, the performance only marginally increases and beyond 16 threads it gradually decreases. This can be explained with decreasing cache locality and increasing communication costs as the test system uses two quad-core processors with Hyper-Threading. Starting with the ninth core, the 2nd processor must constantly communicate with the first. The same effect is mentioned in (Selke, Lofi, & Balke, 2010).

For evaluating the runtime performance of the parallel algorithms in absolute numbers, also the computation time was measured. The results can be found in Figure 9f. The bad performance of pScalagon using more than 256 threads can be explained by a very high locking of the lattice nodes.

Figure 9. Scalagon and its competitors

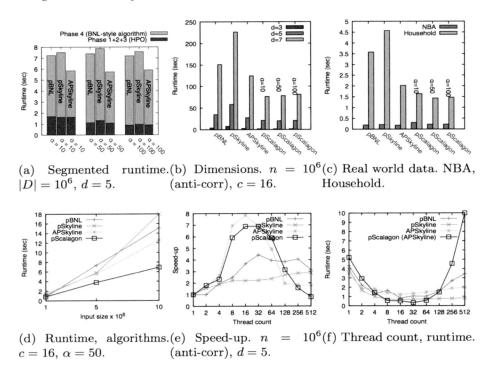

(a) Segmented runtime. $|D| = 10^6$, $d = 5$.

(b) Dimensions. $n = 10^6$ (anti-corr), $c = 16$.

(c) Real world data. NBA, Household.

(d) Runtime, algorithms. $c = 16$, $\alpha = 50$.

(e) Speed-up. $n = 10^6$ (anti-corr), $d = 5$.

(f) Thread count, runtime.

Experiments on SLS

This section presents some experiments for our SLS algorithm.

For our experiments on artificial data, anti-correlated data is used as described in (Börzsönyi, Kossmann, & Stocker, 2001), because this kind of data is most challenging for Skyline queries. The target was to investigate how the chunk size affects the runtime of our algorithm, since this influences the real-time behavior of SLS. In the experiments, chunk sizes from 10 to 100000 objects were used and the algorithm was tested on an input data set of 100000 objects.

Figure 10a evaluates the behavior of SLS for queries with different domains: [2856,1,5], [2,3,5,10,10] and [2,3,7,8,4,10]. The algorithm is significant slower for small chunks (up to 100 objects) than for chunks with more than 100 objects. This can be explained by the frequent repeating of the breadth-first and depth-first traversal in SLS which have to be carried out for each chunk. For the chunk size over 10000 objects the runtime of SLS increases slightly, because the adding of new objects to the BTG (Phase 2 in SLS) is more expensive. Therefore, the claim is, that the optimal chunk size for the best runtime is between 100 and 10000 objects.

Figure 10b shows a Skyline query on the domain [2,3,5,10,10]. Such a setting is typical for "real world" Skyline queries: A few low-cardinality domains are combined with some higher cardinality numerical domains. The SLS algorithm outperforms BNL, but for small chunks (up to 500 objects) and very large chunks (over 10000 objects), the difference is much more significant.

For more comprehensive experiments on synthetic data consider (Endres, Kießling, 2014, 2015), since the presented algorithms are extensions of the lattice algorithms presented in these publications.

Figure 10. SLS on different domains

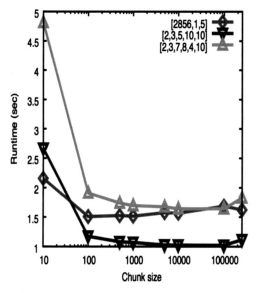

(a) Runtime for different domains.

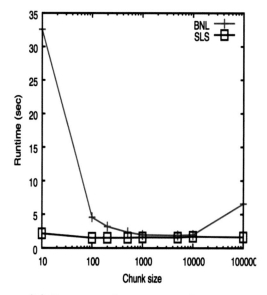

(b) Runtime for 100000 objects.

Experiments on *real-world data* from Twitter were also performed. The test query is based on a three-dimensional Skyline on the Twitter attributes followers_count, status_count, and hashtag. The attribute values were mapped to a numerical domain to apply a *min* Skyline query on these attributes. For the experiment, the chunk sizes from 10 to 1000 objects and the size of the input stream were varied.

Figures 11a and 11b – Real World Data – show our results, which are similar to the results of our previous experiments. For small chunk sizes, up to 200 objects, our SLS algorithm is much better than BNL. From a chunk size of 500 objects on, BNL is nearly as good as SLS, but still worse. This can be explained by the less number of unions which has to be carried out after each chunk evaluation, cp. Equation 4.

Since real-time processing requires high efficient algorithms on few data objects in very short time intervals, our SLS algorithm is superior for real-time preference evaluation as found out in our experiments.

RELATED WORK

There are different models to deal with Skylines, Pareto-optimal objects, or preference queries in general. For example, Kasabov & Song (2002), and Dovzan, Logar, & Skrjanc (2015) handle preferences with fuzzy values, whereas Boutilier, Brafman, Domshlak, Hoos, & Poole (2004), use Ceteris-Paribus (CP-nets) do describe user wishes. Other models as published in (Chomicki, 2003), or (Kießling, 2002, 2005) use strict partial orders to represent preferences in information systems. These models are often more flexible and intuitive than other approaches. This is also shown in (Möller, Roocks, & Endres, 2012).

There are many algorithms for the computation of Skylines and preference queries, see (Chomicki, Ciacia, & Meneghetti, 2013) for an overview. Many of them rely on a tuple-to-tuple comparison ap-

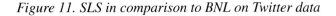

Figure 11. SLS in comparison to BNL on Twitter data

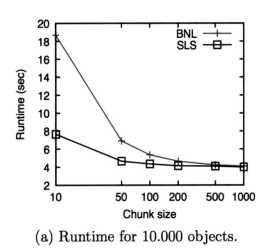

(a) Runtime for 10.000 objects.

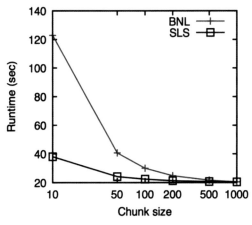

(b) Runtime for 100.000 objects.

proach (e.g., BNL (Börzsönyi, Kossmann, & Stocker, 2001), SFS (Chomicki, Godfrey, Gryz, & Liang, 2003), SaLSa (Bartolini, Ciaccia, & Patella, 2006)). The major advantage of these nested-loop style algorithms is their simplicity and suitability for computing the maxima of *general strict partial orders* due to its tuple-to-tuple comparisons. However, most of these algorithms have a *quadratic* worst-case runtime complexity $O(n^2)$, where n is the size of the input data, cp. (Godfrey, Shipley, & Gryz, 2005). Algorithms having such a runtime complexity can neither be used for real-time data analytics on big data nor for preference evaluation on data streams.

There are also algorithms utilizing an index structure to compute the Skyline, e.g., (Tan, Eng, & Ooi, 2001; Papadias, Tao, Fu, & Seeger, 2003; Lee, Zheng, Li, & Lee, 2007; Endres & Weichmann, 2017). However, index-based algorithms are not capable of processing arbitrary data without any preparations, and hence are not applicable to data streams.

There is also growing interest in distributed Skyline and preference computation. Most of the current approaches partition the input data and distribute it to several cluster nodes for parallel Skyline evaluation. The nodes locally process the partitions in parallel, and finally merge the local Skylines. This approach, e.g., is used by (Balke, Güntzer, & Zheng, 2004; Lo, Yip, Lin, & Cheung, 2006; Wu, Zhang, Feng, Zhao, Agrawal, & Abbadi, 2006; Hose & Vlachou, 2012; Afrati, Koutris, Suciu, & Ullman, 2012; Cosgaya-Lozano, Rau-Chaplin, & Zeh, 2007). The main difference of such a parallel Skyline computation resides in the partitioning schemes of the data. The most used partitioning scheme is grid-based partitioning (Hose & Vlachou, 2012; Rocha-Junior, Vlachou, Doulkeridis, & Nørvåg, 2009). Other work (Vlachou, Doulkeridis, & Kotidis, 2008) focus on an angle-based space partitioning scheme using hyper-spherical coordinates of the data points. In (Köhler, Yang, & Zhou, 2011), the authors partition the space using hyperplane projections to obtain useful partitions of the dataset for parallel processing.

The approach of (Park, Min, & Shim, 2013) is based on MapReduce, and (Bøgh, Assent, & Magnani, 2013; Bøgh, Chester, and Assent, 2015) and (Woods, Alonso, & Teubner, 2013) use emerging hardware like GPUs and FPGAs to evaluate preferences, respectively. When considering parallelization, (Selke, Lofi, & Balke, 2010), (Park, Kim, Park, Kim, & Im, 2009), (Liknes, Vlachou, Doulkeridis, & Nørvåg, 2014), and (Chester, Sidlauskas, Assent, & Bøgh, 2015) developed algorithms which exploit special data structures for high parallel Skyline computation on modern multi-core architectures. However, none of these approaches is efficiently usable for data streams.

On the other hand, there are algorithms which exploit the *lattice structure* induced by a Skyline query for efficient preference evaluation, e.g., (Preisinger & Kießling, 2007, Morse, Patel, & Jagadish, 2007, Lee & Hwang, 2010). Instead of direct comparisons of tuples, a lattice structure represents the better-than relationships. These algorithms offer excellent performance for domains with low-cardinality domains, and, as described in this chapter, for high-cardinality domains as well. They have a *linear runtime complexity*, but the original lattice algorithms can only deal with Skylines / Pareto preferences consisting of preferences that form weak orders on their domains (Davey & Priestley, 2002). Endres & Preisinger (2017) developed a technique to embed arbitrary strict partial orders into lattices. Therefore, all algorithms presented in this chapter can also be applied to arbitrary preference queries, not only Skylines.

Another central aspect in this chapter is stream processing to extract important information from continuous data flows. Babu & Widom (2001), e.g., focus primarily on the problem how to define and evaluate continuous queries over data streams. Ribeiro, Barioni, de Amo, Roncancio, & Labbe (2017) describe an approach for processing data streams according to temporal conditional preferences. In (Lee, Lee, & Kim, 2013) the authors propose a new method for processing multiple continuous Skyline queries over a data stream. Babcok, Babu, Datar, Motwani, & Widom (2002) motivate the need for and research issues arising from stream data processing. Faria, Goncalves, de Carvalho, & Gama (2016) describe various applications of novelty detection in data streams, and Krempl et. al (2016) discuss challenges for data stream mining such as protecting data privacy, handling incomplete and delayed information, or analysis of complex data. In (Kontaki, Papadopoylos, & Manolopoulos, 2010) the authors examine the characteristics of important preference queries (Skyline, top-k and top-k dominating) and review algorithms proposed for the evaluation of continuous preference queries under the sliding window streaming model. However, they do not present any framework for preference-based stream evaluation. The SLS algorithm presented in this chapter is the first algorithm based on the lattice a Skyline query constructs, and hence exploits the linear runtime complexity for evaluation of preferences on data streams.

CONCLUSION

This chapter gives an overview on lattice-based Skyline algorithms. Exploiting the lattice, these algorithms do not rely on tuple-to-tuple comparisons like BNL-style approaches, are independent of any data partitioning, have a linear runtime complexity, and a memory requirement which is linear w.r.t. the size of the lattice. Note that lattice-based algorithms are not restricted only to Skyline computation, they can also be adapted for arbitrary strict partial orders, see (Endres & Preisinger, 2017) for details.

The chapter also describes how to parallelize these algorithms for high-performance Skyline computation on shared-memory multi-processor systems. In addition, Scalagon is presented, which overcomes the low-cardinality restriction the algorithms Hexagon, LS-B, APL-S, and HPL-S suffer from. Furthermore, the SLS algorithm is introduced for real-time Skyline processing on data streams.

In the presented experiments on synthetic and real data, the superior characteristics of these algorithms in different settings are depicted. Exploiting the parallelization on the lattice structure one is able to outperform state-of-the-art approaches for Skyline computation on modern hardware architectures.

Nevertheless, there are still open issues which must be addressed in the future. For example, further development of the SLS algorithm as well as the extension of the lattice-based algorithms for distributed Skyline processing could be a challenging task. Furthermore, the adaption to arbitrary strict partial orders as depicted by (Endres & Preisinger, 2017) is absolutely necessary for efficient real-time Skyline analytics. In addition, the SLS algorithm can be extended with some kind of pruning technique, which allows early pruning of objects from the data stream before adding them to the lattice structure. The idea is based on the approach described in (Preisinger, Kießling, & Endres, 2006). Further directions are the development of a real-time preference-based recommender system based on the theoretical background described in (Satzger, Endres, & Kießling, 2006) in combination with data streams, e.g., from the stock market. Another open issue is how to efficiently detect preference clusters on stream data by exploiting the SLS algorithm. Maybe some ideas from (Kastner, Endres, & Kießling, 2017) might be helpful for this kind of research.

REFERENCES

Afrati, F. N., Koutris, P., Suciu, D., & Ullman, J. D. (2012). Parallel Skyline Queries. In *Proc. of ICDT '12* (pp. 274–284). New York: ACM. 10.1145/2274576.2274605

Babcock, B., Babu, S., Datar, M., Motwani, R., & Widom, J. (2002). Models and Issues in Data Stream Systems. PODS '02, 1-16. doi:10.1145/543613.543615

Babu, S., & Widom, J. (2001). Continuous Queries over Data Streams. *Proceedings of SIGMOD Rec., 30*(3), 109-120.

Balke, W.-T., Güntzer, U., & Zheng, J. X. (2004). Efficient Distributed Skylining for Web Information Systems. *EDBT '04: Proceedings of the 9th International Conference on Extending Database Technology, 256*–273. 10.1007/978-3-540-24741-8_16

Bartolini, I., Ciaccia, P., & Patella, M. (2006). SaLSa: Computing the Skyline without Scanning the Whole Sky. In *Proceedings of CIKM '06* (pp. 405-414). New York, NY: ACM. 10.1145/1183614.1183674

Bøgh, K. S., Assent, I., & Magnani, M. (2013). Efficient GPU-based Skyline computation. In Proc. Of DaMoN '13 (5:1–5:6). New York, NY: ACM.

Bøgh, K. S., Chester, S., & Assent, I. (2015). Work-Efficient Skyline Computation for the GPU. *Proceedings of the Very Large Databases Endowment (PVLDB), 8*(9), 962-973.

Börzsönyi, S., Kossmann, D., & Stocker, K. (2001). The Skyline Operator. In *Proc. of ICDE '01* (pp. 421–430). Washington, DC: IEEE.

Boutilier, C., Brafman, R. I., Domshlak, C., Hoos, H. H., & Poole, D. (2004). CP-nets: A Tool for Representing and Reasoning with Conditional Ceteris Paribus Preference Statements. *Journal of Artificial Intelligence Research, 21*, 135–191.

Chang, C. Y., Jagadish, H. V., Tan, K.-L., Tung, A. K. H., & Zhang, Z. (2006). On High Dimensional Skylines. In *EDBT '06: Proceedings of the 10th International Conference on Extending Database Technology (vol. 3896*, pp. 478–495). Springer.

Chester, S., Sidlauskas, D., Assent, I., & Bøgh, K. S. (2015). Scalable Parallelization of Skyline Computation for Multi-Core Processors. *ICDE '15: 31st IEEE International Conference on Data Engineering, ICDE 2015*, 1083–1094. 10.1109/ICDE.2015.7113358

Chomicki, J., Ciaccia, P., & Meneghetti, N. (2013). Skyline Queries, Front and Back. *SIGMOD Rec., 42*(3), 6–18.

Chomicki, J., Godfrey, P., Gryz, J., & Liang, D. (2003). Skyline with Presorting. *ICDE '03: Proceedings of the 19th International Conference on Data Engineering*, 717–816.

Chomicki, J., Godfrey, P., Gryz, J., & Liang, D. (2003). Skyline with Presorting. *Proceedings of ICDE '03*, 717-816.

Cosgaya-Lozano, A., Rau-Chaplin, A., & Zeh, N. (2007). Parallel Computation of Skyline Queries. *Proc. of HPCS '07*, 12.

Davey, B. A., & Priestley, H. A. (2002). *Introduction to Lattices and Order* (2nd ed.). Cambridge, UK: Cambridge University Press. doi:10.1017/CBO9780511809088

Dovzan, D., Logar, V., & Skrjanc, I. (2015). Implementation of an Evolving Fuzzy Model (eFuMo) in a Monitoring System for a Waste-Water Treatment Process. *IEEE Transactions on Fuzzy Systems, 23*(5), 1761–1776. doi:10.1109/TFUZZ.2014.2379252

Endres, M., & Kießling, W. (2014). High Parallel Skyline Computation over Low-Cardinality Domains. In *Proceedings of ADBIS '14* (pp. 97–111). Springer. 10.1007/978-3-319-10933-6_8

Endres, M. & Kießling, W. (2015). Parallel Skyline Computation Exploiting the Lattice Structure. *JDM: Journal of Database Management, 26*(4).

Endres, M., & Preisinger, T. (2017). Beyond Skylines: Explicit Preferences. In *DASFAA '17* (pp. 327–342). Cham: Springer International Publishing.

Endres, M., Roocks, P., & Kießling, W. (2015). Scalagon: An Efficient Skyline Algorithm for all Seasons. *Proceedings of DASFAA '15*. 10.1007/978-3-319-18123-3_18

Endres, M., & Weichmann, F. (2017). Index Structures for Preference Database Queries. In *FQAS '17: Proceedings of the 12th International Conference on Flexible Query Answering Systems, Lecture Notes in Computer Science*. Springer-Verlag.

Faria, E. R., Goncalves, I. J. C. R., de Carvalho, A. C. P. L. F., & Gama, J. (2016). Novelty Detection in Data Streams. *Artificial Intelligence Review, 45*(2), 235–269. doi:10.100710462-015-9444-8

Godfrey, P., Shipley, R., & Gryz, J. (2005). Maximal Vector Computation in Large Data Sets. In *VLDB '05: Proceedings of the 31st International Conference on Very Large Data Bases* (pp. 229-240). VLDB Endowment.

Godfrey, P., Shipley, R., & Gryz, J. (2007). Algorithms and Analyses for Maximal Vector Computation. *The VLDB Journal*, *16*(1), 5–28. doi:10.100700778-006-0029-7

Hose, K., & Vlachou, A. (2012). A Survey of Skyline Processing in Highly Distributed Environments. *The VLDB Journal*, *21*(3), 359–384. doi:10.100700778-011-0246-6

Kasabov, N. K., & Song, Q. (2002). DENFIS: Dynamic Evolving Neural-Fuzzy Inference System and its Application for Time-Series Prediction. *IEEE Transactions on Fuzzy Systems*, *10*(2), 144–154. doi:10.1109/91.995117

Kastner, J., Endres, M., & Kießling, W. (2017). A Pareto-Dominant Clustering Approach for Pareto-Frontiers. *19th International Workshop on Design, Optimization, Languages and Analytical Processing of Big Data (DOLAP)*.

Kießling, W. (2002). Foundations of Preferences in Database Systems. In *Proceedings of the 28th international conference on Very Large Data Bases* (pp. 311-322). VLDB Endowment. 10.1016/B978-155860869-6/50035-4

Kießling, W. (2005). Preference Queries with SV-Semantics. In *Proceedings of COMAD '05* (pp. 15-26). Computer Society of India.

Kießling, W., Endres, M., & Wenzel, F. (2011). The Preference SQL System - An Overview. *Bulletin of the Technical Committee on Data Engineering*, *34*(2), 11–18.

Köhler, H., Yang, J., & Zhou, X. (2011). Efficient Parallel Skyline Processing Using Hyperplane Projections. *Proceedings of the 2011 ACM SIGMOD International Conference on Management of Data (SIGMOD '11)*, 85-96. 10.1145/1989323.1989333

Kontaki, M., Papadopoulos, A. N., & Manolopoulos, Y. (2010). Continuous Processing of Preference Queries in Data Streams. In SOFSEM '10 (pp. 47-60). Springer. doi:10.1007/978-3-642-11266-9_4

Krempl, G., Zliobaite, I., Brzezinski, D., Hüllermeier, E., Last, M., Lemaire, V., … Stefanowski, J. (2014). Open Challenges for Data Stream Mining Research. SIGKDD '14, Explor. Newsl., 16(1).

Lee, J., & Hwang, S.-W. (2010). BSkyTree: Scalable Skyline Computation Using a Balanced Pivot Selection. *EDBT '10: Proceedings of the 13th International Conference on Extending Database Technology*, 195-206. 10.1145/1739041.1739067

Lee, K., Zheng, B., Li, H., & Lee, W.-C. (2007). Approaching the Skyline in Z Order. In *VLDB '07: Proceedings of the 33rd international conference on Very large data bases* (pp. 279–290). VLDB Endowment.

Lee, Y. W., Lee, K. Y., & Kim, M. H. (2013). Efficient Processing of Multiple Continuous Skyline Queries over a Data Stream. *Information Science*, *221*, 316–337. doi:10.1016/j.ins.2012.09.040

Liknes, S., Vlachou, A., Doulkeridis, C., & Nørvåg, K. (2014). APSkyline: Improved Skyline Computation for Multicore Architectures. *Proc. of DASFAA '14*. 10.1007/978-3-319-05810-8_21

Lo, E., Yip, K. Y., Lin, K.-I., & Cheung, D. W. (2006). Progressive Skylining over Web-accessible Databases. *IEEE TKDE*, *57*(2), 122–147.

Mandl, S., Kozachuk, O., Endres, M., & Kießling, W. (2015). Preference Analytics in EXASolution. *BTW ,15, the 16th Conference on Database Systems for Business, Technology, and Web.*

Möller, B., Roocks, P., & Endres, M. (2012). An Algebraic Calculus of Database Preferences. *MPC '12, the International Conference on Mathematics of Program Construction*, 241-262. 10.1007/978-3-642-31113-0_13

Morse, M., Patel, J. M., & Jagadish, H. V. (2007). Efficient Skyline Computation over Low-Cardinality Domains. In *Proc. of VLDB '07* (pp. 267–278). VLDB.

Papadias, D., Tao, Y., Fu, G., & Seeger, B. (2003). An Optimal and Progressive Algorithm for Skyline Queries. In *SIGMOD '03: Proceedings of the 2003 ACM SIGMOD international conference on Management of data* (pp. 467–478). New York, NY: ACM. 10.1145/872757.872814

Park, S., Kim, T., Park, J., Kim, J., & Im, H. (2009). Parallel Skyline Computation on Multicore Architectures. *Proc. of ICDE '09*, 760–771.

Park, Y., Min, J.-K., & Shim, K. (2013). Parallel Computation of Skyline and Reverse Skyline Queries Using MapReduce. *PVLDB, 6*(14), 2002–2013.

Preisinger, T. (2009). *Graph-based Algorithms for Pareto Preference Query.* Books on Demand.

Preisinger, T., & Kießling, W. (2007). The Hexagon Algorithm for Evaluating Pareto Preference Queries. *Proc. of MPref '07.*

Preisinger, T., Kießling, W., & Endres, M. (2006). The BNL++ Algorithm for Evaluating Pareto Preference Queries. *Proc. of MPref '06.*

Ribeiro, M. R., Barioni, M. C. N., de Amo, S., Roncancio, C., & Labbe, C. (2017). Reasoning with Temporal Preferences over Data Streams. *Proceedings of the Florida Artificial Intelligence Research Society Conference (FLAIRS).*

Rocha-Junior, J., Vlachou, A., Doulkeridis, C., & Nørvåg, K. (2009). AGiDS: A Grid-based Strategy for Distributed Skyline Query Processing. Data Management in Grid and Peer-to-Peer Systems, 12-23. doi:10.1007/978-3-642-03715-3_2

Rudenko, L., & Endres, M. (2017). Personalized Stream Analysis with PreferenceSQL. *PPI Workshop of BTW '17*, 181–184.

Rudenko, L., Endres, M., Roocks, P., & Kießling, W. (2016). A Preference-based Stream Analyzer. *STREAMVOLV Workshop of ECML PKKD'16.*

Satzger, B., Endres, M., & Kießling, W. (2006). A Preference-based Recommender Systems. *Proceedings of EC Web '06, the 7th International Conference on Electronic Commerce and Web Technologies.* 10.1007/11823865_4

Selke, J., Lofi, C., & Balke, W.-T. (2010). Highly Scalable Multiprocessing Algorithms for Preference-Based Database Retrieval. *Proc. of DASFAA '10.* 10.1007/978-3-642-12098-5_19

Shang, H., & Kitsuregawa, M. (2013). Skyline Operator on Anti-correlated Distributions. *Proc. of VLDB '13.*

Tan, K.-L., Eng, P.-K., & Ooi, B. C. (2001). Efficient Progressive Skyline Computation. In *VLDB '01: Proceedings of the 27th International Conference on Very Large Data Bases* (pp. 301–310). San Francisco, CA: Morgan Kaufmann Publishers Inc.

Vlachou, A., Doulkeridis, C., & Kotidis, Y. (2008). Angle-based Space Partitioning for Efficient Parallel Skyline Computation. *Proceedings of the 2008 ACM SIGMOD International Conference on management of Data (SIGMOD '08)*, 227-238. 10.1145/1376616.1376642

Woods, L., Alonso, G., & Teubner, J. (2013). Parallel Computation of Skyline Queries. In *Proc. of the FCCM* (pp. 1–8). Washington, DC: IEEE.

Wu, P., Zhang, C., Feng, Y., Zhao, B. Y., Agrawal, D., & Abbadi, A. E. (2006). Parallelizing Skyline Queries for Scalable Distribution. *Proc. of EDBT '06*.

Chapter 7
Application of Statistical Modelling and Evolutionary Optimization Tools in Resin–Bonded Molding Sand System

Ganesh R. Chate
K. L. S. Gogte Institute of Technology, India

Manjunath Patel G. C.
Sahyadri College of Engineering and Management, India

Mahesh B. Parappagoudar
Padre Conceicao College of Engineering, India

Anand S. Deshpande
K. L. S. Gogte Institute of Technology, India

ABSTRACT

Trial-and-error methods in foundries to determine optimum molding sand properties consume more time and result in reduced productivity, high rejection, and cost. Hence, current research is focused towards development and application of modelling and optimization tools. In foundry, there is requirement of mound properties with conflicting nature (that is, minimize: gas evolution and collapsibility; maximize: compression strength, mound hardness, and permeability) and determining best combination among them is often a difficult task. Optimization of resin-bonded molding sand system is discussed in this book chapter. Six different case studies are considered by assigning different combination of weight fractions for multiple objective functions and corresponding desirability (Do) values are determined for DFA, GA, PSO, and MOPSO-CD. The obtained highest desirability value is considered as the optimum solution. Better performance of non-traditional tools might be due to parallel computing approach. GA and PSO have yielded almost similar results, whereas MOPSO-CD produced better results.

DOI: 10.4018/978-1-5225-5396-0.ch007

INTRODUCTION AND LITERATURE REVIEW

The foundry aims to produce good quality castings at reduced cost, by minimizing the incidence of many possible casting defects. To achieve the said objectives, one should have strong knowledge of process mechanics and dynamics through which the castings are made. Metal casting process involves pattern making, mould preparation, melting and pouring. Sand moulds offer greater technical advantage for the production of large tonnage castings at a low cost. Sand casting is a versatile manufacturing process, as it is used to cast high temperature metals and alloys namely, iron, copper and nickel by Saikaew and Wiengwiset (2012). The process control in casting process is often influenced by a large number of control variables (that is, quantity of binder, sand grain size and shape, degree of ramming, curing time and so on) in sand moulds. The sand mixed with a binder accommodates to hold particles of varied size and shapes,which are being compacted around a pattern to form the cavity in the sand. The casting quality or defects are related directly to sand mould properties namely, compression strength, mould hardness, permeability, gas evolution, and collapsibility. The sand mould properties are to be controlled through a proper choice of moulding sand ingredients and processing method of moulding sand mixture.

Traditional Experimental Method

Trial and error experiments are considered asthe most preferred and widely applied method in major class of the foundries by Acharya and Vadher (2016). Clay bonded sand (i.e. green sand) moulds are most preferred with regard to economic aspects. The possible defects in green sand moulding process are, blow holes, pin hole, gas and shrinkage porosity, poor surface finish and dimensional accuracy, scabs, rat tails, slag inclusion, mis-run, and so on (Kumaravadivel & Natarajan, 2013). The casting defects are related directly to sand mould properties. The type of sand mouldis selected based on the type of metal to be cast, cost, reclaimability of silica sand, casting shape, size and thickness, and dimensional accuracy. Barlow (1966) studied the hardness influence in preventing the mould wall movement. Further, they also tried to develop interrelationship among mould hardness (MH) with permeability (P) and strength in high pressure moulding. Sriganesh, Seshradri and Ramachandran (1966) reported that, the degree of packing (i.e., compaction) of bonded sand grains was dependent mainly on the angularity, shape, and size (i.e. coarse or fine) of sand grains. The results also showed that, a degree of packing had reduced with the addition of bonding material. They failed to include many important factors and provide mathematical support for the analysis.

Resin-boned sand moulds and cores produce better moulding sand properties and dimensionally accurate castings than green sand moulds, provided the technical moulding parameters are optimized accurately by Khandelwal and Ravi (2016). Bargaoui et al., (2017) investigated the resin bonding behavior and foundry sand cores at different temperatures (i.e. 28 ^{0}C to 450 ^{0}C). Sand grain size and mould coating have strong influence on fluidity of the molten alloy, which in turn affects the rate of casting solidification by Jafari et al., (2010). Mould filling ability is influenced directly by section thickness of castings (Jafari et al., 2010). Mould coating had showed a significant impact as compared to the grain size, in yielding better mechanical and metallurgical properties. Philips (1970) had made an attempt to develop the influence of chemicals and mulling time on green compression strength and baked shear strength. It is to be noted that, the distribution of sand grain size play a major role in determining the clay and water requirements in the moulding sand system. However, they failed to provide supportive experimental work in their report. Gardner (1948) investigated the degree of ramming and moisture percentage influence on permeability and tensile strength of the sand mould. Kunsmann (1971) determined the optimum time of sand mix and its sequential operation to gain the minimum retained strength (i.e. collapsibility, CP) and hot strength by conducting large number of experiments. Resin based sand moulds are tested under experimentation and computer simulation (finite element analysis and ProCAST) to know the mechanical behavior of sand under tensile stress and hardness (Lu et al., 2017).Over the past few decades, try-error experiment method was employed to investigate the influence of moulding sand variables on some of casting and moulding sand properties (Caylak & Mahnken, 2010; Ding, Zhang & Zhou, 1997; Jakubski, Dobosz & Major-Gabrys, 2012; Liu, Li, Qu & Liu, 2008; Trinowski, 1999). This method demands extensive experimental work, causes different kinds of waste with regard to material, equipment, labor cost, and energy. To limit the currently adopted try-error method in industries, there has begun a quest to develop more efficient method for the effective control of sand mould system.

Statistical Experimental Methods and Modelling

Great demand led most of the current research work directed towards the development of mathematical model to study and analyze the sand moulding process. Guharaja, Noorul Haq and Karuppannan (2006) optimized the levels of process variables (i.e., moisture content, green compression strength, P and MH) of green sand mould process by utilizing statistical Taguchi's method. Taguchi method adopted in the foundry industry showed that the variation in the casting quality can be minimized by controlling the process variables namely, moisture content, green strength, permeability, mould hardness, and pouring temperature (Kumar, Satsangi & Prajapati, 2011; Tiwari, Singh & Srivastava, 2016). Acharya, Sheladiya and Acharya (2017) used Taguchi method to minimize the casting defects by controlling the parameters namely resin, catalyst and temperature of furan sand moulding system. The major drawbacks of Taguchi method, identified from the literature (Kumar, Satsangi & Prajapati, 2011; Tiwari, Singh & Srivastava, 2016; Senthil & Amirthagadeswaran, 2014; Vijian & Arunachalam, 2007; Benguluri et al., 2011), are listed below.

1. Taguchi method suggests the optimum process variable levels, which may not be a global solution always.
2. Taguchi method fails to provide complete insight of detailed information about input-output behaviour.
3. Accurate process control for foundry-men needs the knowledge of process mechanics and dynamics. Taguchi method fails to do the said task.
4. Taguchi method is used to model and analyse each response individually, although different outputs are measured on the same sample input conditions. This might fail to capture the interdependency among outputs. However, Taguchi method needs only few experiments to model and analyse the process.

Design of Experiments (DOE) and Response Surface Methodology (RSM) restricts few limitations of Taguchi method and provide detailed insight of complete influence of input-output relation and their behaviour. Parappagoudar, Pratihar and Datta (2005) developed linear models for green compression strength and permeability. However, permeability an important mould property had failed to make an accurate prediction. Moreover, bulk density and mould hardness were not considered in their experiments. Parappagoudar, Pratihar and Datta (2007; 2008; 2011) extended their research efforts in similar directions to study, analyze and model the different sand mould systems (i.e. green sand, cement bonded, and sodium silicate bonded sand). Noteworthy that, the developed models were capable enough to provide detailed insight of the process and predict accurately for known set of input variables. Surekha, Hanumanth and Krishnamohan (2013) used DOE and RSM to model the chromite-based sand mould process. DOE and RSM were applied to improve sand mould properties by Kumaravadivel, and Natarajan, (2013) and reduced the possible casting defects by utilizing appropriate set of control parameters by Saikaew, and Wiengwiset, (2012). Following observations are made from the above literature on DOE and RSM.

1. DOE and RSM can able to predict the outputs for known values of input parameters.
2. DOE try to model and analyze individual output, thus failed to capture interdependency among outputs.
3. The model determines the optimal input parameter levels and are not global optimal always.

Realizing the Need for Optimization

The optimized combination of sand mould properties can be obtained with an accurate control of sand mould variables in resin-bonded moulding sand system (i.e. percent of resin, resin-to-hardener ratio, number of strokes, setting time, grain fineness number and so on). Inappropriate combination of sand mould properties (CP, P, MH, compression strength (CS), and gas evolution (GE)) will result in more casting defects such as blow hole, pin hole, porosity, poor surface finish, dimensional variation, scabs, rat tails and misruns etc. Till date, not much significant efforts were made on research and development work to optimize the resin sand mould system and enhance casting quality. Traditional and non-traditional tools have been developed for the optimization of sand mould properties. Non-linear regression equations derived for resin bonded sand mould system using DOE and RSM (Chate et al., 2017) were considered for multiple objective optimization utilizing desirability function approach (DFA), evolutionary genetic algorithm (GA) and particle swarm optimization (PSO). P, MH, CS, CP and GE were treated as objective functions (i.e. responses) expressed as mathematical function of inputs (i.e. process variables) namely, grain fineness number, degree of ramming, percent of resin and resin-to-hardener ratio. Five objective functions, which are considered to be conflict with one another were converted in to a single objective function. GA, PSO and DFA were utilized to optimize the single objective function to gain better and global optimal solution.

Natural Computing

Natural computing also refers to natural computation processes, which are inspired from nature for development of novel problem-solving methods using computers by synthesizing the natural phenomenon (Rozenberg, Back & Kok, 2012; Brabazon, Neill & McGarraghy, 2015). Particle swarm optimization, genetic algorithms, artificial bee colony, neural networks, harmony search, and so on are some of the few natural computing tools. The solutions determined viz. traditional methods may not yield the global optimum solutions always. Thereby, global optimization method is essential to determine the optimal set of parameters for multi modal objective functions. In a single response optimization problem, efforts can be made to gain the best decision or design based on global maxima or minima solutions. It is difficult to determine a single input variable set, for the conflicting requirements (i.e. *maximize:* CS, MH, and P and *minimize:* GE and CP) in a resin bonded sand mould system. To derive global solutions for the said problem there is a need of multiple objective optimization method. Noteworthy that, multiple objective optimization methods can be converted suitably using mathematical formulation to single objective optimization.

Evolutionary algorithms (i.e. GA and PSO) are population based heuristic search methods, and proved as a cost effective tool to locate near optimal solutions in multi-objective optimization problem. Global optimum solutions are expected in evolutionary algorithms be due to stochastic mechanism adopted to carry out search at many distinct spatial locations simultaneously. Early in 1960s, Rosenberg (1967) reported the use of evolutionary computational search to solve various classes of real world problems. The single optimal solution for two or more outputs simultaneously can be obtained by using the concept of multi-evolutionary optimization, introduced in 1985 by Schaffer (1985). In many of the real world problem, the objective functions are found to be conflicting with one another. The efforts are required to optimize a particular solution with regard to individual objective function will always results in a compromised solution (i.e. one solution dominated after sacrificing the other). There is a need for multi-objective optimization problem solutions is to result in a set of solutions, which satisfy an adequate range without dominating the other solution. Two generic approaches are being used to solve the multi-objective optimization problems. Two or more individual objective functions with assigned weight factors are integrated to form a single composite function in the first approach. Important to note that, single composite functions can be formed for the conflicting objective functions after formulating by utilizing suitable methods such as utility theory, weight sum method etc. (Marler & Arora, 2004). However, appropriate choice in selection of weights is still under intensive research study. Pareto optimal solution generation, based on the different trade-off (i.e. weights) is the second approach. In this approach, definite amount of sacrifice is expected in optimizing one objective over the other objective function, while the solutions are moving from one Pareto front to other. The major pitfall lies in the fact that, the size of the Pareto optimal sets increases with an increase in number of objectives. The selection of best solution among many potential solutions is always considered impractical in many industrial applications.

To limit the pitfalls of Pareto optimal set, weight sum method can be adopted for multi-objective optimization to determine distinct solutions after varying weights. Further, to locate single optimal solution that imitates user preferred set of weights can be adopted by Marler and Arora, (2004). Till date many industries are focused to determine the best set of values of the quality characteristics by consulting industry experts and practical data-hand books. The desired quality characteristics and their related input variable set are dependent on the importance assigned to each output quality characteristics. In general, all outputs are relatively dependent as they are measured at different locations on same sample prepared under particular input condition.

Weight Method Based Optimization

In recent years, weighted sum methods are employed by several eminent scholars to identify the optimal parameter settings for electro-discharge machining, tube spinning process and squeeze casting process (Mahapatra & Patnaik, 2007; Vundavilli, Kumar & Parappagoudar, 2013; Patel et al., 2016a; 2016b). The present research work is focussed on multi-objective optimization method based on DFA, GA, PSO and multi-objective particle swarm optimization based crowding distance (MOPSO-CD), applied to resin bonded sand mould process, to evaluate the sand mould properties. Moulding sand properties namely, CP, CS, MH, GE, and P, in resin-bonded moulding sand system are treated as five different objective functions and optimized simultaneously.

Case Study: To Model and Optimize the Resin Sand Mould System

The following objectives are the requirements in foundries to yield best sand mould properties and good quality castings.

1. Identify the critical moulding sand variables that influence sand mould properties.
2. Conduct statistical tests to analyze the significance of moulding sand variables.
3. Surface plot explain the variation of the response surface with input parameters.
4. The models developed for different responses are tested for statistical adequacy.
5. Mathematical input-output relationships are established for the collected experimental data.
6. GA, PSO, DFA, MOPSO-CD models are developed to conduct optimization task for resin sand mould system.
7. Experiments are conducted with the best set of sand mould properties, and tested for practical utility in metal casing industries.

The methodology employed to accomplish the said multi-objective optimization task is presented in Figure 1.

OPTIMIZATION TOOLS

The traditional and non-traditional optimization tools are used to optimize the resin bonded sand mould system. DFA, PSO, GA and MOPSO-CD are the tools utilized to determine the optimal set of sand mould variables and corresponding moulding sand properties. The working principle of optimization tools are discussed below.

Desirability Function Approach (DFA)

DFA was first proposed by Harrington (1965), to optimize multiple outputs simultaneously for a process. This method essentially require to convert the objective functions to a common scale which vary in the ranges of zero and one, integrate them with the geometric mean and optimize composite metric. DFA involves transforming each individual output (Y_i) to corresponding desirability index ($d(y_i)$), which is unit less and vary between zero and one ($0 \leq d(y_i) \geq 1$). The higher desirability value (i.e. $d(y_i) = 1$) indicate the ideal response value, whereas, $d(y_i) = 0$ signifies the completely undesirable response value (Montgomery, 2004). Steps involved in desirability function approach are as follows,

Step 1: Computation of single desirability index $d(y_i)$ for each output function, according to formulae proposed by Derringer and Suich (1980). Noteworthy that, DFA is used according to the output quality characteristics as follows,

For smaller-the-better quality characteristics, the output function required to be minimized as shown below,

Figure 1. Methodology employed for modelling and optimization of resin bonded sand mould system

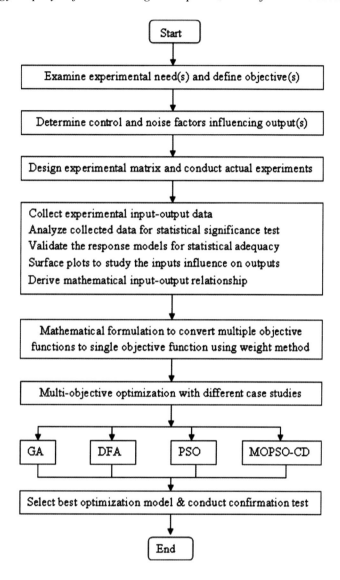

$$d(y_i) = \begin{cases} 1 & \text{if} & y_i < T \\ \left(\dfrac{U - y_i}{U - T}\right) & \text{if} & T \le y_i \le U \\ 0 & \text{if} & y_i > T \end{cases}$$

For larger-the-better quality characteristics, the output function required to be maximized as shown below,

$$d(y_i) = \begin{cases} 0 & \text{if} & y_i < L \\ \left(\dfrac{y_i - L}{T - L}\right) & \text{if} & L \le y_i \le T \\ 1 & \text{if} & y_i > T \end{cases}$$

where, U and L are the upper and lower range values and T correspond to target values.

Step 2: The single desirability indexes of all outputs are combined to gain single value called composite global desirability (D_o) index as shown below:

$$D_o = \sqrt[n]{d(y_1)^{w_1} \times d(y_2)^{w_2} \times d(y_3)^{w_3} \ldots \ldots \times d(y_n)^{w_n}}$$

Terms, w depicts the weight and n indicates the number of outputs.

Genetic Algorithm (GA)

During 1970, Prof. John Holland at University of Michigan introduced the genetic algorithm (mimic the behaviour of biological process observed in natural system), which work with Charles Darwin theory based on survival of fittest among potential population over successive generations. GA optimizes the dynamic control factors of different manufacturing processes. Heuristic mechanism allows conducting search for global solutions at many distinct locations and dimensional space, with set of probabilistic transition rules has gained wide attention during recent past. Tournament selection and bitwise mutation are employed to avoid local minima (if any). GA working cycle is presented in Figure 2.

Particle Swarm Optimization (PSO)

Dr. Russel C. Eberhart and Dr. James Kennedy in 1995 introduced the concept called particle swarm optimization. Particle swarm optimization mimic the movement of foraging behaviour of bird flock. PSO conduct extensive search resulted better than GA and ant colony optimization (ACO) in locating the minimum mean of cost (Adrian, Utamima & Wang, 2015). Simple structure with few tuning particle swarm optimization parameters showed slightly better performance and convergence than genetic algorithm to optimize the fermentation conditions of lipase production (Garlapati, Vundavilli & Banerjee, 2010).

In PSO, swarm is a community which includes many entities known as particles, and each individual particle fly in multi-dimensional search space to locate its optimal solution. Each particle adjusts its own fly path accordingly with self and neighbour particle experience. The working cycle of particle swarm optimization is shown in Figure 3. PSO parameters are adjusted by updating the position and velocity of individual particle using below equations.

$$New \ velocity : V_i^{k+1} = w \times V_i^k + \underbrace{R \ and_1 \left[P \ best_i^k - P_i^k\right]}_{Cognitive \ part} + \underbrace{R \ and_2 \left[G \ best_i^k - P_i^k\right]}_{Social \ part}$$

Figure 2. Schematic representation of working cycle of GA

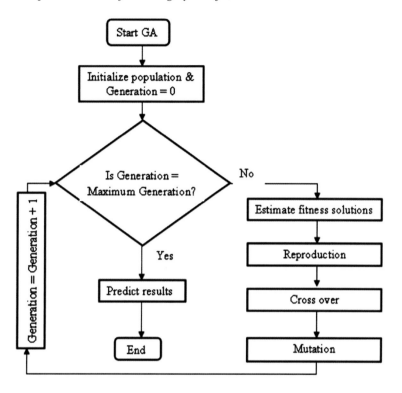

$$New\ Position : P_i^{k+1} = P_i^k + V_i^{k+1}$$

Terms: w refers to inertia weight control the impact of past velocity with the current velocity. High value of inertia weight results enhance the search space and vice versa. V_i^K present velocity of individual particle, i, at iteration, k. V_i^{K+1} define the updated velocity of the individual i, at k + 1, Rand$_1$, Rand$_2$: random number vary in the range of 0 and 1. Pbest$_i^K$ and Gbest$_i^K$ referred to the best positions of each individual particle i, and group till it complete iteration, k. The particle changes its velocity based on self-experience is referred as cognitive leader. Similarly, particle velocity changes according to neighbour particle experience known as social leader.

Multi-Objective Particle Swarm Optimization: Crowding Distance (MOPSO-CD)

MOPSO-CD utilizes the principle of crowding distance with mutation operator to maintain variety of non-dominated solutions stored in an external repository (Raquel and Navel (2005)). Major modifications to basic particle swarm optimization are the choice of cognitive (Pbest) and social (Gbest) leader using Pareto dominance and the crowding distance. MOPSO use external repository to store potential solutions identified at the earlier search. Mutation parameter enhances the search capability of particle swarm optimization to avoid premature convergence (i.e. local minima). The schematic representation of working cycle of MOPSO-CD is shown in Figure 4. Thereby, MOPSO-CD is a tool that handle complex non-linear multiple objective functions which are of conflicting requirements.

Figure 3. Schematic representation of working cycle of PSO

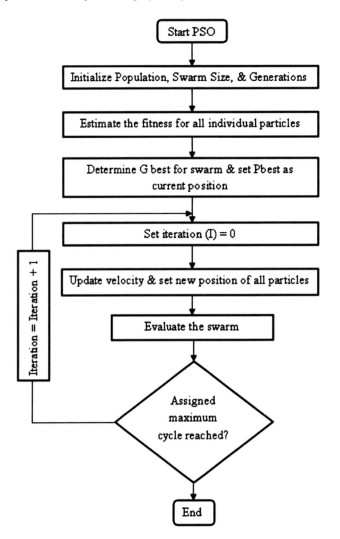

MATERIALS AND METHODS

Resin-bonded moulding sand is prepared by mixing silica sand with adequate quantity of resin and hardener utilizing sand Muller. Test specimens are prepared as per AFS standard and conducted experiments with different combination of sand mould variables with the reference AFS standard.

Sand Mould Property (Response) Measurement

Sand mould properties (CS, CP, MH, P and GE) are measured for the test specimens prepared with different combination of ingredients as per central composite design method.

The samples prepared according to AFS standard are used to determine, permeability with the help of permeability meter (refer Figure 5a), CS and CP using hydraulic strength unit (Figure 5b), MH by mould hardness tester (refer Figure 5c) and GE by utilizing the gas evolution measuring unit (Figure 5d).

Figure 4. Schematic representation of working cycle of MOPSO-CD

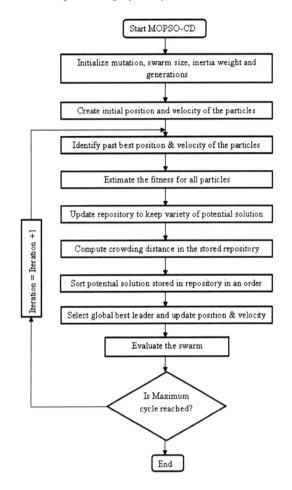

RESULTS AND DISCUSSION

Design of experiments is used to collect input-output experiment data, conduct statistical analysis and develop mathematical input-output relationships. The models developed for each response is tested for statistical adequacy and validate for their practical usefulness. The response equations derived based on statistical design of experiments was used to determine input variables that locate the extreme values of conflicting requirements in sand mould properties. GA, PSO, MOPSO-CD and DFA are used for the said optimization task. The systematic study is conducted to tune the parameters of GA, PSO and MOPSO-CD. Confirmation experiments are conducted to validate the best predicted optimization tool.

Statistical Modeling of Resin Sand Mould System

The quality of castings manufactured in resin-bonded sand mould system depends on the sand mould properties (i.e. CS, CP, MH, P and GE). However, the sand mould properties are largely influenced by grain fineness number (GFN), setting time, amount of resin and hardness. The parameters which influence the properties of resin bonded sand mould system are presented in Figure 6.

Figure 5. (a) Permeability tester, (b) Hydraulic strength testing unit, (c) MH tester, and (d) GE measuring unit

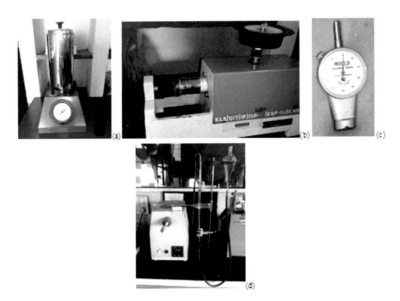

Figure 6. Ishikawa diagram for sand mould and casting quality

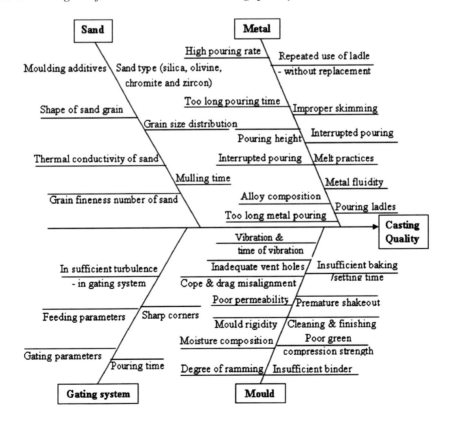

The input-output model of resin-bonded sand mould system is represented schematically as shown in Figure 7. The levels of sand mould variables (i.e. inputs) used in the experimental study are presented in Table 1. Grain fineness number for silica sand is determined after conducting sieve analysis test. Experiments are conducted as per the design matrix of central composite design and the test specimens are prepared and the sand mould properties are measured according to American Foundry Society (AFS) standards (refer Table 2). Important to note that, experiments are conducted at local metal casting industry and three replicates are considered for each set of input conditions. The mathematical input-output relationships developed for the moulding sand properties are represented below.

$$MH = 94.5 - 2.416A - 46.9B + 99.4C + 0.606D + 0.01671A^2 + 14B^2 - 45.4C^2 - 0.003266D^2 + 0.0078AB + 0.0391AC + 0.002031AD - 1.56BC - 0.0521BD + 0.0104CD \tag{1}$$

$$P = 6605 + 87.03A - 8180B - 3876C + 17.42D - 0.6473A^2 + 2215B^2 + 2465C^2 - 0.0016D^2 - 1AB + 1.34AC + 0.0194AD - 87BC - 4.33BD - 8.81CD \tag{2}$$

$$CS = 5723 + 131A - 1680B - 19587C + 10.5D - 1.25A^2 - 185B^2 + 8440C^2 - 0.061D^2 + 26.8AB + 5.08AC - 0.1047AD + 961BC + 5.47BD + 10.36CD \tag{3}$$

$$GE = 73.6 + 0.196A - 80B + 15.6C - 0.1006D\ 0.0025A^2\ 21.25B^2 - 8.75C^2 + 0.0469AB + 0.000556D^2 + 0.1219AC - 0.000125AD - 3.75BC + 0.0063BD - 0.0021CD \tag{4}$$

$$CP = 5592 + 73.7A - 2324B - 11835C - 11.75D - 0.8458A^2 - 208B^2 + 4167C^2 + 0.013D^2 + 23.12AB + 7.5AC - 0.0042AD + 1531BC + 7.71BD + 3.12CD \tag{5}$$

The input-output relations in resin-bonded moulding sand system have been tested for statistical adequacy with the help of analysis of variance. Summary results of analysis of variance are presented in Table 3.

Figure 7. Input and output variables of resin sand mould system

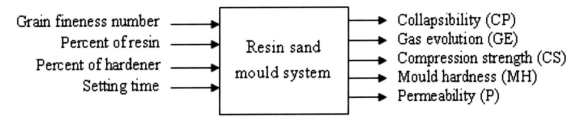

Table 1. Input variables and their corresponding levels

Sl. No	Parameters			Level		
	Source	Unit	Notation	Low	Middle	High
1	Grain fineness number	-	A	50	70	90
2	Percent of resin	-	B	1.8	2.0	2.2
3	Percent of hardener	-	C	0.8	1.0	1.2
4	Setting time	min	D	60	90	120

Table 2. Central composite design experimental matrices for resin sand mould system

Sl. No	Input Parameters				Outputs				
	A	B	C	D	MH(Chate et al., 2017)	P(Chate et al., 2017)	CS, gm/cm²	GE, cc/gm	CP, gm/cm²
1	50	1.8	0.8	120	54.00	510	1080.0	08.7	0780.0
2	50	1.8	1.2	120	58.00	490	1420.0	07.9	0800.0
3	70	2.0	1.0	060	51.00	460	0680.0	10.2	0600.0
4	90	2.2	0.8	120	64.25	450	1485.0	11.9	1280.0
5	50	1.8	1.2	060	55.00	460	0425.0	08.1	0350.0
6	50	1.8	0.8	060	53.50	300	0475.0	08.5	0400.0
7	70	2.0	0.8	090	54.00	600	1630.0	09.9	1100.0
8	90	2.0	1.0	090	66.75	185	0790.0	10.2	0800.0
9	70	2.2	1.0	090	58.50	600	1475.0	12.0	1080.0
10	90	2.2	1.2	120	67.00	410	2075.0	12.6	1720.0
11	50	2.2	0.8	060	54.00	440	0395.0	11.0	0280.0
12	90	1.8	1.2	120	67.25	400	1285.0	10.0	0990.0
13	70	2.0	1.0	090	55.50	490	1250.0	09.6	0950.0
14	90	2.2	1.2	060	62.00	465	1185.0	12.8	1040.0
15	50	2.2	0.8	120	54.50	500	1350.0	11.2	0860.0
16	70	2.0	1.0	120	57.25	540	1750.0	11.0	1350.0
17	90	1.8	0.8	120	62.75	400	1080.0	09.6	0900.0
18	70	2.0	1.0	090	54.50	485	1250.0	10.4	1020.0
19	90	1.8	0.8	060	55.25	194	0495.0	09.9	0500.0
20	50	2.0	1.0	090	60.75	300	0750.0	08.0	0450.0
21	70	2.0	1.2	090	56.50	600	1585.0	09.6	1160.0
22	70	1.8	1.0	090	56.75	580	1050.0	09.9	0830.0
23	90	1.8	1.2	060	61.00	405	0620.0	10.1	0580.0
24	50	2.2	1.2	060	58.00	620	0580.0	08.7	0470.0
25	50	2.2	1.2	120	59.00	460	1640.0	09.0	1090.0
26	90	2.2	0.8	060	58.50	270	1015.0	12.0	0780.0
27	70	2.0	1.0	090	56.75	490	1250.0	10.5	0970.0

Table 3. ANOVA test results for sand mould properties

Response		Permeability (Chate et al., 2017)				Mold Hardness (Chate et al., 2017)			
Source	DF	Adj. SS	Adj. MS	F	P	Adj. SS	Adj. MS	F	P
Model	14	346659	24761	32.30	0.000	491.287	35.092	25.40	0.000
Linear	4	97434	24358	31.78	0.000	326.729	81.682	59.12	0.000
Square	4	190600	47650	62.16	0.000	138.698	34.675	25.10	0.000
Interaction	6	58625	9771	12.75	0.000	25.859	4.310	3.12	0.044
Error	12	9199	767			16.579	1.382		
Lack of fit	10	9182	918	110.19	0.009	14.037	1.404	1.10	0.565
Pure error	2	17	8			2.542	1.271		
Total	26	355858				507.866			
Response		Compression Strength				Gas evolution			
Model	14	5228314	373451	35.59	0.000	46.9089	3.3506	20.13	0.000
Linear	4	3936292	984073	93.78	0.000	37.8789	9.4697	56.88	0.000
Square	4	935726	233931	22.29	0.000	4.1900	1.0475	6.29	0.006
Interaction	6	356297	59383	5.66	0.005	4.8400	0.8067	4.85	0.010
Error	12	125927	10494			1.9978	0.1665		
Lack of fit	10	125927	12593	0.76	0.172	1.5111	0.1511	0.62	0.752
Pure error	2	0	0			0.4867	0.2433		
Total	26	5354241				48.9067			
Response		Collapsibility							
Model	14	2886653	206189	62.57	0.000				
Linear	4	2237128	559282	169.71	0.000				
Square	4	398250	99562	30.21	0.000				
Interaction	6	251275	41879	12.71	0.000				
Error	12	39547	3296						
Lack of fit	10	36947	3695	2.84	0.288				
Pure error	2	2600	1300						
Total	26	2926200							

Most of the linear, square and their relative interaction terms are found to have significant contribution towards all responses, as their corresponding p values are found to be less than 0.05. It is to be noted that, all coefficient of correlation values are found to be close to 1 statistically adequate and further testing of the models for prediction accuracy is carried with by utilizing test cases.

The correlation coefficient values for different sand mould properties are shown in Table 4. It has been observed that significant and insignificant terms for responses (i.e. sand mould properties) are found to be different for different responses. However, the model showed similar insignificant and significant terms for CS and CP, due to the existence of strong dependency among the outputs. Figure 8a shows increase in setting time (i.e. D) does not showed major impact towards GE, as their corresponding p value is found greater than 0.05 (refer Table 4). Table 4 showed the square terms of grain fineness

Table 4. Summary of significance test results for sand mould properties

Output	Coefficient of Correlations		Parameters	
	All Terms	**Exclude Insignificant Terms**	**Significant Terms**	**Insignificant Terms**
MH(Chate et al., 2017)	0.9674	0.9293	A, B, C, D, AA.CC, DD, AD	BB, AB, AC, BC, BD, CD
P(Chate et al., 2017)	0.9741	0.9440	A, B, C, D, AA, BB, CC, BD, CD	DD, AB, AC, AD, BC
CS	0.9765	0.9490	A, B, C, D, AA, CC, AB, AD, CD	BB, DD, AC, BC, BD
CP	0.9865	0.9707	A, B, C, D, AA, CC, AB, BC, BD	BB, DD, AC, AD, CD
GE	0.9592	0.9115	A, B, C, AA, BB, AC	D, CC, DD, AB, AD, BC, BD, CD

number and percent of resin found significant, which signifies the developed relationship is non-linear (refer Figure 8b). Important to note that, GE tends to be in direct relation with the proportion of resin and hardener, (refer Figure 8b and c). Increased values of percent of resin along with an increase in hardener and curing time showed increase in gas evolution (Figure 8d and e). Increase in percent of resin with hardener and sufficient curing time allow strong chemical reactions and burn at high temperature resulting in increased values of gas evolution. Important to note that the impact of resin is found higher as compared to that of hardener and curing time. Increased values of hardener and curing time tend to increase the gas evolution (refer Figure8f). The square term of grain fineness number is found to have significant towards all outputs, indicating the existence of strong non-linear relationship. Percent of resin is found insignificant and thereby resulted in a strong linear relationship with CS, MH and CP. Increase in the percent of resin will result in a strong polymerization reaction with the catalyst which might have helped to develop cohesive bonding between the sand grains. Similar examinations are conducted for the other responses.

Mathematical Formulation for Optimization of Resin Sand Mould System

The present work is an attempt to optimize multiple outputs in a resin-bonded sand mould system by using DFA, GA, PSO, and MOPSO-CD. Weighted sum method is employed to conduct the multi-response optimization tasks. It is to be noted that, five objective functions (CS, CP, GE, P and MH) are normalized to avoid numerical overflows, due to existence of very large and small values of the objectives. The weight sum method is employed to optimize by combining multiple outputs to form single objective function. Five responses in the present work are in conflict with one another. The computation of global desirability (D_o) value is determined as discussed below,

$$D_o = \sqrt[5]{y_{MH}^{w_1} \times y_P^{w_2} \times y_{CS}^{w_3} \times y_{GE}^{w_4} \times y_{CP}^{w_5}}$$

In the present work, CS, P and MH are maximization type of objective functions:

Figure 8. Surface plots of GE with (a) GFN and percent of resin, (b) GFN and percent of hardener, (c) GFN and curing time, (d) percent of resin and percent of hardener, (e) percent of resin and curing time and (f) percent of hardener and curing time.

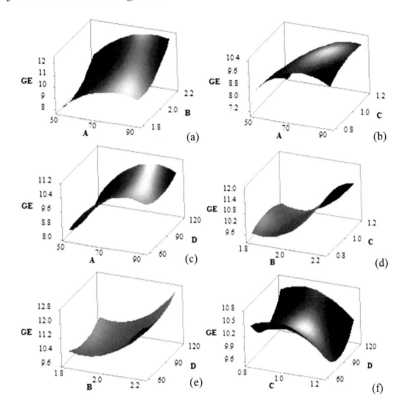

$$Y_{MH} = \frac{MH - MH_{\min}}{MH_{\max} - MH_{\min}}, Y_P = \frac{P - P_{\min}}{P_{\max} - P_{\min}} \, and \, Y_{CS} = \frac{CS - CS_{\min}}{CS_{\max} - CS_{\min}}$$

Similarly, when GE and CP are minimization type of objective function then,

$$Y_{CP} = \frac{CP_{\max} - CP}{CP_{\max} - CP_{\min}} \, and \, Y_{GE} = \frac{GE_{\max} - GE}{GE_{\max} - GE_{\min}}$$

Terms:

- Y_{MH} is the normalized value of mould hardness
- $MH_{\max}$ is maximum values of mould hardness
- $MH_{\min}$ is minimum values of mould hardness
- Y_P is the normalized value of permeability
- $P_{\max}$ is maximum values of permeability
- $P_{\min}$ is minimum values of permeability

- Y_{CS} is the normalized value of compression strength
- CS_{max} is maximum values of compression strength
- CS_{min} is minimum values of compression strength
- Y_{GE} is the normalized value of gas evolution
- GE_{max} is maximum values of gas evolution
- GE_{min} is minimum values of gas evolution
- Y_{CP} is the normalized value of collapsibility
  - CP_{max} is maximum values of collapsibility
- CP_{min} is minimum values of collapsibility.

The present research is focussed to optimize the sand mould variables and sand mould properties utilizing DFA, GA, PSO and MOPSO-CD. The response functions of sand mould properties namely CS, P and MH are to be maximized, while minimizing GE and CP. The present work is posed as a multi objective with conflicting requirements. Weight sum method is employed to convert the multiple conflicting response function to single response function (refer Eq. 6). Important to note that, multiple objective functions have many solutions, due to conflicting requirements. This is considered as tedious task for selection of the best solutions. Hence, different case studies are considered with different weight factors and utilizing the principal component analysis. Weight sum method is employed to formulate objective function by converting multiple response function to single response function.

- Response function $(R_1) = MH$
- Response function $(R_2) = P$
- Response function $(R_3) = CS$
- Response function $(R_4) = 1/GE$
- Response function $(R_5) = 1/CP$

$$\text{Maximize } (F) = w_1 R_1 + w_2 R_2 + w_3 R_3 + w_4 R_4 + w_5 R_5 \tag{6}$$

Subject to control factor constraints

$$50 \leq A \geq 90$$

$$1.8 \leq B \geq 2.2$$

$$0.8 \leq C \geq 1.2$$

$$60 \leq D \geq 120$$

Terms, $w_1 R_1$, $w_2 R_2$, $w_3 R_3$, $w_4 R_4$, and $w_5 R_5$ are the weight fraction and corresponding response functions of MH, P, CS, GE and CP, respectively. Noteworthy that, the weights (i.e., w_1, w_2, w_3, w_4 and w_5) are selected in such a way that their cumulative value will be equal to one. Six case studies are selected based on the weight factor combinations (i.e. assigning equal importance to all outputs and highest importance to individual output one at a time) and corresponding global desirability value is also determined. The summary of the results of optimization obtained by utilizing DFA, GA, PSO and MOPSO-CD are discussed in the following section.

Optimization Using DFA

Experiments are conducted as per the central composite design (CCD) matrix and statistical analysis is conducted and regression equations are developed using ANOVA and response surface methodology respectively. Response optimizer available in the Minitab software has been utilized for conduction of multiple-objective optimization. The summary of results obtained from desirability function approach for six case studies are presented in Table 5. The global desirability values obtained for case 1 to case 6 are found equal to 0.9122, 0.9372, 0.9346, 0.9191, 0.9384 and 0.9299, respectively. DFA recommended the case 5 (GE assigned with highest weight factor, while maintaining the rest at fixed low equal weights) as optimal condition, since its D_o value is found to be highest over other case studies considered.

Optimization Using GA

The variation of fitness value correspond to change in probability of cross over (P_C), with the size of population, probability of mutation and maximum generations at fixed value is shown in Figure9. The present work is focused to maximize the response function value and the value correspond to higher fitness has been selected as an optimal condition. Probability of cross over (Pc*), which is responsible for maximum fitness value is identified. Figure 9b show the variation of fitness value with probability of mutation (P_m) after maintaining the Pc*, population size and number of generation at fixed level. The identified maximum fitness value for the probability of mutation (Pm*) and Pc* were utilized to determine the maximum fitness value for the population size (pop*) as shown in Figure 9c. Moreover,

Table 5. Optimum moulding sand variables for sand mould properties with different weighing factors using DFA

Control Factors and Responses	Optimized Values of Moulding Sand Variables and Sand Mould Properties					
	Case 1(w_1, w_2, w_3,w_4,w_5 = 0.2)	Case 2 (w_1 = 0.6, w_2, w_3,w_4,w_5 = 0.1)	Case 3 (w_2 = 0.6, w_1, w_3,w_4,w_5 = 0.1)	Case 4 (w_3 = 0.6, w_1, w_2,w_4,w_5 = 0.1)	Case 5 (w_4 = 0.6, w_1, w_2,w_3,w_5 = 0.1)	Case 6 (w_5 = 0.6, w_1, w_2,w_3,w_4 = 0.1)
A	53.85	89.59	57.67	58.50	53.63	50.00
B	01.80	01.80	01.80	02.17	01.80	01.80
C	01.20	01.20	01.20	01.20	01.20	01.20
D	101.1	105.5	100.0	110.9	102.4	86.67
MH	58.29	67.28	57.21	57.08	58.33	59.71
P	558.8	416.0	622.6	618.8	554.4	479.8
CS	1306	1190	1424	1934	1315	898.5
GE	07.91	09.93	08.41	09.92	07.89	07.23
CP	783.5	0910	886.7	1328	786.6	526.95
Desirability, D_o	0.9122	0.9372	0.9346	0.9191	0.9384	0.9299

GA parameters namely the number of generations are maintained same as that of previous one. The optimized values of genetic parameters such as P_c*, Pm*, and pop* for higher fitness are maintained at fixed values and conducted to determine the maximum number of generations (gen*) that maximize the fitness (refer Figure9d). The optimized genetic algorithm parameters for the maximum fitness value are given below.

Probability of crossover (Pc*) = 0.85
Probability of mutation (Pm*) = 0.075
Population size (pop*) = 110
Maximum number of generations (gen*) = 90

The maximum fitness and composite desirability values obtained for case 1 to 6 are found to be {0.6194, 0.9035},{0.7238, 0.9296},{0.7440, 0.9350}, {0.7011, 0.9182}, {0.7954, 0.9481} and {0.7039, 0.9242}, respectively. Table 6 shows the optimum sand moulding conditions for multiple outputs obtained for different combination of weight factors. It is to be noted that, Case 5 shows highest fitness and composite desirability value. Hence Case 5 is selected as best case which will produce minimum gas evolution, and collapsibility, while maximizing the permeability, compression strength, and mould hardness.

Figure 9. GA parametric study: (a) Fitness vs. Probability of crossover (Pc), (b) Fitness vs. Probability of mutation (Pm), (c) Fitness vs. Population size and (d) Fitness vs. Generation number

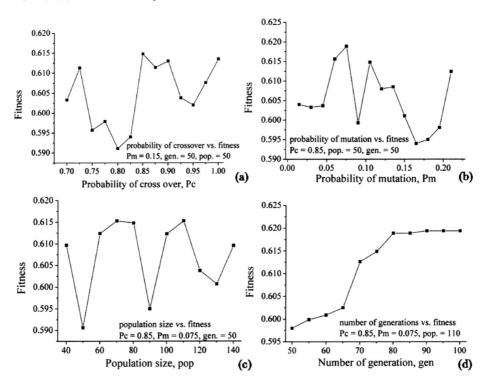

Table 6. Optimum moulding sand variables for sand mould properties with different weighing factors using GA

Control Factors and Responses	Optimized Values of Moulding Sand Variables and Sand Mould Properties					
	Case 1(w_1, w_2, w_3, w_4, w_5 = 0.2)	Case 2 (w_1 = 0.6, w_2, w_3, w_4, w_5 = 0.1)	Case 3 (w_2 = 0.6, w_1, w_3, w_4, w_5 = 0.1)	Case 4 (w_3 = 0.6, w_1, w_2, w_4, w_5 = 0.1)	Case 5 (w_4 = 0.6, w_1, w_2, w_3, w_5 = 0.1)	Case 6 (w_5 = 0.6, w_1, w_2, w_3, w_4 = 0.1)
A	59.4	88.7	65.5	68.1	50.00	50.24
B	1.87	1.87	1.85	1.99	1.84	1.81
C	1.20	1.19	1.20	1.20	1.18	1.11
D	92.0	109	98.0	113.0	91.0	95.0
MH	56.7	66.50	56.40	56.14	59.95	60.4
P	598.9	385.3	657.2	612.4	473.2	398.8
CS	1393	1353	1605	1976	953	795.6
GE	8.38	9.94	9.08	9.70	7.13	7.73
CP	916	1062	1078	1391	573.4	503.5
Desirability, D_o	0.9035	0.9296	0.9350	0.9182	0.9481	0.9242

Optimization Using PSO

PSO conducts heuristic search to determine best solution with optimized the parameters namely, inertia weight, swarm size and generations. Systematic study is employed to maximize the fitness value with the best set of particle swarm optimization parameters. Smaller swarm size and generations always yield solution at very fast convergence and greater probability to get trapped at local solutions, whereas large number of generations and swarm size will require larger computation time over better solution gained. The results of systematic study to optimize parameters of PSO are shown in Figure10. The optimized parameters of particle swarm optimization for maximum fitness value are as follows,

Inertia weight (W*) = 0.4
Swarm size (SS*) = 70
Number of generations (Gen*) = 55

Table 7 shows the optimized sand mould conditions and properties obtained for different combination of weight factors considered under different case studies. Maximum fitness and the composite desirability values obtained for case 1 to 6 are found to be {0.9075, 0.6321}, {0.9333, 0.7395}, {0.9278, 0.7082}, {0.9185, 0.7012}, {0.9397, 0.7681}, and {0.9244, 0.7066}, respectively. PSO also indicates case 5 as optimal condition. Few tuning parameters in particle swarm optimization reduces the computational time and resultsin a fast convergence rate.

Multi-response optimization will yield many solutions and weight factors are selected such that the composite value of all response functions must be equal to one. Noteworthy that, the paramount importance of selection of weight factors are done based on the requirements. Six different case studies with different combination of weighing factors of objectives are shown in Table 7.

Figure 10. Parameter study of PSO: (a) Fitness vs. Inertia weight, (b) Fitness vs. Swarm size and (c) Fitness vs. Maximum number of generations

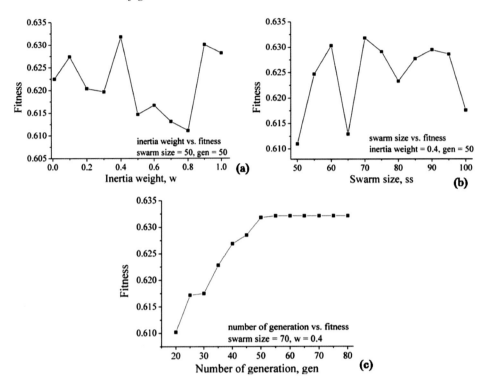

Table 7. Optimum moulding sand variables for sand mould properties with different weighing factors using PSO

Control Factors and Responses	Optimized Values of Moulding Sand Variables and Sand Mould Properties					
	Case 1 (w_1, w_2, w_3, w_4, w_5 = 0.2)	Case 2 (w_1 = 0.6, w_2, w_3, w_4, w_5 = 0.1)	Case 3 (w_2 = 0.6, w_1, w_3, w_4, w_5 = 0.1)	Case 4 (w_3 = 0.6, w_1, w_2, w_4, w_5 = 0.1)	Case 5 (w_4 = 0.6, w_1, w_2, w_3, w_5 = 0.1)	Case 6 (w_5 = 0.6, w_1, w_2, w_3, w_4 = 0.1)
A	55.5	89.3	67.50	68.30	50.19	50.81
B	1.85	1.85	1.86	1.99	1.97	1.87
C	1.20	1.20	1.17	1.20	1.16	1.17
D	92.0	105	97.0	113.0	100.0	81.0
MH	57.7	66.91	56.72	56.17	60.06	59.05
P	552.9	385.8	628.5	614.2	370.8	426.9
CS	1250	1281	1512	1999	1079	783.6
GE	7.91	9.85	9.35	9.75	7.38	7.32
CP	794.7	1000	1050	1409	681.7	511.4
Desirability, D_o	0.9075	0.9333	0.9278	0.9185	0.9397	0.9244

Optimization Using MOPSO-CD

The detailed study (i.e. MOPSO-CD parameters such as inertia weight, swarm size, and number of generations are varied at once) has been conducted to optimize the parameters for maximum fitness values. Note that, the mutation parameter helps to enhance the search capability that prevents premature convergence (i.e. local minima). Small swarm size and number of generations may result in local convergence for global solution. The results of systematic study employed for the present work is shown in Figure11.

The fitness value variation with the change in probability of mutation is shown in Figure11a. The parameters namely, inertia weight, swarm size and number of generations are maintained at fixed values and the maximum fitness value for probability of mutation (Pm*) is determined. Figure 11b shows the study related to inertia weight. Next probability of mutation is set at Pm* and rest of the parameters such as swarm size and number of generations are maintained at fixed level as shown in Figure11a. In this stage, the maximum fitness value and corresponding value of inertia weight (W*) has been identified. The fitness solution with the swarm size has been studied in Figure 11c. During this stage the probability of mutation and inertia weight have been set at Pm* and W* after maintaining the number of generation at fixed level. The study related to solution convergence with number of generation is shown in Figure 11d. The numberof generation (gen*) that yield the maximum fitness value is selected as number of generations. The optimized parameters responsible for better performance are as follows,

Probability of mutation, (Pm*) = 0.09

Figure 11. MOPSO-CD parametric study: (a) Fitness vs. Probability of mutation, (b) Fitness vs. Inertia weight, (c) Fitness vs. Swarm size and (d) Fitness vs. Maximum generations

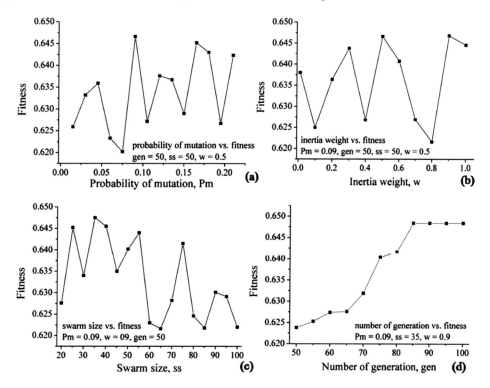

Inertia Weight (W*) = 0.9
Swarm Size (SS*) = 35
Number of Generations (G*) = 85

As mentioned earlier, six different case studies with different combination of weight factors are studied. Table 8 presents the optimized sand mould conditions with combination of different weight factors. Interesting to note that maximum fitness and composite desirability values for case 1 to 6 are found equal to {0.6484, 0.9130}, {0.7619, 0.9383}, {0.7754, 0.9421}, {0.7055, 0.9421}, {0.8161, 0.9512} and {0.7191, 0.9287}, respectively. Case 5 produced the maximum fitness as well as the composite desirability value, and is selected as optimal sand moulding condition.

Summary of Comparison Study of DFA, PSO, MOPSO-CD and GA

The optimization methods namely DFA, GA, PSO and MOPSO-CD are applied to optimize the sand moulding process variables and properties. The nature inspired search techniques determine best set of process variables at many distinct location and multi-dimensional space simultaneously. The swarm size and number of generation are found to be {35, 85} and {70 and 55} for MOPSO-CD and PSO, respectively. Similarly, population size and number of generations obtained for GA are found equal to {110, 90}. This shows that, the genetic algorithm require greater computational effort to gain maximum fitness with regard to speed of convergence than swarm intelligence tools. It is interesting to note that, the desirability value and fitness function value are found to be maximum for Case 5 irrespective of different optimization tools. MOPSO-CD resulted in highest fitness values compared to GA and PSO. The global desirability value obtained for case 5 are found to be 0.9384, 0.9512, 0.9397, and 0.9481 for DFA, MOPSO-CD, PSO and GA. Thereby, MOPSO-CD is capable to yield highest global desirability

Table 8. Optimum moulding sand variables for sand mould properties with different weighing factors using MOPSO-CD

Control Factors and Responses	Optimized Values of Moulding Sand Variables and Sand Mould Properties					
	Case 1(w_1, w_2, w_3,w_4,w_5 = 0.2)	Case 2 (w_1 = 0.6, w_2, w_3,w_4,w_5 = 0.1)	Case 3 (w_2 = 0.6, w_1, w_3,w_4,w_5 = 0.1)	Case 4 (w_3 = 0.6, w_1, w_2,w_4,w_5 = 0.1)	Case 5 (w_4 = 0.6, w_1, w_2,w_3,w_5 = 0.1)	Case 6 (w5 = 0.6, w1, w2,w3,w4 = 0.1)
A	52.0	90.0	68.0	65.0	50.0	50.0
B	1.80	1.80	1.80	2.06	1.95	1.82
C	1.20	1.20	1.20	1.20	1.20	1.18
D	99.0	109.0	90.0	112.0	91.6	85.0
MH	59.08	67.68	56.3	56.06	59.86	59.8
P	523.9	408.6	700.6	618.9	416.8	445.6
CS	1190	1200	1463	2023	1070	811.3
GE	7.62	9.999	9.40	9.76	6.96	7.27
CP	705	931	990	1417	658.6	498.07
Desirability, D_o	0.9130	0.9383	0.9421	0.9194	0.9512	0.9287

(D_o) value to gain best combination of sand mould variables and properties. It is to be noted that, small swarm size and number of generations will result in faster convergence. This might have happened due to the mutation parameter in MOPSO-CD extend the search space to gain maximum fitness.

Confirmation Experimentation

The experiments are conducted with three replicates for the optimized sand mould conditions (i.e. case 5) obtained through MOPSO-CD. Note that, experiment conduction and response measurements are carried out under similar conditions that are used in model development (i.e. CCD and Box-Bhenken Design). The average response values of mould hardness, permeability, compression strength, gas evolution and collapsibility are presented in Table 9. The percent deviation in prediction of different responses such as mould hardness, permeability, compression strength, gas evolution, and collapsibility are found equal to be 2.32%, 3.07%, 4.90%, 5.45%, and 4.54%, respectively.

CONCLUSION

The present work is an attempt to model, analyze and optimize the input-output parameters of resin-bonded sand moulding process. Experiments are conducted as per the design matrices of central composite design considering the input variables such as, grain fineness number, percent of resin, percent of hardener, and curing time. Significant and insignificant parameters are determined for all response functions namely, mould hardness, permeability, compression strength, gas evolution and collapsibility. The models are tested using analysis of variance and are found to be statistically adequate. Surface plots explain the behaviour of input variables on outputs graphically. The response equations developed are utilized to search the optimal input parameters for best combination of responses. The major results are discussed as below,

1.   All individual parameters (except curing time for gas evolution) are found statistically significant towards the sand mould properties. The square terms of grain fineness number and percent of hardener (except for gas evolution) are found to be statistically significant indicating the relationship is non-linear.
2.   All response equations are found to have good correlation coefficients, indicating good fit of polynomials.
3.   Sand mould properties have conflicting requirements (maximize: compression strength, mould hardness, and permeability; and minimize: collapsibility and gas evolution) and determining op-

Table 9. Results of confirmation experiments for the optimized sand mould conditions

Source	Optimized Sand Mould Conditions				Sand Mould Properties				
Parameters	A	B	C	D	MH	P	CS, gm/cm^2	GE, cc/gm	CP, gm/cm^2
Experiment	50	1.95	1.20	92.0	58.50	430.0	1020	6.60	630.0
MOPSO-CD	50	1.95	1.20	91.6	59.86	416.8	1070	6.96	658.6

timal sand mould conditions are difficult for the investigator. Thereby, multiple output functions are converted to single objective function for maximization with different combination of weight factors. Six different case studies are considered with equal weight fraction for all responses in case 1 and assigning maximum importance to individual objective function after maintaining the rest at fixed low weights for case 2-6.

4. GA, PSO and MOPSO-CD parameters are optimized for maximum fitness with the help of parametric study. Case 5, with maximum fitness value and highest desirability function value is considered as the optimal and yielded best sand mould properties as compared to other case studies. MOPSO-CD outperformed GA, PSO and DFA to yield highest desirability value. This might have happened due to the introduced mutation parameter could enhance the search space that locates global solutions.

5. Experiments are conducted for the for the optimized sand mould conditions determined by MOPSO-CD model. The results are in good agreement with model predicted sand mould properties with low percent deviation.

6. The present work might help the foundry personnel that could predict the sand mould properties without requirement of conducting actual experiments. Further, the conflicting requirements in sand mould properties for the foundry personnel are solved which resulted in better quality castings. Furthermore, this research could limit few shortcomings of currently adopted traditional approaches (like try-error-experiment, expert advice, assumption based analytical, numerical, simulation, and so on) in determining the best sand mould conditions, that could improve the casting quality and reduce computation effort and energy consumption.

Future Research Directions

The present research work may be extended in two directions namely, process improvement and application of latest soft computing tools developed in modelling and optimization.

1. The impact of additives such as sawdust, coal dust, wood floor, phosphate and so on, may be studied further, few additives which will enhance the mould properties may be included in modelling the resin bonded moulding sand system.

2. An attempt may be made to relate the sand mould variables, mould properties directly to the quality of the castings (that is, quality charecteristics such as, surface finish, strength, hardness, etc.) This research effort may be more interested for a foundry man.

3. The modelling and optimization tools developed in recent times such Jaya algorithm, cuckoo search optimization, teacher learner based optimization etc. may be applied to get the best operating conditions.

REFERENCES

Acharya, S. G., Sheladiya, M. V., & Acharya, G. D. (2017). Process parameter optimization for sand inclusion defect in furan no-bake casting by grey relational analysis. *IUP Journal of Mechanical Engineering, 10*(4), 7–19.

Acharya, S. G., & Vadher, J. A. (2016). Parametric analyses on compressive strength of furan no bake mould system using ANN. *Archives of Foundry Engineering, 16*(4), 5–10. doi:10.1515/afe-2016-0074

Adrian, A. M., Utamima, A., & Wang, K. J. (2015). A comparative study of GA, PSO and ACO for solving construction site layout optimization. *KSCE Journal of Civil Engineering, 19*(3), 520–527. doi:10.100712205-013-1467-6

Bargaoui, H., Azzouz, F., Thibault, D., & Cailletaud, G. (2017). Thermomechanical behavior of resin bonded foundry sand cores during casting. *Journal of Materials Processing Technology, 246*, 30–41. doi:10.1016/j.jmatprotec.2017.03.002

Barlow, T. E. (1966). Precision green sand molding. *AFS Transactions, 74*, 70–81.

Benguluri, S., Vundavilli, P. R., Bhat, R. P., & Parappagoudar, M. B. (2011). Forward and reverse mappings in metal casting—A step towards quality casting and automation (11-009). *AFS Transactions, 119*, 19.

Brabazon, A., Neill, M. O., & McGarraghy, S. (2015). *Natural Computing Algorithms.* Springer Verlag. doi:10.1007/978-3-662-43631-8

Caylak, I., & Mahnken, R. (2010). Thermo-mechanical characterization of a cold box sand including optical measurements. *International Journal of Cast Metals Research, 23*(3), 176–184. doi:10.1179/174313309X451261

Chate, G. R., Patel, G. C. M., Parappagoudar, M. B., & Deshpande, A. S. (2017). Modeling and optimization phenol formaldehyde resin sand mould system. *Archives of Foundry Engineering, 17*(2), 162–170. doi:10.1515/afe-2017-0069

Derringer & Suich. (1980). Simultaneous optimization of several response variables. *Journal of Quality Technology, 12*, 214-219.

Ding, G., Zhang, Q., & Zhou, Y. (1997). Strengthening of cold-setting resin sand by the additive method. *Journal of Materials Processing Technology, 72*(2), 239–242. doi:10.1016/S0924-0136(97)00174-X

Gardner, G. R. (1948). Physical properties of molding sands. *AFS Transactions, 55*, 331–335.

Garlapati, V. K., Vundavilli, P. R., & Banerjee, R. (2010). Evaluation of lipase production by genetic algorithm and particle swarm optimization and their comparative study. *Applied Biochemistry and Biotechnology, 162*(5), 1350–1361. doi:10.100712010-009-8895-2 PMID:20099046

Guharaja, S., Noorul Haq, A., & Karuppannan, K. M. (2006). Optimization of green sand casting process parameters by using Taguchi's method. *International Journal of Advanced Manufacturing Technology, 30*(11-12), 1040–1048. doi:10.100700170-005-0146-2

Harington, J. (1965). The desirability function. *Industrial Quality Control, 21*, 494–498.

Jafari, H., Idris, M. H., Ourdjini, A., Karimian, M., & Payganeh, G. (2010). Influence of gating system, sand grain size, and mould coating on microstructure and mechanical properties of thin-wall ductile iron. *Journal of Iron and Steel Research International, 17*(12), 38–45. doi:10.1016/S1006-706X(10)60195-1

Jakubski, J., Dobosz, M., & Major-Gabrys, K. (2012). The influence of changes in active binder content on the control system of the moulding sand quality. *Archives of Foundry Engineering, 12*(4), 71–74. doi:10.2478/v10266-012-0109-7

Khandelwal, H., & Ravi, B. (2016). Effect of molding parameters on chemically bonded sand mold properties. *Journal of Manufacturing Processes, 22*, 127–133. doi:10.1016/j.jmapro.2016.03.007

Kumar, S., Satsangi, P. S., & Prajapati, D. R. (2011). Optimization of green sand casting process parameters of a foundry by using Taguchi's method. *International Journal of Advanced Manufacturing Technology, 55*(1-4), 23–34. doi:10.100700170-010-3029-0

Kumaravadivel, A., & Natarajan, U. (2013). Application of six-sigma DMAIC methodology to sand-casting process with response surface methodology. *International Journal of Advanced Manufacturing Technology, 69*(5-8), 1403–1420. doi:10.100700170-013-5119-2

Kunsmann, H. G. F. (1971). Hot strength and collapsibility of CO_2 sand. *AFS Transactions, 79*, 488–492.

Liu, W., Li, Y., Qu, X., & Liu, X. (2008). Study on binder system of CO2 cured phenol formaldehyde resin used in foundry. *68th World Foundry Congress*, 313-317.

Lu, Y., Wang, H., Luo, A. A., & Ripplinger, K. (2017). Process simulation and experimental validation of resin-bonded silica sand mold casting. *AFS Transactions, 125*, 215–220.

Mahapatra, S. S., & Patnaik, A. (2007). Optimization of wire electrical discharge machining (WEDM) process parameters using Taguchi method. *International Journal of Advanced Manufacturing Technology, 34*(9-10), 911–925. doi:10.100700170-006-0672-6

Marler, R. T., & Arora, J. S. (2004). Survey of multi-objective optimization methods for engineering. *Structural and Multidisciplinary Optimization, 26*(6), 369–395. doi:10.100700158-003-0368-6

Marler, R. T., & Arora, J. S. (2010). The weighted sum method for multi-objective optimization: New insights. *Structural and Multidisciplinary Optimization, 41*(6), 853–862. doi:10.100700158-009-0460-7

Montgomery, D. C. (2004). *Design and analysis of experiments* (5th ed.). New York: John Wiley & Sons.

Parappagoudar, M. B., Pratihar, D. K., & Datta, G. L. (2005). Green sand mould system modelling through design of experiments. *Indian Foundry Journal, 51*, 40–51.

Parappagoudar, M. B., Pratihar, D. K., & Datta, G. L. (2007). Non-linear modelling using central composite design to predict green sand mould properties. *Proceedings of the Institution of Mechanical Engineers. Part B, Journal of Engineering Manufacture, 221*(5), 881–895. doi:10.1243/09544054JEM696

Parappagoudar, M. B., Pratihar, D. K., & Datta, G. L. (2008). Linear and non-linear modeling of cement-bonded moulding sand system using conventional statistical regression analysis. *Journal of Materials Engineering and Performance, 17*(4), 472–481. doi:10.100711665-007-9172-6

Parappagoudar, M. B., Pratihar, D. K., & Datta, G. L. (2011). Modeling and analysis of sodium silicate-bonded moulding sand system using design of experiments and response surface methodology. *Journal for Manufacturing Science & Production, 11*(1-3), 1–14. doi:10.1515/jmsp.2011.011

Patel, G. C. M., Krishna, P., Parappagoudar, M. B., & Vundavilli, P. R. (2016b). Multi-objective optimization of squeeze casting process using evolutionary algorithms. *International Journal of Swarm Intelligence Research, 7*(1), 55–74. doi:10.4018/IJSIR.2016010103

Patel, G. C. M., Krishna, P., Vundavilli, P. R., & Parappagoudar, M. B. (2016a). Multi-objective optimization of squeeze casting process using genetic algorithm and particle swarm optimization. *Archives of Foundry Engineering, 16*(3), 172–186. doi:10.1515/afe-2016-0073

Phillips, D. R. (1970). Sand control by independent variables. *AFS Transactions, 78*, 251–258.

Rosenberg, R. S. (1967). *Simulation of genetic populations with biochemical properties* (Ph.D. Thesis). University of Michigan, Ann Arbor, MI.

Rozenberg, G., Back, T., & Kok, J. (2011). *Handbook of Natural Computing.* Springer Verlag.

Saikaew, C., & Wiengwiset, S. (2012). Optimization of molding sand composition for quality improvement of iron castings. *Applied Clay Science, 67*, 26–31. doi:10.1016/j.clay.2012.07.005

Schaffer, J. D. (1985). Multiple objective optimization with vector evaluated genetic algorithm. *Proceedings of 1st International Conference on Genetic Algorithms*, 93–100.

Senthil, P., & Amirthagadeswaran, K. (2014). Experimental study and squeeze casting process optimization for high quality AC2A aluminium alloy castings. *Arabian Journal for Science and Engineering, 39*(3), 2215–2225. doi:10.100713369-013-0752-5

Sriganesh, K., Seshradri, M., & Ramachandran, A. (1966). On the compaction of bonded grains. *AFS Transactions, 74*, 27–36.

Surekha, B., Hanumanth, R. D., & Krishnamohan, R. G. (2013). Application of response surface methodology for modeling the properties of chromite-based resin bonded sand cores. *International Journal of Mechanics, 7*(4), 443–458.

Tiwari, S. K., Singh, R. K., & Srivastava, S. C. (2016). Optimisation of green sand casting process parameters for enhancing quality of mild steel castings. *International Journal of Productivity and Quality Management, 17*(2), 127–141. doi:10.1504/IJPQM.2016.074446

Trinowski, D. M. (1999). New cold box binder system for improved productivity. *AFS Transactions, 107*, 51–57.

Vijian, P., & Arunachalam, V. P. (2007). Modelling and multi objective optimization of LM24 aluminium alloy squeeze cast process parameters using genetic algorithm. *Journal of Materials Processing Technology, 186*(1), 82–86. doi:10.1016/j.jmatprotec.2006.12.019

Vundavilli, P. R., Kumar, J. P., & Parappagoudar, M. B. (2013). Weighted average-based multi-objective optimization of tube spinning process using non-traditional optimization techniques. *International Journal of Swarm Intelligence Research, 4*(3), 42–57. doi:10.4018/ijsir.2013070103

KEY TERMS AND DEFINITIONS

A: Grain fineness number.

A: Cross-sectional area of sand specimen in sq. cm.

AFS: American foundry society.

ANNOVA: Analysis of variance.

B: Percent of resin.

BHN: Brinell hardness number.

C: Percent of hardener.

CCD: Central composite design.

CP: Collapsibility.

CS: Compression strength.

D: Setting time.

d_i: Individual desirability value.

D_o: Overall desirability value.

DFA: Desirability function approach.

DOE: Design of experiments.

GA: Genetic algorithm.

GE: Gas evolution.

GFN: Grain fineness number.

H: Height of specimen in cm.

L: Lower limit.

MH: Mold hardness.

MOPOSO-CD: Multiple-particle-swarm-optimization-based crowding distance.

RSM: Response surface methodology.

P: Permeability.

P: Air pressure in gm/cm^2.

PSO: Particle swarm optimization.

T: Target value.

T: Time in minutes.

U: Upper limit.

UTS: Ultimate tensile strength.

V: Volume of air in cm^3.

W: Weight fraction.

Y_i: Single desirability output value of an objective function.

YS: Yield strength.

Chapter 8
Application of Computational Intelligence in Network Intrusion Detection:
A Review

Heba F. Eid
Al Azhar University, Egypt

ABSTRACT

Intrusion detection system plays an important role in network security. However, network intrusion detection (NID) suffers from several problems, such as false positives, operational issues in high dimensional data, and the difficulty of detecting unknown threats. Most of the problems with intrusion detection are caused by improper implementation of the network intrusion detection system (NIDS). Over the past few years, computational intelligence (CI) has become an effective area in extending research capabilities. Thus, NIDS based upon CI is currently attracting considerable interest from the research community. The scope of this review will encompass the concept of NID and presents the core methods of CI, including support vector machine, hidden naïve Bayes, particle swarm optimization, genetic algorithm, and fuzzy logic. The findings of this review should provide useful insights into the application of different CI methods for NIDS over the literature, allowing to clearly define existing research challenges and progress, and to highlight promising new research directions.

INTRUSION DETECTION SYSTEM

Heady et al. (1990) define an intrusion as any set of actions that attempt to compromise the integrity, confidentiality and availability of host or network resources. James P. Anderson (1980) divides the system intruders into four categories:

1. **External Intruders:** Who are unauthorized users of the machines they attack of.

DOI: 10.4018/978-1-5225-5396-0.ch008

2. **Masquerader:** A user who gained access to the system and attempts to use the authentication information of another user. The masquerader can be either an external penetrator or other authorized user of the system;
3. **Misfeasor:** A user has legitimate access to privileged information but abuses this privilege to violate the security policy of the installation.
4. **Clandestine:** A user operates at a level below the normal auditing mechanisms, perhaps by accessing the machine with supervisory privileges.

In 1980, Anderson proposed the concept of intrusion detection (ID) (Anderson, 1980). ID is based on the assumption that; the behavior of intruders is different from a legal user (Stallings, 2006).

An intrusion detection system (IDS) dynamically monitors the events taking place in a system, and decides whether these events are symptomatic of an attack (intrusion) or constitute a legitimate use of the system (Debar et al., 1999). Figure 1 presents the general structure of an Intrusion detection system.

INTRUSION DETECTION SYSTEM TAXONOMY

There are several ways to categorize an IDS depending on, the location of the IDS in the system, the detection methodology used to generate alerts and respond action to the intrusion, as shown in Figure 2.

Depending on the IDS location, the first type of IDS to appear was the Host-based Intrusion Detection System (HIDS) (Axelsson, 2000). HIDS are installed on the host and monitors the operating system information (e.g. system call sequences and application logs) (Debar et al., 1999). By checking traffic before being sent or just received, HIDS have the advantage of being able to detect attacks from the inside. However, the main problem of HIDSs is that they can only monitor the single host they are

Figure 1. General structure of intrusion detection system

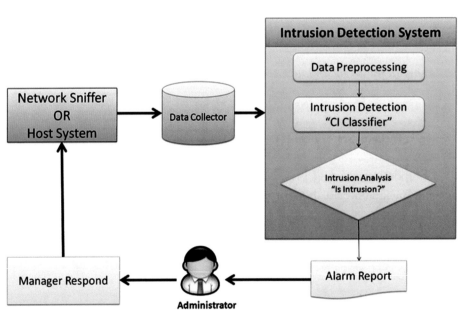

Figure 2. Intrusion detection system taxonomy

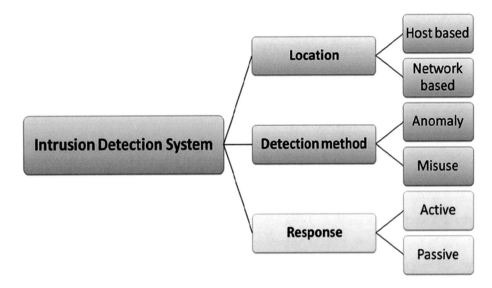

running on, and have to be specifically set up for each host. Thus, scalability is the main problem for HIDSs (Endorf et al., 2004; Bace & Mell, 2001). Network-based Intrusion Detection System (NIDS) identifies intrusions on external interfaces for network traffic among multiple hosts. NIDS gains access to network traffic by placing sniffers at hubs or network switches to monitor packets traveling among various communication mediums. The main advantage of NIDS is that a single system can be used to monitor the whole network. However, NIDS main disadvantages is that they can have difficulties when processing large amount of network packets (Sommers et al., 2004).

Depending on the detection methodology IDSs can be divided into two techniques: misuse detection and anomaly detection (Biermann et al., 2001; Verwoerd & Hunt, 2002). Misuse intrusion detection system (signature-based detection) is the most popular commercial type of IDSs (Zhengbing et al., 2008). A misuse-based detection system contains a database which includes a number of signatures about known attacks. The audit data collected by the IDS is compared with the well-defined patterns of the database and, if a match is found, an alert is generated (Ilgun et al., 1995; Marchette, 1999). The main drawback of misuse-based detection is that it is not able to alert the system administrator in case of new attacks (Bace & Mell, 2001). Anomaly intrusion detection is a behavior-based detection method, it based on the idea of building a normal traffic profiles (Denning, 1987). It identifies malicious traffic based on the deviations from the normal profiles, where the normal patterns are constructed from the statistical measures of the system features (Mukkamala et al., 2002; Brown et al., 2001). One of the key advantages of anomaly based IDS over the misuse detection; is that it can detects new threats, or different versions of known threats (Lundin & Jonsson, 2002; Gong, 2003).

According to the response technique, IDS can be categorized as active IDS and passive IDS. An active IDS is also known as Intrusion Detection and Prevention System (IDPS). The IDPS is configured to automatically block suspected intrusions without any intervention required by an administrator. IDPS has the advantage of providing real-time corrective action in response to an attack. A passive IDS is a system which is configured to monitor and analyze the network traffic activity, then only raises an alert if potential intrusions is found. A passive IDS is not capable of performing any protective or corrective operations on its own (Endorf et al., 2004).

COMPUTATIONAL INTELLIGENCE

Computational intelligence (CI) is a fairly new research field, it was first used in 1990 by the IEEE Neural Networks Council (Dote & Ovaska, 2001). CI provides a combination of methods like learning, adaptation, optimization and evolution to create intelligent systems.

Bezdek (1994) defined CI as: A system is computational intelligent when it: deals with only numerical (low-level) data, has pattern recognition components, and does not use knowledge in the AI sense. Eberhart et al. (1996) define CI as a methodology involving computing that exhibits an ability to learn and/or deal with new situations such that the system is perceived to possess one or more attributes of reason, such as generalization, discovery, association, and abstraction. While, Poole et al. (1998) defined CI as:

Computational Intelligence is the study of the design of intelligent agents. An intelligent agent is a system that acts intelligently. For which, it is flexible to changing environments and changing goals, it learns from experience, and it makes appropriate choices given perceptual limitations and finite computation.

The characteristics of CI methods, such as adaptation, fault tolerance and high computational speed, satisfied the requirements of building IDS.

COMPUTATIONAL INTELLIGENCE METHODS

The intrusion detection problem can be approached by using different computational intelligence methods. This section presents an overview of modern CI methods that have been used to solve the ID problems. These CI methods includes Support vector machine, Hidden naïve bays, Particle Swarm Optimization, Genetic Algorithm and Fuzzy Logic.

SUPPORT VECTOR MACHINES

Support vector machine (SVM) method is a CI classification technique based on Statistical Learning Theory (SLT). It is based on the idea of a hyper plane classifier, or linearly separability. The goal of SVM is to find a linear optimal hyper plane so that the margin of separation between the two classes is maximized (Vapnik, 1998; Burges, 1998). Suppose we have N training data points $\{(x_1, y_1), (x_2, y_2), (x_3, y_3), ..., (x_N, y_N)\}$, where $x_i \in R^d$ and $y_i \in \{+1, -1\}$. Consider a hyper plane defined by (w,b), where w is a weight vector and b is a bias. A new object x can be classified with the following function:

$$f(x) = sign(w.x + b) = sign\left(\sum_{i=1}^{N} \alpha_i y_i (x_i, x) + b\right)$$

(1)

In practice the data is often not linearly separable. However, one can still implement a linear model by transform the data points via a non-linear mapping to another higher feature space, such that the data points will be linear separable. This mapping is done by a kernel function K.

The nonlinear decision function of SVM is given by the following function:

$$f(x) = sign\left(\sum_{i=1}^{N} \alpha_i y_i K(x_i, x) + b\right) \qquad (2)$$

where $K(x_i, x)$ is the kernel function.

SVM has been recently used in many applications, since it has have some advantages compared with conventional machine learning methods (Kim et al., 2005a,b):

1. There are only two free parameters to be chosen, the upper bound and the kernel parameter.
2. The solution of SVM is optimal and global since the training of a SVM is done by solving a linearly constrained quadratic problem.
3. Good generalization performance and Good robustness.

HIDDEN NAÏVE BAYES

Hidden naïve Bayes (HNB) was first proposed by Jiang et al. (2009). HNB inherits its structural from naive Bayes. Where, it creates a hidden parent for each attribute to combine the influences from all other attributes. Hidden parents are defined by the average of weighted one-dependence estimators.

In HNB each attribute Ai has a hidden parent A_{hpi}, i = 1,2,...,n, where C is the class variable and c(E)represent the class of E. The joint distribution represented by an HNB is given by:

$$P(A_1,...,A_n,C) = P(C)\prod_{i=1} P(A_i A_{hpi}, C) \qquad (3)$$

where

$$P(A_i A_{hpi}, C) = \sum_{j=1, j\neq i}^{n} W_{ij} * P(A_i A_j, C) \qquad (4)$$

and

$$\sum_{j=1, j\neq i}^{n} W_{ij} = 1 \qquad (5)$$

The weight W_{ij} is compute directly from the conditional mutual information between two attributes A_i and A_j

$$W_{ij} = \frac{I_p\left(A_i;A_jC\right)}{\sum_{j=1,j\neq i}^{n} I_p\left(A_i;A_jC\right)} \tag{6}$$

where

$$I_p\left(A_i;A_jC\right) = \sum_{a_i,a_j,c} P\left(a_i,a_j,c\right) \log \frac{P\left(a_i,a_jc\right)}{P\left(a_ic\right)P\left(a_jc\right)} \tag{7}$$

The HNB classifier on $E = \left(a_1,...,a_n\right)$ is define as follows

$$c\left(E\right) = \arg\max_{c\in C} P\left(c\right)\prod_{i=1}^{n}P\left(a_i\# \, a_{hpi},c\right) \tag{8}$$

PARTICLE SWARM OPTIMIZATION

Particle Swarm Optimization (PSO) technique was developed by Kennedy and Eberhart (1995). PSO simulates the social behavior of organisms, such as bird flocking. PSO initialize with a random population (swarm) of individuals (particles). Where, each particle of the swarm represents a candidate solution in the d-dimensional search space. To discover the best solution at every iteration of the PSO algorithm, each particle Xi is updated by the two best values pbest and gbest. Where, pbest denotes the best solution the particle Xi has achieved so far, represented by $P_i = \left(p_{i1},p_{i2},...,p_{id}\right)$. While, Wgbest denotes the global best position gained by the swarm so far, represented by $G_i = \left(g_{i1},g_{i2},...,g_{id}\right)$ (Venter & Sobieski, 2003).

The d-dimensional position for the particle i at iteration t can be represented as:

$$x_i^t = x_{i1}^t, x_{i2}^t,...,x_{id}^t \tag{9}$$

While, the velocity; the rate of the position change; for the particle i at iteration t is given by:

$$v_i^t = v_{i1}^t, v_{i2}^t,...,v_{id}^t \tag{10}$$

All of the particles have fitness values, which are evaluated based on a fitness function:

$$Fitness = \alpha.\gamma_R\left(D\right) + \beta\frac{|C|+|R|}{|C|} \qquad (11)$$

where, $\gamma_R\left(D\right)$ is the classification quality of condition attribute set R relative to decision D and |R| is the length of selected feature subset. |C| is the total number of features. While, the parameters α and β are correspond to the importance of classification quality and subset length, $\alpha =[0,1]$ and $\beta = 1 - \alpha$.

GENETIC ALGORITHM

Holland introduced the Genetic algorithm (GA) as an adaptive search technique (Holland, 1975). It is computational model designed to simulate the evolutionary processes in the nature (Duda et al., 2001). GA includes three fundamental operators: selection, crossover and mutation within chromosomes.

1. **Selection:** A population is created with a group of randomly individuals. The individuals in the population are then evaluated by fitness function. Two individuals (offspring) are selected for the next generation based on their fitness.
2. **Crossover:** crossover randomly chooses a point in the two selected parents and exchanging the remaining segments of them to create the new individuals.
3. **Mutation:** mutation randomly changes one or more components of a selected individual. This process continues until a suitable solution has been found or a certain number of generations have passed (Jiang et al., 2008).

Given a well bounded problem GAs can find a global optimum which makes them well suited to feature selection problems.

FUZZY LOGIC

In 1965, Lofti Zadeh introduced the fuzzy sets theory, which allows an element to belong to a set with a degree of membership (not only a binary degree) (Zadeh, 1965). This concept is extended to logic by Zadeh (1975) to introduce Fuzzy logic (FL). Classical logic deals with propositions which are either true or false but not both or in between. However, in real world scenario there are cases where propositions can be partially true and partially false. Fuzzy logic handles such real world uncertainty "vague" by allowing partial truth values.

NETWORK INTRUSION DETECTION DATASETS

Evaluation in intrusion detection system has been based on researchers' proprietary data, thus results are generally not reproducible to be compared and validated. To reduce this problem, commonly used intrusion detection benchmarks have been used in either misuse detection or anomaly detection, Table 1.

Table 1. Network Intrusion Detection benchmarks

Dataset Name	Abbreviation	Dataset Link
1998 DARPA TCPDump Dataset	DARPA98	(DARPA98)
1999 DARPA TCPDump Dataset	DARPA99	(DARPA99)
KDD cup 99 Dataset	KDD99	(KDD99)
NSl-KDD Dataset	NSL-KDD	(NSL-KDD)

(Source: Lincoln Laboratory 2017 a, 2017b; KDD99, n.d.; Canadian Institute for Cybersecurity, n.d.)

In 1998 and 1999 Massachusetts Institute of Technology (MIT), Lincoln Laboratory (LL); under the sponsorship of Defense Advanced Research Projects Agency (DARPA) and Air Force Research Laboratory (AFRL); created the Intrusion Detection Evaluation (IDEVAL) benchmark (Mahoney & Chan, 2003; McHugh, 2000).

The 1998 DARPA dataset includes 7 weeks of training data with labeled test data and 2 weeks of unlabeled test data, it contains over 300 instances of 38 attacks (Fried et al., 2000). The 1999 DARPA dataset presents over 5 million connections over 5 weeks: 2 were attack-free and 3 weeks included attacks. The 1998 and 1999 DARPA dataset has been used to test a large number of host based and network based systems IDS (Durst et al., 1999).

Sal Stofo and Wenke Lee used 1998 DARPA benchmark to prepare the KDD'99 dataset (KDD99). The KDD'99 train dataset is about four gigabytes of compressed binary TCP dump data from seven weeks of network traffic, processed into about five million connections Record each with about 100 bytes. The two weeks of test data have around two million connection records. Each KDD'99 training connection record contains 41 features. There are 38 numeric features and 3 symbolic features, falling into the following four categories:

- **Basic Features:** 9 basic features describe each individual TCP connection.
- **Content Features:** 13 domain knowledge related features which indicate suspicious behavior in the network traffic. This includes features such as the number of failed login attempts.
- **Time-Based Traffic Features:** 9 features used to summarize the connections over 2 second temporal window. Such as the number of connections that had the same destination host or the same service.
- **Host-Based Traffic Features:** 10 features constructed using a window of 100 connections to the same host instead of a time window. It is designed to assess attacks, which span intervals longer than 2 seconds.

Each record is labeled as either normal or an attack, with one specific attack type. The training set contains a total of 22 attack types, while the testing set contains an additional 17 types of attacks. The attacks fall into four categories:

1. **DoS:** Attacker tries to prevent legitimate users from using a service. e.g Neptune, Smurf, Pod and Teardrop.
2. **R2L:** Unauthorized access to local from a remote machine e.g Guess-password, Ftpwrite, Imap and Phf.

3. **U2R:** Unauthorized access to root privileges e.g Buffer-overflow, Load-module, Perl and Spy.
4. Probing e.g. Port-sweep, IP-sweep, Nmap and Satan.

Empirical study conducted by Leung et al (Leung and Leckie, 2005) states important issues which highly affects the performance of evaluated systems and results in a very poor evaluation of anomaly detection approaches.

According to their statistical, two problems are reported in the KDD'99 dataset.

1. KDD'99 dataset contains huge number of redundant records.10% portions of the full dataset contained only two types of DoS attacks (Smurf and Neptune). These two types constitute over 71% of the testing dataset which completely affects the evaluation.
2. Since these attacks consume large volumes of traffic, they are easily detectable by other means and there is no need of using anomaly detection systems to find these attacks.

To solve these problems, the NSL-KDD dataset is suggested (Tavallaee et al., 2009). NSL-KDD consists of selected records of the complete KDD'99 dataset, where the repeated records in the entire KDD'99 train and test set are removed.KDD'99 dataset contains 4898431 records in train set and 311027 records in test set. Table 2 gives statistics of the reduction of repeated records in the KDD train and test sets. The KDD'99 train set is reduced by 78.05% and the test set is reduced by 75.15%.

The NSL-KDD dataset has the following advantages over the original KDD'99 dataset (Tavallaee et al., 2009):

1. The train set does not include redundant records; hence the classifiers will not be biased towards more frequent records.
2. The proposed test sets have no duplicate records; therefore, the performances of the learners are not biased by the methods which have better detection rates on the frequent records.
3. The number of records in the train and test sets is reasonable, which makes it affordable to run the experiments on the complete set without the need to randomly select a small portion. Consequently, evaluation results of different research works will be consistent and comparable.

PERFORMANCE COMPARISON OF KDD99 AND NSL-KDD

Eid et al. (2010) conducted experimental analysis to compare the evolution performance of KDD99 and NSL-KDD dataset (Eid et al., 2010). The SVM classifier is applied on two test sets; the original KDD'99 test set (KDDTest) and NSL-KDD test set (KDDTest+) as shown in Tables 3.

Table 2 KDD'99 dataset reduction statistics

	Train Set		Test Set	
	Repeated Records	**Reduction Rate**	**Repeated Records**	**Reduction Rate**
Intrusion	3663472	93.32%	221058	88.26%
Normal	159967	16.44%	12680	20.92%

Table 3. KDD'99 and NSL-KDD dataset testing accuracy comparison

Class Name	Original KDD'99 Test Set	NSL-KDD Test Set
	Test Accuracy	Test Accuracy
Normal	99.8%	99.5%
DoS	92.5%	97.5%
U2R	5.10%	86.6%
R2L	70.2%	81.3%
Probe	98.3%	92.8%

In Table 3, the redundant records in the original KDD'99 cause the learning algorithms to be biased towards the frequent records (DOS and Prob attacks). Thus prevent the detection algorithms from learning unfrequented records (U2R and R2L attacks).These unbalanced distributions of the KDD'99 testing dataset completely affects the evaluation of the detection algorithms; 5.1% for U2R and 70.2 for R2L. While, NSL-KDD test sets have no redundant records; hence, the performances of the learners are not biased by frequent records.

DATA PRE-PROCESSING

Data Transformation

Symbolic features appear frequently in the network traffic dataset. However, most machine learning methods are designed to work with numerical data only. In order for these methods to use information from symbolic features in detection, some coding schemes are necessary. The most commonly used coding scheme is establishing a correspondence between each category of a symbolic feature and a sequence of integer values.

Yeung and Chow in 2002 proposed unsupervised anomaly NIDS designed to work with numeric data only. They use a coding scheme to transform each symbolic feature of the KDD99 dataset into numeric features. This is done by representing each symbolic feature by a group of binary-valued features. The resulting feature vectors have a total of 119 dimensions (Yeung & Chow, 2002).

Laskov et al. in 2005, apply a data transformation by metric embedding which transforms the data into a metric space (Laskov et al., 2005). The metric embedding is performed in two-stage procedure similar to which is reported in Portnoy et al. (2001) and Eskin et al. (2002).

Pereira et al. (2009) reported that most of machine learning methods used for classification are not able to handle symbolic features directly. They compare three different methods for converting the KDD99 dataset symbolic features into numeric features to be suitable for machine learning methods. The three methods indicator variables, conditional probabilities and the Separability Split Value method are contrasted with the arbitrary conversion method. The results obtained demonstrate that the three conversion methods improve the prediction ability of the classifiers, with respect to the arbitrary and commonly used assignment of numerical values (Pereira et al., 2009).

Data Normalization

The KDD99 dataset features numerical values have significantly varying resolution and ranges. Thus, data normalization is required in order to avoid one feature to dominate another Feature.

Li et al in 2007, proposed an anomaly NIDS. The authors normalized the KDD99 dataset features by replacing each feature value with its distance to the mean of all the values for that attribute in the instance space. In order to accomplish this, the mean and standard deviation vectors are calculated (Li et al., 2007).

Data Discretization

Data discretization is performed by converting the features continuous space into a nominal space (Mizianty et al., 2010). The goal of data discretization process is to find a set of cut points, which split the range into a small number of intervals. The cut-points are real values within the range of the continuous values. These cut-points divides the range into two intervals one greater than the cut-point and other less than or equal to the cut-point value (Kotsiantis & Kanellopoulos, 2006).

Eid et al. (2012) addresses the impact of applying data discretization on building network IDS. The authors conducted several groups of experiments on the NSL-KDD dataset. Experimental results show that data discretization has a positive influence on the detection speed, which is an important factor if real time network IDS is desired (Eid et al., 2013).

Data Reduction

Extraneous network dataset features can make it harder to detect suspicious behavior patterns, leading to the curse of dimensionality problem (Shang & Shen, 2006). Hence, data reduction must be performed to high dimensional data set. Data reduction has been shown to both reduce the build and test time of classifiers, and also improve their detection rate.

Data dimensionality reduction can be achieved by feature extraction or feature selection. Feature extraction methods create a new set of features by linear or nonlinear combination of the original features. While, feature selection methods generate a new set of features by selecting only a subset of the original features (Sung & Mukkamala, 2003).

Feature selection aims to choose an optimal subset of features that are necessary to increase the classifier predictive accuracy (Dash et al., 2002; Koller & Sahami, 1996). Different feature selection methods are proposed to enhance the performance of IDS (Tsang et al., 2007). Based on the evaluation criteria feature selection methods fall into two categories: filter approach (Dash et al., 2002; Yu & Liu, 2003) and wrapper (Kim et al., 2000; Kohavi & John, 1997) approach.

- *Filter approaches* evaluate and select the new set of features depending on the general characteristics of the data without involving any machine algorithm. The features are ranked based on certain statistical criteria, where features with highest ranking values are selected. Frequently used filter methods include chi-square test (Jin et al., 2006), information gain (Ben-Bassat, 1982), and Pearson correlation coefficients (Peng et al., 2005).

- *Wrapper approaches* use a predetermined machine algorithm and use the classification performance as the evaluation criterion to select the new features set. Machine learning algorithms such as ID3 (Quinlan, 1986) and Bayesian networks (Jemili et al., 2009) are commonly used as induction algorithm for wrapper approaches.

Performance Evaluation Criteria

The effectiveness of an ID system is evaluated by its prediction accuracy and detection speed. The prediction accuracy of an IDS is measured by the precision, recall and F − measure. These three measures are calculated based on the confusion matrix, shown in Table 4. The confusion matrix shows the four possible prediction outcomes; True negatives (TN), True positives (TP), False positives (FP) and False negatives (FN) (Duda et al., 2001; Wu & Banzhaf, 2010).

TN and TP indicate that number of normal events and attack events are successfully predicted. While, FP refer to the number of normal events being predicted as attacks, and FN refer the number of attack events are incorrectly predicted as normal.

$$\text{Recall} = \frac{TP}{TP + FN} \tag{12}$$

$$\text{Precision} = \frac{TP}{TP + FP} \tag{13}$$

The commonly used IDS popular metrics include precision and recall, where F-measure is a weighted mean that assesses the trade-off between them.

$$\text{F-measure} = \frac{2 * \text{Recall} * \text{Precision}}{\text{Recall} + \text{Precision}} \tag{14}$$

Support Vector Machine in NID

Sung and Mukkamala in 2003 uses support vector machine classifier to build an intrusion detection system. However, the system totally ignores the relationships and dependencies between the features (Sung & Mukkamala, 2003).

Table 4. Confusion matrix

		Predicted Class	
		Normal	**Intrusion**
Actual Class	Normal	True positives (TP)	False positives (FP)
	Intrusion	False negatives (FN)	True negatives (TN)

Yao et al. (2006) propose an enhanced SVM intrusion detection model with a weighted kernel function. Rough set theory is adopted to perform a feature ranking and selection task of the new model. They proposed intrusion detection model outperformed the conventional SVM in precision, computation time, and false negative rate (Yao et al., 2006).

Shon et al. (2007) propose a new SVM approach for anomaly IDS, named Enhanced SVM. The overall model consist of an enhanced SVM detection engine and its supplement components such as packet profiling using SOFM, packet filtering using PTF, field selection using Genetic Algorithm and packet flow-based data preprocessing. SOFM clustering was used for normal profiling. The Enhanced SVM approach demonstrated an aptitude for detecting novel attacks while Snort and Bro, signature based systems in practice, have well developed detection performance. The SVM approach exhibited a low false positive rate similar to that of real NIDS (Shon & Moon, 2007).

Eid et al. (2010) proposes a novel adaptive IDS based on principal component analysis (PCA) and support vector machines (SVMs). By making use of PCA, the dimension of network data patterns is reduced significantly. Then SVM is employed to construct classification models based on training data processed by PCA. Experimental results on NSL-KDD dataset show that there proposed PCA-SVM NIDS has comparable accuracy as that of conventional SVMs without PCA and is able to speed up the process of intrusion detection and to minimize the memory space and CPU time cost (Eid et al., 2010).

Aburomman and Ibne Reaz (2017) compares several methods for creating SVM-based multiclass ID classifier from a set of binary SVM classifiers. Their research aims to identify the best suited multiclass SVM model for the intrusion detection task. The compared methods include one-against-rest SVM (OAR-SVM), one-against-one SVM (OAO-SVM), directed acyclic graph SVM (DAG-SVM), adaptive directed acyclic graph SVM (ADAGSVM), and error-correcting output code SVM (ECOC-SVM). Also, they propose a novel approach based on weighted one-against-rest SVM (WOAR-SVM). WOAR-SVM model uses differential evaluation as a meta-heuristic generated weight optimizer to define the relationship between the decision rules of the binary SVM classifier. Experiments results on the NSL-KDD dataset indicate that the WOAR-SVM shows an improvement in terms of overall accuracy (Aburomman & Reaz, 2017).

Hidden Naïve Bayes in NID

Valdes et al. (2000) developed an anomaly detection system based on naïve Bayesian networks. The detection model suffers from the problem that the child nodes do not interact between themselves and their output only influences the probability of the root node (Valdes & Skinner, 2000).

Eid et al. (2011) introduced and investigated the performance of a hybrid GA-HNB NIDS, where GA feature selection approach to reduce the data features space and then the hidden naïve bays (HNB) approach were adapted to classify the network intrusion. In order to evaluate the performance of the introduced hybrid GA-HNB NIDS, several experiments are conducted and demonstrated on NSL-KDD dataset. The experimental results show that the proposed GA-HNB NIDS produces consistently better performances on selecting the subsets of features which resulting better classification accuracies about 98.63%. Moreover, the performances results of the authors hybrid NIDS have been compared with the results of five well-known feature selection algorithms such as Chi square, Gain ratio and Principal component analysis (PCA) (Eid et al., 2011).

Koc and Carswell (2015) introduced a binary classifier model based on HNB method as an extension to NB to reduce its naivety assumption. Authors augmented the HNB binary classifier with EMD discretization and CONS feature selection filter methods. Experiment research using classic KDD 1999 Cup ID dataset indicate that the HNB binary classification model has better performance in terms of detection accuracy, error rate and area under ROC curve compared to the traditional NB classifier and can be applied to intrusion detection problem (Koc & Carswell, 2015).

Particle Swarm Optimization in NID

Srinoy (2007) reported that normal operation often produces traffic that matches like attack signature, resulting in false alarms. One main drawback of NIDS is the inability of detecting new attacks which do not have known signatures. The author proposed an IDS model where PSO is used to implement a feature selection, and SVMs with the one-versus-rest method serve as a fitness function of PSO. Experimental result shows that Srinoy's model recognize not only known attacks but also detect suspicious activity that may be the result of a new, unknown attack. The proposed model simplifies features effectively and obtains a higher classification accuracy compared to other methods (Srinoy, 2007).

Wang (2009) proposed PSO–SVM model to intrusion detection. Where, the standard PSO is used to determine free parameters of support vector machine and the binary PSO is to obtain the optimum feature subset at building IDS. The authors developed a series of experiments on KDD99 dataset to examine the effectiveness of their proposed NIDS. The experiment results indicate that PSO–SVM is not only able to achieve the process of selecting important features but also achieve higher detection rate than regular SVM for IDS (Wang et al., 2009).

Kumar et al. (2012) present a new collaborating filtering technique for preprocessing the probe type of attacks. They implemented a hybrid classifiers based on binary PSO and random forests algorithm for the classification of probe attacks in a network. The Collaborative filtering technique and random forests algorithm has been successfully applied to find patterns that are suitable for prediction in large volumes of data. Their experimental result demonstrated that as number of trees used in forest increases, the false positive rate decreases (Kumar et al., 2012).

Bamakan et al. (2015) developed a new model based on multiple criteria linear programming (MCLP) and PSO to enhance the accuracy of attacks detection. In order to improve the performance of MCLP classifier; PSO has been used to tuning the parameters of MCLP. KDD'99 dataset used to evaluate the performance of proposed PSO-MCLP model. The experimental study indicated that the PSO-MCLP model get better performance based on detection rate, false alarm rate and running time compare with MCLP model which its parameters has been chosen by user or by cross validation (Bamakan et al., 2015).

Aburomman and Reaz (2016) proposes a novel ensemble construction method that uses PSO generated weights to create ensemble of classifiers with better accuracy for NID. Authors define an expert as a collection of five binary classifiers that together generate a binary vector of responses. For which, the expert opinions are combined in three ways. (1) PSO approach: generate weights using PSO that is constructed with manually selected behavioral parameters. These weights are then used with the weighted majority voting (WMV) to combine the expert opinions. (2) meta-optimized PSO: is similar to the first approach, except that the PSO behavioral parameters were optimized using Local unimodal sampling (LUS). (3) WMA approach: is to combine the opinions using the WMA. The three approaches were empirically compared using KDD99 datasets. Experimental results showed that the best results obtained for PSO with average accuracy improvement of 0.756% compared to the accuracy of the best base expert; and a relatively short time for PSO based ensemble to complete its task (Aburomman & Reaz, 2016).

GENETIC ALGORITHM IN NID

Crosbie and Spafford (1995) applied the multiple agent technology and Genetic Programming (GP) to detect network intrusions. For both agents they used GP to determine anomalous network behaviors and each agent can monitor one parameter of the network audit data. The proposed model has the advantage when many small autonomous agents are used but it suffers a problem when communicating among the agents (Crosbie & Spafford, 1995).

Stein et al. (2005) uses a genetic algorithm to select a subset of features for decision tree classifiers. The authors intrusion detection model increases the detection accuracy and decreases the false alarm rate (Stein et al., 2005).

Goyal and Kumar (2008) described a GA based algorithm to classify all types of smurf attack. They GA algorithm takes into consideration different features in network connections to generate a classification rule set. The authors were able to generate a rule using the principles of evolution in a GA to classify all types of smurf attack labels in the KDD99 training dataset. Their false positive rate is quite low at 0.2% and accuracy rate is as high as 100% (Goyal & Kumar, 2008).

Khan, in his 2011 study, showed that NIDS on rules formulation is an efficient approach to classify various type of attack. DoS or Probing attack are relatively more common and can be detected more accurately if contributing parameters are formulated in terms of rules. Khan used Genetic algorithm to devise such rule. The author experiments show that the accuracy of rule based learning increases with the number of iteration (Khan, 2011).

Kuang et al. (2014) present a hybrid kernel principal component analysis (KPCA), support vector machine (SVM) and genetic algorithm (GA) model to enhance the detection precision for low-frequent attacks and detection stability. In the proposed model, a multi-layer SVM classifier is adopted, where KPCA is used as a preprocessor to reduce the dimension of feature vectors and shorten training time. GA is employed to optimize the punishment factor C, kernel parameters σ and the tube size ε of SVM. Experimental results on KDD dataset show that the classification accuracies of the proposed hybrid KPCA-SVM-GA model are superior to those of SVM classifiers whose parameters are randomly selected (Kuanga et al., 2014).

Gauthama Raman et al. (2017) introduce an adaptive, and a robust NID technique using Hypergraph based Genetic Algorithm (HG -GA) for parameter setting and feature selection in Support Vector Machine (SVM). For which, the Hyper – clique property of Hypergraph was exploited for the generation of GA initial population to prevent the local minima trap and to fasten the optimal solution search. HG-GA uses a weighted objective function to maintain the trade-off between maximizing the detection rate and minimizing the false alarm rate, along with the optimal number of features. The performance of proposed HGGA-SVM model was evaluated using NSL-KDD dataset under two scenarios. Experimental results show the prominence of HG-GA-SVM model over the existing techniques in terms of classifier accuracy, detection rate, false alarm rate and runtime analysis (Raman et al., 2017).

FUZZY LOGIC IN NID

Dickerson et al. (2000) developed the Fuzzy Intrusion Recognition Engine (FIRE). They applies fuzzy logic rules to the audit data to classify it as normal or intrusion. FIRE process the network input data and generate fuzzy sets for every observed feature. Then, the fuzzy sets are used to define fuzzy rules to detect individual attacks. The FIRE model proofed to be effective against port scans and probes, but its primary disadvantage is the labor intensive rule generation process (Dickerson & Dickerson, 2000).

Orfila et al. (2003) introduce a measure of the IDS prediction skill computed according to the false positives produced. They proposed a model that can quantify the usefulness that a multi-model IDS prediction can bring to the user. The performance obtained from the application of fuzzy thresholds is compared with the corresponding crisp thresholds. The authors results of these comparisons conclude a relevant improvement when fuzzy thresholds are involved instead of crisp logic (Orfila et al., 2003).

Shanmugavadivu and Nagarajan (2012) designed a fuzzy decision-making module for intrusion detection. Where, an effective set of fuzzy rules for inference approach were identified automatically by making use of the fuzzy rule learning strategy. They proposed model at first, the definite rules were for attack data as well as normal data. Then, fuzzy rules were identified by fuzzifying. The definite rules and these rules were given to fuzzy system, which classify the test data (Shanmugavadivu & Nagarajan, 2012).

Elhag et al. (2015) proposed a new methodology for improving the behaviour of misuse NIDS. There new approach consider the use of Genetic Fuzzy Systems (GFS) within a pairwise learning framework for the development of a robust and interpretable NIDS. Specifically, it is based on the combination of the FARCHD algorithm, which is a linguistic fuzzy association rule mining classifier, and the OVO binarization that confronts all pairs of classes in order to learn a single model for each couple. The KD-DCUP'99 has been selected as benchmark dataset for determining the robustness of the proposal approach under different perspectives. Experimental results show that the FARCHD-OVO approach has the best tradeoff among all performance measures, especially in the mean F-measure, the average accuracy and the false alarm rate (Elhag et al., 2015).

REFERENCES

Aburomman, A., & Reaz, M. (2016). A novel svm-knn-pso ensemble method for intrusion detection system. *Applied Soft Computing*, *38*, 360–372. doi:10.1016/j.asoc.2015.10.011

Aburomman, A. A., & Reaz, M. B. I. (2017). A novel weighted support vector machines multiclass classifier based on differential evolution for intrusion detection systems. *Information Sciences*, *414*, 225–246. doi:10.1016/j.ins.2017.06.007

Anderson, J. P. (1980). *Computer security threat monitoring and surveillance. Technical report*. Fort Washington, PA: James P Anderson Co.

Axelsson, S. (2000). *Intrusion detection systems: A survey and taxonomy*. Department of Computer Engineering, Chalmers University of Technology, Tech Rep.

Bace, R., & Mell, P. (2001). *Nist special publication on intrusion detection systems*. National Institute of Standards and Technology, Tech Rep.

Bamakan, S., Amiri, B., Mirzabagheri, M., & Shi, Y. (2015). A new intrusion detection approach using pso based multiple criteria linear programming. *Procedia Computer Science, 55*, 231–237. doi:10.1016/j.procs.2015.07.040

Ben-Bassat, M. (1982). Pattern recognition and reduction of dimensionality, volume 1. Handbook of Statistics II. North-Holland.

Bezdek, J. C. (1994). What is computational intelligence? In *Computational Intelligence Imitating Life*. New York: IEEE Press.

Biermann, E., Cloete, E., & Venter, L. M. (2001). A comparison of intrusion detection systems. *Computers & Security, 20*(8), 676–683. doi:10.1016/S0167-4048(01)00806-9

Brown, D. J., Suckow, B., & Wang, T. (2001). *A survey of intrusion detection systems*. Academic Press.

Burges, C. J. C. (1998). A tutorial on support vector machines for pattern recognition. *Data Mining and Knowledge Discovery, 2*(2), 121–167. doi:10.1023/A:1009715923555

Canadian Institute for Cybersecurity. (n.d.). *NSL-KDD*. Retrieved from http://nsl.cs.unb.ca/NSL-KDD/

Crosbie, M., & Spafford, E. (1995). Applying genetic programming to intrusion detection. *Proceedings of AAAI Fall Symposium on Genetic Programming*, 1–8.

Dash, M., Choi, K., Scheuermann, P., & Liu, H. (2002). Feature selection for clusteringâŁ"a filter solution. *Proceedings of the Second International Conference on Data Mining*, 115-122.

Debar, H., Dacier, M., & Wespi, A. (1999). Towards a taxonomy of intrusion-detection systems. *Computer Networks, 31*(8), 805–822. doi:10.1016/S1389-1286(98)00017-6

Denning, D. (1987). An intrusion detection model. *IEEE Transactions on Software Engineering, 13*(2), 222–232. doi:10.1109/TSE.1987.232894

Dickerson, J., & Dickerson, J. (2000). Fuzzy network profiling for intrusion detection. *19th International Conference of the North American Fuzzy Information Processing Society (NAFIPS)*, 301–306.

Dote, Y., & Ovaska, S. J. (2001). Industrial applications of soft computing: A review. *Proceedings of the IEEE*, 1243–1265. 10.1109/5.949483

Duda, R., Hart, P., & Stork, D. (2001). *Pattern Classification* (2nd ed.). John Wiley & Sons.

Durst, R., Champion, T., Witten, B., Miller, E., & Spagnuolo, L. (1999). Testing and evaluating computer intrusion detection systems. *Communications of the ACM, 42*(7), 53–61. doi:10.1145/306549.306571

Eberhart, R., & Kennedy, J. (1995). A new optimizer using particle swarm theory. *Sixth International Symposium on Micro Machine and Human Science*, 39–43. 10.1109/MHS.1995.494215

Eberhart, R., Simpson, P., & Dobbins, R. (1996). *Computational Intelligence PC Tools*. Boston: Academic Press.

Eid, H. F., Azar, A. T., & Hassanien, A. E. (2013). Improved real-time discretize network intrusion detection system. *Seventh International Conference on Bio-Inspired Computing Theories and Applications (BIC-TA 2012) Advances in Intelligent Systems and Computing*, 99–109. 10.1007/978-81-322-1038-2_9

Eid, H. F., Darwish, A., Hassanien, A. E., & Hoon Kim, T. (2011). *Intelligent hybrid anomaly network intrusion detection system. In International Conference on Future Generation Communication and Networking.* CCIS/ LNCS series, Jeju Island, Korea.

Eid, H. F., Darwish, A., Hassanien, A. E., & Abraham, A. (2010). Principle components analysisand support vector machine based intrusion detection system. *The 10th IEEE international conference in Intelligent Design and Application (ISDA2010).*

Elhag, S., Fernandez, A., Bawakid, A., Alshomrani, S., & Herrera, F. (2015). On the combination of genetic fuzzy systems and pairwise learning for improving detection rates on intrusion detection systems. *Expert Systems with Applications, 42*(1), 193–202. doi:10.1016/j.eswa.2014.08.002

Endorf, C., Schultz, E., & J., M. (2004). *Intrusion Detection and Prevention.* McGraw-Hill.

Eskin, E., Arnold, A., Prerau, M., Portnoy, L., & Stolfo, S. (2002). A geometric framework for unsupervised anomaly detection: detecting intrusions in unlabeled data. In *Data Mining in Computer Security.* Kluwer. doi:10.1007/978-1-4615-0953-0_4

Fried, D. J., Graf, I., Haines, J. W., Kendall, K. R., Mcclung, D., Weber, D., . . . Zissman, M. A. (2000). Evaluating intrusion detection systems: The 1998 darpa off-line intrusion detection evaluation. *Proceedings of the DARPA Information Survivability Conference and Exposition,* 12-26.

Gong, F. (2003). *Deciphering detection techniques: Part ii anomaly-based intrusion detection.* Network Associates.

Goyal, A., & Kumar, C. (2008). *A genetic algorithm based network intrusion detection system.* Academic Press.

Heady, R., Luger, G., Maccabe, A., & Servilla, M. (1990). *The architecture of a network level intrusion detection system. Technical report.* Computer Science Department, University of New Mexico. doi:10.2172/425295

Holland, J. (1975). *Adaptation in Natural and Artificial Systems.* University of Michigan Press.

Ilgun, K., Kemmerer, R. A., & Porras, P. A. (1995). State transition analysis: A rule-based intrusion detection approach. *IEEE Transactions on Software Engineering, 21,* 181–199.

Jemili, F., Zaghdoud, M., & Ahmed, M. (2009). Intrusion detection based on hybrid propagation in Bayesian networks. Proceedings of the IEEE international conference on Intelligence and security informatics, 137–142.

Jiang, B., Ding, X., Ma, L., He, Y., Wang, T., & Xie, W. (2008). A hybrid feature selection algorithm:combination of symmetrical uncertainty and genetic algorithms. *The Second International Symposium on Optimization and Systems Biology OSB'08,* 152–157.

Jiang, L., Zhang, H., & Cai, Z. (2009). A novel Bayes model: Hidden naive Bayes. *IEEE Transactions on Knowledge and Data Engineering, 2*(10), 1361–1371. doi:10.1109/TKDE.2008.234

Jin, X., Xu, A., Bie, R., & Guo, P. (2006). Machine learning techniques and chi-square feature selection for cancer classification using sage gene expression profiles. Lecture Notes in Computer Science, 3916, 106-115. doi:10.1007/11691730_11

KDD99. (n.d.). Retrieved from http://kdd.ics.uci.edu/databases

Khan, M. (2011). Rule based network intrusion detection using genetic algorithm. *International Journal of Computers and Applications, 18*(8), 26–29. doi:10.5120/2303-2914

Kim, S., Shin, K. S., & Park, K. (2005a). An application of support vector machines for customer churn analysis: Credit card case. *Lecture Notes in Computer Science, 3611*, 636–647. doi:10.1007/11539117_91

Kim, S., Yang, S., Seo, K. S., Ro, Y. M., Kim, J.-Y., & Seo, Y. S. (2005b). Home photo categorization based on photographic region templates. *Lecture Notes in Computer Science, 3689*, 328–338. doi:10.1007/11562382_25

Kim, Y., Street, W., & Menczer, F. (2000). Feature selection for unsupervised learning via evolutionary search. *Proceedings of the Sixth ACM SIGKDD International Conference on Knowledge Discovery and Data Mining*, 365-369. 10.1145/347090.347169

Koc, L., & Carswell, A. D. (2015). Network intrusion detection using a hnb binary classifier. In *17th UKSIM-AMSS International Conference on Modelling and Simulation* (pp. 81–85). IEEE. 10.1109/UKSim.2015.37

Kohavi, R., & John, G. H. (1997). Wrappers for feature subset selection. *Artificial Intelligence, 97*(1-2), 273–324. doi:10.1016/S0004-3702(97)00043-X

Koller, D., & Sahami, M. (1996). Toward optimal feature selection. *Proceedings of the Thirteenth International Conference on Machine Learning*, 284-292.

Kotsiantis, S., & Kanellopoulos, D. (2006). Discretization techniques: A recent survey. *GESTS International Transactions on Computer Science and Engineering, 32*, 47–58.

Kuanga, F., Xu, W., & Zhang, S. (2014). A novel hybrid kpca and svm with ga model for intrusion detection. *Applied Soft Computing, 18*, 178–184. doi:10.1016/j.asoc.2014.01.028

Kumar, G. S., Sirisha, C. V. K., Durga, R, K., & Devi, A. (2012). Robust preprocessing and random forests technique for network probe anomaly detection. *International Journal of Soft Computing and Engineering, 6*.

Laskov, P., Dussel, P., Schafer, C., & K., R. (2005). Learning intrusion detection: supervised or unsupervised? *Image Analysis and Processings ICIAP*, 50–57.

Leung, K., & Leckie, C. (2005). Unsupervised anomaly detection in network intrusion detection using clusters. *Proceedings of the Twenty-eighth Australasian conference on Computer Science*, 333–342.

Li, Y., Fang, B., Guo, L., & Chen, Y. (2007). Network anomaly detection based on tcmknn algorithm. In *Proceedings of the 2nd ACM symposium on Information computer and communications security*. ACM.

Lincoln Laboratory, Massachusetts Institute of Technology. (2017a). *1998 DARPA Intrusion Detection Evaluation Data Set*. Retrieved from http://www.ll.mit.edu/mission/communications/cyber/CSTcorpora/ ideval/data/1998data.html

Lincoln Laboratory, Massachusetts Institute of Technology. (2017b). *1999 DARPA Intrusion Detection Evaluation Data Set*. Retrieved from http://www.ll.mit.edu/mission/communications/cyber/CSTcorpora/ ideval/data/1999data.html

Lundin, E., & Jonsson, E. (2002). Anomaly-based intrusion detection: Privacy concerns and other problems. *Computer Networks*, *34*(4), 623–640. doi:10.1016/S1389-1286(00)00134-1

Mahoney, M. V., & Chan, P. K. (2003). An analysis of the 1999 darpa/lincoln laboratory evaluation data for network anomaly detection. In *Sixth International Symposium on Recent Advances in Intrusion Detection* (pp. 220-237). Springer-Verlag.

Marchette, D. (1999). A statistical method for profiling network traffic. *Proceedings of the First USENIX Workshop on Intrusion Detection and Network Monitoring*, 119–128.

McHugh, J. (2000). Testing intrusion detection systems: A critique of the 1998 and 1999 darpa intrusion detection system evaluations as performed by lincoln laboratory. *ACM Transactions on Information and System Security*, *3*(4), 262–294. doi:10.1145/382912.382923

Mizianty, M., Kurgan, L., & Ogiela, M. (2010). Discretization as the enabling technique for the naïve Bayes and semi-naïve Bayes-based classification. *The Knowledge Engineering Review, 25*, 421–449.

Mukkamala, S., Janoski, G., & Sung, A. (2002). Intrusion detection: support vector machines and neural networks. *Proceedings of the IEEE International Joint Conference on Neural Networks (ANNIE)*, 1702–1707. 10.1109/IJCNN.2002.1007774

Orfila, A., Carbo, J., & Ribagorda, A. (2003). Fuzzy logic on decision model for intrusion detection systems. *Proceedings of the 2003 IEEE International Conference on Fuzzy Systems*, 1237–1242. 10.1109/ FUZZ.2003.1206608

Peng, H., Long, F., & Ding, C. (2005). Feature selection based on mutual information criteria of max-dependency, max-relevance, and min redundancy. *IEEE Transactions on Pattern Analysis and Machine Intelligence*, *1226*, 12–38. PMID:16119262

Pereira, H. E. (2009). Conversion methods for symbolic features: A comparison applied to an intrusion detection problem. *Expert Systems with Applications*, *36*(7), 10612–10617. doi:10.1016/j.eswa.2009.02.054

Poole, D., Mackworth, A., & Goebel, R. (1998). *Computational Intelligence: A Logical Approach*. Oxford, UK: Oxford University Press.

Portnoy, L., Eskin, E., & Stolfo, S. (2001). Intrusion detection with unlabeled data using clustering. *Proc. ACM CSS Workshop on Data Mining Applied to Security*.

Quinlan, J. R. (1986). Induction of decision trees. *Machine Learning*, *1*(1), 81–106. doi:10.1007/ BF00116251

Raman, M. R. G., Somu, N., Kirthivasan, K., Liscano, R., & Sriram, V. S. S. (2017). *An efficient intrusion detection system based on hypergraph -genetic algorithm for parameter optimization and feature selection in support vector machine.* Knowledge-Based System.

Shang, C., & Shen, Q. (2006). Aiding classi cation of gene expression data with feature selection: A comparative study. *Computational Intelligence Research, 1,* 68–76.

Shanmugavadivu, R., & Nagarajan, N. (2012). Learning of intrusion detector in conceptual approach of fuzzy towards intrusion methodology. *Int. J. of Advanced Research in Computer Science and Software Engineering, 2.*

Shon, T., & Moon, J. S. (2007). A hybrid machine learning approach to network anomaly detection. *Information Sciences, 177*(18), 3799–3821. doi:10.1016/j.ins.2007.03.025

Sommers, J., Yegneswaran, V., & Barford, P. (2004). A framework for malicious workload generation. In *4th ACM SIGCOMM conference on Internet measurement* (pp. 82-87). ACM.

Srinoy, S. (2007). Intrusion detection model based on particle swarm optimization and support vector machine. Proceeding of Computational Intelligence in Security and Defense Applications. doi:10.1109/CISDA.2007.368152

Stallings, W. (2006). *Cryptography and network security principles and practices.* Prentice Hall.

Stein, G., & Chen, B. W., & K, H. (2005). decision tree classifier for network intrusion detection with ga-based feature selection. *Proceedings of 43rd annual Southeast regional conference, 136*–141. 10.1145/1167253.1167288

Sung, A., & Mukkamala, S. (2003). Identifying important features for intrusion detection using support vector machines and neural networks. *Proceedings of the 2003 Symposium on Applications and the Internet, 209*–216. 10.1109/SAINT.2003.1183050

Tavallaee, M., Bagheri, E., Lu, W., & Ghorbani, A. A. (2009). A detailed analysis of the kdd cup 99 data set. *Proceeding of the 2009 IEEE symposium on computational Intelligence in security and defense application (CISDA).* 10.1109/CISDA.2009.5356528

Tsang, C., Kwong, S., & Wang, H. (2007). Genetic-fuzzy rule mining approach and evaluation of feature selection techniques for anomaly intrusion detection. *Pattern Recognition, 40*(9), 2373–2391. doi:10.1016/j.patcog.2006.12.009

Valdes, A., & Skinner, K. (2000). Adaptive model-based monitoring for cyber attack detection. Recent Advances in Intrusion Detection, 80–92. doi:10.1007/3-540-39945-3_6

Vapnik, V. (1998). *Statistical learning theory.* New York: Wiley.

Venter, G., & Sobieski, J. S. (2003). Particle swarm optimization. *AIAA Journal, 41*(8), 1583–1589. doi:10.2514/2.2111

Verwoerd, T., & Hunt, R. (2002). Intrusion detection techniques and approaches. *Computer Communications, 25*(15), 1356–1365. doi:10.1016/S0140-3664(02)00037-3

Wang, J., Hong, X., Ren, R., & Li, T. (2009). A real-time intrusion detection system based on pso-svm. *Proceeding of the 2009 International Workshop on Information Security and Application*, 319–321.

Wu, S., & Banzhaf, W. (2010). The use of computational intelligence in intrusion detection systems: A review. *Applied Soft Computing, 10*(1), 1–35. doi:10.1016/j.asoc.2009.06.019

Yao, J., Zhao, S., & Fan, L. (2006). An enhanced support vector machine model for intrusion detection. *Proceedings of the First international conference on Rough Sets and Knowledge Technology*, 538–543. 10.1007/11795131_78

Yeung, D., & Chow, C. (2002). Parzen-window network intrusion detectors. *International Conference on pattern recognition*, 385–388. 10.1109/ICPR.2002.1047476

Yu, L., & Liu, H. (2003). Feature selection for high-dimensional data: a fast correlation-based filter solution. *Proceedings of the twentieth International Conference on Machine Learning*, 856-863.

Zadeh, L. (1965). Fuzzy sets. *Information and Control, 8*, 338-352.

Zadeh, L. (1975). Fuzzy logic and approximate reasoning. *Synthese, 30*(3), 407–428. doi:10.1007/BF00485052

Zhengbing, H., Zhitang, L., & Junqi, W. (2008). A novel network intrusion detection system (nids) based on signatures search of data mining. In *1st international conference on Forensic applications and techniques in telecommunications information, and multimedia* (pp. 1-7). ICST.

Chapter 9
Performance Comparison of PSO and Hybrid PSO–GA in Hiding Fuzzy Sensitive Association Rules

Sathiyapriya Krishnamoorthy
PSG College of Technology, India

Sudha Sadasivam G.
PSG College of Technology, India

Rajalakshmi M.
Coimbatore Institute of Technology, India

ABSTRACT

Explosion of data analysis techniques facilitate organizations to publish microdata about individuals. While the released data sets provide valuable information to researchers, it is possible to infer sensitive information from the published non-sensitive data using association rule mining. An association rule is characterized as sensitive if its confidence is above disclosure threshold. These sensitive rules should be made uninteresting before releasing the dataset publicly. This is done by modifying the data that support the sensitive rules, so that the confidence of these sensitive rules is reduced below disclosure threshold. The main goal of the proposed system is to hide a set of sensitive association rules by perturbing the quantitative data that contains sensitive knowledge using PSO and hybrid PSO-GA with minimum side effects like lost rules, ghost rules. The performance of PSO and Hybrid PSO-GA approach in effectively hiding fuzzy association rule is also compared. Experimental results demonstrate that hybrid approach is efficient in terms of lost rules, number of modifications, hiding failure.

DOI: 10.4018/978-1-5225-5396-0.ch009

1. INTRODUCTION

Data or knowledge mining aims at discovering previously unknown knowledge from large collection of data items. Association rule mining is a popular technique in data mining to find frequent patterns, associations, correlations among set of items or objects in transactional databases. An association rule is an implication of the form X→Y, where both X and Y are set of attributes (items) from the database. X is called as the body (Left Hand Side (LHS)) of the rule and Y is called as the head (Right Hand Side (RHS)) of the rule. For example, an association rule in a market data may be defined as, Pen=> ink (support = 50%, confidence =65%). In 50% of the transactions, 65% of the people buying pen also buy ink in the same transaction; 50% and 65% represent the support and the confidence, respectively. Support is the percentage of number of transactions that contain both X and Y. Confidence is the ratio of the support of XUY to the support of X (Sathiyapriya Sudhasadasivam & Suganya 2014).

The Apriori algorithm was the common algorithm that uses the concept of frequent item sets to mine association rules in transaction data (Srikant & Agrawal,1995). The Apriori algorithm generates large number of candidate item set. The Frequent-Pattern-tree structure (FP-tree) efficiently mines association rules without generation of candidate item sets (Han & Fu, 1995).

But most databases in real world contains numerical, categorical and integer values. The binary algorithm cannot be applied directly. One way of mining quantitative rules is to treat them like categorical attributes and generate rules for all potential values. This would result in the explosion of number of rules generated and also specific numerical value will not appear frequently. So the domain of each quantitative attribute is divided into intervals and rules are generated from these intervals. This is called discretization (Srikant & Agrawal, 1996). Choosing intervals for numeric attributes is sensitive to support and confidence measures.

As it is possible that the data set may be skewed, intervals cannot be formed randomly. It was shown that if the range of the attribute is divided into equal intervals it leads to two problems of minsupport and minconfidence (Srikant & Agrawal, 1996). If large number of small intervals is chosen then the support of some of the interval becomes low. This is called "Minsupport" issue. Building larger intervals results in information loss and rules mined are different from that in original data. This is called "Minconfidence" issue. Another problem with discretization is sharp boundary problem. For example, consider the rule, if experience >=2 and bonus points >= 5000 then credit = approved. If a customer has a job for two years and bonus point of 4,990 then the application for credit approval may be rejected. Such a precise cut-off seems unfair. So, in order to avoid the sharp boundary problem the data is fuzzified.

In this example, the bonus point can be discretized into categories like low, medium, high and fuzzy logic can be applied to allow fuzzy threshold or boundaries to be defined for each category. Unlike the crisp sets where an element either belongs to a set S or its complement, in fuzzy set theory, each element can belong to more than one fuzzy set. In this example, the bonus point 4,990 belongs to both medium and high fuzzy sets, but to different degrees. In order to avoid sharp boundary problem numerous fuzzy mining approaches have been proposed to mine interesting association rules from quantitative values.

Motivation

The data published by organizations for research and mining purpose may contain information identifiable to individuals. Though the released data sets contain useful information to researchers, they may also contain sensitive information about individuals or business organization whose privacy may be at risk. Using data mining techniques like association rule mining it is possible to extract personal or sensitive information which are actually hidden in the data. This would provide an advantage for the business competitors. An association rule is characterized as sensitive is its confidence is above disclosure threshold. These sensitive rules should be made uninteresting before releasing the dataset to the public. That is the data supporting these rules should be modified in such a way that the confidence of these sensitive rules is reduced below disclosure threshold.

Hence, a number of techniques have been proposed for modifying or transforming the data to preserve privacy without compromising the knowledge being mined. Sensitive information can be hidden using distortion based technique or blocking based technique (Saygin, Verykios & Clifton, 2001). The distortion based technique distorts the data in such a way that the support and confidence of sensitive association rule is reduced below threshold. This technique has side effects of 'Lost Rules' and 'Ghost Rules'. Lost Rules refers to non-sensitive association rules that are hidden due to data modification. Ghost rules are non-interesting association rules which become interesting after sanitization. Distortion based technique reduces these side effects but the complexity of theses algorithms increase with dataset size. This technique have a severe restriction in some specific situations like medical database where deleting a part of dataset may infer to a wrong prescription. Blocking based technique is characterized by introducing uncertainty without distorting the database. It also suffers from side effects of lost item, lost rule and ghost rule.

The problem of sanitizing the database in such a way to provide an appropriate balance between privacy and knowledge discovery is proved to be NP-Hard (Saygin et al., 2001). Research in this area is focused on perturbation of original database heuristically which in turn reduces the accuracy of database. In addition to the accuracy, the privacy is also not warranted in most of the heuristics approaches. While hiding quantitative sensitive association rules, the search space is infinite. The goal is to find a finite set of interesting solutions, close to optimal solution. So, new approaches is essential for hiding sensitive association rules using metaheuristics. The motivation of this research is to design information hiding method for quantitative data which continue to be effective, without compromising security.

In order to hide sensitive association rule, it is possible to perturb the data in different ways resulting in numerous solutions in the solution space. Each solution provides different degree of compromise between the knowledge mined and the security of private information. It is necessary to choose an optimal solution that maximizes the knowledge mined without compromising security. In Particle Swarm Optimization, it is possible for the particles to exhaustively explore search space for finding better global solution. So PSO is applied for effective hiding of sensitive information.

The genetic algorithm technique (Sathiyapriya, Sudha & Karthikeyan, 2012) proposed earlier makes perturbation in multiple data resulting in side effects of lost rule, ghost rule and large number of modification to original data. The experimental results also show hiding failure which is unacceptable in most cases. The proposed method clusters the transactions and PSO is run in the cluster one by one till the support goes below minimum support. This would reduce number of modifications.

The contribution of this paper is as follows:

1. Most of the approaches proposed in literature hides sensitive information in binary data. Hiding binary association rules require only insertion and deletion of items (changing 1 to 0 and vice versa) whereas hiding quantitative rules requires changing the magnitude of quantity of item without compromising knowledge and security.

2. The evolutionary methods proposed earlier makes perturbation in multiple data resulting in side effects of lost rule, ghost rule and large number of modification to original data. The proposed method clusters the transactions and PSO is run in the cluster one by one till the support goes below minimum support. This reduces number of modifications.

3. A novel method of updating the position of the particle and the objective function, helps to reduce the side effects. Hybrid approach using PSO and Genetic Algorithm (GA) is proposed and its performance is compared with the PSO approach.

The proposed approach uses fuzzification to mine association rules from quantitative data. Then Particle Swarm Optimization (PSO) and Hybrid PSO-GA are used to hide sensitive association rules. Experimental results show that the hybrid approach is more effective in preserving the privacy of sensitive data present in quantitative database.

2. RELATED WORK

A method for hiding fuzzy association rules in quantitative data was proposed to hide critical fuzzy association rules from quantitative data (Berberoglu & Kaya, 2008). For this purpose, support value of Left Hand Side (LHS) of the rule to be hidden is increased. It employs fuzzy set concept. However the fuzzy association rule mining approaches require the membership function to be defined by human experts. In absence of expertise, the membership functions cannot be accurately defined which reduces system performance (Sathiyapriya, Sudha Sadasivam & Celin, 2011).

Wang et al. (2005) introduced two strategies for hiding sensitive association rules. The first strategy, called ISL (Increasing the Support of LHS), decreases the confidence of a rule by increasing the support of the item set in its antecedent. The second approach, called DSR (Decreasing the Support of Right Hand Side (RHS)), reduces the confidence of the rule by decreasing the support of the item set in its consequent. Both algorithms rely on the distortion of a portion of the database transactions to lower the confidence of the association rule. But DSR require reduced number of database scans and are useful when the sensitive items have high support.

A method for hiding sensitive association rule using Heuristic approach (Verykios, Elmagarmid, Bertino, Saygin, & Dasseni, 2004) marks the representative rules among the sensitive rules and hides them. The confidence of the sensitive rules is reduced while maintaining the support. The disadvantage of this method is that it has computational overhead associated with the computation of confidence of the rules.

Many algorithms were proposed in literature that applied genetic algorithm for hiding sensitive association rules. Dehkordi et al. (2009) adapted genetic algorithm for hiding sensitive association rules with the intention of reducing the hiding failure while increasing the number of non-sensitive rules mined from sanitized dataset. Narmadha et al. (2011) proposed genetic algorithm technique for protecting sensitive rules from malicious data miner. Based on the fitness value, chromosomes are selected and the genes representing the sensitive items in these chromosomes are modified with crossover and mutation operations without any loss of data. This helped to reduce the side effects of hiding. Shah et al. (2014) proposed privacy preserving genetic algorithm in which the database is sanitized repeatedly until the support or confidence of the restricted rules dropped below the user specified threshold. It hides sensitive fuzzy association rules derived from the quantitative dataset, while the techniques proposed by Dehkordi et al. (2009) and Narmadha et al. (2011) are only applicable on binary dataset. A new method for preserving privacy in quantitative association rules using Genetic Algorithm (Sathiyapriya, Sudha & Karthikeyan, 2012) mines fuzzified data using modified apriori algorithm in order to extract the rules and identify sensitive rules. The sensitive rules are hidden by using DSR approach with genetic algorithm in order to ensure high level of security and utility of the database.

Map reduce version of rough set has been used for attribute set reduction and in the resultant attribute set DSR technique has been applied using Particle Swarm Optimization (PSO) for hiding sensitive rules (Sudha, Sangeetha & Sathiyapriya,2012).

Cheng and Shyang, (2014) employed the concept of Evolutionary Multi-Objective optimization (EMO) to modify the original database. Sensitive rules were hidden by deleting identified transactions/ tuples. Khan et al., (2014) proposed Improved Genetic Algorithm Approach that Uses fitness function for hiding sensitive rules by reducing loss of information, lost rules and generation of ghost rules. Shah and Asghar (2014) applied Genetic algorithm to hide sensitive rules. The Fitness function has two parts: i) Transaction sensitivity and ii) Transaction priority and the transactions that contain the maximum number of sensitive items and minimum number of data items are chosen for modification.

Bonam and Reddy, (2014) used Particle Swarm Optimization (PSO) to recognize the most sensitive transactions for hiding the given sensitive association rules. Cheng et al., (2015) applied Evolutionary Multi-Objective optimization (EMO) and achieved rule hiding by selectively inserting items into the database.

The existing methods for hiding the sensitive rules lead to computational overhead. Some of the methods fail to hide all the desired rules which are supposed to be hidden in minimum number of passes and generates more side effects. The proposed method overcomes these disadvantages by hiding maximum number of sensitive rules in minimum number of generations using PSO. The proposed PSO based approach reduces hiding failure and avoids generation of ghost rules. But increases the number of modification to actual data. So a hybrid PSO – GA approach is proposed and the performance is compared with PSO approach.

The paper is organized as follows: Section 3 describes the proposed work and the proposed algorithm. The experimental analysis and the conclusion are provided in section 4 and 5 respectively.

3. PROPOSED WORK

Let I = {i_1, i_2, i_3} be the set of items called item set. Every i_j is a quantity of the item where $1 \leq j \leq m$. Given a database D= {t_1, t_2,...., t_n}. Each t_j is a transaction with itemset I. Let us consider P = {p_1, p_2,... ,p_x} and Q = {q_1, q_2,....., q_y} which are disjoint subset of I as two large itemsets. Then, the fuzzy association rule can be given as: A→B where A= {f1, f_2,...f_p} and B ={g_1, g_2,..... g_q} where f_i is the set containing fuzzy regions related to item p_i and g_j is set containing fuzzy regions related to item q_j. A and B contain the fuzzy sets associated with the corresponding itemset in P and Q (Gupta M. & Joshi R. C. 2009)

A fuzzy set A for the item X is defined as

$$A = \left\{ \left(X, \ \mu_A \left(X \right) \right) | X \in A, \mu_A \left(X \right) \in \left[0, 1 \right] \right\}$$ (1)

where $\mu_A(X)$ is a membership function that takes value in the interval [0, 1] and it is referred as the membership grade or degree of membership.

Assume that x_1 to x_n are the elements in fuzzy set A, and μ_1 to μ_n respectively are their grades of membership in A. A is then usually represented as $A = \dfrac{\mu_1}{x_1} + \dfrac{\mu_2}{x_2} + \ldots\ldots \dfrac{\mu_n}{x_n}$. The support of the fuzzy set A is given by the scalar cardinality of a fuzzy set A which is the summation of the membership grades of all the elements of X in A. Thus

$$|A| = \sum_{i=1}^{n} \mu_A(x_i) \tag{2}$$

The combined support of two fuzzy sets X and Y is denoted as Supp(X∩Y), and it can be found by fuzzy intersection as given below

$$\mu_{X \cap Y}(P) = min\{\mu_X(i), \mu_Y(i)\} \tag{3}$$

where i denotes the region of membership in the corresponding fuzzy set.

The major steps in the proposed approach includes

1. Fuzzification
2. Rule Generation
3. Clustering
4. Hiding sensitive rules using PSO and Hybrid PSO-GA as described in the following sections.

Fuzzification

The proposed work uses the approach proposed by Hong et al. (1999) for mining fuzzy association rule.

The quantitative value V_{ij} of each transaction data T_i, i = 1 to n, for each item Ij, j = 1 to m, is transformed into a fuzzy set f_{ij} using triangular membership function represented as

$$\left(\frac{f_{ij1}}{Z_{j1}} + \frac{f_{ij2}}{Z_{j2}} + \ldots\ldots + \frac{f_{ijl}}{Z_{jl}}\right) \tag{4}$$

where Z_{jk} is the kth fuzzy region of item I_j. f_{ijk} is V_{ij} 's fuzzy membership value in region Z_{jk}, and l is the number of fuzzy regions for I_j.

Rule Generation

The count of each attribute region Z_{jk} is given as

$$\text{count}_{jk} = \sum_{i=1}^{n} f_{ijk} \tag{5}$$

For each item, the region with maximum count is used to represent it for further mining. Let $Maxcount_j = \text{MAX}_{K=1}^{l}(\text{count}_{jk})$, for j= 1 to m, where l is the number of fuzzy regions for Ij. If $Maxcount_j$ is equal to or greater than predefined minimum support value S, put it in the set of large 1-itemsets (L1).

The L1 itemset is joined to form Candidate itemset C2 in the way similar to Apriori algorithm. Consider the dataset given in Table 1. The dataset is fuzzified using triangular membership function in equation (6) into three regions z, o, b as shown in the Figure 1. The fuzzified data is shown in Table 2.

$$\mu = Max \left(Min \left(\frac{x-a}{b-a}, \frac{c-x}{c-b} \right), 0 \right) \tag{6}$$

where a is the left end of the triangle, b is the peak of the triangle and c is the right end of the triangle (values are the corresponding x axis values).

Do the following sub steps for each newly formed r +1 item sets with items (I1, I2,. . . Ir+1) in the candidate set Cr+1:

1.   Calculate the fuzzy value of each transaction data T_i as

$$f_{iz} = f_{iz_1} , f_{iz_2} , \dots, f_{iz_{r+1}} \tag{7}$$

Where f_{izj} is the membership value of T_i in region Zj. The intersection of the items in the item set is found using the minimum operator. This represent the combined support of the items in the itemset for each Ti.

$$f_{iz} = \min_{j=1}^{r+1} f_{izj} \tag{8}$$

Table 1. A sample dataset

T	A0	A1	A2	A3	A4
T1	5	1	1	1	2
T2	1	4	4	5	7
T3	3	1	1	1	2
T4	8	8	8	1	3
T5	0	1	1	3	2

Figure 1. Triangular membership function

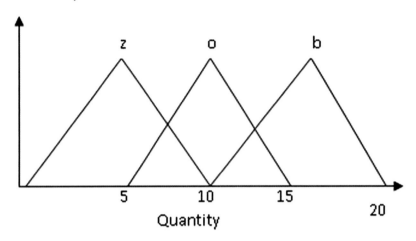

2. The sum of the combined support of each transaction data Ti is found as:

$$count_i = \sum_{i=1}^{n} f_{iz}$$

3. If counti is greater or equal to the pre-defined minimum support value S, put I in Lr+1.

Frequent items are identified using Apriori algorithm based on min support and rules are generated based on minimum confidence. Calculate the support count of each attribute region on the transaction data by summing up the fuzzy values of all the transactions in the fuzzified transaction data as in Table 2. Check whether the count of each attribute is greater than or equal to the predefined minimum support value. If an attribute satisfies the above condition, put it in the set of large-2 itemsets (L_2). Consider the minimum support to 2.0 and minimum confidence to 85%. The regions A0z, A3z and A4z have their support value greater than minimum support, so are considered in forming the rules and finding the corresponding confidence value. The rules can be A0z→A4z, A0z→A3z, A4z→A3z, A4z→A0z, A3z→A0z, A3z→A4z. Interesting rules are the rules for which the confidence value is greater than or equal to minimum confidence value. For each two large itemsets, based on user specified minimum confidence value, rules are extracted. The confidence of a rule A→B is computed as follows:

$$\text{Confidence (A→B)} = \frac{\text{Support}\left(AB\right)}{\text{Support}\left(A\right)} \qquad (9)$$

Only interesting rules that is sensitive needs to be hidden. From the above rules, one of the interesting rules is A3z→A0z, since the confidence of the given rule is Confidence (A3z→A0z) = 2.2 / 2.2 = 100% which is greater than minimum confidence. The fuzzy values of the attributes A3z, A0z are shown in table 3. If this rule is considered as sensitive, then its confidence has to be reduced below the threshold confidence.

Clustering

To hide a rule $A \Rightarrow B$, only the transaction values of the items in the rule to be hidden are considered and these transactions are clustered using K-Means clustering. Euclidean distance is used as the distance metric, and the distance between two transactions T_i and T_j is defined as given in Equation (10)

$$d\left(T_i, T_j\right) = \sqrt{\sum_{k=1}^{m}\left(T_{ik} - T_{jk}\right)} \tag{10}$$

where k is the number of items present in the transaction. $\sqrt{\sum_{k=1}^{n}\left(I_{ik} - I_{jk}\right)}$ A Cluster $C = \{ T_1, T_{2,\ldots} T_n \}$ is a set of transactions and the center of the cluster Cg is defined as

$$C_g = \frac{1}{n}\sum_{i=1}^{n} T_i \tag{11}$$

Table 2. Fuzzified dataset

T	A0			A1			A2			A3			A4		
N	A0z	A0o	A0b	A1z	A1o	A1b	A2z	A2o	A2b	A3z	A3o	A3b	A4z	A4o	A4b
T1	1.0	0.0	0.0	0.2	0.0	0.0	0.2	0.0	0.0	0.2	0.0	0.0	0.4	0.0	0.0
T2	1.0	0.0	0.0	0.8	0.0	0.0	0.8	0.0	0.0	1.0	0.0	0.0	0.6	0.4	0.0
T3	0.6	0.0	0.0	0.2	0.0	0.0	0.2	0.0	0.0	0.2	0.0	0.0	0.4	0.0	0.0
T4	0.8	0.2	0.0	0.4	0.6	0.0	0.4	0.6	0.0	0.2	0.0	0.0	0.6	0.0	0.0
T5	0.8	0.0	0.0	0.2	0.0	0.0	0.2	0.0	0.0	0.6	0.0	0.0	0.4	0.0	0.0
count	4.2	0.2	0.0	1.8	0.6	0.0	1.8	0.6	0.0	2.2	0.0	0.0	2.4	0.4	0.0

Table 3. Fuzzy values of A3z and A0z

Transaction	A3z	A0z	Support
T1	0.2	1.0	0.2
T2	1.0	1.0	1.0
T3	0.2	0.6	0.2
T4	0.2	0.8	0.2
T5	0.6	0.8	0.6
Count	2.2	4.2	2.2

Algorithm of K-Means clustering is as follows:

Step 1: Input k the number of clusters to be formed.
Step 2: Initially find means for k cluster centers.
Step 3: Find Euclidean distance between transaction and cluster center using Equation (10)
Step 4: Each transaction is put into a cluster for which the distance between the transaction and corresponding cluster's mean is minimum.
Step 5: Calculate new mean for each cluster as transactions may be added or removed from the cluster using Equation (11).
Step 6: Steps 3, 4, 5 are repeated until two iterations have the same result. From the clusters formed identify the local best positions for PSO.

Particle Swarm Optimization

In PSO, the current position of each particle stands for one possible solution. So each transaction in the database is represented as particles. Therefore, a swarm represents a number of candidate solutions for perturbation. Each particle is represented as a vector $V_i = (I_1, I_2, I_3, \ldots I_m)$, where I_i represents the ith item and m is the number of items. Each particle in the swarm has its own position and velocity. Each particle movement is bound by its velocity. The term v (t+1) represents the new velocity of the particle t. The particle's new position in every generation is computed by adding the particle's current velocity v (t+1) to its position x (t) using Equation (12) and Equation (13) (Kennedy & Eberhart, 1995) and thus the velocity of the particle is updated.

$$v\left(t+1\right) = w*v\left(t\right) + c_1*rand_1*\left(lbest\left[\ \right] - x\left(t\right)\right) + c_2*rand_2*\left(gbest\left[\ \right]\right) - x\left(t\right)) \qquad (12)$$

$$x\left(t+1\right) = x\left(t\right) + v\left(t+1\right) \qquad (13)$$

where t is the generation number, v is the velocity of the particle, w is the weight, c_1 and c_2 are the acceleration coefficients, rand is the random number and x is the fitness value. Each particle stores the personal and global best position in the search space. The personal best position of ith particle is the best position the particle has visited until the current time and is denoted as $lbest_i(t)$. Let f be the objective function, the personal best of the particle at time t is updated using Equation (14).

$$lbest_i(t+1) = \begin{cases} lbest_i(t) & if & f(x_i(t+1) \leq f(lbest_i(t)) \\ x_i(t+1) & if & f(x_i(t+1) > f(lbest_i(t)) \end{cases} \qquad (14)$$

The global best solution is represented as gbest. For the gbest, the personal best that is best among all the particle in the entire swarm is chosen which is updated based on the best known position of the swarm using Equation (15).

$$gbest(t) \in \left\{ lbest_0, lbest_1, ...lbest_k \right\} = \min \left\{ f(lbest_0(t), ...lbest_k(t) \right\} \tag{15}$$

In Equation (12), the random values $rand_1$ and $rand_2$ are used for an extensive search. The factor w represents the inertia random value. The values of c_1 and c_2 specifies the weight that decide the particle's next movement. The PSO algorithm needs an objective function to evaluate each particle performance which is given as

$$\text{Objective function } X_i\left(t\right) = min\left(TL_i, TR_i\right) \tag{16}$$

where TL is the Left Hand Side of the rule and TR is the Right Hand Side of the rule and i is the transaction number.

The steps of the PSO algorithm are as follows:

Step 1: Randomly initialize the particle velocity and particle position. The K cluster centroids are selected and particles are clustered around these centroids.
Step 2: Evaluate the fitness for each particle in each cluster. Compute the confidence of the sensitive rule. If the confidence of sensitive rule less is than minimum confidence, then break, else continue.
Step 3: Find lbest = min ($x_{ij}\left(t\right)$) where i is the ith particle and j is the jth cluster. Gbest is found using Equation 15.
Step 4: Each particle's new velocity is found using Equation 12 and their positions are updated using Equation 13.

Sensitive rules are obtained from the user. The transaction data of attributes that appear in the sensitive rules is extracted and clustered. Then PSO is applied to hide the sensitive rules where each transaction is considered as a particle. For each particle fitness function is evaluated as given in Equation (16).

The lbest particle with a minimum fitness value in a cluster is identified in each cluster. The lbest particle is the particle with minimum fitness value in a cluster. The gbest value is the best of lbest value of the swarm. The velocity of each particle is calculated using Equation 12 and the position of each particle is updated using Equation 13. After updating the position of the particle, check the confidence of the rule. If the confidence of the rule is not less than the minimum confidence, modified transactions are taken to the next generation. This process is repeated until the sensitive rule is hidden.

Abbreviations used in the proposed algorithm are given as follows:

- D: Original database
- F: Fuzzified database
- f: Fuzzy items in databasc
- r_i: Rule
- $R_{h:}$ Sensitive rules
- csr: count of sensitive rules
- LHS: Left Hand Side of the rule
- RHS: Right Hand Side of the rule
- TL: Transactions belong to LHS item of the rule

- TR: Transactions belong to RHS item of the rule
- Curr_iter: Current iteration
- D': Sanitized database
- C: Number of cluster
- Nog: Number of Generations
- t: Generation number
- v: Velocity of the particle
- w: Weight
- c1, c2: the acceleration coefficients,
- rand: the random number
- X: Fitness value.

Input:

1. The original database D
2. Minimum support value (min_support)
3. Minimum confidence value (min_confidence)
4. Set of sensitive rules to hide (R_h)

Output:
The sanitized database D' so that R_h cannot be mined

Algorithm PSO-FSH

```
1.       Start
2.       Call FRM() // from chapter 3
3.       Get the sensitive rules Rₕ from user
4.       ∀ sr_i in Rₕ            where i = 1 to csr
5.       Read C
6.       Cluster the transactions in F    //using K-means clustering
7.       Compute β (sr_i)
8.       Curr_iter = 0;
     REPEAT UNTIL β (sr_i)>  δ and curr_iter < NoG THEN
        ∀C_i ∈ C
            lbest=  minimum (X(t))
               // X_i(t) =min (TL_i,TR_i), i = number of particles in the
cluster.
          gbest = minimum(lbest)
        ∀C_i, P_i ∈ C,
          v_i (t+1) = w * v(t) + c1 * rand1 * (lbest - X(t)) + c2* rand2 *
(gbest - X(t))
             //Update the position of the particle
```

```
IF  TL_i ≤  TR_i  THEN
        TL_i = TL_i + v_i  (t+1)
                    ELSE
                        TR_i = TR_i + v_i  (t+1)
            END IF
              Compute β  ( sr_i )
            IF β  ( sr_i ) <   δ
                Break
            Curr_iter = curr_iter+1;
    END REPEAT
9.        Transform updated database F to D' and return D'
10.       End
```

Fuzzification causes some transactions of sensitive item to have zero membership in the corresponding fuzzy region that has support above the minimum support. Since the objective is a minimization function that is, decreasing the support of sensitive items, these values with zero membership will be the lbest in the clusters they belong. As gbest is the best of lbest, even the lbest with higher values tend to move towards zero value. This results in the movement of all the particles having value greater than zero towards the corresponding lbest and consequently towards the gbest resulting in more number of modifications to the original data. Consequence of this movement is the generation of more number of lost rules.

Hybrid PSO-GA Technique for Hiding Fuzzy Sensitive Rules

PSO-FSH has 0% hiding failure and does not generate any false knowledge. But its performance with respect to lost rule generation and data quality is less significant when compared with GA-FSH (Sathiyapriya, Sudha. & Karthikeyan, 2012). This is due to the objective function which is the minimum of LHS and RHS of the rule. If for any particle, this value is zero, then it results in premature convergence. To prevent the premature convergence, position of the global best particles is changed. The position update is done through hybrid mechanism with GA. The idea behind GA is its genetic operators crossover and mutation. The crossover operation allows two particles to exchange information and enables them to move to new search area. Applying mutation to gbest particle in PSO increases the range of the population and helps to circumvent the local minima. So in order to improve the performance of PSO-FSH, Hybrid PSO-GA FSH is proposed. In order to avoid zero value of lbest and gbest, crossover is applied on lbest if it is zero and mutation is executed on gbest if it has zero value.

Abbreviations used in the proposed algorithm are given as follows:

- D: Original database
- F: Fuzzified database
- f: Fuzzy items in database
- r_i: Rule
- R_h: Sensitive rules
- Csr:count of sensitive rules

- LHS: Left Hand Side of the rule
- RHS: Right Hand Side of the rule
- TL: Transactions belong to LHS item of the rule
- TR: Transactions belong to RHS item of the rule
- D': Sanitized database
- Curr_iter: Current iteration
- C: Number of cluster
- Nog: Number of Generations
- T: Generation number
- v:Velocity of the particle
- w: Weight
- c1, c2: the acceleration coefficients,
- rand: the random number
- X: Fitness value.
- x_{ij} :jth fuzzy item in ith particle

Input:

1. The original database D
2. Minimum support value (min_support)
3. Minimum confidence value (min_confidence)
4. Set of sensitive rules to hide (R_h)

Output:
The sanitized database D' so that R_h cannot be mined

Algorithm PSO-GA-FSH

```
1.         Start
2.         Call FRM() // from chapter 3
3.         Get the sensitive rules Rₕ from user
4.         ∀ srᵢ in Rₕ            where i = 1 to csr
5.         Read C
6.         Cluster the transactions in F     //using K-means clustering
7.         Compute β ( srᵢ)
8.         Curr_iter = 0;
        REPEAT UNTIL β ( srᵢ)> δ and curr_iter < NoG THEN
          ∀Cᵢ ∈ C
            lbest=  minimum (X(t) )
```

$$X_i\left(t\right) = \sum_{j=1}^{n}\frac{x_{ij}}{\alpha\left(f_j\right)}, \quad i = \text{number of particles in the cluster.}$$

```
            gbest = minimum(lbest)
```

```
            IF lbest = 0 then
                    Choose parent using roulette wheel selection
                Perform crossover
                go to step 8
        IF gbest = 0 then
                    Perform mutation
                    go to step 8
```

$\forall C_{i,} P_i \in C,$

```
v (t+1) = w * v(t) + c1 * rand1 * (lbest - X(t)) + c2* rand2 * (gbest - X(t))
 i
            //Update the position of the particle
```

IF $TL_i \le TR_i$ THEN

$\qquad TL_i = TL_i + v_i$ (t+1)

```
                ELSE
```

$\qquad\qquad TR_i = TR_i + v_i$ (t+1)

```
            END IF
              Compute β (
```
sr_i
```
)
            IF β (
```
sr_i
```
) <   δ
                Break
            Curr_iter = curr_iter+1;
        END REPEAT
    9. Transform updated database F to D' and return D'
    10. End
```

4. EXPERIMENTAL RESULTS AND DISCUSSION

The proposed techniques are tested using the Breast cancer dataset taken from University of California at Irvine Repository (UCI Repository) (Lichman, 2013) and the traffic accidents dataset obtained from the National Institute of Statistics (NIS) in the region of Flanders (Belgium) for the period 1991-2000 (Geurts, 2003). The experiments were carried out on a PC with Intel core i5 processor with a clock rate of 2.67 GHz and 8 GB of main memory.

Parameters Used to Evaluate the Performance

Let D be the transactional database and R be the set of interesting fuzzy association rules mined from the database D under given threshold association measure. Let R_h be the set of sensitive rules to be hidden and R_n the set of non-sensitive rules mined from D then $R_h \cup R_n = R$. R' is the set of rules mined from sanitized database D'.

The proposed fuzzy association rule hiding methods are evaluated using the following parameters.

1. **Number of Lost Rules:** A lost rule is a non-sensitive association rule that can be discovered from the original database but cannot be mined from the released database.

$$\left\{ lost\ Rule\ q | q \in R_n \cap q \notin R' \right\}$$

2. **Number of Ghost Rules:** A ghost rule is a non-sensitive association rule that cannot be discovered from the original database but can be mined from the released database.

$$\left\{ Ghost\ Rule\ q | q \in R' \cap q \notin R \right\}$$

3. **Hiding Failure:** A false rule is a sensitive association rule that cannot be hidden by hiding process. Number of false rules denotes the hiding failure.

$$\left\{ False\ Rule\ q | q \in R_h \cap q \in R' \right\}$$

4. **Percentage of Modification:** Percentage of modification refers to the distortions to the total data items in the original database expressed in percentage.

$$\text{Percentage of modification} = \frac{D - D'}{D} \times 100$$

5. **Execution Time:** Execution time also called "running time" is the length of time required to implement hiding algorithm.

Lost Rules

Table 4 and Table 5 show the number of rules lost when PSO-FSH and Hybrid PSO-GA FSH are applied on breast cancer dataset and traffic accidents dataset respectively for hiding three ($R_h = 3$) and five rules ($R_h = 5$).

In PSO-FSH 18% and 21% of interesting rules are lost while hiding three and five rules respectively in breast cancer dataset. It has also recorded 20% and 24% of lost rules for hiding three and five rules

Table 4. Number of rules lost in breast cancer dataset

Minimum Confidence in %	Breast Cancer Dataset			
	$R_h = 3$		$R_h = 5$	
	PSO- FSH	PSO-GA-FSH	PSO- FSH	PSO- GA-FSH
20	31	28	36	33
30	27	24	33	28
40	22	21	24	21
50	16	13	17	13
60	10	10	11	9

Table 5. Number of rules lost in traffic accidents dataset

Minimum Confidence in %	Traffic Accidents Dataset			
	$R_h = 3$		$R_h = 5$	
	PSO- FSH	PSO-GA-FSH	PSO- FSH	PSO-GA-FSH
20	321	260	382	291
30	280	252	336	280
40	201	171	265	204
50	176	146	224	165
60	151	94	173	128

respectively in accidents dataset. The number of rules lost is higher in PSO-FSH as more number of particles move towards global minimum.

With hybrid PSO-GA FSH, 16% and 18% of interesting non sensitive rules are lost as a side effect of hiding three sensitive and five sensitive rules respectively, when the algorithm is tested with breast cancer dataset. When tested with accidents dataset, it results in 17% and 20% of interesting rules being lost while hiding three and five rules respectively. When comparing the results with PSO based approach, hybrid PSO-GA approach reduced the number of lost rules by 3% on an average.

Ghost Rules

Table 6 and Table 7 show the side effect of hiding sensitive rules in terms of ghost rules generated under different confidence setting for breast cancer and accidents dataset respectively for hiding three ($R_h = 3$) and five rules ($R_h = 5$).

PSO-FSH does not generate any ghost rule for hiding three and five rules in both the datasets. As fuzzification of dataset generates zero membership for some items in the chosen fuzzy region, this zero value will become the lbest for the cluster to which the item belongs. Consequently this value will be the gbest and all the particles tend to move towards it. As a result support of all items tends to decrease. Ghost rules are generated only when the support of some items increase as a side effect of sanitization. So no ghost rules are generated in PSO-FSH.

Table 6. Number of ghost rules generated in breast cancer dataset

Minimum Confidence in %	Breast Cancer Dataset			
	$R_h = 3$		$R_h = 5$	
	PSO- FSH	PSO-GA-FSH	PSO- FSH	PSO-GA-FSH
20	0	10	0	12
30	0	8	0	8
40	0	7	0	7
50	0	7	0	6
60	0	5	0	3

Table 7. Number of ghost rules generated in traffic accidents dataset

Minimum Confidence in %	Traffic Accidents Dataset			
	$R_h = 3$		$R_h = 5$	
	PSO- FSH	PSO-GA-FSH	PSO- FSH	PSO-GA-FSH
20	0	91	0	123
30	0	70	0	98
40	0	63	0	84
50	0	49	0	68
60	0	45	0	59

Hybrid PSO-GA generated 5% and 6% ghost rules while hiding three and five sensitive rules in breast cancer dataset and 6% and 8% ghost rules while hiding the said rules in accidents dataset. The ghost rule generated was increased by 6% on an average in hybrid PSO-GA approach when compared with PSO approach and decreased by an average of 2% when compared with GA approach. In hybrid PSO-GA approach crossover operation is applied to lbest particle with the fitness value of zero and mutation is applied to gbest particle with fitness value of zero, thus avoiding movement of all the particles towards this value.

Percentage of Modification

In PSO, the movement of the particles with values greater than zero towards global best (zero) results in more modification to the original data, which can be observed in Figure 2. The percentage of modification to the original dataset is less in hybrid PSO-GA technique when compared to PSO-FSH technique as evident in Figure 2. Consequently, the number of lost rules in hybrid PSO-GA FSH is less than in PSO-FSH technique but the application of crossover and mutation operators to the particles result in generation of ghost rules.

Hiding Failure

PSO-FSH does not show any hiding failure. PSO –FSH is efficient with respect to hiding failure and ghost rule generation as it completely avoids ghost rule generation with 0% hiding failure. *PSO -GA-FSH has 0% hiding failure* like PSO-FSH.

Execution Time

Figure 3 and Figure 4 shows the execution time required to hide sensitive rules for various minimum confidence thresholds for breast cancer dataset and traffic accidents dataset respectively.

The running time of PSO-GA is almost same as PSO with a marginal increase of 3 seconds on an average when compared to PSO approach.

Figure 2. Percentage of entries modified due to sanitization

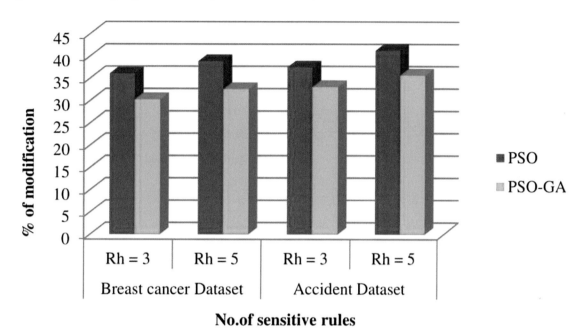

Figure 3. Execution time for breast cancer dataset

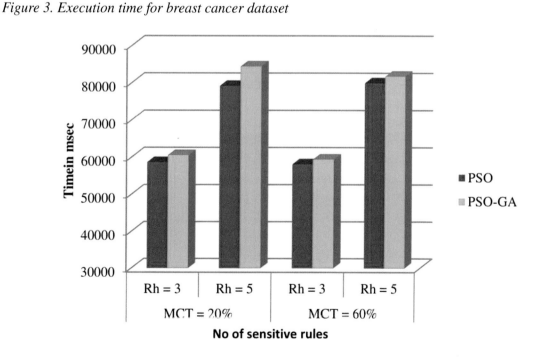

Figure 4. Execution time for traffic accidents dataset

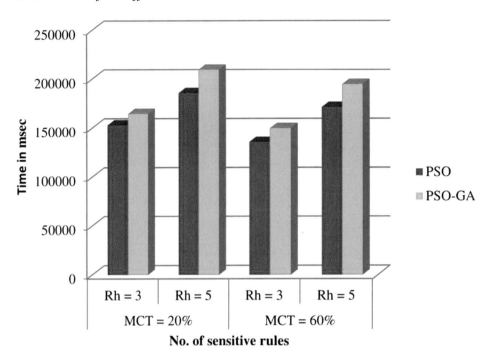

5. CONCLUSION

This paper analyzed the performance of particle swarm optimization and Hybrid PSO- GA for hiding sensitive fuzzy association rules. PSO approach was proposed in which all the particles would move towards the particle with smallest fuzzy value between LHS and RHS items in the sensitive rule. This movement of the particles helped to achieve 0% hiding failure and ghost rules but increased the data distortion by 12% and consequently lost rules by 6%. In PSO technique, the minimum value among the RHS and LHS items of the rule is set as objective value for the corresponding particle. If a particle in a cluster has zero as its objective value, then this particle becomes the lbest for the corresponding cluster and consequently becomes gbest. The movement of all the particles towards this value result in increase in data distortion.

In order to get the benefit of both GA and PSO approach, hybrid PSO-GA FSH algorithm was proposed if any lbest has zero value for fitness then cross over operation is applied on it and mutation was applied on gbest particle. The experimental results showed that lost rules were reduced by 3% and data distortion were reduced by 5% when compared with PSO approach. The ghost rule generation increases to 6% in hybrid approach when compared to 0% in PSO-FSH. Hybrid PSO-GA also does not have hiding failure. Thus hybrid PSO-GA FSH provided better performance when compared with PSO-FSH. In future, this work can be extended for distributed databases and a new objective function can be designed so that the number of modifications can be reduced further.

REFERENCES

Abdullah, Z., Herawan, T., Noraziah, A., & Deris, M. M. (2014). A scalable algorithm for constructing Frequnt pattern Tree. *International Journal of Intelligent Information Technologies, 10*(1), 42–56. doi:10.4018/ijiit.2014010103

Anbumani, K., & Nedunchezhian, R. (2006). Rapid Privacy preserving algorithms for large databases. *International Journal of Intelligent Information Technologies, 2*(1), 68–81. doi:10.4018/jiit.2006010104

Ashrafi, M. Z., Taniar, D., & Smith, K. (2005). PPDAM: Privacy Preserving Distributed Association Rule - Mining Algorithm. *International Journal of Intelligent Information Technologies, 1*(1), 49–69. doi:10.4018/jiit.2005010104

Berberoglu, T., & Kaya, M. (2008), Hiding Fuzzy Association Rules in Quantitative Data. *The 3rd International Conference on Grid and Pervasive Computing – Workshops,* 387-392.

Bonam, J., Reddy, A. R., & Kalyani, G. (2014), Privacy Preserving in Association Rule Mining by Data Distortion Using PSO, ICT and Critical Infrastructure. In *Proceedings of the 48th Annual Convention of Computer Society of India.* Springer International Publishing.

Cai, C. H., Fu, W. C., Cheng, C. H., & Kwong, W. W. (1998). Mining association rules with weighted items. *Proceedings of the International Database Engineering and Applications Symposium,* 68–77.

Cheng, P., & Shyang, J. (2014), Completely Hide Sensitive Association Rules using EMO by Deleting Transactions. *Proceedings 2014 Annual Conference on Genetic and Evolutionary Computation,* 167-168.

Dehkordi, M. N., Badie, K., & Zadeh, A. K. (2009). A Novel Method for Privacy Preserving in Association Rule Mining Based on Genetic Algorithms. *Journal of Software, 4*(6), 555–562. doi:10.4304/jsw.4.6.555-562

Duraiswamy, K., Manjula, D., & Maheswari, N. (2010). A New Approach to Sensitive Rule Hiding. *CCSENET Journal, 1*(3), 107-111.

Evfimievski, A. (2002). Randomization in privacy preserving data mining. *ACM SIGKDD Explorations Newsletter, 4*(2), 43–48. doi:10.1145/772862.772869

Evfimievski, A., Srikant, R., Agrawal, R., & Gehrke, J. (2002). Privacy preserving mining of association rules. *8th ACM SIGKDD International Conference on Knowledge Discovery and Data Mining,* 217–228.

Frank, A., & Asuncion, A. (2010). *UCI Machine Learning Repository.* Irvine, CA: University of California, School of Information and Computer Science.

Geurts, K., Wets, G., Brijs, T., & Vanhoof, K. (2003). Profiling High Frequency Accident Locations Using Association Rules. *Electronic Proceedings of the 82th Annual Meeting of the Transportation Research Board,* 18.

Giannotti, F., Lakshmanan, L., Monreale, A., Pedreschi, D., & Wang, H. (2013). Privacy-preserving mining of association rules from outsourced transaction databases. *IEEE Systems Journal, 7*(3), 385–395. doi:10.1109/JSYST.2012.2221854

Guo, Y. (2007). Reconstruction-Based Association Rule Hiding. *Proceedings of SIGMOD2007 Ph.D. Workshop on Innovative Database Research 2007*, 51-56.

Gupta, M., & Joshi, R. C. (2009). Privacy Preserving Fuzzy Association Rules in Quantitative Data. *International Journal of Computer Theory and Engineering*, *1*(4), 382–388. doi:10.7763/IJCTE.2009.V1.60

Han, J., & Fu, Y. (1995). Discovery of multiple-level association rules from large database. *Proceedings of the 21st International Conference on Very Large Data Bases*, 420–431.

Hong, T. P., Kuo, C. S., & Chi, S. C. (1999). Mining association rules from quantitative data. *Intelligent Data Analysis*, *3*(5), 363–376. doi:10.1016/S1088-467X(99)00028-1

Kargupta, H., Datta, S., Wang, Q., & Sivakumar, K. (2003). On the privacy preserving properties of random data perturbation techniques. *3rd Int'l Conference on Data Mining*, 99–106. 10.1109/ICDM.2003.1250908

Kennedy, J., & Eberhart, R. (1995). Particle Swarm Optimization. *Proceedings of IEEE Conference on Neural Networks*, *4*, 1942 – 1948.

Khan, A., Qureshi, M. S., & Hussain, A. (2014). Improved Genetic Algorithm Approach for Sensitive Association Rules Hiding. *World Applied Sciences Journal*, *31*(12), 2087–2092.

Krishnamoorthy, S., Sadasivam, S., Rajalakshmi, M., Kowsalyaa, K., & Dhivya, M. (2017). Privacy Preserving Fuzzy Association Rule Mining in Data Clusters Using Particle Swarm Optimization. *International Journal of Intelligent Information Technologies*, *13*(2), 1–20. doi:10.4018/IJIIT.2017040101

Lichman, M. (2013). *UCI Machine Learning Repository*. Irvine, CA: University of California, School of Information and Computer Science.

Narmadha, S., & Vijayarani, S. (2011). Protecting sensitive association rules in privacy preserving data mining using genetic algorithms. *International Journal of Computers and Applications*, *33*(7), 37–34.

Rajalakshmi, M., Purusothaman, T., & Pratheeba, S. (2010). Collusion free privacy preserving Data Mining. *International Journal of Intelligent Information Technologies*, *6*(4), 30–45. doi:10.4018/jiit.2010100103

Renjit, K., & Shunmuganathan, K. (2010). Mining the data from distributed database using an improved mining algorithm. *International Journal of Computer Science and Information Security*, *7*(3), 116–121.

Sathiyapriya, K., Sudha, G., & Karthikeyan, V.B. (2012). A New Method for Preserving Privacy in Quantitative Association Rules using Genetic Algorithm. *International Journal of Computer Applications, 60*(12), 12-19.

Sathiyapriya, K., & Sudha Sadasivam, G. (2016). Hybrid Evolutionary Algorithm for Preserving Privacy of sensitive data in Quantitative Databases. *Journal of Scientific and Industrial Research*, *75*(7), 399–403.

Sathiyapriya, K., Sudhasadasivam, G., & Celin, N. (2011). A New Method for preserving privacy in Quantitative Association Rules Using DSR Approach with Automated Generation of Membership Function. *Proceedings of World Congress on Information and Communication Technologies*, 48-153.

Sathiyapriya, K., Sudhasadasivam, G., & Suganya, C. J. P. (2014). Hiding Sensitive Fuzzy Association rules Using Weighted Item Grouping and Rank Based Correlated Rule Hiding Algorithm. *WSEAS Transactions on Computers*, *13*, 78–89.

Saygin, Y., Verykios, V., & Clifton, C. (2001). Using Unknowns to Prevent Discovery of Association Rules. *SIGMOD Record*, *30*(4), 45–54. doi:10.1145/604264.604271

Shah, R. A., & Asghar, S. (2014). Privacy preserving in association rules using genetic algorithm. *Turkish Journal of Electrical Engineering and Computer Sciences*, *22*(2), 434–450. doi:10.3906/elk-1206-66

Srikant, R., & Agrawal, R. (1995). Mining generalized association rules. *Proceedings of the 21st International Conference on Very Large Data Bases*, 407–419.

Srikant, R., & Agrawal, R. (1996). Mining Quantitative Association Rules in Large Relational Tables. *Proceedings of the ACM SIGMOD International Conference on Management of Data*, 1-12. 10.1145/233269.233311

Sudha, G., Sangeetha, S., & Sathiyapriya, K., (2012). Privacy Preservation with Attribute Reduction in Quantitative Association Rules using PSO and DSR. *International Journal of Computer Applications*, 19-30.

Verykios, V., Elmagarmid, A. K., Bertino, E., Saygin, Y., & Dasseni, E. (2004). Hiding Sensitive Association Rule using Heuristic Approach. *IEEE Transactions on Knowledge and Data Engineering*, *16*(4), 434–447. doi:10.1109/TKDE.2004.1269668

Wang, S. L., & Jafari, A. (2005). Using unknowns for hiding sensitive predictive association rules. *Proceedings of the 2005 IEEE International Conference on Information Reuse and Integration (IRI 2005)*, 223–228. 10.1109/IRI-05.2005.1506477

Wang, S. L., Parikh, B., & Jafari, A. (2007, August). Hiding Sensitive Association Rules without Altering the Support of Sensitive Item. *Expert Systems with Applications*, *33*(2), 316–323. doi:10.1016/j.eswa.2006.05.022

Weng, C. C., Chen, S. T., & Chang, Y. C. (2007). A Novel Algorithm for Completely Hiding Sensitive Frequent Itemset. *Proceedings of the eighth International Symposium on Advanced Intelligent Systems*, 753-757.

Weng, C. C., Chen, S. T., & Lo, H. C. (2008). A Novel Algorithm for Completely Hiding Sensitive Association Rules. *Eighth International Conference on Intelligent Systems Design and Applications*, *3*, 202-208. 10.1109/ISDA.2008.180

Wu, Y. H., Chiang, C. M., & Chen, A. L. P. (2007). Hiding Sensitive Association Rules with Limited Side Effects. *IEEE Transactions on Knowledge and Data Engineering*, *19*(1), 29–42. doi:10.1109/TKDE.2007.250583

Yang, Z., Zhong, S., & Wright, R. N. (2005). Privacy-Preserving Classification of Customer Data without Loss of Accuracy. *Proceedings of the Fifth SIAM International Conference on Data Mining*, 92-102. 10.1137/1.9781611972757.9

Yao, A. C. (1986). How to generate and exchange secrets. *27th IEEE Symposium on Foundations of Computer Science*, 162–167.

Yi, X., & Zhang, Y. (2007). Privacy-preserving distributed association rule mining via semi-trusted mixer. *Data & Knowledge Engineering*, *63*(2), 550–567. doi:10.1016/j.datak.2007.04.001

Zadeh, L. A. (1965). Fuzzy Sets. *Information and Control*, *8*(3), 338–353. doi:10.1016/S0019-9958(65)90241-X

Zhang, N., Li, M., & Lou, W. (2011). Distributed data mining with differential privacy. *Proceedings of the IEEE International Conference on Communications (ICC)*, 1.

Chapter 10
Modeling Fish Population Dynamics for Sustainability and Resilience

Nayem Rahman
Portland State University, USA

Mahmud Ullah
University of Dhaka, Bangladesh

ABSTRACT

Conservation of any living creature is very vital to maintain the balance of ecosystem. Fish is one of the most regularly consumed living creatures, and hence its conservation is essential for sustainable fish population to help maintain a balanced ecosystem. It is possible to keep a sustainable fish population only if a balance between consumption and growth of fish population can be ensured. Developing a model on fish population dynamics is needed to achieve this objective. In this chapter, the authors present a system dynamics model. This model will provide the scientific tools for determining fish population, its growth, and harvesting. The model's sensitivity to changes in key parameters and initial values resulting from the changes in basic scenarios and boundary conditions was tested several times. Model results show that fish birth, growth, stocks, and catch can be controlled timely and effectively in different real-world changing conditions to maintain a sustainable fish population.

INTRODUCTION

Fish and fisheries provides basic food supplies and make essential contributions to human well-being. This resource needs to be maintained judiciously. If not sufficiently controlled and managed that might cause extinction of fish population and lead to damage to the ecosystem (Cochrane & Garcia, 2009). This speaks for developing a mechanism to maintain a sustainable fish population. Sustainability is an import filed of studies in our time from the standpoint of business, ecological, economic and social, to name a few. In all aspects of human activities sustainability considerations need to be made to make sure living things and human civilization is not in danger. Maintaining an ecological balance is imperative. So,

DOI: 10.4018/978-1-5225-5396-0.ch010

governments, policy makers, scientists and general public need to make adequate measure individually and collectively to ensure sustainability. This paper deals with fish population ecological balance and sustainability. The goal here is to see how we can simulate fish population growth and maintain a balance.

Systems modeling is an extremely powerful technique that easily lends itself as a tool to understand the complexity found in scientific and business world today. It allows us to understand the reason for certain behavior of a system and how it might change over a period of time. Models enable to see how a real-world activity will perform under different conditions and test various hypotheses at a fraction of the cost of performing the actual activity (Laguna & Markland, 2005). Finding the behavior of certain activity through real world scenarios might take longer time and by that time it might be difficult or impossible to make correction or take correct course of action. System dynamics modeling have been applied in different areas. Now a days, the dynamics of a project management risk is evaluated through the approaches of systems dynamics. Simulation is quite often used in performance improvement of a new technology or finding design flaws of a complex technology.

Eliciting and mapping of mental model is always necessary but it is far from sufficient to visualize or address complex real word problems (Sterman, 2000). Mental modeling helps a bit in understanding an activity or user's world to a certain degree. But it is not practical to think through when we need to deal with a lot of constraints as well as data. And sometimes it is even cumbersome to present. The mental models are runnable in which there is a sense of deriving answers via mental simulation rather than logical reasoning (Forbus & Gentner, 1997). With mental model we cannot take into consideration many aspects of a real-world problems. The mental models are dynamically deficient, omitting feedbacks, time delays, accumulations, and nonlinearities (Sterman, 2000). In fact mental modeling does not provide use with all kinds of if-then-else scenario results. Simulation is a practical way to test any model (Lindenmayer et al., 2000; Rahman, 2018a). It provides us with results or behavior of a system without building it. Thus it provides practical feedback during design of a system. Simulation is a running model in order to estimate or project its behavior, either by solving the equations in the case of systems dynamics, or by generating random numbers representing events and decisions in the case of discrete system simulation (Rahman, 2014).

System dynamics is a powerful method to gain useful insight into situations of dynamic complexity (Pruyt, 2006b) and policy resistance. In case of dynamic complexity it gives the architect or decision maker some kind of confidence or assurance that might work. In case of policy resistance it will let stakeholders put an end to differences of opinion and come to a conclusion. It is increasingly used to design more successful policies in companies and public policy settings (Sterman, 2000). In this chapter, we demonstrate a sustainable fish population growth model with help from a system dynamics modeling tool (Vensim, Inc., 2012). With the growth of world population, increasing demand for fish, continuous over-catch of fish, and the waste of natural resources sustainability of fish population is at risk (Rahman, 2014). Industrial revolution has provided human society with enormous capability to manufacture goods and services by virtue of machineries and equipment. In case of fisheries excessive number of fishing fleets might be one of the reasons for overfishing. In many cases overfishing causes wasting and discarding this valuable God-gifted resource. In its 2015 report, the World Wildlife Fund (WWF) reported that the amount of fish has decreased to fifty percent since 1970 (CBS News, 2015). The WWF also mentioned that the most impacted group of fish includes tuna, mackerel, and bonito, 75% decreased since 1970. Governments, authorities, and regulatory bodies have become concerned about declining fish population in ponds, rivers, and oceans. Nielsen at al. (2017) developed a model for the Northeast Atlantic pelagic fisheries. Their goal is to develop a welfare-optimal value chain toward the management of fisheries. In their research he authors found that to be optimal the number of vessels must be reduced from 156 to 80. In line with real-world problem of fish population decline we make an attempt to come up with a dynamic model to maintain sustainability.

Different aspects of dynamic models for fish population have been investigated by researchers (Hallam et al., 2000; Wakeland et al., 2003; Pruyt, 2006; Flottmann, 2014; Rose et al., 2001). The Population Dynamics and Modeling group of the Southwest Fisheries Science Center conducts different kinds of dynamics model of fish population to understand dynamics of fish populations, stock assessment, sensitivity analysis, and development of population model (NOAA, 2015).

As part of building a dynamic model for fish population growth we take several constraints into consideration. First, there is a carrying capacity, that is, K. Should the population rise above K, population should begin to decline to eventually stay within the maximum capacity limit. Second, the birth and death rates have been specified for the fish population growth model. When a population is near zero, the maximum birth rate would be expected. As population approaches the carrying capacity, the birth rate might fall by a factor of four or five but, never entirely to zero, even in situations where the population exceeds the carrying capacity K. When a population is near zero, the minimum death should be at least 10% of the fish population in any time period. If the population ever exceeds the carrying capacity, the death rate might be expected to be even high, as great as 3-4 times the minimum. The birth rates and death rates are closely linked to population density (N/K) which is the ratio of the total population (N) to the carrying capacity (K). Given the constraints, the 'goal seeking' behavior of fish population growth will be explored. The key idea is to construct a model that employs the concept of population density as a factor that influences both birth and death rates. Goal seeking behavior is a system that is strongly influenced by the presence of one or more goal-seeking feedback loops (Abdelbari & Shafi, 2017).

LITURATURE REVIEW

Simulation consists of several basic steps. They include formulating a problem, requirements analysis, set and specify boundary conditions of the model, design and development of the model, formulate and collect data, validate the model, perform simulation, analyze the performance measures, and evaluate alternative scenarios (Rahman, 2018a; Laguna & Markland, 2005). With the advent of software and computer engineering there are plenty of simulation software available on the market. As a result, dynamic simulation modeling tools (Richardson, 2013; Martinez-Moyano & Richardson, 2013) are being used to measure sustainability of various ecological (Thakker et al., 2013; Rahman, 2016), economic (Pierson & Sterman, 2013; Wyburn & Roach, 2013; Rahman, 2018b), social (Abdel-Hamid, 1989; Onggo, 2012; Black, 2013; Eberlein & Thompson, 2013; Morrison et al., 2013), technological (Rahman, 2016; Jones et al., 2002; Morrison, 2012; Ng et al., 2012; Jammoussi et al., 2013) and natural phenomena (Barker, 2008).

System dynamics approaches have been applied in various disciplines. Celine et al. (2011) examine the economic and business impacts of automating information management in clinical trials in new drug development using system dynamics model. Loebbecke (2011) examines the global system of mobile (GSM) communication using system dynamics to capture the complexity. This is an important real world problem being solved by simulation techniques. Choi et al. (2008) present the impact of potential staffing strategies under various conditions using a system dynamics model. The model provides guidance for staffing decisions. Wyburn and Roach (2013) employ system dynamics model by employing different dynamic hypotheses to analyze the price history of comic book market. Bhushan (2012, 2013) applies systems dynamic model this helps in streamlining the structural complexity of innovation diffusion. Thakker et al. (2013) use a system dynamics approach to quantitatively analyze the effects of mobile broadband ecosystem's variables on demands and allocation of wireless spectrum for the cellular industry. Onggo (2013) present that system dynamics modeling can be used to analyze the dynamics of the social care workforce. Abdelsalam (2012) developed a system dynamic model to simulate the complex multi-channel structure and factors that affect the demand and channel conflict. Pierson and Sterman (2013) developed a cyclical dynamics model of airline industry earnings. All these models speak for use of system dynamic approaches to solve or provide insights on varieties of real world problems.

Sivertson (2018) developed a system dynamics model to make a balance between predator and prey fish population in the Western Lake Superior. The experiments of his model suggest that current high rates of predator stockings need to be reduced by moderately increasing the predator harvesting which will allow for a sustainable population growth and stability of both predator and prey fish population. Hayes et al. (2009) develop a model to determine fish population in terms of birth and death by linking it to fish habitat conditions. Qin et al. (2016) state that fish population stability and sustainability could be impacted by environmental factors of coastal ecosystem. The authors develop a model to determine how environmental factors influence fish population dynamics. Levhari and Mirman (1980) uses a dynamic Cournot-Nash equilibrium model to depict the conflict between fishing regulators and fishing right advocates. This model shows that fish population change is the outcome of the actions taken by both parties. Their model tries to determine a steady-state situation of fish population based on above mentioned parties' interactions. Shelton and Mangel (2011) make attempts to understand to root causes of fish population fluctuations. They came up with three hypotheses including species' interactions, environmental variations, and single-species dynamics. The authors take the single-species and environmental factors into consideration to assess as to how their interaction with human exploitation contributes to fish population variations. They conclude that single-species dynamics are less likely to cause deterministic fluctuations in fish population.

Fishery is an important area from environmental sustainability standpoint. Over the last three decades, awareness of sustainability (Rahman & Akhter, 2010) has increased significantly among government, industry, and the general public. Policymakers worldwide have sought to incorporate sustainability considerations into urban and industrial development (Fiksel, 2006). In the fishery sector, sustainability could be achieved by better managing fish harvesting and stocks (Rahman, 2014).

It is important to explore the possibilities as to how we can prudently use these resources without exceeding limits which cause burdens on Earth's carrying capacity. Economist Herman Daly has offered three simple but practical rules to help define the sustainable limits to material and energy throughput (Meadows et al., 2004): (i) for renewable materials he suggested that sustainable rate of natural resources consumption cannot be greater than the rate it could be regenerated; (ii) in regards to nonrenewable materials the sustainable rate of use cannot be greater than the rate of substitute renewable resources; and (iii) for pollutants, 'the sustainable rate of emission cannot be greater than the rate at which that pollutant can be recycled, absorbed, or rendered harmless in its sink.' Any activity that causes a renewable resources stock to fall, pollution sink to rise and non-renewable resources stock to fall without a renewable replacement insight cannot be sustained (Meadows et al., 2004). This is true for fisheries as well because they use natural resources.

We assert that advances toward sustainability could be achieved by considering system dynamic approaches. In this chapter, we use system dynamics modeling in maintaining a stable fish population. In fishery, system dynamics model (Wakeland et al., 2003) could be used to control fish population growth, fish stocks and catch. We make an attempt to develop a system dynamics model for a sustainable fishery and show that there are opportunities for this technique to achieving sustainability in fishery.

MODELING FISH POPULATION DYNAMICS

A model is a representation of reality which is frequently mathematical. It is used to study a system of interest in order to predict, understand and/or improve its behavior. System dynamics is a method of specifying the modeled system as a set of simultaneous, ordinary differential equations and then simulating the system behavior by numerically integrating those equations. In order to build a system dynamics model, we are making certain simplifying assumptions based on the constraints laid out in the fish population growth scenarios. Time is measured in terms of months. There will be an initial population number which reaches the carrying capacity of a certain number within a total simulation time of a certain number of months. The birth percentage increase is different than the death increase. Also, the birth decrease is different than the death increases. With the population growth the birth fraction decreases while the death fraction decreases. There is an inverse relationship between the birth and death fractions increase and decrease. We put certain hypothetical boundary conditions for population growth model: the birth rate must not be more than 50% even if the population density is near zero and it cannot be less than 10% even if the population density goes above 1. The death fraction cannot be less than 10% even if the population density is near zero.

Population growth should be stable must comply with carrying capacity. However, population should not be static. With all factors changing the population might increase or decrease as long as it complies with the carrying capacity. It will remain a little below or over the carrying capacity. If for some reason, the population exceeds the carrying capacity significantly, some dynamic activity should trigger to reach equilibrium state very fast. A dynamic equilibrium occurs when the flows into storages match the flows out of storages so the values of the storages no longer change. The model implements a feedback loop. The birth and death fractions increase or decrease causes population growth increase or decrease which in turn causes birth and death fractions to change as a result of continuous change of population density.

In system dynamics modeling, all dynamics arise from the interaction of just two types of feedback loops, positive (or self-reinforcing) and negative (or self-correcting) loops. Positive loops tend to reinforce or amplify whatever is happening in the system. Positive loops tend to move the system away from equilibrium position. Negative loops counteract and oppose change (Sterman, 2000). Positive loops are self-reinforcing. Negative loop occurs in response to certain stimulus which causes a decrease in function. In this case, more fish lay more eggs, which hatch and add to the fish population, leading to still more eggs, and so on. Negative loops are self-correcting. They counteract change. As the fish population grows, various negative loops with act to balance the fish population with its carrying capacity (Sterman, 2000).

Based on the model in Figure 1 we have developed some equations to test for these assumptions. For density-dependent birth factors (bf) we have used below equation:

birth percentage = 0.15/population density

The equation was apparently working well with initial population of 100 (N) and carrying capacity (K) of 1,000. However, when we attempted to check the sensitivity of the model by resetting the initial

Figure 1. Initial fish population growth model

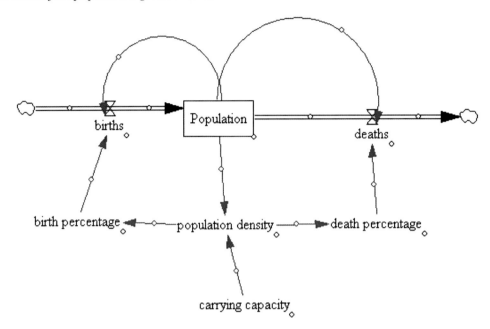

population (N) to 4,000 and keeping the K as-is (1,000), we found the birth rate for the month 1 was calculated as low as 3% although it should never fall below 10%. This is not what we intended.

As for density-dependent death factors (df) we have used below equation:

death percentage = 0.1*population density

The equation seemed work well with N=100 and K=1,000 and with N=4,000 and K=1,000 as well.

The graph in Figure 2 shows the birth and death percentages change as expected and the population growth seems to be stable as expected.

But the model equation seems to have a problem with birth and death rates when population exceeds carrying capacity. We checked the sensitivity analysis by setting the Initial population to 4,000. In Table 1, we can see that birth fraction came down to 0.03 although it should never be less than 0.10.

In our initial model, the equation for birth percentage did not work as expected. Our expectation was to see the minimum birth rate stays 10% in case the population density goes above 1.0 and maximum birth rate stays 50% even if the population density falls zero.

In order to make sure that the birth fraction does not fall below 10%, we have added one parameter called "population density max" which resets population density to 1.0 in case it goes above 1.0.

population density max = IF THEN ELSE (population density >= 1, 1, population density)

So, we have changed the equation for birth rate fraction. We have derived below equation:

birth percentage = IF THEN ELSE (population density max <= 0.1, 0.5, (0.5 (ABS(0.1 - population density max) * 100000 * .00000445)))

Figure 2. The graph of bf, df and K with initial N=100 and K=1000

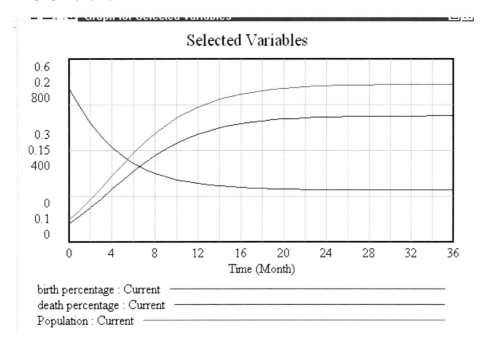

birth percentage : Current

death percentage : Current

Population : Current

Table 1. The bf and df with initial N = 4,000 and K=1000

Time (Month)	Selected	birth percentage	death percentage	Population
0	Variables	0.0357143	0.5	4000
1	Variables	0.0640244	0.314286	2142.86
2	Variables	0.0830297	0.260658	1606.58
3	Variables	0.0986059	0.232121	1321.21
4		0.11154	0.214481	1144.81
5		0.122253	0.202696	1026.96
6		0.131079	0.194435	944.349
7		0.13831	0.188452	884.518
8		0.144208	0.184017	840.167
9		0.148999	0.180672	806.721
10		0.152879	0.178117	781.169
11		0.156014	0.176145	761.454
12		0.158541	0.174612	746.125
13		0.160577	0.173413	734.134
14		0.162213	0.172471	724.71
15		0.163528	0.171728	717.276

One other constraint was to make sure birth rate does not go beyond 50%. We have set the condition in the equation that sets birth fraction to 0.50 in case population density is less than 0.10. So, birth rate stays 0.50 when population density below 0.10 and birth rate stays 0.10 when population density is greater than or equal to 1.0.

So, the range of birth rate is 50% to 10%. When the population is thin the birth rate is 50% maximum and when the population is near and above carrying capacity the birth rate would fall up to 10%. Our analyses show that when population density increases 10% the birth rate decreases about 4.5%. In birth calculation, to achieve the finest granularity after decimal points if have used 8 digits after decimal (.00000445). With the increase of population growth the birth rate is designed to fall from 0.50 to 0.10. Our equation made sure that it works accordingly. To check the sensitivity of birth rate calculation with any values of N and K, we turned off the death fraction equation before running the simulation. We did the same check on the sensitivity of death rate calculation. We found everything worked as expected. So, the results are more or less what we expected. We expected the population growth fall immediately, after it exceeds the carrying capacity.

MODEL TESTING AND RESULTS

The graph in Figure 4 shows the result with initial population 100 and carrying capacity 1,500.

Table 2 shows that the new equation for birth fraction works well with N=100 and K=1,000.

The graph in Figure 5 shows the result with initial population 100 and carrying capacity 1,500.

Compared to Figure 4, the equilibrium in Figure 5 was achieved a little late with the same initial population but, with carrying capacity of 1,500. This was expected.

Table 3 shows that the new equation for birth fraction works well with N = 100 and K is changed to 1,500 as well.

The graph in Figure 6 shows result with initial value greater than carrying capacity (1,000) – 4,000.

Table 4 also shows that the new equation for birth fraction works well with N is changed to 4,000 and K = 1,000. The population comes down to near carrying capacity very fast and equilibrium achieved.

Figure 3. Final fish population growth model

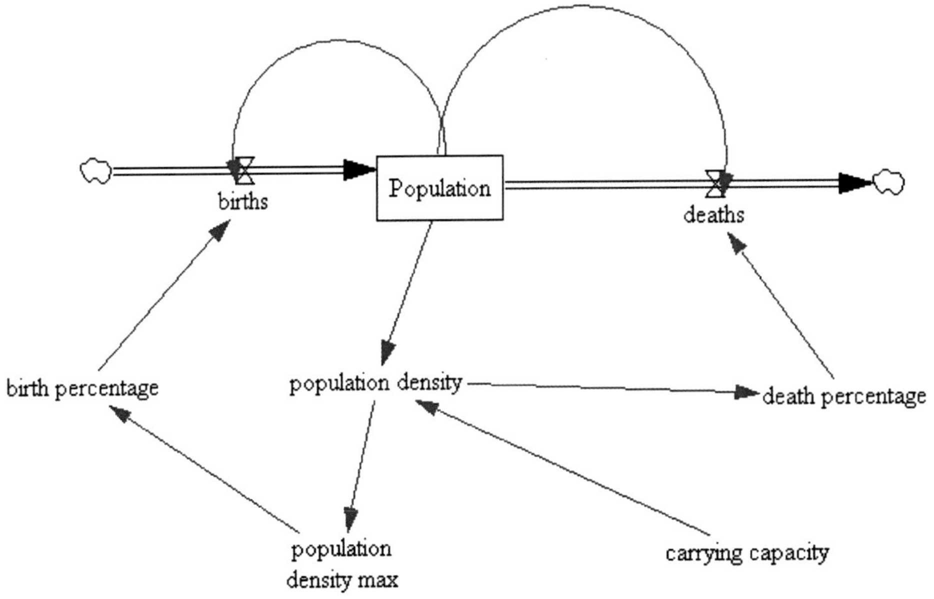

Figure 4. Based on starting point information given

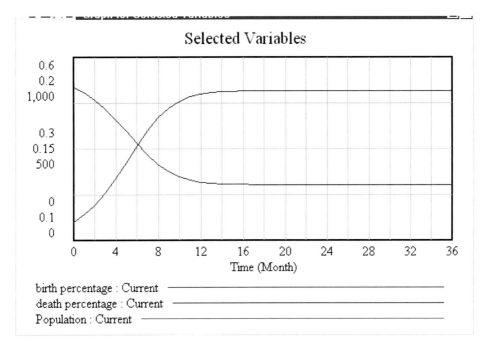

Table 2.

Time (Month)	Selected	birth percentage	death percentage	Population
0	Variables	0.5	0.11	100
1	Runs:	0.482645	0.1139	139
2	Current	0.459836	0.119026	190.256
3		0.430982	0.12551	255.097
4		0.396305	0.133302	333.022
5		0.35733	0.142061	420.607
6		0.317038	0.151115	511.151
7		0.279297	0.159596	595.963
8		0.247552	0.16673	667.3
9		0.223552	0.172123	721.232
10		0.207046	0.175832	758.324
11		0.196513	0.178199	781.994
12		0.19014	0.179631	796.315
13		0.186416	0.180468	804.683
14		0.184286	0.180947	809.469
15		0.183083	0.181217	812.172
16		0.182409	0.181369	813.688
17		0.182032	0.181453	814.534
18		0.181822	0.181501	815.006
19		0.181706	0.181527	815.268
20		0.181641	0.181541	815.414

Figure 5. The graph of bf, df and K with initial N=100 and K=1500

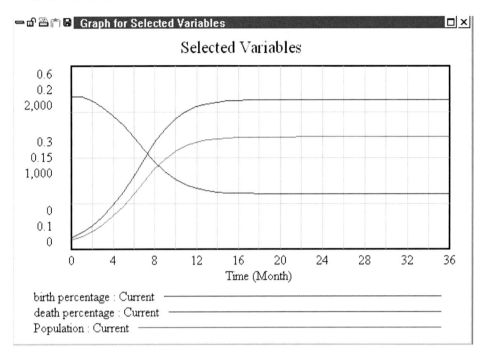

Table 3. The bf and df with initial N = 100 and K=1,500

Time (Month)	Selected	birth percentage	death percentage	Population
0	Variables	0.5	0.106667	100
1	Variables	0.5	0.109289	139.333
2	Variables	0.487014	0.112918	193.772
3	Variables	0.465509	0.117751	266.262
4		0.438039	0.123924	358.857
5		0.404598	0.131439	471.579
6		0.366383	0.140026	600.395
7		0.326065	0.149087	736.299
8		0.287406	0.157774	866.607
9		0.254079	0.165263	978.948
10		0.228285	0.17106	1065.89
11		0.210189	0.175126	1126.89

Figure 6. The graph of bf, df and K with initial N=4,000 and K=1,000

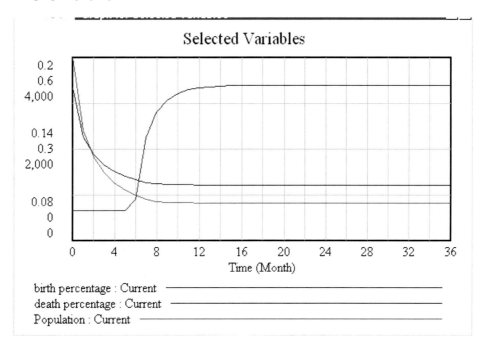

Table 4. The bf and df with initial N = 4,000 and K=1,000

Time (Month)	Selected	birth percentage	death percentage	Population
0	Variables	0.0995	0.5	4000
1	Runs:	0.0995	0.3398	2398
2	Current	0.0995	0.282176	1821.76
3		0.0995	0.248897	1488.97
4		0.0995	0.226652	1266.52
5		0.0995	0.210548	1105.48
6		0.10719	0.198272	982.719
7		0.147021	0.189321	893.211
8		0.163834	0.185543	855.428
9		0.172098	0.183686	836.858
10		0.176413	0.182716	827.161
...				
...				
31		0.18156	0.18156	815.596
32		0.18156	0.18156	815.596
33		0.18156	0.18156	815.596
34		0.18156	0.18156	815.596
35		0.18156	0.18156	815.596
36		0.18156	0.18156	815.596

ANALYSIS AND RECOMMENDATIONS

We did a thorough validation and verification of our model. The validation is the process of establishing that the modeler's mental model matches reality. Verification is the process of establishing that the computer model correctly implements the modeler's model. Verification compares implemented model to conceptual model. Model validation is the process of reaching an acceptable level of confidence that the inferences drawn from the model are correct and applicable to the real-world system being represented.

Based on testing the final model we can see that the model can predict the fish population exceeds the carrying capacity. In order to make sure the birth and death rates change with correct proportion, we ran the model setting the initial fish population to more than carrying capacity and results matched the expected output. We successfully performed the testing of an offset between N (population) and K (carrying capacity) at equilibrium. In Table 2 shows that initial population was 100 and carrying capacity was 1,000. Within a 36-month period the offset between N and K was reached at 815. We also performed testing of equilibrium between births and deaths in which the model-run comes to equilibrium between births and deaths established. It took about 6 to 7 months for the equilibrium to be reached. Table 2 shows the equilibrium between births and deaths was established when birth rate was between 0.27 and 0.31 and death rate was 0.15.

As part of testing, we did a significant amount of sensitivity analysis of the model. Sensitivity analysis (SA) is the systematic variation of input parameters and cataloging of how the key output indicators respond, in order to determine which input parameters must be further verified, and to assess if the response to changes is reasonable (Sterman, 2000; Pannell, 1997a, 1997b; Walrave, 2016). As for sensitivity analysis, we have taken a few measures to see population growth and equilibrium. We have changed the initial population from 100 to 4,000 to see how birth and death factors work when population is greater than the carrying capacity. We have also changed the carrying capacity from 1,000 to 1,500 to see how it changes birth and death fractions and how population growth works.

We also performed testing of the model to see how the model dynamics change dramatically if we significantly change carrying capacity (K). We increased K significantly from 1,000 to 50,000 while keeping the initial population (N) at 100. If we compare simulation results shown in Table 2 above and Table 5 below we will see that in Table 2 (with N=100 and K=1000), the model equilibrium achieved at 12 month whereas in Table 5 the equilibrium achieved at 24th month of 36 months period. But the pattern of initial birth and death fractions contain pretty much the same trend. The initial birth rates for the first few months remain high (50%) and death fraction remain low (10%).

We also conducted a thorough testing of density-dependent functions. We tried to change birth fraction by removing the "population density max" constraints mentioned in *Modeling Fish Population Dynamics* above. We also had set the initial value of population (N) to 4,000 (as opposed to 100) to see how birth and death fraction re-calculates and influences population growth. We kept the carrying capacity (K) at 1,000. This resulted in birth fraction dropping down as low as 0.03 (as opposed to 10% minimum rate threshold). The death rate went up to 0.5 which was consistent with expectations of the model. The dramatic impact was it took only 4 months to bring down population from 4,000 to near the carrying capacity of 1,000. This happened due to extreme low birth fraction (3%) and significantly higher death fraction (50%). With these birth and death fractions the model became in equilibrium state with a population of 700 to 800 after the first 10 months.

We tested the model's prediction capability both in the equilibrium values of fish population and birth/death rates. Based on our model test with significant number of initial population (e.g., 4,000) and

Table 5. The bf and df with initial N = 100 and K=50,000

Time (Month)	Selected	birth percentage	death percentage	Population
0	Variables	0.5	0.1002	100
1	Runs:	0.5	0.10028	139.98
2	Current	0.5	0.100392	195.933
3		0.5	0.100548	274.229
4		0.5	0.100768	383.77
5		0.5	0.101074	536.984
6		0.5	0.101502	751.201
7		0.5	0.102101	1050.55
8		0.5	0.102937	1468.57
9		0.5	0.104103	2051.68
10		0.5	0.105728	2863.93
11		0.5	0.107986	3993.1
12		0.49503	0.111117	5558.45
13		0.476038	0.115385	7692.41
14		0.451346	0.120933	10466.7
15		0.420567	0.12785	13925
...				
...				
24		0.188731	0.179948	39974.1
25		0.185606	0.18065	40325.2
26		0.183827	0.18105	40525
27		0.182826	0.181275	40637.6
28		0.182265	0.181401	40700.6
29		0.181952	0.181471	40735.7
30		0.181778	0.181511	40755.3
31		0.181681	0.181532	40766.2
32		0.181627	0.181545	40772.3
33		0.181597	0.181551	40775.6
34		0.18158	0.181555	40777.5
35		0.181571	0.181557	40778.5
36		0.181566	0.181558	40779.1

by keeping the carrying capacity unaltered, we noticed the initial birth fraction was calculated to 0.10 but the death fraction was calculated as 50% as intended. This has led population to drop dramatically in each of the first few months. In month 1 the birth rate was 0.0995 and the death fraction was calculated to 0.5 which is five times higher than birth rate. With these birth and death fractions changes, the model became relatively stable after the first seven months.

CONCLUSION AND FUTURE WORK

Human society is continuously facing reduction of fish population growth in rivers and oceans. This is happening because of overfishing, environmental destruction and pollution. In fact commercial nature of fish catching ends up with overfishing and some cases wasting and discarding this vital source of food for human and well as other creatures in the ecosystem of the ocean. Irresponsible fishing practices need to be controlled. Researcher suggests that recovery of fish population deficit could be reversed and brought to a stable and sustainable state. It could be achieved through management and regulations around fish cultivation and consumption. We need to make sure our fishing spree does not exceed the sustainable limit.

Sustainable exploitation of fish population could be achieved by conserving, harvesting and adjusting fishing growth and fishing capacity. To achieve a balanced exploitation, fish growing, stocks and harvesting need to be managed in accordance with the principle of sustainability (Cochrane and Garcia, 2009). In this chapter we presented a system dynamic model that shows how system dynamics modeling could be applied to help test options for improving fish population growth. In our model, we used a few equations to accurately calculate the dynamic behavior of fish birth, death, and harvest which match real-world population observations. Our equations and built-in functions used in this model accurately calculate the birth and death factors and represent the growth of fish population under the mentioned assumptions. The feedback loop worked as expected, in terms of birth and death fractions and population growth. We used mathematical equation to control the birth and death fractions and population growth.

One of the major strengths of simulation modeling as a tool is that it can help reduce the risks inherent in any type of change (Laguna and Markland, 2005). In our model building, we did simulation with a small number of population (N) and carrying capacity (K) scenarios. In our simulation runs we found the birth and death fractions and population growth worked properly. A future improvement could be done by adding a few more constraints to address other known 'real-world' factors and testing with a large number of initial population and carrying capacity, perhaps, with millions. As part of future research it needs to be seen as to how fish cultivation could be diversified.

REFERENCES

Abdel-Hamid, T. K. (1989). The dynamics of software project staffing: A system dynamics based simulation approach. *IEEE Transactions on Software Engineering, 15*(2), 109–119. doi:10.1109/32.21738

Abdelbari, H., & Shafi, K. (2017). A computational intelligence-based method to 'Learn' causal loop diagram-like structures from observed Data. *System Dynamics Review, 33*(1), 3–33. doi:10.1002dr.1567

Abdelsalam, H. M., & El-Tagy, A. O. (2012). A simulation model for managing marketing multi-channel conflict. *International Journal of System Dynamics Applications, 1*(4), 59–76. doi:10.4018/ijsda.2012100103

Barker, T. (2008). The economics of avoiding dangerous climate change. An Editorial Essay on *The Stern Review. Climatic Change, 89*(3-4), 173–194. doi:10.100710584-008-9433-x

Bhushan, S. (2012). System dynamics integrative modeling and simulation for mobile telephony innovation diffusion: A study of emerging Indian telecom market. *International Journal of System Dynamics Applications, 2*(3), 84–121. doi:10.4018/ijsda.2012070103

Bhushan, S. (2013). Capturing structural complexity of innovation diffusion through system dynamics: A discussion on model development, calibration and simulation results. *International Journal of System Dynamics Applications, 2*(1), 59–96. doi:10.4018/ijsda.2013010104

Black, L. J. (2013). When visuals are boundary objects in system dynamics work. *System Dynamics Review, 29*(2), 70–86. doi:10.1002dr.1496

CBS News. (2015). Ocean fish numbers on 'brink of collapse,' WWF reports. Science and Technology. *CBS News*. Retrieved on 1/23/2018 from: http://www.cbc.ca/news/technology/ocean-fish-wwf-1.3230157

Céline Bérard, C. (2005). Performance evaluation of management information systems in clinical trials: A system dynamics approach. In *Proceedings of the 2005 System Dynamics Conference*. The System Dynamics Society.

Choi, J., Nazareth, D. L., & Jain, H. K. (2008). Information technology skill management: A systems dynamics approach. *Proceedings of the 41st Hawaii International Conference on System Sciences*. 10.1109/HICSS.2008.206

Cochrane, K. L., & Garcia, S. M. (2009). *A fishery manager's guidebook* (2nd ed.). Wiley-Blackwell. doi:10.1002/9781444316315

Eberlein, R. L., & Thompson, J. P. (2013). Precise modeling of aging populations. *System Dynamics Review*, *29*(2), 87–101. doi:10.1002dr.1497

Fiksel, J. (2006). Sustainability and resilience: Toward a systems approach. *Sustainability: Science, Practice, & Policy, 2*(2).

Flottmann, M. (2014). *Population dynamics: A catastrophe model for fishing*. Retrieved on 01/23/2018 from: http://jaguar.biologie.hu-berlin.de/~wolfram/pages/seminar_theoretische_biologie_2007/ausar-beitungen/floettmann.pdf

Forbus, K., & Gentner, D. (1997). Qualitative mental models: Simulations or memories? *Proceedings of the 11th International Workshop on Qualitative Reasoning*.

Hallam, T. G., Lassiter, R. R., & Henson, S. M. (2000). Modeling fish population dynamics. *Nonlinear Analysis*, *40*(1-8), 227–250. doi:10.1016/S0362-546X(00)85013-0

Hayes, D., Jones, M., Lester, N., Chu, C., Doka, S., Netto, J., ... Collins, N. (2009). Linking fish population dynamics to habitat conditions: Insights from the application of a process-oriented approach to several Great Lakes species. *Reviews in Fish Biology and Fisheries*, *19*(3), 295–312. doi:10.100711160-009-9103-8

Jammoussi, H., Franchek, M., Grigoriadis, K., & Books, M. (2013). Closed-loop system identification based on data correlation. *Journal of Dynamic Systems, Measurement, and Control*, *136*(1), 014507. doi:10.1115/1.4025158

Jones, Q., Ravid, G., & Rafaeli, S. (2002). An empirical exploration of mass interaction system dynamics: Individual information overload and Usenet discourse. *Proceedings of the 35th Hawaii International Conference on System Sciences*. 10.1109/HICSS.2002.994061

Laguna, M., & Markland, J. (2005). *Business process modeling, simulation, and Design*. Upper Saddle River, NJ: Pearson Education, Inc.

Levhari, D., & Mirman, L. J. (1980). The Great Fish War: An example using a dynamic Cournot-Nash solution. *The Bell Journal of Economics*, *11*(1), 322–334. doi:10.2307/3003416

Lindenmayer, D. B., Lacy, R. C., & Pope, M. L. (2000). Testing a simulation model for population variability analysis. *Ecological Applications*, *10*(2), 580–597. doi:10.1890/1051-0761(2000)010[0580:TASMFP]2.0.CO;2

Loebbecke, C. (1997). A system dynamics approach to modeling a nationwide mobile communication market. *IFAC, Symposium Automated Systems Based on Human Skill - Joint Design of Technology and Organization*, 27-42.

Martinez-Moyano, I. J., & Richardson, G. P. (2013). Best practices in system dynamics modeling. *System Dynamics Review*, *29*(2), 102–123. doi:10.1002dr.1495

Meadows, D., Randers, J., & Meadows, D. (2004). *Limits to growth: The 30-Year Update*. Chelsea Green.

Morrison, J. B. (2012). Process improvement dynamics under constrained resources: Managing the work harder versus work smarter balance. *System Dynamics Review*, *28*(4), 329–350. doi:10.1002dr.1485

Morrison, J. B., Rudolphb, J. W., & Carrollc, J. S. (2013). Dynamic modeling as a multidiscipline collaborative journey. *System Dynamics Review*, *29*(1), 4–25. doi:10.1002dr.1492

Ng, T. S., Sy, C. L., & Loo Hay Lee, L. H. (2012). Robust parameter design for system dynamics models: A Formal approach based on goal-seeking behavior. *System Dynamics Review*, *28*(3), 230–254. doi:10.1002dr.1475

Nielsen, M., Andersen, P., Ravensbeck, L., Laugesen, F., Kristofersson, D. M., & Ellefsen, H. (2017). Fisheries management and the value chain: The Northeast Atlantic pelagic fisheries case. *Fisheries Research*, *186*, 36–47. doi:10.1016/j.fishres.2016.08.004

NOAA Fisheries. (2015). *Fish population dynamics and modeling*. Southwest Fisheries Science Center, NOOA Fisheries. Retrieved on 1/23/2018 from: https://swfsc.noaa.gov/textblock.aspx?Division=FRD&id=1111

Onggo, S. (2012). Adult social care workforce analysis in England: A system dynamics approach. *International Journal of System Dynamics Applications*, *1*(4), 1–20. doi:10.4018/ijsda.2012100101

Pannell, D. J. (1997a). Sensitivity Analysis of Normative Economic Models: Theoretical Framework and Practical Strategies. *Agricultural Economics*, *16*(2), 139–152. doi:10.1016/S0169-5150(96)01217-0

Pannell, D. J. (1997b). *Sensitivity analysis: strategies, methods, concepts, examples*. Retrieved on 01/23/2018 from: http://dpannell.fnas.uwa.edu.au/dpap971f.htm

Pierson, K., & Sterman, J. D. (2013). Cyclical dynamics of airline industry earnings. *System Dynamics Review*, *29*(3), 129–156. doi:10.1002dr.1501

Pruyt, E. (2006a). System dynamics and decision-making in the context of dynamically complex multi-dimensional societal issues. *Proceedings of the 2006 Conference of the System Dynamics Society*.

Pruyt, E. (2006b). What is system dynamics? A paradigmatic inquiry. *Proceedings of the 2006 Conference of the System Dynamics Society*.

Qin, Y., Nakatani, N., & Tsukahara, Y. (2016). Study on the formulation of fish population dynamics model using statistical data. *Proceedings of the Techno-Ocean (Techno-Ocean) Conference*. 10.1109/Techno-Ocean.2016.7890654

Rahman, N. (2014). A system dynamics model for a sustainable fish population. *International Journal of Technology Diffusion*, *5*(2), 39–53. doi:10.4018/ijtd.2014040104

Rahman, N. (2016). Toward achieving environmental sustainability in the computer industry. *International Journal of Green Computing*, 7(1), 37–54. doi:10.4018/IJGC.2016010103

Rahman, N. (2018a). A simulation model for application development in data warehouses. *International Journal of Operations Research and Information Systems*, 9(1), 66–80. doi:10.4018/IJORIS.2018010104

Rahman, N. (2018b). Environmental sustainability in the computer industry for competitive advantage. In Green Computing Strategies for Competitive Advantage and Business Sustainability. IGI Global. Doi:10.4018/978-1-5225-5017-4.ch006

Rahman, N., & Akhter, S. (2010). Incorporating sustainability into information technology management. *International Journal of Technology Management & Sustainable Development*, 9(2), 95–111. doi:10.1386/tmsd.9.2.95_1

Richardson, J. (2013). The past is prologue: Reflections on forty-plus years of system dynamics modeling practice. *System Dynamics Review*, 29(3), 172–187. doi:10.1002dr.1503

Rose, K. A., Cowan, J. H. Jr, Winemiller, K. O., Myers, R. A., & Hilborn, R. (2001). Compensatory density dependence in fish populations: Importance, controversy, understanding and prognosis. *Fish and Fisheries*, 2(4), 293–327. doi:10.1046/j.1467-2960.2001.00056.x

Shelton, A. O., & Mangel, M. (2011). Fluctuations of fish populations and the magnifying effects of fishing. *Proceedings of the National Academy of Sciences of the United States of America*, 108(17), 7075–7080. doi:10.1073/pnas.1100334108 PMID:21482785

Sivertson, S. (2018). A system dynamics model of fish populations in Western Lake Superior. *Semantics Scholar*. Retrieved on 1/23/2018 from: https://pdfs.semanticscholar.org/2385/9916484ba4c2a318720e e4e092c368a91276.pdf

Sterman, J. D. (2000). *Business dynamics: Systems thinking and modeling for a complex world*. McGraw-Hill Higher Education.

Thakker, R., Eveleigh, T., Holzer, T., & Sarkani, S. (2013). A system dynamics approach to quantitatively analyze the effects of mobile broadband ecosystem's variables on demands and allocation of wireless spectrum for the cellular industry. *International Journal of System Dynamics Applications*, 2(3), 73–93. doi:10.4018/ijsda.2013070105

Ventana Systems, Inc. (2011). *Vensim® from Ventana Systems, Inc.* Retrieved on 1/30/2018: http://www.vensim.com/

Wakeland, W., Cangur, O., Rueda, G., & Scholz, A. (2003). A system dynamics model of the pacific coast rockfish fishery. *Proceedings of the 21st International Conference of the System Dynamics Society*.

Walrave, B. (2016). Determining intervention thresholds that change output behavior patterns. *System Dynamics Review*, 32(3-4), 261–278. doi:10.1002dr.1564

Wyburn, J., & Roach, P. A. (2013). A system dynamics model of the American collectable comic book market. *International Journal of System Dynamics Applications*, 2(1), 37–58. doi:10.4018/ijsda.2013010103

APPENDIX

The *model diagram* is shown in Figure 1 (initial) and 3 (final) above.
We have included two listings of the *equations*. ***First***, generated based on Initial Model (Figure 1):

```
(01)        birth percentage=
                0.15/population density
        Units: **undefined**


(02)        births=
                Population*birth percentage
        Units: **undefined**


(03)        carrying capacity=
                1000
        Units: **undefined**


(04)        death percentage=
                0.1*population density
        Units: **undefined**


(05)        deaths=
                Population *death percentage
        Units: **undefined**


(06)        FINAL TIME  = 36
        Units: Month
        The final time for the simulation.
(07)        INITIAL TIME  = 0
        Units: Month
        The initial time for the simulation.
(08)        Population= INTEG (
                births-deaths,
                        100)
        Units: **undefined**


(09)        population density=
                Population/carrying capacity
        Units: **undefined**


(10)        SAVEPER  =
                TIME STEP
        Units: Month [0,?]
```

```
            The frequency with which output is stored.
(11)        TIME STEP  = 1
        Units: Month [0,?]
        The time step for the simulation.
```

Second, the equation generated based on Final Model (Figure 3): Here the birth percentage equation is different from the first equation. Also a new parameter, called "population density max", added to make sure population density is reset to 1 when it goes above 1.0. This helps keep birth percentage 0.10, minimum, even if the population density is well above 1.

```
(01)        birth percentage=
                IF THEN ELSE (population density max <= 0.1, 0.5, (0.5 -
(ABS(0.1 - population density max) * 100000 * .00000445)))
        Units: **undefined**
(02)        births=
                Population*birth percentage
        Units: **undefined**


(03)        carrying capacity=
                1500
        Units: **undefined**


(04)        death percentage=
                0.1+0.1*population density
        Units: **undefined**


(05)        deaths=
                Population *death percentage
        Units: **undefined**


(06)        FINAL TIME  = 36
        Units: Month
        The final time for the simulation.
(07)        INITIAL TIME  = 0
        Units: Month
        The initial time for the simulation.
(08)        Population= INTEG (
                births-deaths,
                        100)
        Units: **undefined**


(09)        population density=
                Population/carrying capacity
```

Units: **undefined**

(10)   population density max=
          IF THEN ELSE (population density >= 1, 1, population density)
Units: **undefined**

(11)   SAVEPER =
          TIME STEP
Units: Month [0,?]
The frequency with which output is stored.

(12)   TIME STEP = 1
Units: Month [0,?]
The time step for the simulation.

Chapter 11
Search for an Optimal Solution to Vague Traffic Problems Using the PSK Method

P. Senthil Kumar
Jamal Mohamed College (Autonomous), India

ABSTRACT

There are several algorithms, in literature, for obtaining the fuzzy optimal solution of fuzzy transportation problems (FTPs). To the best of the author's knowledge, in the history of mathematics, no one has been able to solve transportation problem (TP) under four different uncertain environment using single method in the past years. So, in this chapter, the author tried to categories the TP under four different environments and formulates the problem and utilizes the crisp numbers, triangular fuzzy numbers (TFNs), and trapezoidal fuzzy numbers (TrFNs) to solve the TP. A new method, namely, PSK (P. Senthil Kumar) method for finding a fuzzy optimal solution to fuzzy transportation problem (FTP) is proposed. Practical usefulness of the PSK method over other existing methods is demonstrated with four different numerical examples. To illustrate the PSK method different types of FTP is solved by using the PSK method and the obtained results are discussed.

1. INTRODUCTION

Resource allocation is used to assign the available resources in an economic way. When the resources to be allocated are scarce, a well-planned action is necessary for a decision-maker (DM) to attain the optimal utility. If the supplying sources and the receiving agents are limited, the best pattern of allocation to get the maximum return or the best plan with the least cost, whichever may be applicable to the problem, is to be found out. This class of problems is termed as 'allocation problems' and is divided into 'transportation problems (TPs)' and 'assignment problems (APs)'. The TPs and APs both are also called optimization problems.

DOI: 10.4018/978-1-5225-5396-0.ch011

TPs play an important role in logistics and supply chain management for reducing cost and improving service. In today's highly competitive market, the pressure on organizations to find better ways to create and deliver products and services to customers becomes stronger. How and when to send the products to the customers in the quantities which they want in a cost-effective manner becomes more challenging. Transportation models provide a powerful framework to meet this challenge. They ensure the efficient movement and timely availability of raw materials and finished goods.

The TP is a special class of linear programming problem (LPP) which deals with the distribution of single homogeneous product from various origins (sources) to various destinations (sinks). The objective of the TP is to determine the optimal amount of a commodity to be transported from various supply points to various demand points so that the total transportation cost is minimum for a minimization problem or total transportation profit is maximum for a maximization problem.

The unit costs, that is, the cost of transporting one unit from a particular supply point to a particular demand point, the amounts available at the supply points and the amounts required at the demand points are the parameters of the TP. Efficient algorithms have been developed for solving TPs when the cost coefficients, the demand and supply quantities are known precisely.

In the history of mathematics, Hitchcock (1941) originally developed the basic TP. Charnes and Cooper (1954) developed the stepping stone method which provides an alternative way of determining the simplex method information. Appa (1973) discussed several variations of the TP. Arsham et al. (1989) proposed a simplex type algorithm for general TPs. An Introduction to Operations Research Taha (2008) deals the TP. Aljanabi and Jasim (2015) presented an approach for solving TP using modified Kruskal's algorithm. Ahmed et al. (2016) developed a new approach to solve TPs. Akpan and Iwok (2017) presented a minimum spanning tree approach of solving a TP.

In today's real world problems such as in corporate or in industry many of the distribution problems are imprecise in nature due to variations in the parameters. To deal quantitatively with imprecise information in making decision, Zadeh (1965) introduced the fuzzy set theory and has applied it successfully in various fields. The use of fuzzy set theory becomes very rapid in the field of optimization after the pioneering work done by Bellman and Zadeh (1970). The fuzzy set deals with the degree of membership (belongingness) of an element in the set. In a fuzzy set the membership value (level of acceptance or level of satisfaction) lies between 0 and 1 where as in crisp set the element belongs to the set represent 1 and the element not belongs to the set represent 0.

The occurrence of randomness and imprecision in the real world is inevitable owing to some unexpected situations. To deal quantitatively with imprecise information in making decisions, Bellman and Zadeh (1970) and Zadeh (1978) introduced the notion of fuzziness. There are cases that the cost coefficients (or profit coefficients for the maximization TP) or/and the supply and demand quantities of a TP may be uncertain due to some uncontrollable factors. Such TPs are known as FTPs. The objective of the FTP is to determine the shipping schedule that optimizes the total fuzzy transportation cost / fuzzy transportation profit while satisfying fuzzy supply and fuzzy demand limits. In the history of mathematics, various efficient algorithms were developed for solving FTPs using fuzzy linear programming techniques, crisp conversion techniques, or the parametric programming technique. Some of the studies provide an optimal solution for FTPs, which is not a fuzzy number, but a crisp value. If the obtained results are crisp values, then it might lose some helpful information.

Various effective methods were developed for solving TPs with the assumption that the coefficients of the objective function and the demand and supply values are specified in a precise manner. However, these conditions may not be satisfied always. For example, the unit transportation costs are rarely constant. To deal with ambiguous coefficients in mathematical programming, inexact, fuzzy and interval programming techniques have been proposed. Interval TP is a generalization of the TP in which input data are expressed as intervals instead of point values. This problem can arise when uncertainty exists in the problem and decision-makers (DMs) are more comfortable expressing it as intervals. FTP is also a generalization of the crisp TP in which input values are expressed as fuzzy numbers. FTP arises when the DM has some vague information about the problem, that is, the DM has some lack of precision and then the coefficients defining the problem can be modelled by means of fuzzy sets.

Due to the applications of fuzzy set theory, several authors like Oheigeartaigh (1982) presented an algorithm for solving TPs where the availabilities and requirements are fuzzy sets with linear or triangular membership functions. Chanas et al. (1984) presented a fuzzy linear programming model for solving TPs with fuzzy supply, fuzzy demand and crisp costs. Chanas et al. (1993) formulated the FTPs in three different situations and proposed method for solving the formulated FTPs. Chanas and Kuchta (1996) proposed the concept of the optimal solution for the TP with fuzzy coefficients expressed as fuzzy numbers, and developed an algorithm for obtaining the optimal solution.

Chanas and Kuchta (1998) developed a new method for solving fuzzy integer TP by representing the supply and demand parameters as L-R type fuzzy numbers. Saad and Abbas (2003) proposed an algorithm for solving the TPs under fuzzy environment. Liu and Kao (2004) presented a method for solving FTPs based on extension principle. Chiang (2005) proposed a method to find the optimal solution of TPs with fuzzy requirements and fuzzy availabilities. Gani and Razak (2006) obtained a fuzzy solution for a two stage cost minimizing FTP in which availabilities and requirements are TrFNs using a parametric approach. A parametric approach is used to obtain a fuzzy optimal solution and the aim is to optimize the total transportation cost in the two stages. Das and Baruah (2007) discussed Vogel's approximation method to find the fuzzy initial basic feasible solution of FTP in which all the parameters (supply, demand and cost) are represented by TFNs. Li et al. (2008) proposed a new method based on goal programming approach for solving FTPs with fuzzy costs.

Chen et al. (2008) proposed the methods for solving TPs on a fuzzy network. Lin (2009) used genetic algorithm for solving TPs with fuzzy coefficients. Dinagar and Palanivel (2009) investigated the TP in fuzzy environment using TrFNs. Pandian and Natarajan (2010) presented a new method called, fuzzy zero point method for finding a fuzzy optimal solution for a FTPs, where the transportation cost, supply and demand quantities are represented by TrFNs. Recently, Rao et al. (2016) proposed a perfect mathematical formulation of FTP provides an optimal solution speedily and solved the same numerical example which was proposed by Pandian and Natarajan (2010). Rao et al. (2016) presented two stage method for finding a fuzzy optimal solution for a FTPs and they compared proposed result with fuzzy zero point method. From this comparative study, the result states that the values of the variables as obtained by Pandian and Natarajan (2010) are same as what obtain by the researchers Rao et al. (2016), but the optimal fuzzy transportation cost by the researchers Rao, Mudaliar, Hasan and Alam's method is 121 whereas, as obtained by Pandian and Natarajan (2010) method the solution obtained is 132.17. From this comparative result, the author conclude that the proposed study is not new in the history of mathematics. Since, the proposed result is already obtained by the eminent researchers Mohideen and Kumar (2010) and presented a paper titled " a comparative study on TP in fuzzy environment", where the numerical example is taken from Pandian and Natarajan (2010). De and Yadav (2010) modified the existing method (Kikuchi 2000) by using TrFNs instead of TFNs. Mohideen and Kumar (2010) presented a comparative study on TP in fuzzy environment. Sudhakar et al. (2011) proposed a different approach for solving two stage FTPs in which supplies and demands are TrFNs. Basirzadeh (2011) discussed an approach for solving FTP, where all the parameters are represented by TrFNs. Gani et al. (2011) presented simplex type algorithm for solving FTP, where all the parameters are TFNs. Nasseri and Ebrahimnejad (2011) did sensitivity analysis on linear programming problems with trapezoidal fuzzy variables.

Biswas and Modak (2012) studied using fuzzy goal programming technique to solve multiobjective chance constrained programming problems in a fuzzy environment. Saati et al. (2012) presented a two-fold linear programming model with fuzzy data. Ebrahimnejad (2012) discussed cost efficiency measures with TrFNs in data envelopment analysis based on ranking functions: application in insurance organization and hospital. Kumar and Kaur (2013) developed methods for solving fully fuzzy transportation problems (FFTPs) based on classical transportation methods. Rani et al. (2014) presented a method for unbalanced TPs in fuzzy environment taking all the parameters are TrFNs. Solaiappan and Jeyaraman (2014) did a new optimal solution method for trapezoidal FTP. Liao (2015) presented decision method of optimal investment enterprise selection under uncertain information environment. Pattnaik (2015) presented decision making approach to fuzzy linear programming problems with post optimal analysis. Vimala and Prabha (2016) presented fuzzy transportation problem through monalisha's approximation method. Kumar (2016a, b) solved TPs under four different situations using the PSK Method. Sahoo et al. (2016) presented solution of FTP by using ranking function. Christi and Malini (2016) developed an approach to solve transportation problems with octagonal fuzzy numbers using best candidates method and different ranking techniques. Ebrahimnejad (2016a) developed fuzzy linear programming approach for solving TPs with interval-valued TrFNs. Rajarajeswari and Sangeetha (2016) proposed new similarity performance measures of fuzzy transportation and its application. Mathur et al. (2016) presented trapezoidal fuzzy model to optimize TP. Ebrahimnejad (2016b) developed new method for solving FTPs with L-R flat fuzzy numbers. Reddy et al. (2016) discussed unclear carrying problem of triangular numbers with α–slash and position method. Kumar (2017a) presented PSK method for solving type-1 and type-3 FTPs. Maity and Roy (2017) developed multiobjective TP using fuzzy decision variable through multi-choice programming. Singh and Saxena (2017) have proposed a new data transfer approach through fuzzy Vogel's Approximation Method (VAM). Samuel and Raja (2017a) developed algorithmic approach to unbalanced FTP. Hunwisai and Kumam (2017) presented a method for solving a FTP via Robust ranking technique and allocation table method (ATM). Agustina et al. (2017) proposed PMZ method for solving fuzzy transportation. Baykasoğlu and Subulan (2017) developed constrained fuzzy arithmetic approach to FTPs with fuzzy decision variables. Ali and Faraz (2017) studied solving fuzzy triangular transportation problem using fuzzy least cost method with ranking approach. Samuel and Raja (2017b) developed an advanced approximation method for finding an optimal solution of unbalanced fuzzy transportation problems. AnithaKumari et al. (2017) presented fuzzy transportation problems with new kind of ranking function. Anuradha and Sobana (2017) presented a survey on fuzzy transportation problems. Purushothkumar and Ananathanarayanan (2017) developed fuzzy transportation problem of trapezoidal fuzzy numbers with new ranking technique.

Atanassov (1983) introduced a concept of intuitionistic fuzzy sets (IFSs), which is a generalization of fuzzy sets (FSs) introduced by Zadeh (1965). In fuzzy set, only, the level of satisfaction (degree of acceptance) is considered by a membership function but it does not consider the degree of rejection (degree of non-acceptance) for the non-membership function. On the other hand, in intuitionistic fuzzy set (IFS), not only the degree of acceptance is considered by a membership function, but also the degree of rejection (degree of non-acceptance) is defined by a non-membership function so that the sum of both degrees should be less than or equal to one (i.e., not beyond unity). Therefore the numerous applications of IFS theory, Hussain and Kumar (2012a; 2012b; 2012c; 2013) solved different types of IFTPs. Kumar and Hussain (2014a; 2014b; 2014c; 2015; 2016a; 2016b; 2016c) solved different types of allocation problems under intuitionistic fuzzy environment successfully. Kumar (2017b) proposed algorithmic approach for solving allocation problems under intuitionistic fuzzy environment, which is based on PSK method. Kumar (2017a; 2018a; 2018b) solved various types of optimization problems under uncertain environment. Kumar (2018c) developed linear programming approach for solving balanced and unbalanced intuitionistic fuzzy transportation problems. Recently, Kumar (2018d, e) has solved different types of intuitionistic fuzzy solid transportation problems by using two different methods.

Therefore, the number of authors has solved TPs and other real life oriented problems under fuzzy environment. To the best of the author's knowledge, no one has to illustrate the solution procedure for mixed FTP. But some of the authors discussed simple method for solving FTP also none of them proved mathematically the solution obtained by simple method for solving FTP is optimal. In addition to that all the existing literature deals with conversion of FTP into crisp TP and it finds only the occupied cells but they couldn't find out how to allot the maximum possible value (supply or demand) to the occupied cells. So, the existing literature offers solution for limited number of sources and destinations only through inspection. But in our real life there is always a fair chance to have large number of sources and destinations. To counter this difficulty, in this chapter proposed a solution by using PSK method.

Ranking of fuzzy numbers plays a vital role in optimization and decision making problems. Chen and Hsieh (1999) discussed graded mean integration representation of generalized fuzzy numbers which is used to compare any two TrFNs. Shankar et al. (2013) presented fuzzy critical path method based on a new approach of ranking fuzzy numbers using centroid of centroids. Thus, many researchers have studied fuzzy numbers and analyzed its properties.

In this chapter, a new and efficient method called PSK method is proposed to find the optimal objective value of type-1, type-2, type-3 and type-4 FTP in single stage. The existing ranking procedure of Liou and Wang (1992) is used to transform the type-1, type-2, type-3 and type-4 FTP into a crisp one so that the conventional method may be applied to solve the TP. The occupied cells of crisp TP that the author / researcher obtained are as same as the occupied cells of type-1, type-2, type-3 and type-4 FTP, but the value of occupied cells for type-1, type-2, type-3 and type-4 FTP is the maximum possible value of crisp supply (or fuzzy supply/ mixed fuzzy supply) and crisp demand (or fuzzy demand / mixed fuzzy demand). On the basis of this idea the solution procedure is differs from TP to type-1, type-2, type-3 and type-4 FTP in allocation step only. From this idea, the author conclude that the PSK method is easy to understand and to apply for finding the fuzzy optimal solution of different types of FTPs occurring in real life situations. Therefore, the innovative method called PSK method and new multiplication operation on trapezoidal fuzzy number (TrFN) is proposed to find the optimal solution in terms of mixture of crisp numbers, TFNs and TrFNs. The necessary theorems are proved for the solution obtained by PSK method for solving a type-1, type-2, type-3 and type-4 FTP with equality constraints is an optimal solution (or fuzzy optimal solution / mixed fuzzy optimal solution) for the type-1, type-2, type-3 and type-4 FTP. Hence, the proposed method gives the optimal solution not only in terms of crisp numbers and fully fuzzy numbers but also mixed fuzzy numbers. Moreover, the proposed method gives the opportunity to the DM to solve all the types of FTP and it is much easier to apply the proposed method when compared to all the existing methods.

Rest of the chapter is organized as follows: section 2 deals with some terminology and new multiplication operation, section 3 consists of ranking procedure and ordering principles of TrFN. Section 4 provides the definition of type-1, type-2, type-3 and type-4 FTP and its mathematical formulation, section 5 consists of the PSK Method, section 6 provides the numerical examples, results and discussion, finally the conclusion and future work is given in section 7.

2. PRELIMINARIES

In this section the author review the basic definitions and results on FSs and related topics. Further, the author present a very basic but brief discussion on FSs, fuzzy numbers and arithmetic operations on TrFN. Since ranking of fuzzy numbers is an important aspect in the study of FTP, the author shall continue their discussion on this topic in later sections as well.

2.1. Definition: Fuzzy Set

Let A be a classical set $\mu_A(x)$ be a function from A to [0, 1]. A fuzzy set A* with the membership function $\mu_A(x)$ is defined by, $A* = \{(x, \mu_A(x)): x \in A \text{ and } \mu_A(x) \in [0, 1]\}$.

2.2. Definition: Fuzzy Number

The fuzzy number $\tilde{A}$ is an extension of a regular number in the sense that it does not refer to one single value but rather to a connected set of possible values, where each possible values has its own weight between 0 and 1. The weight (membership function) denoted by $\mu_A(x)$ that satisfies the following conditions:

1. $\mu_A(x)$ is piecewise continuous;
2. $\mu_A(x)$ is a convex fuzzy subset;
3. 3. $\mu_A(x)$ is the normality of a fuzzy subset, implying that for at least one element x_o the membership grade must be 1:

i.e., $\mu_A(x_0) = 1$

2.3. Definition: TrFN

A real fuzzy number $\tilde{a} = (a_1, a_2, a_3, a_4)$ is a fuzzy subset from the real line R with the membership function $\mu_{\tilde{a}}(a)$ satisfying the following conditions.

1. $\mu_{\tilde{a}}(a)$ is a continuous mapping from R to the closed interval [0, 1];
2. $\mu_{\tilde{a}}(a) = 0$ for every $a \in (-\infty, a_1]$;
3. $\mu_{\tilde{a}}(a)$ is strictly increasing and continuous on $[a_1, a_2]$;
4. $\mu_{\tilde{a}}(a) = 1$ for every $a \in [a_2, a_3]$;
5. $\mu_{\tilde{a}}(a)$ is strictly decreasing and continuous on $[a_3, a_4]$;
6. $\mu_{\tilde{a}}(a) = 0$ for every $a \in [a_4, + \infty)$.

Particular Cases

Let $\tilde{A} = [a_1, a_2, a_3, a_4]$ be a TrFN. Then the following cases arise.

Case 1: If $a_2 = a_3 = a_2 \left(\text{say}\right)$ then $\tilde{A}$ represent Tringular Fuzzy Number (TFN).

It is denoted by $\tilde{A} = \left(a_1, a_2, a_4\right)$.

Case 2: If $a_1 = a_2 = a_3 = a_4 = m \left(\text{say}\right)$ then $\tilde{A}$ represent a real number m.

2.4. Definition: Arithmetic Operations on TrFN

Let $\tilde{A} = [a_1, a_2, a_3, a_4]$ and $\tilde{B} = [b_1, b_2, b_3, b_4]$ be two TrFNs then the arithmetic operations on $\tilde{A}$ and $\tilde{B}$ are as follows:

1. Addition:

$$\tilde{A} \oplus \tilde{B} = \left[a_1 + b_1, a_2 + b_2, a_3 + b_3, a_4 + b_4\right]$$

2. Subtraction:

$$\tilde{A} \ominus \tilde{B} = [a_1 - b_4, a_2 - b_3, a_3 - b_2, a_4 - b_1]$$

3. New Multiplication:

$$\tilde{A} \otimes \tilde{B} = [a_1 \, \Re\left(\tilde{B}\right) a_2 \, \Re\left(\tilde{B}\right) a_3 \, \Re\left(\tilde{B}\right) a_4 \, \Re\left(\tilde{B}\right), \text{ if } \Re\left(\tilde{B}\right) \geq 0$$

$$\tilde{A} \otimes \tilde{B} = [a_4 \, \Re\left(\tilde{B}\right) a_3 \, \Re\left(\tilde{B}\right) a_2 \, \Re\left(\tilde{B}\right) a_1 \, \Re\left(\tilde{B}\right), \text{ if } \Re(\tilde{B}) < 0$$

4. Scalar multiplication:

$$k\tilde{A} = \left[ka_1, ka_2, ka_3, ka_4\right], for \; k \geq 0$$

$$k\tilde{A} = [ka_4, ka_3, ka_2, ka_1], for \; k < 0$$

3. COMPARISON OF TrFN

Ranking of fuzzy numbers is an important problem in the study of fuzzy set theory. In this section, some basic and important definitions, ranking of fuzzy numbers and its related theorems are presented.

Definition 3.1.

A TrFN $\tilde{A} = \left[a_1, a_2, a_3, a_4\right]$ is said to be non negative TrFN if and only if $\Re(\tilde{A}) \geq 0$.

Definition 3.2.

A TrFN $\tilde{A} = \left[a_1, a_2, a_3, a_4\right]$ is said to be zero TrFN if and only if $\Re(\tilde{A}) \geq 0$.

Definition 3.3.

Two TrFNs $\tilde{A} = \left[a_1, a_2, a_3, a_4\right]$ and $\tilde{B} = \left[b_1, b_2, b_3, b_4\right]$ are said to be equal TrFN if and only if $\Re\left(\tilde{A}\right) = \Re\left(\tilde{B}\right)$.

Definition 3.4. (Liou and Wang 1992)

A ranking function is a function $\Re : F(R) \rightarrow R$, where F(R) is a set of fuzzy numbers defined on set of real numbers, which maps each fuzzy number into the real line.

Let $\tilde{A} = \left[a_1, a_2, a_3, a_4\right]$ be a TrFN then:

$$\Re\left(\tilde{A}\right) = \left(\frac{\sigma_1 + \sigma_2 + \sigma_3 + \sigma_4}{4}\right)$$

Let $\tilde{A} = \left[a_1, a_2, a_3, a_4\right]$ and $\tilde{B} = \left[b_1, b_2, b_3, b_4\right]$ be two TrFNs.
Then:

1. $\Re(\tilde{A}) > \Re(\tilde{B})$ *iff* $\tilde{A} > \tilde{B}$
2. $\Re(\tilde{A}) < \Re(\tilde{B})$ *iff* $\tilde{A} < \tilde{B}$
3. $\Re(\tilde{A}) = \Re(\tilde{B})$ *iff* $\tilde{A} \approx \tilde{B}$

where:

$$\left(\tilde{A}\right) = \left(\frac{a_1 + a_2 + a_3 + a_4}{4}\right)., \left(\tilde{B}\right) = \left(\frac{b_1 + b_2 + b_3 + b_4}{4}\right).$$

Theorem: 1 The ranking function $\Re : F(R) \rightarrow R$ is a linear function
Proof: Let $\Re(\tilde{A}) = \left[\sigma_1, \sigma_2, \sigma_3, \sigma_4\right]$ and $\Re(\tilde{B}) = \left[\tau_1, \tau_2, \tau_3, \tau_4\right]$ two TrFNs. Then, for all $c \geq 0$ we have:

$$\Re\left(c\tilde{A} \oplus \tilde{B}\right) = \Re\left[c\left(\sigma_1, \sigma_2, \sigma_3, \sigma_4\right) \oplus \left(\tau_1, \tau_2, \tau_3, \tau_4\right)\right]$$

We know that (Wkt):

$$c\tilde{A} = \left[c\sigma_1, c\sigma_2, c\sigma_3, c\sigma_4\right], \ for \ c \geq 0$$

$$\Re\left(c\tilde{A} \oplus \tilde{B}\right) = \Re\left(\left(c\sigma_1, c\sigma_2, c\sigma_3, c\sigma_4\right) \oplus \left(\tau_1, \tau_2, \tau_3, \tau_4\right)\right)$$

Wkt $\tilde{A} \oplus \tilde{B} = \left[\sigma_1 + \tau_1, \sigma_2 + \tau_2, \sigma_3 + \tau_3, \sigma_4 + \tau_4\right]$

$$\Re\left(c\tilde{A} + \tilde{B}\right) = \Re\left(\left(c\sigma_1 + \tau_1, c\sigma_2 + \tau_2, c\sigma_3 + \tau_3, c\sigma_4 + \tau_4\right)\right)$$

Wkt $\Re\left(\tilde{A}\right) = \left(\dfrac{\sigma_1 + \sigma_2 + \sigma_3 + \sigma_4}{4}\right)$

$$\Re\left(c\tilde{A} \oplus \tilde{B}\right) = \left(\dfrac{c\sigma_1 + \tau_1 + c\sigma_2 + \tau_2 + c\sigma_3 + \tau_3 + c\sigma_4 + \tau_4}{4}\right)$$

$$\Re\left(c\tilde{A} \oplus \tilde{B}\right) = \left(\dfrac{c\sigma_1 + c\sigma_2 + c\sigma_3 + c\sigma_4 + \tau_1 + \tau_2 + \tau_3 + \tau_4}{4}\right)$$

$$\Re\left(c\tilde{A} \oplus \tilde{B}\right) = \left(\dfrac{c\sigma_1 + c\sigma_2 + c\sigma_3 + c\sigma_4}{4}\right) + \left(\dfrac{\tau_1 + \tau_2 + \tau_3 + \tau_4}{4}\right)$$

$$\Re\left(c\tilde{A} \oplus \tilde{B}\right) = c\left(\dfrac{\sigma_1 + \sigma_2 + \sigma_3 + \sigma_4}{4}\right) + \left(\dfrac{\tau_1 + \tau_2 + \tau_3 + \tau_4}{4}\right)$$

$$\Re\left(c\tilde{A} \oplus \tilde{B}\right) = c\Re\left(\tilde{A}\right) \oplus \Re\left(\tilde{B}\right)$$

Similarly, it can be proved for $c < 0$. This implies that the ranking function $\Re$ is a linear function.

4. FULLY FUZZY TRANSPORTATION PROBLEM (FFTP) AND ITS MATHEMATICAL FORMULATION

In this section, the author discusses different types of FTP, some necessary and important definitions and mathematical formulation of the fully fuzzy transportation problem.

4.1. Definition: FTP

If the TP has at least one of the parameter (cost) or two of the parameters (supply and demand) or all of the parameters (supply, demand and cost) are in fuzzy numbers then the problem is called FTP.
Further, FTP can be classified into four categories. They are:

Type-1 FTP.
Type-2 FTP.
Type-3 FTP (Mixed FTP).
Type-4 FTP (FFTP).

4.1.1. Definition: Type-1 FTP

A TP having fuzzy availabilities and fuzzy demands but crisp costs is termed as FTP of type-1.

4.1.2. Definition: Type-2 FTP

A TP having crisp availabilities and crisp demands but fuzzy costs is termed as FTP of type-2.

4.1.3. Definition: Type-3 FTP (Mixed FTP)

The TP is said to be the type-3 FTP or mixed FTP if all the parameters of the TP (such as supplies, demands and costs) must be in the mixture of crisp numbers, TFNs and TrFNs.

4.1.4. Definition: Type-4 FTP (FFTP)

The TP is said to be the type-4 FTP or FFTP if all the parameters of the TP (such as supplies, demands and costs) must be in fuzzy numbers.

4.2. Definition: Balanced Fuzzy Transportation Problem (BFTP)

The TP is said to be BFTP if total fuzzy supply is equal to total fuzzy demand.

That is, $\sum_{i=1}^{m} \tilde{a}_i = \sum_{j=1}^{n} \tilde{b}_j$

4.3. Definition: Unbalanced FTP

The TP is said to be an unbalanced FTP if total fuzzy supply is not equal to total fuzzy demand.

That is, $\sum_{i=1}^{m} \tilde{a}_i \neq \sum_{j=1}^{n} \tilde{b}_j$

4.4. Definition: Fuzzy Feasible Solution

A set of fuzzy non negative allocations $\tilde{x}_{ij} > \tilde{0}$ satisfies the row and column restriction is known as fuzzy feasible solution.

4.5. Definition: Fuzzy Basic Feasible Solution

Any feasible solution is a fuzzy basic feasible solution if the number of non negative allocations is at most $(m + n - 1)$ where m is the number of rows and n is the number of columns in the $(m \times n)$ transportation table.

4.6. Definition: Fuzzy Degenerate Solution

If the fuzzy basic feasible solution contains less than $(m + n - 1)$ non negative allocations in $(m \times n)$ transportation table, it is said to be degenerate.

4.7. Definition: Fuzzy Non Degenerate Solution

Any fuzzy feasible solution to a TP containing m origins and n destinations is said to be fuzzy non degenerate, if it contains exactly $(m + n - 1)$ occupied cells.

4.8. Definition: Fuzzy Optimal Solution

The fuzzy basic feasible solution is said to be fuzzy optimal solution if it minimizes the total fuzzy transportation cost (or) it maximizes the total fuzzy transportation profit.

4.9. Definition: Mathematical Formulation

A FTP is a TP in which the transportation costs, supply and demand quantities are fuzzy numbers. Let us consider TP with m fuzzy origins (rows) and n fuzzy destinations (columns). Let $\tilde{c}_{ij} = \left[c_{ij}^1, c_{ij}^2, c_{ij}^3, c_{ij}^4 \right]$ be the uncertain cost of transporting one unit of the product from ith fuzzy origin to jth fuzzy destination, $\tilde{a}_i = \left[a_i^1, a_i^2, a_i^3, a_i^4 \right]$ be the uncertain quantity of commodity available at fuzzy origin i and $\tilde{b}_j = \left[b_j^1, b_j^2, b_j^3, b_j^4 \right]$ be the uncertain quantity of commodity required at fuzzy destination j. Let $\tilde{x}_{ij} = \left[x_{ij}^1, x_{ij}^2, x_{ij}^3, x_{ij}^4 \right]$ be the uncertain quantity of commodity transported from ith fuzzy origin to jth fuzzy destination. Our aim is to determine the shipping schedule that minimizes the total fuzzy transportation cost while satisfying fuzzy supply and fuzzy demand limits.

Now, the mathematical formulation of the above fully fuzzy transportation problem (FFTP) is defined as follows:

(P) Minimize $\tilde{Z} = \displaystyle\sum_{i=1}^{m}\sum_{j=1}^{n} \tilde{c}_{ij} \otimes \tilde{x}_{ij}$

subject to:

$$\sum_{j=1}^{n} \tilde{x}_{ij} \approx \tilde{a}_i, \text{ for } i = 1, 2, \ldots, m \tag{1}$$

$$\sum_{i=1}^{m} \tilde{x}_{ij} \approx \tilde{b}_j, \text{ for } j = 1, 2, \ldots, n \tag{2}$$

$$\tilde{x}_{ij} \succeq \tilde{0}, \text{ for } i = 1, 2, \ldots, m \text{ and } j = 1, 2, \ldots, n \tag{3}$$

where:

m = the number of supply points
n = the number of demand points.

When the supplies, demands and costs are fuzzy numbers, then the total cost becomes the fuzzy number. Symbolically, it can be noted as $\tilde{Z}^I$ where $\tilde{Z} = \displaystyle\sum_{i=1}^{m}\sum_{j=1}^{n} \tilde{c}_{ij}\tilde{x}_{ij}$.

Hence it cannot be minimized directly. For solving the problem the author convert the fuzzy supplies, fuzzy demands and the fuzzy costs into crisp ones by a fuzzy number ranking method.

Consider the TP with m origins (rows) and n destinations (columns). Let c_{ij} be the cost of transporting one unit of the product from ith origin to jth destination, a_i be the quantity of commodity available at origin i, b_j the quantity of commodity needed at destination j, x_{ij} is the quantity transported from ith origin to jth destination, so as to minimize the total transportation cost:

(P*) Minimize $\Re\left(\tilde{Z}^*\right) = \displaystyle\sum_{i=1}^{m}\sum_{j=1}^{n} \Re\left(\tilde{c}_{ij}\right) \otimes \Re(\tilde{x}_{ij})$

subject to:

$$\sum_{j=1}^{n} \Re(\tilde{x}_{ij}) \approx \Re(\tilde{a}_i), \text{ for } i = 1, 2, \ldots, m \tag{4}$$

$$\sum_{i=1}^{m} \Re(\tilde{x}_{ij}) \approx \Re\left(\tilde{b}_{j}\right), \text{for } j = 1, 2, \ldots, n \tag{5}$$

$$\Re(\tilde{x}_{ij}) \succeq \Re\left(\tilde{0}\right), \text{ for } i = 1, 2, \ldots, m \tag{6}$$

and

$$j = 1, 2, \ldots, n$$

Since $\Re(\tilde{c}_{ij}), \Re(\tilde{x}_{ij}), \Re(\tilde{a}_{ij}), \Re(\tilde{b}_{ij})$, all are crisp values, this problem (P*) is obviously the crisp TP of the form (P) which can be solved by the conventional method namely the Zero Point Method, Modified Distribution Method or any other software package such as LINGO 17.0, TORA and so on. Once the optimal solution x^* of Model (P*) is found, the optimal fuzzy objective value $\tilde{Z}^*$ of the original problem can be calculated as:

$$\tilde{Z}^* = \sum_{i=1}^{m}\sum_{j=1}^{n} \tilde{c}_{ij} \otimes \tilde{x}_{ij}^{\ *}$$

where $\tilde{c}_{ij} = \left[c_{ij}^1, c_{ij}^2, c_{ij}^3, c_{ij}^4 \right]$, $\tilde{x}_{ij}^{\ *} = \left[x_{ij}^1, x_{ij}^2, x_{ij}^3, x_{ij}^4 \right]$

The above FFTP and its equivalent crisp TP can be stated in the tabular form as shown in Tables 1 and 2.

Now a new method is proposed, namely, PSK method for finding an optimal solution to the FTP.

Table 1. Tabular representation of FFTP

Source	Destination				Fuzzy Availability $\tilde{a}_i$
	D_1	D_2	$\cdots$	D_n	
S_1	$\tilde{c}_{11}$	$\tilde{c}_{12}$	$\cdots$	$\tilde{c}_{1n}$	$\tilde{a}_1$
S_2	$\tilde{c}_{21}$	$\tilde{c}_{22}$	$\cdots$	$\tilde{c}_{2n}$	$\tilde{a}_2$
$\vdots$	$\vdots$	$\vdots$	$\cdots$	$\vdots$	$\vdots$
S_m	$\tilde{c}_{m1}$	$\tilde{c}_{m2}$	$\cdots$	$\tilde{c}_{mn}$	$\tilde{a}_m$
Fuzzy Demand $\tilde{b}_j$	$\tilde{b}_1$	$\tilde{b}_2$	$\cdots$	$\tilde{b}_n$	$\sum_{i=1}^{m}\tilde{a}_i = \sum_{j=1}^{n}\tilde{b}_j$

Table 2. Tabular representation of crisp TP

Source	Destination				Availability $\Re(\tilde{a}_i)$
	D_1	D_2	$\cdots$	D_n	
S_1	$\Re\left(\tilde{c}_{11}\right)$	$\Re\left(\tilde{c}_{12}\right)$	$\cdots$	$\Re\left(\tilde{c}_{1n}\right)$	$\Re\left(\tilde{a}_1\right)$
S_2	$\Re\left(\tilde{c}_{21}\right)$	$\Re\left(\tilde{c}_{22}\right)$	$\cdots$	$\Re\left(\tilde{c}_{2n}\right)$	$\Re\left(\tilde{a}_2\right)$
$\vdots$	$\vdots$	$\vdots$	$\cdots$	$\vdots$	$\vdots$
S_m	$\Re\left(\tilde{c}_{m1}\right)$	$\Re\left(\tilde{c}_{m2}\right)$	$\cdots$	$\Re\left(\tilde{c}_{mn}\right)$	$\Re\left(\tilde{a}_m\right)$
Demand $\Re\left(\tilde{b}_j\right)$	$\Re\left(\tilde{b}_1\right)$	$\Re\left(\tilde{b}_2\right)$	$\cdots$	$\Re\left(\tilde{b}_n\right)$	$\sum_{i=1}^{m}\Re\left(\tilde{a}_i\right)=\sum_{j=1}^{n}\Re\left(\tilde{b}_j\right)$

5. PSK METHOD

The PSK method proceeds as follows:

Step 1: Construct the transportation table in which costs, supplies and demands are must be a mixture of crisp numbers, TFNs and TrFNs such TP is called MFTP then convert the MFTP into a balanced mixed fuzzy transportation problem (BMFTP), if it is not, by using ranking method.

Step 2: After using step 1, convert BMFTP into balanced fully fuzzy transportation problem (BFFTP) using the following steps:

1. If any one or more in the supplies/demands/costs of a TP having a real number say a_1 that can be expanded as a TrFN $a_1 = \left(a_1, a_1, a_1, a_1\right)$;
2. If any one or more in the supplies/demands/costs of a TP having a TFN say $\left(a_1, a_2, a_3\right)$ that can be expanded as a TrFN $\left(a_1, a_2, a_3\right) = \left(a_1, a_2, a_2, a_3\right)$;
3. If any one or more in the supplies /demands/costs of a TP having a TrFN say $\left(a_1, a_2, a_3, a_4\right)$ that can be kept as it is. That is $\left(a_1, a_2, a_3, a_4\right) = \left(a_1, a_2, a_3, a_4\right)$.

Step 3: After using step 2, transform the BFFTP into its equivalent crisp TP using the ranking procedure as mentioned in section 3.

Step 4: Now, the crisp TP having all the entries of supply, demand and costs are in integers then kept as it is. Otherwise at least one or all of the supply, demand and costs are not in integers then rewrite its nearest integer value.

Step 5: After using step 4 of the proposed method, now solve the crisp TP by using any one of the existing methods (MODI, Zero Point Method) or software packages such as LINGO 17.0, TORA and so on. This step yields the optimal allocation and optimal objective value of the crisp TP (The optimal allotted cell in crisp transportation table is referred as occupied cells. The remaining cells are called unoccupied cells. The numbers of occupied cells in crisp TP which are exactly $m + n - 1$ and all have zero cost. Similarly in FFTP also have the same $m + n - 1$ number of occupied cells but its corresponding costs are fuzzy zeros). Now, construct the new fully fuzzy transportation table (FFTT) whose occupied cells costs are fuzzy zeros and the remaining cells costs are its original cost. Subtract each row entries for the current table from the row minimum. Next subtract each column entries of the reduced table from the column minimum. Clearly, each row and each column of the resulting table has at least one fuzzy zero. The current resulting table is the allotment table.

Step 6: After using step 5 of the proposed method, now we check the allotment table if one or more rows/columns having exactly one occupied cell (fuzzy zero) then allot the maximum possible value to that cell and adjust the corresponding supply or demand with a positive difference of supply and demand. Otherwise, if all the rows/columns having more than one occupied cells then select a cell in the α - row and β - column of the transportation table whose cost is maximum (If the maximum cost is more than one i.e., break ties arbitrarily) and examine which one of the cells is minimum cost (If the minimum cost is more than one i.e., ties are broken arbitrarily) among all the occupied cells in that row and column then allot the maximum possible value to that cell. In this manner proceeds selected row and column entirely. If the entire row and column of the occupied cells having fully allotted then select the next maximum cost of the transportation table and examine which one of the cells is minimum cost among all the occupied cells in that row and column then allot the maximum possible value to that cell. Repeat this process until all the fuzzy supply points are fully used and all the fuzzy demand points are fully received. This allotment yields the fully fuzzy solution to the given FFTP.

Remark 5.1: Allot the maximum possible value to the occupied cells in type-1 and type-3 FTP which is the most preferable row/column having exactly one occupied cell.

Remark 5.2: From the MODI method, the author conclude that the TP have exactly $m + n - 1$ number of non-negative independent allocations.

Remark 5.3 From the Zero Point Method, we can make exactly $m + n - 1$ number of zeros (zero referred to as zero cost) in the cost matrix. All these zeros (costs) are in independent positions.

Remark 5.4: From Remark 5.2 and Remark 5.3, we can directly replace the fuzzy zeros instead of original costs in the occupied cells in the original FTP. This modification does not affect the originality of the problem

Remark 5.5: The proposed method may be called as PSK's (P.Senthil Kumar) method for finding the fuzzy optimal solution of type-1, type-2, type-3 and type-4 FTPs. PSK is the lovely son of Periyasamy. He was born in 1985 at Elayaperumal Patty in Karur. Now he is working as an Assistant Professor, PG and Research Department of Mathematics, Jamal Mohamed College, Tiruchirappalli.

Now, the author prove the following theorems which are used to derive the solution to a FTP obtained by the PSK method is a fuzzy optimal solution to the FFTP.

5.1. Theorem

Any optimal solution to the fully fuzzy transportation (P_1) where

$$(P_1) \text{ Minimize } \tilde{Z}^* = \sum_{i=1}^{m}\sum_{j=1}^{n}(\tilde{c}_{ij} \ominus \tilde{u}_i \ominus \tilde{v}_j)\tilde{x}_{ij}$$

subject to (1) to (3) are satisfied, where $\tilde{u}_i$ (minimum of ith row of the newly constructed transportation table $\tilde{c}_{ij}$) and $\tilde{v}_j$ (minimum of jth column of the resulting transportation table $[\tilde{c}_{ij} \ominus \tilde{u}_i]$)are some real TrFNs, is an optimal solution to the problem (P) where

$$(P) \text{ Minimize } \tilde{Z} = \sum_{i=1}^{m}\sum_{j=1}^{n}\tilde{c}_{ij} \otimes \tilde{x}_{ij}$$

subject to (1) to (3) are satisfied.

Proof: Let $\tilde{u}_i$ be the minimum of ith row of the newly constructed transportation table $[\tilde{c}_{ij}]$. Now, we subtract $\tilde{u}_i$ from the ith row entries so that the resulting table is $[\tilde{c}_{ij} \ominus \tilde{u}_i]$. Let $\tilde{v}_j$ be the minimum of jth column of the resulting table $[\tilde{c}_{ij} \ominus \tilde{u}_i]$. Now, we subtract $\tilde{v}_j$ from the jth column entries so that the resulting table is $\left(\tilde{c}_{ij} \ominus \tilde{u}_i \ominus \tilde{v}_j\right)$. It may be noted that $\left(\tilde{c}_{ij} \ominus \tilde{u}_i \ominus \tilde{v}_j\right) \succeq \tilde{0}$, for all i and j. Further each row and each column having at least one fuzzy zero.

Now:

$$\tilde{Z}^* \approx \sum_{i=1}^{m}\sum_{j=1}^{n}(\tilde{c}_{ij} \ominus \tilde{u}_i \ominus \tilde{v}_j)\tilde{x}_{ij}$$

$$\tilde{Z}^* \approx \sum_{i=1}^{m}\sum_{j=1}^{n}\tilde{c}_{ij} \otimes \tilde{x}_{ij} \ominus \sum_{i=1}^{m}\sum_{j=1}^{n}\tilde{u}_i \otimes \tilde{x}_{ij} \ominus \sum_{i=1}^{m}\sum_{j=1}^{n}\tilde{v}_j \otimes \tilde{x}_{ij}$$

$$\tilde{z}^* \approx \tilde{z}\Theta\sum_{i=1}^{m}\tilde{\mu}_i \otimes \tilde{b}_j\Theta\sum_{j=1}^{n}\tilde{v}_j \otimes \tilde{a}_i$$

Since $\sum_{i=1}^{m}\tilde{u}_i \otimes \tilde{b}_j$ and $\sum_{j=1}^{n}\tilde{v}_j \otimes \tilde{a}_i$ are independent of $\tilde{x}_{ij}$, for all i and j. According to the obtained result, the author conclude that any optimal solution to the problem (P_1) is also a fuzzy optimal solution to the problem (P). Hence the theorem.

5.2. Theorem

If $\left\{ \tilde{x}_{ij}^{o}, i = 1, 2, \ldots, m \text{ and } j = 1, 2, \ldots n \right\}$ is a feasible solution to the problem (P) and $\left(\tilde{c}_{ij} \ominus \tilde{u}_{i} \ominus \tilde{v}_{j} \right) \succeq \tilde{0}$, for all i and j where $\tilde{u}_{i}$ and $\tilde{v}_{j}$ are some real TrFNs, such that the minimum $\sum_{i=1}^{m} \sum_{j=1}^{n} (\tilde{c}_{ij} \ominus \tilde{u}_{i} \ominus \tilde{v}_{j}) \tilde{x}_{ij}$ subject to (1) to (3) are satisfied, is fuzzy zero, then $\left\{ \tilde{x}_{ij}^{o}, i = 1, 2, \ldots, m \text{ and } j = 1, 2, \ldots n \right\}$ is a fuzzy optimal solution to the problem (P).

Proof: From the Theorem 5.1, the result follows.

Hence the theorem.

Now, the author prove that the solution to the FFTP (or mixed FTP) obtained by the PSK method is a fully fuzzy optimal solution (or mixed fuzzy optimal solution) to the FFTP (or mixed FTP).

5.3. Theorem (PSK Theorem)

A solution obtained by the PSK's method for a FFTP (or mixed FTP) with equality constraints (P) is a fully fuzzy optimal solution (or mixed fuzzy optimal solution) for the FFTP (P) (or mixed FTP).

Proof: We, now describe the PSK's method in detail.

We construct the transportation table in which costs, supplies and demands are must be a combination of crisp numbers, TFNs and TrFNs such TP is called MFTP. Next, transform the MFTP into a balanced mixed fuzzy transportation problem (BMFTP), if it is not balanced, by using ranking method and convert BMFTP into balanced fully fuzzy transportation problem (BFFTP) using the following steps:

1. If any one or more in the supplies/demands/costs of a TP having a real number say a_1 that can be expanded as a TrFN $a_1 = \left(a_1, a_1, a_1, a_1 \right)$.
2. If any one or more in the supplies/demands/costs of a TP having a TFN say $\left(a_1, a_2, a_3 \right)$ that can be expanded as a TrFN $\left(a_1, a_2, a_3 \right) = \left(a_1, a_2, a_2, a_3 \right)$.
3. If any one or more in the supplies /demands/costs of a TP having a TrFN say $\left(a_1, a_2, a_3, a_4 \right)$ that can be kept as it is. That is $\left(a_1, a_2, a_3, a_4 \right) = \left(a_1, a_2, a_3, a_4 \right)$.

After using above steps, we get the fully fuzzy transportation table $[\tilde{c}_{ij}]$ then, transform the FFTP into its equivalent crisp TP using the ranking procedure of Liou and Wang.

Now, the crisp TP having all the entries of supply, demand and costs are integers then kept as it is. Otherwise at least one or all of the supply, demand and costs are not in integers then rewrite its nearest integer value because decimal values in TP has no physical meaning (such a TP referred as crisp TP).

Now, solve the crisp TP by using any one of the existing methods (MODI, Zero Point Method) or software packages such as LINGO 17.0, TORA and so on. This process will yield the optimal allotment and optimal objective value of the crisp TP (The optimal allotted cells in crisp transportation table is referred to as occupied cells which are exactly $m + n - 1$. All the decision variables in this occupied cells are basic feasible with zero cost. Clearly, each row and each column have at least one zero cost which corresponds to the occupied cells. The remaining cells are called unoccupied cells. All the decision variables in these unoccupied cells are non basic. The value of decision variables in this unoccupied cells are at zero level).

By the definitions, occupied cells in crisp TP is same as that of occupied cells in FFTP but the value of occupied cells for FFTP is the maximum possible value of fuzzy supply and fuzzy demand. Therefore, we need not further investigate the occupied cells in FFTP. But only we claim that how much quantity (fuzzy supply, fuzzy demand) to allot the occupied cells subject to (1),(2) and (3) are satisfied. The occupied cells in crisp TP is exactly $m + n - 1$ and all are having zero cost. Similarly in FFTP also have the same $m + n - 1$ number of occupied cells but its corresponding cost is fuzzy zeros. Now, construct the new FFTT whose occupied cells costs are fuzzy zeros and the remaining cells costs are its original cost. Let $\tilde{u}_i$ be the minimum of ith row of the current table $[\tilde{c}_{ij}]$. Now, we subtract $\tilde{u}_i$ from the ith row entries so that the resulting table is $[\tilde{c}_{ij} \ominus \tilde{u}_i]$. Let $\tilde{v}_j$ be the minimum of jth column of the resulting table $[\tilde{c}_{ij} \ominus \tilde{u}_i]$. Now, we subtract $\tilde{v}_j$ from the jth column entries so that the resulting table is $\left(\tilde{c}_{ij} \ominus \tilde{u}_i \ominus \tilde{v}_j \right)$. It may be noted that $\left(\tilde{c}_{ij} \ominus \tilde{u}_i \ominus \tilde{v}_j \right) \succeq \tilde{0}$ for all i and j. Clearly, each row and each column have at least one fuzzy zero. The current resulting table is the allotment table.

Now, we check the allotment table if one or more rows/columns having exactly one occupied cell then allot the maximum possible value to that cell and adjust the corresponding supply or demand with a positive difference of supply and demand. Otherwise, if all the rows/columns having more than one occupied cells then select a cell in the α row and β column of the transportation table whose cost is maximum (If the maximum cost is more than one i.e., a tie occurs then select arbitrarily) and examine which one of the cells is minimum cost (If the minimum cost is more than one i.e., a tie occurs then select arbitrarily) among all the occupied cells in that row and column then allot the maximum possible value to that cell. In this manner proceeds selected row/column entirely. If the entire row and column of the occupied cells having fully allotted then select the next maximum cost of the transportation table and examine which one of the cells is minimum cost among all the occupied cells in that row and column then allot the maximum possible value to that cell. Repeat this process until all the fuzzy supply points are fully used and all the fuzzy demand points are fully received. This step yields the optimum fuzzy allotment.

Clearly, the above process satisfies all the rim requirements (row and column sum restriction). If all the rim requirements are satisfied then automatically it satisfies, total fuzzy supply is equal to total fuzzy demand i.e., the necessary and sufficient condition for a FFTP/MFTP is satisfied.

Finally, we have a solution $\left\{ \tilde{x}_{ij}, i = 1, 2, \ldots, m \text{ and } j = 1, 2, \ldots n \right\}$ for the FFTP/MFTP whose cost matrix is $[\tilde{c}_{ij} \ominus \tilde{u}_i \ominus \tilde{v}_j]$ such that $\tilde{x}_{ij} \approx \tilde{0}$ for $(\tilde{c}_{ij} \ominus \tilde{u}_i \ominus \tilde{v}_j) \succeq \tilde{0}$ and $\tilde{x}_{ij} \succ \tilde{0}$ for $(\tilde{c}_{ij} \ominus \tilde{u}_i \ominus \tilde{v}_j) \approx \tilde{0}$.

Therefore, the minimum $\sum\limits_{i=1}^{m} \sum\limits_{j=1}^{n} (\tilde{c}_{ij} \ominus \tilde{u}_i \ominus \tilde{v}_j) \tilde{x}_{ij}$ subject to (1) to (3) are satisfied, is fuzzy zero.

Thus, by the Theorem 5.2, the solution $\left\{ \tilde{x}_{ij}, i = 1, 2, \ldots, m \text{ and } j = 1, 2, \ldots n \right\}$ is obtained by the PSK method for a FFTP (or mixed FTP) with equality constraints is a fully fuzzy optimal solution (or mixed fuzzy optimal solution) for the FFTP (or mixed FTP). Hence the theorem.

The procedure for the solution is illustrated with the following numerical example.

6. ILLUSTRATIVE EXAMPLES

Example: 1 Type-1 FTP

A firm has three factories S_1, S_2, and S_3 that manufacture the same product of air coolers in three different places. The firm manager would like to transport air coolers from three different factories to four different warehouses D_1, D_2, D_3 and D_4. All the factories are connected to all the warehouses by roads and air coolers are transported by trucks/lorries. The availability (availability/supply of air coolers are depends on its production but production depends on machine, men etc.) of air coolers are not known exactly due to long power cut, unexpected failures in machine, labour's over time work etc. The demand/requirement of air coolers is not known exactly due to seasonal changes (in sunny days the sale of air coolers are more when compared to rainy days). The shipping costs (rupees in hundreds) of an air cooler from three different factories (or origins) to four different warehouses (or destinations) are given in exactly. Hence, from the past experience fuzzy supply, fuzzy demand, and crisp costs are given in Table 3.

Find the optimal allocation which minimizes total fuzzy transportation cost.

Solution by proposed method:

Now using step 2 we get, $\sum_{i=1}^{m} \tilde{a}_i = \sum_{j=1}^{n} \tilde{b}_j = 60$, the given problem is a balanced type-1 FTP.

Now, using the step 3 of proposed method, in conformation to Model (P*) FFTP can be transformed into its equivalent crisp TP by using the ranking method $\Re\left(\tilde{A}\right) = \left(a_1 + a_2 + a_3 + a_4\right)/4$. Crisp version of type-1 FTP corresponding to example 1 is shown in Table 4.

Since in TPs supplies, demands and costs are not in decimal values because no physical meaning of fractional value. Therefore whenever the rank values occur in the form of decimal then we convert it into its nearest integer value. Otherwise, all the rank values of the type-1 FTP are in integers then kept as it is.

Table 3. Type-1 FTP

Factories	Warehouses				Fuzzy Availability $\tilde{a}_i$
	D_1	D_2	D_3	D_4	
S_1	2	2	2	1	[0, 2, 4, 6]
S_2	10	8	5	4	[2, 4, 9, 13]
S_3	7	6	6	8	[2, 4, 6, 8]
Fuzzy Demand $\tilde{b}_j$	[1, 3, 5, 7]	[0, 2, 4, 6]	[1, 3, 5, 7]	[1, 3, 5, 7]	

Table 4. Crisp version of type-1 FTP

Factories	Warehouses				Availability $\tilde{a}_i$
	D_1	D_2	D_3	D_4	
S_1	2	2	2	1	3
S_2	10	8	5	4	7
S_3	7	6	6	8	5
Demand $\tilde{b}_j$	4	3	4	4	

After using step 5 of the proposed method, the optimal allotment of the above problem (Crisp version of type-1 FTP) is shown in Table 5.

The optimum solution is: $x_{11} = 3$, $x_{23} = 3$, $x_{24} = 4$, $x_{31} = 1$, $x_{32} = 3$, $x_{33} = 1$
The minimum objective value is: Z= (2×3) + (5×3) + (4×4) + (7×1) + (6×3) + (6×1) =68(Rupees in hundreds)

After using step 5 of the proposed method, now using step 6, we get the optimal allotment directly for the type-1 FTP is shown in the following table (refer to Table 6).

The fuzzy optimal solution in terms of TrFN is:

$\tilde{x}_{11}$ =[0,2,4,6], $\tilde{x}_{23}$ =[-5,-1,6,12], $\tilde{x}_{24}$ =[1,3,5,7], $\tilde{x}_{31}$ =[-5,-1,3,7], $\tilde{x}_{32}$ =[0,2,4, 6], $\tilde{x}_{33}$ =[-11,-3,6,12]

Table 5. Crisp optimum table of type-1 FTP

Factories	Warehouses				Availability $\tilde{a}_i$
	D_1	D_2	D_3	D_4	
S_1	0(3)	2	2	1	3
S_2	10	8	0(3)	0(4)	7
S_3	0(1)	0(3)	0(1)	8	5
Demand $\tilde{b}_j$	4	3	4	4	

Table 6. Fuzzy optimum table of type-1 FTP

Factories	Warehouses				Fuzzy Availability $\tilde{a}_i$
	D_1	D_2	D_3	D_4	
S_1	**[0,2,4, 6]** 0	2	2	1	[0,2, 4, 6]
S_2	10	8	**[-5,-1,6,12]** 0	**[1,3,5,7]** 0	[2,4,9,13]
S_3	**[-5,-1,3,7]** 0	**[0, 2, 4, 6]** 0	**[-11,-3,6,12]** 0	8	[2,4, 6, 8]
Fuzzy Demand $\tilde{b}_j$	[1, 3, 5, 7]	[0, 2, 4, 6]	[1, 3, 5, 7]	[1, 3, 5, 7]	

Hence, the total fuzzy transportation cost is:

Min $\tilde{Z} = 2 \otimes [0,2,4, 6] \oplus 5 \otimes [-5,-1,6,12] \oplus 4 \otimes [1,3,5,7] \oplus 7 \otimes [-5,-1,3,7] . \oplus 6 \otimes [0, 2, 4, 6] \oplus 6 \otimes [-11,-3,6,12]$.

Min $\tilde{Z} = [0,4,8,12] \oplus [-25,-5,30,60] \oplus [4,12,20,28] \oplus [-35,-7,21,49] \oplus [0,12,24,36] \oplus [-66,-18,36,72]$.

Min $\tilde{Z} = [-122,-2,139,257]$ (Rupees in hundreds)

$\Re(\tilde{Z}) = [12,55,88,117] = \dfrac{-122 - 2 + 139 + 257}{4} = 68$ (Rupees in hundreds)

Example: 2 Consider the 3×3 MFTP (Type-3 FTP)

A company has three factories S_1, S_2, and S_3 that manufacture the same product of umbrellas in three different places. The company manager would like to transport umbrellas from three different factories (or origins) to three different retail stores (or destinations) D_1, D_2, and D_3. All the factories are connected to all the retail stores by roads and umbrellas are transported by trucks/lorries/motorcycles. The availability (availability of umbrellas are depends on its production but production depends on machine, men etc.) of umbrellas are not known exactly due to long power cut, unexpected failures in machine, labour's over time work etc. The demand of an umbrella is not known exactly due to seasonal changes (in rainy days the sale of an umbrella is more when compared to sunny days). Similarly, the transportation cost is not known exactly due to variations in rates of diesel or petrol, weather in hilly areas, traffic jams etc. So, all the parameters of the TP are given in mixture of crisp numbers, TFNs and TrFNs. The transportation cost for an umbrella from different factories to different retail stores are given in Table 7 from the past experience.

Table 7. Type-3 FTP

Source	Destination			Mixed Fuzzy Supply $\tilde{a}_i$
	D_1	D_2	D_3	
S_1	6	[1,2,3]	[5,7,9,11]	10
S_2	[1,2,3]	[4, 8,16,20]	10	[10,16,24,30]
S_3	[1,3,5,7]	3	[6, 8, 10]	[8,16,24]
Mixed Fuzzy Demand $\tilde{b}_j$	[11,22,30,41]	[5,8,11]	12	[28,42,50,64]

Find the optimal allocation which minimizes total fuzzy transportation cost.

Solution by proposed method:

After using step1 of the proposed method now, then using step 2 we get the following type-4 FTP which is shown in Table 8.

Now using step 2 we get, $\sum_{i=1}^{m} \tilde{a}_i = \sum_{j=1}^{n} \tilde{b}_j = 184$, the given problem is balanced FFTP.

Now, using the step 3 of proposed method, in conformation to Model (P*) FFTP can be transformed into its equivalent crisp TP by using the ranking method $\Re\left(\tilde{A}\right) = \left(a_1 + a_2 + a_3 + a_4\right) / 4$. Crisp version of type-4 FTP corresponding to type-3 FTP is shown in Table 9.

Since in TPs supplies, demands and costs are not in decimal values because no physical meaning of fractional value. Therefore whenever decimal values occur in crisp TP we convert it into its nearest integer value. Here, the ranking method gives the integer values therefore we need not apply the step 4.

Table 8. Modified form of type-3 FTP to type-4 FTP

Source	Destination			Fuzzy Supply $\tilde{a}_i$
	D_1	D_2	D_3	
S_1	[6,6,6,6]	[1,2,2,3]	[5,7,9,11]	[10,10,10,10]
S_2	[1,2,2,3]	[4, 8,16,20]	[10,10,10,10]	[10,16,24,30]
S_3	[1,3,5,7]	[3,3,3,3]	[6,8,8,10]	[8,16,16,24]
Fuzzy Demand $\tilde{b}_j$	[11,22,30,41]	[5,8,8,11]	[12,12,12,12]	[28,42,50,64]

Table 9. Crisp version of type-4 FTP

Source	Destination			Supply $\tilde{a}_i$
	D_1	D_2	D_3	
S_1	6	2	8	10
S_2	2	12	10	20
S_3	4	3	8	16
Demand $\tilde{b}_j$	26	8	12	46

After using step 5 of the proposed method, the optimal allotment of the above problem is given in Table 10.

From the Table 10, the optimal objective value is:

$$Z= (0\times8) + (0\times2) + (0\times20) + (0\times6) + (0\times10) =0 \text{ (we could not minimize cost below zero)}$$

Therefore, the optimum solution is:

$$x_{12} = 8, x_{13} = 2, x_{21} = 20, x_{31} = 6, x_{33} = 10$$

The minimum objective value is:

$$Z= (2\times8) + (8\times2) + (2\times20) + (4\times6) + (8\times10) =176$$

Table 10. Crisp optimum table of type-3 FTP

Source	Destination			Supply $\tilde{a}_i$
	D_1	D_2	D_3	
S_1	6	0(8)	0(2)	10
S_2	0(20)	12	10	20
S_3	0(6)	3	0(10)	16
Demand $\tilde{b}_j$	26	8	12	46

After using step 5 of the PSK, now using step 6, we get the optimal allotment directly for the FFTP is shown in the following table (see Table 11).

From the Table 11, the optimal objective value is:

Min $\tilde{Z}$ = [-2,-1,1,2]$\otimes$ [5,8,8,11] + [-2,-1,1,2] $\otimes$ [-1,2,2,5] + [-2,-1,1,2] $\otimes$ [10,16,24,30] + [-2,-1,1,2] $\otimes$ [-19,-2,14,31] + [-2,-1,1,2] $\otimes$ [7,10,10,13]

Min $\tilde{Z}$ =[-2,-1,1,2]$\otimes$ 8+[-2,-1,1,2]$\otimes$ 2+ [-2,-1,1,2] $\otimes$20+ [-2,-1,1,2] $\otimes$6+ [-2,-1,1,2] $\otimes$ 10

Min $\tilde{Z}$ =[-16,-8,8,16]+[-4,-2,2,4]+ [-40,-20,20,40]+ [-12,-6,6,12] + [-20,-10,10,20]

Min $\tilde{Z}$ =[-92,-46,46,92] = $\tilde{0}$ (we could not minimize fuzzy cost below $\tilde{0}$).

Therefore, the fuzzy optimal solution in terms of TrFN is

$\tilde{x}_{12} = \left[5,8,8,11\right]$, $\tilde{x}_{13} = \left[-1,2,2,5\right]$, $\tilde{x}_{21} = \left[10,16,24,30\right]$, $\tilde{x}_{31} = \left[-19,-2,14,31\right]$

$\tilde{x}_{33} = \left[7,10,10,13\right]$.

The above solution can be written in the mixed solution form, which is given in below:

$\tilde{x}_{12} = \left[5,8,11\right]$, $\tilde{x}_{13} = \left[-1,2,5\right]$, $\tilde{x}_{21} = \left[10,16,24,30\right]$, $\tilde{x}_{31} = \left[-19,-2,14,31\right]$, $\tilde{x}_{33} = \left[7,10,13\right]$.

Hence, the total fuzzy transportation minimum cost is:

Table 11. Fuzzy optimum table of type-3 FTP

Source	Destination			Fuzzy Supply $\tilde{a}_i$
	D_1	D_2	D_3	
S_1	[6,6,6,6]	**[5,8,8,11]** [-2,-1,1,2]	**[-1,2,2,5]** [-2,-1,1,2]	[10,10,10,10]
S_2	**[10,16,24,30]** [-2,-1,1,2]	[4, 8,16,20]	[10,10,10,10]	[10,16,24,30]
S_3	**[-19,-2,14,31]** [-2,-1,1,2]	[3,3,3,3]	**[7,10,10,13]** [-2,-1,1,2]	[8,16,16,24]
Fuzzy Demand $\tilde{b}_j$	[11,22,30,41]	[5,8,8,11]	[12,12,12,12]	[28,42,50,64]

Min $\tilde{Z}$ =[1,2,2,3] $\otimes$ [5,8,8,11]+[5,7,9,11] $\otimes$ -1,2,2,5]+[1,2,2,3] $\otimes$ [10,16,24,30]+ [1,3,5,7] $\otimes$ [-19,-2,14,31] + [6,8,8,10] $\otimes$ [7,10,10,13].

Min $\tilde{Z}$ =[1,2,2,3] $\otimes$ [8]+[5,7,9,11] $\otimes$ 2]+[1,2,2,3] $\otimes$ [20]+ [1,3,5,7] $\otimes$ [6] +[6,8,8,10] $\otimes$ [10].

Min $\tilde{Z}$ =[8,16,16,24] +[10,14,18,22] +[20,40,40,60] + [6,18,30,42] +[60,80,80,100].

Min $\tilde{Z}$ = [104,168,184,248]

$$\Re\left(\tilde{Z}\right)= \Re\,[104,168,184,248]= \frac{104+168+184+248}{4}=176\,.$$

Example: 3 Type-4 FTP

A firm has three factories S_1, S_2, and S_3 that manufacture the same product of air coolers in three different places. The firm manager would like to transport air coolers from three different factories to four different warehouses D_1, D_2, D_3 and D_4. All the factories are connected to all the warehouses by roads and air coolers are transported by lorries/trucks. The availability (availability of air coolers are depends on its production but production depends on men, machine, etc.) of air coolers are not known exactly due to long power cut, labour's over time work, unexpected failures in machine etc. The demand of air coolers is not known exactly due to seasonal changes (in sunny days the sale of air coolers are more when compared to rainy days). Similarly, the transportation cost is not known exactly due to variations in rates of gas or diesel, traffic jams, weather in hilly areas etc. So, all the parameters of the TP are in uncertain quantities which are given in terms of TrFN. The transportation costs (rupees in hundreds) for each air cooler from different factories to different warehouses are given in Table 12, from the past experience.

Find the optimal allocation which minimizes total fuzzy transportation cost.

Solution by proposed method:

Table 12. Type-4 FTP

Factories	Warehouses				Fuzzy Availability $\tilde{a}_i$
	D_1	D_2	D_3	D_4	
S_1	[0, 1, 3, 4]	[0, 1, 3, 4]	[0, 1, 3, 4]	[0, 0, 2, 2]	[0,2, 4, 6]
S_2	[4,8,12, 16]	[4, 7, 9, 12]	[2, 4, 6, 8]	[1, 3, 5, 7]	[2,4,9,13]
S_3	[2, 4, 9, 13]	[0, 6, 8, 10]	[0, 6, 8, 10]	[4, 7, 9, 12]	[2,4, 6, 8]
Fuzzy Demand $\tilde{b}_j$	[1, 3, 5, 7]	[0, 2, 4, 6]	[1, 3, 5, 7]	[1, 3, 5, 7]	

By solving this problem using PSK method, we get the following fuzzy optimal solution:
The fuzzy optimal solution in terms of TrFN is:

$$\tilde{x}_{11}=[0,2,4,6], \ \tilde{x}_{31}=[-5,-1,3,7], \ \tilde{x}_{23}=[-5,-1,6,12], \ \tilde{x}_{32}=[0,2,4,6], \ \tilde{x}_{24}=[1,3,5,7], \ \tilde{x}_{33}=[-11,-3,6,12]$$

and its optimal fuzzy transportation cost is:

Min $\tilde{Z} = [12, 55, 88, 117]$ (Rupees in hundreds)

$$\Re\left(\tilde{Z}\right) = \ \Re\ [12,55,88,117] = \frac{12 + 55 + 88 + 117}{4} = 68 \ \text{(Rupees in hundreds).}$$

Example: 4 Type-2 FTP

There are three sources (rows) and four destinations (columns), all the sources are connected to all the destinations by roads and the goods are transported by lorries/trucks. The supply and demand of goods are well known crisp quantities but the transportation cost is not known exactly (due to variations in rates of petrol/gas, traffic jams, weather in hilly areas etc). Hence crisp supply, crisp demand and unit transportation cost (given in terms of TrFNs) are given, in Table 13. Find the optimal allocation which minimizes total fuzzy transportation cost (FTC).
Solution by PSK method:
By solving this problem using PSK method, we get the following optimal solution:
Hence, the optimal solution is:

$$x_{13} = 3, \ x_{24} = 5, \ x_{31} = 5, \ x_{32} = 4, \ x_{33} = 0, \ x_{34} = 3$$

and its optimal fuzzy transportation cost is:

Min $\tilde{Z} = [3,6,10,13] \times \oplus \ [1,4,8,11] \times 5 \ \oplus [2,4,6,8] \times 5 \ \oplus [4,6,10,12] \times 4 \ \oplus [0,10,20,30] \times 0$
$\oplus [4,8,12,16] \times 3$

Table 13. Type-2 FTP

	D_1	D_2	D_3	D_4	Availability
O_1	[1, 2,4, 5]	[1,4,6,9]	[3,6,10,13]	[5,8,16,19]	3
O_2	[0, 2,4, 6]	[2,4,10,12]	[7,10,12,15]	[1,4, 8, 11]	5
O_3	[2, 4,6, 8]	[4,6,10,12]	[0,10,20,30]	[4,8,12,16]	12
Demand	5	4	3	8	

=[9,18,30,39] $\oplus$ [5,20,40,55] $\oplus$ [10,20,30,40] $\oplus$ [16,24,40,48] $\oplus$ [0,0,0,0] $\oplus$ [12,24,36,48]

Min $\tilde{Z}$ =[52,106,176,230]

$$\text{Min Z = Min } \Re\left(\tilde{Z}\right) = \Re\left[52, 106, 176, 230\right] = \frac{52 + 106 + 176 + 230}{4} = 141$$

Solution by LINGO 17.0:

Now, by applying the ranking method to the given type-2 FTP, then we get the following crisp TP (see Table 14).

We can write the above problem (see Table 14) as an LLP, which is as follows:

Minimize

$$Z = 3x_{11} + 5x_{12} + 8x_{13} + 12x_{14} + 3x_{21} + 7x_{22} + 11x_{23} + 6x_{24} + 5x_{31} + 8x_{32} + 15x_{33} + 10x_{34}$$

subject to the constraints

$$x_{11} + x_{12} + x_{13} + x_{14} = 3$$

$$x_{21} + x_{22} + x_{23} + x_{24} = 5$$

$$x_{31} + x_{32} + x_{33} + x_{34} = 12$$

$$x_{11} + x_{21} + x_{31} = 5$$

$$x_{12} + x_{22} + x_{32} = 4$$

$$x_{13} + x_{23} + x_{33} = 3$$

$$x_{14} + x_{24} + x_{34} = 8$$

Table 14. Crisp version of type-2 FTP

	D_1	D_2	D_3	D_4	Availability
O_1	3	5	8	12	3
O_2	3	7	11	6	5
O_3	5	8	15	10	12
Demand	5	4	3	8	

$$x_{11}, \ x_{12}, \ x_{13}, \ x_{14}, \ x_{21}, \ x_{22}, \ x_{23}, \ x_{24}, \ x_{31}, \ x_{32}, \ x_{33}, \ x_{34} \geq 0$$

By applying LINGO 17.0 software to this problem (see Table 14), we get the following optimal solution and optimal objective value.

The optimal solution and the total transportation cost are

$$x_{13} = 3, \ x_{24} = 5, \ x_{31} = 5, \ x_{32} = 4, \ x_{33} = 0, \ x_{34} = 3 \text{ and Min Z} = 141$$

From the obtained solution, we can write the optimal objective value for the given type-2 FTP as follows:

$$\text{Min } \tilde{Z} = [52, 106, 176, 230]$$

From the obtained objective value of the given type-2 FTP, we can write the optimal objective value for the crisp type-2 FTP as follows:

$$\text{Min Z} = \text{Min } \Re\left(\tilde{Z}\right) = \Re\left[52, 106, 176, 230\right] = \frac{52 + 106 + 176 + 230}{4} = 141$$

From Figure 1, the optimal solution and optimal objective value of the given type-2 FTP and its crisp TP have been verified by using both the proposed method and the existing method.

Results and Discussion

A comparative study of the proposed method over existing methods is given in the following table (refer to Table 15).

The minimum total FTC of problem 2 is:

$$\tilde{Z} = [104, 168, 184, 248] \tag{7}$$

The result in (7) can be explained (Refer to Figure 2) as follows:

1. Transportation cost lies in [104,248];
2. 100% expect are in favour that the transportation cost is [168,184] as $\mu_{\tilde{z}}\left(c\right) = 1$ $c = 168 \text{ to } 184$
3. Let $\mu_{\tilde{z}}\left(c\right)$ be a membership value at c. Then $100\,\mu_{\tilde{z}}\left(c\right)\%$ experts are in favour that the transportation cost is c..

Values of $\mu_{\tilde{z}}\left(c\right)$ at different values of c can be determined using the following equation (8):

Figure 1. Output summary for type-2 FTP and its crisp TP: LPP approach (LINGO 17.0)

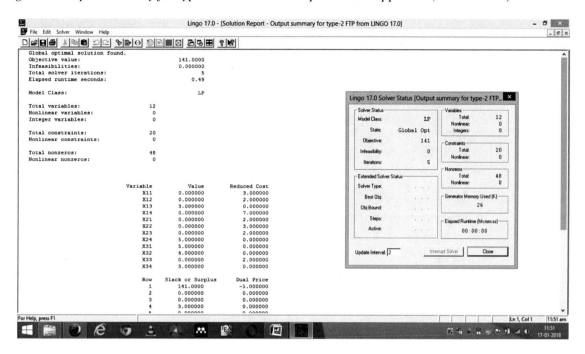

Table 15. Comparative analysis

Problem Number	Ranking method	Solution Methods						
	Liou and Wang (1992)	VAM	MODI	Zero Point Method	LINGO 17.0	Fuzzy Zero Point Method Pandian and Natarajan (2010)	Fuzzy Modified Distribution Method Dinagar and Palanivel (2009)	PSK Method Kumar (2016a, b; 2017a)
1		68 (Rupees in hundreds)	68 (Rupees in hundreds)	68 (Rupees in hundreds)	68 (Rupees in hundreds)	[-122,-2,139,257] 68 (Rupees in hundreds)	[-122,-2,139,257] 68 (Rupees in hundreds)	[-122,-2,139,257] 68 (Rupees in hundreds)
2		176	176	176	176	[104,168,184,248] 176	[104,168,184,248] 176	[104,168,184,248] 176
3		68 (Rupees in hundreds)	68 (Rupees in hundreds)	68 (Rupees in hundreds)	68 (Rupees in hundreds)	[12,55,88,117] 68 (Rupees in hundreds)	[12,55,88,117] 68 (Rupees in hundreds)	[12,55,88,117] 68 (Rupees in hundreds)
4		141	141	141	141	[52,106,176,230] 141	[52,106,176,230] 141	[52,106,176,230] 141

Figure 2. Graphical representation of type-3 fuzzy transportation cost

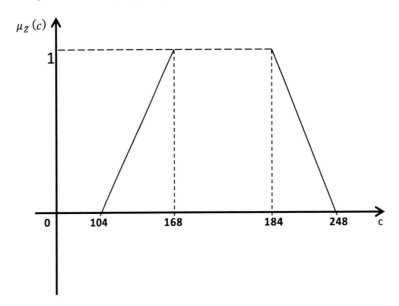

$$
\mu_{\tilde{Z}}\left(c\right) =
\begin{cases}
0, & for\ c \leq 104 \\
\dfrac{c - 104}{64}, & for\, 104 \leq c \leq 168 \\
1, & for\, 168 \leq c \leq 184 \\
\dfrac{248 - c}{64}, & for\, 184 \leq c \leq 248 \\
0, & for\ c \geq 248
\end{cases}
\tag{8}
$$

Advantages of the PSK method

By using the proposed method a DM has the following advantages:

1. The proposed method gives the optimal solution in terms of mixed fuzzy numbers. Moreover, the proposed method give the opportunity to the DM to solve all the types of FTP.
2. The PSK method is easy to understand and computationally very simple.
3. Both the maximization and minimization FTP can be solved by using PSK method.
4. The PSK method gives the new ideas for solving the variety of optimization problems.
5. The PSK method reduces the computation time of the decision maker.

7. CONCLUSION AND FUTURE WORK

On the basis of the present study, it can be concluded that the type-1, type-2, type-3 or mixed FTP and type-4 FTP which can be solved by the existing methods (Pandian and Natarajan (2010), Dinagar and Palanivel (2009), Rani, Gulathi, and Kumar (2014), Basirzadeh (2011), Ahmed et al. (2015), Gani and Razak (2006)) can also be solved by the proposed method. However, it is much easier to apply the proposed method as compared to all the existing methods. Also, new method and new multiplication operation on TrFN is proposed to compute the optimal objective values in terms of TrFNs which are very simple and easy to understand and it can be easily applied by DM to solve type-1, type-2, type-3 and type-4 FTP. The PSK method gives the optimal solution in terms of mixed fuzzy numbers. Hence the PSK method give the opportunity to the DM to solve all the types of FTP and computationally very simple when compared to all the existing methods. Further, the optimal solution and optimal objective value of the proposed type-2 FTP and its crisp TP have been verified by using both the proposed method and the LINGO 17.0 software tool. My future research will extend the proposed method here to deal with the transportation problems under intuitionistic fuzzy environment. In addition, the author would like to develop the software package for solving fuzzy transportation problems by using PSK method.

ACKNOWLEDGMENT

The author sincerely thanks the anonymous reviewers and Editor-in-Chief Professor Maki Habib for their careful reading, constructive comments and fruitful suggestions. The author would also like to acknowledge Dr.S.Ismail Mohideen, Additional Vice Principal, My Guide and Associate Professor Dr.R.Jahir Hussain, Dr.A.Nagoor Gani, Associate Professor, Dr.K.Ramanaiah, Associate Professor (retired), Mr.N.Shamsudeen, Associate Professor (retired), Jamal Mohamed College (Autonomous), Tiruchirappalli, Tamil Nadu, India for their motivation and kind support.

REFERENCES

Agustina, F., Lukman, & Puspita, E. (2017, May 30). PMZ method for solving fuzzy transportation. In AIP Conference Proceedings. Melville, NY: American Institute of Physics (AIP) Publishing. doi:10.1063/1.4983945

Ahmed, M. M., Khan, A. R., Uddin, M. S., & Ahmed, F. (2016). A new approach to solve transportation problems. *Open Journal of Optimization*, 5(01), 22–30. doi:10.4236/ojop.2016.51003

Ahmed, N. U., Khan, A. R., & Uddin, M. S. (2015). Solution of mixed type transportation problem: A fuzzy approach. *Bul. Ins. Pol. Din Iasi, Romania. Secţia Automatica si Calculatoare, 61*(2), 19–32.

Akpan, N. P., & Iwok, I. A. (2017). A minimum spanning tree approach of solving a transportation problem. *International Journal of Mathematics and Statistics Invention, 5*(3), 8-17.

Ali, A. M., & Faraz, D. (2017). Solving fuzzy triangular transportation problem using fuzzy least cost method with ranking approach. *International Journal of Current Research in Science and Technology, 3*(7), 15–20.

Aljanabi, K. B., & Jasim, A. N. (2015). An approach for solving transportation problem using modified Kruskal's algorithm. *International Journal of Science and Research, 4*(7), 2426–2429.

AnithaKumari, T., Venkateswarlu, B., & Murthy, A. S. (2017). Fuzzy transportation problems with new kind of ranking function. *International Journal of Engineering Science, 6*(11), 15–19.

Anuradha, D., & Sobana, V. E. (2017, November). A survey on fuzzy transportation problems. In IOP Conference Series: Materials Science and Engineering (Vol. 263, No. 4, p. 042105). IOP Publishing. doi:10.1088/1757-899X/263/4/042105

Appa, G. M. (1973). The transportation problem and its variants. *The Journal of the Operational Research Society*, *24*(1), 79–99. doi:10.1057/jors.1973.10

Arsham, H., & Kahn, A. B. (1989). A simplex-type algorithm for general transportation problems: An alternative to stepping-stone. *The Journal of the Operational Research Society*, *40*(6), 581–590. doi:10.1057/jors.1989.95

Atanassov, K.T. (1983). Intuitionistic fuzzy sets. *Library of Bulg. Acad. of Sci.*, *1697*(84).

Basirzadeh, H. (2011). An approach for solving fuzzy transportation problem. *Applied Mathematical Sciences*, *5*(32), 1549–1566.

Baykasoğlu, A., & Subulan, K. (2017). Constrained fuzzy arithmetic approach to fuzzy transportation problems with fuzzy decision variables. *Expert Systems with Applications*, *81*, 193–222. doi:10.1016/j.eswa.2017.03.040

Bellman, R. E., & Zadeh, L. A. (1970). Decision-making in a fuzzy environment. *Management Science*, *17*(4), B-141–B-164. doi:10.1287/mnsc.17.4.B141

Biswas, A., & Modak, N. (2012). Using fuzzy goal programming technique to solve multiobjective chance constrained programming problems in a fuzzy environment. *International Journal of Fuzzy System Applications*, *2*(1), 71–80. doi:10.4018/ijfsa.2012010105

Chanas, S., Delgado, M., Verdegay, J. L., & Vila, M. A. (1993). Interval and fuzzy extensions of classical transportation problems. *Transportation Planning and Technology*, *17*(2), 203–218. doi:10.1080/03081069308717511

Chanas, S., Kołodziejczyk, W., & Machaj, A. (1984). A fuzzy approach to the transportation problem. *Fuzzy Sets and Systems*, *13*(3), 211–221. doi:10.1016/0165-0114(84)90057-5

Chanas, S., & Kuchta, D. (1996). A concept of the optimal solution of the transportation problem with fuzzy cost coefficients. *Fuzzy Sets and Systems*, *82*(3), 299–305. doi:10.1016/0165-0114(95)00278-2

Chanas, S., & Kuchta, D. (1998). Fuzzy integer transportation problem. *Fuzzy Sets and Systems*, *98*(3), 291–298. doi:10.1016/S0165-0114(96)00380-6

Charnes, A., & Cooper, W. W. (1954). The stepping stone method of explaining linear programming calculations in transportation problems. *Management Science*, *1*(1), 49–69. doi:10.1287/mnsc.1.1.49

Chen, M., Ishii, H., & Wu, C. (2008). Transportation problems on a fuzzy network. *International Journal of Innovative Computing, Information, & Control*, *4*(5), 1105–1109.

Chen, S. H., & Hsieh, C. H. (1999). Graded mean integration representation of generalized fuzzy numbers. *Journal of the Chinese Fuzzy Systems Association*, *5*(2), 1–7.

Chiang, J. (2005). The optimal solution of the transportation problem with fuzzy demand and fuzzy product. *Journal of Information Science and Engineering*, *21*(2), 439–451.

Christi, M. S. A., & Malini, D. (2016). An approach to solve transportation problems with octagonal fuzzy numbers using best candidates method and different ranking techniques. *International Journal of Computers and Applications*, *6*(1), 71–85.

Das, M., & Baruah, H. K. (2007). Solution of the transportation problem in fuzzified form. *Journal of Fuzzy Mathematics*, *15*(1), 79–95.

De, P. K., & Yadav, B. (2010). Approach to defuzzify the trapezoidal fuzzy number in transportation problem. *International Journal of Computational Cognition*, *8*(4), 64–67.

Dinagar, D. S., & Palanivel, K. (2009). The transportation problem in fuzzy environment. *International Journal of Algorithms. Computing and Mathematics*, *2*(3), 65–71.

Ebrahimnejad, A. (2012). Cost efficiency measures with trapezoidal fuzzy numbers in data envelopment analysis based on ranking functions: Application in insurance organization and hospital. *International Journal of Fuzzy System Applications*, *2*(3), 51–68. doi:10.4018/ijfsa.2012070104

Ebrahimnejad, A. (2016a). Fuzzy linear programming approach for solving transportation problems with interval-valued trapezoidal fuzzy numbers. *Sadhana*, *41*(3), 299–316.

Ebrahimnejad, A. (2016b). New method for solving fuzzy transportation problems with LR flat fuzzy numbers. *Information Sciences*, *357*, 108–124. doi:10.1016/j.ins.2016.04.008

Gani, A. N., & Razak, K. A. (2006). Two stage fuzzy transportation problem. *The Journal of Physiological Sciences; JPS*, *10*, 63–69.

Gani, A. N., Samuel, A. E., & Anuradha, D. (2011). Simplex type algorithm for solving fuzzy transportation problem. *Tamsui Oxford Journal of Information and Mathematical Sciences*, *27*(1), 89–98.

Hasan, M. K. (2012). Direct methods for finding optimal solution of a transportation problem are not always reliable. *International Refereed Journal of Engineering and Science*, *1*(2), 46–52.

Hitchcock, F. L. (1941). The distribution of a product from several sources to numerous localities. *Journal of Mathematics and Physics*, *20*(2), 224–230. doi:10.1002apm1941201224

Hunwisai, D., & Kumam, P. (2017). A method for solving a fuzzy transportation problem via Robust ranking technique and ATM. *Cogent Mathematics*, *4*(1), 1283730. doi:10.1080/23311835.2017.1283730

Hussain, R. J., & Kumar, P. S. (2012a). The transportation problem with the aid of triangular intuitionistic fuzzy numbers. In *Proceedings in International Conference on Mathematical Modeling and Applied Soft Computing (MMASC-2012)*. Coimbatore Institute of Technology.

Hussain, R. J., & Kumar, P. S. (2012b). The transportation problem in an intuitionistic fuzzy environment. *International Journal of Mathematics Research*, *4*(4), 411–420.

Hussain, R. J., & Kumar, P. S. (2012c). Algorithmic approach for solving intuitionistic fuzzy transportation problem. *Applied Mathematical Sciences*, *6*(80), 3981–3989.

Hussain, R. J., & Kumar, P. S. (2013). An optimal more-for-less solution of mixed constraints intuitionistic fuzzy transportation problems. *International Journal of Contemporary Mathematical Sciences*, *8*(12), 565–576. doi:10.12988/ijcms.2013.13056

Kikuchi, S. (2000). A method to defuzzify the fuzzy number: Transportation problem application. *Fuzzy Sets and Systems*, *116*(1), 3–9. doi:10.1016/S0165-0114(99)00033-0

Kumar, A., & Kaur, A. (2013). Methods for solving fully fuzzy transportation problems based on classical transportation methods. In J. Wang (Ed.), *Optimizing, Innovating, and Capitalizing on Information Systems for Operations* (pp. 328–347). Hershey, PA: IGI Global. doi:10.4018/978-1-4666-2925-7.ch017

Kumar, A., Kaur, A., & Gupta, A. (2011). Fuzzy linear programming approach for solving fuzzy transportation problems with transhipment. *Journal of Mathematical Modelling and Algorithms*, *10*(2), 163–180. doi:10.100710852-010-9147-8

Kumar, P. S. (2016a). PSK method for solving type-1 and type-3 fuzzy transportation problems. *International Journal of Fuzzy System Applications*, *5*(4), 121–146. doi:10.4018/IJFSA.2016100106

Kumar, P. S. (2016b). A simple method for solving type-2 and type-4 fuzzy transportation problems. *International Journal of Fuzzy Logic and Intelligent Systems*, *16*(4), 225–237. doi:10.5391/IJFIS.2016.16.4.225

Kumar, P. S. (2017a). PSK method for solving type-1 and type-3 fuzzy transportation problems. In I. Management Association (Ed.), Fuzzy Systems: Concepts, Methodologies, Tools, and Applications (pp. 367-392). Hershey, PA: IGI Global. doi:10.4018/978-1-5225-1908-9.ch017

Kumar, P. S. (2017b). *Algorithmic approach for solving allocation problems under intuitionistic fuzzy environment* (Unpublished doctoral dissertation). Jamal Mohamed College (Autonomous), Tiruchirappalli, India.

Kumar, P. S. (2018a). A note on 'a new approach for solving intuitionistic fuzzy transportation problem of type-2'. *International Journal of Logistics Systems and Management*, *29*(1), 102–129. doi:10.1504/IJLSM.2018.088586

Kumar, P. S. (2018b). Linear programming approach for solving balanced and unbalanced intuitionistic fuzzy transportation problems. *International Journal of Operations Research and Information Systems*, *9*(2), 73–100. doi:10.4018/IJORIS.2018040104

Kumar, P. S. (2018c). Intuitionistic fuzzy zero point method for solving type-2 intuitionistic fuzzy transportation problem. *International Journal of Operational Research*.

Kumar, P. S. (2018d). PSK method for solving intuitionistic fuzzy solid transportation problems. *International Journal of Fuzzy System Applications*.

Kumar, P. S. (2018e). A simple and efficient algorithm for solving type-1 intuitionistic fuzzy solid transportation problems *International Journal of Operations Research and Information Systems*.

Kumar, P. S., & Hussain, R. J. (2014a). *New algorithm for solving mixed intuitionistic fuzzy assignment problem. In Elixir Applied Mathematics* (pp. 25971–25977). Salem, Tamilnadu, India: Elixir Publishers.

Kumar, P. S., & Hussain, R. J. (2014b). A systematic approach for solving mixed intuitionistic fuzzy transportation problems. *International Journal of Pure and Applied Mathematics*, *92*(2), 181–190. doi:10.12732/ijpam.v92i2.4

Kumar, P. S., & Hussain, R. J. (2014c) A method for finding an optimal solution of an assignment problem under mixed intuitionistic fuzzy environment. In *Proceedings in International Conference on Mathematical Sciences (ICMS-2014)*. Elsevier.

Kumar, P. S., & Hussain, R. J. (2015). A method for solving unbalanced intuitionistic fuzzy transportation problems. *Notes on Intuitionistic Fuzzy Sets*, *21*(3), 54–65.

Kumar, P. S., & Hussain, R. J. (2016a). An algorithm for solving unbalanced intuitionistic fuzzy assignment problem using triangular intuitionistic fuzzy number. *The Journal of Fuzzy Mathematics*, *24*(2), 289–302.

Kumar, P. S., & Hussain, R. J. (2016b). Computationally simple approach for solving fully intuitionistic fuzzy real life transportation problems. *International Journal of System Assurance Engineering and Management*, *7*(1), 90–101. doi:10.100713198-014-0334-2

Kumar, P. S., & Hussain, R. J. (2016c). A simple method for solving fully intuitionistic fuzzy real life assignment problem. *International Journal of Operations Research and Information Systems*, *7*(2), 39–61. doi:10.4018/IJORIS.2016040103

Li, L., Huang, Z., Da, Q., & Hu, J. (2008, May). A new method based on goal programming for solving transportation problem with fuzzy cost. In Information Processing (ISIP), 2008 International Symposiums on (pp. 3-8). IEEE. doi:10.1109/ISIP.2008.9

Liao, X. (2015). Decision method of optimal investment enterprise selection under uncertain information environment. *International Journal of Fuzzy System Applications*, *4*(1), 33–42. doi:10.4018/IJFSA.2015010102

Lin, F. T. (2009, August). Solving the transportation problem with fuzzy coefficients using genetic algorithms. In *Fuzzy Systems, 2009. FUZZ-IEEE 2009. IEEE International Conference on* (pp. 1468-1473). IEEE. 10.1109/FUZZY.2009.5277202

Liou, T. S., & Wang, M. J. J. (1992). Ranking fuzzy numbers with integral value. *Fuzzy Sets and Systems*, *50*(3), 247–255. doi:10.1016/0165-0114(92)90223-Q

Maity, G., & Roy, S. K. (2017). Multiobjective transportation problem using fuzzy decision variable through multi-choice programming. *International Journal of Operations Research and Information Systems*, *8*(3), 82–96. doi:10.4018/IJORIS.2017070105

Mathur, N., Srivastava, P. K., & Paul, A. (2016). Trapezoidal fuzzy model to optimize transportation problem. *International Journal of Modeling, Simulation, and Scientific Computing, 7*(3). DOI: 10.1142/S1793962316500288

Mohideen, S. I., & Kumar, P. S. (2010). A comparative study on transportation problem in fuzzy environment. *International Journal of Mathematics Research*, *2*(1), 151–158.

Mohideen, S. I., & Kumar, P. S. (2010). *A comparative study on transportation problem in fuzzy environment* (Unpublished master's thesis). Jamal Mohamed College (Autonomous), Tiruchirappalli, India.

Nasseri, S. H., & Ebrahimnejad, A. (2011). Sensitivity analysis on linear programming problems with trapezoidal fuzzy variables. *International Journal of Operations Research and Information Systems*, *2*(2), 22–39. doi:10.4018/joris.2011040102

Oheigeartaigh, M. (1982). A fuzzy transportation algorithm. *Fuzzy Sets and Systems*, *8*(3), 235–243. doi:10.1016/S0165-0114(82)80002-X

Pandian, P., & Natarajan, G. (2010). A new algorithm for finding a fuzzy optimal solution for fuzzy transportation problems. *Applied Mathematical Sciences*, *4*(2), 79–90.

Pattnaik, M. (2015). Decision making approach to fuzzy linear programming (FLP) problems with post optimal analysis. *International Journal of Operations Research and Information Systems*, *6*(4), 75–90. doi:10.4018/IJORIS.2015100105

Ping, J. I., & Chu, K. F. (2002). A dual-matrix approach to the transportation problem. *Asia-Pacific Journal of Operational Research*, *19*(1), 35–45.

Purushothkumar, M.K., & Ananathanarayanan, M. (2017). Fuzzy transportation problem of trapezoidal fuzzy numbers with new ranking technique. *IOSR Journal of Mathematics, 13*(6), 6-12.

Rajarajeswari, P. & Sangeetha, M. (2016). New similarity performance measures of fuzzy transportation and its application. *International Journal of Innovative Research in Computer and Communication Engineering, 4*(4), 6353-6360. DOI: .040400910.15680/IJIRCCE.2016

Rani, D., Gulati, T. R., & Kumar, A. (2014). A method for unbalanced transportation problems in fuzzy environment. *Indian Academy of Sciences Sadhana*, *39*(3), 573–581. doi:10.100712046-014-0243-8

Rao, K. R., Mudaliar, R. K., Hasan, M. K., & Alam, M. K. (2016, December). A perfect mathematical formulation of fuzzy transportation problem provides an optimal solution speedily. In *Computer Science and Engineering (APWC on CSE), 2016 3rd Asia-Pacific World Congress on* (pp. 271-278). IEEE. 10.1109/APWC-on-CSE.2016.051

Reddy, M. R., Raman, P. V., & Kumar, M. V. (2016). Unclear carrying problem of triangular numbers with α–slash and position method. *International Journal of Mathematical Archive*, *7*(10), 66–68.

Saad, O. M., & Abass, S. A. (2003). A parametric study on transportation problem under fuzzy environment. *Journal of Fuzzy Mathematics*, *11*(1), 115–124.

Saati, S., Hatami-Marbini, A., Tavana, M., & Hajiahkondi, E. (2012). A two-fold linear programming model with fuzzy data. *International Journal of Fuzzy System Applications*, *2*(3), 1–12. doi:10.4018/ijfsa.2012070101

Sahoo, P. K., Behera, S. K., & Nayak, J. R. (2016). Solution of fuzzy transportation problem by using ranking function. *Advanced Science Letters*, *22*(2), 564–566. doi:10.1166/asl.2016.6864

Samuel, A. E., & Raja, P. (2017a). Algorithmic approach to unbalanced fuzzy transportation problem. *International Journal of Pure and Applied Mathematics*, *113*(5), 553–561.

Samuel, A. E., & Raja, P. (2017b). Advanced approximation method for finding an optimal solution of unbalanced fuzzy transportation problems. *Global Journal of Pure and Applied Mathematics*, *13*(9), 5307–5315.

Shankar, N. R., Saradhi, B. P., & Babu, S. S. (2013). Fuzzy critical path method based on a new approach of ranking fuzzy numbers using centroid of centroids. *International Journal of Fuzzy System Applications*, *3*(2), 16–31. doi:10.4018/ijfsa.2013040102

Singh, R., & Saxena, V. (2017). A new data transfer approach through fuzzy Vogel's approximation method. *International Journal of Advanced Research in Computer Science*, *8*(3), 515–519.

Solaiappan, S., & Jeyaraman, K. (2014). A new optimal solution method for trapezoidal fuzzy transportation problem. *International Journal of Advanced Research*, *2*(1), 933–942.

Sudhakar, V. J., & Kumar, V. N. (2011). A different approach for solving two stage fuzzy transportation problems. *International Journal of Contemporary Mathematical Sciences*, *6*(11), 517–526.

Taha, H. A. (2008). *Operations Research: An Introduction* (8th ed.). Pearson Education.

Vimala, S., & Prabha, S. K. (2016). Fuzzy transportation problem through monalisha's approximation method. *British Journal of Mathematics & Computer Science*, *17*(2), 1–11. doi:10.9734/BJMCS/2016/26097

Zadeh, L. A. (1965). Fuzzy sets. *Information and Control*, *8*(3), 338–353. doi:10.1016/S0019-9958(65)90241-X

Zadeh, L. A. (1978). Fuzzy sets as a basis for a theory of possibility. *Fuzzy Sets and Systems*, *1*(1), 3–28. doi:10.1016/0165-0114(78)90029-5

APPENDIX

Global optimal solution found.
Objective Value: 141.0000
Infeasibilities: 0.000000
Total Solver Iterations: 5
Elapsed Runtime Seconds: 0.49
Model Class: LP
Total Variables: 12
Nonlinear Variables: 0
Integer Variables: 0
Total Constraints: 20
Nonlinear Constraints: 0
Total Nonzeros: 48
Nonlinear Nonzeros: 0

Box 1.

Variable	Value	Reduced Cost
X11	0.000000	3.000000
X12	0.000000	2.000000
X13	3.000000	0.000000
X14	0.000000	7.000000
X21	0.000000	2.000000
X22	0.000000	3.000000
X23	0.000000	2.000000
X24	5.000000	0.000000
X31	5.000000	0.000000
X32	4.000000	0.000000
X33	0.000000	2.000000
X34	3.000000	0.000000

Box 2.

Row	Slack or Surplus	Dual Price
1	141.0000	-1.000000
2	0.000000	0.000000
3	0.000000	0.000000
4	3.000000	0.000000
5	0.000000	0.000000
6	0.000000	0.000000
7	0.000000	0.000000
8	0.000000	0.000000
9	5.000000	0.000000
10	5.000000	0.000000
11	4.000000	0.000000
12	0.000000	0.000000
13	3.000000	0.000000
14	0.000000	0.000000
15	0.000000	-1.000000
16	0.000000	-5.000000
17	0.000000	0.000000
18	0.000000	-3.000000
19	0.000000	-8.000000
20	0.000000	-5.000000

Chapter 12
Design Patterns for Social Intelligent Agent Architectures Implementation

Manuel Kolp
Université catholique de Louvain, Belgium

Yves Wautelet
KU Leuven, Belgium

Samedi Heng
Université catholique de Lovuain, Belgium

ABSTRACT

Multi-agent systems (MAS) architectures are popular for building open, distributed, and evolving software required by today's business IT applications such as e-business systems, web services, or enterprise knowledge bases. Since the fundamental concepts of MAS are social and intentional rather than object, functional, or implementation-oriented, the design of MAS architectures can be eased by using social patterns. They are detailed agent-oriented design idioms to describe MAS architectures as composed of autonomous agents that interact and coordinate to achieve their intentions like actors in human organizations. This chapter presents social patterns and focuses on a framework aimed to gain insight into these patterns. The framework can be integrated into agent-oriented software engineering methodologies used to build MAS. The authors consider the broker social pattern to illustrate the framework. The mapping from system architectural design (through organizational architectural styles), to system detailed design (through social patterns), is overviewed with a data integration case study.

DOI: 10.4018/978-1-5225-5396-0.ch012

1. INTRODUCTION

This section introduces and motivates the research. In Section 1.1, we describe the advantages of using multi-agent systems over traditional systems. Section 1.2 presents the importance of *patterns* for designing information systems. We formulate our research proposal in Section 1.3. The Section 1.4 introduces elements for work validation. The context of the research and an overview of the state of the art are given in Section 1.5. Finally, Section 1.6 presents the organization of the chapter.

1.1. Advantages of Multi-Agent Systems

The meteoric rise of Internet and World-Wide Web technologies has created overnight new application areas for enterprise software, including eBusiness, web services, ubiquitous computing, knowledge management and peer-to-peer networks. These areas demand software that is robust, can operate within a wide range of environments, and can evolve over time to cope with changing requirements. Moreover, such software has to be highly customizable to meet the needs of a wide range of users, and sufficiently secure to protect personal data and other assets on behalf of its stakeholders.

Not surprisingly, researchers are looking for new software designs that can cope with such requirements. One promising source of ideas for designing such business software is the area of multi-agent systems. Multi-agent system architectures appear to be more flexible, modular and robust than traditional including object-oriented ones. They tend to be open and dynamic in the sense they exist in a changing organizational and operational environment where new components can be added, modified or removed at any time.

Multi-agent systems are based on the concept of agent which is defined as "a software component situated in some environment that is capable of flexible autonomous action in order to meet its design objective" (Aridor & Lange, 1998). An agent exhibits the following characteristics:

- **Autonomy:** An agent has its own internal thread of execution, typically oriented to the achievement of a specific task, and it decides for itself what actions it should perform at what time.
- **Situateness:** Agents perform their actions in the context of being situated in a particular environment. This environment may be a computational one (e.g., a Web site) or a physical one (e.g., a manufacturing pipeline). The agent can sense and affect some portion of that environment.
- **Flexibility:** In order to accomplish its design objectives in a dynamic and unpredictable environment, the agent may need to act to ensure that its goals are achieved (by realizing alternative plan). This property is enabled by the fact that the agent is autonomous in its problem solving.

An agent can be useful as a stand-alone entity that delegates particular tasks on behalf of a user (e.g., a learning environment in a Massive Open Online Course (Wautelet et al., 2016a), or a goal-driven office delivery mobile device (Castro, Kolp & Mylopoulos, 2002)). However, in the overwhelming majority of cases, agents exist in an environment that contains other agents. Such environment is a multi-agent system (MAS).

In MAS, the global behavior derives from the interaction among the constituent agents: they cooperate, coordinate or negotiate with one another. A multi-agent system is then conceived as a society of autonomous, collaborative, and goal-driven software components (agents), much like a social organization. Each role an agent can play has a well defined set of responsibilities (goals) achieved by means of an agent's own abilities, as well as its interaction capabilities.

This sociality of MAS is well suited to tackling the complexity of today's organization software systems for a number of reasons:

- It permits a better match between system architectures and its organizational operational environment for example a public organization, a corporation, a non-profit association, a local community, …
- The autonomy of an agent (i.e., the ability an agent has to decide what actions it should take at what time (Aridor & Lange, 1998)) reflects the social and decentralized nature of modern enterprise systems (Wautelet et al., 2016a) that are operated by different stakeholders (Miller et al., 2014).
- The flexible way in which agents operate to accomplish its goals is suited to the dynamic and unpredictable situations in which business software is now expected to run (see Zambonelli, Jennings, Omicini & Wooldridge, 2000, Zambonelli, Jennings & Wooldridge, 2000).

MAS architectures become rapidly complicated due to the ever-increasing complexity of these new business domains and their human or organizational actors. As the expectations of the stakeholders change day after day, as the complexity of the systems, communication technologies and organizations continually increases in today's dynamic environments, developers are expected to produce architectures that must handle more difficult and intricate requirements that were not taken into account ten years ago, making thus architectural design a central engineering issue in modern enterprise information system life-cycle (Liu, Deters, & Zhang, 2010).

1.2. Patterns for Designing Systems

An important technique that helps to manage this complexity when constructing and docu-menting such architectures is the reuse of development experience and know-how. Over the past few years, *design patterns* have significantly contributed to the reuse of design expertise, improvement application documentation and more flexible and adaptable designs (Juziuk, Weyns & Holvoet, 2014; Gamma, Helm, Johnson & Vlissides, 1995; Buschmann, Meunier, Rohnert, Sommerlad & Stal, 1996; Bosch, 1998). The idea behind a pattern is to record the essence of a solution to a design problem so as to facilitate its reuse when similar problems are encountered (Cockburn, 1996; Pree 1994; Riehle & Züllighoven, 1996).

Considerable work has been done in software engineering on defining design patterns (Gamma, Helm, Johnson & Vlissides, 1995; Buschmann, Meunier, Rohnert, Sommerlad & Stal, 1996; Bosch, 1998). Unfortunately, they focus on object-oriented (Fernandez & Pan, 2001) rather than agent-oriented systems. In the area of MASs, little emphasis has been put on social and intentional aspects. Moreover, the proposals of agent patterns that could address those aspects (see e.g., Aridor & Lange, 1998; Deugo, Oppacher, Kuester & Otte, 1999; Hayden, Carrick & Yang, 1999) are not aimed at the design level, but rather at the implementation of lower-level issues like agent communication, information gathering, or connection setup. For instance, the Foundation for Intelligent Physical Agents (FIPA, 2017) identified and defined a set of agent's interaction protocols that are only restricted to communication. This research fills this gap by propping a series of social patterns for the detailed design phase of Tropos so that pattern-oriented development can be fully integrated at higher level development stages.

1.3. A Framework for Mas Detailed Design

Since there is a fundamental mismatch between the concepts used by the object-oriented paradigm (and other traditional mainstream software engineering approaches) and the agent-oriented approach (Jennings & Wooldridge, 2001), there is a need to develop high level patterns that are specifically tailored to the development of (multi-)agent systems using agent-oriented primitives.

Research objective is to take the principles of a social organization-based approach that contributes to reduce the distance between the system and the real world together with the important role of design patterns to help to reuse design experience. This research proposes a design framework and develops a catalogue of social patterns for making MAS design more efficient. Research contributions include:

- A framework composed of a set of complementary dimension for designing MAS. The concepts and notions used for each dimension are introduced and illustrated;
- A catalogue of social patterns to help the designer's tasks so that development time is reduced. Each social pattern in the catalogue will be designed in detail through this framework;
- A tool for designing MAS. It allows the designer to: (i) design the components of a MAS to-be constructed in a graphical way, (ii) reuse the catalogue of patterns to construct the MAS, and (iii) generate the code for automating the programmer task.

The research also brings secondary contributions:

- A set of predefined predicates integrated into an extended version of Formal Tropos for formalizing each pattern;
- The illustration of concepts introduced in our framework through a case study.

1.4. Validation

The social patterns for developing a business data integration application have been applied to multiple case studies. The reusability of these patterns and the code generation help to reduce the development tasks of the application on both designer and programmer sides.

Furthermore, an empirical experience to evaluate the benefits of pattern-oriented development should be to achieve similar case studies with and without the use of patterns and to evaluate the results on the basis of software metrics. To focus on the contribution of the design-patterns we point to structural complexity evaluation. Indeed, structural complexity focuses on MAS architecture and agent relationships, features that should be enriched using patterns.

Due to the poorness of literature concerning agent-oriented software metrics evaluating structural complexity, we point to the use of existing object-oriented ones. As a preliminary tests suite, we claim for the use of the metrics proposed by Chidamber and Kemerer (1994). Those include:

- The Depth of Inheritance Tree (DIT)

This metric measures the maximum level of the inheritance hierarchy of a class. The root of the inheritance tree inherits from no class and has a DIT count of 0. Chidamber and Kemerer suggest that DIT can be used to indicate the complexity of the design, potential for reuse;

- The Number of Children (NOC)

This metric counts the number of immediate subclasses belonging to a class. NOC was intended to indicate the level of reuse in a system and a possible indicator of the level of testing required;

- The Lack of Cohesion in Methods (LCOM)

This metric is intended to measure the lack of cohesion in the methods of a class. It is based on the principle that different attributes occurring in different methods of a class causes that class to be less cohesive than one where the same attribute is used in few methods of the class. It is viewed that a lack of cohesiveness as undesirable as it is against encapsulation. Lack of cohesion could imply that the class should probably be split into two or more subclasses;

- The Weighted Methods per Class (WMC)

The sum of the complexities of the methods in a class;

- The Coupling Between Objects (CBO)

The number of other classes whose methods or instance attribute(s) are used by methods of this class;

- The Response for a Class (RFC)

The sum of the number of methods in the class and the number of methods called by each of these methods, where each called method is counted once.

1.5. Context of the Research and Limitations

Design patterns are generally used during the *detailed design* phase of software methodologies. Agent-oriented methodologies such as TROPOS (Castro, Kolp & Mylopoulos, 2002), GAIA (Woodridge, Jennings & Kinny, 2000), MASE (Wood, DeLoach & Sparkman, 2001) and MESSAGE (Caire et al., 2002) span the following steps of software engineering:

- **Early Requirements:** Concerned with the understanding of a problem by studying an organizational setting; the output is an organizational model which includes relevant actors, their goals and their interdependencies.
- **Late Requirements:** Where the system-to-be is described within its operational environment, along with relevant functions and qualities.
- **Architectural Design:** Where the system architecture is defined in terms of subsystems, interconnected through data, control, and dependencies.
- **Detailed Design:** Where the behavior of each architectural components is defined in detail.

The catalogue of social patterns proposed in Kolp, Giorgini, and Mylopoulos (2002) constitutes a contribution to the definition of agent-oriented design patterns. This chapter focuses on these patterns, conceptualizes a framework to explore them and facilitate the building of MAS during detailed design as well as the generation of code for agent implementation. It models and introspects the patterns along different complementary dimensions.

As pointed out above, the patterns proposed into this chapter take place at Tropos' detailed design step. The process described hereafter is part of a broader methodology called I-Tropos (Wautelet, 2008) based on Tropos, driven by i* diagrams and organized following an iterative software development life cycle. This methodology is conceived to bring Agent-Oriented development to be adopted into real life development of huge enterprise information systems. Due to lack of space, we only present the detailed design discipline in the form of a workflow, more details can be found in Kolp, Wautelet and Faulkner (2011), and Faulkner et al., (2008). Figure 1 describes the workflow of the detailed design discipline using the *Software Process Engineering Metamodel* (*SPEM*) notation (see OMG, 2005). The Software Architect selects the most appropriate Social Patterns for the components under development from the catalogue overviewed in the chapter. New goals are included to the Strategic Dependency Model (Social Dimension) according to the semantics of the pattern. The Agent Designer identifies services provided by each agent to achieve the goal dependencies. Each service belongs to an agent and is represented with an NFR goal analysis to refine the Strategic Rationale Diagram (Intentional Dimension). The structure of each agent and its components such as Plans, Events and Beliefs are then specified with an agent UML class diagram (Structural Dimension). Agents communicate through events exchanged in the system and modeled in a temporal manner with extended Agent UML sequence diagrams (Communicational Dimension). The synchronization and the relationships between plans and events are designed through agent oriented activity diagrams (Dynamic Dimension).

We nevertheless point out some important limitations of our research:

- We only consider the design of cooperative MASs. Indeed, MAS may be either cooperative or competitive. In a cooperative MAS, the agents cooperate together in order to achieve common goals. Inversely, a competitive MAS is composed of agents that pursue personal goals and defend their own interests. The design of competitive MAS is left for future developments;
- The patterns need to gain experience with their use. In this dissertation, we have applied them on a case study. By doing so, we have explored the applicability of patterns and shown how our framework can help the design of MAS. However, it should be tested on more case studies;
- The dissertation only considers a MAS composed of more than one pattern as an "addition" of them. However, the combination of multiple patterns in a MAS is more complicated than that, and the emergence of conflicts remains possible. This issue needs further investigation.

1.6. Chapter Organization

The chapter is organized as follows. In Section 2, we describe the patterns. Section 3 proposes the framework and illustrates its different modeling dimensions through the Broker pattern. A *data integrator* case study that illustrates the mapping from organizational styles (architectural design phase) to social patterns (detailed design phase), is presented in Section 4. The automation of social patterns is overviewed in Section 5 while Section 6 overviews related work on software patterns. Finally, Section 7 points to some conclusions.

Figure 1. The detailed design workflow

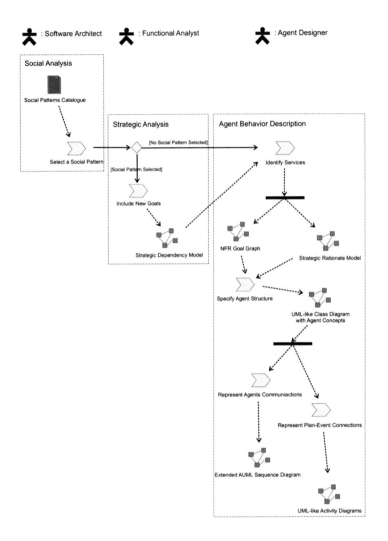

2. SOCIAL PATTERNS

Social patterns can be classified in two categories. The *Pair* patterns describe direct interactions between negotiating agents. The *Mediation* patterns feature intermediate agents that help other agents to reach agreement about an exchange of services.

In the following, we briefly model patterns using i* (Kolp & Wautelet, 2015) and communication diagrams respectively to represent the social and communicational dimensions of each pattern (Wautelet & Kolp, 2016b). In i*, agents are drawn as circles and their intentional dependencies as ovals. An agent (the *depender*) depends upon another agent (the *dependee*) for an intention to be fulfilled (the *dependum*). Dependencies have the form *depender → dependum → dependee*. Note that i* also allows to model other kind of dependencies such as resource, task or strategic ones respectively represented as rectangles, hexagons and clouds as we will see in Figure 13. AUML extends classical sequence diagrams for agent oriented modeling. For instance, the diamond symbol indicates alternative events.

The broker, as well as the subscription and call-for-proposal patterns that are both part of the broker pattern, will be modeled in detail to explain the framework in Section 3.

2.1. Pair Patterns

The Booking pattern (Figure 2) involves a client and a number of service providers. The client issues a request to book some resource from a service provider. The provider can accept the request, deny it, or propose to place the client on a waiting list, until the requested resource becomes available when some other client cancels a reservation.

The Subscription pattern involves a yellow-page agent and a number of service providers. The providers advertise their services by subscribing to the yellow pages. A provider that no longer wishes to be advertised can request to be unsubscribed.

The Call-For-Proposals pattern involves an initiator and a number of participants. The initiator issues a call for proposals for a service to all participants and then accepts proposals that offer the service for a specified cost. The initiator selects one participant to supply the service.

The Bidding (Figure 3) pattern involves a client and a number of service providers. The client organizes and leads the bidding process, and receives proposals. At each iteration, the client publishes the current bid; it can accept an offer, raise the bid, or cancel the process.

2.3. Mediation Patterns

In the Monitor pattern (Figure 4), subscribers register for receiving, from a monitor agent, notifications of changes of state in some subjects of their interest. The monitor accepts subscriptions, requests information from the subjects of interest, and alerts subscribers accordingly.

In the Broker pattern, the broker agent is an arbiter and intermediary that requests services from providers to satisfy the request of clients.

In the Matchmaker pattern (Figure 5), a matchmaker agent locates a provider for a given service requested by a client, and then lets the client interact directly with the provider, unlike brokers, who handle all interactions between clients and providers.

In the Mediator pattern (Figure 6), a mediator agent coordinates the cooperation of service provider agents to satisfy the request of a client agent. While a matchmaker simply matches providers with clients, a mediator encapsulates interactions and maintains models of the capabilities of clients and providers over time.

Figure 2. Social and communicational diagrams for the booking pattern

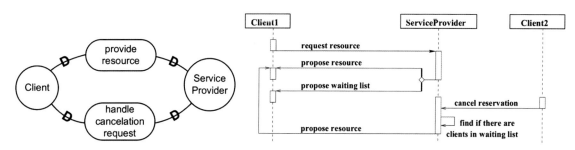

Figure 3. Social and communicational diagrams for the bidding pattern

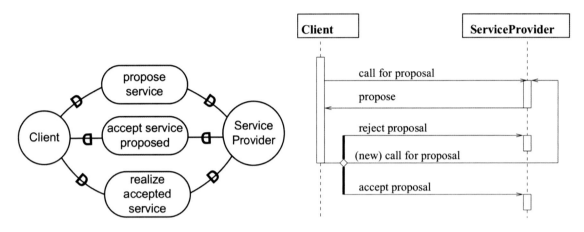

Figure 4. Social and communicational diagrams for the monitor pattern

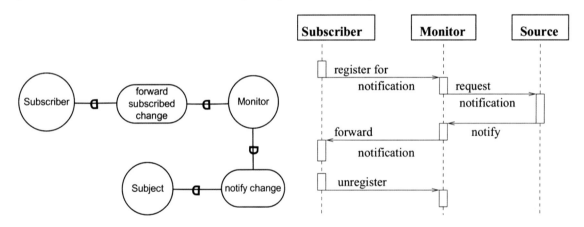

Figure 5. Social and communicational diagrams for the matchmaker pattern

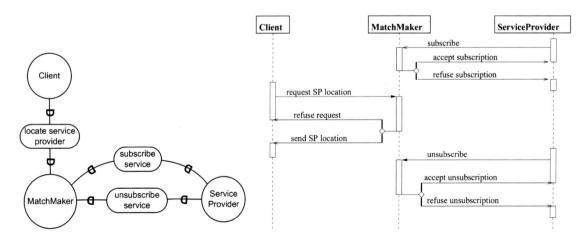

Figure 6. Social and communicational diagrams for the mediator pattern

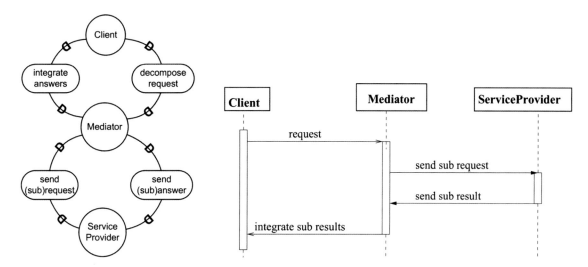

In the Embassy pattern, an embassy agent routes a service requested by an external agent to a local agent. If the request is granted, the external agent can submit messages to the embassy for translation in accordance with a standard ontology. Translated messages are forwarded to the requested local agent and the result of the query is passed back out through the embassy to the external agent.

The Wrapper pattern (Figure 7) incorporates a legacy system into a multi-agent system. A wrapper agent interfaces system agents with the legacy system by acting as a translator. This ensures that communication protocols are respected and the legacy system remains decoupled from the rest of the agent system.

3. A SOCIAL PATTERNS FRAMEWORK

This section describes a conceptual framework based on five complementary modeling dimensions, to investigate social patterns. The framework has been applied in the context of the Tropos development

Figure 7. Social and communicational diagrams for the wrapper pattern

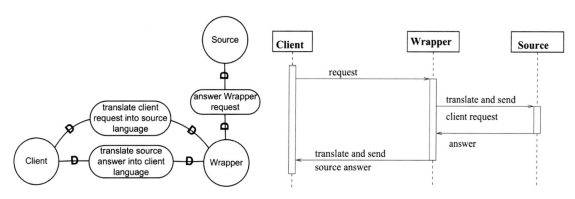

methodology (Castro, Kolp & Mylopoulos, 2002). Each dimension reflects a particular aspect of a MAS architecture, as follows.

- The *social dimension* identifies the relevant agents in the system and their intentional interdependencies.
- The *intentional dimension* identifies and formalizes services provided by agents to realize the intentions identified by the social dimension, independently of the plans that implement those services. This dimension answers the question: "What does each service do?"
- The *structural dimension* operationalizes the services identified by the intentional dimension in terms of agent-oriented concepts like beliefs, events, plans, and their relationships. This dimension answers the question: "How is each service operationalized?"
- The *communicational dimension* models the temporal exchange of events between agents.
- The *dynamic dimension* models the synchronization mechanisms between events and plans.

The social and the intentional dimensions are specific to MAS. The last three dimensions (structural, communicational, and dynamic) of the architecture are also relevant for traditional (non-agent) systems, but we have adapted and extended them with agent-oriented concepts. They are for instance the modeling dimensions used in object-oriented visual modeling languages such as UML.

The rest of this section details the five dimensions of the framework and illustrates them through the Broker pattern (Yu et al., 2011).

This pattern involves an arbiter intermediary that requests services from providers to satisfy the request of clients. It is designed through the framework as follows.

3.1. Social Dimension

The social dimension specifies a number of agents and their intentional interdependencies using the i* model (Kolp & Wautelet 2015). Figure 8 shows a social diagram for the Broker pattern.

The Broker pattern can be considered as a combination of (1) a Subscription pattern (shown enclosed within dashed boundary (a)), that allows service providers to subscribe their services to the Broker agent and where the Broker agent plays the role of a yellow-page agent, (2) one of the other pair patterns - Booking, Call-for-Proposals, or Bidding - whereby the Broker agent requests and receives services from service providers (in Figure 13, it is a Call-for-Proposals pattern, shown enclosed within dotted boundary (b)), and (3) interaction between the broker and the client: the Broker agent depends on the client for sending a service request and the client depends on the Broker agent to forward the service.

To formalize intentional interdependencies, we use Formal Tropos (Fuxman, Pistore, Mylopoulos, & Traverso, 2001), a first-order temporal-logic language that provides a textual notation for i* models and allows to describe dynamic constraints. A *forward service* dependency can be defined in Formal Tropos as follows.

```
Dependum Forward Service
        Mode: Achieve
        Depender: Client cl
        Dependee: Broker br
        Fulfillment:
```

Figure 8. Social diagram for the broker pattern

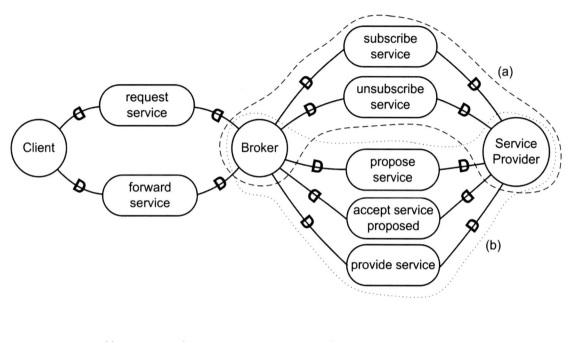

$$(\forall \; sr: \texttt{ServiceRequest}, \; st: \texttt{ServiceType})$$
$$\texttt{request}(cl, \; br, \; sr) \land \texttt{provide}(br, \; st) \land \texttt{ofType}(sr, \; st)$$
$$\rightarrow \diamond \; \texttt{received}(cl, \; br, \; st)$$

[Broker *br* successfully provides its service to client *cl* if all requests *sr* from *cl* to *br*, that are of a type *st* that *br* can handle, are eventually satisfied]

3.2. Intentional Dimension

While the social dimension focuses on interdependencies between agents, the intentional dimension aims at modeling agent rationale. It is concerned with the identification of *services* provided by agents and made available to achieve the intentions identified in the social dimension. Each service belongs to one agent. Service definitions can be formalized by its fulfillment condition.

Table 1 lists several services of the Broker pattern with an informal definition. With the FindBroker service, a client finds a broker that can handle a given service request. The request is then sent to the broker through the SendServiceRequest service. The broker can query its belief knowledge with the QuerySPAvailability service and answer the client through the SendServiceRequestDecision service. If the answer is negative, the client records it with its RecordBRRefusal service. If the answer is positive, the broker records the request (RecordClientServiceRequest service) and then broadcasts a call (Call-ForProposals service) to potential service providers. The client records acceptance by the broker with the RecordBRAcceptance service.

The Call-For-Proposals pattern could be used here, but this presentation omits it for brevity.

The broker then selects one of the service providers among those that offer the requested service. If the selected provider successfully returns the requested service, it informs the broker, that records the information and forwards it to the client (RecordAndSendSPInformDone service).

Table 1. Some services of the Broker pattern

Service Name	Informal Definition	Agent
FindBroker	Find a broker that can provide a service	Client
SendServiceRequest	Send a service request to a broker	Client
QuerySPAvailability	Query the knowledge for information about the availability of the requested service	Broker
SendService RequestDecision	Send an answer to the client	Broker
RecordBRRefusal	Record a negative answer from a broker	Client
RecordBRAcceptance	Record a positive answer from a broker	Client
RecordClient ServiceRequest	Record a service request received from a Client	Broker
CallForProposals	Send a call for proposals to service providers	Broker
RecordAndSend SPInformDone	Record a service received from a service provider	Broker

Services can be formalized in Formal Tropos as illustrated below for the FindBroker service.

```
Service FindBroker (sr: ServiceRequest)
      Mode: Achieve
      Agent: Client cl
      Fulfillment:
            (∃ br: Broker, st: ServiceType)
            provide(br, st) ∧ ofType (sr, st)
                  → ◊ known(cl, br)
```

[*FindBroker* is fulfilled when client *cl* has found (*known* predicate) *Broker br* that is able to perform (*provide* predicate) the service requested.]

3.3. Structural Dimension

While the intentional dimension answers the question "What does each service do?", the structural dimension answers the question "How is each service operationalized?". Services are operationalized as *plans*, that is, sequences of actions.

The knowledge that an agent has (about itself or its environment) is stored in its *beliefs*. An agent can act in response to the *events* that it handles through its plans. A plan, in turn, is used by the agent to read or modify its beliefs, and send events to other agents or post events to itself.

The structural dimension is modeled using a UML style class diagram extended for MAS engineering.

The required agent concepts extending the class diagram model are defined below.

3.3.1. Structural Concepts

Figure 9 depicts the concepts and their relationships needed to build the structural dimension. Each concept defines a common template for classes of concrete MAS (for example, Agent in Figure 9. is a template for the Broker agent class of Figure 10).

A Belief describes a piece of the knowledge that an agent has about itself and its environment. Beliefs are represented as tuples composed of a key and value fields.

Events describe stimuli, emitted by agents or automatically generated, in response to which the agents must take action. As shown in Figure 9, the structure of an event is composed of three parts: declaration of the attributes of the event, declaration of the methods to create the event, declaration of the beliefs and the condition used for an automatic event. The third part only appears for automatic events. Events can be described along three dimensions:

- *External or Internal* **Event:** External events are sent to other agents while internal events are posted by an agent to itself. This property is captured by the *scope* attribute.
- *Normal or BDI* **Event:** An agent has a number of alternative plans to respond to a BDI (Belief-Desire-Event) event and only one plan in response to a normal event. Whenever an event occurs, the agent initiates a plan to handle it. If the plan execution fails and if the event is a normal event, then the event is said to have failed. If the event is a BDI event, a set of plans can be selected for execution and these are attempted in turn. If all selected plans fail, the event is also said to have failed. The event type is captured by the *type* attribute.

Figure 9. Structural diagram template

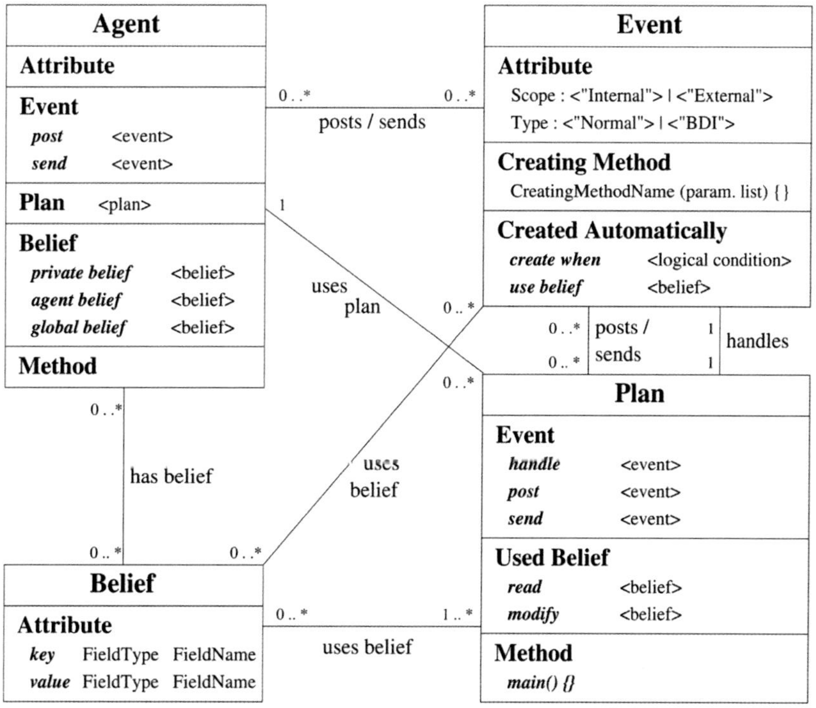

- *Automatic or Nonautomatic* **Event:** An automatic event is automatically created when certain belief states arise. The *create when* statement specifies the logical condition which must arise for the event to be automatically created. The states of the beliefs that are defined by *use belief* are monitored to determine when to automatically create events.

A *Plan* describes a sequence of actions that an agent can take when an event occurs. As shown by Figure 9, plans are structured in three parts: the Event part, the Belief part, and the Method part. The Event part declares events that the plan handles (i.e., events that trigger the execution of the plan) and events that the plan produces. The latter can be either posted (i.e., sent by an agent only to itself) or sent (i.e., sent to other agents). The Belief part declares beliefs that the plan reads and those that it modifies. The Method part describes the plan itself, that is, the actions performed when the plan is executed.

The Agent concept defines the behavior of an agent, as composed of five parts: the declaration of its attributes, of the events that it can post or send explicitly (i.e., without using its plans), of the plans that it uses to respond to events, of the beliefs that make up its knowledge, and of its methods.

The beliefs of an agent can be of type *private*, *agent*, or *global*. A *private* access is restricted to the agent to which the belief belongs. *Agent* access is shared with other agents of the same class, while *global* access is unrestricted.

3.3.2. Structural Model for the Broker Pattern

Figure 10 depicts the Broker pattern components. For brevity, each construct described earlier is illustrated only through one component. Each component can be considered as an instantiation of the (corresponding) template in Figure 9.

Broker is one of the three agents composing the Broker pattern. It has plans such as QuerySPAvailability, SendServiceRequestDecision, etc. When there is no ambiguity, by convention, the plan name is the same as the as the name of the service that it operationalizes. The private belief SPProvidedService stores the service type that each service provider can provide. This belief is declared as private since the broker is the only agent that can manipulate it. The ServiceType belief stores the information about types of service provided by service providers and is declared as global since its must be known both by the service provider and the broker agent.

The constructor *method* allows to give a name to a broker agent when created. This method may call other methods, for example loadBR(), to initialize agent beliefs.

SendServiceRequestDecision is one of the plans that the broker uses to answer the client: the BRRefusalSent event is sent when the answer is negative, BRAcceptanceSent when the broker has found service provider(s) that may provide the requested service. In the latter case, the plan also posts the BRAcceptancePosted event to invoke the process of recording the service request and the 'call for proposals' process between the broker and services providers. The SendServiceRequestDecision plan is executed when the AvailabilityQueried event (containing the information about the availability of the service provider to realize the client's request) occurs.

SPProvidedService is one of the broker's beliefs used to store the services provided by the service providers. The service provider code sPCode and the service type code serviceTypeCode form the belief key. The corresponding quantity attribute is declared as value field.

BRAcceptanceSent is an event that is sent to inform the client that its request is accepted.

At a lower level, each plan could also be modeled by an activity diagram for further detail if necessary.

Figure 10. Structural diagram: Some components of the broker pattern

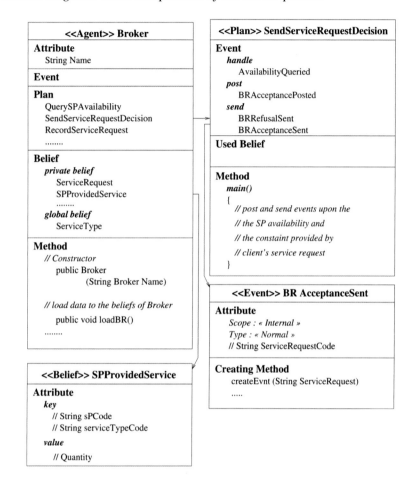

3.4. Communication Dimension

Agents interact with each other by exchanging events. The communicational dimension models, in a temporal manner, events exchanged in the system. We adopt the sequence diagram model proposed in AUML (Wautelet & Kolp, 2016b) and extend it: *agent_name/role:pattern_name* expresses the role (*role*) of the agent (*agent_name*) in the pattern; the arrows are labeled with the name of the exchanged events.

Figure 11 shows a sequence diagram for the Broker pattern. The client (customer1) sends a service request (ServiceRequestSent) containing the characteristics of the service it wishes to obtain from the broker. The broker may alternatively answer with a denial (BRRefusalSent) or a acceptance (BRAcceptanceSent).

In the case of an acceptance, the broker sends a call for proposal to the registered service providers (CallForProposalSent). The call for proposal (CFP) pattern is then applied to model the interaction between the broker and the service providers. The service provider either fails or achieves the requested service. The broker then informs the client about this result by sending a InformFailureServiceRequestSent or a ServiceForwarded, respectively.

Figure 11. Communication diagram: Broker

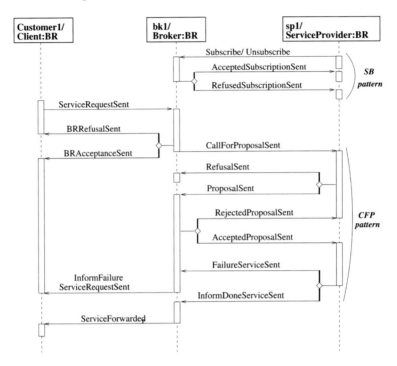

The communication dimension of the subscription pattern (SB) is given at the top-right and the communication dimension of the call-for- proposals pattern (CFP) is given at the bottom-right part of Figure 11. The communication specific for the broker pattern is given in the left part of the figure.

3.5. Dynamic Dimension

As described earlier, a plan can be invoked by an event that it handles and it can create new events. Relationships between plans and events can rapidly become complex. To cope with this problem, we propose to model the synchronization and the relationships between plans and events with activity diagrams extended for agent-oriented systems. These diagrams specify the events that are created in parallel, the conditions under which events are created, which plans handle which events, and so on.

An internal event is represented by a dashed arrow and an external event by a solid arrow. As mentioned earlier, a BDI event may be handled by alternative plans. They are enclosed in a round-corner box. Synchronization and branching are represented as usual.

We omit the dynamic dimension of the Subscription and the CFP patterns, and only present in Figure 12 the activity diagram specific to the Broker pattern. It models the flow of control from the emission of a service request sent by the client to the reception by the same client of the realized service result sent by the broker. Three swimlanes, one for each agent of the Broker pattern, compose the diagram. In this pattern, the FindBroker service described in Section 3.2.2, is either operationalized by the FindBR or the FindBRWithMM plans (the client finds a broker based on its own knowledge or via a matchmaker).

Figure 12. Dynamic diagram: Broker

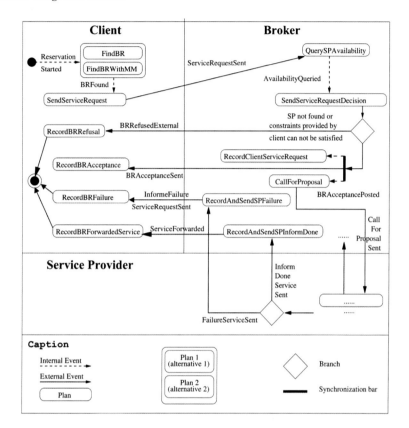

4. FROM ORGANIZATIONAL ARCHITECTURAL STYLES TO SOCIAL DESIGN PATTERNS

A key aspect to conduct MAS architectural design is the specification and use of *organizational styles* (Castro, Kolp & Mylopoulos, 2002; Kolp, Giorgini & Mylopoulos, 2002; Do, Faulkner, & Kolp, 2003) that are socially-based architectural designs inspired from models and concepts from organization theory (e.g., Mintzberg, 1992; Scott, 1998; Yoshino & Srinivasa Rangan, 1995) and strategic alliances (e.g., Dussauge & Garrette, 1999; Morabito, Sack & Bhate, 1999; Segil, 1996) that analyze the structure and design of real-world human organization. These are for instance the structure-in-fives, the matrix, the joint-venture, the hierarchical contracting.

As described in (Castro, Kolp & Mylopoulos, 2002; Zambonelli, Jennings & Wooldridge, 2000), in MAS architectural design, organizational styles are used to give information about the system architecture to be: every time an organizational style is applied, it allows to easily point up, to the designer, the required organizational actors and roles. Then the next step needs to detail and relate such (organizational) actors and roles to more specific agents in order to proceed with the agent behavior characterization. Namely, each actor in an organization-based architecture is much closer to the real world system actor behavior that we consequently aim to have in software agents. As a consequence, once the organizational architectural reflection has figured out the MAS global structure in terms of actors, roles, and their intentional relationships, a deepener analysis is required to detail the agent behaviors and their interdependencies necessary to accomplish their roles in the software organization. To effectively deal with such a purpose, developers can be guided by social patterns proposed in this chapter.

Social patterns offer a microscopic view of the MAS at the *detailed design* phase to express in deeper detail organizational styles during the architectural design. To explain the necessary relationship between *styles* and *patterns* we consider an original *data integrator* case study and overview how a MAS designed from some style at the architectural level is decomposed into social patterns at the detailed design level.

The data integrator allows users to obtain information that come from different heterogeneous and distributed sources. Sources range from text file systems agent knowledge bases. Information from each source that may be of interest is extracted, translated and filtered as appropriate, merged with relevant information from other sources to provide the answer to the users' queries (Widom, 1995).

Figure 13 shows a MAS architecture in i* for the data integrator that applies the *joint-venture* style (Castro, Kolp & Mylopoulos, 2002; Do, Faulkner, & Kolp, 2003) at the architectural design level. In a few words, the joint venture organizational style is a meta-structure that defines an organizational system that involves agreement between two or more independent partners to obtain the benefits of larger scale, shared investment and lower maintenance costs. A specific joint management actor coordinates tasks and manages the sharing of resources between partner actors. Each partner can manage and control itself on a local dimension and may interact directly with other partners to exchange resources, such as data and knowledge. However, the strategic operation and coordination of such a system, and its actors on a global dimension, are the only responsibility of the joint management actor in which the original actors possess equity participations.

Joint-venture's roles at the architectural design level are expressed in the detailed design level in terms of patterns, namely the broker, the matchmaker, the monitor, the mediator and the wrapper. The *joint management private interface* is assumed by a mediator, the joint-venture partners are the *wrapper*, the *monitor*, the *multi-criteria analyzer* and the *matchmaker*. The *public interface* is assumed by the *broker*.

Figure 13. A Joint-Venture MAS architecture expressed in terms of social patterns: A data integration example

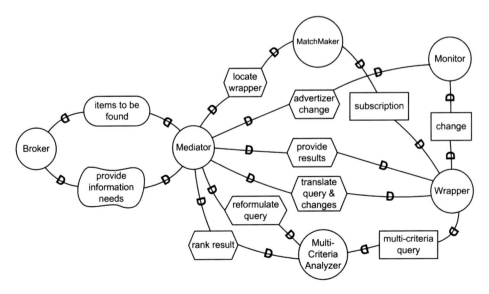

The system works as follows. When a user wishes to send a request, she contacts the *broker* agent which is an intermediary to select one or many *mediator(s)* that can satisfy the user information needs. Then, the selected mediator(s) decomposes the user's query into one or more subqueries to the sources, synthesizes the source answers and return the answers to the broker.

If the mediator identifies a recurrent user information request, the information that may be of interest is extracted from each source, merged with relevant information from other sources, and stored as knowledge by the mediator. This stored information constitutes a materialized view that the mediator will have to maintain up-to-date.

A *wrapper* and a *monitor* agents are connected to each information source. The *wrapper* is responsible for translating the subquery issued by the mediator into the native format of the source and translating the source response in the data model used by the mediator.

The *monitor* is responsible for detecting changes of interest (e.g., change which affects a materialized view) in the information source and reporting them to the mediator. Changes are then translated by the wrapper and sent to the mediator.

It may be also necessary for the mediator to obtain the information concerning the localization of a source and its connected wrapper that are able to provide current or future relevant information. This kind of information is provided by the *matchmaker* agent which then lets the mediator interacts directly with the correspondant wrapper.

Finally, the multi-c*riteria analyzer* can reformulate a subquery (sent by a mediator to a wrapper) through a set of criteria in order to express the user preferences in a more detailed way, and refine the possible domain of results.

5. AUTOMATION

The main motivation behind design patterns is the possibility of reusing them during system detailed design and implementation. Numerous CASE tools such as Rational Rose (IBM Rational Rose, 2007) and Together (Borland Together, 2007) include code generators for object-oriented design patterns. Programmers identify and parameterize, during system detailed design, the patterns that they use in their applications. The code skeleton for the patterns is then automatically generated and programming is thus made easier.

For agent-oriented programming, SKwyRL (Kolp & Wautelet, 2015), for instance, proposes a code generator to automate the use of social patterns introduced in Section 2. Figure 13 shows the main window of the tool. It has been developed in Java and produces code for JACK (JACK Intelligent Agents, 2006), an agent-oriented development environment built on top of Java. JACK extends Java with specific capabilities to implement agent behaviors. On a conceptual point of view, the relationship of JACK to Java is analogous to that between C++ and C. On a technical point of view, JACK source code is first compiled into regular Java code before being executed.

In SKwyRL's code generator, the programmer first chooses which social pattern to use, then the roles for each agent in the selected pattern (e.g. the E_Broker agent plays the *broker* role for the Broker pattern but can also play the *initiator* role for the CallForProposals pattern and the *yellow page* role for the Subscription pattern in the same application). The process is repeated until all relevant patterns have been identified. The code generator then produces the generic code for the patterns (.agent, .event, .plan, .bel JACK files).

The programmer has to add the particular JACK code for each generated files and implement the graphical interface if necessary.

Figure 15 shows an example of the (e-business) broker for the data integrator presented in Section 4. It was developed with JACK and the code skeleton was generated with SKwyRL's code generator using the Broker pattern explained in the chater. The bottom half of the figure shows the interface between the customer and the broker. The customer sends a service request to the broker asking for buying or sending DVDs. He chooses which DVDs to sell or buy, selects the corresponding DVD titles, the quantity and the deadline (the time-out before which the broker has to realizes the requested service). When receiving the customer's request, the broker interacts with the media shops to obtain the DVDs. The interactions between the broker and the media shops are shown on the bottom-right corner of this figure. The top half of the figure shows the items that are provided by each media shop.

6. RELATED WORK

As already said, a lot of work has been devoted to software patterns these last fifteen years. Patterns for software development are one of software engineering problem-solving discipline that has its roots in a design movement in contemporary architecture and the documentation of best practices and lessons learned in all vocations. The goal of patterns is to create a body of literature to help software developers resolve recurring problems encountered throughout all of software development. Patterns help create a shared language for communicating insight and experience about these problems and their solutions.

Figure 14. JACK code generation

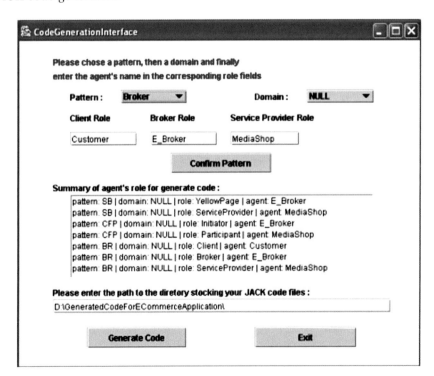

Figure 15. An e-business broker

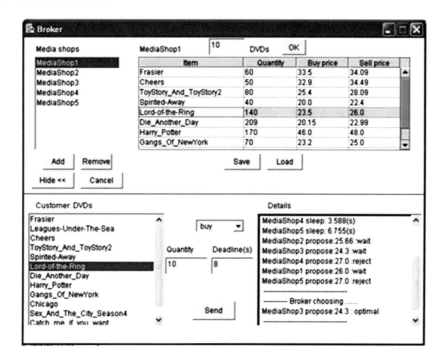

Ward Cunningham and Kent Beck developed a small set of five patterns (Beck & Cunningham, 1987), for guiding Smalltalk programmers to design user interface. Jim Coplien introduced a catalog of for C++ patterns, called *idioms* (Coplien, 1991). Software patterns then became popular with the wide acceptance of the Gang of Four or GoF (Erich Gamma, Richard Helm, Ralph Johnson, and John Vlissides) book (Gamma, Helm, Johnson, & Vlissides, 1995).

However, the patterns in the GoF book are only one kind of pattern – the object-oriented *design patterns*. There are many other kinds of patterns. For example, Martin Fowler's "*Analysis Patterns*" (Fowler, 1997) describe the models of business processes that occur repeatedly in the analysis phase of software development; *organizational patterns* (Coplien & Schmidt, 1995) are about software-development organizations and about people who work in such organizations. *Process patterns* (Ambler, 1998) relate to the strategies that software professionals employ to solve problems that recur across organizations. Frank Buschmann, Regine Meunier, Hans Rohnert, Peter Sommerlad, and Michael Stal, helped popularize these kinds of patterns (organizational and process patterns) (Buschmann, Meunier, Rohnert, Sommerlad & Stal, 1996).

Contrary to pattern, that represents a "best practice", an *anti-pattern* represents a "lesson learned". There are two kinds of "anti-patterns": those that describe a bad solution to a problem which resulted in a bad situation and those that describe how to get out of a bad situation and how to proceed from there to a good solution. Anti-pattern is initially proposed by Andrew Koenig. Anti-patterns extend the field of software patterns research into exciting new areas and issues, including: refactoring, reengineering, system extension, and system migration (Chen & al, 2014; Webster, 1995; Brown, Malveau, Hays, McCormick Iii & Mowbray, 1998; Love, 1997).

Recent popularity of autonomous agents and agent-oriented software engineering has led to the discovery of agent patterns (Kolp & Wautelet, 2015; Aridor & Lange, 1998; Deugo, Oppacher, Kuester, & Otte, 1999; Hayden, Carrick & Yang, 1999; Do, Faulkner & Kolp, 2003; Mouratidis, Giorgini & Manson, 2003), that capture good solutions to common problems in agent design in many aspect such as security, architecture, organization, etc. However, as pointed out earlier, little focus has been put on social and intentional considerations and these agent patterns rather aim at the implementation level. The framework presented in the chapter should add more detail to the design process of agent oriented software engineering (Kolp & Wautelet, 2015; Do, Faulkner & Kolp, 2003).

7. CONCLUSION

Nowadays, software engineering for new enterprise application domains such as eBusiness, knowledge management, peer-to-peer computing or web services is forced to build up open systems able to cope with distributed, heterogeneous, and dynamic information issues. Most of these software systems exist in a changing organizational and operational environment where new components can be added, modified or removed at any time. For these reasons and more, Multi-Agent Systems (MAS) architectures are gaining popularity in that they do allow dynamic and evolving structures which can change at run-time.

An important technique that helps to manage the complexity of such architectures is the reuse of development experience and know-how. Like any architect, software architects use patterns to guide system development. Over the years, patterns have become an attractive approach to reusing architectural design knowledge in software engineering. Patterns describe a problem commonly found in software designs and prescribe a flexible solution for the problem, so as to ease the reuse of that solution.

As explored in this chapter, MAS architectures can be considered social structures composed of autonomous and proactive agents that interact and cooperate with each other to achieve common or private goals. Since the fundamental concepts of multi-agent systems are intentional and social, rather than implementation-oriented, social abstractions could provide inspiration and insights to define patterns for designing MAS architectures.

This chapter has focused on social patterns. With real-world social behaviors as a metaphor, social patterns are agent-oriented design patterns that describe MAS as composed of autonomous agents that interact and coordinate to achieve their intentions, like actors in human organizations.

The chapter has described such patterns, a design framework to introspect them and formalize their "code of ethics", answering the question: what can one expect from a broker, mediator, embassy, etc. It aims to be used during the detail design phase of any agent-oriented methodology detailing the patterns following different point of views.

REFERENCES

Ambler, S. W. (1998). *Process patterns: building large-scale systems using object technology*. Cambridge University Press.

Aridor, Y., & Lange, D. B. (1998, May). Agent design patterns: elements of agent application design. In *Proceedings of the second international conference on Autonomous agents* (pp. 108-115). ACM. 10.1145/280765.280784

Beck, K., & Cunningham, W. (1987). Using Pattern Languages for Object-Oriented Programs. *Workshop on the Specification and Design for Object-Oriented Programming (OOPSLA'87)*.

Borland Together. (2007). Available at: http://www.borland.com/downloads/download_together.html

Bosch, J. (1998). Design Patterns as Language Constructs. *Journal of Object-Oriented Programming, 11*(2), 18–32.

Brown, W. J., Malveau, R. C., Hays, W., McCormick Iii, H., & Mowbray, T. J. (1998). *AntiPatterns: Refactoring Software, Architectures, and Projects in Crisis*. John Wiley & Sons.

Buschmann, F., Meunier, R., Rohnert, H., Sommerlad, P., & Stal, M. (1996). *Pattern-Oriented Software Architecture - A System of Patterns*. John Wiley & Sons.

Caire, J., & ... . (2002). Agent-oriented analysis using MESSAGE/UML. *Proceedings of the 2nd Int. Workshop on Agent-Oriented Software Engineering*, 119-135. 10.1007/3-540-70657-7_8

Castro, J., Kolp, M., & Mylopoulos, J. (2002). Towards Requirements-Driven Information Systems Engineering: The Tropos Project. *Information Systems, 27*(6), 365–389. doi:10.1016/S0306-4379(02)00012-1

Chen, T. H., Shang, W., Jiang, Z. M., Hassan, A. E., Nasser, M., & Flora, P. (2014). Detecting performance anti-patterns for applications developed using object-relational mapping. In *Proceedings of the 36th International Conference on Software Engineering* (pp. 1001-1012). ACM. 10.1145/2568225.2568259

Chidamber, S.R., & Kemerer, C.F. (1994). A Metrics Suite for Object-Oriented Design. *IEEE Transactions on Software Engineering, 20*(6), 476-493.

Cockburn, A. (1996). The Interaction of Social Issues and Software Architecture. *Communications of the ACM, 39*(10), 40–49. doi:10.1145/236156.236165

Coplien, J., & Schmidt, D. (1995). *Pattern Languages of Program Design*. Addison-Wesley.

Coplien, O. (1991). *Advanced C++ Programming Styles and Idioms*. Addison-Wesley International.

Deugo, D., Oppacher, F., Kuester, J., & Otte, I. V. (1999). Patterns as a Means for Intelligent Software Engineering. *Proceedings of the Int. Conf. on Artificial Intelligence*, 605-611.

Do, T. T., Faulkner, S., & Kolp, M. (2003). Organizational Multi-Agent Architectures for Information Systems. *Proceedings of the 5th International Conference on Enterprise Information Systems, ICEIS 2003*, 89-96.

Dussauge, P., & Garrette, B. (1999). *Cooperative Strategy: Competing Successfully Through Strategic Alliances*. Wiley and Sons.

Faulkner, S., Kolp, M., Wautelet, Y., & Achbany, Y. (2008). A formal description language for multi-agent architectures. *Agent-Oriented Information Systems, IV*, 143–163. doi:10.1007/978-3-540-77990-2_9

Fernandez, E. B., & Pan, R. (2001). A Pattern Language for Security Models. *Proceedings of the 8th Conference on Pattern Language of Programs.*

FIPA. (2017). *The Foundation for Intelligent Physical Agent (FIPA).* Retrieved from http://www.fipa.org/

Fowler, M. (1997). *Analysis Patterns: Reusable Object Models.* Addison-Wesley.

Fuxman, A., Pistore, M., Mylopoulos, J., & Traverso, P. (2001). Model Checking Early Requirements Specifications in Tropos. *Proc. of the 5th IEEE Int. Symposium on Requirements Engineering*, 174-181.

Gamma, E., Helm, R., Johnson, R., & Vlissides, J. (1995). *Design Patterns: Elements of Reusable Object-Oriented Software.* Addison-Wesley.

Hayden, S., Carrick, C., & Yang, Q. (1999). Architectural Design Patterns for Multiagent Coordination. *Proceedings of the 3rd Int. Conf. on Agent Systems.*

IBM Rational Rose. (2007). Available at: http://www-306.ibm.com/software/rational

JACK Intelligent Agents. (2006). Retrieved from http://www.agent-software.com

Jennings, N. R., & Wooldridge, M. (2001). Agent-Oriented Software Engineering. In *Handbook of Agent Technology.* AAAI/ MIT Press.

Juziuk, J., Weyns, D., & Holvoet, T. (2014). Design patterns for multi-agent systems: a systematic literature Review. In *Agent-Oriented Software Engineering* (pp. 79–99). Springer Berlin Heidelberg. doi:10.1007/978-3-642-54432-3_5

Kolp, M., Giorgini, P., & Mylopoulos, J. (2002). Information Systems Development through Social Structures. *Proceedings of the 14th Int. Conference on Software Engineering and Knowledge Engineering*, 183-190.

Kolp, M., & Wautelet, Y. (2015). Human organizational patterns applied to collaborative learning software systems. *Computers in Human Behavior*, *51*, 742–751. doi:10.1016/j.chb.2014.11.094

Kolp, M., Wautelet, Y., & Faulkner, S. (2011). Social-Centric Design of Multi-Agent Architectures. In E. Yu, P. Giorgini, N. Maiden, & J. Mylopoulos (Eds.), *Social Modeling for Requirements Engineering.* MIT Press.

Liu, D., Deters, R., & Zhang, W. J. (2010). Architectural design for resilience. *Enterprise Information Systems*, *4*(2), 137–152. doi:10.1080/17517570903067751

Love, T. (1997). *Object Lessons.* Cambridge University Press.

Miller, T., Lu, B., Sterling, L., Beydoun, G., & Taveter, K. (2014). Requirements elicitation and specification using the agent paradigm: The case study of an aircraft turnaround simulator. *IEEE Transactions on Software Engineering*, *40*(10), 1007–1024. doi:10.1109/TSE.2014.2339827

Mintzberg, H. (1992). *Structure in fives: designing effective organizations.* Prentice-Hall.

Morabito, J., Sack, I., & Bhate, A. (1999). *Organization modeling: innovative architectures for the 21st century.* Prentice Hall.

Mouratidis, H., Giorgini, P., & Manson, G. (2003). Modelling Secure Multiagent Systems. *Proceedings of the 2nd International Joint Conference on Autonomous Agents and Multiagent Systems*, 859-866.

OMG. (2005). *The Software Process Engineering Metamodel Specification*. Version 1.1. OMG.

Pree, W. (1994). *Design Patterns for Object Oriented Development*. Addison Wesley.

Riehle, D., & Züllighoven, H. (1996). Understanding and Using Patterns in Software Development. Theory and Practice of Object Systems, 2(1), 3-13. doi:10.1002/(SICI)1096-9942(1996)2:1<3::AID-TAPO1>3.0.CO;2-#

Scott, W. R. (1998). *Organizations: Rational, natural, and open systems*. Prentice Hall.

Segil, L. (1996). *Intelligent business alliances: how to profit using today's most important strategic tool*. Times Business.

Wautelet, Y. (2008). *A goal-driven project management framework for multi-agent software development: The case of i-tropos* (PhD Thesis). Université Catholique de Louvain, Belgium.

Wautelet, Y., Heng, S., Kolp, M., Penserini, L., & Poelmans, S. (2016a). Designing an MOOC as an agent-platform aggregating heterogeneous virtual learning environments. *Behaviour & Information Technology*, *35*(11), 980–997. doi:10.1080/0144929X.2016.1212095

Wautelet, Y., & Kolp, M. (2016b). Business and model-driven development of BDI multi-agent systems. *Neurocomputing*, *182*, 304–321. doi:10.1016/j.neucom.2015.12.022

Webster, B. F. (1995). *Pitfalls of Object Oriented Development*. John Wiley & Sons Inc.

Widom, J. (1995). Research Problems in Data Warehousing. *Proceedings of the Fourth Int. Conf. on Information and Knowledge Management*, 25-30.

Wood, M., DeLoach, S. A., & Sparkman, C. (2001). Multi-Agent System Engineering. *International Journal of Software Engineering and Knowledge Engineering*, *11*(3), 231–258. doi:10.1142/S0218194001000542

Woodridge, M., Jennings, N. R., & Kinny, D. (2000). The Gaia Methodology for Agent-Oriented Analysis and Design. *Autonomous Agents and Multi-Agent Systems*, *3*(3), 285–312. doi:10.1023/A:1010071910869

Yoshino, M. Y., & Srinivasa Rangan, U. (1995). *Strategic alliances: an entrepreneurial approach to globalization*. Harvard Business School Press.

Yu, E., Giorgini, P., Maiden, N., & Mylopoulos, J. (2011). *Social Modeling for Requirements Engineering*. MIT Press.

Zambonelli, F., Jennings, N. R., Omicini, A., & Wooldridge, M. (2000). Agent-Oriented Software Engineering for Internet Applications. In *Coordination of Internet Agents: Models, Technologies and Applications* (pp. 326–346). Springer Verlag.

Zambonelli, F., Jennings, N. R., & Wooldridge, M. (2000). Organizational abstractions for the analysis and design of multi-agent systems. *Proceedings of the 1st International Workshop on Agent-Oriented Software Engineering*, 243-252.

Chapter 13
Agent-Based Software Engineering, Paradigm Shift, or Research Program Evolution

Yves Wautelet
KU Leuven, Belgium

Christophe Schinckus
Royal Melbourne Institute of Technology, Australia

Manuel Kolp
Université catholique de Lovuain, Belgium

ABSTRACT

Information systems are deeply linked to human activities. Unfortunately, development methodologies have been traditionally inspired by programming concepts and not by organizational and human ones. This leads to ontological and semantic gaps between the systems and their environments. The adoption of agent orientation and multi-agent systems (MAS) helps to reduce these gaps by offering modeling tools based on organizational concepts (actors, agents, goals, objectives, responsibilities, social dependencies, etc.) as fundamentals to conceive systems through all the development process. Moreover, software development is becoming increasingly complex. Stakeholders' expectations are growing higher while the development agendas have to be as short as possible. Project managers, business analysts, and software developers need adequate processes and models to specify the organizational context, capture requirements, and build efficient and flexible systems.

INTRODUCTION

Information systems are deeply linked to human activities. Unfortunately, development methodologies have been traditionally inspired by programming concepts and not by organizational and human ones. This leads to ontological and semantic gaps between the systems and their environments. The adoption of agent orientation and Multi-Agent Systems (MAS) helps to reduce these gaps by offering modeling

DOI: 10.4018/978-1-5225-5396-0.ch013

tools based on organizational concepts (actors, agents, goals, objectives, responsibilities, social dependencies, etc.) as fundamentals to conceive systems through all the development process. Moreover, software development is becoming increasingly complex. Stakeholders' expectations are growing higher while the development agendas have to be as short as possible. Project managers, business analysts and software developers need adequate processes and models to specify the organizational context, capture requirements and build efficient and flexible systems.

We propose, in this paper, a modern epistemological validation of the emergence of Object-Orientation (OO) and Agent-Orientation (AO). The latter will be put into perspective through the Lakatosian approach. Related work and contributions to the epistemological position of OO and AO will first be explicated. The emerging context of the conceptual frameworks of OO and AO is then briefly described. The validation of our epistemological reading will be done on the basis of OO and AO operationalization of some critical theoretical concepts derived from the Kuhnian and Lakatosian theories. We finally discuss the adoption of the Lakatosian research programme concept to characterize both OO and AO. Implications of this epistemological position on everyday work have been distinguished both for software engineering researchers and practitioners. For researchers, it mostly has an implication on how agent ontologies are built and for practitioners it has an implication on how software problems are envisaged.

This paper is organized as follows. Section 2 presents the contributions as well as the research context. We point out the emergence of OO and AO. Section 3 focuses on our epistemological approach: AO is successively considered as a paradigm and a research programme. On the basis of how some relevant concepts of the Kuhnian and Lakatosian frameworks are operationalized by OO and AO, we provide a Lakatosian reading of those modeling concepts. Conclusions are summarized in Section 4.

STATE OF THE ART

This section presents the contributions of an epistemological reading for the computer science researcher.

Related Work and Contributions

Basili (1992) defines Software Engineering (SE) as "the disciplined development and evolution of software systems based upon a set of principles, technologies and processes". These theoretical frameworks are expected to solve practical problems by proposing software solutions. SE is a practice-oriented field (where empiricism often plays an important role) and constantly evolving; however, one must dispose of a framework to build common (and preferably best) practices improvement. Kaisler (2005) points out that "We develop more experience, we not only continue to learn new practices, but we refine and hone the practices that we have already learned". SE is the genuine discipline that emerged from this interconnection between practices and software solutions. Today's software development has become a very complex task and no one has the required skills or time to resolve a sophisticated problem on his or her own. Software development phases need the input from lots of people having to use concepts and ideas for which they share a common understanding. This can be referred as SE's key role: providing some common theoretical entities to allow specialists to develop software solutions.

Few papers in specialized literature point to an in depth questioning of SE knowledge evolution. As (Kaisler, 2005) emphasizes, the literature is mainly technical or practical and focused on the software design processes. Research methodologies, however, need to be conscientiously built to favour the development and improvement of software solutions. To this end, an epistemological analysis is of primary importance as pointed out by (Boehm et al., 2005): "The goal is to develop the conceptual scientific foundations of software engineering upon which future researchers can build".

In this paper, we mostly focus on a specific aspect of SE: OO and AO which are modelling and programming ontologies rather than development processes. A few papers have discussed the evolution of knowledge in SE but encompass a broader range of aspects of this discipline than the current paper.

In the book titled Software Paradigms, Kaisler (2005) uses the notion of a paradigm to characterize the way of solving problems in software development. Though he explicitly quotes Kuhn's work to define the concept of paradigm, he explains that he includes in this definition the "concepts of law, theory, application and instrumentation: in, effect, both the theoretical and the practical". The practical dimension being a key issue in computer science, it must be integrated into the paradigm when this concept is used in engineering software. Kaisler's work is based on an empirical process: "We are going to apply the notion of paradigm to the investigation of programming languages and software architectures to determine how well we can solve different types of problems". On the basis of this study, he proposes a problem typology which would determine the programming approach: "For a given problem class, we'd like to be able to create software that solves the problem or parts of it efficiently. There are two aspects to creating such software: the software's architecture and the choice of programming language." Kaisler uses the term paradigm in a very large sense since he applies the concept to the whole "top-down analysis." The problem typology defines a software typology which finally determines a specific implementation.

Even if we do not assign the same meaning as Kaisler to the paradigm concept, our analysis can be related to his work. By proposing an epistemological reading of the evolution toward AO, we only focus on the last step of Kaisler's view. Indeed, the emergence of AO can be seen as a broadening of the unit of implementation and consequently to the amount of problems that can be solved. This is in line with the vision developed in Zeigler (2014), and Jennings and Wooldridge (2001). AO is the best suited to solve complex problems because it refers to a higher abstraction level and it provides some advantages for solution programming. Jennings and Wooldridge use the term "paradigm" to characterize the evolution from OO to AO. They paradoxically emphasize the continuity between these two paradigms. Indeed, as far as the Kuhnian discussion is concerned, if two theoretical frameworks can be compared they cannot be quoted as paradigms; this will be explained in the following sections.

Göktürk and Akkok (2004) point out that: "One of the most recent (and widely accepted) examples to a "rescuer new paradigm" in software engineering is the object-orientation paradigm,…" and recalls that the evolution from OO toward AO is often presented in terms of paradigm shift (Conte, 2014; Jennings & Wooldridge, 2001). A very important point discussed by Göktürk and Akkok, (2004) is that the choice of a paradigm is similar to the choice of a conceptualization/communication language; consequently mixing two different paradigms could be counter productive. What Göktürk et al. (2004) emphasize indirectly is what epistemologists call the "incommensurability thesis". Following this line of argument, two paradigms are totally incomparable since they represent two different set of knowledge.

The work of Software Engineers is cognitive since a significant part of their work is devoted to build and understand artefacts of different nature. Cognitive computing is the discipline in charge of understanding these cognitive aspects. Chentouf (2014) argues that Cognitive Software Engineering is a Lakatosian problem shift rather than a Kunhian paradigm shift. This means that it is a natural evolution, rather than a conceptual one. More specifically, "it is complementary to Software Engineering and represents a widening of the conceptual belt of Software Engineering through introducing the cognitive dimension as part of the scientific problematic" (Chentouf 2014).

Based on these related works, our contribution is multiple:

- We emphasize on the epistemological reasons why the paradigm concept is inappropriate to explain the differences between OO and AO. To be considered as paradigm, two theoretical frameworks need to be incomparable and "incommensurable";
- We propose a new epistemological analysis of the evolution toward AO by using a Lakatosian framework which can explain and justify the effectiveness of this framework. In this paper, AO will be presented as a new research programme widening and improving the knowledge in SE. This improvement cannot be seen as discontinuity of knowledge but rather as continuity since AO could encapsulate object technology;
- By proposing an epistemological reading of the emergence of the AO, we try to reduce what Jennings and Woolridge (2001) call the "gap" between knowledge and applications. We prove that this evolution can be explained in line with the conventional standards to justify the scientific status of the SE discipline. The paradigm-concept cannot justify the scientific status whereas the research programme-concept can.

Towards Agent Orientation

The meteoric rise of the online and mobile technologies has created new application areas for enterprise software, including eBusiness, web services, ubiquitous computing, knowledge management and peer-to-peer networks. These areas demand software design that is robust, can operate within a wide range of environments, and can evolve over time to cope with changing requirements. Moreover, such software has to be highly customizable to meet the needs of a wide range of users, and sufficiently secure to protect personal data and other assets on behalf of its stakeholders.

Not surprisingly, researchers are looking for new software designs that can cope with such requirements. One promising source of ideas for designing such business software is the area of multi-agent systems. They appear to be more flexible, modular and robust than traditional systems including object-oriented ones. They tend to be open and dynamic in the sense that they exist in a changing organizational and operational environment where new components can be added, modified or removed at any time.

Multi-agent systems are based on the concept of agent and are defined as "a computer system, situated in some environment that is capable of flexible autonomous action in order to meet its design objective" (Woodridge & Jennings, 1995). An agent exhibits the following characteristics:

- **Autonomy:** An agent has its own internal thread of execution, typically oriented to the achievement of a specific task, and it decides for itself what actions it should perform at what time.
- **Situateness:** Agents perform their actions in the context of being situated in a particular environment. This environment may be a computational one (e.g., a Web site) or a physical one (e.g., a manufacturing pipeline). The agent can sense and affect some portion of that environment.
- **Flexibility:** In order to accomplish its design objectives in a dynamic and unpredictable environment, the agent may need to act to ensure that its goals are achieved (by realizing alternative plan). This property is enabled by the fact that the agent is autonomous in its problem solving.

Agents can be useful as stand-alone entities that delegate particular tasks on behalf of a user (e.g., personal digital assistants and e-mail filters (Dimarogonas et al., 2012), or business and goal-driven software entities (Wautelet & Kolp, 2016). However, in the overwhelming majority of cases, agents exist in an environment that contains other agents. Such an environment is called a multi-agent system (MAS).

In MAS, the global behavior is derived from the interaction among the constituent agents: they cooperate, coordinate or negotiate with one another. A multi-agent system is conceived as a society of autonomous, collaborative, and goal-driven software components (agents), much like a social organization. Each role an agent can play has a well-defined set of responsibilities (goals) achieved by means of an agent's own abilities, as well as its interaction capabilities.

This sociality of MAS is well suited to tackle the complexity of an organization's software systems for a number of reasons:

- It permits a better match between system architectures and their operational environment (e.g. a public organization, a corporation, a non-profit association, a local community, etc.);
- The autonomy of an agent (i.e., the ability an agent has to decide what actions it should take at what time (Fortino & Trunfio, 2014)) reflects the social and decentralized nature of modern enterprise systems (Wautelet & Kolp, 2016) that are operated by different stakeholders (Gascueña et al., 2012);
- The agent social abilities have been successfully applied to mimic real-life social environments like for example to manage MOOC architectures in e-learning environments (Kolp & Wautelet, 2015; Wautelet, Heng, Penserini & Kolp, 2016);
- The flexible way in which agents operate to accomplish their goals is suited to the dynamic and unpredictable situations in which business software is now expected to run (Wautelet & Kolp, 2016; Chen & Cheng, 2010).

EPISTEMOLOGICAL APPROACH

We argue that a Lakatosian vision should be adapted for an epistemological reading of the emergence of AO. To develop our argumentation, we first consider its use in the literature dealing with the "paradigm" concept to characterize the evolution from OO to AO. We then explain why the Lakatosian "research programme" concept is more adequate than the Kuhnian "paradigm" concept to illustrate the evolution of modeling and programming concepts.

The Traditional Kuhnian Perspective of Software Engineering

The Paradigm-Concept: A Definition

The word "paradigm" comes directly from philosophy where its meaning remains surprisingly rather vague. Plato and Aristotle were the first authors to introduce this concept. According to them, the paradigm is a kind of explanatory model, which allows people to understand, in terms of causality, the changes imposed by Nature. However, the paradigm is not, strictly speaking, a logic. For Aristotle, the "paradigm" was "different from both deduction, which goes from universal to particular, and induction, which goes from particular to universal, in the sense that the paradigm goes from particular to particular." (Göktürk & Akkok, 2004).

The term "paradigm" has not really been used before the 20th century when Thomas Kuhn developed a specific epistemology based on this concept. The paradigm is defined as "a constellation of concepts, values, perceptions and practices shared by a community and which forms a particular vision of reality that is the basis of the way a community organizes itself " (Kuhn, 1996). Nevertheless, Kuhn himself admits that the use of the word remains rather vague: it is possible to identify twenty-two different meanings of the "paradigm" concept used in Kuhnian epistemology (Masterman, 1970). In the last edition of his book, Kuhn even recognized that the "paradigm" concept is vague but he explained that it is close to what he calls a "disciplinary matrix".

This leads us to consider in this paper the "paradigm" as a way of representing the world, which necessarily includes conceptual tools and methods (the conjunction of these two elements forming what Kuhn called a disciplinary matrix), such that an observer can create models. Each paradigm refers to a particular ontology and represents a subset of "what is representable". The representation abilities of a paradigm are basically related to the conceptual tools, to the modeling methodology and the use of these two elements by theoreticians.

Paradigms and Software Engineering

The first paradigm to be introduced in SE was the procedural paradigm (Göktürk & Akkok, 2004). It was based on the use of algorithms to execute particular tasks. The second paradigm was the data-hiding paradigm, which focused on the data's organization and introduced the concept of modules (to hide the data's). This paradigm was followed by the data-abstraction paradigm, which concentrated on the types and on the operations defined on these types. Next was the object-oriented paradigm, "built upon the data-abstraction" paradigm but introducing new concepts like inheritance and polymorphism. Finally, using the flexibility of the component-oriented logic, the agent-oriented paradigm has divided software into independent and communicating entities called "agents" (Zeigler, 2014). This last paradigm has been described in detail in *Towards Agent Orientation*.

Programming languages and modeling paradigms are interdependent. The "chicken and egg" metaphor could be used to characterize their reciprocal relationship (Göktürk & Akkok, 2004): sometimes, specific needs for a programming language lead to a better implementation of a modeling paradigm and sometimes, the evolution of the modeling paradigm influences and improves the development of a specific programming language. However, even if programming languages and modeling paradigms are interdependent, the agent-oriented paradigm differs in the sense that it is not formally related to specific programming languages. The concepts used in AO have been inspired from the organizational structures found in the real world. In the beginning, agent-oriented models were implemented in object-oriented languages but further evolutions allow to support and directly implement multi-agent systems in terms of full-fledged agent concepts such as Beliefs, Desires and Intentions (BDI) (see Wautelet & Kolp, 2016).

A Lakatosian Perspective of Software Engineering

In the following sections, we will propose to review the Kuhnian vision of OO and AO to demonstrate that it is not best suited to describe the evolution in SE. With respect to the research programme concept developed by Lakatos, we will explain why a Lakatosian understanding of the evolution to AO is more appropriate than a Kuhnian one.

"Research Programme" Concept: A Definition

In the continuity of the Popperian philosophy (which will be briefly presented in the following section), Imre Lakatos has developed in 1974 an original approach of science. He considers scientific theories as general structures he calls "research programmes". A Lakatosian research programme is a kind of scientific construction, a theoretical framework which guides future research (in a specific field) in a positive or negative way. Each research programme is constituted by a hard core, a protective belt of auxiliary hypotheses, a positive and a negative heuristic.

The hard core is composed of general theoretical assumptions which constitute the basic knowledge for the programme development. In other words, these axioms are the assumptions the theorists will not challenge in their research. This hard core is surrounded with a protective belt composed of the auxiliary hypotheses, which complete the hard core and with assumptions related to the description of the initial conditions of a specific problem. These auxiliary hypotheses will be thoroughly studied again, widened and completed by theorists in their further studies within the programme. This widening of the protective belt hypotheses contributes to the evolution of the research programme without calling into question the basic knowledge shared by a scientific community.

The positive heuristic represents the agreement among the theoreticians over the scientific evolution of the research programme. It is a kind of "problem solving machinery" composed by proposals and indications on the way to widen and enrich the research programme. The negative heuristic is the opposite of the positive one. Within each research programme, it is important to maintain the basic assumptions unchanged. It means that all the questions or methodologies that are not in accordance with the basic knowledge must be rejected. All doubts appearing about the basic knowledge of the main theoretical framework become a kind of negative heuristic of the research programme. When the negative heuristic becomes more and more important, a research programme can become "degenerative" (i.e. it has more and more empirical anomalies). This means that theoreticians have to reconsider the basic knowledge of the programme, which can lead to the creation of another research programme. Let us mention that this revision is always a very slow process.

According to Lakatos, we can characterize the evolution of knowledge as a series of "problems shifts" which allow the scientific theories to evolve without rejecting the basic axioms shared by theorists within a specific research programme. The concept of "research programme" represents a descriptive and minimal unit of knowledge, which allows for a rational reconstruction of the history of science.

At first glance, the "research programme" concept seems rather close to the "paradigm" concept. Indeed, it is, in both cases, a matter of "disciplinary matrix" used to describe a particular ontology of the external world. However, differences exist between these two concepts especially in the evolution of science and knowledge in a large sense.

According to Kuhn, the evolution of science does not follow a straight line and does not converge towards something, which would be the "truth". In the Kuhnian vision, the evolution of science could be represented by a broken line where discontinuity would mark the passage from one paradigm to another. From this point of view, different paradigms cannot be compared. Moreover, Kuhn specifies that a paradigm always emerges within a discipline facing a methodological crisis (characterized by the absence of a dominating theoretical framework) (Kuhn, 1996). Following a crisis undergone by a previously dominating paradigm, a new paradigm emerges with a new language and a new rationality. This new way of thinking does not allow a comparison between the old and the new paradigm. Given that a new paradigm is a new way of thinking about the world, there is no basis for comparison. The "paradigms incommensurability" thesis has become a very well known issue in the philosophy of sciences (Sankey, 1994).

Lakatos decomposes the evolution of science into successive methodological and epistemological steps. These steps form a kind of vertical structure built with a multitude of "layers of knowledge" and where each layer represents a particular research programme. In the Lakatosian vision, the emergence of a new research programme is induced by an empirical degeneration of a previously dominating research programme. The new research programme will constitute a superior layer of knowledge, which will integrate the same conceptual tools as the former but which would be able to solve its empirical anomalies through what Lakatos calls a "problem shift". The latter is characterized by an extension or a redefinition of the protective belt of the preceding programme. In this vision, research programmes remain comparable to each other (in both conceptual and empirical terms). The language and rationality of the new research programme result from a progressive evolution of knowledge and from the resolution of the empirical anomalies of the previous research programme. In contrast to the kuhnian vision, Lakatos explains that there is no discontinuity between the different research programmes.

Agent-Orientation: Paradigm vs. Research Programme

In this section, we present three main arguments for the use of the Lakatosian research programme to understand the shift from OO to AO.

Kuhnian Crisis or Lakatosian Problem Shift?

As discussed in the first part of this paper, a SE-crisis has been observed due to the fact that few software projects successfully manage to fully satisfy users' requirements. In the Kuhnian vision, this crisis could be considered as a favourable argument for the emergence of a new paradigm. In this perspective, a crucial question raises: "does the current crisis characterize the end of a dominating paradigm or is it simply the result of a pre-paradigmatic step specific to "young sciences" which have not found a dominating paradigm yet?" Using the Kuhnian rhetoric to analyse this crisis, we can consider the situation as a paradigm evolution. Indeed, the pre-paradigmatic step was rather characterized by the procedural framework (which was defined by an algorithmic and sequential, i.e., a strictly computer/mathematical logic) as well as the data-hiding and the data-abstraction frameworks. This pre-paradigmatic period was essential to the evolution process towards OO. However, the crisis situation observed in SE must be carefully analysed. Even if the "SE-crisis" diagnosis has been noted for several years, we think that the context in which AO has emerged cannot be considered as a crisis in the Kuhnian sense. Indeed, most of the methodological rules existed before AO and the current software development process does not seem to be so chaotic: IT specialists dispose of analysis methods and methodological tools with a high level of abstraction (see for example Wautelet & Kolp, 2016). These elements tend to show that what looks like a crisis is rather an (animated but normal) evolution of knowledge in SE (see del Aguila, 2014), which could be interpreted as a "problem shift" in the Lakatosian vision.

Kuhnian Discontinuity or Lakatosian Continuity?

We consider that the Kuhnian discontinuity between paradigms is not appropriate to explain the emergence of AO because there is no real "fracture" between OO and AO. Indeed, in some software solutions, communicating objects are used and are completely relevant and sufficient. In software problems where no learning skills are valuable, the use of agents would not bring crucial advantages: they would just transfer messages and would not behave like learning and collaborating agents pursuing goals (Zeigler, 2014). In this special case, there is no contribution of the agent concept to the software solution in comparison to object technology. We can see that the cohabitation within the same application between modules exploiting object technology and others exploiting agent technology can thus be an "optimal" solution (see Zeigler, 2014). In a Lakatosian vision, this cohabitation represents a progressive evolution of knowledge in SE. Indeed, the Lakatosian epistemology implies that the transition between research programmes is not clear and depends on the specific aspects of the experiment conducted (the software solution is the experiment in our case). A hybrid solution between modules developed on the basis of objects and others on the basis of agents can thus be explained by the continuity between research programmes inherent to the Lakatosian vision of knowledge applied to SE.

Kuhnian Incommensurability or Lakatosian Commensurability ?

Another drawback of the adoption of the Kuhnian epistemology in SE is the incommensurability between paradigms. OO and AO can be compared since collaborating agents can be used as communicating objects and, more important, agents can be implemented using object-oriented languages (see for example Bellifemine et al., 2007). In this perspective, agents can be considered as "super objects" i.e. objects possessing skills as collaboration, intentionality, learning, autonomy, reasoning, etc. If we consider SE development as a history of "raising the level of abstraction", AO can be seen as an evolution of OO because it raises that level a little higher (see Skarmeas, 1999). In this perspective, research programmes preceding OO can also be considered as lower layered than the later. This vision perfectly matches with the Lakatosian concept of layers of knowledge introduced earlier. Indeed, considering SE evolution, each new research programme raises the abstraction level and constitutes a higher layer of knowledge. These layers are comparable so that OO and AO are said to be commensurable.

Lessons Learned

AO is based on the basic knowledge that existed before its emergence. We could say that agent-oriented modelling and programming has a hard core composed of the concepts defined in the previous research programmes (procedural, data hiding and data abstraction) on the one hand, and the artificial intelligence field on the other hand. The protective belt of the AO research programme would be characterized by the evolution towards a widely used SE methodology allowing the development of large projects.

Table 1 summarizes the contrast between the Kuhnian and Lakatosian epistemologies applied to the evolution from OO to AO. The lessons learned are:

- The context in which AO has emerged cannot be considered as a Kuhnian crisis because of the existence of strong methodological rules that emerged within OO preceding the emergence of AO. We claim there is a problem shift;
- AO seems to be based on the evolution of the previous methodological rules so that we point to continuity between OO and AO;
- OO and AO are directly commensurable since the latter can be conceptualized as a knowledge layer upon the first.

Table 1. Kuhnian and Lakatosian visions of AO emergence

		Kuhnian Paradigm	**Lakatosian Research Programme**
Evolution Steps	**Knowledge Emergence**	Crisis	Problem shift
	Knowledge Evolution	Discontinuity	Continuity
	Knowledge Maturity	Incommensurability	Commensurability

In the light of the arguments presented above, we contend that the Kuhnian epistemology often referred to in the literature is not appropriate to provide a correct epistemological analysis of the knowledge in SE. We rather propose to use the Lakatosian epistemology to characterize the emergence of AO.

We argue that the Lakatosian epistemology is directly in line with the idea of computer knowledge depicted as a "structure in layers". We have represented this architecture in the following Figure 1.

Implications

In this section, we briefly discuss the implications of using the concept of research programme rather than paradigm to characterize OO and AO for both software engineering researchers and practitioners.

Our work provides SE researchers a complementary view and the specific nature of the research area they are working on. Moreover, the impact of this nuance is important due to the fact that, as we have pointed out, no fundamental departure was observed when evolving from OO to AO. Therefore, concepts developed in OO and other related research areas can be adapted to AO with some consequence on the process of building agent ontologies.

Managers and other SE practitioners will learn that AO should be envisaged as a natural evolution rather than as a complete revolution. AO can be seen as complementary to OO and leads to the fact that the modularity of software solutions resulting from several techniques can be utilized when developing new systems. Software modeling techniques can then be considered as problem oriented, i.e., modeling, design and implementation techniques are driven by the problem specificities, rather than solution

Figure 1. Evolution of Knowledge in SE

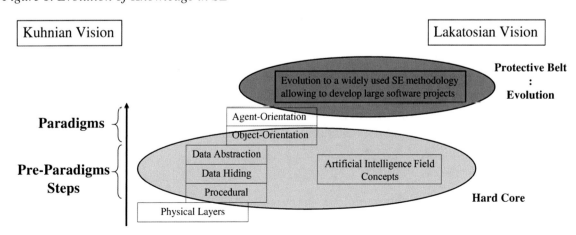

oriented (where those should be driven by an ex ante methodological/technical choice). This conclusion can be taken at different levels:

- At the analysis stage where organizational modeling can be better performed using models representing collaborative agents (see for example the i* diagrams in Yu et al. (2011) while purely functional requirements can be simply modeled using object modeling languages such as UML use cases or business use-cases (Wautelet & Poelmans, 2017);
- At the design stage, entities required to collaborate and learn can be designed as agents while others requiring less sophisticated behavior can be designed as objects;
- At the implementation level, modules can be implemented using agent technologies that facilitates communication with modules implemented in object technology.

Finally, our new conceptualization has a profound impact on the SE development life cycles. Indeed, the literature on the evolution of software engineering life cycles is rich and the adoption of mature development life cycles such as the spiral model, the Rational Unified Process, or agile methodologies traditionally operationalized by OO technologies can be adapted to AO development without revising the fundamental concepts.

CONCLUSION

The importance of modern IT solutions and the complexity of software ecosystems lead computer science to completely rethink software development models. Persistent solutions can be found at different levels, and among those, OO at the first level and AO at the second level constituted definite progress. AO furnishes concepts to model the organization more precisely, thus enabling analysts to create more accurate models.

This paper has presented an epistemological analysis of these improvements. AO is a promising innovation in tools allowing analysts to model the organization and user requirements. We have shown in this paper that the emergence of this innovation can be better studied using Lakatosian ideas rather than Kuhnian ones. In this vision, AO would be considered as a research programme rather than a paradigm. Even if it seems to be just a matter of terminology, the differences between these two epistemological concepts is clear and profound so that they should not be confused. The paper also advocates that the approaches taken by both researchers and practitioners to software problems and their possible solutions is influenced by the vision of OO and AO as a research programme.

More work should be carried out in SE fundamentals by studying other methodological frameworks and epistemological foundations to provide the computer science researcher a more accurate conscience of the research field that he or she is working on. Software development life cycles such as waterfall or iterative development can also be studied from such a point of view. The latter is, for example, strongly inspired by Herbert Simon's bounded rationality principle as well as Popper's knowledge growth theory.

REFERENCES

Basili, V. (1992). The experimental paradigm in software engineering. In *Experimental Software Engineering Issues: Critical Assessment and Future Directives*. Springer-Verlag.

Bellifemine, F. L., Caire, G., & Greenwood, D. (2007). *Developing multi-agent systems with JADE* (Vol. 7). John Wiley & Sons. doi:10.1002/9780470058411

Boehm, B., Rombach, H. D., & Zelkowitz, M. V. (Eds.). (2005). *Foundations of empirical software engineering: The legacy of Victor R. Basili*. Springer Science & Business Media. doi:10.1007/3-540-27662-9

Chen, B., & Cheng, H. H. (2010). A review of the applications of agent technology in traffic and transportation systems. *IEEE Transactions on Intelligent Transportation Systems*, *11*(2), 485–497. doi:10.1109/TITS.2010.2048313

Chentouf, Z. (2014). Cognitive software engineering: A research framework and roadmap. *Journal of Software Engineering and Applications*, *7*(6), 530–539. doi:10.4236/jsea.2014.76049

Conte, R., & Paolucci, M. (2014). On agent-based modeling and computational social science. *Frontiers in Psychology*, 5. PMID:25071642

del Águila, I. M., Palma, J., & Túnez, S. (2014). Milestones in software engineering and knowledge engineering history: A comparative review. *The Scientific World Journal*. PMID:24624046

Dimarogonas, D. V., Frazzoli, E., & Johansson, K. H. (2012). Distributed event-triggered control for multi-agent systems. *IEEE Transactions on Automatic Control*, *57*(5), 1291–1297. doi:10.1109/TAC.2011.2174666

Fortino, G., & Trunfio, P. (Eds.). (2014). *Internet of things based on smart objects: Technology, middleware and applications*. Springer Science & Business Media. doi:10.1007/978-3-319-00491-4

Gascueña, J. M., Navarro, E., & Fernández-Caballero, A. (2012). Model-driven engineering techniques for the development of multi-agent systems. *Engineering Applications of Artificial Intelligence*, *25*(1), 159–173. doi:10.1016/j.engappai.2011.08.008

Göktürk, E., & Akkok, N. (2004). Paradigm and software engineering. Proceedings of Impact of Software Process on Quality.

Jennings, N. R., & Wooldridge, M. (2001). Agent-Oriented Software Engineering. In *Handbook of Agent Technology*. AAAI/ MIT Press.

Kaisler, S.H. (2005). *Software Paradigms*. John Wiley & Son.

Kolp, M., & Wautelet, Y. (2015). Human organizational patterns applied to collaborative learning software systems. *Computers in Human Behavior*, *51*, 742–751. doi:10.1016/j.chb.2014.11.094

Kuhn, T. (1996). *The structure of scientific revolutions* (3rd ed.). University of Chicago Press. doi:10.7208/chicago/9780226458106.001.0001

Masterman, M. (1970). The nature of paradigm. In I. Lakatos & A. Musgrave (Eds.), *Criticism and the Growth of Knowledge*. Cambridge University Press. doi:10.1017/CBO9781139171434.008

Sankey, H. (1994). *The Incommensurability Thesis*. Ashgate.

Wautelet, Y., Heng, S., Kolp, M., Penserini, L., & Poelmans, S. (2016). Designing an MOOC as an agent-platform aggregating heterogeneous virtual learning environments. *Behaviour & Information Technology*, *35*(11), 980–997. doi:10.1080/0144929X.2016.1212095

Wautelet, Y., & Kolp, M. (2016). Business and model-driven development of BDI multi-agent systems. *Neurocomputing*, *182*, 304–321. doi:10.1016/j.neucom.2015.12.022

Wautelet, Y., & Poelmans, S. (2017). An Integrated Enterprise Modeling Framework Using the RUP/UML Business Use-Case Model and BPMN. In *IFIP Working Conference on The Practice of Enterprise Modeling* (pp. 299-315). Springer. 10.1007/978-3-319-70241-4_20

Woodridge, M., & Jennings, N. R. (1995). Intelligent agents: Theory and practice. *The Knowledge Engineering Review*, *10*(2), 115–152. doi:10.1017/S0269888900008122

Yu, E., Giorgini, P., Maiden, N., & Mylopoulos, J. (2011). *Social modeling for requirements engineering*. MIT Press.

Zeigler, B. P. (2014). *Object-oriented simulation with hierarchical, modular models: intelligent agents and endomorphic systems*. Academic Press.

Chapter 14
Application of Fuzzy Sets and Shadowed Sets in Predicting Time Series Data

Mahua Bose
University of Kalyani, India

Kalyani Mali
University of Kalyani, India

ABSTRACT

In recent years, several methods for forecasting fuzzy time series have been presented in different areas, such as stock price, student enrollments, climatology, production sector, etc. Choice of data partitioning technique is a central factor and it highly influences the forecast accuracy. In all existing works on fuzzy time series model, cluster with highest membership is used to form fuzzy logical relationships. But the position of the element within the cluster is not considered. The present study incorporates the idea of fuzzy discretization and shadowed set theory in defining intervals and uses the positional information of elements within a cluster in selection of rules for decision making. The objective of this work is to show the effect of the elements, lying outside the core area on forecast. Performance of the presented model is evaluated on standard datasets.

1. INTRODUCTION

Fuzzy time series (FTS) is comparatively new research area. Decisions that involve factor of uncertainty of the future, fuzzy time series models have been found one of the most effective methods of forecasting. The traditional time series methods cannot deal with forecasting problems where the values of time series are linguistic terms represented by fuzzy sets. Theory of fuzzy time series has been presented in order to overcome this drawback. In this approach, the values of fuzzy time series are fuzzy sets and, there is a relationship between the observations at present time and those at previous times. Another advantage of fuzzy time series model is that it can forecast with little number of data.

DOI: 10.4018/978-1-5225-5396-0.ch014

In last twenty-five years, several methods have been developed for forecasting fuzzy time series in different research areas, like student enrollment, weather, stock price, agricultural production, etc. Fundamental idea of Fuzzy time series forecasting model was first conceived by Song and Chissom (1993a, 1993b, 1994). A significant drawback of this model is high computational overheads due to complex matrix operations. Chen (1996) proposed a simplified model including only simple Arithmetic Operations. This model is considered as most important milestone in this particular field of research. Later many researchers contributed for the development and advancement of research on fuzzy time series forecasting.

The main motivation behind this proposed work is to investigate the effect of positional information of each element within an interval/cluster on forecast accuracy. In this study two fuzzy time series models are presented. First method is the modification of difference parameters-based model proposed by Singh (2009) and the second method is a new algorithm applying the concept of shadowed set.

This paper is organized as follows: Section 2 summaries previous works in this direction. In Section 3, the basic concept of fuzzy time series is discussed. Section 4 presents the methodology along with the basic concept of fuzzy discretization and Shadowed Set theory. Section 5 shows comparison of the experimental results. Conclusion is presented in Section 6.

2. LITERATURE SURVEY

In Fuzzy time series models, partitioning of universe of discourse is a crucial issue. There are two types of interval generation techniques: (1) equal-sized intervals and (2) unequal-sized intervals. In the studies made by earlier researchers, universe of discourse is directly partitioned into equal-sized intervals. Gradually, researchers shift their focus towards variable length intervals. These techniques can be classified into different categories depending upon the methodology adopted for the creation of intervals/clusters. Clusters can be created by applying (1) clustering algorithm directly (2) generating mathematical models (3) Using Evolutionary techniques namely genetic algorithms, particle swarm optimization. It is observed from literature review that unequal-sized partitioning techniques produce better forecasting accuracy than equal-sized partitioning techniques.

Studies that attempt variable sized data partitioning techniques include Distribution-and average-based partitioning (Huarng, 2001), recursive partition level by level (Li & Chen, 2004), two-phase partitioning (Chen & Hsu, 2004) "ratio-based" partitioning (Huarng & Yu, 2006), automatic clustering algorithm (Chen & Tanuwijaya, 2011), "minimize entropy principle approach" and "Trapezoid fuzzification approach" (Cheng et al., 2006), "Mean-Based Discretization" (Singh & Borah, 2013a), and "Re-Partitioning Discretization'' approach (Singh & Borah, 2013b), "Dynamic time warping distance (Wang et al., 2015) have been proposed. Recently, many forecasting models using the concept of information granule have been presented by Wang et al. (2013, 2014), Wang et al. (2015), Lu et al. (2014, 2015) and Chen and Chen (2015). Entropy discretization techniques (Chen and Chen, 2014) have also been presented.

Application of evolutionary algorithm for partitioning universe of discourse improved the performance of forecasting models. Chen and Kao (2013) employed PSO for data partitioning and SVM for prediction. Singh and Borah (2014b) presented a multivariate model using PSO based partitioning. Cai et al. (2015) developed a high order ACO-AR technique. Fuzzy time series forecasting based K-means algorithm and PSO has been devised by Cheng et al. (2016). Bas et al. (2015) also presented a novel PSO based model. In addition to that different clustering algorithms such as fuzzy –c-means (Egrioglu et al., 2013; Sun et al., 2015), Gustafson-Kessel (Egrioglu et al., 2011), Fuzzy C-Medoid (Izakian et al., 2015), Fuzzy c-means based on dynamic time warping (Wang et al., 2015) have significant contribution in this field. Some researchers namely Aladag et al. (2014), Bas et al. (2014), Cai et al. (2013) applied genetic algorithm to partition the universe of discourse.

Formulation of fuzzy relationships has significant role in forecast accuracy. Fuzzy logical relationships can be established using Mathematical Models, Data mining techniques and Hybrid Models. A variety of Difference parameters-based approaches (Kumar & Gangwar, 2012; Singh, 2009; Joshi & Kumar, 2013), Index-based weights (Singh & Borah 2013a) technique. Different fuzzy forecasting models using Markov Chain theory (Tsaur, 2012) and Rough sets theory (Cheng, 2010; Askari & Montazerin, 2015), Type-2 Fuzzy logic (Huarng & Yu, 2005; Bajestani & Zare, 2011; Singh & Borah, 2014b) have been developed to forecast fuzzy time series.

Integration of Artificial Neural Network with the fuzzy forecast model improved forecasting results especially for nonlinear data. Back propagation Neural Network based models (Singh & Borah, 2013; Egrioglu et al., 2013; Yu & Huarng, 2008, 2010) have been widely used.

Multiplicative neuron model (Aladag, 2013) and Self-Organizing Feature Map (2014a, 2016b) based fuzzy time series forecasting models have been designed also. A variety of other hybrid models using neural network such as ANFIS–PSO model (Wei et al., 2014), Neuro-fuzzy model with Entropy Discretization (Singh, 2016a) have been attempted successfully. A brief review of recent developments has been prepared by Singh (2015).

In order to investigate the effect of the border elements in forecasting, (1)"w-step fuzzy predictor" algorithm (Singh, 2009) is applied with the modified intervals defined by the authors and (2) a new forecasting model is presented using Shadowed Set theory. In the first model, initially we have equal length intervals of length in each dataset. Using fuzzy discretization, these lower bound and upper bound of the intervals are modified where group and affinity values are different (Table1) and final prediction is done on the basis of affinity value and the error rate is reduced.

Advance knowledge about future event is essential for policy planning, decision making and disaster management. But limitation of first method is that it can't predict out-of-sample data. Second method overcomes this difficulty. Novelty of the second (proposed) model is that, the concept of shadow set theory will be applied to separate the core and boundary regions. Performance of both of the models, for different orders, is evaluated and compared with the other related works. It is observed that suggested technique gives best result.

3. THEORY OF FUZZY TIME SERIES

A fuzzy set A of the universe of discourse U, $U = \{u_1, u_2, \ldots, u_n\}$, is defined as follows (Zadeh, 1965):

$$A = f_A(u_1)/u_1 + f_A(u_2)/u_2 + \ldots\ldots\ldots\ldots + f_A(u_n)/u_n$$

where, f_A is the membership function of the fuzzy set A, $f_A : U \to [0, 1]$, $f_A(u_i)$ denotes the grade of membership of u_i in the fuzzy set A, and $1 \leq i \leq n$.

Let $Z(t)$ $(t = \ldots, 0, 1, 2, \ldots)$, a subset of R(Real time), be the universe of discourse on which fuzzy sets $f_i(t)(i = 1, 2, \ldots)$ are defined and let F(t) consist of $f_1(t), f_2(t), \ldots$ Then, F(t) is called a fuzzy time series defined on $Z(t)$ $(t = \ldots, 0, 1, 2, \ldots)$ (Chen, 1996; Lee et al., 2006b; Song & Chissom, 1993a, 1993b, 1994).

If F(t) is caused by F(t - 1) only, i.e., F(t - 1)->F(t), then the it is called first-order forecasting model, where ''F(t- 1)'' and ''F(t)'' are called the present state and the next state, respectively. If F(t) is caused by F(t- 1), F(t - 2), . . ., and F(t - n), then this fuzzy logical relationship (FLR) is represented by F(t - n), . . . F(t – 2), F(t – 1)-> F(t) is called n-th order fuzzy time series forecasting model, where ''F(t - n), . . .,F(t - 2),F(t - 1)'' and ''F(t)'' are called the current state and the next state, respectively (Chen, 1996; Lee et al., 2006b; Song & Chissom, 1993a).

Most of the existing fuzzy time series forecasting methods use the following steps for forecasting problems (Chen, 1996): (1) Partition of the universe of discourse into intervals, (2) Fuzzification of the past data,(3) establishing fuzzy logical relationships (FLR) and fuzzy logical relationship groups (FLRG) (4) Calculation of forecast.

4. METHODOLOGY

4.1. Forecasting Model Using Modified W-Step Fuzzy Predictor Algorithm

"W-step fuzzy predictor algorithm" (Singh, 2009) is a Mathematical Model developed for forecasting Fuzzy Time Series using Difference parameters. The basic version of "W-step fuzzy predictor algorithm" used fixed length data partitioning approach. Bose and Mali (2016) improved the work by introducing a modified version of the basic algorithm where intervals are calculated by fuzzy discretization method (Roy & Pal, 2003).

In fuzzy discretization procedure, intervals are formed between two consecutive cuts C_i and C_{i+1}, where the positions of cuts are fuzzy. Thus a continuous value 'v' is converted, after fuzzy discretization, into a triplet {m; g; a}, where membership value, group number and affinity are represented by m, g and a, respectively. Here, affinity means closeness of an element to any cut. An element in a group may have strong affinity to its own group or any adjacent group satisfying a particular criterion. Elements in the core area have affinity to its own group. But elements around the edge of a Group/Interval may have affinity to other Group/Interval.

Modified Algorithm (Bose & Mali, 2016)

Step 1: Define Universe of discourse U for the data set. Let D_{max} and D_{min} be the maximum and minimum value, respectively. Then,

$U = [D_{min} – D_1, D_{max +} D_2]$,where, D_1 and D_2 are two positive numbers.

For Lahi Production data, D_{min}=440 and D_{max}=1067. Here, D_1 =40 and D_2 =33. So, U= [400 -1100].

Step 2: Partition U into n equal intervals: u_i i=1, 2…., n. Let us consider, n fuzzy sets A_1, A_2, …, A_n having linguistic values on the universe of discourse U. Each u_i belongs to a particular A_j j=1, 2…., n.

Step 3: There are seven intervals of length 100 in Lahi production data: u1= [400-500], u2= [500-600], u3= [600-700], u4= [700-800], u5= [800-900], u6= [900-1000], u7= [1000-1100].

Seven fuzzy sets A_1, A_2, …, and A_7 having linguistic values on the universe of discourse U is defined as:

A_1 poor production
A_2 below normal production
A_3 normal production
A_4 good production
A_5 very good production
A_6 high production
A_7 very high production

Step 4: Using the concept of fuzzy discretization, for each data value, its membership and affinity in the appropriate interval has been calculated. Here, For n intervals (given by u_i, i=1,2....,n), there are n+1 cuts. A trapezoidal membership function is considered between the cuts. In this function, membership value varies between 0.2 and 1. According to the algorithm proposed by Roy and Pal (2003):

$$t = s*\left(C_{i+1}-C_i\right) \tag{1}$$

where, 't' and 's' represent the fraction of the flat and slanted portion of the trapezoid function, w.r.t the width of the base, respectively.

If the data value 'p' for a particular year belongs to the interval/group 3, then it is to be fuzzified into A_3. Its membership value m is calculated (Roy and Pal, 2003).

$$m=\left(base\left(1-base\right)*\left(\frac{c_{i+1}-v}{t}\right)\right) \tag{2}$$

There are eight 'cuts' {400, 500, ...,1100}. In each interval, after fuzzy discretization, triplet is obtained (Table 1). Affinity of a datapoint for any particular group has been computed. Points near the cuts (outside core area) have affinity to other groups.

In this algorithm, s= 0.25 and base=0.2. Thus for interval with lower bound 500 and upper bound 600 and t=25, left= C_i + t = 525 and right= C_{i+1} −t = 575. In case of, data values within 525-575, both affinity and group is same but points within the range 575-600 have affinity for the next group. Similarly, data points within the range 500-525 have affinity for the previous group (Figure 1).

Let us consider two values 635 and 502 in Table 1. First one is within the range 625-675 and its affinity value and group is 3 (membership value is 1) and second one is less than 575, its affinity value is 1 and group is 2. So, membership value is calculated using equation 2 and m.26.

Step 5: Establish fuzzy logical relationships. If the fuzzified value of the yeat 'n-1' and 'n' are A_i and A_j respectively, the relationship will be represented by A_i -> A_j

L us consider, a model of order two utilizing the historical data of years n - 2, n - 1 to implement fuzzy logical relation, A_{i1}, A_i -> A_j, where the fuzzified value of the year 'n-2', 'n-1' and 'n' are A_{i1}, A_i and A_j respectively.

Step 6: Modify the intervals where group number (g) not equal to affinity value (a).

For a data point, where group id and affinity is not equal (element lying outside the core area), lower and upper bound of the interval used in the forecasting algorithm are modified, otherwise it will remain unaltered.

Moreover, it is also observed that, membership value is always equal to 1, where its affinity value and group are same. But in some cases, membership value may be equal to 1, where its affinity value and group are not same. In these cases the lower bound and upper bound of the interval are needed to be modified also. The positions of cuts are significant effect towards the forecast accuracy.

Let us consider an interval defined by two cuts C_i and C_{i+1}.

1. If a<g and m<1, then $L(*A_j)= C_i -t, U(*A_j)= C_i + t$
2. If a>g and m<1, then $L(*A_j)= C_{i+1} - t, U(*A_j) = C_{i+1} + t$
3. If a<g and m=1, then $L(*A_j)= C_i - t, U(*A_j)= C_{i+1}$
4. If a>g and m=1, then $L(*A_j)= C_i , U(*A_j)= C_{i+1} + t$

Lower bound, upper bound, middle value of the modified interval u_j are represented by $L(*A_j)$, $U(*A_j)$, $M(*A_j)$, respectively. Middle value in all above cases are computed by taking average of $L(*A_j)$ and $U(*A_j)$.

Data values, for which, group id and affinity is not equal, lower and upper bound of the intervals are adjusted (table 1). For the data value 512, values of lower bound and upper bound should be 500-t and 500+t. There may be some cases, where membership value is equal to 1, but its affinity value and group are not same. Let us consider the data point 775. Its affinity is 5, group is 4. In this case, only upper bound is only changed to 800+t.

Step 6: Apply "w-step fuzzy predictor" algorithm (Singh, 2009) with modified intervals obtained from previous step.

A fuzzy difference parameter d^m; m = 2, 3, 4, . . . of different orders, has been proposed, where,

$$d^m E_i = | d^{m-1} E_i - d^{m-1} E_{i-1} | \qquad (3)$$

E_i is the actual enrollments of year n -1
E_{i-1} is the actual enrollments of year n – 2
E_j is the actual enrollments of year n

For a second order model, forecast for the year 't' is computed as

F(t) = F(t-1) * R (t-1, t-2),

where fuzzy relation R is considered a numeric and is calculated as difference between differences in the consecutive values of year t-1 with t - 2.

The fuzzy parameters are used as w-step (N= 1, 2, ...,w) fuzzy predictors:

Table 1. Computation of intervals after discretization (Lahi Production)

Year	Production	Membership	Production in Linguistic Variables	Group	Affinity	Modified Intervals	
						LB	UB
1981	1025	1	A_7	7	7	1000	1100
1982	512	0.58	A_2	2	1	475	525
1983	1005	0.36	A_7	7	6	975	1025
1984	852	1	A_5	5	5	800	900
1985	440	1	A_1	1	1	400	500
1986	502	0.26	A_2	2	1	475	525
1987	775	1	A_4	4	5	700	825
1988	465	1	A_1	1	1	400	500
1989	795	0.36	A_4	4	5	775	825
1990	970	1	A_6	6	6	900	1000
1991	742	1	A_4	4	4	700	800
1992	635	1	A_3	3	3	600	700
1993	994	0.39	A_6	6	7	975	1025
1994	759	1	A_4	4	4	700	800
1995	883	0.74	A_5	5	6	875	925
1996	599	0.23	A_2	2	3	575	625
1997	499	0.23	A_1	1	2	475	525
1998	590	0.52	A_2	2	3	575	625
1999	911	0.55	A_6	6	5	875	925
2000	862	1	A_5	5	5	800	900
2001	801	0.23	A_5	5	4	775	825
2002	1067	1	A_7	7	7	1000	1100
2003	917	0.74	A_6	6	5	875	925

Figure 1. Fuzzy Discretization (example)

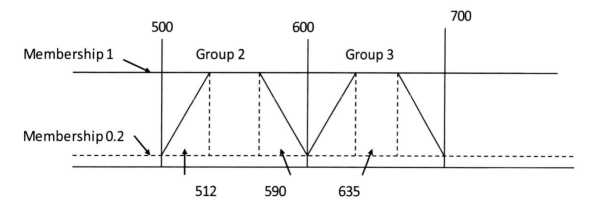

303

$$E_i \pm N * d_{E_i}^m . \text{ and } E_i \pm \left(\frac{1}{N}\right) * d_{E_i}^m .$$

Number of steps w = int (number of intervals/2).

For model of order two, $d^2 E_i = \left|512 - 1025\right| . = 513$

For model of order three, $d^3 E_i = \left\|\left|1005 - 512\right| - \left|512 - 1025\right|\right\| . = 20$

If number of intervals = 7, then w = 3.

When calculating forecast for any year, values $E_i \pm N * d_{E_i}^m .$ and $E_i \pm \left(\frac{1}{N}\right) * d_{E_i}^m$ within modified interval (lower and upper bound), should be considered.

4.2. Forecasting Model Using Shadowed Set

The shadowed sets were proposed by Pedrycz (1998) for representing uncertainty in fuzzy sets. Let us consider a fuzzy set A defined in X. Shadow set B (induced by A) maps elements of X into 0,1,[0, 1].

The method for construction a shadow set from fuzzy set is proposed by Pedrycz as follows: First a pair of thresholds $\alpha \in [0,0.5], \beta \in [0.5,1]$ are chosen; Next, low membership is reduced to 0 and high membership grades is raised to 1; Then, membership grades between α and β are converted to unit interval [0,1]. In practical applications, β can be represented by (1- α).

Shadowed sets are established by selecting the threshold $\alpha \in (0, 0.5)$ and constructing three areas as the core area which is created from the elements that almost certainly belonging to a fuzzy set, the shadow area is formed from the elements possibly belonging to a fuzzy set. The excluded area which is composed of the elements excluded from a fuzzy set cluded area is formed by the elements with all membership values less than the threshold α to 0. Core area formed by the elements whose membership value is greater than 1-α to 1 and for the elements in the shadow area, membership values are around 0.5. the process of constructing a shadow set, the threshold α has a crucial role. Let us consider a dataset with 'c' clusters. Membership value of an element is $u_i \in [0,1]$, i = 1, 2, ..., c.

Reduction of membership, Elevation of membership and shadow formation are represented by Ω_1, Ω_2 and Ω_3, respectively.

$$\Omega_1 = \sum_{(u_i \leq \alpha)} u_i \tag{4}$$

$$\Omega_2 = \sum_{(u_i > (1-\alpha))} 1 - u_i \tag{5}$$

$$\Omega_{3=}\text{card}\ \{\ u_i\ |\ \alpha \le u_i < 1\text{-}\ \alpha\ \} \qquad (6)$$

Optimal α satisfies the following condition:

$$\text{Minimize}\ V(\alpha) = \left| \Omega 1 + \Omega 2 - \Omega 3 \right| \qquad (7)$$

Algorithm

Step 1: Apply Fuzzy –c-means (FCM) algorithm (Bezdek, 1981).
Step 2: Calculate α value of each cluster using equation 7.

On Lahi Production data, FCM is applied taking seven clusters and α value for each cluster is calculated (Table 2). Position of each element in the clusters is shown in Table 3. From the table is seen that, element 1, i.e. 1025 is in the Shadow area of cluster 6 and 7. Element 8, i.e., 465 is in the Shadow area of cluster 1 and cluster 2. Shadow area of cluster 5 contains 852 and 917.

Step 3: Establish fuzzy logical relationship and calculate firing strength of the rule.

Let us consider a third order FLR: $A_i\ A_k\ A_p\text{->}A_j$

Table 2. Cluster centres and α values (Lahi Production)

Cluster Number	Centre	α value
1	451.59	0.1
2	504.26	0.1
3	606.84	0.2
4	774.81	0.2
5	883.37	0.2
6	992.92	0.2
7	1058.81	0.1

Table 3. Description of clusters (Lahi Production)

Cluster Number	Elements in Core Area	Elements in Shadow Area
1	5	8
2	2, 6, 17	8
3	12, 16, 18	-
4	7, 9, 11, 14, 21	-
5	15, 19, 20	4, 23
6	3, 10, 13	1
7	22	1

Firing strength of the rule is $\mu_{A_i}(x).*\mu_{A_k}(x).*\mu_{A_p}(x)$, where, a data element is denoted by x. In this expression, * denotes minimum or product t - norm.

Step 4: Defuzzification and Forecasting

For every successful match, compare its firing strength. Rule with nearest firing strength is selected for defuzzification. Elements which are in the core region of a cluster, corresponding centre value are used in defuzzification. But for the elements in the shadow region different strategy is adopted.

- **Principle 1:** If the data value is in the core area of the cluster, then the centre of the cluster (fuzzy set) in the R.H.S of the FLR is the predicted value.
- **Principle 2:** If the data value is in the shadowed area of two adjacent clusters, then mean value of the corresponding centres is the predicted value.

For example, Data element 1025 is in the shadow region of cluster 6 and cluster 7. Using Principle 2, average values of these two centres (992.92 and 1058.81) are calculated and it is 1025.87. Data element 465 is in the shadow region of cluster 1 and cluster 2. Similarly, corresponding centre is 477.92.

- **Principle 3:** If the data value is in the shadowed area of a single cluster, then a weighted average technique is applied to compute the predicted value.

Let A_m be the fuzzy set (cluster) with highest membership μ_x. Find the cluster with second highest membership μ_y.

Defuzzified value = $((\mu_x * c_1) + (\mu_y * c_2)) / (\mu_x + \mu_y)$, c_1 and c_2 are the corresponding cluster centres.

Data element 852 is in the shadow area of cluster 5 and its highest membership value is 0.788378. Its next highest membership value (obtained from FCM) is 0.13 in cluster 4. But it is less than corresponding α value (α =0.2). So, it is in the exclusion region. In this case, using Principle 3, centre is computed as:

((0.13*774.81) + (883.37*0.788)) / (774.81+883.37) =867.98

Similarly, data element 917 is in the shadow area of cluster 5 and its highest membership value is 0.75. Its next highest membership value is 0.14 in cluster 6. But it is less than corresponding α value (α = 0.2). This is in the exclusion region. In this case, centre is calculated as:

((0.14*992.93) + (883.37*0.75)) / (992.93+883.37) =901.33.

- **Principle 4:** If no maching rule is found, reduce the order (Chen, 2002) and repeat step 4 until order is equal to 1.

Step 5: If, $A_i \rightarrow \varphi$, then Centre value of cluster 'i' is chosen as predicted value.

Step 6: Stop.

In Table 4, for the elements in the core region of a cluster and corresponding centre values are shown and these centres are used in defuzzification. But for the elements in the shadow region, it is calculated using principle 2 and 3. These values are displayed in bold font.

5. RESULTS AND DISCUSSION

5.1. Description of Datasets

Experiments are carried on three datasets:

1.   Lahi production data from 1981 to 2003.

Table 4. Cluster with highest membership (Lahi Production)

Sl .No.	Actual Production	Cluster -id	Highest Membership	Centre/ Middle Value
1	1025	6	0.505093	**1025.873**
2	512	2	0.975759	504.2588
3	1005	6	0.939108	992.9338
4	852	5	0.788378	**867.98**
5	440	1	0.961527	451.5876
6	502	2	0.997394	504.2588
7	775	4	0.999994	774.8128
8	465	1	0.885177	**477.9232**
9	795	4	0.918927	774.8128
10	970	6	0.862855	992.9338
11	742	4	0.852914	774.8128
12	635	3	0.881855	606.8418
13	994	6	0.999597	992.9338
14	759	4	0.960786	774.8128
15	883	5	0.999969	883.373
16 .	599	3	0.987052	606.8418
17	499	2	0.984802	504.2588
18	590	3	0.936306	606.8418
19	911	5	0.829009	883.373
20	862	5	0.899418	883.373
21	801	4	0.860885	774.8128
22	1067	7	0.984547	1058.813
23	917	5	0.750817	**901.33**

2. Historical Enrollment data from 1971 to 1992.
3. Yearly Rainfall data of India for the month of August (1930-1980) has been used for training and dataset of the same month for the year 1981-2006 is used for testing.

5.2. Error Estimation

In this section, performance of the proposed work is evaluated for different orders. Error estimation is done using Root Mean Square Error (RMSE) and Mean absolute percentage error (MAPE). Let us consider n number of observations. Then, RMSE and MAPE values are defined as follows:

$$\text{RMSE} = \sqrt{\sum_{i=1}^{n} \left(\left(Actual - predicted \right) * \left(Actual - predicted \right) \right) / n} \qquad (8)$$

$$\text{MAPE} = \left(\sum_{i=1}^{n} \left(Actual - predicted \right) / Actual \right) * 100 / n \qquad (9)$$

In FCM algotithm, number of iterations =25 and Fuzzy Parameters m is 2.

For enrolment data, D_{min}=13055 and D_{max}=19332. Here, U= [13000 -20000]. For the model using fuzzy discretization technique, seven fuzzy sets having linguistic values L_1, L_2, L_3 .. L_7 have been created on the universe of discourse. For the second model (using Shadowed Set) eight clusters are created. Comparative analysis of the proposed technique with previous works is shown in Tables 5-6.

Proposed model using Shadowed Set theory produces minimum error at order 3 whereas Fuzzy discretization based model gives best performance at order 5.

For Lahi Production data, Performance of the models is shown in the following tables 7-8. For, dataset 1 and 2, Fixed length partitioning has been applied creating seven equal length partitions in Chen (1996), Singh (2009) and Kumar and Gangwar (2012). Proposed model using the concept of Shadowed Set theory produces minimum error at order 2 whereas Fuzzy discretization based model gives best performance at order 5.

For Rainfall Forecasting, using first model three fuzzy sets having linguistic values L_1, L_2, L_3 have been created on the universe of discourse U. Here, U= [190 -340]. For the second model, five clusters are created. Using training dataset, second order model is the best for both of the cases (Table 9-10). For test data performance of the Shadowed Set based model are recorded up to fourth order (table 11), as no significant change is observed. Minimum error is obtained at order 3.

Table 5. RMSE values (Enrollment data)

Methods	Order 2	Order 3	Order 4	Order 5	Order 6	Order 7
Singh(2009)	345.62	311.73	355.92	336.78	403.9	385.51
Bose and Mali (2016)	165.03	142.91	160.17	**141.66**	194.86	169.47
Proposed model using Shadowed Set	111.66	**105.95**	108.63	111.59	114.9	114.85

Table 6. Comparison using enrollment data

Models	RMSE
AR(1)	542.46
Chen(1996)	638.5
Cheng et al. (2006)	515.66
Chen and Tanuwijaya (2011)	349.4
Singh and Borah (2013)	325.61
Kumar and Gangwar (2012)	250.97
Tsaur (2012)	295.96
Joshi et al. (2013)	260.65
Lu et al. (2015)	120.6
Bose and Mali (2016)	141.66
Proposed model (using Shadowed Set)	**105.95**

Figure 2. Forecasting enrollment

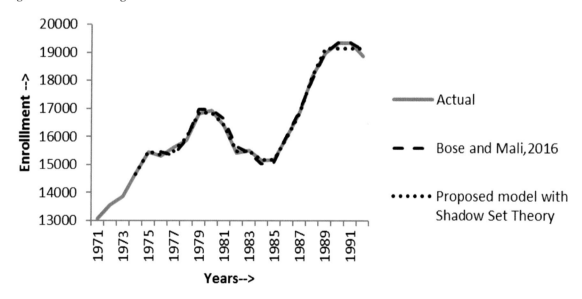

Table 7. RMSE values (Lahi Production)

Methods	Order 2	Order 3	Order 4	Order 5	Order 6	Order 7
Singh(2009)	33.01	30.23	34.35	36.21	39.96	34.74
Bose and Mali (2016)	12.87	11.57	12.26	**10.27**	10.56	11.32
Proposed model using Shadowed Set	**17.39**	17.61	17.7	17.98	18.49	19.06

Table 8. Results of Lahi production data in kg/ha (using other methods)

Methods	AR(1)	Chen (1996)	Cheng et al. (2006)	Kumar and Gangwar (2012)	Chen and Tanuwijaya (2011)	Singh and Borah (2013)	Bose and Mali (2016)	Proposed Model Using shadowed Set
RMSE	189.76	175.76	187.41	36.68	141.5	141.4	**10.27**	17.39
MAPE	24.75	22.5	24.71	4.4	17.58	16.1	1.21	1.97

Figure 3. Forecasting Lahi production

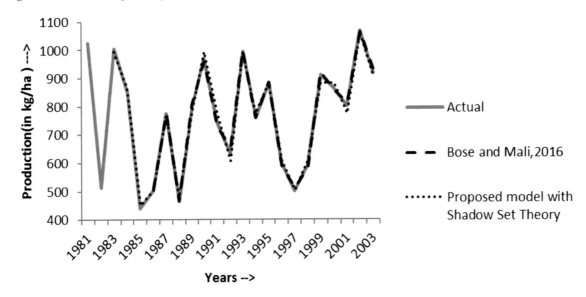

Table 9. Rainfall prediction error (RMSE)

Methods	Order 2	Order 3	Order 4	Order 5	Order 6	Order 7
Singh(2009)	29.3	33.04	33.04	30.6	35.11	26.42
Bose and Mali (2016)	**15.81**	16.92	16.71	19.69	18.65	19.22
Proposed model using Shadowed Set	**5.85**	5.91	5.96	6.02	6.06	6.13

It is revealed from comparative analysis of the results that in case of Enrollment data and Rainfall data (training set), proposed model using the concept of Shadowed Set theory gives best performance but for Lahi Production data, Fuzzy discretization based model (Bose & Mali, 2016) is the best. Performances of the methods up to order seven are recorded. Result can further be improved by changing number of intervals or clusters.

Table 10. Rainfall prediction error (MAPE)

Methods	Order 2	Order 3	Order 4	Order 5	Order 6	Order 7
Singh(2009)	9.72	10.75	10.81	9.65	11.59	11.98
Bose and Mali (2016)	**4.79**	5.22	5.1	5.97	5.5	5.53
Proposed model using Shadowed Set	**1.54**	1.57	1.59	1.61	1.62	1.65

Table 11. Error estimation for test dataset (Rainfall data)

Error	Order 2	Order 3	Order 4
RMSE	46.29	**43.43**	43.6
MAPE	15.16	**14.21**	14.2

Figure 4. Rainfall graph

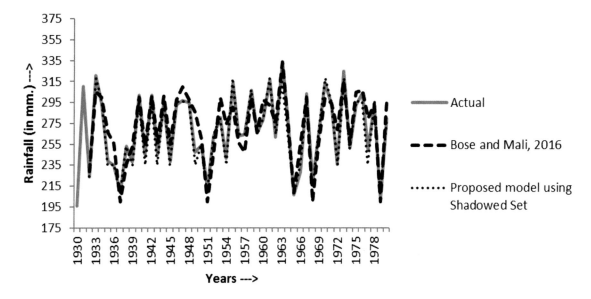

6. CONCLUSION

In Fuzzy Time Series forecasting model, length of the interval and establishing fuzzy logical relationship have significant role on forecasting accuracy. In this study using affinity, wider range is divided into small fragments (Table 1). Final prediction is done by applying "w-step fuzzy predictor" algorithm (Singh, 2009) with modified intervals and the error rate is reduced. But the limitation of the technique is that it can't be extended for out-of-sample data prediction. Using the idea of shadowed set a new forecasting model is presented which overcomes this difficulty. Accuracy in forecast values of proposed model with the actual observations and other models is made on the basis MAPE and RMSE value. In future similar experiment can be done using rough set.

REFERENCES

Aladag, C. H. (2013). Using multiplicative neuron model to establish fuzzy logic relationships. *Expert Systems with Applications*, *40*(3), 850–853. doi:10.1016/j.eswa.2012.05.039

Aladag, C. H., Yolcu, U., & Egrioglu, E. (2010). A high order fuzzy time series forecasting model based on adaptive expectation and artificial neural networks. *Mathematics and Computers in Simulation*, *81*(4), 875–882. doi:10.1016/j.matcom.2010.09.011

Aladag, C. H., Yolcu, U., Egrioglu, E., & Bas, E. (2014). Fuzzy lagged variable selection in fuzzy time series with genetic algorithms. *Applied Soft Computing*, *22*, 465–473. doi:10.1016/j.asoc.2014.03.028

Askari, S., & Montazerin, N. (2015). A high-order multi-variable fuzzy time series forecasting algorithm based on fuzzy clustering. *Expert Systems with Applications*, *42*(4), 2121–2135. doi:10.1016/j.eswa.2014.09.036

Bajestani, N. S., & Zare, A. (2011). Forecasting TAIEX using Improved Type-2 Fuzzy Time Series. *Expert Systems with Applications*, *38*(5), 5816–5821. doi:10.1016/j.eswa.2010.10.049

Bas, E., Egrioglu, E., Aladag, C. H. & Yolcu, U. (2015). Fuzzy-time-series network used to forecast linear and nonlinear time series, *Applied Intelligence*, *43*, 343–355.

Bas, E., Uslu, V. R., Yolcu, U., & Egrioglu, E. (2014). A modified genetic algorithm for forecasting fuzzy time series. *Applied Intelligence*, *41*(2), 453–463. doi:10.100710489-014-0529-x

Bezdek, J. C. (1981). *Pattern recognition with fuzzy objective function algorithms*. New York: Plenum Press. doi:10.1007/978-1-4757-0450-1

Bose, M., & Mali, K. (2016). High order time series forecasting using fuzzy discretization. *International Journal of Fuzzy System Applications*, *5*(4), 147–164. doi:10.4018/IJFSA.2016100107

Cai, Q., Zhang, D., Wu, B., & Leung, S. C. H. (2013). A novel stock forecasting model based on fuzzy time series and genetic algorithm, The 13th International Conference on Computational Science (2013 ICCS). *Procedia Computer Science*, *18*, 1155–1162. doi:10.1016/j.procs.2013.05.281

Cai, Q., Zhang, D., Wu, B., & Leung, S. C. H. (2015). A new fuzzy time series forecasting model combined with ant colony optimization and auto-regression. *Knowledge-Based Systems*, *74*, 61–68. doi:10.1016/j.knosys.2014.11.003

Chen, M. Y., & Chen, B. T. (2014). Online fuzzy time series analysis based on entropy discretization and a fast fourier transform. *Applied Soft Computing*, *14*, 156–166. doi:10.1016/j.asoc.2013.07.024

Chen, M. Y., & Chen, B. T. (2015). A hybrid fuzzy time series model based on granular Computing for stock price forecasting. *Information Sciences*, *294*(2), 227–241. doi:10.1016/j.ins.2014.09.038

Chen, M. Y., & Chen, B. T. (2015). A hybrid fuzzy time series model based on granular computing for stock price forecasting. *Information Sciences*, *294*, 227–241. doi:10.1016/j.ins.2014.09.038

Chen, S. M. (1996). Forecasting enrollments based on fuzzy time series. *Fuzzy Sets and Systems*, *81*(3), 311–319. doi:10.1016/0165-0114(95)00220-0

Chen, S. M. (2002). Forecasting enrollments based on high-order fuzzy time series. *Cybernetics and Systems: An International Journal, 33*(1), 1–16. doi:10.1080/019697202753306479

Chen, S. M., & Hsu, C. C. (2004). A new method to forecast enrollments using fuzzy time series. *International Journal of Applied Sciences and Engineering, 2*(3), 234–244.

Chen, S. M., & Kao, P. Y. (2013). TAIEX forecasting based on fuzzy time series, particle Swarm optimization techniques and support vector machines. *Information Sciences, 247*, 62–71. doi:10.1016/j.ins.2013.06.005

Chen, S.-M., & Tanuwijaya, K. (2011). Fuzzy forecasting based on high-order fuzzy logical relationships and automatic clustering techniques. *Expert Systems with Applications, 38*(12), 15425–15437. doi:10.1016/j.eswa.2011.06.019

Cheng, C. H., Chen, T. L., & Wei, L. Y. (2010). A hybrid model based on rough sets theory and genetic algorithms for stock price forecasting. *Information Sciences, 180*(9), 1610–1629. doi:10.1016/j.ins.2010.01.014

Cheng, S.-H., Chen, S.-M., & Jian, W.-S. (2016). Fuzzy time series forecasting based on fuzzy logical relationships and similarity measures. *Information Sciences, 327*, 272–287. doi:10.1016/j.ins.2015.08.024

Egrioglu, E., Aladag, C., Basaran, M., Yolcu, U., & Uslu, V. (2011). A new approach based on the optimization of the length of intervals in fuzzy time series. *Journal of Intelligent & Fuzzy Systems, 22*(1), 15–19.

Egrioglu, E., Aladag, C., & Yolcu, U. (2013). Fuzzy time series forecasting with a novel hybrid approach combining fuzzy c-means and neural networks. *Expert Systems with Applications, 40*(3), 854–857. doi:10.1016/j.eswa.2012.05.040

Egrioglu, E., Aladag, C. H., Yolcu, U., Uslu, V. R., & Erilli, N. A. (2011). Fuzzy time series forecasting method based on Gustafson–Kessel fuzzy clustering. *Expert Systems with Applications, 38*(8), 10355–10357. doi:10.1016/j.eswa.2011.02.052

Huarng, K. (2001). Effective lengths of intervals to improve forecasting in fuzzy time series. *Fuzzy Sets and Systems, 123*(3), 387–394. doi:10.1016/S0165-0114(00)00057-9

Huarng, K., & Yu, T. H. K. (2005). A Type-2 Time Series Model for Stock Index Forecasting. *Physica A, 353*, 445–462. doi:10.1016/j.physa.2004.11.070

Huarng, K., & Yu, T. H. K. (2006). Ratio-based lengths of intervals to improve fuzzy time series forecasting. *IEEE Transactions on Systems, Man, and Cybernetics. Part B, Cybernetics, 36*(2), 328–340. doi:10.1109/TSMCB.2005.857093 PMID:16602593

Izakian, H., Pedrycz, W., & Jamal, I. (2015). Fuzzy clustering of time series data using dynamic time warping distance. *Engineering Applications of Artificial Intelligence, 39*, 235–244. doi:10.1016/j.engappai.2014.12.015

Joshi, B.P. & Kumar, S.(2013) A Computational method for fuzzy time series forecasting based on difference parameters. *International Journal of Modeling, Simulation and Scientific Computing, 4*(1), 1250023-11250023-12.

Kumar, S., & Gangwar, S. S. (2012). Partitions based computational method for high-order Fuzzy time series forecasting. *Expert Systems with Applications, 39*(15), 12158–12164. doi:10.1016/j.eswa.2012.04.039

Lee, L. W., Wang, L. H., Chen, S. M., & Leu, Y. H. (2006b). Handling forecasting problems based on two-factors high-order fuzzy time series. *IEEE Transactions on Fuzzy Systems, 14*(3), 468–477. doi:10.1109/TFUZZ.2006.876367

Li, S. T., & Chen, Y. P. (2004). Natural partition-based forecasting model for fuzzy time series. *IEEE International Conference on Fuzzy Systems*, 25–29.

Lu, W., Chen, X., Pedrycz, W., Liu, X., & Yang, J. (2015). Using interval information granules to improve forecasting in fuzzy time series. *International Journal of Approximate Reasoning, 57*, 1–18. doi:10.1016/j.ijar.2014.11.002

Lu, W., Pedrycz, W., Liu, X., Yang, J., & Li, P. (2014). The modeling of time series based on fuzzy information granules. *Expert Systems with Applications, 41*(8), 3799–3808. doi:10.1016/j.eswa.2013.12.005

Pedrycz, W. (1998). Shadowed sets: Representing and processing fuzzy sets. *IEEE Transactions on Systems, Man, and Cybernetics. Part B, Cybernetics, 28*(1), 103–109. doi:10.1109/3477.658584 PMID:18255928

Roy, A., & Pal, S. K. (2003). Fuzzy discretization of feature space for a rough set classifier. *Pattern Recognition Letters, 24*(6), 895–902. doi:10.1016/S0167-8655(02)00201-5

Singh, P. (2015). A brief review of modeling approaches based on fuzzy time series. *International Journal of Machine Learning and Cybernetics*, 1–24.

Singh, P. (2016a). High-order fuzzy-neuro-entropy integration-based expert system for time series forecasting. *Neural Computing & Applications*, 1–18.

Singh, P. (2016b). Rainfall and financial forecasting using fuzzy time series and neural networks based model. *International Journal of Machine Learning and Cybernetics*. doi:10.100713042-016-0548-5

Singh, P., & Borah, B. (2013a). An efficient time series forecasting model based on fuzzy time series. *Engineering Applications of Artificial Intelligence, 26*(10), 2443–2457. doi:10.1016/j.engappai.2013.07.012

Singh, P., & Borah, B. (2013b). High-order fuzzy-neuro expert system for time series forecasting. *Knowledge-Based Systems, 46*, 12–21. doi:10.1016/j.knosys.2013.01.030

Singh, P., & Borah, B. (2014a). An effective neural network and fuzzy time series-based hybridized model to handle forecasting problems of two factors. *Knowledge and Information Systems, 38*(3), 669–690. doi:10.100710115-012-0603-9

Singh, P., & Borah, B. (2014b). Forecasting stock index price based on m-factors fuzzy time series and particle swarm optimization. *International Journal of Approximate Reasoning, 55*(3), 812–833. doi:10.1016/j.ijar.2013.09.014

Singh, S. R. (2009). A computational method of forecasting based on high-order fuzzy time series. *Expert Systems with Applications, 36*(7), 10551–10559. doi:10.1016/j.eswa.2009.02.061

Song, Q., & Chissom, B. S. (1993a). Fuzzy time series and its models. *Fuzzy Sets and Systems, 54*(3), 269–277. doi:10.1016/0165-0114(93)90372-O

Song, Q., & Chissom, B. S. (1993b). Forecasting enrollments with fuzzy time series – part I. *Fuzzy Sets and Systems*, *54*(1), 1–9. doi:10.1016/0165-0114(93)90355-L

Song, Q., & Chissom, B. S. (1994). Forecasting enrollments with fuzzy time series – part II. *Fuzzy Sets and Systems*, *62*(1), 1–8. doi:10.1016/0165-0114(94)90067-1

Sun, B., Guo, H., Karimi, H. R., Ge, Y., & Xiong, S. (2015). Prediction of stock index futures prices based on fuzzy sets and multivariate fuzzy time series. *Neurocomputing*, *151*, 1528–1536. doi:10.1016/j.neucom.2014.09.018

Tsaur, R.-C. (2012). A fuzzy time series-markov chain model with an Application to forecast the exchange rate between the Taiwan and us dollar. *International Journal of Innovative Computing, Information, & Control*, *8*(7B), 4931–4942.

Wang, L., Liu, X., & Pedrycz, W. (2013). Effective intervals determined by information granules to improve forecasting in fuzzy time series. *Expert Systems with Applications*, *40*(14), 5673–5679. doi:10.1016/j.eswa.2013.04.026

Wang, L., Liu, X., Pedrycz, W., & Shao, Y. (2014). Determination of temporal information granules to improve forecasting in fuzzy time series. *Expert Systems with Applications*, *41*(6), 3134–3142. doi:10.1016/j.eswa.2013.10.046

Wang, W., Pedrycz, W., & Liu, X. (2015). Time series long-term forecasting model based on information granules and fuzzy clustering. *Engineering Applications of Artificial Intelligence*, 4117–4124.

Wei, L. Y., Cheng, C. H., & Wu, H. H. (2014). A hybrid ANFIS based on n-period moving Average model to forecast TAIEX stock. *Applied Soft Computing*, *19*, 86–92. doi:10.1016/j.asoc.2014.01.022

Yu, T. H. K., & Huarng, K. H. (2008). A bivariate fuzzy time series model to forecast the TAIEX. *Expert Systems with Applications*, *34*(4), 2945–2952. doi:10.1016/j.eswa.2007.05.016

Yu, T. H. K., & Huarng, K. H. (2010). A neural network- based fuzzy time series model to improve forecasting. *Expert Systems with Applications*, *37*(4), 3366–3372. doi:10.1016/j.eswa.2009.10.013

Zadeh, L. A. (1965). Fuzzy sets. *Information and Control*, *8*(3), 338–353. doi:10.1016/S0019-9958(65)90241-X

Zadeh, L. A. (1975). The concept of a linguistic variable and its application to approximate reasoning. – Part I. *Information Sciences*, *8*(3), 199–249. doi:10.1016/0020-0255(75)90036-5

Chapter 15

Fuzzy–DSS Human Health Risk Assessment Under Uncertain Environment

Palash Dutta
Dibrugarh University, India

ABSTRACT

It is always utmost essential to accumulate knowledge on the nature of each and every accessible data, information, and model parameters in risk assessment. It is noticed that more often model parameters, data, information are fouled with uncertainty due to lack of precision, deficiency in data, diminutive sample sizes. In such environments, fuzzy set theory or Dempster-Shafer theory (DST) can be explored to represent this type of uncertainty. Most frequently, both types of uncertainty representation theories coexist in human health risk assessment and need to merge within the same framework. For this purpose, this chapter presents two algorithms to combine Dempster-Shafer structure (DSS) with generalized/ normal fuzzy focal elements, generalized/normal fuzzy numbers within the same framework. Computer codes are generated using Matlab M-files. Finally, human health risk assessment is carried out under this setting and it is observed that the results are obtained in the form of fuzzy numbers (normal/gener- alized) at different fractiles.

INTRODUCTION

Uncertainty plays an imperative role in decision making course of action. Therefore, it is really entailed to know the temperament of all available information, data or components of models in risk assessment. Usually, two kinds of uncertainties occurs viz., *aleatory uncertainty* arises due to inherent variability, natural stochasticity, environmental or structural variation across space or time, due to heterogeneity or the random character of natural processes and *epistemic uncertainty* transpires due to scarce or incomplete information or data, measurement error or data obtain from expert judgment or subjective interpretation of available data or information. Generally probability theory (PT) is considered as a well-recognized Mathematical tool to deal with *aleatory uncertainty* and therefore, available information/data are con-

DOI: 10.4018/978-1-5225-5396-0.ch015

strued in terms of probabilistic sense. However, it is well known that not all available information, data or components of models are affected by *aleatory uncertainty* and can directly be handled by conventional PT. *Epistemic uncertainty* also more often occurs in real world situations/problems. Thus, if components of models, data/information are affected by such kind of (*epistemic*) uncertainty conventional PT is improper to represent *epistemic uncertainty*. To prevail over the limitation of PT, Zadeh (1965) set up a new theory called FST. Dempster (1967) put forward another theory which is known as DST. FST is more appropriate in such circumstances where *epistemic uncertainty* is generally involved. On the other hand, the use of DST in risk assessment has numerous advantages upon the usual PT approaches. DST is especially useful for modelling uncertainty when we don't have enough data and need to depend on specialist judgment. The elementary objects of DST are called focal elements and the primitive function associated with it is called basic probability assignment (BPA). A DSS can be depicted by focal elements and its corresponding BPA. Experts' judgments are needed when encountering uncertainty, ignorance and complexity are involved in the system. It is needed to deal with the circumstances where cost of technical difficulties involved or uniqueness of the situation under study make it difficult/impossible to make enough observations to quantify the models with real data. Sometimes, these are also used to refine the estimate obtained from real data as well. Generally in DST, specialists provide BPA for interval focal elements. However, in real world problem it can be easily observed that data/information are imprecise or incomplete due to insufficient knowledge (Dutta et al., 2011b) and therefore, due to the occurrence of uncertainty, data/information can be treated as generalized triangular/normal triangular fuzzy number (TFN) because TFN encodes only most likely value (mode) and the spread (confidence interval). Hence, a comprehensive form of DST can be obtained.

Problem Statements

Components of health risk assessment models are frequently fouled with *epistemic uncertainties*. In such circumstances, it may occur that depictions of some uncertain input components of models are of DSS with fuzzy focal elements while depictions of some other components of models are fuzzy numbers (FNs). To deal with such situation, one has to develop a new efficient coalesce technique. Thus, coexistence of DSS and FNs make the situation complex to perform health risk assessment. Situations become more and more complex when GFNs are involved in the system. Hybridization of FNs and DSS with fuzzy focal elements of different shapes, technique yet not encountered to carry out risk assessment.

Motivations

As components of the models representing real world problems, in general are tainted with *epistemic uncertainty,* and as a consequence, representations of some uncertain model parameters are of DSS with fuzzy focal elements and some others are TFNs. In such circumstances, it is important to develop a new efficient amalgamate technique. In literature no any such approaches have been seen to unite DSS and FNs. This motivates us to device an efficient technique to unite DSS with fuzzy focal elements of different shapes and FNs with different shapes and types within the same framework.

Objective

The foremost objective of this article is to accomplish health risk assessment via the amalgamation of DSSs with normal/generalized fuzzy focal elements together with GFNs and normal FNs within the same framework. Furthermore, strengths and opportunities of this study will be addressed.

RELATED WORKS

In risk assessment, more often epistemic uncertainty exist and so FST has been successfully applied to deal with uncertainty such as Alguliyev and Abdullayeva (2015) performed fuzzy risk evaluation for dynamic federation of clouds, Wessiani and Sarwoko (2015) presented fuzzy risk analysis of poultry feed production, Zararsız (2015) carried out fuzzy risk analysis via similarity measures of sequence of fuzzy numbers, Dutta (2016) studied risk assessment via arithmetic operations of generalized fuzzy numbers, e Silva et al., (2016) studied assessment of earth dams using fuzzy numbers, Zhang et al., (2016) presented a risk assessment approach based on fuzzy 3D risk matrix for network device, Pamučar et al., (2017) proposed a risk assessment method of natural disasters using fuzzy logic system of type 2, Buchanan et al., (2017) performed risk assessment using fuzzy multiple criteria evaluation, Liu et al., (2017) studied risk evaluation in failure mode and effects analysis using fuzzy measure and fuzzy integral, Kuchta and Ptaszyńska (2017) carried out construction project risk assessment using fuzzy set.

But in some situations, it is seen that more often both *aleatory* and *epistemic uncertainties* co-exist. Therefore, joint propagation of probability distributions and fuzzy sets and their application in risk assessment is a common trend in risk analysis such as Guyonnet et al., (1999, 2003) discussed hybrid uncertainty modelling, Kentel and Aral (2004) studied on probalistic-fuzzy health risk modeling, Baudrit and Dubois(2006), Baudrit, Dubois, and Guyonnet (2006) and Baudrit et al. (2008) studied probability-fuzzy based uncertainty modeling, Anoop et al.,(2008) discussed safety assessment of austenitic steel nuclear power plant pipelines against stress corrosion cracking in the presence of hybrid uncertainties, Baraldi et al., (2008) combined Monte Carlo and possibilistic approach to uncertainty propagation in event tree analysis, Limbourg et al., (2010) studied uncertainty analysis using evidence theory – confronting level-1and level-2 approaches with data availability and computational constraints, Chen and Lee (2010) proposed hybrid fuzzy-stochastic modelling approach in environmental risk assessment of offshore produced water discharges, Flage et al., (2010, 2011), discussed probabilistic and Possibilistic treatment of epistemic uncertainties, Karami et al., (2013) discussed Fuzzy logic and adaptive neuro-fuzzy inference system for characterization of contaminant exposure, Pedroni et al., (2012, 2013) studied propagation of aleatory and epistemic uncertainties, Arunraj and Mandal (2013) proposed an integrated approach with fuzzy set theory and Monte Carlo simulation for uncertainty modeling in risk assessment, Pastoor et al., (2014) studied roadmap for human health risk assessment in 21st century, Farakos et al., (2013, 2014, 2016) studied risk assessment for Salmonella in tree nuts, Salmonella in low-water activity foods and Salmonella in low-moisture foods, Zwietering (2015) studied uncertainty modelling for risk assessment and risk management for safe foods, Alyami et al. (2016) studied advanced uncertainty modelling for container port risk analysis, Innal et al. (2016) studied uncertainty handling in safety instrumented systems according to IEC and new proposal based on coupling Monte Carlo analysis and fuzzy sets, Abdo and Flaus (2016) proposed a new approach with randomness and fuzzy theory for uncertainty quantification in dynamic system risk assessment, Zhang et al., (2016) discussed risk assessment of shallow groundwater contamination under irrigation and fertilization conditions, Jie et al., (2016) studied uncertainty analysis based on probability bounds in probabilistic risk assessment of high microgravity science experiment system, Zhang et al., (2017) presented a fuzzy probability Bayesian network approach for dynamic cyber security risk assessment in industrial control systems, Olawoyin (2017) performed risk and reliability evaluation of gas connector systems using fuzzy theory and expert elicitation, Jiang et al., (2017) studied probability-interval hybrid uncertainty analysis for structures with both aleatory and epistemic uncertainties, Qi and Cheng (2017) presented imprecise reliability assessment of generating systems involving interval probability, Rębiasz et al., (2017) studied joint treatment of imprecision and randomness in the appraisal of the effectiveness and risk of investment projects, Dutta (2017) devised a technique for joint propagation of aleatory and epistemic uncertainty, Liu et al.,(2017) discussed possibilistic-probabilistic programming approach to identify water quality management policy of watershed system, Nadiri et al., (2017) presented an assessment of groundwater vulnerability to combine fuzzy logic models. Though, joint promulgation of probability distributions and fuzzy sets is a common phenomenon in risk assessment, but combination of DST and FST in risk assessment is very atypical. Dutta (2015) proposed an approach to deal with DSS focal elements as normal/generalized triangular type fuzzy numbers, Dutta (2016) presented an approach to carry out human health risk assessment via DST-fuzzy number, Straszecka (2003, 2006a, 2006b) studied the basic framework of DST with fuzzy focal elements and used in medical diagnosis. Every disease is associated with a set of symptoms. The symptoms are usually of fuzzy nature (e.g., low blood pressure, high body temperature etc.) and so, use of fuzzy focal elements in DST is justifiable. Membership functions for these symptoms can be defined in consultation with an expert (a physician) or during training data investigation. Then BPAs are assigned to the focal elements. In the calculation of belief and plausibility for the disease only those focal elements (symptoms) will take part for which the membership value corresponding to the observed value (laboratory test), exceeds some given threshold value. [Bel(D), Pl(D)] determines the credibility of the diagnosis. Dutta et al. (2011b) studied DST with fuzzy focal elements and proposed arithmetic operations on DSTs. Dutta et al. (2011c) also discussed DST with fuzzy focal elements and devised a method for obtaining belief and plausibility measure from BPA's assigned to fuzzy focal elements. Further, Dutta (2015) studied DST with generalized/normal fuzzy focal elements and an approach was devised to combine DSTs using possibilistic sampling technique. Helton et al. (2005) presented failure risk analysis based on DST, Khatibi and Montazer (2009) performed coronary heart disease risk assessment using DST, Xu et al. (2010) performed risk analysis of system security via DST, Yang et al. (2011) provided risk evaluation in failure mode and effects analysis of aircraft turbine rotor blades using DST under uncertainty, Kronprasert and Thipnee (2016) studied fault tree analysis for road safety inspection using DST, Mezaal et al. (2017) studied DST based automatic landslide detection, Gündüz et al. (2017) presented driving pattern fusion using DST for fuzzy driving risk level assessment, Deng and Jiang (2017) carried out fuzzy risk evaluation in failure mode and effects analysis using a D numbers based multi-sensor information fusion method, Zhou et al.(2017) presented an improved belief entropy and its application in decision-making, and Leung et al. (2017) applied of extended DST in accident probability estimation for dangerous goods transportation. Bauer, (1997), Beynon et al., (2000), Beynon et al., (2001), Beynon, (2002), Beynon, (2005), Mercier et al., (2007), Srivastava & Liu, (2003), Wu, (2009), Yager, (2008), Yang and Sen, (1997), Yang and Xu, (2002), and Deng and Chan, (2011) applied DST in decision making. Some amalgamation of fuzzy with other theory and their applications can be seen in Elshazly et al. (2013), Jothi et al. (2013), Sahu et al. (2015), Kharola et al. (2016), Subramanian and Savarimuthu (2016), Ng and Zhang (2016), and Faquir et al. (2017).

Preliminaries

Environmental/human health risk assessment is an important element in any decision-making process in order to minimize the effects of human activities on the environment. Unfortunately, often environmental data tends to be vague and imprecise, so uncertainty is associated with any study related with these kinds of data. FST and DST provide ways to characterize the imprecisely defined variables, define relationships between variables based on expert human knowledge and use them to compute results. In this section, some necessary backgrounds and notions of fuzzy set theory (Dutta et al., 2011a; Zadeh, 1965) that will be required in the sequel are reviewed.

FUZZY SET THEORY (FST)

- **Definition:** Let X be a universal set. Then the fuzzy subset A of X is defined by its membership function

$$\mu_A : X \to [0,1]$$

Which assign a real number $\mu_A(x)$ in the interval [0, 1], to each element $x \in A$, where the value of $\mu_A(x)$ at x shows the grade of membership of x in A.

- **Definition:** Given a fuzzy set A in X and any real number $\alpha \in [0, 1]$. Then the α-cut or α-level or cut worthy set of A, denoted by $^\alpha A$ is the crisp set

$$^\alpha A = \left\{ x \in X : \mu_A(x) \geq \alpha \right\}$$

- **Definition:** The height of a fuzzy set A, denoted by $h(A)$ is the largest membership grade obtain by any element in the set and it is denoted as

$$h(A) = \sup_{x \in X} \mu_A(x)$$

- **Definition:** The core of a fuzzy set A defined on X is a crisp set defined as

$$\mathrm{Supp}h(A) = \left\{ x \in X : \mu_A(x) > 0 \right\}$$

- **Definition:** The support of a fuzzy set A defined on X is a crisp set defined as

$$\mathrm{Supp}(A) = \left\{ x \in X : \mu_A(x) > 0 \right\}$$

- **Definition:** A fuzzy number is a convex normalized fuzzy set of the real line R whose membership function is piecewise continuous.

- **Definition:** A trapezoidal fuzzy number (TrFN) A can be expressed as $[a, b, c, d]$ and its MF is defined as:

$$\mu_A(x) = \begin{cases} \dfrac{x-a}{b-a}, a \leq x \leq b \\ 1, b \leq x \leq c \\ \dfrac{d-x}{d-c}, c \leq x \leq d \end{cases}$$

- **Definition:** A triangular fuzzy number (TFN) A can be defined as a triplet $[a, b, c]$. Its membership function (MF) is defined as:

$$\mu_A(x) = \begin{cases} \dfrac{x-a}{b-a}, a \leq x \leq b \\ \dfrac{c-x}{c-b}, b \leq x \leq c \end{cases}$$

- **Definition:** A trapezoidal generalized fuzzy numbers (TrGFN) (Chen, 1985 & Chen, 1999) can be expressed $A = \left[a, b, c, d; w\right]$ where $a \leq b \leq c \leq d, 0 < w < 1$ and its MF is defined as

$$\mu_A(x) = \begin{cases} 0, x < a \\ w\dfrac{x-a}{b-a}, a \leq x \leq b \\ w, \quad b \leq x \leq c \\ w\dfrac{x-c}{d-c}, c \leq x \leq d \\ 0, x > d \end{cases}$$

- **Definition:** A triangular generalized fuzzy numbers (TGFN) (Chen, 1985 & Chen, 1999) can be expressed $A = \left[a, b, c; w\right]$ where $a \leq b \leq c, 0 < w < 1$ and its MF is defined as

$$\mu_A(x) = \begin{cases} 0, x < a \\ w\dfrac{x-a}{b-a}, a \leq x \leq b \\ w, \quad b \leq x \leq c \\ w\dfrac{x-c}{d-c}, c \leq x \leq d \\ 0, x > d \end{cases}$$

Compared to normal fuzzy number the GFN can deal with uncertain information in a more flexible manner because of the parameter w that represent the degree of confidence of opinions of decision maker's.

DEMPSTER -SHAFER THEORY OF EVIDENCE (DST)

DST (Shafer, 1976) is extensively used to model both epistemic and aleatory uncertainty. The fundamental underlying set considered in DST is called a frame of discernment Θ which is a set of mutually exclusive and exhaustive propositional hypotheses, one and only one of them is true.

DST is based on belief measure and plausible measure. The primitive function in DST used to define belief measure and plausible measure is known as basic probability assignment (BPA) and it is usually denoted by m.

Mathematically, BPA is a function $m : 2^\Theta \to [0,1]$ such that

$$\left. \begin{array}{l} m(\phi) = 0 \\ \displaystyle\sum_{A \subseteq \Theta} m(A) = 1 \end{array} \right\}$$

where ϕ is an empty set and A is any subset of Θ.

Given a frame, Θ, for each source of evidence, a BPA assigns a mass to every subset of Θ, which represents the degree of belief that one of the hypotheses in the subset is true in the, given the source of evidence.

A subset A of frame Θ is called the focal element of m, if $m(A) > 0$.

Using the BPA, belief measure and plausibility measure are respectively defined as

$$Bel(A) = \sum_{B \subseteq A} m(B), A \subseteq \Theta \text{ and } Pl(A) = \sum_{B \cap A \neq \phi} m(B)$$

Here $m(B)$ is the degree of evidence in the set B alone, whereas $Bel(A)$ is the total evidence in set A and all subset B of A and the plausibility of an event A is the total evidence in set A, plus the evidence in all sets of the universe that intersect with A.

Where $Bel(A)$ and $Pl(A)$ represent the lower bound and upper bound of belief in A. Hence, interval $[Bel(A), Pl(A)]$ is the range of belief in A.

If two DSS m_1 and m_2 are obtained from two different evidence sources, then the following Dempster's combination rule is used to combine them as:

$$m(C) = \frac{\displaystyle\sum_{A \cap B = C} m_1(A) m_2(B)}{1 - \displaystyle\sum_{A \cap B = \phi} m_1(A) m_2(B)}$$

Sampling Technique for DST

In the sampling technique for DST, at first uniformly distributed random number between 0 and 1 is created. Random variables are produced by comparing this uniformly created numbers to belief function and plausibility function. Two numbers are produced in this procedure, one consequent to belief function (x_b) and the other consequent to the plausibility function (x_p). For example, consider a uniformly distributed random number r the uncertain variable x_n and uncertainty variable x_p are obtained as

$x_n = Bel^{-1}(r)$ and $x_p = Pl^{-1}(r)$.

Suppose Figure 1 is the graphical representation of cumulative belief and plausibility measures whose DSS is provided by an expert. For the uniformly distributed random number 0.75, using DST sampling 25 and 35 are obtained as the values of the uncertain variable corresponding to plausibility measure and belief measure respectively.

FUZZY FOCAL ELEMENTS

A subset A of frame Θ is called the fuzzy focal element of m if A is a fuzzy number. Here, a discussion being made to show how the belief and plausibility measures can be constructed when focal elements are fuzzy numbers. Suppose Θ is a universe of discourse and information regarding some parameter, say, X, experts providing DSS of fuzzy focal elements (normal/generalized triangular fuzzy numbers).

Figure 1. Cumulative belief and plausibility

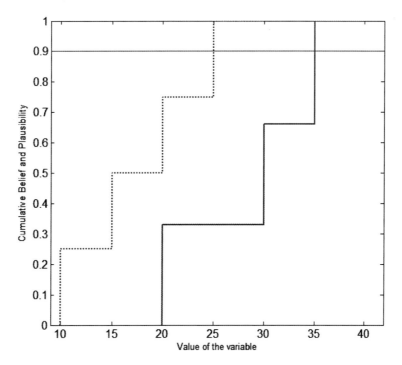

Let's suppose $m([a_i, b_i, c_i; w_i]) = p_i, i = 1, 2, 3, \ldots n$ satisfying $\sum_{i=1}^{n} p_i = 1$ where $w_i \in (0, 1]$ is a DSS.

Now, α-cut of GFN is $[a_i, b_i, c_i; w_i]$ is $[a_i + (b_i - a_i)\alpha / w_i, c_i - (c_i - b_i)\alpha / w_i]$ for $\alpha \in [0, w_i]$.

It is known to us that α-cut is a bridge between fuzzy set & crisp set, and it produces closed interval and accordingly cumulative belief and plausibility measure for each α-cut can be evaluated using typical DST. If focal elements are normal FNs then it is easy to obtain cumulative belief and plausibility for all α-cuts, but if it is GFNs, it is unfeasible to obtain the same. To get rid of this problem, heights of GFNs are truncated at the minimum height of all the GFNs. i.e., it is considered that $\alpha \in [0, \min(w_i)]$. Then, a collection of cumulative belief and plausibility distributions is obtained for all α-cuts from 0 to $\min(w_i)$ using classical DST. For instance, if we consider $\alpha = 0 : \frac{\min(w_i)}{10} : \min(w_i)$, (i.e., if α takes 11 values) a family of 22 cumulative distribution functions (cdfs); 11 cumulative belief measures, 11 cumulative plausibility measures are obtained. From these cumulative belief and plausibility measures, MF (fuzzy numbers) at different fractiles can be generated (Dutta and Ali, 2011b).

However, if focal elements are normal fuzzy number instead of generalized fuzzy numbers, then for $\alpha = 0 : 0.1 : 1$ (if α takes 11 values) then a collection of 21 cumulative distribution functions (cdfs) are obtained; 10 cumulative belief measures, 10 cumulative plausibility measures, while there is one CDF where both belief and plausibility measure coincide and which corresponds to 1-cut. From these cumulative belief and plausibility measures also, MFs of risk at different fractiles can be generated and that will be normal fuzzy numbers.

Example

Suppose for an uncertain variable *X*, the DSS with normal fuzzy focal elements is obtained and given in Table 1. Require to evaluate their cumulative belief and plausibility.

These TFNs can be transformed into intervals using α-cuts and accordingly classical DSS will be obtained, given in Table 2.

Then, using typical DST, cumulative belief and plausibility of the DSS can be obtained. For straightforward and apparent representation of belief and plausibility measures, $\alpha = 0, 0.5$ and 1 are considered and the graphical representation of the same is depicted in Figure 2.

Table 1. BPA of the fuzzy focal elements

Focal Elements	BPA
[15, 22.5, 30]	0.05
[30, 37.5, 45]	0.1
[30, 45, 60]	0.2
[45, 60, 70]	0.3
[75, 82.5, 90]	0.1
[60, 75, 90]	0.2
[90, 97.5, 105]	0.05

Table 2. Alpha-cuts of fuzzy focal elements

Focal Elements	BPA
[15+7.5α, 30-7.5α]	0.05
[30+7.5α, 45-7.5α]	0.1
[30+15α, 60-15α]	0.2
[45+15α, 75-15α]	0.3
[75+7.5α, 90-7.5α]	0.1
[60+15α, 90-15α]	0.2
[90+7.5α, 105-7.5α]	0.05

Figure 2. Cumulative Bel and Pl of fuzzy focal elements for α=0, 0.5 and 1

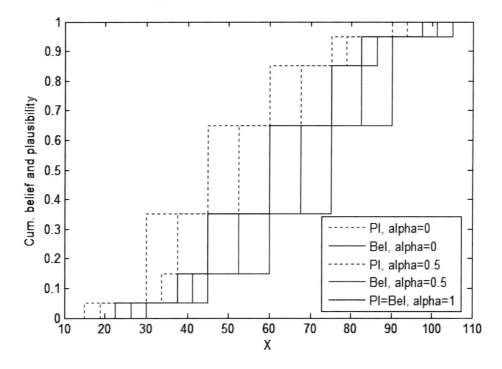

Now, MFs of the resultant FNs can be evaluated at different fractiles. For example, at 90th fractile, for α = 0, 0.5 & 1, the values obtained from cumulative belief and plausibility measures are 75 & 90, 78.75 & 86.25 and 82.5 respectively (Figure 3).

The resultant FN at 90th fractile is depicted in Figure 4.

On the other hand, if representation of the variable X is DSS with generalized fuzzy focal elements where heights of the GFNs are 0.75, 0.80, 0.85, 0.90, 0.95, 0.70, and 0.75 respectively (Table 3) and to construct the cumulative belief and plausibility measures, minimum heights of all the GFNs (i.e., 0.7)is considered. For α=0, 0.35 and 0.7 cumulative belief and plausibility are depicted in Figure 5.

Then, from this collection of CDFs, MF of X at 90th fractile is generated and given in the Figure 6.

Figure 3. Bel & Pl of X for α=0.0, 0.5 & 1.0

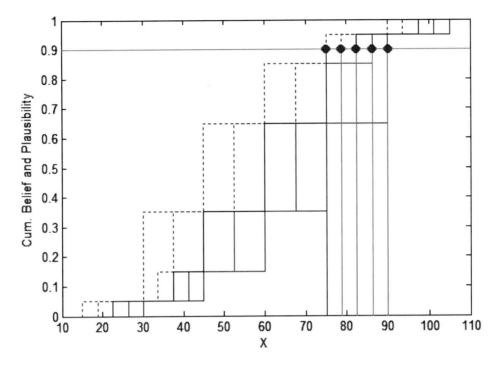

Figure 4. The membership function of X at 90ᵗʰ fractile

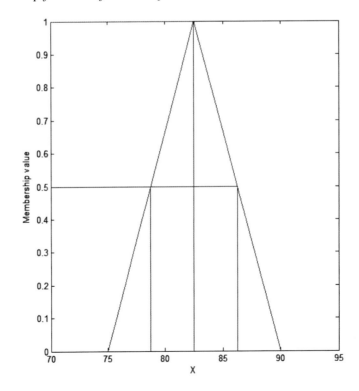

Table 3. Basic probability assignment of the fuzzy focal elements

Focal Elements	Basic Probability Assignment
[15, 22.5, 30;0.75]	0.05
[30, 37.5, 45;0.80]	0.1
[30, 45, 60;0.85]	0.2
[45, 60, 700;.90]	0.3
[75, 82.5, 90;0.95]	0.1
[60, 75, 90;0.70]	0.2
[90, 97.5, 105;0.75]	0.05

Figure 5. Bel & Pl of X for α=0.0, 0.35 & 0.7

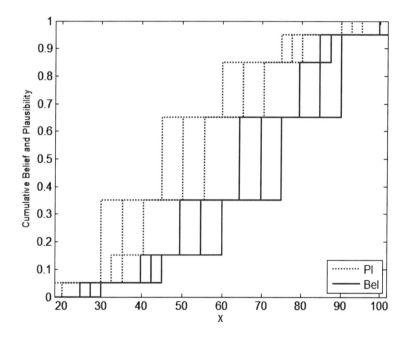

Proposed Approach

It is palpable that components of human health risk assessment model are tainted with *epistemic uncertainty* and consequently certain model parameters are reasonably represented by DSS with fuzzy (normal/GFN) focal elements while others are better represented by FNs of different shapes. Then, the question may arise as to how these two modes of uncertainty representation techniques can be united for the purpose of assessing the risk. In uncertainty modelling via DSS, generally focal elements are considered as crisp (intervals), but due to occurrence of uncertainty/imprecision it can be taken as FNs of different shapes. A special procedure is indeed required to lever hybrid uncertainties (*i.e.,* hybridization of fuzzy and DSS), to perform health risk assessment.

Consider any arbitrary Mathematical model

Figure 6. The membership function of X at 90ᵗʰ fractile

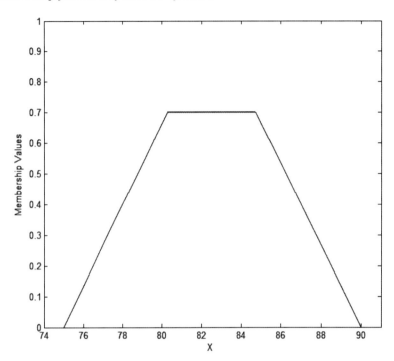

$M = f(D_j, G_k), j = 1, 2, 3, ..., r; k = 1, 2, 3, ..., s;$ which is a function of some parameters ξ_j and ζ_k where representations of ξ_j are DSS in which focal elements are considered as normal/GFNs; also representations of ζ_k are normal/GFNs. It should be noted that number of focal elements for each DSS is not necessarily same; it may vary from DSS to DSS.

Here, two algorithms have been formulated to amalgamate DSS with fuzzy focal elements and FNs in which interval computation has been employed.

A brief description of interval computation in terms of this study has been depicted here.

Interval Computation

Suppose $\lambda = [\lambda_1, \lambda_2]$ and $\eta = [\eta_1, \eta_2]$ are two given intervals and $f(\lambda, \eta) = \lambda * \eta$ where $* \in \{+, -, \times, \div\}$. Then, $f(\lambda, \eta) = \lambda + \eta = [\lambda_1, \lambda_2] + [\eta_1, \eta_2] = [\lambda_1 + \eta_1, \lambda_2 + \eta_2]$,

$$f(\lambda, \eta) = \lambda - \eta = [\lambda_1, \lambda_2] - [\eta_1, \eta_2] = [\lambda_1 - \eta_2, \lambda_2 - \eta_1]$$

$$f(\lambda, \eta) = \lambda * \eta = [\lambda_1, \lambda_2] * [\eta_1, \eta_2] = [\min(\lambda_1 \eta_1, \lambda_2 \eta_1, \lambda_2 \eta_1, \lambda_2 \eta_2), \max(\lambda_1 \eta_1, \lambda_2 \eta_1, \lambda_2 \eta_1, \lambda_2 \eta_2)]$$

and

$$f(\lambda, \eta) = \lambda \div \eta = [\lambda_1, \lambda_2] \div [\eta_1, \eta_2] = [\min(\lambda_1 / \eta_1, \lambda_2 / \eta_1, \lambda_2 / \eta_1, \lambda_2 / \eta_2), \max(\lambda_1 / \eta_1, \lambda_2 / \eta_1, \lambda_2 / \eta_1, \lambda_2 / \eta_2)]$$

If $\lambda = [\lambda_1, \lambda_2]$, $\eta = [\eta_1, \eta_2]$ and $\mu = [\mu_1, \mu_2]$ are given intervals. Suppose we need to compute the followings $g(\lambda, \eta, \mu) = \dfrac{\lambda + \eta}{\mu}$, $g(\lambda, \eta, \mu) = \dfrac{\lambda - \eta}{\mu}$ and $g(\lambda, \eta, \mu) = \dfrac{\lambda \eta}{\mu}$.

Then, to compute the required functions, we need to insert all the combinations of the initial and end points of the intervals in the respective functions.

i.e.,

$$g(\lambda, \eta, \mu) = \frac{\lambda + \eta}{\mu} \left[\begin{matrix} \min\left(\dfrac{\lambda_1 + \eta_1}{\mu_1}, \dfrac{\lambda_1 + \eta_2}{\mu_1}, \dfrac{\lambda_2 + \eta_1}{\mu_1}, \dfrac{\lambda_2 + \eta_2}{\mu_1}, \dfrac{\lambda_1 + \eta_1}{\mu_2}, \dfrac{\lambda_1 + \eta_2}{\mu_2}, \dfrac{\lambda_2 + \eta_1}{\mu_2}, \dfrac{\lambda_2 + \eta_2}{\mu_2} \right), \\ \max\left(\dfrac{\lambda_1 + \eta_1}{\mu_1}, \dfrac{\lambda_1 + \eta_2}{\mu_1}, \dfrac{\lambda_2 + \eta_1}{\mu_1}, \dfrac{\lambda_2 + \eta_2}{\mu_1}, \dfrac{\lambda_1 + \eta_1}{\mu_2}, \dfrac{\lambda_1 + \eta_2}{\mu_2}, \dfrac{\lambda_2 + \eta_1}{\mu_2}, \dfrac{\lambda_2 + \eta_2}{\mu_2} \right) \end{matrix} \right],$$

$$g(\lambda, \eta, \mu) = \frac{\lambda - \eta}{\mu} \left[\begin{matrix} \min\left(\dfrac{\lambda_1 - \eta_1}{\mu_1}, \dfrac{\lambda_1 - \eta_2}{\mu_1}, \dfrac{\lambda_2 - \eta_1}{\mu_1}, \dfrac{\lambda_2 - \eta_2}{\mu_1}, \dfrac{\lambda_1 - \eta_1}{\mu_2}, \dfrac{\lambda_1 - \eta_2}{\mu_2}, \dfrac{\lambda_2 - \eta_1}{\mu_2}, \dfrac{\lambda_2 - \eta_2}{\mu_2} \right), \\ \max\left(\dfrac{\lambda_1 - \eta_1}{\mu_1}, \dfrac{\lambda_1 - \eta_2}{\mu_1}, \dfrac{\lambda_2 - \eta_1}{\mu_1}, \dfrac{\lambda_2 - \eta_2}{\mu_1}, \dfrac{\lambda_1 - \eta_1}{\mu_2}, \dfrac{\lambda_1 - \eta_2}{\mu_2}, \dfrac{\lambda_2 - \eta_1}{\mu_2}, \dfrac{\lambda_2 - \eta_2}{\mu_2} \right) \end{matrix} \right]$$

and

$$g(\lambda, \eta, \mu) = \frac{\lambda \eta}{\mu} \left[\begin{matrix} \min\left(\dfrac{\lambda_1 \eta_1}{\mu_1}, \dfrac{\lambda_1 \eta_2}{\mu_1}, \dfrac{\lambda_2 \eta_1}{\mu_1}, \dfrac{\lambda_2 \eta_2}{\mu_1}, \dfrac{\lambda_1 \eta_1}{\mu_2}, \dfrac{\lambda_1 \eta_2}{\mu_2}, \dfrac{\lambda_2 \eta_1}{\mu_2}, \dfrac{\lambda_2 \eta_2}{\mu_2} \right), \\ \max\left(\dfrac{\lambda_1 \eta_1}{\mu_1}, \dfrac{\lambda_1 \eta_2}{\mu_1}, \dfrac{\lambda_2 \eta_1}{\mu_1}, \dfrac{\lambda_2 \eta_2}{\mu_1}, \dfrac{\lambda_1 \eta_1}{\mu_2}, \dfrac{\lambda_1 \eta_2}{\mu_2}, \dfrac{\lambda_2 \eta_1}{\mu_2}, \dfrac{\lambda_2 \eta_2}{\mu_2} \right) \end{matrix} \right]$$

Algorithm I

In this algorithm, depictions of a few uncertain model parameters are taken to be DSS where each focal element of DSS is normal fuzzy numbers. Again, depictions of several other uncertain model parameters are considered as normal fuzzy numbers. To amalgamate both mode of representation of uncertainty, first certain alpha-cut of the fuzzy for focal elements are calculated which produces crisp focal elements from which cumulative belief and plausibility measure are evaluated using existing DST. Then DST can be performed to obtain two values (close interval) corresponding to plausibility measure and belief measure respectively. Again same alpha value is considered for other fuzzy numbers and calculated alpha-cut, then assigned all combinations of interval values in the model. Then minimum and maximum value of the risk model can be calculated and process is repeated for **N** times. The cumulative distribution functions (CDFs) of model values are plotted. Process is repeated for other alpha cuts. Thus, a collection of CDFs will be obtained and from theses collection of MFs are generated CDFs at different fractiles which will be available in the form of normal FNs.

Here, it should be remembered that ξ_j are DSS in which focal elements are considered as normal FNs; also representations of ζ_k are normal FNs.

The details procedure is summarized by the steps below:

Step 1: Acquire all the uncertain components of the Mathematical model (**R**) whose representations are DSS where focal elements are normal fuzzy numbers.

Step 2: Contemplate $\alpha = \left[0, \dfrac{1}{q}, \dfrac{2}{q}, ...1\right], q \in \mathbb{N},$ and gauge α -cut for α -value 0 of each fuzzy focal element of each DSS which produces crisp (interval) focal elements.

Step 3: Then, p duos of cumulative Belief and Plausibility measures are obtained.

Step 4: Create p number of uniformly distributed random numbers in between 0 and 1. Then, executing DST sampling procedure produces p number of closed intervals i.e., $2p$ number of (end points) real numbers.

Step 5: Consider every uncertain components of the model **R** whose representations are FNs.

Step 6: Evaluate α -cut for the same α -value (as in step 1) for each fuzzy numbers which produce q numbers of closed intervals i.e., $2q$ number of (end points) real numbers.

Step 7: Insert all the combinations of all the $2p$ and $2q$ real values in the risk model **R**.

Step 8: Gauge infimum and supremum values of the model **R** (compute using the interval computation technique).

i.e., $M_1^{Inf} = Inf(M)$ and $M_1^{Sup} = Sup(M)$.

Step 9: Reiterate step 1 to step 7 for **N** times.

Step 10: Plot CDFs of $(R_1^{inf}, R_2^{inf}, ..., R_N^{inf})$ and $(R_1^{sup}, R_2^{sup}, ..., R_N^{sup})$.

Step 11: Compute other α -cut for other α -values and reiterate step 3 to step 10.

Then, it produces a collection of cumulative belief and plausibility measures. For illustration, taking $\alpha = 0 : 0.1 : 1$ (i.e., for 11 α -values) and the execution of the algorithm-I gives 21 CDFs; 10 cumulative belief measures, 10 cumulative plausibility measures, while there is one CDF where both belief and plausibility measure coincide that corresponds to 1-cut. From this collection of cumulative belief and plausibility measures, MFs (normal fuzzy numbers) of risk value can be generated at different fractiles (Dutta & Ali, 2011b; Dutta, 2016).

Algorithm II

In this algorithm, depictions of several uncertain input components of the Mathematical model are DSS where each focal element of DSS is in the form of normal/GFNs. Furthermore, depictions of a few other uncertain input components of the model are too normal/GFNs. Since heights of GFNs are different so to execute the Mathematical model minimum of all heights of GFNs is taken into consideration and subsequently another algorithm is being generated. Here also a collection of CDFs will be obtained and from theses family of CDFs and at different fractiles MFs can also be generated which will be obtained in the form of GFNs with each of height will be the minimum of all the heights of input fuzzy numbers.

Here also, it should noted that ξ_j are DSS in which focal elements are considered as normal/GFNs; also representations of ξ_k are normal/GFNs.

The procedure is summarized by the steps below:

Step 1: Contemplate those uncertain input components of **R** whose depictions are DSS with focal elements as normal/ GFNs.

Step 2: Take $\alpha = \left[0 : \dfrac{w}{q} : w\right], q \in \mathbb{N},$ and gauge α-cut for α-value 0 for each focal element (GFN or normal FN).

Step 3: Using classical DST p pairs of cumulative Belief and Plausibility measures are obtained.

Step 4: Create p number of uniformly distributed random numbers in between 0 & 1. Then execution of DST sampling technique produces p numbers of closed intervals i.e., $2p$ number of (end points) real numbers.

Step 5: Consider every uncertain components of the model **R** whose representations are normal/GFNs.. Gauge α-cut for the same α-value (as in step 1) for each FNs. Then, q numbers of closed intervals i.e., $2s$ number of (end points) real numbers will be obtained.

Step 6: Insert all the combinations of all $2p$ and $2q$ number of values in the risk model **R**.

Step 7: Estimate infimum and supremum value of the risk model **R**(compute using the interval computation technique).

i.e., $M_1^{Inf} = Inf(M)$ and $M_1^{Sup} = Sup(M)$.

Step 8: Reiterate step 1 to step 7 for **N** times.

Step 9: Plotting CDFs of $(R_1^{inf}, R_2^{inf}, \ldots, R_N^{inf})$ and $(R_1^{sup}, R_2^{sup}, \ldots, R_N^{sup})$ give a pair of CDF i.e., one lower and one upper probability.

Step 10: Gauging other α-cuts for other α-values (remember that $\alpha \in [0, w]$) and reiterating step 2 to step 9 produces a family of cumulative belief and plausibility measures. In the same way as algorithm-I, for $\alpha = 0 : \dfrac{w}{q} : w$, 22 CDFs (for 11 values); 11 cumulative belief measures, 11 cumulative plausibility measures are obtained. From these cumulative belief and plausibility measures, MFs (GFNs) at different fractiles can be generated with each of height w. It is because consideration of minimum heights of all the GFNs.

In both the algorithm, 11 α-values are taken and same have been observed for *N*=5000 simulations which are adequate. However, if one feels the necessity of any increment in numbers of α values and simulations values to acquire further smoothness of the results that can also be done.

HYPOTHETICAL CASE STUDY

In this segment, human health risk assessment has been carried out with hypothetical data.

In view of the fact that the beginning of the earth's continuation; human being has always been exposed to radiation from natural sources or manmade/artificial sources of radiation.

There is an extensive assortment of fonts of natural radiation to which individual being incessantly exposed (National Radiation Laboratory Report). Amongst these fonts, the most well-known to us is the sun which fabricates infrared radiation that people feel as warmth, visible light, and ultraviolet light. Radioactive materials are also obtained throughout nature. They are available in the soil, water, and vegetation. Low levels of uranium, thorium, and their decay products are found everywhere. Some of these materials are ingested with food and water, while others, such as radon, are inhaled. Cosmic and terrestrial sources are also sources of radiation (Dutta, 2016).

On the other hand, artificial radiation is a kind of radiation produced in devices, such as x-ray machines, and artificially produced radioisotopes made in a reactor or accelerator. Main users of man-made radiation include: medical facilities, such as hospitals and pharmaceutical facilities; research and teaching institutions; nuclear reactors and their supporting facilities, such as uranium mills and fuel preparation plants; and federal facilities involved in nuclear weapons production (USEPA, 2007). Radiation accidents involved radiation devices, radioisotopes, and criticality incidents. It must be emphasized that radiation accidents could involve either high- or low-level radiation exposures. Furthermore, pollutions may also occur from different industries. When human being is exposed, in general, the amount and duration of radiation exposure affects the severity or type of health affect such as acute radiation sickness, cancer, teratogenic (fetal) damage, hereditary changes etc. Therefore when hazardous substances are released into the environment, an evaluation or assessment is necessary to determine possible impact these substances may have on human health and environment.

In this case study, it is assumed that water turn out to be contaminated due to the discharge of radionuclide/hazardous materials into the water and as a consequence human being may be directly or indirectly affected owing to intake of such contaminated water, fish etc., so it is important to assess risk.

Health Risk Assessment Model

It is well known that health risk assessment is performed using models and models are function of parameters which are affected by uncertainties. The well validated risk assessment model due to the ingestion of radionuclide in water as provided by (EPA, 2001) is as follows

$$Risk = \frac{C \times IR \times EF \times ED}{BW \times AT} \times CSF \tag{1}$$

Abbreviation of terms of the risk model and their full forms are given in the Table 4.
Here two scenarios have been considered to carry out the risk assessment.

Table 4. Abbreviation of terms and their full names

Sl. No.	Abbreviation	Full Form
1.	*C*	concentration (mg/L)
2.	*IR*	ingestion rate (L/day)
4.	*EF*	Exposure frequency (day/year)
5.	*ED*	Exposure duration (years)
7.	*BW*	Body weight (kg)
8.	*AT*	Averaging time (days)
9.	*CSF*	Cancer slope or potency factor $(mg/kg\text{-}day)^{-1}$.
10	*PEC*	Predicted environmental concentration (mg/l)

Scenario 1

In this scenario, depiction of the uncertain input parameters Concentration (*C*), Exposure frequency (EF) are taken as DSSs with normal fuzzy focal elements and Cancer slope factor (*CSF*) is normal FN respectively besides other parameters are keeping constant. Values of the parameters for the calculation of health risk are given in the Table 5.

Given that here, focal elements of each DDS as well as some other model parameters are normal FNs and as an upshot algorithm-I can be directly employed to estimate the health risk. Assume that $\alpha = 0 : 0.1 : 1$ (i.e., 11 α values are taken gradually from 0 to 1) and consequently, CDFs are obtained; 10 cumulative belief measures (blue coloured), 10 cumulative plausibility measures (red coloured), while there is one CDF (green coloured) where both belief and plausibility measure coincide and which corresponds to 1-cut and that are depicted in the following Figure 7.

From this collection of 21 cumulative belief measures and cumulative plausibility measures, MFs (fuzzy numbers) of risk at different fractiles can be estimated and obtained in the form of normal FNs (Detail analysis are given in results and discussion section).

Table 5. Parameter values used in the risk assessment

Parameter	Units	Type of Variable	Value/Distribution
C	mg/L	DSS	Given in Table 6
IR	L/day	Constant	5
EF	Days/year	DSS	Given in Table 7
ED	Years	Constant	30
AT	Days	Constant	25550
BW	Kg	Constant	70
CSF	$(mg/kg\text{-}day)^{-1}$	Fuzzy	[0.14, 0.15, 0.16]

Table 6. DSS for concentration (C)

Fuzzy Focal Elements	BPA
[0.02,0.055,0.09]	0.15
[0.07,0.12,0.17]	0.20
[0.12, 0.18,0.24]	0.35
[0.22,0.24,0.26]	0.20
[0.26,0.27,0.28]	0.10

Table 7. DSS for Exposure Frequency (EF)

Fuzzy Focal Elements	BPA
[330, 337.5, 345]	0.15
[340, 350, 360]	0.60
[350, 360, 370]	0.25

Figure 7. Cumulative belief and plausibility of risk for $\alpha = 0 : 0.1 : 1$

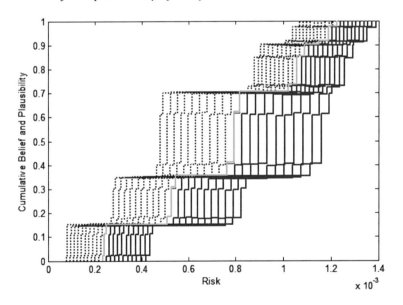

Scenario 2

Here, depiction of the uncertain input model parameter *Concentration (C)* is DSS with generalized fuzzy focal elements, besides depiction of the uncertain input model parameter *Exposure frequency (EF)* is also DSS with normal fuzzy focal elements. On the other hand, depiction of *Body weight (BW)* and *cancer slope factor (CSF)* are normal and GFN respectively. Other parameters are taken as deterministic. Required values of the parameters for the calculation of cancer risk are given in the Table 8.

Table 8. Parameters used in the risk assessment

Parameter	Units	Type of Variable	Value/Distribution
C	mg/L	Probabilistic	Given in Table 9
IR	L/day	IVFN	5
EF	Days/year	Constant	Given in Table 10
ED	Years	Constant	30
AT	Days	Constant	25550
BW	Kg	Fuzzy	[60, 70, 80]
CSF	(mg/kg-day)$^{-1}$	GFN	[0.14, 0.15, 0.16; 0.8]

Table 9. DSS for concentration (C)

Fuzzy Focal Elements	BPA
[0.02,0.055,0.09;0.74]	0.15
[0.07,0.12,0.17;0.81]	0.20
[0.12, 0.18,0.24;0.0.94]	0.35
[0.22,0.24,0.26;0.86]	0.20
[0.26,0.27,0.28;0.70]	0.10

Table 10. DSS for Exposure Frequency (EF)

Fuzzy Focal Elements	BPA
[330, 337.5, 345]	0.15
[340, 350, 360]	0.60
[350, 360, 370]	0.25

In view of the fact that GFNs are involved in uncertain model parameters algorithm- I is inadequate to achieve the risk assessment while algorithm-II is well enough for the same. Here also we consider α takes 11 values i.e., $\alpha = 0 : 0.1 : \min(w_j)$, execution of algorithm-II provides 22 CDFs; 11 cumulative belief measures (blue coloured); 11 cumulative plausibility measures (red colours) which are depicted in the following Figure 10. Here the same CDF will not be obtained as minimum height i.e., 0.7-cut of all the fuzzy focal elements give interval focal elements and consequently belief and plausibility measures. However, in algorithm-I heights of all the FNs were same i.e., 1-cut of each fuzzy focal element gives single values and subsequently we got same CDF (as both belief and plausibility measure coincide and which corresponds to 1-cut).

In a similar fashion as algorithm-I, from this collection of 22 CDFs, MFs of risk at different fractiles can be generated which are obtained in the form of GFNs with height 0.7 (Details results are depicted in results and discussions section).

Figure 8. Cumulative belief and plausibility of risk for $\alpha = 0 : 0.1 : 1$

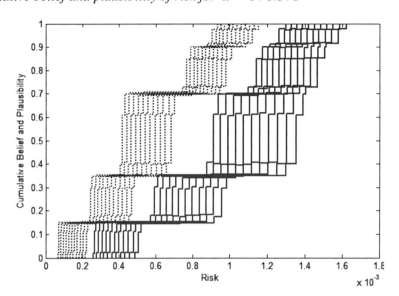

RESULTS AND DISCUSSION

In general the most of the health risk assessment problem employs treating with uncertainties. Researchers/ Scientists should be conscientious of all such kind of uncertainties and attempt to include all the necessary information into the investigation. The aim of risk assessment is to estimate the severity and likelihood of harm to human health from exposure to a substance or activity that under plausible circumstances can cause harm to human health. The assessment is generally performed using 'model' and a model is a function of parameters which are usually affected by uncertainty. Uncertainties have different representations viz. probabilistic and possibilistic, DSS etc. In this study it is considered that some components of health risk model are DSS with normal/generalized fuzzy focal elements while a few are normal/GFNs besides rest are deterministic. To deal with such situations a novel combine technique has been developed in which two algorithms have been proposed. Using these two algorithms a hypothetical case study has been performed where two scenarios have been considered. In scenario 1, depiction of the uncertain parameters *Concentration (C)*, *Exposure frequency (EF)* are considered as DSSs with focal element as normal FNs and *Cancer slope factor (CSF)* as normal FN respectively and other parameters are taken as constant. Employing algorithm-I, risk has been assessed and obtained as a collection of cumulative belief and plausibility measures. Then, risk value is derived in terms of FNs at different fractiles. For instance, at 95th fractile, risk is the fuzzy number around 1.1888e-03 i.e. [1.0380e-03, 1.1888e-03, 1.3526e-03], on the other hand, risk at 90th fractile is the fuzzy number [8.7828e-04, 1.0568e-03, 1.2560e-03] which are deliberated and MFs of risk are depicted in Figure 8 and 9 respectively.

Details evaluation of results obtained at different fractiles by using algorithm-I is depicted in Table 11.

In the same way, in scenario 2, depiction of the uncertain input model component *Concentration (C)* is DSS with generalized fuzzy focal elements while depiction of the uncertain model components *Exposure frequency (EF)* is also DSS with normal fuzzy focal elements. On the other hand, depiction of *Body weight (BW)* and *cancer slope factor (CSF)* are normal FN and GFN respectively and other parameters are chosen as deterministic. Here, algorithm-I will not work, so it is necessary to employ algorithm II to

Figure 9. MF of Risk at 95ᵗʰ fractile

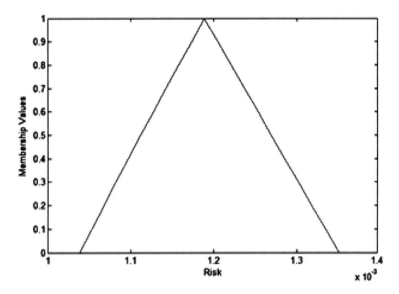

Figure 10. MF of Risk at 90ᵗʰ fractile

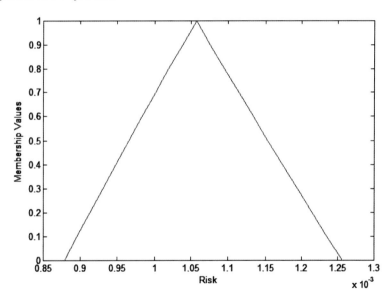

evaluate risk. Here also a collection of cumulative belief and plausibility measures has been obtained. Then, risk value is evaluated at different fractiles and obtained in the form of GFNs.

For example, in this scenario, at 95ᵗʰ fractile, risk is the GFN [9.0822e-004, 1.1208e-003, 1.2632e-003, 1.5781e-003; 0.7], and risk at 90ᵗʰ fractile is the GFN [7.6849e-004, 9.8082e-004, 1.1402e-003, 1.4654e-003; 0.7]. These are depicted in Figure 11 and 12 respectively.

For the second scenario a detailed evaluation of results obtained at different fractiles by using algorithm-I is depicted in Table 12.

Table 11. Fractiles of risk value of the resultant FNs

Fractiles	Core Value	Range
95th	1.1888e-03	[1.0380e-03, 1.3526e-03]
90th	1.0568e-03	[8.7828e-04, 1.2560e-03]
80h	1.0158e-03	[8.5239e-04, 1.2162e-03]
70th	1.0014e-03	[8.3813e-04, 1.1928e-03]
60th	7.9381e-04	[4.6251e-04, 1.14918-03]
50th	7.9379e-04	[4.6250e-04, 1.14915-03]
40th	7.4948e-04	[4.4891e-04, 1.09576-03]
30th	5.4786e-04	[2.7195e-04, 8.3821e-04]
20th	5.2782e-04	[2.7082e-04, 8.0928e-04]
10th	2.2371e-04	[8.324e-05, 4.48491e-04]

Figure 11. MF of Risk at 95th fractile

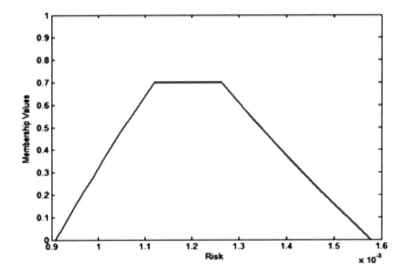

CONCLUSION

DST and FST are imperative Mathematical apparatus of uncertainty modelling when basically *epistemic uncertainty* is present in the problem under consideration. In the absence of experiential data, specialists in allied areas offer essential information and same are construed in terms of FNs and DSS. The foremost contribution of this manuscript is to establish an amalgamate technique to accomplish human health risk assessment. The motive for preferring DSS and FNs for the reason that of their capability to tackle imprecision, uncertainty and vagueness in their own crazing which are generally involved in health risk assessment models. For this purpose, a novel technique has been devised and that was supported by two algorithms. A case study has been performed via two scenarios. In scenario 1, depiction of the uncertain input model parameter *Concentration (C)* is DSS with generalized fuzzy focal elements, besides depic-

Figure 12. MF of Risk at 90th fractile

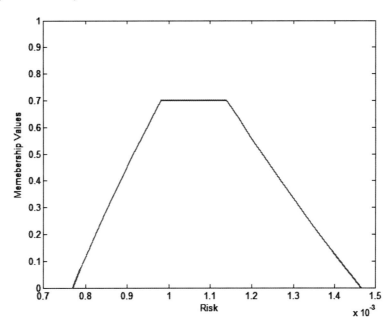

Table 12. Fractiles of risk value of the resultant GFNs

Fractiles	Height	Core Value	Range
95th	0.7	[1.1208e-03, 1.2632e-03]	[9.0822e-04, 1.5781e-03]
90th	0.7	[9.8082e-04, 1.1402e-03]	[7.6849e-04, 1.4654e-03]
80h	0.7	[9.4972e-04, 1.2416e-03]	[7.4172e-04, 1.4193e-03]
70th	0.7	[6.9271e-04, 9.1853e-04]	[4.1813e-04, 1.388e-03]
60th	0.7	[6.8251e-04, 9.0012e-04]	[3.9682e-04, 1.3291e-03]
50th	0.7	[6.8251e-04, 9.0001e-04]	[3.9678e-04, 1.3290e-03]
40th	0.7	[6.7581e-04, 8.4968e-04]	[3.8831e-04, 1.2931e-03]
30th	0.7	[4.4782e-04, 5.9531e-04]	[2.1693e-04, 9.7384e-04]
20th	0.7	[4.4775e-04, 5.9529-04]	[2.7080e-04, 8.0923e-04]
10th	0.7	[2.009e-05, 2.5872e-04]	[7.1932e-05, 5.0093e-04]

tion of the uncertain input model parameter *Exposure frequency* (*EF*) is also DSS with normal fuzzy focal elements. On the other hand, depiction of *Body weight* (*BW*) and *cancer slope factor* (*CSF*) are normal and GFN respectively. Other parameters are taken as deterministic. In scenario 2, depiction of the uncertain input model component *Concentration* (*C*) is DSS with generalized fuzzy focal elements while depiction of the uncertain model components *Exposure frequency* (*EF*) is also DSS with normal fuzzy focal elements. On the other hand, depiction of *Body weight* (*BW*) and *cancer slope factor* (*CSF*) are normal FN and GFN respectively and other parameters are chosen as deterministic.

The MFs of risk at different fractiles are FNs as the focal elements are taken as FNs. MFs of risks are construed as the risk being around the most likely value. It provides significant information to the analyst also. MF indicates the possibility of happening of risk values having zero membership values for a certain fractile are zero, while the risk value with a membership value of one is the most likely risk. The support of the MF of risk presents the feasible assortments of the risk at the corresponding fractile. On the other hand, the shape also presents additional information about the resulting uncertainty.

In brief the foremost strength of this study can be pointed as the proposed approach has the capability to characterize imprecision, uncertainty of human health risk assessment model in its own crazing, it can be applied for extensive assortment of perilous substances, it is a researchers' affable apparatus to comprehend, less extra exertion necessitated etc.

The opportunities of this study can be pointed out as it provides support to scientists, environmentalists, specialists to accomplish health risk assessment providing enhanced efficiency to the yield, individuals live in the neighbourhood of industries, nuclear power plant *etc.* from where emission exposed will be benefited, even though this swot up is carried out in health risk assessment model, but it can be successfully applied where model components are tainted with *epistemic uncertainty*, all uncertainty modelling commune of researchers can espouse these techniques, software module can be prepared for such types of study *etc.*

FUTURE RESEARCH DIRECTIONS

As uncertainty is an integral part of risk assessment process and it is generally characterized by triangular/trapezoidal FNs. It is also observed that focal elements of DSS are always considered as TFNs but there is no evidences of taking bell shaped fuzzy Numbers (BFNs), because it creates the risk assessment process more complicated. Similarly, representation of other uncertain model parameters may be of BFNs numbers with different types based on gathered information or data set. Hence, as an extension of this work, an effort will be made to combine DSS with fuzzy focal elements of different types and FNs of various types and shapes within the same framework.

Furthermore, existence of different types of uncertainties leads to imprecise fuzzy set MFs and as a result ordinary FST is inappropriate to model such types of uncertainties. IVFS and type-II fuzzy sets are competent to model uncertainties. Therefore, as an extension of this work IVFSs and type-II fuzzy sets of different types and shapes will be studied through DSS.

Finally a detail of (strength-weakness-opportunity-threat) SWOT analysis will be made for these types of studies.

REFERENCES

Abdo, H., & Flaus, J. M. (2016). Uncertainty quantification in dynamic system risk assessment: A new approach with randomness and fuzzy theory. *International Journal of Production Research*, *54*(19), 5862–5885. doi:10.1080/00207543.2016.1184348

Alguliyev, R., & Abdullayeva, F. (2015). Development of Fuzzy Risk Calculation Method for a Dynamic Federation of Clouds. *Intelligent Information Management*, *7*(04), 230–241. doi:10.4236/iim.2015.74018

Alyami, H., Yang, Z., Riahi, R., Bonsall, S., & Wang, J. (2016). Advanced uncertainty modelling for container port risk analysis. *Accident; Analysis and Prevention.* doi:10.1016/j.aap.2016.08.007 PMID:27530609

Anoop, M. B., Rao, K. B., & Lakshmanan, N. (2008). Safety assessment of austenitic steel nuclear power plant pipelines against stress corrosion cracking in the presence of hybrid uncertainties. *International Journal of Pressure Vessels and Piping, 85*(4), 238–247. doi:10.1016/j.ijpvp.2007.09.001

Arunraj, N. S., Mandal, S., & Maiti, J. (2013). Modeling uncertainty in risk assessment: An integrated approach with fuzzy set theory and Monte Carlo simulation. *Accident; Analysis and Prevention, 55*, 242–255. doi:10.1016/j.aap.2013.03.007 PMID:23567215

Baraldi, P., & Zio, E. (2008). A combined Monte Carlo and possibilistic approach to uncertainty propagation in event tree analysis. *Risk Analysis, 28*(5), 1309–1326. doi:10.1111/j.1539-6924.2008.01085.x PMID:18631304

Baudrit, C., & Dubois, D. (2006). Practical representations of incomplete probabilistic knowledge. *Computational Statistics & Data Analysis, 51*(1), 86–108. doi:10.1016/j.csda.2006.02.009

Baudrit, C., Dubois, D., & Guyonnet, D. (2006). Joint propagation and exploitation of probabilistic and possibilistic information in risk assessment. *IEEE Transactions on Fuzzy Systems, 14*(5), 593–608. doi:10.1109/TFUZZ.2006.876720

Baudrit, C., Dubois, D., & Perrot, N. (2008). Representing parametric probabilistic models tainted with imprecision. *Fuzzy Sets and Systems, 159*(15), 1913–1928. doi:10.1016/j.fss.2008.02.013

Bauer, M. (1997). Approximation algorithms and decision making in the Dempster-Shafer theory of evidence—An empirical study. *International Journal of Approximate Reasoning, 17*(2-3), 217–237. doi:10.1016/S0888-613X(97)00013-3

Beynon, M. (2002). DS/AHP method: A mathematical analysis, including an understanding of uncertainty. *European Journal of Operational Research, 140*(1), 148–164. doi:10.1016/S0377-2217(01)00230-2

Beynon, M., Cosker, D., & Marshall, D. (2001). An expert system for multi-criteria decision making using Dempster Shafer theory. *Expert Systems with Applications, 20*(4), 357–367. doi:10.1016/S0957-4174(01)00020-3

Beynon, M., Curry, B., & Morgan, P. (2000). The Dempster–Shafer theory of evidence: An alternative approach to multicriteria decision modelling. *Omega, 28*(1), 37–50. doi:10.1016/S0305-0483(99)00033-X

Beynon, M. J. (2005). A method of aggregation in DS/AHP for group decision-making with the non-equivalent importance of individuals in the group. *Computers & Operations Research, 32*(7), 1881–1896. doi:10.1016/j.cor.2003.12.004

Buchanan, S., Huang, J., & Triantafilis, J. (2017). Salinity risk assessment using fuzzy multiple criteria evaluation. *Soil Use and Management, 33*(2), 216–232. doi:10.1111um.12301

Chen, S. H. (1985). Operations on fuzzy numbers with function principal. *Tamkang Journal of Management Sciences, 6*(1), 13–25.

Chen, S. H. (1999). Ranking generalized fuzzy number with graded mean integration. *Proceeding 8th International Fuzzy Systems Association World Congress, 2*, 899-902.

Chen, Z., Zhao, L., & Lee, K. (2010). Environmental risk assessment of offshore produced water discharges using a hybrid fuzzy-stochastic modeling approach. *Environmental Modelling & Software, 25*(6), 782–792. doi:10.1016/j.envsoft.2010.01.001

Deng, X., & Jiang, W. (2017). Fuzzy risk evaluation in failure mode and effects analysis using a D numbers based multi-sensor information fusion method. *Sensors (Basel), 17*(9), 2086. doi:10.339017092086 PMID:28895905

Deng, Y., & Chan, F. T. S. (2011). A new fuzzy Dempster MCDM method and its application in supplier selection. *Expert Systems with Applications, 38*(8), 9854–9861. doi:10.1016/j.eswa.2011.02.017

Dutta, P. (2011). Arithmetic operations of fuzzy focal elements in evidence theory. *International Journal of Latest Trends in Computing, 2*(4).

Dutta, P. (2015). Uncertainty modeling in risk assessment based on Dempster–Shafer theory of evidence with generalized fuzzy focal elements. *Fuzzy Information and Engineering, 7*(1), 15–30. doi:10.1016/j.fiae.2015.03.002

Dutta, P. (2016). Comparison of arithmetic operations of generalized fuzzy numbers: Case study in risk assessment. *Cybernetics and Systems, 47*(4), 290–320. doi:10.1080/01969722.2016.1182354

Dutta, P. (2016). Dempster shafer structure-Fuzzy number based uncertainty modeling in human health risk assessment. *International Journal of Fuzzy System Applications, 5*(2), 96–117. doi:10.4018/IJFSA.2016040107

Dutta, P. (2017). Modeling of variability and uncertainty in human health risk assessment. *MethodsX, 4*, 76–85. doi:10.1016/j.mex.2017.01.005 PMID:28239562

Dutta, P., & Ali, T. (2011). Fuzzy focal elements in dempster-shafer theory of evidence: Case study in risk analysis. *International Journal of Computers and Applications, 34*, 46–53.

Dutta, P., Boruah, H., & Ali, T. (2011a). Fuzzy arithmetic with and without using α -cut method: A comparative study. *International Journal of Latest Trends in Computing, 2*(1), 99–108.

Elshazly, H. I., Azar, A. T., Hassanien, A. E., & Elkorany, A. M. (2013). Hybrid system based on rough sets and genetic algorithms for medical data classifications. *International Journal of Fuzzy System Applications, 3*(4), 31–46. doi:10.4018/ijfsa.2013100103

Faquir, S., Yahyaouy, A., Tairi, H., & Sabor, J. (2017). Implementing a fuzzy logic based algorithm to predict solar and wind energies in a hybrid renewable energy system. In Renewable and Alternative Energy: Concepts, Methodologies, Tools, and Applications (pp. 1220-1235). IGI Global. doi:10.4018/978-1-5225-1671-2.ch040

Farakos, S. M. S., Pouillot, R., Anderson, N., Johnson, R., Son, I., & Van Doren, J. (2016). Modeling the survival kinetics of Salmonella in tree nuts for use in risk assessment. *International Journal of Food Microbiology, 227*, 41–50. doi:10.1016/j.ijfoodmicro.2016.03.014 PMID:27062527

Farakos, S. S., Frank, J. F., & Schaffner, D. W. (2013). Modeling the influence of temperature, water activity and water mobility on the persistence of Salmonella in low-moisture foods. *International Journal of Food Microbiology*, *166*(2), 280–293. doi:10.1016/j.ijfoodmicro.2013.07.007 PMID:23973840

Farakos, S. S. M., Schaffner, D. W., & Frank, J. F. (2014). Predicting survival of Salmonella in low–water activity foods: An analysis of literature data. *Journal of Food Protection*, *77*(9), 1448–1461. doi:10.4315/0362-028X.JFP-14-013 PMID:25198835

Flage, R., Baraldi, P., Zio, E., & Aven, T. (2010, September). Possibility-probability transformation in comparing different approaches to the treatment of epistemic uncertainties in a fault tree analysis. In Reliability, Risk and Safety-Proceedings of the European Safety and Reliability (ESREL) 2010 Conference, Rhodes, Greece (pp. 5-9). Academic Press.

Flage, R., Baraldi, P., Zio, E., & Aven, T. (2013). Probabilistic and possibilistic treatment of epistemic uncertainties in fault tree analysis. *Risk Analysis*, *33*(1), 121–133. doi:10.1111/j.1539-6924.2012.01873.x PMID:22831561

Gündüz, G., Yaman, Ç., Peker, A. U., & Acarman, T. (2017, June). Driving pattern fusion using dempster-shafer theory for fuzzy driving risk level assessment. In *Intelligent Vehicles Symposium (IV)*, 2017 IEEE (pp. 595-599). IEEE. 10.1109/IVS.2017.7995783

Guyonnet, D., Bourgine, B., Dubois, D., & Fargier, H., Coⱪ me, B., & Chilès, J. P. (2003). Hybrid approach for addressing uncertainty in risk assessments. *Journal of Environmental Engineering*, *129*(1), 68–78. doi:10.1061/(ASCE)0733-9372(2003)129:1(68)

Guyonnet, D., Côme, B., Perrochet, P., & Parriaux, A. (1999). Comparing two methods for addressing uncertainty in risk assessments. *Journal of Environmental Engineering*, *125*(7), 660–666. doi:10.1061/(ASCE)0733-9372(1999)125:7(660)

Helton, J. C., Oberkampf, W. L., & Johnson, J. D. (2005). Competing failure risk analysis using evidence theory. *Risk Analysis*, *25*(4), 973–995. doi:10.1111/j.1539-6924.2005.00644.x PMID:16268945

Innal, F., Chebila, M., & Dutuit, Y. (2016). Uncertainty handling in safety instrumented systems according to IEC 61508 and new proposal based on coupling Monte Carlo analysis and fuzzy sets. *Journal of Loss Prevention in the Process Industries*, *44*, 503–514. doi:10.1016/j.jlp.2016.07.028

Jiang, C., Zheng, J., & Han, X. (2017). Probability-interval hybrid uncertainty analysis for structures with both aleatory and epistemic uncertainties: A review. *Structural and Multidisciplinary Optimization*, 1–18.

Jie, Y., Wang, W., Bai, X., & Li, Y. (2016, October). Uncertainty analysis based on probability bounds in probabilistic risk assessment of high microgravity science experiment system. In *Reliability, Maintainability and Safety (ICRMS), 2016 11th International Conference on* (pp. 1-6). IEEE. 10.1109/ICRMS.2016.8050109

Jothi, G., Inbarani, H. H., & Azar, A. T. (2013). Hybrid Tolerance Rough Set: PSO Based Supervised Feature Selection for Digital Mammogram Images. *International Journal of Fuzzy System Applications*, *3*(4), 15–30. doi:10.4018/ijfsa.2013100102

Kentel, E., & Aral, M. M. (2004). Probabilistic-fuzzy health risk modeling. *Stochastic Environmental Research and Risk Assessment*, *18*(5), 324–338. doi:10.100700477-004-0187-3

Kharola, A. (2017). Design of a hybrid adaptive neuro fuzzy inference system (ANFIS) controller for position and angle control of inverted pendulum (IP) systems. *Fuzzy Systems: Concepts, Methodologies, Tools, and Applications: Concepts, Methodologies, Tools, and Applications*, 308.

Khatibi, V., & Montazer, G. A. (2009, October). Coronary heart disease risk assessment using dempster-shafer theory. In *Computer Conference, 2009. CSICC 2009. 14th International CSI* (pp. 361-366). IEEE. 10.1109/CSICC.2009.5349607

Kronprasert, N., & Thipnee, N. (2016, September). Use of Evidence Theory in Fault Tree Analysis for Road Safety Inspection. In *International Conference on Belief Functions* (pp. 84-93). Springer International Publishing. 10.1007/978-3-319-45559-4_9

Kuchta, D., & Ptaszyńska, E. (2017, July). Fuzzy based risk register for construction project risk assessment. In AIP Conference Proceedings: Vol. 1863. *No. 1* (p. 230006). AIP Publishing. doi:10.1063/1.4992391

Leung, Y., Li, R., & Ji, N. (2017). Application of extended Dempster–Shafer theory of evidence in accident probability estimation for dangerous goods transportation. *Journal of Geographical Systems*, 1–23.

Limbourg, P., & De Rocquigny, E. (2010). Uncertainty analysis using evidence theory–confronting level-1 and level-2 approaches with data availability and computational constraints. *Reliability Engineering & System Safety*, *95*(5), 550–564. doi:10.1016/j.ress.2010.01.005

Liu, H., Deng, X., & Jiang, W. (2017). Risk Evaluation in Failure Mode and Effects Analysis Using Fuzzy Measure and Fuzzy Integral. *Symmetry*, *9*(8), 162. doi:10.3390ym9080162

Liu, J., Li, Y., Huang, G., Fu, H., Zhang, J., & Cheng, G. (2017). Identification of water quality management policy of watershed system with multiple uncertain interactions using a multi-level-factorial risk-inference-based possibilistic-probabilistic programming approach. *Environmental Science and Pollution Research International*, 1–21. doi:10.100711356-017-9106-2 PMID:28488149

Mercier, D., Cron, G., Denoeux, T., & Masson, M. H. (2007). Postal decision fusion based on the transferable belief model. *Traitement Du Signal*, *24*(2), 133–151.

Mezaal, M. R., Pradhan, B., Shafri, H. Z. M., & Yusoff, Z. M. (2017). Automatic landslide detection using Dempster–Shafer theory from LiDAR-derived data and orthophotos. *Geomatics, Natural Hazards & Risk*, *8*(2), 1935–1954. doi:10.1080/19475705.2017.1401013

Mofarrah, A., & Hussain, T. (2010). Modeling for uncertainty assessment in human health risk quantification: A fuzzy based approach. *International congress on environmental modeling and soft modeling for environment's sake*.

Nadiri, A. A., Gharekhani, M., Khatibi, R., & Moghaddam, A. A. (2017). Assessment of groundwater vulnerability using supervised committee to combine fuzzy logic models. *Environmental Science and Pollution Research International*, *24*(9), 8562–8577. doi:10.100711356-017-8489-4 PMID:28194673

National Radiation Laboratory. (n.d.). *Radiation in the environment*. Retrieved from www.nrlmoh.govtnz/fq/radiationintheenvironment.asp.

Ng, P. S., & Zhang, F. (2016). An Improved Hybrid Model for Order Quantity Allocation and Supplier Risk Exposure. *International Journal of Fuzzy System Applications*, *5*(3), 120–147. doi:10.4018/IJFSA.2016070107

Olawoyin, R. (2017). Risk and reliability evaluation of gas connector systems using fuzzy theory and expert elicitation. *Cogent Engineering*, *4*(1), 1372731. doi:10.1080/23311916.2017.1372731

Pamučar, D. S., Božanić, D., & Komazec, N. (2017). Risk assessment of natural disasters using fuzzy logic system of type 2. *Management: Journal of Sustainable Business and Management Solutions in Emerging Economies*, *21*(80), 23–34.

Pastoor, T. P., Bachman, A. N., Bell, D. R., Cohen, S. M., Dellarco, M., Dewhurst, I. C., ... Moretto, A. (2014). A 21st century roadmap for human health risk assessment. *Critical Reviews in Toxicology*, *44*(sup3), 1-5.

Pedroni, N., Zio, E., Ferrario, E., Pasanisi, A., & Couplet, M. (2012, June). Propagation of aleatory and epistemic uncertainties in the model for the design of a flood protection dike. In PSAM 11 & ESREL 2012 (pp. 1-10). Academic Press.

Pedroni, N., Zio, E., Ferrario, E., Pasanisi, A., & Couplet, M. (2013). Hierarchical propagation of probabilistic and non-probabilistic uncertainty in the parameters of a risk model. *Computers & Structures*, *126*, 199–213. doi:10.1016/j.compstruc.2013.02.003

Qi, X., & Cheng, Q. (2017). Imprecise reliability assessment of generating systems involving interval probability. *IET Generation, Transmission & Distribution*, *11*(17), 4332–4337. doi:10.1049/iet-gtd.2017.0874

Rębiasz, B., Gaweł, B., & Skalna, I. (2017). Joint Treatment of Imprecision and Randomness in the Appraisal of the Effectiveness and Risk of Investment Projects. In *Information Systems Architecture and Technology: Proceedings of 37th International Conference on Information Systems Architecture and Technology–ISAT 2016–Part IV* (pp. 21-31). Springer International Publishing. 10.1007/978-3-319-46592-0_2

Sahu, A. K., Sahu, N. K., & Sahu, A. K. (2015). Benchmarking CNC Machine Tool Using Hybrid-Fuzzy Methodology: A Multi-Indices Decision Making (MCDM) Approach. *International Journal of Fuzzy System Applications*, *4*(2), 28–46. doi:10.4018/IJFSA.2015040103

Shafer, G. (1976). *A Mathematical Theory of Evidence*. Princeton University Press.

Silva, A. V., Neto, S. A. D., & de Sousa Filho, F. D. A. (2016). A Simplified Method for Risk Assessment in Slope Stability Analysis of Earth Dams Using Fuzzy Numbers. *The Electronic Journal of Geotechnical Engineering*, *21*(10), 3607–3624.

Srivastava, R. P., & Liu, L. (2003). Applications of belief functions in business decisions: A review. *Information Systems Frontiers*, *5*(4), 359–378. doi:10.1023/B:ISFI.0000005651.93751.4b

Straszecka, E. (2003). An interpretation of focal elements as fuzzy sets. *International Journal of Intelligent Systems*, *18*(7), 821–835. doi:10.1002/int.10118

Straszecka, E. (2006a). A Model of a Diagnostic Rule in the Dempster-Shafer Theory. *ICAISC, 8th international conference on Artificial intelligence and soft computing.*

Straszecka, E. (2006b). Combining uncertainty and imprecision in models of medical diagnosis. *Information Sciences*, *176*(20), 3026–3059. doi:10.1016/j.ins.2005.12.006

Subramanian, T., & Savarimuthu, N. (2016). Cloud Service Evaluation and Selection Using Fuzzy Hybrid MCDM Approach in Marketplace. *International Journal of Fuzzy System Applications*, *5*(2), 118–153. doi:10.4018/IJFSA.2016040108

Wessiani, N. A., & Sarwoko, S. O. (2015). Risk analysis of poultry feed production using fuzzy FMEA. *Procedia Manufacturing*, *4*, 270–281. doi:10.1016/j.promfg.2015.11.041

Wu, D. D. (2009). Supplier selection in a fuzzy group setting: A method using grey related analysis and Dempster–Shafer theory. *Expert Systems with Applications*, *36*(5), 8892–8899. doi:10.1016/j.eswa.2008.11.010

Xu, P., Deng, Y., Xu, J., & Su, X. (2010, June). Risk analysis of system security based on evidence theory. In *Computer Design and Applications (ICCDA), 2010 International Conference on* (Vol. 5, pp. V5-610). IEEE.

Yager, R. R. (2008). A knowledge-based approach to adversarial decision making. *International Journal of Intelligent Systems*, *23*(1), 1–21. doi:10.1002/int.20254

Yang, J., Huang, H. Z., He, L. P., Zhu, S. P., & Wen, D. (2011). Risk evaluation in failure mode and effects analysis of aircraft turbine rotor blades using Dempster–Shafer evidence theory under uncertainty. *Engineering Failure Analysis*, *18*(8), 2084–2092. doi:10.1016/j.engfailanal.2011.06.014

Yang, J. B., & Sen, P. (1997). Multiple attribute design evaluation of complex engineering products using the evidential reasoning approach. *Journal of Engineering Design*, *8*(3), 211–230. doi:10.1080/09544829708907962

Yang, J. B., & Xu, D. L. (2002). On the evidential reasoning algorithm for multiple attribute decision analysis under uncertainty. *IEEE Transactions on Systems, Man, and Cybernetics. Part A, Systems and Humans*, *32*(3), 289–304. doi:10.1109/TSMCA.2002.802746

Zadeh, L. A. (1965). Information and control. *Fuzzy Sets, 8*(3), 338-353.

Zararsız, Z. (2015). Similarity measures of sequence of fuzzy numbers and fuzzy risk analysis. *Advances in Mathematical Physics*. http://dx.doi.org/10.1155/2015/724647.

Zhang, D., Han, J., Song, J., & Yuan, L. (2016, October). A risk assessment approach based on fuzzy 3D risk matrix for network device. In *Computer and Communications (ICCC), 2016 2nd IEEE International Conference on* (pp. 1106-1110). IEEE.

Zhang, Q., Zhou, C., Tian, Y. C., Xiong, N., Qin, Y., & Hu, B. (2017). A Fuzzy Probability Bayesian Network Approach for Dynamic Cybersecurity Risk Assessment in Industrial Control Systems. *IEEE Transactions on Industrial Informatics*.

Zhang, X., Sun, M., Wang, N., Huo, Z., & Huang, G. (2016). Risk assessment of shallow groundwater contamination under irrigation and fertilization conditions. *Environmental Earth Sciences*, *75*(7), 603. doi:10.100712665-016-5379-x

Zhou, D., Tang, Y., & Jiang, W. (2017). An improved belief entropy and its application in decision-making. *Complexity*.

Zwietering, M. H. (2015). Risk assessment and risk management for safe foods: Assessment needs inclusion of variability and uncertainty, management needs discrete decisions. *International Journal of Food Microbiology*, *213*, 118–123. doi:10.1016/j.ijfoodmicro.2015.03.032 PMID:25890788

Chapter 16
Enhanced Complex Event Processing Framework for Geriatric Remote Healthcare

V. Vaidehi
VIT University, India

C. Sweetlin Hemalatha
VIT University, India

Ravi Pathak
Striim Inc., India

A. Annis Fathima
VIT University, India

Renta Chintala Bhargavi
VIT University Chennai, India

P. T. V. Bhuvaneswari
Madras Institute of Technology, India & Anna University, India

Kirupa Ganapathy
Saveetha University, India

Sibi Chakkaravarthy S.
Madras Institute of Technology, India & Anna University, India

Xavier Fernando
Ryerson University, Canada

ABSTRACT

Advances in information and communication technology (ICT) have paved way for improved healthcare and facilitates remote health monitoring. Geriatric remote health monitoring system (GRHMS) uses WBAN (wireless body area network) which provides flexibility and mobility for the patients. GRHMS uses complex event processing (CEP) to detect the abnormality in patient's health condition, formulate contexts based on spatiotemporal relations between vital parameters, learn rules dynamically, and generate alerts in real time. Even though CEP is powerful in detecting abnormal events, its capability is limited due to uncertain incoming events, static rule base, and scalability problem. To address the above challenges, this chapter proposes an enhanced CEP (eCEP) which encompasses augmented CEP (a-CEP), a statistical event refinement model to minimize the error due to uncertainty, dynamic CEP (DCEP) to add and delete rules dynamically into the rule base and scalable CEP (SCEP) to address scalability problem. Experimental results show that the proposed framework has better accuracy in decision making.

DOI: 10.4018/978-1-5225-5396-0.ch016

1. INTRODUCTION

Monitoring the health condition of elderly people and sharing the information with remote health care providers or hospitals is of great demand with increasing population of senior citizens choosing to live independently. A number of physiological sensors can be integrated into a wearable Wireless Body Area Network (WBAN), which can be used for computer-assisted rehabilitation or early detection of medical conditions (Pantelopoulos et al., 2010; Patel et al., 2012). The use of wireless sensors within a body area network makes continuous health monitoring seamless and easy.

Full utilization of WBAN occurs only when the events of interest are detected and respective action is taken in minimum time. Some of the challenges in developing a GRHMS are:

1. The number of sensed events is high as every sensor observation generates an event.
2. The latency in detecting an abnormal event should be as small as possible to allow appropriate actions to be taken during emergency.

This relies on the feasibility of placing very small biosensors on the human body that are comfortable and do not impair the regular activities of the patient. These sensors worn on the human body collect various physiological changes in order to monitor the health status of a person irrespective of their location. The collected health information is transmitted wirelessly in real time to the doctor. If any emergency is detected, then the physician is immediately informed about the patient's status by sending appropriate alert message.

Vital sign monitoring plays an important role in detecting abnormalities in physiological parameters such as heart rate, respiration rate, blood pressure etc. Besides vital parameters, the activity of the patient is required to be monitored as it acts as context information to decide the health condition of the patient. Fall of an elderly person is of major concern in healthcare application as most of the unexpected and unpredictable falls leads to death and critical conditions. Hence, early detection of fall activity is required to treat such patients on time. Human activity recognition enables detection of sudden fall of the elderly person.

The vital parameters are highly correlated as any change in the health condition of a patient relates change in other two physiological parameters. Therefore, abnormality detection algorithms that identify the abnormal patterns need to be false proof. CEP based GRHMS proves to be very efficient (Vaidehi et al., 2012; Sanjana et al., 2013; Bhargavi et al., 2013; Ravi Pathak et al., 2015). The earlier work on CEP based IRHMS is extended and integrated in the proposed eCEP.

A data stream is a sequence of data generated continuously by a source (i.e., Sensor(s)). There are several challenges in collecting and processing these data streams as they are continuous and unbounded. Moreover, timely detection of interesting and complex events or patterns and response generation is critical and it depends upon the application. Traditional data processing paradigm does not fully meet the requirements such as response time, memory and throughput.

Most of the existing CEP systems are based on event driven architecture and use stream processing engines and database system to support continuous querying, pattern recognition and response generation in real time. Esper and Drools are a few examples of generic CEP engines. Bhargavi and Vaidehi (2013) have proposed the basic framework of CEP for handling the data streams from distributed sources. The existing CEP engines consider the event stream received from the event sources is precise and certain. Also, application developers neglect the issue of uncertainty in the events. Hence, these applications fail to handle various types of uncertainties in the received events and also affect the complex events derived from them (Diao et al., 2009; Wasserkrug, Gal, Etzion & Turchin, 2012). But the issues related to event refinement are more severe in real time streaming data. Moreover, they support initial configuration of rules and occasionally support addition of rules at regular intervals of time using the polling mechanism. However, there are several applications which demand dynamic rule engine to support adaptability. To achieve the objective of low latency and high throughput, the CEP framework must process the data on the fly without a need for memory. Polling the data continuously for checking the conditions of interest or event materialization introduces additional delay. Hence, active systems must avoid polling and use event or data driven processing capability. The system must support a high level query language with built-in stream oriented primitives to filter, merge, aggregate and correlate for complex data transformations. A stream processing system must guarantee predictable and repeatable outcomes for fault tolerance and recovery.

Another requirement is the capability to efficiently store, access and modify state information and combine it with live streaming data. This is to meet the need for frequent switching between stored data and live data for analysis. A proactive architecture which exploits historical data using machine learning for prediction in conjunction with CEP is proposed by Akbar et al. (2017). The proposed architecture combines the power of real-time and historical data processing using CEP and ML, respectively. High availability at all times, despite failures is another important concern for stream processing systems. To achieve better performance, it is important to adapt distributed processing with automatic and transparent distribution across the processors. Stream processing systems should also support multi-threaded operation to take advantage of modern multi-processor or multi core computer architectures. Even on a single-processor machine, multi-threaded operation avoids system blocking for external events. Stream processing system has to be highly-optimized with minimal-overhead execution engine to deliver real-time response for high-volume healthcare applications.

Initially, rule engine or the expert system is preconfigured with all the rules that need to be matched against the input data streams. Once the rules are defined and configured, the system freezes i.e. rules cannot be added/deleted dynamically at run time. But there are several applications in which new rules need to be added to the system after few hours or weeks or months or years of deployment. For example suppose medical diagnosing system like MYCIN is initially configured for identifying cold, cough and fever. At a later point of time, the system may need to identify cases of pneumonia too. There arises the need to add new rules in knowledge base to make the rule engine to identify pneumonia. To overcome the limitation of user based rule specification, Mousheimish et al. (2016) have proposed autoCEP, which learns predictive CEP rules from historical sources based on data mining approach. Automatic rule generation based on sequence clustering and probabilistic graphical modeling is proposed for mining history of domain experts (Lee & Jung, 2017).

This paper also proposes an eCEP framework for RHMS. The web enabled sensor data are processed within enhanced CEP framework to generate alarm in case of any abnormality in the physiological parameters. The events are correlated from prior generated rules in the rule engine. Besides the initial configuration of rules, the proposed framework uses event driven or push based approach for updating the rules dynamically in the CEP system at runtime.

However, the existing CEP needs enhancement in terms of flexibility and scalability. This paper proposes an eCEP framework with DCEP to support dynamic rule addition and SCEP to handle more patients and rules efficiently.

The remaining sections in this paper are organized as follows: Section II discusses the related work in the area of Complex Event Processing. Section III presents the architecture of eCEP framework with DCEP and SCEP for RHMS. Section IV discusses the results of the proposed work. Section V concludes the paper with the scope for future work.

2. RELATED WORK

There are several existing solutions for monitoring activity and health status of a person. In literature, various health monitoring systems (Gatton & Lee, 2010; Huang et al., 2009; Occhiuzzi & Marrocco, 2010) have been modeled, experimented and tested. Nowadays, data mining and soft computing based machine learning approaches are preferably used for anomaly detection, prediction and decision making (Liu et al., 2012; Ye et al., 2012). Figure 1 shows the taxonomy of the classification and prediction algorithms used for decision making.

OGC Sensor Web Enablement (SWE) is used for Taiwan Debris Flow Monitoring System (TDFMS) (Yu et al., 2009). The use of open standards such as OGC takes the system into an interoperable environment.

The popular data driven methods are Support Vector Machines, Neural Networks, Decision Trees, Gaussian Mixture Model, Hidden Markov Model, Rule based Methods, Bayesian Network, Fuzzy classifier, Logistic regression, association rules etc. However, the existing system lacks on accuracy by using complex learning model, which increases the overall system complexity.

Complex Event Processing system based on production rules is very flexible and well integrated with existing programming languages. Business rule management systems like Drools or ILOG JRules (ILOG, y2002) use production rules. The rules are tightly coupled with a host programming language (e.g., Java) and actions to be executed upon entering certain states are specified. Whenever an event occurs, the corresponding fact must be created in the working memory. The states are expressed as conditions on the facts. The incremental evaluation (e.g., with Rete) makes production rules suitable for CEP. However, the production rules have the reputation to be less efficient than data stream query languages.

A logic-based homogenous reaction rule language and event-based middleware called RuleML are proposed by Paschke et al. (2007) which combines technologies from declarative rule-based programming with enterprise application technologies for CEP and SOC. The authors have defined interval-based event algebra with event definition, event selection and event consumption. Also, the authors have proposed a homogenously integrated event messaging reaction rule language, called Prova AA.

This model is further extended, where the general framework for CEP is proposed to handle uncertainty (Wasserkrug et al., 2008). The sources of uncertainty are captured and uncertainty in events and rules are considered for modeling. A Bayesian Network model is constructed with events of interest (Moller et al., 2009). Bayesian network updates itself whenever a new primitive event arrives. In such a model, performance is a concern as the methodology requires partial rebuilding of Bayesian network on introduction of new primitive event and hence the model has significant impact on processing time. Kawashima, Kitagawa and Li (2010) proposed a simple way to solve issue of uncertainty in CEP. The authors proposed a system which works by building a deterministic automaton for each query by developing a matching tree. Branches of the tree below the given threshold are pruned early for optimization purposes. The events are considered as independent and are incorporated with probability. Although throughput values reached hundreds of events per second, but the experiments were done with single query with lower complexity and no shared variables.

Figure 1. Taxonomy of existing classification and prediction algorithms

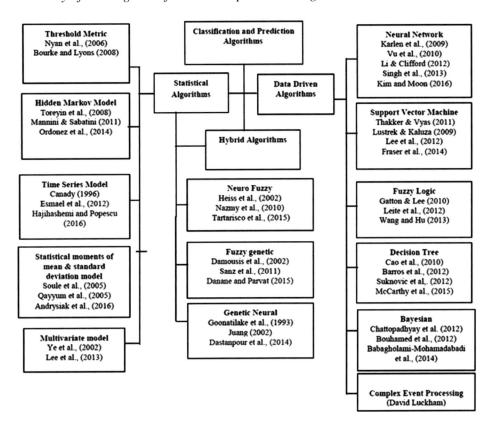

Wang, Cao and Zhang (2013) attempted to address two issues in uncertainty of CEP. The first is the inability to express Complex Event hierarchies in Nondeterministic Finite Automaton based methods, the second is the performance issue. The author has proposed a CEP system which is probabilistic and distributed. The Complex Event recognition depends on another special data structure called Active Instance Stack. A data partitioning methodology is adopted to distribute different part of event to different computing nodes. The local results are later merged to find an overall result. Event hierarchies are constructed by connecting events across different nodes via channels forming an Event Processing Network.

A model and a mechanism are presented by Turchin et al., (2009) for deriving rule parameters automatically. Their model provides one-time parameter derivation mechanism as well as continuous adjustment of parameters using machine learning techniques preferably based on a correct-predict paradigm. The approach follows Kalman estimators which are modified to take into account indirect rather than direct feedback. This model acts as a domain expert providing feedback on the accuracy of event materialization rather than on the parameter values.

Anomaly management using Complex Event Processing is proposed by Hoßbach and Seeger (2013). The authors have discussed the need for a dynamic CEP with several applications. They proposed a framework for CEP infrastructure to support dynamism by incorporating anomaly identification. However, their work does not handle rule management.

Cheung et al. (2010) proposed a load balancing framework for content based publish/ subscribe systems. The load balancing framework used brokers based strategy to balance load between its different resources efficiently. Ma et al. (2014) proposed an event matching framework for attribute based publish subscribe. They used hierarchical multi attribute space partitioning algorithm for event matching. Esposito et al. (2014) proposed automatic schema mapping algorithm for serialization to avoid problems related to data heterogeneity in high volume stream processing applications.

To overcome the challenges in handling data with high velocity with volume and variety, there are some potential works like Scalable Internet Event Notification Architecture (SIENA) (Carzaniga et al., 2001), Distributed Heterogeneous Event Processing (DHEP) (Schilling et al., 2012), High Performance Complex Event Processing (HPCEP) (Wang & Yang 2010) and Scalable Context Delivery Platform (SCTXPF) (Isoyama et al., 2011). SIENA achieved high performance and scalability by utilizing overlay networks. However, SIENA has not considered balancing of event processing loads among different network nodes. DHEP achieved automatic rule deployment, i.e., which event processing rule is to be executed on which engine and on which node in the network. However, it did not consider scalability relative to the number of CEP rules. HPCEP decomposed the processes of CEP and allocates them to multiple CEP processors. It focused on decomposition of a few complicated CEP rules. However, it did not support a large number of CEP rules. The SCTXPF is a scalable CEP and places importance on scalability factors in terms of number of CEP rules and volume of incoming event traffic by proposing Rule allocation algorithm.

To overcome the issues of event allocation with state management, Lakshmanan et al. (2009), Neumeyer et al (2010), and Gulisano et al. (2010) used hash table based technique to distribute events arriving into the system. All the events having same hash value arrive into the same server. Hash function is based on some attributes values in the event.

Event Refinement Model Augmented Complex Event Processing (Ravi Pathak & Vaidehi, 2015) is used to handle the uncertainty in the input event streams. The uncertainty of the incoming event streams is handled by augmenting the events with statistical approaches that refine the events and facilitates better decision making.

An efficient rule balancing for Scalable Complex Event Processing (Ravi Pathak & Vaidehi, 2015) performs state management and efficient rule distribution for design of distributed framework for CEP. This work also proposes a novel way of indexing CEP rules based on Geometric series for better flexibility.

In summary, a CEP framework is needed to address scalability, rule distribution and dynamic rule updation. Hence, to overcome the challenges of scalability due to huge number of events and large number of CEP rules, this paper proposes an eCEP framework consisting of augmented CEP (a-CEP), Scalable CEP (SCEP) and Dynamic CEP (DCEP) for online rule addition and deletion.

3. PROPOSED eCEP FRAMEWORK FOR GERIATRIC REMOTE HEALTHCARE MONITORING SYSTEM

The system architecture of proposed eCEP framework for Geriatric Remote Healthcare Monitoring System (GRHMS) is shown in Figure 2.

Figure 2. Architecture of CEP framework for geriatric remote health monitoring system

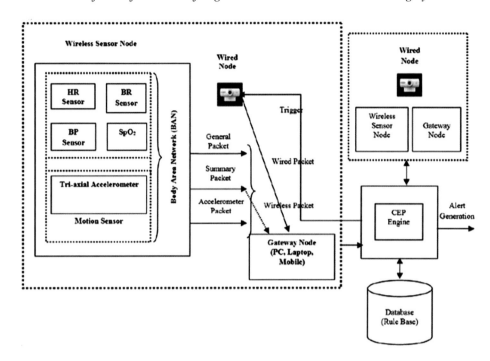

Data generated from Biosensor measuring Heart Rate (HR), Breathing Rate (BR), Blood Pressure (BP) and oxygen saturation level (SPO_2), motion sensors such as tri-axial accelerometer, and wired sensor nodes such as camera reach the gateway node which may be a PC, laptop or mobile phone. The sensors are worn in the body as shown in Figure 3.

Bio sensors give information about vital signs like blood pressure, cardiovascular disorders using HR data and ECG data, percentage of oxygen in blood, respiration rate as number of breaths per minute. The ambiguity in the data is removed using CEP. Accelerometer sensor is used for monitoring the movement and identifying the activity of person at home. Environmental sensor such as image sensor (camera) is

Figure 3. Data collection of Vital Parameters

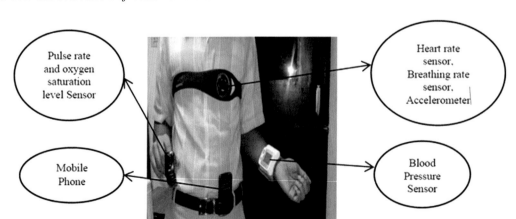

used to detect and confirm human fall event. Accelerometer data, physiological data and environmental data get collected in the sink node which is the PC at home. Activity recognition module in PC processes the accelerometer data and classifies the sensor data as one of normal events such as sitting, standing, lying, walking or as an abnormal event, fall using associative classification (Hemalatha & Vaidehi, 2013).

The Flow diagram of proposed eCEP framework for Geriatric Remote Health Monitoring is shown in Figure 4. The collective data from the sensors reach the central server where the enhanced eCEP framework comprising of Dynamic CEP (DCEP) and Scalable CEP (S-CEP) are running. DCEP has the facility to add or delete rules dynamically. DCEP module processes the physiological data for detecting abnormal patterns using rules. It detects abnormality in vital parameter or identifies the activity pattern as "fall" or both. DCEP uses these values for generating new rules and updating the knowledge base dynamically.

3.1 Sensor Web Enablement

OGC SWE is applicable to different sensor systems including medical sensor networks. The aim is to provide the data in an open & interoperable manner, and reduce data redundancy. Fixed specification is used for exchange of sensor data globally for all sensor networks. A standard format is used to document sensor descriptions and encapsulate data.

The Open Geospatial Consortium's SWE activities are executed through the OGC Web Services (OWS) (OpenGIS Sensor Model Language). OGC solves the interoperability problem, establishes the interfaces and protocols to enable "Sensor Webs" through which applications and services access body

Figure 4. Flow diagram of proposed eCEP framework for geriatric remote health monitoring

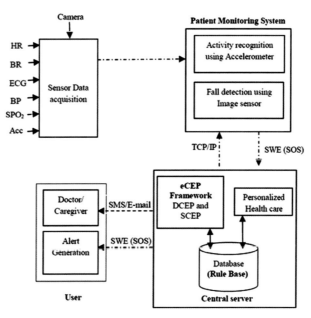

HR – Heart Rate Sensor, BR – Breathing Rate Sensor, ECG – Electrocardiogram sensor

BP - Blood Pressure Sensor, SPO2- Pulse oximeter, Acc – Accelerometer Sensor,
SWE (SOS) – Sensor Web Enablement (Sensor Observation Service)

sensors. These standards can be utilized to wrap and transport medical data in a universally reachable and acceptable manner (Yu et al., 2009).

The four major services provided by SWE are Sensor Observation Service (SOS), Sensor Planning Service (SPS), Web Notification Service (WNS), and Sensor Alert Service (SAS). All sensor data is described in XML format and Simple Object Access protocol (SOAP) is used by each service to provide communication for each service. The description of sensors includes the sensor location, sampling rate, time stamp, sensor id and sensor data. The end user is given the entire information about the sensor availability, observations and measurements as a service. The common traditional model for observation metadata combines unambiguously across heterogeneous environment. In remote healthcare, highly sensitive health data need to be discovered properly for quality data estimation.

Figure 5 shows the O&M document for a single observed value from a respiration sensor with sensor id/procedure and the observed respiration rate of 15 breath/sec.

O&M is used for the transport of observed measurements to client applications. O&M formatted results can be requested by a web client using the GetObservation query. The request is formulated as filter observations by observed phenomenon, time, sensor or location. SOS also presents enhanced operations such as Get Result, Get Feature-Of Interest, Get Feature of Interest Time and Describe Observation Type. Based on the query, the observation response is spatial and temporal information.

Figure 5. XML based O&M encoding format for respiration rate sensor

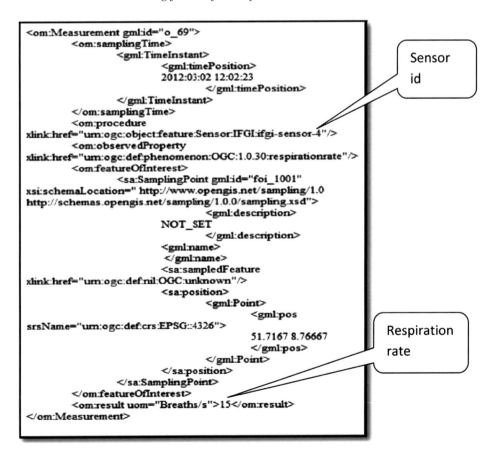

3.2 Augmented CEP for Healthcare Application

Figure 6a and Figure 6b show the design of augmented complex events and basic/primitive events respectively. Precision layer is augmented to the basic and complex events. The precision layer function is to filter imprecise events. Precision layer applies statistical models on overlapping where size of windows of events is predefined. The augmented primitive events refer Figure 6 (b) filter the noise on raw event streams to obtain higher precise values for event processing in event hierarchy. Similarly, augmented complex events takes input from precise augmented primitive events (placed lower in event hierarchy) and transform them to precise complex event. Figure 7 shows Event interaction between 2 levels (level 1 and level 2) of events in event hierarchy of a-CEP. The input of any level 'l' is represented by 'x_{li}'. 'l' is number of level starting from bottom to top in event hierarchy and 'i' is the index of event at particular level 'l' of event hierarchy. Here, 'i' lies between (0 < i < (n,k,m)) where 'n', 'k' and 'm' represent number of events at any level 'l'.

The precision layer of augmented events accumulates the input stream of raw events based on the window size. Figure 8 shows an overlapped sliding window of size 4 inside precision layer. Statistical parameters like median (M) and expectations (E[x]) are determined on windowed streams inside the precision layer for obtaining precise events as output. These precise events are then used for CEP operations like correlation and assertions.

For example, consider one stream of events X= $x_1,x_2,x_3,x_4,x_5,x_6, \cdots,x_n$, where 'n' is the last received event index. For a window of size 'l' (l<n) when event 'n' is received, the event ranges from $x_{(n-l)}$ to x_n {$x_{(n-l)}, x_{(n-l+1)}, x_{(n-l+2)}, \cdots,x_n$}.

Let, E[X] represents the expectation of the events present in window of size 'l'.

$$E[X] = x(n-l)p(n-l) + x(n-l+1)p(n-l+1) + x(n-l+2)p(n-l+2) + \ldots + x(n)p(n)$$

(1)

Figure 6. Augmented events

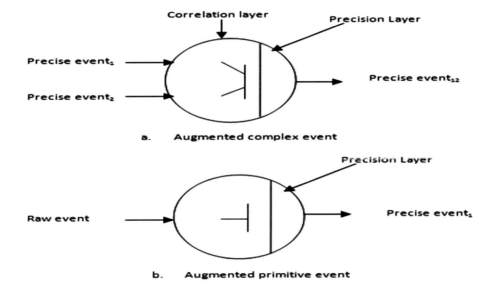

Figure 7. Event Interaction at a level of event hierarchy in a-CEP

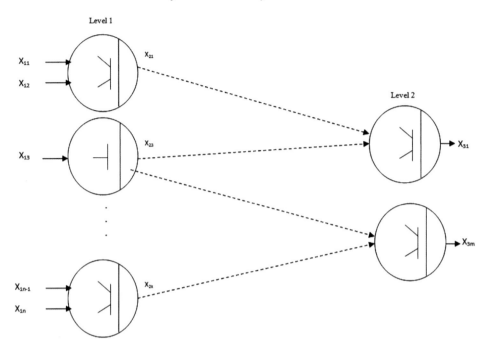

Figure 8. Overlapping of sliding window

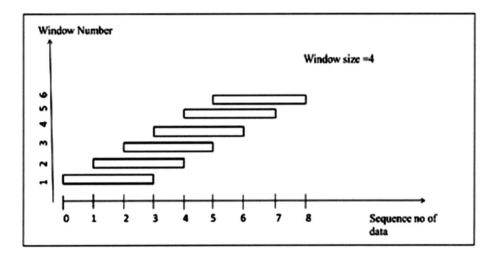

where, 'p(n)' represents probability density function at 'n' in the window (l). Let 'M' represent the median for events that are present in window of size 'l' in sorted order.

$$M = \{ \begin{array}{l} x\left[\dfrac{low+high}{2}\right], \wedge window\ is\ odd \\ \\ \dfrac{x\left[\dfrac{low+high}{2}\right] + x\left[\dfrac{low+high}{2}+1\right]}{2}, \wedge window\ is\ even \end{array} \tag{2}$$

Window size 'l' contains events from $x_{(n-1)}$ to x_n.

Precision layer enables the events to be consistent and keeps check on the number of events entering the CEP and exiting are same. The use of statistical parameters like M, and E[X] reduce the noise from the raw noisy event streams. The derived precise event helps in efficient decision making when it goes higher in event hierarchy.

3.3 Dynamic CEP for Healthcare Application

The CEP engine runs in the central server which processes the raw sensed physiological data and activity data. The general packet specifies the general event structure which contains pat_id, time stamp of occurrence of basic event, sensor name whose sensor value obtained at given time stamp and unit of sensor value measurement.

The summary packet specifies the summary event structure which is similar to the general event structure except it adds few more attributes namely variation, rate, mean value and deviation. The format and example of general event and summary event are shown below:

Example:

(1, 1374677443722, Respiration rate, 7.9, Breaths/sec)
(1, 1374677443722, Heart rate, 72, Beats/min)

Example:

(1, 1374677443722, Heart rate, increasing, 1.2, 69, 2.3)
(1, 1374677443722, Heart rate, decreasing, 1.2, 59, 1.3)

The general packet and summary packet are sent to the forwarding unit where sampling rate is set according to the user requirement. The general and summary packets act as basic events for the CEP module placed in remote server at Hospital. The prototype system uses JBoss Drools as CEP system. Rules are formulated to filter, aggregate and correlate the events in time and space domains to identify the higher and complex events which represent the abnormalities in the health condition of the patients. Every rule has associated action to be executed such as sending SMS to the care giver or doctor or patient. These rules are stored in the rule base or in the knowledgebase. Whenever the events from the sensors or the internally generated events arrive at the engine, all the rules involving those events are executed by the CEP engine for checking the conditions or pattern match corresponding to possible health abnormality.

Figure 9. Basic rule format

```
rule "<rule name>"
when
        <conditional element>
then
        <action>
end
```

On identifying alarming situations like abnormal health condition or fall, the caregiver or doctor is alerted by sending SMS. Figure 9 shows the format of a rule. A rule indicates that *when* a particular set of conditions occur, specified as the "conditional element", *then* do the specified list of actions. These rules work on the streaming events or facts. Each condition in the rule acts as a filter to the event stream and the aggregation of all the conditions leads to identification of the desired complex events.

For the proposed healthcare application, a simple rule that captures the abnormal SPO_2 in blood by filtering out the normal values is shown in Figure 10.

Another rule that filters the normal heart rate data and captures only the abnormal or alarming hear rate of a patient is shown in Figure 11. When the abnormal heart rate is identified, a new event called abnormalHR is created and is fed back to the CEP engine. These abnormalHR events form a new stream called abnormalHR stream. Thus, rules are formulated based on these internally generated streams to create the next higher level events. Similarly rules are formulated to detect the abnormalities in the blood pressure (systolic and diastolic).

The basic events to detect the fall of a person due to abnormal health condition are abnormalHR, abnormalBP, and the activity from the accelerometer. The rule capturing the fall event is given in Figure 12.

If the heart rate or BP or both of a person are found to be abnormal and accelerometer indicates that the activity of the person is "FALL" within a time of 10 minutes, then there is a high probability that the person had a fall and it is alerted to the doctor. At the same time, using the web services, camera in

Figure 10. Rule capturing the abnormality in oxygen saturation level

```
rule "abnormal oxygenSaturation level"
when (curpid = $oxySaturation.pid) (curtime = $ oxySaturation.time)
listSat = accumulate(oxySaturation.value &&  oxySaturation.pid == curpid)
avgSat = avg(listSat)
avgSat < 90
then
sendMsgToDoctor()
end
```

Figure 11. Rule capturing the abnormality in heart rate value

```
rule "abnormal heart rate"
when  (curpid = $HeartRate.pid)    (curtime = $HeartRate.time)
listHR = accumulate(HeartRate.value &&HeartRate.pid == curpid)
                    avgHR = avg(listHR)
                    avgHR< 60 && avgHR >100
then
            insert abnormalHR (curpid, avgHR, curtime)
end
```

Figure 12. Rule capturing the fall event

```
rule "probable fall"
when (curpid = $accelerometer.pid)
(abnormalHRpid == curpid)
&&( abnormalBP.pid == curpid)
&& ($acccelerometer.activity = "fall") over window:
time (10 m)
then
sendMsgToDoctor()
triggerCamera()
end
```

the person's house is triggered to capture the image of the person and it is sent to the doctor to confirm the critical situation.

The system is initially configured with all the rules which define the complex events or patterns to be identified and alerted. These domain experts need to provide the set of basic events which serves as input to the rule, their interrelationships, and the parameters of the events that determine the complex event. However, rules may change over time, due to the dynamic nature of the application.

There are two approaches to dynamically update the rule base at run time without stopping or restarting the system such as:

1. First approach is to poll a resource (directory or URL) at regular intervals of time to check if new rules need to be added, if needed then create new processing agents and add to inference engine and interface them with the corresponding input streams and output listeners.
2. Second approach is event driven approach in which the system gets notified whenever a new rule is to be added and then update the rule base by creating and adding new processing agents to inference engine and interfacing them with the corresponding input streams and output listeners.

The second approach is more efficient than the first approach as the system is notified whenever there is a need to update the rule base rather than polling the resource again and again. Figure 13 shows the proposed dynamic rule engine architecture based on event driven approach (Bhargavi et al., 2013). Following are the functions of the proposed dynamic rule engine components:

- **Expert:** It is a user interface which interacts with experts and Knowledge Engineer to create new rules. Rules are entered in the specific format.
- **Knowledge Source:** Knowledge source is responsible for generating the knowledge update event. This module lies in between Expert and Knowledge Listener.
- **Knowledge Event:** Knowledge Event is an event object instance. Knowledge event triggers the Knowledge Base update.
- **Knowledge Listener:** The Knowledge Base acts like a Knowledge Listener interface. It listens to the Knowledge event, and updates the Knowledge Base. This module uses the rules given by the expert in the Expert Interface and creates a knowledge package instance and adds it to the knowledge Base.

Thus, the rule base is updated dynamically. The steps involved in dynamic rule update are as follows:

Step 1: Enter and submit the new rules to be added in the Expert Interface.
Step 2: Generate Knowledge Event instance which has all the needed information for creating the new rule.
Step 3: Notify Knowledge Listener about the occurrence of Knowledge event.
Step 4: Create knowledge package with the information collected from the Knowledge event.
Step 5: Add the knowledge package to the Knowledge base which is updated with the new rules as added knowledge package.

Figure 13. Proposed dynamic rule engine for DCEP

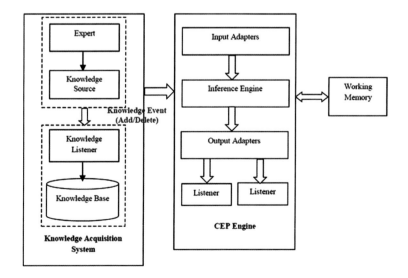

3.3 Scalable CEP for Healthcare Application

Scalable CEP consists of 5 major components: Load Balancer, Event Dispatcher, Event Routing Service (ERS), Context Management Service (CMS) and Complex Event Processors (CEP).

- **Event Dispatchers:** Event Dispatchers are stateless rule engines which perform routing decision of events arriving from publishers.
- **Complex Event Processors:** Event Processors (EP) are state full Complex Event Processing Engines which apply CEP rules on incoming events and keep state of the events updated in their working memory.
- **Event Routing Service (ERS):** ERS is a metadata repository which stores metadata of all the event routing rules mapped with Event Dispatcher identifiers. Event Routing Service is implemented as an In-Memory Cache with hash table as data structure and it provides lookup service for load balancing module to take decision for routing event.
- **Context Management Service (CMS):** Context Management Service is a metadata repository of the entire Context (CEP rules) in the system mapped with subscribers.
- **Load Balancer:** Load Balancer in SCEP is responsible for receiving subscriptions and distributes CEP rules dynamically, based on subscription to EP layer of SCEP.

The steps for adding new subscription in the SCEP are:

1. New subscription arrives at load balancer; Load balancer identifies the CEP rule for subscription.
2. Check if the context of CEP rule is available in CMS. If context is available, add new subscriber to CMS list with the same context.
3. If the context is unavailable then run the rule allocation algorithm.

Figure 14. Rule allocation algorithm

```
Rule Allocation Algorithm
• Given: initialized list of all event processors, EPlist;
• Input: p: Point(x,y)  Context Identifier of new CEP rule
• Input: max: maximum number of rules allowed per EP
• Output: id: Epid for Event Processor in which allocation has to be done

start
    Double sim[]=new double[EPList.size()];
    for(i=0;i<sim.length;i++)
    sim[i] =euclediandistance(p,Eplist[i].getCentroid());
    End for
    Double thresh= (max(sim)+min(sim))/2;
    For (i=0;i<sim.length;i++)
    if(sim[i]<thresh & Eplist[i].getSize()<max) return Eplist[i].getId();
    End for
    Print "Add new resource"
    Return null;
end
```

Load balancing in SCEP basically consists of two parts: distributing CEP rules on Event Processors and writing rules for allocating events from Event Dispatcher to Event Processors. In SCEP rules are allocated based on the Rule allocation algorithm as shown in Figure 14.

- **Event Route Identifier (ERI) Identifier:** CEP rule from its syntax in the antecedent part is composed of patterns. ERI is a 2D point index value depicting a pattern in the CEP rule. It assures that no two similar patterns can have same ERI value. The index ERI is represented as shown in Equation 3:

$$X = (ObjectOf, Id);$$ (3)

"ObjectOf" field in X is assigned the class of the pattern. The class is similar as that of class concept in Object Oriented Language. "Id" is generated from the pattern and it is attribute specific. The uniqueness of "Id" is derived from the property of geometric series up-to infinity given by Equation 2. The value of ith term in the series is always greater than sum of $i+1^{th}$ to ∞ as shown in Equation 5.

$$\frac{1}{2^0} + \frac{1}{2^1} + \frac{1}{2^2} + \frac{1}{2^3} + \ldots + \frac{1}{2^\infty}$$ (4)

$$\frac{1}{2^i} > \sum_{j=i+1}^{\infty} \frac{1}{2^j}$$ (5)

This property of geometric series helps to identify unique index for a given type of pattern.

- **Context Identifier:** The index of complete antecedent part of CEP rule is called Context Identifier (CI). It is a 2D point depicting an antecedent of CEP rule. It assures that no two CEP rules having different patterns can have the same Context Identifier. The index CI is also given by Equation 1. CI is calculated as sum of ERI of all unique patterns available in an antecedent part of rule as given by Equation 6.

$$CI = \sum_{i=1}^{n} ERI_i,$$ (6)

where, value of *i* is the number of patterns in a CEP rule.

4. IMPLEMENTATION DETAILS

The experiment was carried out in a Windows based environment with 4 core Intel-i3 processor and 3GB RAM. Drools Fusion 5.4 software is used as CEP engine (An enhanced implementation of RETE algorithm (Forgy, 1982)), Java7 is used for the development of proposed eCEP framework. Netbeans 7.0

IDE is used for software development and MySQL 5.5 as backend database. The system implementation is divided into two parts as patient side client application and hospital side CEP server application.

The proposed eCEP framework has been evaluated using 7 VMs and 3 PCs. 1PC is used to run the VMs. 2 VMs are assigned as event dispatcher, 5 VMs run the CEP rules. 1 PC is used for event generation and 1PC acts as control server with ERS and CMS. The event generator application sends the records one by one, in the form of events.

4.1 Client Application

A chest worn sensing device (Zephyr-Bioharness) is used to collect the vital parameters which comprises of sensors to measure heart rate, breathing rate and a tri-axial accelerometer for measuring body movements. The sampling rate of the sensors is given in Table 1.

The client application receives and sends only the abnormal data to remote hospital CEP server for processing. Figure 15 shows client app running in patient side indicating the Heart Rate (HR) to be 118 BPM, Respiration Rate (RR) to be 12.8 BPM and Activity to be Normal.

Table 1. Sampling rate of sensors

Sensor	Sampling Rate	Data Rate(ms)
ECG	252 ms/ data packet and 63 data/ Packet	4ms/data
Accelerometer	400ms/data packet 20 data/packet	20 ms/data
Breathing rate	1.008s/data packet 18 data/packet	56ms/data
Heart rate	1.008s/data packet 18 data/packet	56ms/data

Figure 15. Patient side client app

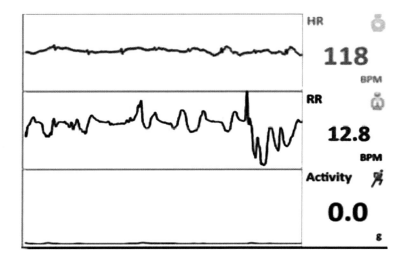

4.2 eCEP Server

Server side system is implemented using java language and JBoss Drools Fusion 5.4.0 (Bali, 2009) CEP Engine. It is open source software for expert system as well as CEP. It provides an integrated platform for modeling rules, events, and processes.

The eCEP server contains a Web server and CEP engine for alert generation. The rules made to identify abnormality are formulated and then implemented using drools rule language. Web server provides authentication control for doctor and caretaker so as to see their patient's related information and activity.

5. RESULTS AND DISCUSSION

The validation of the idea of proposed a-CEP was performed on models constructed by using Ozone Detection Sensor Dataset (https://archive.ics.uci.edu/ml/datasets/Ozone+Level+Detection), Glass Identification Dataset (https://archive.ics.uci.edu/ml/datasets/Glass+Identification) and Activity Identification dataset (http://www.cis.fordham.edu/wisdm/dataset.php). These models are not 100% accurate and hence their accuracy is compared with deterministic approach and the proposed approaches. These dataset are multivariate, numerical attribute with categorical values in class attribute suitable for classification problem.

5.1 Augmented CEP

The proposed a-CEP performance is analysed for varying noise levels. The compared models are:

1. **Deterministic Model:** Deterministic model is a model where no uncertainty handling is considered during Complex Event Identification.
2. **a-CEP Expectation:** A-CEP model is used for uncertainty handling on Complex Event with statistical Expectation is used as model for determining precise events.
3. **a-CEP Median:** A-CEP model is used for uncertainty handling on Complex Event with statistical Median is used as model for determining precise events.
4. **Max Possible Deterministic:** It is the theoretical threshold calculated using equation 3, which determines the maximum accuracy attainable under best event conditions and uncertainty is not handled.

The results are compared with Conventional (Traditional) CEP system and Maximum possible accuracy when % of noise or uncertainty is known, results are presented in Figure 16. For analysis, comparison between traditional CEP and proposed a-CEP with Median and Expectation is performed in terms of classification accuracy for varying noise levels (10%, 20%, and 30%) and event processing time (time when event arrives till it is recognized).

Figure 16 shows the graph of accuracy of decision making with noise in datasets when Complex Event model is not 100% accurate. From the analysis in (Figure 16) Ozone Detection Dataset Figure 16(a), the accuracy of classification for deterministic system (traditional CEP) starts dropping from accuracy of 95% without noise to 65% for 30% noise. The use of proposed precision layer reduces these

Figure 16. a) Noise vs accuracy for ozone detection dataset, b) noise vs accuracy for activity detection dataset, c) noise vs accuracy for glass identification dataset

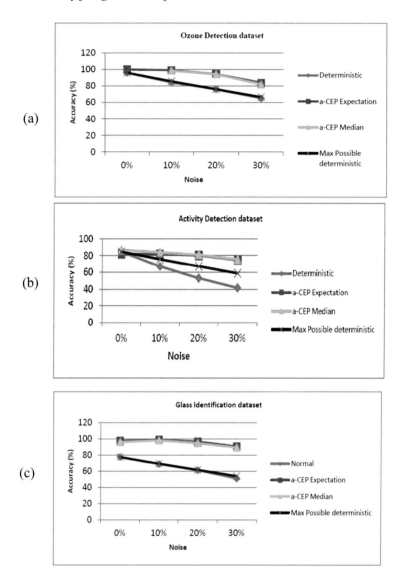

false alarms from 99% accuracy without noise to 83% accuracy with 30% noise. However, the theoretical max possible accuracy with noise in dataset is similar to deterministic CEP accuracies.

For Activity detection dataset in Figure 16(b), for increase in noise from 0% to 30% the accuracy declines from 84% to 41% when CEP was deterministic. The proposed precision layer reduced the false alarms and gives better accuracy ranging from 82% to 74% for 0% and 30% noise respectively.

Glass Identification dataset in Figure 16(c) shows the same trend where the precision layer reduces false events with 96% accuracy for 0% noise and 89% accuracy for 30% noise. The value is fairly higher than deterministic CEP approach which lies in range of 77% to 54% for increasing noise levels.

The usage of Expectation and Median with overlapping sliding window for streams proves to give better accuracy for noisy events thus making CEP model more accurate.

Figure 17 shows the analysis of event processing time of proposed a-CEP. The event processing time of a-CEP is increased due to precision layer. Precision layer which performs statistical models on overlapped window of incoming aw event streams to generate precise events. It can be seen that traditional CEP processes 2567 events in 1000 ms while a-CEP took 2000 ms for same size of events.

Table 2 shows the comparison of accuracy of the Traditional CEP, a-CEP with median and a-CEP with Expectation on varied noise levels of event streams for Remote health monitoring system. From Table 2 the accuracy of basic events for varied level of noise are low. Column HR& AY and BR & AY are complex events their accuracy is higher in comparison to basic events HR, BR and AY. Similarly accuracy increases as hierarchy increases and the accuracy of SK is highest.

The accuracy obtained from a-CEP is better than traditional CEP at 5% and 10% noise levels. Precision layer helps a-CEP to improve accuracy with noise level in event streams. While comparing a-CEP Median (M) and a-CEP Expectation (E[x]), the later performs poorly due to fact that the expectation of

Figure 17. Comparison of event processing time for ozone detection dataset

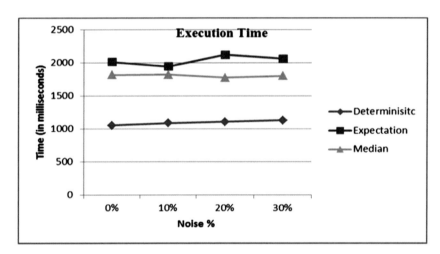

Figure 18. Event processing time for remote health monitoring system

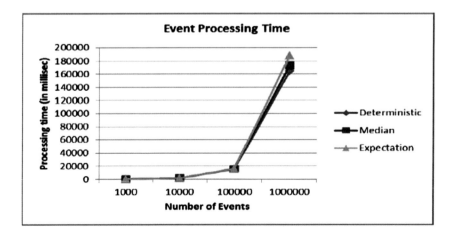

Table 2. Accuracy of the proposed system for GRHMS application

Event Approach	Accuracy																	
	HR			AY			BR			HR & AY			BR & AY			SK		
Noise levels	0%	5%	10%	0%	5%	10%	0%	5%	10%	0%	5%	10%	0%	5%	10%	0%	5%	10%
Traditional CEP	100	95	90	100	95	90	100	95	90	100	97.64	95.22	100	98.3	96.74	100	98.7	97.4
Median based a-CEP	100	99.94	99.92	99.97	99.5	99.2	99.98	99.97	99.93	100	99.97	99.94	100	100	100	**100**	**100**	**100**
Expectation based a-CEP	100	64	55	99.7	82.5	75	99.73	70	55	100	73.5	65.3	99.08	78.2	62.6	100	79.5	69.3

a sample depends on outlier values. If outliers are found in a particular window the accuracy of event identification reduces. However, a-CEP overall accuracy is improved when event hierarchy is increased.

Figure 18 shows Event Processing time of traditional (Deterministic) CEP and proposed a-CEP Median and a-CEP Expectation methods for Remote health monitoring system. Event processing time increases with number of events. It is seen that deterministic CEP is faster compared to a-CEP in Figure 16. Figure 17 shows that with increase in number of events the event processing time for a-CEP comes closer to deterministic CEP time. The event processing time difference between deterministic and proposed a-CEP starts from 1000 events (31%) and slowly reduces for 10 lakh events (13%). Hence, a-CEP outperforms deterministic CEP with better accuracy and competitive event processing time.

The performance of the proposed CEP framework system is tested in real time. The analysis between number of packets arrived and the rule execution time (in milliseconds) is done to compute the average execution time as shown in Figure 19. The average execution time of packets arriving at the server is approximately 131ms for the first 1000 packets and it increases approximately to 600ms when the number of packets increases. Therefore, the proposed framework can identify the abnormality in close to 131ms or 600ms after the events reaches the CEP server.

5.2 Dynamic CEP

The screenshot of the user interface for viewing, adding or deleting the rules and interface after addition of rule is shown in the Figure 20 and Figure 21 respectively. Table 3 shows the execution time for adding and deleting rules respectively.

5.3 Scalable CEP

The performance of the Scalable CEP (SCEP) system and existing system is evaluated based on Throughput, Multicasts, and Latencies which is presented in Figure 22, Figure 23 and Table 4 respectively.

Figure 22 presents the Throughput achieved by proposed eCEP framework for given number of EPs.

Throughput of the system is better by using SCEP when compared to Round Robin (RR) rule distribution, as the RR-rule distribution could not efficiently reduce the number of multicasts. Figure 23 indicates that the increase in number of EPs, also increases the number of multicasts in the system. The average multicasts are 2.02 and 1.86 for Round Robin and proposed SCEP respectively.

Figure 19. Relationship between number of events and event processing time (ms)

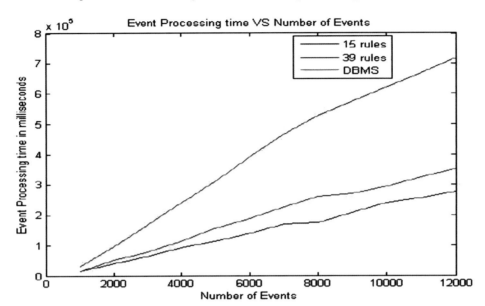

Figure 20. CEP rule addition and deletion

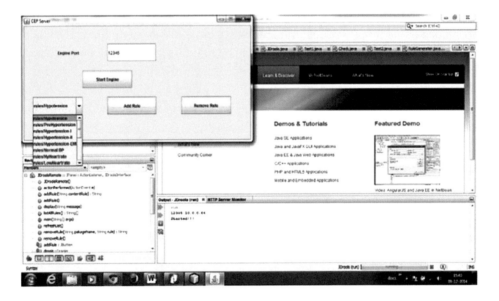

Table 4 presents the observation of latency of events executed in Event Processors for the proposed eCEP framework. The latency measure is compared for all the systems. The latency shows similar trends with lowest value for SCEP compared to Round Robin.

The average latencies of Round Robin and SCEP are 6.3ms and 4.33ms respectively. This indicates that there is a significant reduction in latency in proposed SCEP when compared to RR.

Figure 21. CEP abnormal heart rate detection

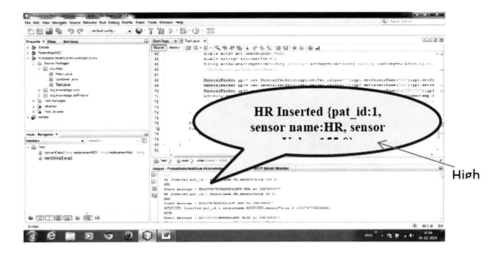

Table 3. Execution time for rule addition and deletion

Operation	Average Time (ms)
Addition	3.69
Deletion	0.203

Figure 22. Throughput comparison of RR and SCEP

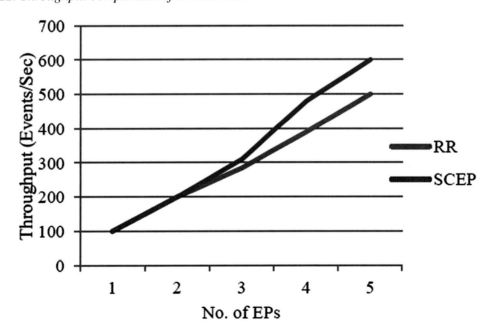

Figure 23. Multicasts comparison of RR and SCEP

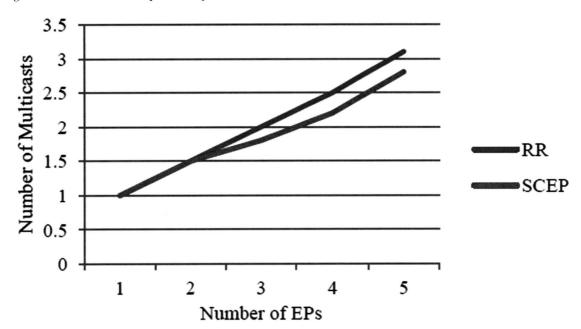

Table 4. Latency in milliseconds for eCEP with RR and SCEP

Scheme	Number of Eps				
	1	2	3	4	5
RR	3.508	1.66	1.258	1.252	0.915
SCEP	3.5	1.7	0.758	0.3973	0.4593

6. CONCLUSION AND FUTURE WORK

An enhanced Complex Event Processing (eCEP) Framework for Geriatric Remote Healthcare is proposed with Augmented Complex Event Processing (a-CEP), Dynamic Complex Event Processing (DCEP) and Scalable Complex Event Processing (SCEP) techniques. The collective information from various biosensors are aggregated and sent to the gateway node for processing. Patterns representing abnormal events are modeled as complex events which in turn are aggregated from base events and other complex events using logical and spatiotemporal relations.

Accuracy of decision making in CEP system depends on the veracity of events received and the complex event model used. The proposed a-CEP approach augments the CEP events with a statistical reasoning layer such that all raw sensor streams pass through this layer before applying on CEP rules models.

The CEP framework is initially configured with all the rules which define the complex events or patterns to be identified and alerted. To support dynamic addition and deletion of the rules at run time, a DCEP rule engine is implemented. It is observed that the proposed event driven dynamic rule engine performs better than polling based rule engines.

However, the accuracy of decision making in CEP system depends on the volume of events received to derive the complex event. Hence, SCEP approach is implemented such that the throughput of the system remains intact with the increase in number of rules. The experimental result shows that the proposed eCEP framework is very much scalable when compared conventional data streaming systems reduces the time taken for abnormality detection.

In future, the proposed CEP framework can be made to include effective data mining approaches to update the system with new CEP rules. Data visualisation of the healthcare system can be improved to get higher level of information. In addition, the CEP can be streamlined with machine learning algorithms for effective predictions of diseases. Further, data in the database at hospital cloud server can be used for personalisation of patient vital parameters and to formulate CEP rules in order to enhance the system performance by reducing false alarms.

ACKNOWLEDGMENT

This research project is funded by NRDMS, Department of Science and Technology, Government of India, New Delhi. The authors would like to extend their sincere thanks to NRDMS for their support.

REFERENCES

Akbar, A., Khan, A., Carrez, F., & Moessner, K. (2017). *Predictive Analytics for Complex IoT Data Streams*. IEEE Internet of Things.

Andrysiak, T., Saganowski, Ł., Choraś, M., & Kozik, R. (2016). Proposal and comparison of network anomaly detection based on long-memory statistical models. *Logic Journal of the IGPL, 24*(6), 944–956. doi:10.1093/jigpal/jzw051

Babagholami-Mohamadabadi, B., Jourabloo, A., Zarghami, A., & Kasaei, S. (2014). A bayesian framework for sparse representation-based 3-d human pose estimation. *IEEE Signal Processing Letters, 21*(3), 297–300. doi:10.1109/LSP.2014.2301726

Babu, S., Chandini, M., Lavanya, P., Ganapathy, K., & Vaidehi, V. (2013). Integrating Wireless Sensor Network with Sensor Web Enablement for Remote Health Care Decision Making in Cloud. *International Conference on Recent Trends in Information Technology, ICRTIT 2013.*

Bali, M. (2009). *Drools JBoss Rules 5.0 Developer's Guide*. Packt Publishing Ltd.

Barros, R. C., Basgalupp, M. P., De Carvalho, A. C. P. L. F., & Freitas, A. A. (2012). A survey of evolutionary algorithms for decision-tree induction. *Systems, Man, and Cybernetics, Part C: Applications and Reviews. IEEE Transactions on, 42*(3), 291–312.

Bhargavi, R., & Vaidehi, V. (2013). Semantic intrusion detection with multisensor data fusion using complex event processing. *Sadhana, 38*(2), 169–185.

Bhargavi, R., Ravi Pathak, Vaidehi, V. (2013). Dynamic Complex Event Processing – Adaptive Rule Engine. *International Conference on Recent Trends in Information Technology, ICRTIT 2013.*

Bouhamed, H., Masmoudi, A., Lecroq, T., & Rebaï, A. (2012). A new approach for Bayesian classifier learning structure via K2 Algorithm. In *Emerging Intelligent Computing Technology and Applications* (pp. 387–393). Springer Berlin Heidelberg. doi:10.1007/978-3-642-31837-5_56

Bourke, A. K., & Lyons, G. M. (2008). A threshold-based fall-detection algorithm using a bi-axial gyroscope sensor. *Medical Engineering & Physics*, *30*(1), 84–90. doi:10.1016/j.medengphy.2006.12.001 PMID:17222579

Cannady, J., & Harrell, J. (1996, May). A comparative analysis of current intrusion detection technologies. *Proceedings of the Fourth Technology for Information Security Conference*, 96.

Carzaniga, A., Rosenblum, D. S., & Wolf, A. L. (2001). Design and evaluation of a wide-area event notification service. *ACM Transactions on Computer Systems*, *19*(3), 332–383. doi:10.1145/380749.380767

Chattopadhyay, S., Davis, R. M., Menezes, D. D., Singh, G., Acharya, R. U., & Tamura, T. (2012). Application of Bayesian classifier for the diagnosis of dental pain. *Journal of Medical Systems*, *36*(3), 1425–1439. doi:10.100710916-010-9604-y PMID:20945154

Cheung, A. K. Y., & Jacobsen, H. A. (2010). Load balancing content-based publish/subscribe systems. *ACM Transactions on Computer Systems*, *28*(4), 9. doi:10.1145/1880018.1880020

Damousis, I. G., Satsios, K. J., Labridis, D. P., & Dokopoulos, P. S. (2002). Combined fuzzy logic and genetic algorithm techniques—application to an electromagnetic field problem. *Fuzzy Sets and Systems*, *129*(3), 371–386. doi:10.1016/S0165-0114(01)00137-3

Danane, Y., & Parvat, T. (2015, January). Intrusion detection system using fuzzy genetic algorithm. In *Pervasive Computing (ICPC), 2015 International Conference on* (pp. 1-5). IEEE. 10.1109/PERVASIVE.2015.7086963

Dastanpour, A., Ibrahim, S., Mashinchi, R., & Selamat, A. (2014, October). Comparison of genetic algorithm optimization on artificial neural network and support vector machine in intrusion detection system. In *Open Systems (ICOS), 2014 IEEE Conference on* (pp. 72-77). IEEE. 10.1109/ICOS.2014.7042412

Diao, Y., Li, B., Liu, A., Peng, L., Sutton, C., Tran, T., & Zink, M. (2009). *Capturing data uncertainty in high-volume stream processing.* arXiv preprint arXiv:0909.1777

Esmael, B., Arnaout, A., Fruhwirth, R. K., & Thonhauser, G. (2012). *Improving time series classification using Hidden Markov Models* (pp. 502–507). HIS. doi:10.1109/HIS.2012.6421385

Esposito, C., Ficco, M., Palmieri, F., & Castiglione, A. (2014). A knowledge-based platform for Big Data analytics based on publish/subscribe services and stream processing. *Knowledge-Based Systems*.

Fathima, A. A., Vaidehi, V., & Selvaraj, K. (2014). Fall detection with part-based approach for Indoor Environment. *International Journal of Intelligent Information Technologies*, *10*(4), 51–69. doi:10.4018/ijiit.2014100104

Forgy, C. L. (1982). Rete: A fast algorithm for the many pattern/many object pattern match problem. *Artificial Intelligence*, *19*(1), 17–37. doi:10.1016/0004-3702(82)90020-0

Fraser, G. D., Chan, A. D., Green, J. R., & MacIsaac, D. T. (2014). Automated biosignal quality analysis for electromyography using a one-class support vector machine. *IEEE Transactions on Instrumentation and Measurement*, *63*(12), 2919–2930. doi:10.1109/TIM.2014.2317296

Ganapathy, Vaidehi, & Raghuraman. (2015). An Efficient Remote Healthcare using Parallel Genetic approach. *International Journal of Applied Engineering Research*, *9*(21), 4961–4966.

Gatton, T. M., & Lee, M. (2010). Fuzzy logic decision making for an intelligent home healthcare system. In *Future Information Technology (FutureTech), 2010 5th International Conference on* (pp. 1-5). IEEE. 10.1109/FUTURETECH.2010.5482667

Gaynor, M., Moulton, S. L., Welsh, M., LaCombe, E., Rowan, A., & Wynne, J. (2004). Integrating wireless sensor networks with the grid. *IEEE Internet Computing*, *8*(4), 32–39. doi:10.1109/MIC.2004.18

Goonatilake & Khebbal. (1993). *Genetic programming of Neural Networks: Theory and practice. Intelligent hybrid systems*. John Wiley & Sons.

Gulisano, Jimenez-Peris, Patino-Martinez, & Valduriez. (2010). Streamcloud: A large scale data streaming system. In *Distributed Computing Systems (ICDCS), 2010 IEEE 30th International Conference on*. IEEE.

Hajihashemi, Z., & Popescu, M. (2016). A Multidimensional Time-Series Similarity Measure With Applications to Eldercare Monitoring. *IEEE Journal of Biomedical and Health Informatics*, *20*(3), 953–962. doi:10.1109/JBHI.2015.2424711 PMID:25910260

Heiss, J. E., Held, C. M., Estevez, P. A., Perez, C. A., Holzmann, C. A., & Perez, J. P. (2002). Classification of sleep stages in infants: A neuro fuzzy approach. *Engineering in Medicine and Biology Magazine, IEEE*, *21*(5), 147–151. doi:10.1109/MEMB.2002.1044185 PMID:12405069

Hemalatha, C. S., & Vaidehi, V. (2013). Associative Classification based Human Activity Recognition and Fall Detection using Accelerometer. *International Journal of Intelligent Information Technologies*, *9*(3), 20–37. doi:10.4018/jiit.2013070102

Hoßbach, B., & Seeger, B. (2013). Anomaly management using complex event processing: extending data base technology paper. In *Proceedings of the 16th International Conference on Extending Database Technology* (pp. 149-154). ACM.

Huang, Y. M., Hsieh, M. Y., Chao, H. C., Hung, S. H., & Park, J. H. (2009). Pervasive, secure access to a hierarchical sensor-based healthcare monitoring architecture in wireless heterogeneous networks. *Selected Areas in Communications. IEEE Journal on*, *27*(4), 400–411.

IEEE-BAN. (n.d.). Retrieved from http://www.ieee802.org/15/pub/TG6.html

ILOG JRules. (2002). ILOG, Inc. Retrieved from http://www.ilog.com/products/jrules/whitepapers/index.cfm?filename=WPJRules4.0.pdf

Isoyama, K., Kobayashi, Y., Sato, T., Kida, K., Yoshida, M., & Tagato, H. (2012, July). A scalable complex event processing system and evaluations of its performance. In *Proceedings of the 6th ACM International Conference on Distributed Event-Based Systems* (pp. 123-126). ACM. 10.1145/2335484.2335498

Juang, C. F. (2002). A TSK-type recurrent fuzzy network for dynamic systems processing by neural network and genetic algorithms. *Fuzzy Systems. IEEE Transactions on, 10*(2), 155–170.

Karlen, W., Mattiussi, C., & Floreano, D. (2009). Sleep and wake classification with ECG and respiratory effort signals. *Biomedical Circuits and Systems. IEEE Transactions on, 3*(2), 71–78. PMID:23853198

Kawashima, H., Kitagawa, H., & Li, X. (2010, November). Complex event processing over uncertain data streams. In *P2P, Parallel, Grid, Cloud and Internet Computing (3PGCIC), 2010 International Conference on* (pp. 521-526). IEEE. 10.1109/3PGCIC.2010.89

Kim, Y., & Moon, T. (2016). Human detection and activity classification based on micro-Doppler signatures using deep convolutional neural networks. *IEEE Geoscience and Remote Sensing Letters, 13*(1), 8–12. doi:10.1109/LGRS.2015.2491329

Lakshmanan, Rabinovich, & Etzion. (2009). A stratified approach for supporting high throughput event processing 99 applications. In *Proceedings of the Third ACM International Conference on Distributed Event-Based Systems*. ACM.

Lee, K. H., Kung, S. Y., & Verma, N. (2012). Low-energy formulations of support vector machine kernel functions for biomedical sensor applications. *Journal of Signal Processing Systems for Signal, Image, and Video Technology, 69*(3), 339–349. doi:10.100711265-012-0672-8

Lee, O. J., & Jung, J. E. (2017). Sequence clustering-based automated rule generation for adaptive complex event processing. *Future Generation Computer Systems, 66*, 100–109. doi:10.1016/j.future.2016.02.011

Lee, S. X., & McLachlan, G. J. (2013). *Modelling asset return using multivariate asymmetric mixture models with applications to estimation of Value-at-Risk*. Academic Press.

Leite, R. M. C., Sizilio, G. R. M. A., Ribeiro, A. G. C. D., Valentim, R., Pedro, F. R., & Ana Guerreiro, M. G. (2012). *Mobile Technologies Applied to Hospital Automation, Advances and Applications in Mobile Computing*. Retrieved from http://www.intechopen.com/books/advances-and-applications-in-mobilecomputing/mobile-technologies-applied-to-hospital-automation

Li, Q., & Clifford, G. D. (2012). Dynamic time warping and machine learning for signal quality assessment of pulsatile signals. *Physiological Measurement, 33*(9), 1491–1501. doi:10.1088/0967-3334/33/9/1491 PMID:22902950

Liu, Y., Yi, T. H., & Wang, C. Q. (2012). Investment Decision Support for Engineering Projects Based on Risk Correlation Analysis. *Mathematical Problems in Engineering*.

Ma, X., Wang, Y., Qiu, Q., Sun, W., & Pei, X. (2014). Scalable and elastic event matching for attribute-based publish/subscribe systems. *Future Generation Computer Systems, 36*, 102–119. doi:10.1016/j.future.2013.09.019

Mannini, A., & Sabatini, A. M. (2011). Accelerometry-based classification of human activities using markov modeling. *Computational Intelligence and Neuroscience, 2011*, 4. doi:10.1155/2011/647858 PMID:21904542

McCarthy, M. W., James, D. A., Lee, J. B., & Rowlands, D. D. (2015). Decision-tree-based human activity classification algorithm using single-channel foot-mounted gyroscope. *Electronics Letters*, *51*(9), 675–676. doi:10.1049/el.2015.0436

Moller, S., Engelbrecht, K. P., Kuhnel, C., Wechsung, I., & Weiss, B. (2009, July). A taxonomy of quality of service and quality of experience of multimodal human-machine interaction. In *Quality of Multimedia Experience, 2009. QoMEx 2009. International Workshop on* (pp. 7-12). IEEE. 10.1109/QOMEX.2009.5246986

Mousheimish, R., Taher, Y., & Zeitouni, K. (2016, June). Automatic learning of predictive rules for complex event processing: doctoral symposium. In *Proceedings of the 10th ACM International Conference on Distributed and Event-based Systems* (pp. 414-417). ACM. 10.1145/2933267.2933430

Nazmy, T. M., El-Messiry, H., & Al-Bokhity, B. (2010, March). Adaptive neuro-fuzzy inference system for classification of ECG signals. In *Informatics and Systems (INFOS), 2010 The 7th International Conference on* (pp. 1-6). IEEE.

Neumeyer, Robbins, Nair, & Kesari. (2010). S4: Distributed stream computing platform. In *Data Mining Workshops (ICDMW), 2010 IEEE International Conference*. IEEE.

Nonin-Pulse oximeter. (n.d.). Retrieved from http://www.nonin.com/pulseoximetry/fingertip/onyx9550

Nyan, M. N., Tay, F. E., Tan, A. W. Y., & Seah, K. H. W. (2006). Distinguishing fall activities from normal activities by angular rate characteristics and high-speed camera characterization. *Medical Engineering & Physics*, *28*(8), 842–849. doi:10.1016/j.medengphy.2005.11.008 PMID:16406739

Occhiuzzi, C., & Marrocco, G. (2010). The RFID technology for neurosciences: Feasibility of limbs' monitoring in sleep diseases. *Information Technology in Biomedicine. IEEE Transactions on*, *14*(1), 37–43. PMID:19726273

Ordonez, F. J., Englebienne, G., De Toledo, P., Van Kasteren, T., Sanchis, A., & Krose, B. (2014). In-home activity recognition: Bayesian inference for hidden Markov models. *IEEE Pervasive Computing*, *13*(3), 67–75. doi:10.1109/MPRV.2014.52

Pantelopoulos, A., & Bourbakis, N. G. (2010). A survey on wearable sensor-based systems for health monitoring and prognosis. *Systems, Man, and Cybernetics, Part C: Applications and Reviews. IEEE Transactions on*, *40*(1), 1–12.

Paschke, A., Kozlenkov, A., & Boley, H. (2007). *A homogeneous reaction rule language for complex event processing*. Academic Press.

Patel, S., Park, H., Bonato, P., Chan, L., & Rodgers, M. (2012). A review of wearable sensors and systems with application in rehabilitation. *Journal of Neuroengineering and Rehabilitation*, *9*(1), 21. doi:10.1186/1743-0003-9-21 PMID:22520559

Pathak, R., & Vaidehi, V. (2014). Event Refinement Model Augmented Complex Event Processing for efficient decision making. In *International Conference on Intelligent Information Technology, ICIIT 2014*. Anna University.

Pathak, R., & Vaidehi, V. (2015). An efficient rule balancing for scalable complex event processing. *Electrical and Computer Engineering (CCECE), 2015 IEEE 28th Canadian Conference on*, 190-195. 10.1109/CCECE.2015.7129184

Qayyum, A., Islam, M. H., & Jamil, M. (2005, September). Taxonomy of statistical based anomaly detection techniques for intrusion detection. In *Emerging Technologies, 2005. Proceedings of the IEEE Symposium on* (pp. 270-276). IEEE. 10.1109/ICET.2005.1558893

Sanz, J., Fernández, A., Bustince, H., & Herrera, F. (2011). A genetic tuning to improve the performance of fuzzy rule-based classification systems with interval-valued fuzzy sets: Degree of ignorance and lateral position. *International Journal of Approximate Reasoning, 52*(6), 751–766. doi:10.1016/j.ijar.2011.01.011

Schilling, B., Koldehofe, B., Pletat, U., & Rothermel, K. (2012). Distributed heterogeneous event processing. In Computer-based medical consultations: MYCIN. Elsevier.

Singh, R. R., Conjeti, S., & Banerjee, R. (2013). A comparative evaluation of neural network classifiers for stress level analysis of automotive drivers using physiological signals. *Biomedical Signal Processing and Control, 8*(6), 740–754. doi:10.1016/j.bspc.2013.06.014

Soule, A., Salamatian, K., & Taft, N. (2005, October). Combining filtering and statistical methods for anomaly detection. In *Proceedings of the 5th ACM SIGCOMM conference on Internet Measurement* (pp. 31-31). USENIX Association. 10.1145/1330107.1330147

Suknovic, M., Delibasic, B., Jovanovic, M., Vukicevic, M., Becejski-Vujaklija, D., & Obradovic, Z. (2012). Reusable components in decision tree induction algorithms. *Computational Statistics, 27*(1), 127–148. doi:10.100700180-011-0242-8

Tartarisco, G., Carbonaro, N., Tonacci, A., Bernava, G. M., Arnao, A., Crifaci, G., ... Tognetti, A. (2015). Neuro-fuzzy physiological computing to assess stress levels in virtual reality therapy. *Interacting with Computers, 27*(5), 521–533. doi:10.1093/iwc/iwv010

Thakker, B., & Vyas, A. L. (2011). Support vector machine for abnormal pulse classification. *International Journal of Computers and Applications, 22*(7), 13–19. doi:10.5120/2597-3610

Toreyin, B. U., Soyer, E. B., Onaran, I., & Cetin, A. E. (2008). Falling person detection using multisensor signal processing. *EURASIP Journal on Advances in Signal Processing, 2008*, 29.

Turchin, Y., Gal, A., & Wasserkrug, S. (2009, July). Tuning complex event processing rules using the prediction-correction paradigm. In *Proceedings of the Third ACM International Conference on Distributed Event-Based Systems* (p. 10). ACM. 10.1145/1619258.1619272

Vaidehi, V., Bhargavi, R., Ganapathy, K., & Sweetlin Hemalatha, C. (2012). Multi-sensor based in-home health monitoring using Complex Event Processing. In *Proceedings of IEEE International Conference on Recent Trends in Information Technology (ICRTIT 2012)*. MIT, Anna University.

Walter, K., & Nash, E. (2009, June). Coupling wireless sensor networks and the Sensor Observation Service—bridging the interoperability gap. *Proceedings of 12th AGILE International Conference on Geographic Information Science 2009*.

Walzer, K., Breddin, T., & Groch, M. (2008, July). Relative temporal constraints in the Rete algorithm for complex event detection. In *Proceedings of the second international conference on Distributed event-based systems* (pp. 147-155). ACM. 10.1145/1385989.1386008

Wang, Y., & Hu, X. (2013). Fuzzy reasoning of accident provenance in pervasive healthcare monitoring systems. *IEEE Journal of Biomedical and Health Informatics, 17*(6), 1015–1022. doi:10.1109/JBHI.2013.2274518 PMID:24240719

Wang, Y., & Yang, S. (2010, July). High-performance complex event processing for large-scale RFID applications. In *Signal Processing Systems (ICSPS), 2010 2nd International Conference on* (Vol. 1, pp. V1-127). IEEE. 10.1109/ICSPS.2010.5555586

Wang, Y. H., Cao, K., & Zhang, X. M. (2013). Complex event processing over distributed probabilistic event streams. *Computers & Mathematics with Applications (Oxford, England), 66*(10), 1808–1821. doi:10.1016/j.camwa.2013.06.032

Wasserkrug, S., Gal, A., Etzion, O., & Turchin, Y. (2008, July). Complex event processing over uncertain data. In *Proceedings of the second international conference on Distributed event-based systems* (pp. 253-264). ACM. 10.1145/1385989.1386022

Wasserkrug, S., Gal, A., Etzion, O., & Turchin, Y. (2012b). Efficient processing of uncertain events in rule-based systems. *Knowledge and Data Engineering. IEEE Transactions on, 24*(1), 45–58.

Ye, N., Emran, S. M., Chen, Q., & Vilbert, S. (2002). Multivariate statistical analysis of audit trails for host-based intrusion detection. *Computers. IEEE Transactions on, 51*(7), 810–820.

Ye, X. W., Ran, L., Yi, T. H., & Dong, X. B. (2012). Intelligent risk assessment for dewatering of metro-tunnel deep excavations. *Mathematical Problems in Engineering.*

Yu, H. C. J., Lee, Z. H., Ye, C. F., Chung, L. K., & Fang, Y. M. (2009). *SWE Application for Debris Flow Monitoring System in Taiwan.* OGC 09-082 Version: 0.3.0, OGC® Discussion Paper.

Zephyr-Bioharness. (n.d.). Retrieved from http://www.zephyr-technology.com/, http://www.zephyranywhere.com/healthcare/zephyrlife/

Zephyr-Pressure Monitor. (n.d.). Retrieved from http://www.zephyranywherestore.com/Automatic-Bluetooth-Pressure-Monitor-HPL-108/dp/B009ZUG2Z8

Chapter 17
CASPL:
A Coevolution Analysis Platform for Software Product Lines

Anissa Benlarabi
Mohamed V University, Morocco

Amal Khtira
Mohammed V University, Morocco

Bouchra El Asri
Mohamed V University, Morocco

ABSTRACT

Software product line engineering is a development paradigm based on reuse. It builds a common platform from which a set of applications can be derived. Despite its advantage of enhancing time to market and costs, it presents some complications. Among them, the complexity of its evolution because all the components are shared between the derived products. For this reason, the change impact analysis and the evolution understanding in software product lines require greater focus than in single software. In this chapter, the authors present CASPL platform for co-evolution analysis in software product lines. The platform uses evolutionary trees that are mainly used in biology to analyze the co-evolution between applications. The major goal is to enhance the change understanding and to compare the history of changes in the applications of the family, at the aim of correcting divergences between them.

INTRODUCTION

Software development tends currently to improve costs and resources reuse because of the huge amount of data managed by applications. Software product line (SPL) engineering (Pohl, Bockle, & Van der Linden, 2005) is a reuse based approach aimed at reducing costs and time to market. It consists on developing a set of assets for a specific domain, customizable to be reused in the development in many applications (Clements & Northrop, 2002).

DOI: 10.4018/978-1-5225-5396-0.ch017

In order to achieve the main goal of reuse, software product lines must cope with technology evolution and new business needs without risk on the safety of early-derived systems. However, the evolution activity in SPLs is more complex than evolution of single software because the assets are shared between many applications. For this reason, the change impact analysis and the evolution understanding in SPL require greater focus. Recent works on SPL evolution aimed mainly on enhancing the rigor and the reliability of the change. We separated them into many research areas. The main ones are change impact analysis (Ferreira, Borba, Soares & Gheyi, 2012; Ter Beek, Muccini & Pelliccione, 2011; Schubanz et al., 2013), and post-evolution verification (Sabouri & Khosravi, 2011; Dintzner, 2015). These approaches are time consuming and use human knowledge, which is error prone in practice.

In this paper, we introduce our framework for coevolution analysis in software product lines (CASPL). It automates the coevolution analysis approach that we introduced earlier (Benlarabi, Khtira, & El Asri, 2015). Coevolution is extensively used in biology (Ehrlich & Raven, 1964) to show how organisms influence each other during their evolution. Similarly, to biological co-evolution, we intend to study the similarities and the divergences between the platform and the products evolution histories of a SPL. The aim of this study is improving the change understanding and evolution trends. The major advantage of the co-evolution analysis is its reliance on the features of the studied organisms instead of human knowledge.

CASPL is composed of four tools. The first one receives feature models of platform and applications releases and transforms them to instances of our proposed features meta-model. The second tool extracts features from the instances established in the first step. The third tool process data of the two previous steps to construct feature databases for applications and platform. The coevolution analysis starts in the fourth tool, which applies the cladistics method we described before to deal with the coevolution analysis. The output of the platform is a set of evolutionary trees that we compare in Mesquite tool (Maddison & Maddison, 2001).

The remainder of this paper is divided into five sections. In section 2 we outline the major works done in our area of research and we introduce our approach for coevolution analysis. In section 3, we present the CASPL platform to improve the understanding of SPL evolution and to help identifying its evolution trends. In section 4, the example of Mobile Media SPL is discussed through the results found in the platform. We give assessment and future work in section 5.

SPL CO-EVOLUTION ANALYSIS: MOTIVATIONS AND BACKGROUND

From our literature, we identified the main research areas of software product lines evolution that are: dealing with SPL evolution, documenting the SPL evolution, post-evolution verification of SPL, change impact analysis in SPL, SPL re-engineering, predictive analysis of SPL evolution trends. Nevertheless, recent works focus on the verification and the change impact analysis. In the following subsections, we will present major works done in the two areas, and then we introduce our coevolution-based analysis to study the software product lines evolution.

Change Impact Analysis

The Impact analysis is a challenge in software development and maintenance, especially in software product lines. According to Livingood (2011), some changes have a great and complicated impact, which makes them unsafe. Works that study the change impact analysis are divided in two techniques, dependencies analysis and traceability analysis.

The dependency analysis aims at selecting all the products related to the components concerned by the evolution and verifying their coherence. In Ferreira, Borba, Soares, and Gheyi (2012) and Ter Beek, Muccini and Pelliccione (2011) authors propose a platform for SPL evolution with four verification tools that take into consideration the impact of the change through a dependency analysis. Another approach (Yazdanshenas & Moonen, 2012) makes a map of dependencies between the platform and the derived products through their common components. The same technique is used in Michalik and Weyns (2011), however when a component is impacted, only some derived products are selected depending on criteria fixed by the authors. This technique is interesting to define the impact of a change. Even though it present a risk because of the hidden inter-dependencies between components.

Approaches based on traceability techniques, trace the history of changes, sometimes they include versioning using configuration management tools or other specific tools. In Schubanz et al. (2013) an approach proposed to manage the versioning and the traceability of feature models, the approach in Dhungana, Grünbacher, Rabiser and Neumayer (2010) do likewise by dividing the features model to fragments. Another method proposed in Anquetil et al. (2010) considers four levels for the traceability, and provide a tool that implements them.

Post-Evolution Verification

The post-evolution verification approaches aim at ensuring the reliability and the coherence of a SPL after its evolution. They encompass verification tools, the assessment of development techniques and stability measurement. A platform was proposed by Ferreira, Borba, Soares and Gheyi (2012) containing four verification tools that assess the behavior at four levels: the changed components, the impacted products, all the products and the whole family. In Sabouri and Khosravi (2011), authors define a set of properties with values indicating the correctness of the family, after each change the values are recalculated and compared with the default values for only the impacted products which implicates a rigorous impact analysis. Other works (Figueiredo et al., 2008; Krishnan et al., 2013; Gaia et al., 2014) focus on the stability of development techniques and made a comparison of development techniques such the object oriented programming and the aspect oriented programming, they affirm that the choice of the development techniques affects the stability of the SPL during its maintenance and evolution. Metrics are widely used to assess the stability of SPLs (Dintzner, 2015). The metrics typically inspired from those used to assess single software with adaptation to the context of SPL. Most Verification approaches made a complete verification after each change, which is costly in time and resources.

Discussion

Unlike the presented works, our approach deals with the challenge of evolution understanding, it allows for improving the change understanding through a synthesis of the history of the SPL evolution and helps predicting future changes by considering changes that were implemented at products level and may be propagated to the common platform and then to the other products. Through our coevolution analysis (Benlarabi, Khtira, & El Asri, 2015), we discuss also the evolution trends on the family to give developers the ability to anticipate future Changes. To the best of our knowledge, there is still no research work for introducing the concept of co-evolution of domain and application engineering in SPLs. This principal used widely in biology gives a basis for understanding the evolution of a population using concrete data extracted from existing organisms. We presented earlier (Benlarabi, Khtira, & El Asri, 2015) our cladistique method for studying the coevolution. We rely on feature models of all the releases of the platform and the derived applications. Then we extract a database of feature and we build matrices of characters states that show features of the database that exist in a release and those that do not exist. The matrices are used to build evolutionary tree for each application and for the platform. Finally, trees are compared to deduce their co-evolution degree. In the next section, we present in details the CASPL (Coevolution Analysis for Software Product Lines) platform, which automates our approach.

OVERVIEW OF CASPL

The CASPL platform is composed of four main modules. The first is the *data collection* which receives the feature models of the population chosen, and creates instances of our FM meta-model. The second module is *data preparation* which uses the instances generated and transforms them to instances of the class Feature Figure 1. The third module is *data persistence*, which constructs features database by filtering features from the objects instantiated from the class Feature_. The final module includes data manipulation tools to construct evolutionary trees and analysis tools to study the coevolution within the population studied.

Figure 1. Overview of CASPL platform

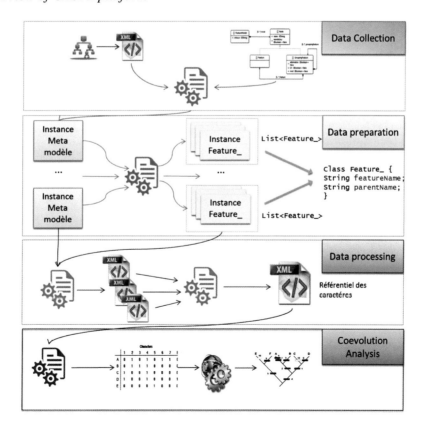

Data Collection

The input of our study is a population of software applications, to study their coevolution we focus on their features, we started by creating a feature model of each application in the featureIDE tool (Kastner et al., 2009), the tool gives two views of the model: the graphical view and the text view in the XML format.

Before extracting data from the models, it was necessary to format them into instances of a single meta-model. For this reason we studied the different feature meta-models and we found that they respect commonly the concepts meta-model proposed by Pohl (Pohl, Bockle, and Van der Linden, 2005). We adopt a new meta-model illustrated in Figure 2. which we constructed on the basis of the meta-model cited (Pohl, Bockle, and Van der Linden, 2005). We changed the concepts of variant and variation point to feature and grouped feature, a feature model is composed several nodes that can be simple features or grouped features, the nodes can be mandatory or optional, and the grouped features can have three relations: alternative, or, and.

We programmed a java class, which creates instances of the class feure model of Figure 2. For all the feature models based on their XML view and we persist them in a list of objets. In the Figure 3. We depict a set of features and grouped features extracted from a feature model of a mobile media application.

Data Preparation

In this intermediate stage, we aim to prepare the instances of feature models for the coevolution analysis. We have to learn from these instances the history of features and their evolution. A list of all the patterns of features evolution in a feature model was already established (Alves et al., 2006), in this step we tried to prepare the necessary data to capture the evolution history of features. After an analysis of the patterns, we found that the hierarchy of a feature in the feature model is important to build its evolution history. Hence, we must consider the couple (feature, node parent). For that purpose we programmed a new class Feature_ illustrated in Figure 4. which represents for each feature this couple.

The following items will then represent each feature:

- The name of the feature
- The name of the parent node

Figure 2. Feature Meta-model

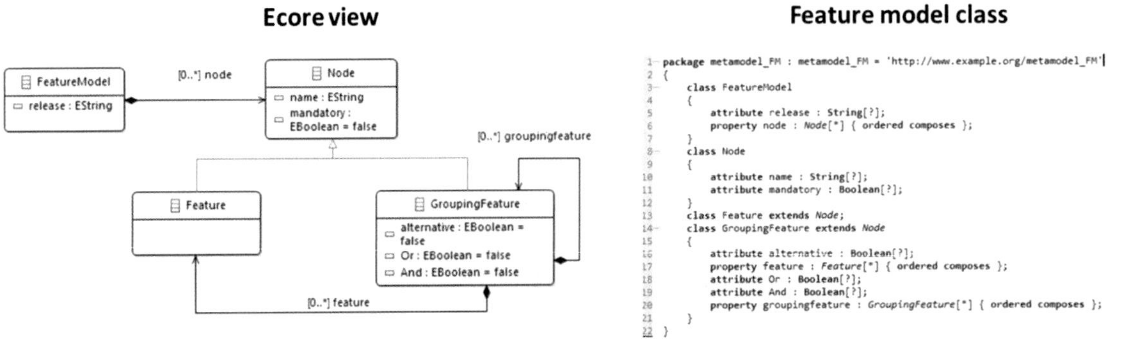

Figure 3. Creation of meta-model instances

```java
public static void main(String[] args) {
    // TODO Auto-generated method stub
    FeatureModelTest fm = new FeatureModelTest("FM.xml");
    System.out.println(fm.createFeatureModel.getRelease());
    for(Node e : fm.createFeatureModel.getNode())
    {
        GroupingFeature gf = (GroupingFeature)e;
        for(GroupingFeature gfe : gf.getGroupingfeature())
        {
            afficher(gfe);
        }
    }
}
public static void afficher(GroupingFeature g)
{
    if(g.getGroupingfeature() == null)
    {
        for(Feature f : g.getFeature())
        {
            System.out.println(f.getName());
        }
    }
    else
    {
        for(GroupingFeature gfe : g.getGroupingfeature())
        {
            System.out.println(gfe.getName());
            afficher(gfe);
        }
    }
}
```

```
EClass Hierarchy    EClass References    Console

<terminated> Program [Java Application] C:\Program Files\Java\j
file:/D:/4eme_annee_doct/rapport%20de%20these/fran
struct null
and MobileMedia
alt PhotoManagement
feature CreateAlbum
feature DeleteAlbum
and AlbumManagement
feature Favourites
feature Sorting
and BasicPhotoOperations
feature Create
feature Delete
feature View
feature EditLabel
constraints null
comments null
```

- The relation between the feature and the parent node: mandatory, optional, alternative (see Figure 4)

In the following illustration Figure 5. we present an example of an instance of Feature_ extracted from the feature model of mobile media application.

Data Processing

The purpose of this stage is to build a database of features based on the feature meta-model instances. We gathered discrete features from the releases of applications derived from a software product line. Then we compared their feature models after transforming them into instances of our meta-models as described in the two previous stages. To make a comparison between feature models, we start by transforming their features to a list of the class Feature's objects presented in the data preparation section, and we compare each object with the rest in order to build a list of the discrete features only. We save the list obtained in XML file, which represents the feature's database of the population.

*Figure 4. Class Feature_*

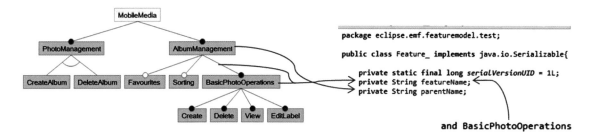

Figure 5. Extraction of features from feature model

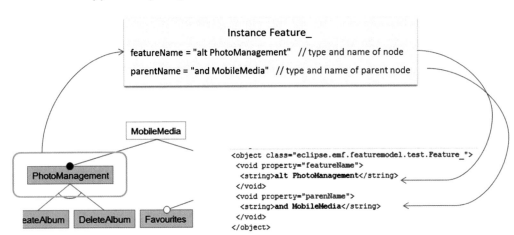

We developed a tool called *Feature Comparer* which respects a set of rules in order to give reliable results and to avoid data duplication or lost in the database. In Figure 6. we show how the comparer works.

The comparer detects duplication and remove the duplicated features, the tool was validated by many tests on different sets of mobile media feature models, the following figure illustrate a database of feature resulted from a test done on two releases of mobile media applications.

Coevolution Analysis

In this stage, we build evolutionary trees for the population in the aim of comparing them. The results of the comparison will provide conclusions about the coevolution level between the applications and the software common platform, and the evolution trends of the family.

Figure 6. Comparer of feature models

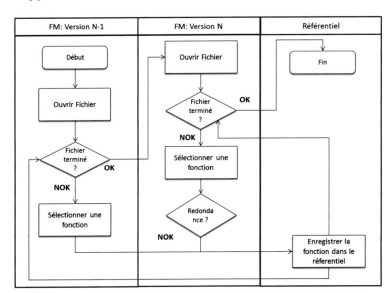

Figure 7. Extraction of features database

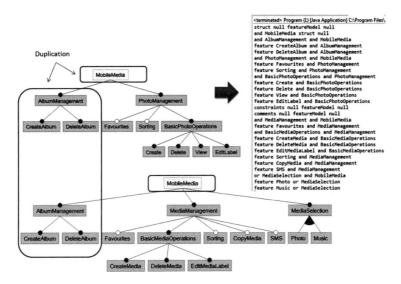

The coevolution analysis takes place in three steps: the creation of character's states matrices for all the applications and for the common platform, then the creation of evolutionary trees and finally their analysis and comparison. We use Mesquite tool for evolutionary biology (Maddison & Maddison, 2001), particularly coevolution analysis. It is composed of modules for the coevolution analysis based on genetic sequences, and others that concern evolutionary analysis based on characters description. We worked with the second type. The tool allows for drawing the character's states matrices and generates the evolutionary trees relevant to the matrices. It also enables to explore the trees with many analysis tools.

Character's States Matrices

The character's states matrix is built for each application of the population. The matrix represents the states of the database features in the application, each feature or character has two states: exists or not. In some cases, characters may have more than two states, for example the size which can be small, medium or large. Concretely, the coevolution analysis tools use input files that describe the matrices, these files have a standard format illustrated in Figure 8. The first line contains the number of releases and the number of characters, the following lines start with the name of the release and contain the sequences of the states of characters. Each code in the sequence represents a state 1 for the state exist and 0 for the state do not exist.

We programmed the necessary functions to create these files from the features database and the application's features lists generated in the previous stages. The three functions work as follows:

- Create a text file
- Access to the directory containing the lists of features for an application releases, each list is saved in an XML file. Their names start all with REF_FN.

Figure 8. Characters states matrix format

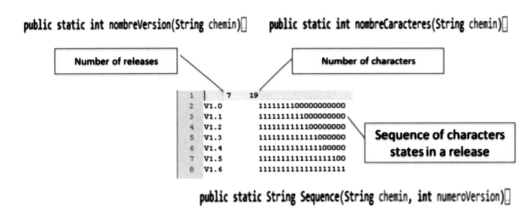

- Calculate the number of file and put the result in the text file as the number of releases
- Access to the features database, it is an XML file named REF_CARACTERES
- Calculate the number of feature or characters and put the result in the text file
- For each release file, calculate the sequence of characters states and put it in the text file respectively.

Then, the matrix is imported in the Mesquite tool as shown in Figure 9., which creates an evolutionary tree or cladogram for the matrix.

Figure 9. Importation of matrices in Mesquite

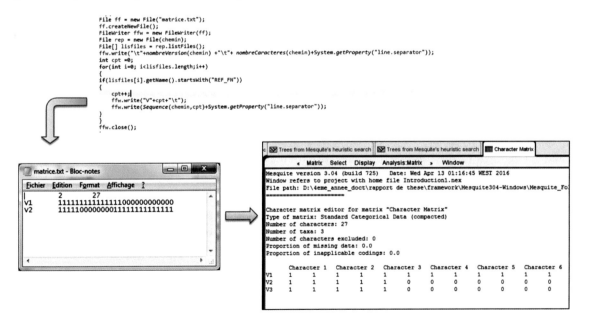

Coevolution Analysis

We present the analysis tools provided by Mesquite, there are two types of tools: tools dedicated for trees based on characters and tools dedicated for tree based on genes and ADN sequences. The first type is the one we present here:

- The tool of character's evolution analysis
- The tool of diversification analysis
- The tool of molecular data analysis
- The tool of simulation
- The tool of character's continuity analysis
- The tool of trees topology analysis

We focused on the character's evolution and the diversification.

Character's Evolution Analysis

We separate this part according to two objectives: the study of the evolution history of characters, and the study of interdependence between characters.

Evolution History

Mesquite allows for exploring the character's evolution with two ways:

- Trace a character on the cladogram: we can select a character and explore the tree in order to see his states in all the branches. A legend represents the different states, hence when exploring the tree the current state is written in Observed states are as shown in Figure 10
- Trace all the characters on the cladogram in a table similar to the matrix. In this table we find the states of the characters in all the internal and the external nodes of the tree (see Figure 11).

Interdependence Between Characters

Mesquite provides a summary of the changes of the states in the tree for all the characters, this analysis is done by branch, we have to select the branch then we trace the changes of characters. It is valuable when we have many populations that share the same characters because we can follow the changes of characters in many different populations.

Diversification Analysis

The diversification identifies the speciation and the disappearance of characters by branch. Mesquite provides a model named BISSE. It calculates the speciation and disappearance rates on the basis of six parameters: transition rate from the state 0 to the state 1, the transition rate from the state 1 to the state 0, the speciation rate caused by the state 0, the speciation rate caused by the state 1, the disappearance rate

Figure 10. trace character on tree

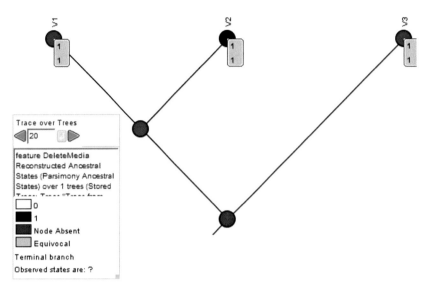

Figure 11. trace all characters on tree

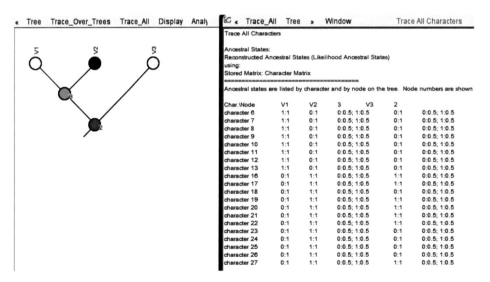

caused by the state 0, and the disappearance rate caused by the state 1. The calculation and the results of Mesquite analysis modules will be presented with examples in the following section

RESULTS

In this section, we describe an experiment done on mobile media software product line using CASPL. The mobile Media SPL manipulates photo, music, and video on mobile devices such as mobile phones and has many derived products (Tizzei et al., 2011). Since its creation in 2008, Many evolution scenarios

Figure 12: trace changes in characters

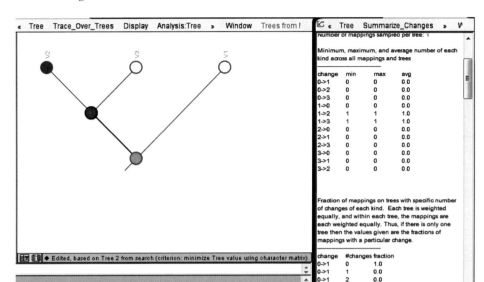

were performed on the SPL. We studied in an early work (Benlarabi, Khtira, & El Asri, 2015) the co-evolution in the mobile media SPL without using a specific tool, we applied the same method to create cladograms then we analyze them using a mathematical analysis.

Population of the Study

In the experiment, we consider a population of two families. The first family described in Table 1 represents seven releases of the common platform, in each release an evolution scenario was applied. The second family described in Table 2 represents seven releases of a derived application from the software product line. Likewise, each release was subject to modifications compared to the previous release.

Mobile Media Coevolution Analysis

From the feature models of the different releases of the two populations, we constructed their matrices in Mesquite with the CASPL data preparation and transformation tools. The matrix of the common platform contains 31 characters and 7 releases as illustrated in Figure 13., the names of characters are composed by the word feature and the names of features extracted from feature models, these names are not the same names of features in the derived application. The matrix of the applications is composed by 19 characters and 7 releases as illustrated in Figure 14.

On the basis of the two matrices we created their cladograms at the aim of studying their coevolution. Mesquite provides the following analysis tool to achieve this purpose:

- **Trace Over Trees:** The tool traces the path of each character in the cladogram, it allows for exploring the history of characters in the cladogram. We relied on the names of features in order to compare their histories in the two cladograms. We show and example in the Figure 15. we present

Table 1. Mobile media platform population

Version	Description
V1.0	The first release of the mobile media SPL, this release encompasses the following features: Manage photos ($F_{1,1}$), Create album ($F_{1,2}$), Delete album($F_{1,3}$), Create media ($F_{1,4}$), Delete media ($F_{1,5}$), View media ($F_{1,6}$), Sort media ($F_{1,7}$), Edit media label ($F_{1,8}$)
V1.1	The second release of the mobile media SPL, in which the following features were added: Set favorites ($F_{1,9}$) and See favorites ($F_{1,10}$)
V1.2	The third release of the mobile media SPL, in which the feature Copy media ($F_{1,11}$) was added
V1.3	The fourth release of the mobile media SPL, in which the following features were added: Send media ($F_{1,12}$) and Receive media ($F_{1,13}$)
V1.4	The fifth release of the mobile media SPL, in which the feature Add music media management ($F_{1,14}$) was added
V1.5	The sixth release of the mobile media SPL, in which the following features were added: Add video media management ($F_{1,15}$), Capture videos ($F_{1,16}$) and Capture photos ($F_{1,17}$)
V1.6	The seventh release of the mobile media SPL, in which the following features were added: Play videos ($F_{1,18}$) and Play music ($F_{1,19}$)

Table 2. Derived product population

Version	Description
V2.0	The first release of the product, this release encompasses the following features: Manage photos (F2, 1), Create album ($F_{2,2}$), Delete album ($F_{2,3}$), Create Photo ($F_{2,4}$), Delete Photo ($F_{2,5}$), View Photo ($F_{2,6}$), Sort media ($F_{2,7}$), Edit media label ($F_{2,8}$)
V2.1	The second release of the product, in which the following features were added: Set favorites ($F_{2,9}$) and See favorites ($F_{2,10}$)
V2.2	The third release of the product, in which the feature Copy media ($F_{2,11}$) was added
V2.3	The fourth release of the mobile media product, in which the following features were added: Send media ($F_{2,12}$) and Receive media ($F_{2,13}$)
V2.4	The fifth release of the product, in which the feature Print photo ($F_{2,14}$) was added
V2.5	The sixth release of the product, in which, the feature Capture photos ($F_{2,15}$) was added
V2.6	The seventh release of the product, in which, the feature Share photo in social websites ($F_{2,16}$) was added

the history of the feature "favorites", the result was that the feature has the same history in the two cladograms.

Character Associated Diversification Analysis: the tool calculates a set of important measures, which serves in studying evolution history. It calculate the speciation rate, which means the appearance of characters in the tree, also their disappearance. By comparing the measures in the two trees we deduce the similarity degree between the history of a character in the two tree. In the example showed in the Figure 16. the hypothesis done about the feature "favorites" is validated because measures have the same values with a high accuracy degree.

Through a deep investigation with the traceability and the diversification analysis tools we obtain the following results:

Figure 13. Characters matrix of the population

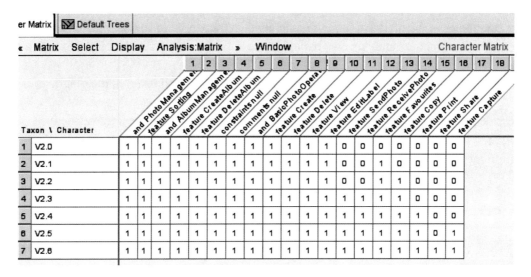

Figure 14. Characters matrix of the application

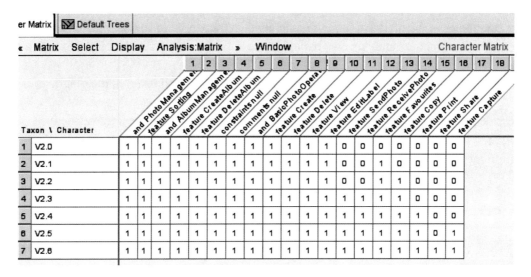

Figure 15. Comparison of characters history in trees

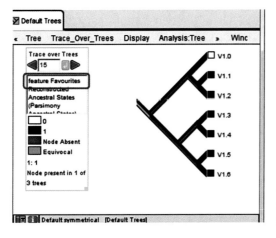

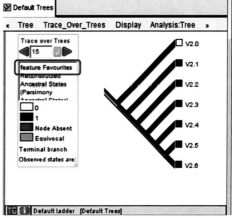

Figure 16. Comparison of diversification of characters in trees

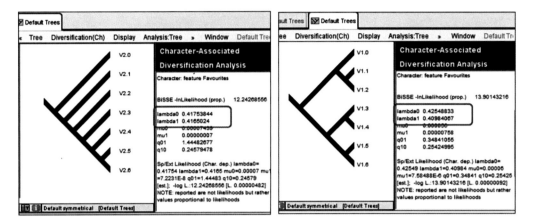

- Features related to media management does not exist in all the application releases because they appeared later in the platform with the emergence of new type of media
- Features "send photo" and "receive photo" in the application exist in the platform with a different name "sms"
- Features "print" and "share" exist in the application but does not exist in the platform

Others results concerning the evolution trends of the software product line was deduced from the observation of the cladogram without the use of special tools (Benlarabi, Khtira, & El Asri, 2015). This observation focus on the users needs and aims at anticipating their future needs.

ASSESSMENT AND FUTURE WORK

In this paper, we introduced a framework for software product line coevolution analysis (CASPL), which encompasses many tools that receive and prepare data from feature models in order to build evolutionary trees for the common platform and the derived applications. The trees were compared in the tool Mesquite to deduce the coevolution degree between them. We evaluated our approach on Mobile Media SPL. We worked on the platform and one derived product. Their features databases and characters states matrices were built by the processing data tools. Then, the two evolutionary trees were realized and compared in Mesquite. Through the analysis modules of Mesquite, we were able to trace the evolution path of each character. We discovered features of the platform that are absent from the application, also the opposite. Other results were deduced without using Mesquite proving that Management media features are the most concerned by the evolution. As perspective, we envisage taking into consideration fine levels in the coevolution analysis. Currently, we focus on feature models, this level does not allow a thorough view because some changes are done on more fine levels. Hence, we target in future work technical components and classes of code for more rigorous results.

REFERENCES

Alves, V., Gheyi, R., Massoni, T., Kulesza, U., Borba, P., & Lucena, C. (2006). Refactoring product lines. In *Proceedings of the 5th international conference on Generative programming and component engineering* (pp. 201–210). ACM. doi:10.1109/ICSE.2009.5070568

Anquetil, N., Kulesza, U., Mitschke, R., Moreira, A., Royer, J.-C., Rummler, A., & Sousa, A. (2010). A model-driven traceability framework for software product lines. *Software & Systems Modeling*, *9*(4), 427–451. doi:10.100710270-009-0120-9

Benlarabi, A., Khtira, A., & El Asri, B. (2015). A co-evolution analysis for software product lines: An approach based on evolutionary trees. *International Journal of Applied Evolutionary Computation*, *6*(3), 9–32.

Clements, P. P., & Northrop, L. (2002). *Software product lines: Practices and patterns*. Academic Press.

Dhungana, D., Grünbacher, P., Rabiser, R., & Neumayer, T. (2010). Structuring the modeling space and supporting evolution in software product line engineering. *Journal of Systems and Software*, *83*(7), 1108–1122. doi:10.1016/j.jss.2010.02.018

Dintzner, N. (2015). Safe evolution patterns for software product lines. In *Proceedings of the 37th International Conference on Software Engineering* (vol. 2, pp. 875–878). IEEE Press.

Ehrlich, P. R., & Raven, P. H. (1964). Butterflies and plants: A study in coevolution. *Evolution; International Journal of Organic Evolution*, *18*(4), 586–608. doi:10.1111/j.1558-5646.1964.tb01674.x

Figueiredo, E., Cacho, N., Sant'Anna, C., Monteiro, M., Kulesza, U., Garcia, A., . . . Dantas, F. (2008). Evolving software product lines with aspects. In *2008 ACM/IEEE 30th International Conference on Software Engineering* (pp. 261–270). IEEE.

Fondo Xavier Clavigero, S. J., Ferreira, F., Borba, P., Soares, G., & Gheyi, R. (2012). Making software product line evolution safer. In *Software Components Architectures and Reuse (SBCARS), 2012 Sixth Brazilian Symposium on* (pp. 21–30). IEEE.

Gaia, G. N., Ferreira, G. C. S., Figueiredo, E., & Maia, M. A. (2014). A quantitative and qualitative assessment of aspectual feature modules for evolving software product lines. *Science of Computer Programming*, *96*, 230–253. doi:10.1016/j.scico.2014.03.006

Kastner, C., Thum, T., Saake, G., Feigenspan, J., Leich, T., Wielgorz, F., & Apel, S. (2009) Featureide: A tool framework for feature-oriented software development. In *Proceedings of the 31st International Conference on Software Engineering* (pp. 611–614). IEEE Computer Society.

Krishnan, S., Strasburg, C., Lutz, R. R., Goseva-Popstojanova, K., & Dorman, K. S. (2013). Predicting failure-proneness in an evolving software product line. *Information and Software Technology*, *55*(8), 1479–1495. doi:10.1016/j.infsof.2012.11.008

Livingood, S. (2011). Issues in software product line evolution: complex changes in variability. *PLEASE '11 Proceedings of the 2nd International Workshop on Product Line Approaches in Software Engineering*.

Michalik, B., & Weyns, D. (2011). Towards a solution for change impact analysis of software product line products. In *Software Architecture (WICSA), 2011 9th Working IEEE/IFIP Conference on* (pp. 290–293). IEEE. 10.1109/WICSA.2011.45

Pohl, K., Bockle, G., & Van der Linden, F. J. (2005). *Software product line engineering: foundations, principles and techniques.* Springer. doi:10.1007/3-540-28901-1

Sabouri, H., & Khosravi, R. (2011). Efficient verification of evolving software product lines. In *International Conference on Fundamentals of Software Engineering* (pp. 351–358). Springer.

Schubanz, M., Pleuss, A., Pradhan, L., Botterweck, G., & Thurimella, A. K. (2013). Model-driven planning and monitoring of long-term software product line evolution. In *Proceedings of the Seventh International Workshop on Variability Modelling of Softwareintensive Systems* (p. 18). ACM. 10.1145/2430502.2430527

Ter Beek, M. H., Muccini, H., & Pelliccione, P. (2011). Guaranteeing correct evolution of software product lines: setting up the problem. In *International Workshop on Software Engineering for Resilient Systems* (pp. 100–105). Springer. 10.1007/978-3-642-24124-6_9

Wayne, P. M., & David, R. M. (2001). *Mesquite: a modular system for evolutionary analysis.* Retrieved from: http://www.cs.mcgill.ca/~birch/doc/mesquite/doc/MesquiteManual.pdf

Yazdanshenas, A. R., & Moonen, L. (2012). Fine-grained change impact analysis for component-based product families. In *Software Maintenance (ICSM), 2012 28th IEEE International Conference on* (pp. 119–128). IEEE. 10.1109/ICSM.2012.6405262

Chapter 18
Hybrid Term–Similarity–Based Clustering Approach and Its Applications

Banage T. G. S. Kumara
Sabaragamuwa University of Sri Lanka, Sri Lanka

Incheon Paik
University of Aizu, Japan

Koswatte R. C. Koswatte
Sri Lanka Institute of Information Technology, Sri Lanka

ABSTRACT

With the large number of web services now available via the internet, service discovery, recommendation, and selection have become a challenging and time-consuming task. Organizing services into similar clusters is a very efficient approach. A principal issue for clustering is computing the semantic similarity. Current approaches use methods such as keyword, information retrieval, or ontology-based methods. These approaches have problems that include discovering semantic characteristics, loss of semantic information, and a shortage of high-quality ontologies. Thus, the authors present a method that first adopts ontology learning to generate ontologies via the hidden semantic patterns existing within complex terms. Then, they propose service recommendation and selection approaches based on proposed clustering approach. Experimental results show that the term-similarity approach outperforms comparable existing clustering approaches. Further, empirical study of the prototyping recommendation and selection approaches have proved the effectiveness of proposed approaches.

DOI: 10.4018/978-1-5225-5396-0.ch018

INTRODUCTION

Service Oriented Architecture (Endrei et al., 2004) has been a widely accepted paradigm to facilitate distributed application integration and interoperability. Web services, which share business logic, data and processes through a programmatic interface, are a popular implementation of the service-oriented architecture. Web services are loosely coupled software components and represent an important way for businesses to communicate with each other and with clients. Existing technologies for Web services have been extended to give value-added customized services to users through service composition (Paik et al., 2014). Developers and users can then solve complex problems by combining available basic services such as travel planners. Web service discovery, which aims to match the user request against multiple service advertisements and provides a set of substitutable and compatible services by maintaining the relationship among services, is a crucial part of service composition. Now most of the business organizations are moving towards the Web services. Hence, numbers of Web services publish on the Internet are being increased in recent years (Al-Masri & Mahmoud, 2008). With this proliferation of Web services, service discovery, selection and recommendation are becoming a challenging and time-consuming task because of unnecessary similarity calculations in the matchmaking process within repositories such as Universal Description, Discovery and Integrations (UDDIs) and Web portals. Clustering Web services into similar groups, which can greatly reduce the search space, is an efficient approach to improving performance of service discovery, selection and recommendation. Clustering the Web services enables the user to identify appropriate and interesting services according to his or her requirements while excluding potential candidate services outside the relevant cluster and thereby limiting the search space to that cluster alone. Further, it enables efficient browsing for similar services within the same cluster.

In our previous work, we classified service clustering into several categories by considering the properties used in the clustering process: (i) functionally based clustering (ii) non-functionally based clustering and (iii) social-criteria-based clustering. Most previous works focus on the functionally based clustering approaches, considering the semantics of functional properties such *input*, *output*, *precondition*, and *effect* (Dasgupta et al., 2011; Nayak & Lee, 2007; Elgazzar et al., 2010). Non-functionally based clustering approaches reduce the computational time and complexity for Web service processes by considering quality-of-service (QoS) properties such as *cost* and *reliability*. Social-criteria-based clustering approaches consider social properties of services such as *sociability* (Chen et al., 2013). In our works, we mainly focused on functionally based clustering. A principal issue for clustering is computing the semantic similarity between services. Recent studies have proposed several approaches to calculating functional similarity. Simple approaches include checking the one-to-one matching of features such as the *service name* and checking the matching of service signatures such as the *messages* (Elgazzar et al., 2010). In some studies, information retrieval (IR) techniques are used (Platzer et al., 2009). These include similarity-measuring methods such as search-engine-based (SEB) methods (Liu & Wong 2009) and cosine similarity (Chen et al., 2010; Ma et al., 2008). Some researchers have used logical relationships such as *exact* and *plug-in* (Wagner et al., 2011) or edge-counting-based techniques (Xie et al., 2011; Sun, 2010) to increase the semantics in the similarity calculations via ontologies.

However, one-to-one matching, structure matching or a vector-space model may not accurately identify the semantic similarity among terms because of the heterogeneity and independence of service sources. These methods consider terms only at the syntactic level, whereas different service providers may use the same term to represent different concepts or may use different terms for the same concept. Furthermore, IR techniques such as cosine similarity usually focus on plain text, whereas Web services contain much more complex structures, often with very little textual description. This means that depending on IR techniques is very problematic. Moreover, there can be a loss of the machine-interpretable semantics found in service descriptions when converting data provided in service descriptions into vectors in IR techniques. In SEB similarity-measuring methods such as normalized Google distance (NGD), there is no guarantee that all the information needed to measure the semantic similarity between a given pair of words is contained in the top-ranking snippets. On the other hand, although ontologies help to improve semantic similarity, defining high-quality ontologies is a major challenge. Several methods have been used to develop ontologies in current approaches, including obtaining assistance from domain expertise, using resources such as WordNet (http://wordnet.princeton.edu/, n.d.) and using ontologies already available via the Internet (Xie et al., 2011). Developing ontology by obtaining assistance from domain expertise is a time-consuming task that requires considerable human effort. In addition, the lack of up-to-date information in a resource might fail to capture the latest concepts and relationships in a domain. Further, the lack of standards for integrating and reusing existing ontologies also hampers ontology-based (OB) semantics matching. Thus, we proposed hybrid term similarity (HTS) based clustering approach. In the approach first, we use an ontology-learning method. If this fails to calculate the similarities, we then use an IR-based method. Our ontology learning uses Web service description language (WSDL) documents to generate ontologies by examining the hidden semantic patterns that exist within the complex terms used in service features. In IR method, we use both thesaurus-based and SEB term similarities. We presented the method in (Kumara et al., 2014). This paper is extended version of the paper. After proposing the HTS based clustering approach we apply the method to solve some hot issues in service computing research area such as service recommendation and selection.

The remainder of this paper is organized as follows. Section 2 describes the background to service clustering and the proposed clustering approach. Section 3 explains service-feature calculations. Section 4 describes our proposed term-similarity approach. Section 5 presents the integration of the extracted features and the clustering algorithm. In section 6, we discuss the application of HTS based clustering. Section 7 discusses our experiments and their evaluation. In section 8, we present the related work. Finally, Section 9 concludes the study.

BACKGROUND

Service Clustering and Motivation

Calculating the semantic similarity between services has been a critical issue for clustering. Over recent decades, several approaches have been developed for the improved measurement of service similarity. We consider keyword-matching (Elgazzar et al., 2010; Liu & Wong, 2009), IR methods (Platzer et al., 2009; Chen et al., 2010) and OB methods (Wagner et al., 2011; Xie et al., 2011) as important methods. Table 1 provides the summary of issues that affect the clustering approaches in existing clustering approaches.

Description of service features in WSDL or OWL-S usually consists of complex terms. The current approaches simply split them into token terms and enter the analysis phase directly. This results in a simple mechanical analysis of the terms and hinders the accurate calculation of service similarity. In a real situation, complex terms contain ontological relationships that should be utilized. Our research analyzed these ontological relationships by ontology learning from a service data set. Capturing ontological concepts in complex terms improved the performance of the similarity calculation significantly. Then, if

Table 1. Summary of issues in current clustering approaches

Current Approaches	Problem for Clustering Performance
One-to-one and Structure Matching	• Consider terms only at the syntactic level • Loss of the machine-interpretable semantics found in service descriptions • Lack of up-to-date knowledge • Failed to identify synonyms or variations of terms
IR-based methods (ex., Cosine similarity)	• Usually focus on plain text, whereas Web services contain much more complex structures, often with very little textual description. • Loss of the machine-interpretable semantics found in service descriptions • Lack of up-to-date knowledge • Failed to identify synonyms or variations of terms
OB method	• Shortage of high quality ontology (defining high-quality ontologies is a major challenge), • Lack of up-to-date knowledge
SEB (ex., NGD)	• Do not encode fine grained information

the similarity calculation procedure fails, in terms of the generated ontologies, it will hand over to calculation by an IR-based method. Therefore, although ontologies may fail in calculating similarities, our approach can calculate a reasonable semantic similarity for services via an IR-based method. This hybrid of ontology learning and an IR-based method optimized the similarity calculation in a natural fashion.

Motivating Example for Ontology Learning

Consider the calculation of similarity between *ScienceFictionNovel* and *RomanticNovel* services. To calculate the similarity, we first tokenize the complex terms and calculate pair similarities (e.g., (*Science, Romantic*), (*Science, Novel*), (*Fiction, Romantic*)). Existing approaches consider only the distance between pairs of tokenized terms and cannot catch completely the semantics of the complex term. When we analyze the complex terms, we can identify hidden semantic patterns that may exist between tokenized terms in complex terms (e.g., *RomanticNovel* is a subclass of *Novel*). We can use this semantic pattern by generating ontologies for the service domain. Figure 1 shows the generated ontology for the above two services. Figure 2 shows the extended ontology with more services.

Figure 1. Ontology for two web services

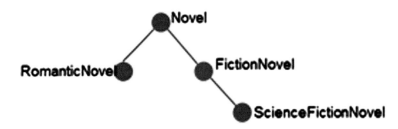

Figure 2. Extended ontology

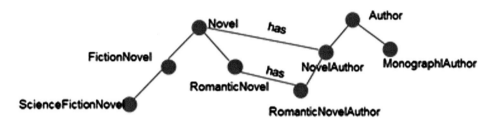

Proposed Ontology Learning Based Clustering Approach

The architecture of the proposed ontology learning based clustering approach is illustrated in Figure 3. We used WSDL files to cluster the services. First, we mined the WSDL documents to extract features that describe the functionality of services in the feature-extraction phase. In the ontology-learning Phase, we used ontology learning method to generate ontologies for all of the extracted features. We then computed the similarity of individual features in the similarity-calculation phase using the HTS method which uses ontology learning and IR based term similarity. Next, features were integrated in the feature-integration phase. Finally, in the clustering phase, an agglomerative clustering algorithm was used to cluster the services.

Figure 3. Overview of the clustering approach

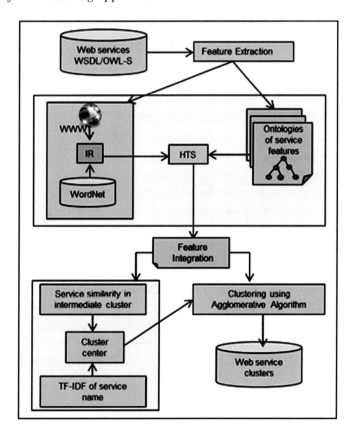

FEATURE EXTRACTION

As the first step of the functional based clustering procedure, we need to extract service features from the Web service description documents. As we mentioned, we used WSDL documents to cluster the Web services. As is usual in the literature (Elgazzar et al., 2010), we used *service name, operation, domain name, input* and *output messages* as the service features. Selected features of WSDL file describe and reveal the functionality of its Web services.

We extracted the *service name* and *domain name* used in the service and definition elements of WSDL documents. Figure 4 shows location of *service name* in the WSDL file. The figure is part of *ScienceFictionNovelPublisher* service's WSDL document. *Operations* give an abstract description of the actions supported by the service, which are listed in the main element <portType>. Operation has several parameters such as *name* and another optional attributes specifying the order of the parameters used in that operation. As an example, we can define an operation called "*GetSymbol*" that has the "*GetSymbolInput*" massage as an *input* that produce the "*GetSymbolOutput*" massage as an output. We extract the *operation name* as a feature.

Message elements describe the data being exchanged between the Web service providers and consumers. Messages are composed of part elements, one for each parameter of the Web service's function. We considered the part elements for measuring the similarity of *input* and *output* messages. Multiple part names are used in the messages when the message has multiple logic units. For example, a *get_Book_PriceResponse* output message in an *AuthorBook-price* service would have *Book* and *Price* part elements. Then average similarity value for the input or output messages is calculated as follows:

$$Sim_m(S_i, S_j) = \sum_{p=1}^{k} \sum_{q=1}^{n} \frac{\max\_sim(s_p, r_q)}{(k+n)}$$

Here, s_p and r_q denote the individual part elements of input or output messages in services S_i and, S_j respectively. Parameters k and n are the number of part elements in input or output messages.

Figure 4. Part of a WSDL document

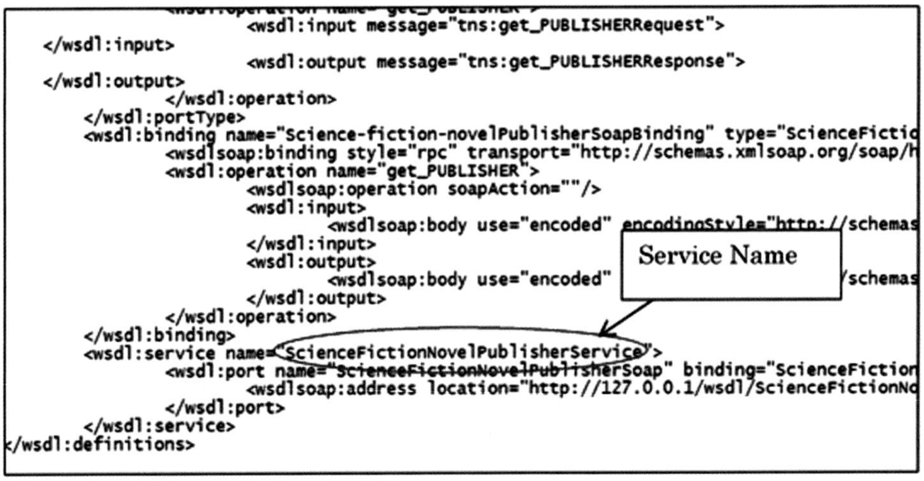

ONTOLOGY GENERATION AND FEATURE SIMILARITY CALCULATION

After extracting the features, we need to generate the ontologies from service documents. Here, ontologies were generated for each service feature type (*service name*) separately. After generating the ontologies, service feature similarity values were computed using HTS approach. In calculating the similarity of the relevant feature (*service name*) of two Web services, we did not split the complex terms as in usual literature, but considered the ontologies that generated by ontology learning method for those complex terms to check for the existence of concepts. If there were any concepts that relate to service features of the two Web services in the same ontology, then we computed the degree of semantic matching for the given pair of service features by applying different filters. Otherwise, we used the IR method to calculate the similarity.

Ontology Learning Method

As mentioned, developing high-quality ontology is a difficult and time-consuming task and also IR loss semantic found in service description. Therefore, the clustering accuracy of existing approaches has reached a saturation point and cannot be improved further. We therefore proposed an ontology learning method that analyzes service features to recognize their semantics more precisely. We used the complex terms used in service features and their underling semantics to generate the ontologies automatically. First, we extracted the relevant feature (e.g., *service name*) from the service data set. If the feature is a complex term, we then split it into individual terms based on several assumptions. For example, the *ComedyFilm* name would be divided into two parts (*Comedy*, *Film*) based on the assumption that the capitalized characters indicate the start of a new word. Stop-word filtering was then performed to remove any stop words (e.g., of). In the next step after this preprocessing, we calculated the TF–IDF value of all the tokenized words. The terms were ranked according to their TF–IDF values, with the highest-ranking word having the highest TF–IDF value and a threshold TF–IDF value being defined. This is because we need to identify only service-specific terms relevant to the service domain and the more meaningful terms in generating the upper-level concepts.

Ontology is an explicit specification of a conceptualization. Relations describe the interactions between concepts or a concept's properties. We consider two types of relations, namely concept hierarchy (Subclass–Superclass) and triples (Subject–Predicate–Object). Let C be a set of concepts $\{C_1, C_2, ..., Cn\}$ in the ontology. Here, C_i represents S_iF, which is a feature F (e.g., *service name*) of service S_i. $\mathrm{LSC}(C_i)$ is the set of least specific concepts (direct children) C_x of C_i. That is, C_x is an immediate sub-concept of C_i in the concept hierarchy. $\mathrm{LGC}(C_x)$ is the set of least generic concepts (direct parents) C_i of C_x. $\mathrm{PROP}(C_i)$ is the set of properties of concept C_i.

Definition 1 (Subclass–Superclass Relationship)

If $C_i{\in}LSC(C_j) \bigwedge C_j{\in}LGC(C_i)$, then there exists a Subclass–Superclass relationship between concepts C_i and C_j .

Concept C_i can be an individual term (*Employee*) or a complex term (*OrganizationEmployee*). If a concept is a complex term, then its rightmost term is the head of the concept (*Employee*) and the element to the left is the modifier term of the concept (*Organization*).

- **Rule 1 (Head–Modifier Relation Rule):** *Heads and modifiers express Subclass–Superclass relations between lexical items. This identifies a set of terms related through hyponymy with the head of the compound constituting the hypernym (Hippisley, Cheng et al., 2005).*
- **Example 1 (Subclass–Superclass relationship):** Let us consider the complex term *RomanticNovel*. Here, *Novel* is modified by the term *Romantic*. Therefore, *RomanticNovel* is a subclass of *Novel*.

We consider two types of properties, namely *data* and *object* in this research. The *data* property refers to the *data* in a concept *(Organization name)*. The *object* property is used to relate a concept to another concept *(Organization* has *Organization Employee)*.

Definition 2 (Property Relationship)

If there exists $C_j \in PROP(C_i)$, then C_j has a property relation (triple relation) with C_i. Here, the target entity of the property could be either an object or data.

Definition 2.1 (Data Property Relationship)

If $p_i \in PROP(C_j)$ and p_i is data in concept C_j, then there exists a data property relationship between p_i and concept C_j.

- **Rule 2 (Compound Noun Rule):** *If the individual terms in complex term t are nouns and if there is no concept in the ontology that is equal to head term H_t and if there is a concept that is equal to modifier term M_t, then there exists a data property relationship between concept M_t and data t.*
- **Example 2 (Data Property Relationship):** Let us consider the complex term *PhysicianName*. If *Name* is not a concept and *Physician* is a concept, then *PhysicianName* is a data property of *Physician*.

Definition 2.2 (Object Property Relationship)

If $(C_i \in PROP(C_j)) \bigwedge (C_j \in PROP(C_i))$, then there exists an object property relationship between concepts C_i and C_j.

- **Rule 3 (Concept and Modifier Rule):** *If concept C_i is equal to a modifier term of concept C_j, then there exists an object property relationship between C_i and C_j.*
- **Example 3 (Object Property Relationship):** If concept C_i is *Hospital* and concept C_j is *HospitalEmployee*, then the relationship can be expressed as *HospitalEmployee* has *Hospital* and *Hospital* has *HospitalEmployee*.
- **Rule 4 (Modifier Only Rule):** *If a modifier term of concept C_i is equal to a modifier term of concept C_j and if there is no concept in the ontology that is equal to that modifier term, then there exists an object property relationship between C_i and C_j*
- **Example 4 (Object Property Relationship):** Let us consider two concepts *MedicalEmployee* and *MedicalOrganization*. If term *Medical* is not a concept, then the relationship can be expressed as *MedicalEmployee* has *MedicalOrganization* and *MedicalOrganization* has *MedicalEmployee*.

Ontology Construction Algorithm

Algorithm 1 describes the ontology-construction process for complex service terms. We generated the concepts and relationships between concepts using the TF–IDF value ranking and rules. We selected a word of the highest rank and generated a concept for that term. We then selected all complex terms that make use of that word to build the complex term by taking it as its head. We considered all levels in the subsumption hierarchy of the complex term as show in Figure 5. We generated concepts for all levels of the particular complex term (Lines 3–7). We then applied Rule 1 to generate a Subclass–Superclass relation (Line 8). This process was repeated for all tokenized words that have TF–IDF values greater than the defined threshold value. Next, we generated a data property relation by applying Rule 2 (Lines 11–17). Finally, we applied Rules 3 and 4 to generate object property relations (Lines 18–23).

IR-Based Term Similarity

As IR-based term-similarity methods, we used two approaches, namely thesaurus-based term similarity and SEB term similarity.

- **Thesaurus-Based Term Similarity:** This method can be considered as a knowledge-rich similarity-measuring technique. We used WordNet as the knowledge base. To calculate the semantic similarity of two terms we used an edge-count-based approach (Qu et al., 2009).
- **SEB Term Similarity:** One main issue for the above method is that some terms used in Web services may not be included in the thesaurus. We may therefore fail to obtain a reasonable similarity value for features (e.g., "*IphonePrice*" and "*NokiaPrice*"). However, the SEB method can overcome this problem because it analyzes Web-based documents. Further, it can identify the latent semantics in the terms (e.g., the semantic similarity between "*Apple*" and "*Computer*").

We considered three algorithms called Web-Jaccard, Web-Dice and Web-PMI, as described in (Bollegala et al., 2007).

$$Web - Jaccard\left(P, Q\right) = \begin{cases} 0, & if(H\left(P \cap Q\right)) \leq c \\ \dfrac{H\left(P \cap Q\right)}{H\left(P\right) + H\left(Q\right) - H\left(P \cap Q\right)}, & otherwise \end{cases}$$

Figure 5. Sub-subsumption hierarchy of the complex term

Level 1 ● Organization

Level 2 ● EducationalOrganization

Level 3 ● HigherEducationalOrganization

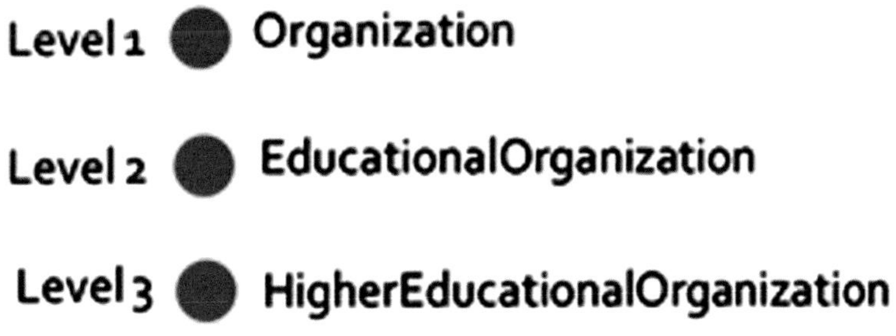

Algorithm 1 Ontology Construction

Input T_c: Array of complex terms
Input T_t: Array of tokenized terms
Input θ: Threshold TF-IDF value
Output O: Ontology
1. **for** each tokenized term t_t, where TF-IDF value > θ in T_t **do**
2.   generate Concept(t_t);
3.   **for** each complex term t in T_c **do**
4. H_t = get Head Term(t);
5.   **if** (t_t.equals (H_t))
6.   generate Concepts for All Level-Complex Terms(t);
7.   **end**
8.   generate Sub Super Relationship (); // By Rule 1.
9.   **end-for**
10. **end-for**
11. **for** each complex term t in T_c **do**
12. H_t = get Head Term(t);
13. M_t = get Modifier Term(t);
14.   **If** (H_t is not a concept and M_t is a concept)
15.   generate Data Property (); //By Rule 2.
16.   **end**
17. **end-for**
18. **for** each concept C_i **do**
19.   **for** each concept C_j **do**
20.   generate Object Property for Concept Modifier (); // By Rule 3.
21.   generate Object Property for Modifier Only (); //By Rule 4.
22.   **end-for**
23. **end-for**

$$Web-Dice\left(P,Q\right) = \begin{cases} 0, & if(H\left(P \cap Q\right)) \leq c \\ \dfrac{2H(P \cap Q)}{H\left(P\right)+H\left(Q\right)}, & otherwise \end{cases}$$

$$Web-PMI\left(P,Q\right) = \begin{cases} 0, & if(H\left(P \cap Q\right)) \leq c \\ \log_2(\dfrac{\dfrac{H(P \cap Q)}{N}}{\dfrac{H\left(P\right)}{N}\dfrac{H\left(Q\right)}{N}}), & otherwise \end{cases}$$

Here, $H(P)$ and $H(Q)$ are page counts for the queries P and Q, respectively. $H\left(P \cap Q\right)$ is the conjunction query P AND Q. All the coefficients are set to zero if $H\left(P \cap Q\right)$ is less than a threshold, c, because two terms may appear by accident on the same page. N is the number of documents indexed by the search engine.

First, we computed the pair similarity of the individual terms used in complex terms to calculate the feature similarity as follows:

$$Sim\left(T_1, T_2\right) = \alpha Sim_T\left(T_1, T_2\right) + \beta Sim_{SE}\left(T_1, T_2\right)$$

Here, $Sim_T\left(T_1, T_2\right)$ is the thesaurus-based term-similarity score and $Sim_{SE}\left(T_1, T_2\right)$ is the SEB similarity score. Parameters α and β are real values between 0 and 1, with $\alpha + \beta = 1$.

We then calculated the feature similarity value:

$$Sim_F\left(S_i, S_j\right) = \sum_{p=1}^{l}\sum_{q=1}^{m}\frac{\max\_ sim(x_p, y_q)}{(l + m)}.$$

where x_p and y_q denote the individual terms, with l and m being the number of individual terms in a particular feature of services S_i and S_j respectively.

Similarity Computation

In calculating the similarity of two Web services, we first extracted the relevant feature from two WSDL files. We did not split the complex terms, but considered the ontologies for those complex terms to check for the existence of concepts. If there were any concepts that relate to service features in the same ontology, then we computed the degree of semantic matching for the given pair of service features by applying different filters.

We use the *Exact, Plug-in* and *Subsumes* filters defined in Klusch et al. (2006). If one concept is a property of another concept, then those concepts are semantically closer to each other. We therefore introduce three new filters, namely *Property-&-Concept, Property-&-Property* and *Sibling*, in this research.

- **Exact:** If $C_i \equiv C_j$ then S_iF perfectly matches S_jF.
- **Property-&-Concept:** If $C_i \in PROP\left(C_j\right)$, then the S_iF property-&-concept matches S_jF.
- **Property-&-Property:** If $C_i \in PROP\left(C_k\right) \wedge C_j \in PROP\left(C_k\right)$, then S_iF property-&-property matches S_jF.
- **Plug-in Match:** If $C_i \in LSC\left(C_j\right)$, then S_iF.plugs into S_jF.
- **Sibling Match:** If $C_i \in LSC\left(C_k\right) \wedge C_j \in LSC\left(C_k\right)$, then S_iF sibling-matches S_jF.
- **Subsumes Match:** If $C_j > C_i$ (C_i is more specific than C_j, then S_jF subsumes S_iF.

- **Logic Fail and Fail:** If C_i and C_j are in the same ontology O_p, but fail in the above six matches, then S_iF logic-fails to match S_jF. If the two concepts are in heterogeneous ontologies, then S_iF fails to match S_jF.

We applid the filters in the following order, based on the degree of strength for logic-based matching: *Exact > Property-&-Concept > Property-&-Property > Plug-in > Sibling > Subsumes > Logic Fail > Fail.*

If there is an *Exact* match between two concepts, then the similarity is equal to the highest value 1. If the matching filter is *Property-&-Concept, Property-&-Property, Sibling, Plug-in, Subsumes, or Logic Fail,* then we calculate the similarity as follows:

$$Sim\left(C_i, C_j\right) = W_m + W_e Sim_E\left(C_i, C_j\right)$$

Here, W_m and W_e are weights for matching filter and edge-base similarity respectively, with $W_m + W_e = 1$. $Sim_E\left(C_i, C_j\right)$ is the edge-based similarity and calculated by using following equation (Zhang et al., 2007).

$$Sim_E\left(C_i, C_j\right) = -\log \frac{d\left(C_i, C_j\right)}{2D}$$

Here, $d\left(C_i, C_j\right)$ is the shortest distance between concepts C_i and C_j and parameter D is the maximum depth of the ontology.

If two concepts are in heterogeneous ontologies (the services fail to match using any matching filter except *Fail*), then the IR-based term-similarity method was used to calculate the feature similarity.

In this research, we did not generate and train from labeled data, but just generated ontology for helping more exact term similarity calculation from the existing Web service set by defining the rules. Our method created some standard for answer from the existing problem sets before examination.

FEATURE INTEGRATION AND CLUSTERING

Feature Integration

The final service similarity value $Sim_S\left(S_i, S_j\right)$ to be used for service clustering was calculated by integrating the feature-similarity values for Web services S_i and S_j as follows:

$$Sim_S\left(S_i, S_j\right) = W_N Sim\left(Name_i, Name_j\right) + W_{OP} Sim(Op_i, Op_j) + W_D Sim(Domain_i, Domain_j)$$
$$+ W_O Sim(Out_i, Out_j) + W_I Sim(Ini, Inj)$$

Here, weights for each feature elements, $W_N \cdot W_{OP} \cdot W_D, W_O$ .nd W_I .are real values between 0 and 1, with $W_N \cdot W_{OP} \cdot W_D + W_O + W_I = 1$..

Clustering

We used an agglomerative clustering algorithm in Algorithm 2 that can handle any form of similarity or distance easily, can obtain the main structure of the data and has a low computation cost. This bottom-up hierarchical clustering method starts by assigning each service to its own cluster (Lines 1 in Algorithm 2). It then starts merging the most similar clusters, based on proximity of the clusters at each iteration, until the stopping criterion is met (e.g., number of clusters) (Lines 4–10 in Algorithm 2). Several methods have been used to merge clusters, such as single-link and complete-link (Murtagh, 1985). We use a centroid-based method where, for the proximity value, we use $Sim_S\left(S_i, S_j\right)$ .between cluster centers.

We proposed novel cluster center identification approach in previous paper (Kumara et al., 2014). Figure 6 and Figure 7 show an example of the clustering steps, with Figure 8 showing a tree representation.

APPLICATIONS OF SERVICE CLUSTERING

Cluster-Based Web Service Recommendation

As the abundance of Web services on the internet increase, designing effective approaches for Web service recommendation has become more and more important. Current recommendation approaches can be categorized into three categories: content-based (Pazzani & Billsus, 2007), collaborative filtering (CF) (Ma et al., 2007) and hybrid approach (Burke, 2007). Content-based approach aims at inferring similarities among services by analyzing service's functionalities. The approaches use features of the services as the background data for the recommendation. CF based approaches focus on recommending end-users services that other similar end-users interacted with and appreciated in the past, depending

Figure 6. Web Services

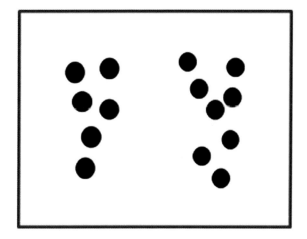

Figure 7. Clustering

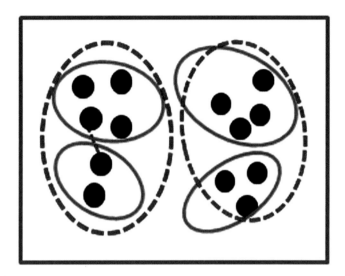

Figure 8. Tree representation

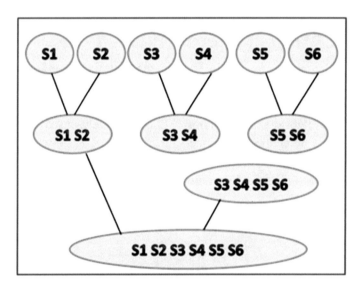

on the similarity between their profiles, preferences, interest and past ranking. Hybrid approaches use both CF and content-based approaches.

In our next work, we proposed cluster based service recommendation approach. In that approach, we clustered the services based on two factors. CF approach is not appropriate in some context, where the users do not want to interact with services that have totally different functionalities, which they used to interact. Therefore, we considered functionality of services to address the issue as the first factor. Further, Web services are intended to be composed together and user may be interesting to identify the appropriate services to generate value-added service. Thus, we considered the association between services as the second factor. As the first factor, semantic similarities values between services were calculated. To

Algorithm 2 Clustering Algorithm

```
Input    S: Array of service similarity values
Input    n: Number of required clusters
Output   C: Service clusters
1. Let each service be a cluster;
2. Compute Proximity Matrix (S);
3. k = No Of Services;
4. while k ! = n do
5.     Merge two closest clusters;
6.     k = get No Of Current Clusters ();
7.     Calculate center value of all services in all   clusters;
8.     Select service with highest value of each cluster as cluster centers;
9.     Update Proximity Matrix ();
10. end while
```

calculate the semantic similarity, we used HTS method. To calculate the second factor, service's past social interactions were used. By analyzing past workflows, we can find usage patterns to know with whom the service has worked in the past and with whom it would prefer to work in the future. Here, we used association rules mining technique to calculate the second factor.

Proposed Approach

Figure 9 shows the architecture of the proposed cluster based recommendation approach. We used the structure of WSDL files as usual and past workflows information to recommend services. First, we clustered the services considering functionality and association between services. Then, we calculated the affinity of currently invoked service (CIS) with cluster representatives of all the clusters to select the candidate cluster. After selecting the candidate cluster, affinity values between CIS and cluster members were calculated. To calculate similarity values, HTS method and association rule mining techniques (Chen et al., 2006) were used. Then, we ranked the services according to the similarities and finally, services with the top ranks and better Quality of Service (QoS) attributes were selected as the candidate services. We presented the approach in our previous paper (Kumara et al., 2016).

Web Service Selection

As we mentioned in introduction section, Web services have been extended to give value-added customized services to users through service composition Service Composition consists of four stages: planning, discovery, selection, and execution (Paik et al., 2014).. In the planning stage, an abstract workflow is constructed. For each workflow task, the discovery stage tries to identify available related services as candidates. Set of functionally equivalent services with varying QoS values can be identified. In the selection stage, a QoS-aware service selection algorithm selects optimal services for each task. In the execution stage, the selected services are operated in the workflow. In our next work, we proposed QoS aware Web service selection approach.

Figure 9. Architecture of proposed recommendation approach

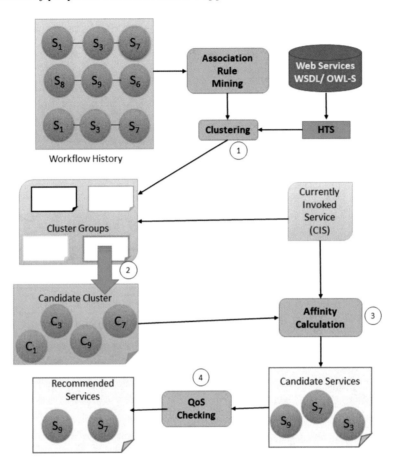

Proposed Approach

Figure 10 shows a block diagram of the architecture of the proposed approach. First, we clustered the services by considering the services functionality. Here, HTS method was used to compute the semantic similarity between the services. SASKS algorithm (Sasaki et al., 2012) was used as the clustering algorithm. Then as the next step, we extracted the clusters and compute the QoS similarity values between the services in each cluster. To calculate the QoS similarity, first we generated QoS vector for each service and employed Euclidean distance based similarity calculation approach. Next, affinity matrix was generated using the QoS similarity values. Finally, services are clustered and plotted onto the sphere using the SASKS algorithm according to the QoS similarity values. We presented our approach in (Kumara et al., 2017).

EXPERIMENTS AND EVALUATION

The experimental platform used Microsoft Windows 7, an Intel Core i7-3770 at 3.40 GHz and 4 GB RAM. Java was used as the programming language, and the Jena Framework was used to build the ontologies.

Figure 10. Architecture of proposed selection approach

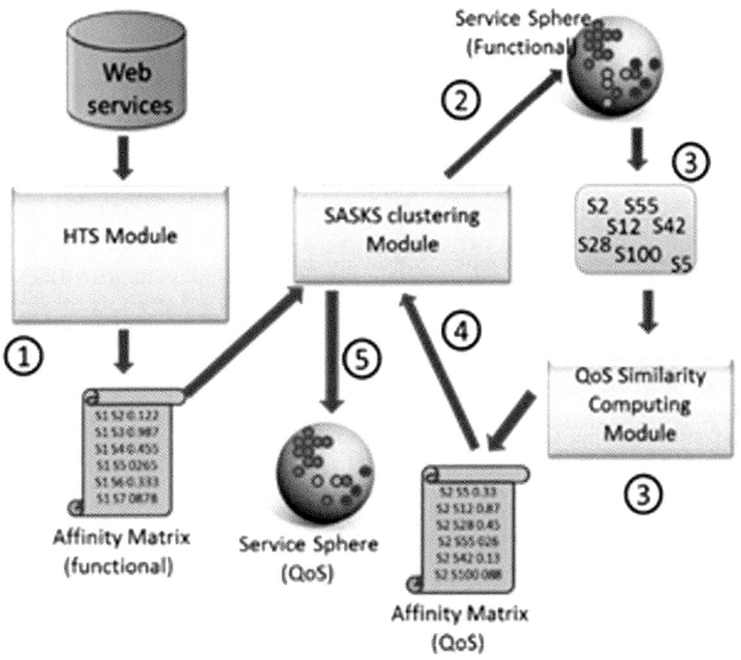

The Jena Framework provides a collection of tools and Java libraries for developing ontologies. WSDL documents were gathered from real-world Web service repositories, and the OWL-S (http://projects. semwebcentral.org/projects/owls-tc/) test collection to act as the services dataset.

HTS Based Cluster Evaluation

We first performed a manual classification to categorize the Web service data set for comparison purposes. The categories identified were *Book, Medical, Food, Film* and *Vehicle*. For the evaluation of cluster quality, we first used purity and entropy, which are external evaluation criteria. Purity determines how pure each of the clusters is and is defined as:

$$Purity = \frac{1}{n} \sum_{j=1}^{k} \max_{c} \left\{ n_j^i \right\}.$$

Here, n is the total number of services and n_j^i is the number of services in cluster j belonging to domain class i.

Entropy measures how the various semantic classes are distributed within each cluster. Smaller entropy values indicate better clustering solutions. The entropy of a cluster is given by:

$$E\left(C_r\right) = -\frac{1}{\log q} \sum_{i=1}^{q} \frac{n_r^i}{n_r} \log \frac{n_r^i}{n_r}.$$

Here, q is the number of domain classes in the data set, n_r^i .s the number of services of the i .ᵗʰ domain class that were assigned to the r .ᵗʰ cluster and n_r .s the number of services in cluster r . The entropy of the entire cluster is:

$$Entropy = \sum_{r=1}^{k} \frac{n_r}{n} E\left(C_r\right).$$

We evaluated the cluster performance by changing the weight values in IR based term similarity equation to measure the effect of the term-similarity methods. We used two methods. For Method 1, if two terms were in the WordNet database, we assigned 1 for α .and 0 for β .(otherwise 0 for α .and 1 for β). For Method 2, we assigned the same value of 0.5 for both α .nd β . Figure 11 shows the variation in purity when the number of Web services is increased.

We can therefore determine that, by using Method 1, we can improve the performance of the clustering process.

In the next evaluation procedure, we evaluated our HTS approach, which uses both ontology learning and IR-based term similarity. We implemented a clustering approach using only the edge-count-based method that uses WordNet to calculate similarities for comparison. Figure 12 shows the purity and entropy values for the two approaches with respect to the number of services.

According to the results, purity decreases and entropy increases when increasing the number of services in both approaches. However, our approach obtained lower entropy and higher purity values throughout. Moreover, the rate of entropy increase is greater in the edge-count-based method and the rate of purity-value decrease is smaller in the HTS approach. According to these results, we can see that our HTS approach improves the clustering performance.

As additional evaluation criteria for our HTS clustering approach, we used precision, recall and F-measure. Precision is the fraction of a cluster that comprises services of a specified class. Recall is the fraction of a cluster that comprises all services of a specified class. The F-measure measures the extent to which a cluster contains only services of a particular class and all services of that class.

Figure 11. Contribution of term-similarity methods

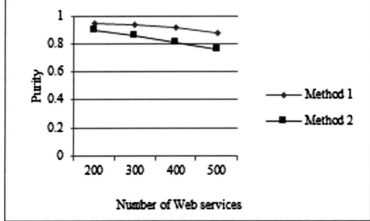

Figure 12. Cluster performance with HTS approach

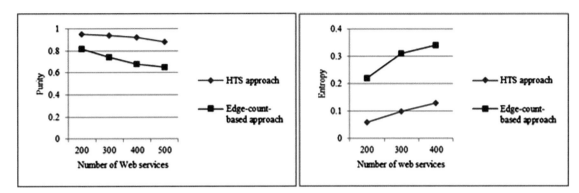

Following Equations are used to calculate these three criteria.

$$\text{Precision}\left(i, j\right) = \frac{NM_{ij}}{NM_j}.$$

$$\text{Recall}\left(i, j\right) = \frac{NM_{ij}}{NM_i}.$$

Here, NM_{ij} .is the number of members of class i .in cluster j . NM_j .s the number of members of cluster j .and NM_i .s the number of members of class i .

The F-measure of cluster i .with respect to class j .is,

$$F\left(i, j\right) = \frac{2 \times \text{Precision}\left(i, j\right) \times \text{Recall}\left(i, j\right)}{\text{Precision}\left(i, j\right) + \text{Recall}\left(i, j\right)}$$

According to the experimental results in Table 2, there are no false positives for the *Medical* cluster in either approach, the precision values for both approaches being 100%. For all other clusters, however, our approach obtained higher precision values. For example, our approach improved the precision value for the *Food* cluster by 41%. However, the *Medical* cluster obtained the lowest recall. When we analyzed the WSDL documents, we observed that some extracted features failed to identify their ontology. For example, the *CheckRoomAvailability* service belonging to the medical domain was not successfully placed in the *Medical* cluster. In this case, the service failed to join with other services, such as *MedicalOrganization, HospitalClinic* and many others in the medical domain, in generating the ontology. Moreover, the IR-based method in the HTS approach also failed to identify the correct domain from the terms used in the *CheckRoomAvailability* service. As for the precision values, our approach obtained higher values for both recall and F-measure. The recall value for the *Book* cluster improved by 38.7% and obtained a 100% value by placing all services correctly.

Table 2. Performance measures of clusters

Cluster	HTS Approach			Edge-Count-Based Term-Similarity Using WordNet		
	Precision %	Recall %	F-Measure %	Precision %	Recall %	F-Measure%
Book	86.7	100	92.9	67.1	61.3	64.1
Medical	100	83.1	90.8	100	70.0	82.4
Food	96.0	91.3	93.6	55.0	60.0	57.4
Film	91.0	88.0	89.5	77.7	50.0	60.8
Vehicle	81.6	94.8	87.7	56.0	80.9	66.2

Evaluation of Recommendation Approach

First, we considered only the functionality of the services to cluster the services. Figure 13 shows the sample output of our clustering based recommendation approach. Here, the approach recommended the services to *EmergencyPhysian* service according to the functionality. According to the results, we can observe that our approach listed most functionally similar in the top of the list. To provide a comparison, we implemented a recommendation approach without using clustering. WordNet and the edge-count-based (ECB) methods were used to calculate similarity between *CIS* and services in the dataset. Figure 14 show the outputs of ECB approach. Figure 14 also we can see the *HospitalPhysian* as the top service as in clustering based approach. However, there are some invalid members such as *TitleMedia* in the recommended list.

Next, we considered both association rule mining techniques and HTS method to calculate affinity values in clustering process. Here, service were clustered according to their past patterns of the transactions. The clustered are different from the functional based clusters. For an example, services of the Hotel domain such as *city_luxuryhotel_service* and *village_hotel_service*, services of the Geography domain such as *calculateDistanceInMiles* and *calculateSunriseTime*, and services of Sport domain such as *sports_beach_service* and *hiking_ruralarea_service* were in same clusters. When we analyze the past workflows, we show that those services worked together to generate composite services. The services can be used to generate travel plan. But in functional based clustering the services were not in same cluster. In functional clustering, we do not consider the workflow patterns and consider only the

Figure 13. Sample output of Clustering based recommendation approach (Functional based clustering)

Currently Invoked Service: *EmergencyPhysianService*
Recommended Services
HospitalPhysian
CheckDoctoravailability
CareorganizationDiagnosticprocesstimeinterval
CareorganizationDiagnosticprocesstimemeasure
CheckHospitalavailability
InformHospital

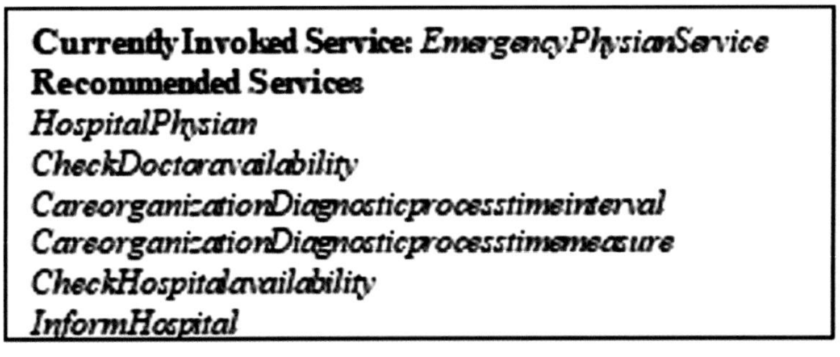

Figure 14. Sample output of recommendation approach without service clustering

Currently Invoked Service: *EmergencyPhysianService*
Recommended Services
HospitalPhysian
CheckDoctaravailability
TitleMedia
CareorganizationDiagnosticprocesstimemeasure
CheckHospitalavailability
MaxpriceLiquid

semantic similarity. For an example, functionalities of *calculateSunriseTime*, service and *city_luxury-hotel_*service are different from each other. Thus, similarity value is low value. As a result of this, the services are clustered into different clusters.

Figure 15 shows the sample output of cluster-based recommendation approach of above evaluation step. Here, the approach recommended the services to *ActivityNationalpark* service. When we analyzed the pattern, we show that to *ActivityNationalpark* service was worked together with recommended services such as *Location-MapService* to construct composite services

However, if a service is an isolated service or new service, then the service will not be able to find a suitable cluster under the Association rule mining based clustering due to lack of interaction with other services in the history. Further, semantic similarity value of two services may be low value. But those services may be frequently interact with each other in history. Thus, by considering the both factors we can overcome above issues.

Evaluation of Service Selection Approach

This sub section discusses the visualization results of the proposed selection method. In this method, we identified four main regions. Figure 16 shows the services sphere, part of the profit based cluster PC1 and part of the profit based cluster PC2.

Figure 15. Sample output of Clustering based recommendation approach (association rule mining techniques band HTS based clustering)

Currently Invoked Service: *ActivityNationalpark*
Recommended Services
Location-MapService
CalculateDistanceInMiles
countrycity_hotel_service
ActivityDestination
luxuryhotel_service

Figure 16. Visualization results of the profit based QoS aware clustering

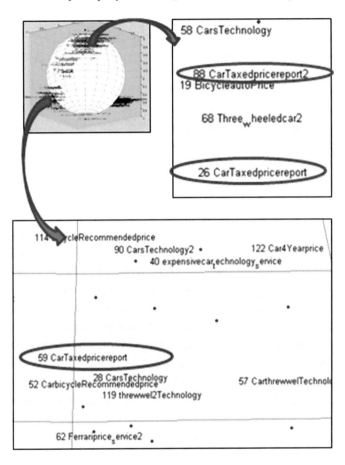

Here we observed that some services with high functional similarity are in different clusters. For example, there are services with service ID 88, 26 and 59 (see highlighted areas in Figure 8). Name (*CarTaxedPriceReport*) and functionality of the services are functionally identical and functional similarity is 1. But, service with ID 59 is in cluster PC2 and others are in PC1 due to the QoS variation. Furthermore, *CarsTechnology* service with ID 58 is in PC1 and *CarsTechnology2* service with ID 90 is in PC2. When we analyzed the QoS profit vectors of the services, we observed that the services have totally different QoS profit values. QoS profit vector of service 58 is {0.88, 0.13, 1.0, 0.88} and vector {0.25, 0.88, 0.25, 0.25} is the QoS profit vector of service 90. Here, service 58 has high QoS profit values for all QoS attributes except cost. But, service 90 has low QoS profit values for all QoS attributes except cost. As a result of this, the services are placed into two separate clusters. We provided detail evaluation in our previous paper

RELATED WORK

In this section, we discuss work related to Web service clustering. Calculating the semantic similarity between services has been a critical issue for functional based service clustering. Over recent decades, several approaches have been developed for the improved measurement of service similarity. The similarity methods such as cosine similarity, SEB methods and ontology methods again can be categorized into several categories: (i) string based approaches (ii) corpus based approaches (iii) knowledge based approaches and (iv) hybrid approaches. String based approaches operate on string sequences and character composition. The approaches measure similarity or dissimilarity between two text strings for approximate string matching or comparison. Similarity methods such as cosine similarity (Platzer et al., 2009) are belonging to this category. Cosine similarity usually focuses on plain text, whereas Web services can contain much more complex structures, often with very little textual description. This makes the method very problematic. Corpus based similarity is a semantic similarity measure that determines the similarity between terms according to information gained from large corpora. Knowledge-based similarity is a semantic similarity measure that determines the degree of similarity between terms using information derived from semantic network such as ontologies and knowledge based such as WordNet. Hybrid approaches used combination of above approaches

(Liu & Wong, 2009) combined a string-based similarity method such as structure matching with a corpus-based method to measure the similarity of Web service. However, structure matching may not accurately identify the semantic similarity among terms because of the heterogeneity and independence of service sources. These methods consider terms only at the syntactic level. Wen et al. (2011) presented a Web service discovery method based on semantics and clustering. Similarities among services were computed by using knowledge-based methods based on WordNet and ontologies. Wagner et al. (2011) arranged Web services in a functionality graph based on the Exact and Plug-in relationships. Logic-based filters were used to calculate the service similarity. Chifu et al. (2010) proposed an approach to service clustering inspired by the behavior of ants. They defined a set of metrics to evaluate the semantic similarity between services. The proposed metrics considered ontology hierarchies of concepts and properties. However, by using fixed ontologies and fixed knowledge bases, these approaches failed to capture reasonable similarity values for different domains. Further, developing ontology by obtaining assistance from domain expertise is a time-consuming task that requires considerable human effort. In our ontology learning approach, we automatically generate ontologies by examine the service description files.

Huynh et al. (2017) proposed a quality-controlled logic-based clustering approach for web service composition and verification. In the approach, Web service was represented as a logical expression. Then, Web services were grouped into clusters based on the calculation of the similarity between their logical expressions. Finally, they combined hierarchical agglomerative clustering and k-means to ensure the quality of generated clusters. To improve the performance of discovery, Surianarayanan et al. (2016) presented a clustering based approach. They used two similarity models namely, Output Similarity Model and Total Similarity Model. First model computed similarity between two services based on their output parameters and second method computed similarity between services using both the input and output parameters. Further, Kotekar and Kamath (2018) proposed another clustering approach based on Meta-heuristic Cat Swarm Optimization Algorithm, further optimized by Principle Component Analysis dimension reduction technique to increase the service discovery. Jiang et al. (2017) extracted service goals from service description documents by using natural language processing technologies. Then, they calculated similarity between two service goals and clustered the services by the K-means algorithm.

Current approaches do not consider the domain-specific context in measuring similarity and this has affected their clustering performance. Therefore, we proposed a context-aware similarity (CAS) method that learns domain context by machine learning to produce models of context for terms retrieved from the Web (Kumara et al., 2014). The CAS method analyzes the hidden semantics of services within a particular domain, and the awareness of service context helps to find cluster tensors that characterize the cluster elements. Experimental results show that CAS based approach works efficiently for the domain-context-aware clustering of services. Rupasingha et al. (2017) proposed a novel ontology-based approach for Web service clustering. It was an extended version of our ontology generation method. Authors focused on the similarity and specificity of terms for ontology generation. The amount of domain-specific information included in a term is used to define the specificity of that term.

CONCLUSION

Similarity computing approaches that use in current clustering approaches have problems that include a lack of semantic characteristics. This results in a loss of semantic information caused by the shortage of proper ontologies. To address this issue, we proposed ontology learning based clustering approach. The approach uses ontology learning in calculating the similarities. In the ontology learning step, we investigated the use of latent semantic patterns in the complex terms used for service features to generate the ontologies. Current approaches measure only the similarity of individual terms, thereby failing to identify hidden semantics in complex terms. Ontology learning based approach is able to capture the hidden semantics via an ontology learning phase that generates ontologies for service domains. However, if the concepts belong to different ontologies, the ontology learning method fails to measure similarities. We therefore needed to include an alternative approach to capture the semantics in services. Thus, we hybridized ontology learning with an IR-based method. Experimental results showed that the HTS approach performed better than an approach that used only edge-count-based term similarity, improving the average precision value by 19.9%. Then, we proposed clustering based recommendation and selection approaches. To cluster services in proposed recommendation approach, we have considered service semantic similarity and association between services. HTS method was used to calculate the semantic similarity and association rule mining technique was used to analyse the service association. According to the user interest, our approach recommend services for the currently invoked service of the user. User can get the functionally similar services for his currently invoked service by getting the advantage of semantic similarity value and user can identify members for generate workflow using service association factor. In proposed selection approach, first clustered the services using HTS method, Then, we extracted the clusters and compute the QoS similarity values between the services in each cluster. Then, affinity matrix was generated based on QoS profit values. Finally, the SASKS algorithm was used to cluster the Web services. Experimental results show that our recommendation approach and selection approach work effectively.

In future work, experiments will be carried out to improve the performance of Web service discovery and composition of services. Further, we plan to conduct a thorough evaluation of our proposed recommendation approach and selection approach.

REFERENCES

Al-Masri, E., & Mahmoud, Q. H. (2008). Investigating Web services on the World Wide Web. *Proceeding of the 17th International Conference on the World Wide Web*, 795-804. 10.1145/1367497.1367605

Bollegala, D., Matsuo, Y., & Ishizuka, M. (2007). Measuring Semantic Similarity between Words using Web Search Engines. *Proceeding of the 16th International World Wide Web Conference*, 757-766.

Burke, R. (2007). Hybrid Web Recommender Systems. In P. Brusilovsky, A. Kobsa, & W. Nejdl (Eds.), *The Adaptive Web: Methods and Strategies of Web Personalization. In LNCS, 4321* (pp. 377–408). Heidelberg, Germany: Springer. doi:10.1007/978-3-540-72079-9_12

Chen, G., Liu, H., Yu, L., Wei, Q., & Zhang, X. (2006). A new approach to classification based on association rule mining. *Decision Support Systems*, *42*(2), 674–689. doi:10.1016/j.dss.2005.03.005

Chen, L., Yang, G., Zhang, Y., & Chen, Z. (2010). Web services clustering using SOM based on kernel cosine similarity measure. *Proceeding of the 2nd International Conference on Information Science and Engineering*, 846–850. 10.1109/ICISE.2010.5689254

Chen, W., Paik, I., & Hung, P. C. K. (2014). Constructing a Global Social Service Network for Better Quality of Web Service Discovery. *IEEE Transactions on Services Computing*, *26*(5), 1466–1476.

Chifu, V. R., Pop, C. B., Salomie, I., Dinsoreanu, M., Acretoaie, V., & David, T. (2010). An ant-inspired approach for semantic web service clustering. *Proc. 9th Roedunet International Conference (RoEduNet)*, 145–150.

Dasgupta, S., Bhat, S., & Lee, Y. (2011). Taxonomic clustering and query matching for efficient service discovery. *Proceeding of the 9th IEEE International Conference on Web Services*, 363–370. 10.1109/ICWS.2011.112

Elgazzar, K., Hassan, A. E., & Martin, P. (2010). Clustering WSDL Documents to Bootstrap the Discovery of Web Services. *Proceeding of the 8th IEEE International Conference on Web Services*, 147-154. 10.1109/ICWS.2010.31

Endrei, M., Ang, J., Arsanjani, A., Chua, S., Comte, P., Krogdahl, P., Luo, M., & Newling, T. (2004, April). Patterns: Service-Oriented Architecture and Web Services. *IBM Redbooks*.

Hippisley, A., Cheng, D., & Ahmad, K. (2005). The head-modifier principle and multilingual term extraction. *Natural Language Engineering*, *11*(2), 129–157. doi:10.1017/S1351324904003535

Huynh, K. T., Quan, T. T., & Bui, T. H. (2017). A quality-controlled logic-based clustering approach for web service composition and verification. *International Journal of Web Information Systems*, *13*(2), 173–198. doi:10.1108/IJWIS-12-2016-0068

Jiang, B., Ye, L., Wang, J., & Wang, Y. (2017). A Semantic-Based Approach to Service Clustering from Service Documents. *Services Computing (SCC), 2017 IEEE International Conference on*, 265-272.

Klusch, M., Fries, B., & Sycara, K. (2006). Automated semantic Web service discovery with OWLS-MX. *Proceeding of the 5th International Conference on Autonomous Agents and Multi-Agent Systems*, 915-922. 10.1145/1160633.1160796

Kotekar, S., & Kamath, S. S. (2018). Enhancing Web Service Discovery Using Meta-heuristic CSO and PCA Based Clustering. *Progress in Intelligent Computing Techniques: Theory, Practice, and Applications*, 393-403.

Kumara, B. T. G. S., Paik, I., Chen, W., & Ryu, K. (2014). Web Service Clustering using a Hybrid Term-Similarity Measure with Ontology Learning. *International Journal of Web Services Research, 11*(2), 24–45. doi:10.4018/ijwsr.2014040102

Kumara, B. T. G. S., Paik, I., & Koswatte, K. R. C. (2016). Cluster-Based Web Service Recommendation. *Proceedings on IEEE International Conference on Service Computing.* 10.1109/SCC.2016.52

Kumara, B. T. G. S., Paik, I., Ohashi, H., Yaguchi, Y., & Chen, W. (2014). (accepted). Context Aware Filtering and Visualization of Web Service Clusters. *International Journal of Web Services Research.*

Kumara, B. T. G. S., Paik, I., Siriweera, T. H. A. S., & Koswatte, K. R. C. (2017) QoS Aware Service Clustering to Bootstrap the Web Service Selection. *Proceedings on IEEE International Conference on Service Computing.* 10.1109/SCC.2017.37

Liu, W., & Wong, W. (2009). Web service clustering using text mining techniques, International Journal of Agent-*oriented. Software Engineering, 3*(1), 6–26.

Ma, H., King, I., & Lyu, M. R. (2007). Effective missing data prediction for collaborative filtering. *SIGIR,* 39–46.

Ma, J., Zhang, Y., & He, J. (2008). Efficiently finding Web services using a clustering semantic approach. *Proceeding of the International Workshop on Context-enabled Source and Service Selection, Integration and Adaptation, organized with the 17th International World Wide Web Conference,* 1–8. 10.1145/1361482.1361487

Nayak, R., & Lee, B. (2007). Web service discovery with additional semantics and clustering. *Proc. IEEE/WIC/ACM International Conference on Web Intelligence,* 555–558. 10.1109/WI.2007.82

Paik, I., Chen, W., & Huhns, M. N. (2014). A scalable architecture for automatic service composition. *IEEE Transactions on Services Computing, 7*(1), 82–95. doi:10.1109/TSC.2012.33

Pazzani, M. J, Billsus, D., (2007). Content-based recommendation systems. *The Adaptive Web,* 325–341.

Platzer, C., Rosenberg, F., & Dustdar, S. (2009). Web service clustering using multidimensional angles as proximity measures. *ACM Transactions on Internet Technology, 9*(3), 1–26. doi:10.1145/1552291.1552294

Qu, X., Sun, H., Li, X., Liu, X., & Lin, W. (2009). WSSM: A WordNet-Based Web Services Similarity Mining Mechanism. *Proceeding of the Future Computing, Service Computation, Cognitive, Adaptive, Content, Patterns,* 339–345. 10.1109/ComputationWorld.2009.96

Rupasingha, R. A., Paik, I., & Kumara, B. T. (2017). Improving Web Service Clustering through a Novel Ontology Generation Method by Domain Specificity. *Web Services (ICWS), 2017 IEEE International Conference on,* 744-751.

Sasaki, T., Yaguchi, Y., Watanobe, Y., & Oka, R. (2012). Extracting a Spatial Ontology from a Large Flickr Tag Dataset. *IEEE on 4th International Conference on Awareness Science and Technology (iCAST).*

Sun, P. (2010). Service Clustering Based on Profile and Process Similarity. *Proceeding of the International Symposium on Information Science and Engineering,* 535–539. 10.1109/ISISE.2010.151

Surianarayanan, C., & Ganapathy, G. (2016). An Approach to Computation of Similarity Inter-Cluster Distance and Selection of Threshold for Service Discovery using Clusters. *IEEE Transactions on Services Computing*, *9*(4), 524–536. doi:10.1109/TSC.2015.2399301

Wagner, F., Ishikawa, F., & Honiden, S. (2011). QoS-aware Automatic Service Composition by Applying Functional Clustering. *Proceeding of the 9th IEEE International Conference on Web Services*, 89–96. 10.1109/ICWS.2011.32

Wen, T., Sheng, G., Li, Y., & Guo, Q. (2011). Research on Web service discovery with semantics and clustering. *Proceeding of the 6th IEEE Joint International Information Technology and Artificial Intelligence Conference*, 62–67. 10.1109/ITAIC.2011.6030151

Xie, L., Chen, F., & Kou, J. (2011). Ontology-based semantic Web services clustering. *Proceeding of the 18th IEEE International Conference on Industrial Engineering and Engineering Management*, 2075–2079.

Zhang, X., Jing, L., Hu, X., Ng, M., & Zhou, X. (2007). A comparative study of ontology based term similarity measures on PubMed document clustering. *Proceeding of the 12th International Conference on Database Systems for Advanced Applications*, 115-126. 10.1007/978-3-540-71703-4_12

Chapter 19
Deep Model Framework for Ontology-Based Document Clustering

U. K. Sridevi
Sri Krishna College of Engineering and Technology, India

P. Shanthi
Sri Krishna College of Engineering and Technology, India

N. Nagaveni
Coimbatore Institute of Technology, India

ABSTRACT

Searching of relevant documents from the web has become more challenging due to the rapid growth in information. Although there is enormous amount of information available online, most of the documents are uncategorized. It is a time-consuming task for the users to browse through a large number of documents and search for information about the specific topics. The automatic clustering from these documents could be important and has great potential to improve the efficiency of information seeking behaviors. To address this issue, the authors propose a deep ontology-based approach to document clustering. The obtained results are encouraging and in implementation annotation rules are used. The work compared the information extraction capabilities of annotated framework of using ontology and without using ontology. The increase in F-measure is achieved when ontology as the distance measure. The improvement of 11% is achieved by ontology in comparison with keyword search.

INTRODUCTION

The increase in the growth of text documents in the Web is a great challenge to information retrieval system. The searching and indexing systems are available for accessing the information but the retrieval of relevant information is still a problem. One current problem of information retrieval is that it is not really possible to extract relevant documents automatically. An information retrieval system uses index-

DOI: 10.4018/978-1-5225-5396-0.ch019

ing and the system's performance depends on the quality of the indexing. The two main challenges in indexing are to create representative internal descriptions of documents and to organize these descriptions for fast retrieval. Descriptions of documents in information retrieval are supposed to reflect the documents content and establish the foundation for the retrieval of information when requested by users. The documents are marked with the description in indexing for easy retrieval.

Ontology has good conceptual structure representation and can be combined with the knowledge representation. The model makes use of annotation and indexing. The ontology model depends on the semantic index terms but the vector space model depends on the keyword index. The semantics of the concepts are used to build a concept term representation. The ontology similarity measure improves the concept relevance score. The semantically related terms gain more weights and it will improve the term importance in indexing process. The semantic analysis should somehow recognize concepts in the documents and then map them into the ontologies. The indexing process maps information found in documents into the ontology, identifying concepts and their positions in the ontology. Information in queries can similarly be mapped into the ontology and thus in addition to retrieving the exact match, the structure of the ontology can be used to retrieve semantically related documents. Semantic similarity and indexing focuses on the similarity measure using ontology. It also compares the vector space model with semantic information retrieval model. The methods are integrated to find the concept relation information, while these concepts are considered to be independent in the term vector space method. Using the ontology similarity method given in Euzenat and Shvaiko (2007), the cosine similarity between concept are measured. The term reweighting approaches based on ontology is used in information retrieval applications (Varelas et al., 2005). The semantic annotation process includes the creation of domain ontology and the ontology maps into the concept terms of the documents. In this model, the weight of the concepts is computed using their semantic similarity to other concepts in the document. The concept vector is generated in the document annotation process and the concept index is built. To improve the recognition of important indexing terms, it is possible to weight the concepts of a document in different ways (Valkeapaa et al., 2007).

Text mining algorithm can handle the real-world data that come in a diversity of forms and can be tremendously bulky (Pankaj et al., 2015). The work provides ontology framework based on text analytics and social media analytics. Social tagging system improves the personalized document clustering. The knowledge gained from social tagging system should be tremendous assets for conducting and improving various business intelligent applications (Yang et al., 2015).

In text clustering there exist some issues to tackle such as feature extraction and data dimension reduction. To overcome these problems, Yi et al (2017) presented a novel approach named deep-learning vocabulary network. Deep learning is used to extract the features of the text document and in the d in the process of clustering and extract features of text documents. Yan et al. (2015) has used semantic representation and deep belief network for document classification and retrieval. However, there are very few publications addressing semantic indexing with deep learning. Yan et al. (2016) included the semantic indexing in biomedical literature by including a vast amount of semantic labels from automatically annotating MeSH terms for MEDLINE.

Chen et al. (2016) proposed a deep learning based framework to identify and categorize topics related to diabetes in online Chinese articles. The experiments use the datasets with over 19,000 online articles showed that the framework achieved a higher effectiveness and accuracy in categorizing diabetes related topic. Deep learning techniques are applied in the classification of texts for the enhanced construction regulated documents (Zhou & Ei-Gohary, 2015). They have developed domain specific ontology to represent the hierarchy of topics along with the associated relationships. The classification into topics is done based on the similarity thresholds.

DEEP LEARNING FRAMEWORK FOR ONTOLOGY BASED SIMILARITY

The Information Extraction methodologies identify the semantic entities represented in the documents. The ontology entities within the documents are identified by semantic annotation. The contents are pieces of raw text that need a meaning and which are linked with ontological concepts. Annotate every instance of the class through manual process or automatic annotation process. Our research explores (i) semantic similarity representation (ii) deep model framework document clustering. The methodology is summarized in Figure 1.

Semantic Similarity Representation

The mathematical representation of similarity measure is given based on Euzenat and Shvaiko (2007) the similarity measures. Let S be the set of all synset, I denote the set of all entries in the index and C denote set of concepts. T1 is the set of term. The semantic similarity function R1 is given as follows

$$R1 : T1 \times S \rightarrow \{0,1\} \tag{1}$$

Figure 1. Ontology based deep model framework

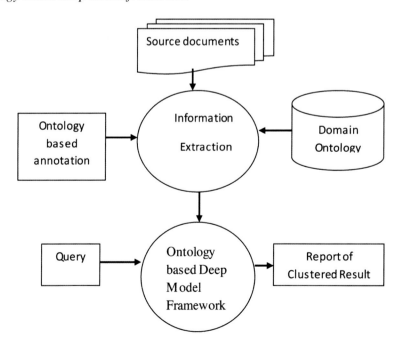

$$R1(a,b) = \begin{cases} 1 & if\ synset(a) \cap synset(b) \neq 0 \\ 0 & otherwise \end{cases} \tag{2}$$

The indexing of corpus is done using

$$I : T1 \rightarrow S \tag{3}$$

$$I(a) = \left\{ b \mid \quad b \in S \quad and \quad R(a,b) \quad \right\} \tag{4}$$

The semantic annotation process includes the creation of domain ontology and ontology mapping of concept terms from the documents. The relations between entities are discovered through the measure of the similarity between the entities of ontology.

Deep Model Framework

Hinton and Salakhutdinov (2006) showed that Deep Belief Networks (DBN) are generative neural network models with many layers of hidden explanatory factors. A restricted Boltzmann machines (RBMs) can be stacked and trained in a greedy manner to form so called Deep Belief Networks. DBN models extract a deep representation of the training data. The training consists of layer pre-training and fine turning. DBN contains the input layer (visible layer), the hidden layers, and the output layer. There are connections between a layer and adjacent layer, but no connections among units in each layer.

Restricted Boltzmann machines (RBMs) are Boltzmann machines that are constrained to two fully-connected non-recurrent layers called the visible layer, where salient inputs clamp nodes to output levels of either zero or one, and the hidden layer, where associations between input vectors are learned. All nodes in the visible layer and all nodes in the hidden layer are connected by undirected edges, and there no connections between nodes in the same layer. RBM uses the energy function to determine the probability of the hidden/visible states.

Visible units are multinomial over word counts. The concept detectors are in hidden units. The energies of the joint configurations are optimized by Gibbs sampling that learns the parameters by minimizing the lowest energy function of the RBM.

The energy function $E(v,h)$ of an RBM is defined as:

$$E(v,h) = -b'v - c;h - h'Wv$$

where w represents the weights connecting hidden and visible units and, b, c are the offsets of the visible v and hidden h layers respectively.

This translates directly to the following free energy formula:

$$F(v) = -b'v - \sum_i \log \sum_{h_i} e^{h_i(c_i + w_i v)}$$

Figure 2. General RBM: 2 layer model

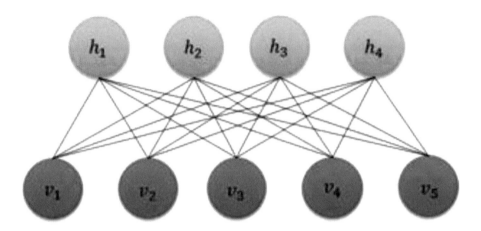

The deep model framework automatically determines the topics of cluster from the document collections. The framework includes the training of the DBN model for clustering. The annotated words are adapted as the features for the deep learning. Each document was presented as a vector with the features as dimension. All of the features were binary and if the corresponding word appeared in the document is represented as 1 otherwise 0. The nodes of the network represent the words and an edge represents the relations between the words. The relationship of the words is useful in document clustering.

EXPERIMENTAL RESULTS

Test Data

The semantic similarity analysis collects the set of keywords or terms that occur frequently together and then finds the relationship among them. The semantic information retrieval uses domain ontology to describe the concepts and builds information base. The query model can find and manipulate the needful data from the annotated documents. The performances of the proposed methods are evaluated using web documents collected from USGS. According to USGS the major kinds of topics are environmental contamination, health and human impacts. The concepts will be defined as the class and some attributes, which describe the document information

Once the experimental setting has been set up, the retrieval is tested with IR functionality in GATE. GATE comes with a full-featured information retrieval subsystem. Using the GATE tool the annotation features are assigned as the class or instance annotation. The weight for the query term is assigned and the query is run against the document taken forms USGS and returns the relevant information available.

The user query is translated into SPARQL query in order to perform an exact retrieval of documents annotated with the instances found, either matched against the semantic annotation which represents the document's meaning in order to perform an approximate retrieval, ranked with matching measures. The ontology describes the document and RDF annotations example is as follows

```
<rdf:Description ID=''AIRPollution''>
<rdf:type resource=''http://www.w3.org/
TR/1999/PR-rdf-schema-19990303#Class''/>
<rdfs:subClassOf rdf:resource=''http://
www.geolog.org#POLLUTION''/>
<rdfs:subClassOf rdf:resource=''http://
www.hydrolg.org#AIRQUALITY''/><!} -- >
<rdf:Description ID=''IndoorAirQuality''>
<rdf:type resource=''http://www.w3.org/
1999/02/22-rdf-syntax-ns#Property''/>
<!} IndoorAirQuality  is a property-- >
```

The document contains an instance of event that contains an instance of topic which contains the term air pollution. If the query is given as, "Air pollution caused by California fire in 2007". The query is transformed as follows

Q1: AirPollution∩ causeBy.Fire∩ takePlacein.California hasTime.2007

The query has the following rewriting in SPARQL:

```
PREFIX cfp: <http://corpusCFP/thiam/ontology#>
SELECT ?name
WHERE { ?c cfp:hasNamePollution?name .
?c cfp:hasEvent ?e .
?e cfp:hasSetOfTopic ?st .
?st cfp:hasTopic ?t .
FILTER regex(?t, "airpollution", "i")
```

The querying system can suggest all possible instances by setting a relevance weighting measure for each one according to the semantic annotations associated to the structural units in which these instances are located.

The precision (P) and recall (R) is computed as follows

$$P = \frac{Good\,annotation \quad retrieved}{Good\,annotation \quad retrieved \quad + \quad Bad \quad annotation} \tag{3.1}$$

$$R = \frac{Good\,annotation \quad retrieved}{Good\,annotation \quad retrieved \quad + \quad Missed\_Goodannotations} \tag{3.2}$$

Table 1 shows the extraction of traditional information extraction and Table 2 shows the performance of ontology based extraction. The average comparison of the performance of the system over the set of twenty queries is performed and the performance of ontology approach is better than traditional approach. Table 3 shows the comparison of query evaluation results between the ontology and statistical models.

Comparison of Information Extraction (IE) Model

The statistical model based on the rule based approach is compared with ontology based information extraction method. The result of the precision measure based on the rule base approach alone is very satisfactory but the recall measure is quite disappointing. This shows that the approach is able to extract information which is mostly relevant.

The following are the statistic obtained from the rule based results without using ontology.

Total relation(s) from manually extracted information = 6
Total relation(s) from rule based information extraction = 3
Correct relations from rule based information extraction = 3

The precision for Rule based approach is 100% because of the fact that whatever relations have been extracted are correct whereas recall is 50% because this approach could not extract 50% of the relations that should have been extracted.

The following are the statistic obtained from the results of ontology based extraction with rules

Table 1. Extraction results without ontology

Concept	Correctly Identified	Incorrectly Identified	Recall	Precision
C1	70	63	0.51	0.52
C2	101	26	0.84	0.82
C3	93	23	0.82	0.8
C4	15	56	0.25	0.22
C5	41	59	0.73	0.41

Table 2. Extraction results using ontology

Concept	Correctly Identified	Incorrectly Identified	Recall	Precision
C1	121	7	0.88	0.95
C2	104	17	0.83	0.86
C3	108	19	0.96	0.85
C4	46	5	0.75	0.9
C5	50	52	0.91	0.49

Table 3. Query evaluation results

Type of Queries	No. of queries	Recall		Precision	
		Ontology Model %	Statistical Model%	Ontology Model%	Statistical Model%
General	20	100	20	100	100
General	5	91	7	84	62
Specific	13	92	80	82	74
Specific	11	90	75	91	100
Specific	10	92	75	90	82
Average		93	51	89	84

Total relation(s) from manually extracted information = 6
Total relation(s) from ontology based information extraction = 4
Correct relations from ontology based information extraction = 4

The Table 4 presents the comparative analysis of the rule based and ontology based approaches.

It shows that precision measure for ontology based approach is higher than rule based approach. It shows that rules developed for ontology approach is only extracting information for which are relevant since domain concepts and rules are combined together. Experimental results indicate that a semantic annotation improves the retrieval performance.

Table 4. Comparison of IE results

Method	Precision	Recall
Statistical IE	95%	64%
Ontology based IE	97%	50%

Table 5. Top-5 search ratings for 5 queries

Category	Similarity Distance Comparison		
	Tf-idf	ONTOVSM	DEEPONTO
minedrainage:Coal	13.02	10.49	9.17
Contamination pollution:Water Quality	12.85	13.47	13.59
content:Acid Rain	15.93	15.86	16.87
environmental pollution	14.68	14.61	14.72
Toxic	11.39	11.33	12.07
minedrainage:Coal	15.56	16.49	16.58
	13.69	14.03	18.41

The documents were annotated and stored. Table 5 shows the search rating for the queries. The similarity degree of each document was evaluated. The result shows the performance of semantic information retrieval combined with keyword based retrieval. The similarity distance is compared with TF-IDF (Term Frequency–Inverse Document Frequency) and ONTOVSM (Ontology Vector Space Model).

Table 6 shows the comparison of the keyword and ontology retrieval. The Table 7 shows that the method can improve precision by 11% from 0.3761 to 0.4119 in relevant measure. The performance of the two methods is compared using precision and recall. The F measure is defined using precision and recall shows the accuracy of the methods. Table 8 shows the F-measure value of the similarity measure and the ontology based similarity has improved results than keyword based similarity.

Figure 3 shows the performance of retrieval on document annotation and without annotation. Instead of simple keyword index lookup, the semantic search system processes a semantic query against the KB, which returns the relevant document. Semantic retrieval is achieved by implementing a document ranking for Lucene indices so that documents containing ontological information get higher rates Better precision is achieved by using structured document annotation weight and the average precision for the top 10 and 20 documents is shown in Table 6. Table 7 concludes the ontology distances are more accurate compared to keyword and the F-measure value is improved from 0.685 to 0.768 in relevant measure.

Figure 4 shows the average execution time depends on the number of documents. Figure 5 shows the comparison of F-measure based on the number of document and similarity measures.

The approach shows how the semantic annotated model can be used to formulate and to approximate queries in order to adapt them to the various levels of precision of the annotation. The results suggest that ontology based information extraction performs significantly better than traditional IE on selected data. The experimental results show that the reweighting improves the document illustrates that the ontology based VSM has the higher F-measure value then traditional VSM. Higher F-measure shows the high accuracy. The traditional VSM cannot identify the semantic relationship between words, which is important in representing the text documents. The improvement of 11% is achieved by VSM+Ontology in comparison with VSM+ keyword search.

Table 6. Comparisons of average precision

Average Precision	Keyword Similarity	Ontology Similarity	Ratio
Top 10	0.3761	0.4119	1.09519
Top 20	0.1983	0.2074	1.04589

Table 7. Comparison of keyword and ontology distance measure

Methods	Precision	Recall	F-Measure	Time in Minutes
Keyword Similarity	0.737	0.640	0.685	17.37
Ontology Similarity	0.768	0.727	0.747	15.59

Figure 3. Comparison of precision and recall for similarity measure

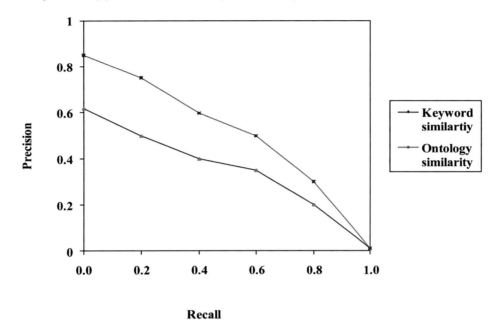

Figure 4. Average execution time

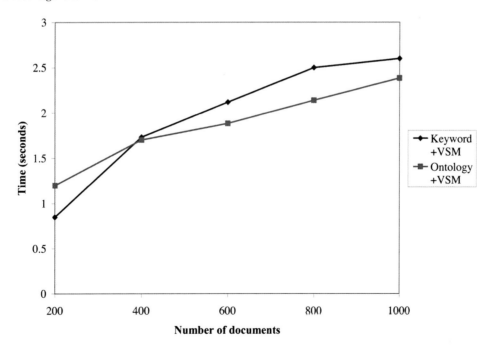

Figure 5. Performance comparison of F-measure

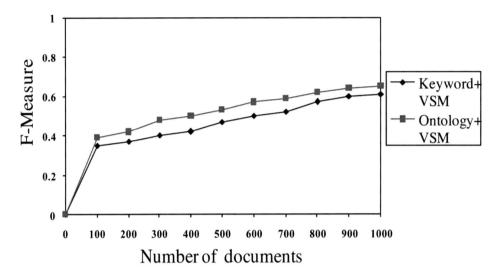

CONCLUSION

Semantic Web provides a structured data and knowledge representation framework for Web information. The techniques to generate metadata that semantically annotating a web page will help improving lack of semantic information. The semantic relations between the classes are analyzed. This work introduces an annotation scheme that combines the semantic similarity measures and indexing in the document. The approach can be seen as a evolution of the keyword indices that are replaced by ontology knowledge base and a semiautomatic document annotation weighting procedure that improves the retrieval performance. The semantic indexing and retrieval framework includes all the aspects of Semantic Web, namely, ontology development, information extraction, ontology population, inference, semantic rules, semantic indexing and retrieval. When these technologies are combined with the comfort of keyword-based search interface, high performance and scalable semantic retrieval system is obtained. Evaluation results show that the proposed approach can easily outperform both the traditional approach.

REFERENCES

Chen, X., Zhang, Y., Xu, J., Xing, C., & Chen, H. (2016). Deep learning based topic identification and categorization: Mining diabetes-related topics on Chinese health website. In Lecture Notes in Computer Science: *Vol. 9642* (pp. 481–500). Springer Verlag. doi:10.1007/978-3-319-32025-0_30

Euzenat, J., & Shvaiko, P. (2007). *Ontology matching*. Berlin: Springer-Verlag.

Kaur, Sharma, & Vohra. (2015). An Ontology Based Text Analytics on Social Media. *International Journal of Database Theory and Application*, 8(5), 233–240.

Valkeapaa, O., Alm, O., & Hyvonen, E. (2007). An adaptable framework for ontology-based content creation on the semantic web. *J. UCS*, *13*(12), 1825–1853.

Varelas, G., Voutsakis, E., Raftopoulou, P., Petrakis, E. G., & Milios, E. E. (2005). Semantic similarity methods in wordnet and their application to information retrieval on the web. *Proceedings of the 7th annual ACM International Workshop on Web Information and Data Management*, 10-16. 10.1145/1097047.1097051

Yan, Yin, & Li, Yang, & Hao. (2015). Learning Document Semantic Representation with Hybrid Deep Belief Network. *Computational Intelligence and Neuroscience*, 9.

Yan, Yin, Zhang, Yang, & Hao. (2016). Semantic indexing with deep learning: A case study. *Big Data Analytics, 1*(7).

Yang, C. S., & Chang, P. C. (2015). Mining Social Media for Enhancing Personalized Document Clustering. In F. Fui-Hoon Nah & C. H. Tan (Eds.), Lecture Notes in Computer Science: Vol. 9191. *HCI in Business. HCIB 2015*. Cham: Springer. doi:10.1007/978-3-319-20895-4_18

Yi, J., Zhang, Y., Zhao, X., & Wan, J. (2017). A Novel Text Clustering Approach Using Deep-Learning Vocabulary Network. *Mathematical Problems in Engineering*, 13.

Zhou, P., & El-Gohary, N. (2015). Domain-specific hierarchical text classification for supporting automated environmental compliance checking. *Journal of Computing in Civil Engineering*. doi:10.1061/(ASCE)CP.1943-5487

Compilation of References

Abaas, T., Shibghatullah, A. S., Yusof, R., & Alaameri, A. (2014). Importance and Significance of Information Sharing in Terrorism Field. *International Symposium on Research in Innovation and Sustainability (ISoRIS '14)*, 1719-1725.

Abdelbari, H., & Shafi, K. (2017). A computational intelligence-based method to 'Learn' causal loop diagram-like structures from observed Data. *System Dynamics Review, 33*(1), 3–33. doi:10.1002dr.1567

Abdel-Hamid, T. K. (1989). The dynamics of software project staffing: A system dynamics based simulation approach. *IEEE Transactions on Software Engineering, 15*(2), 109–119. doi:10.1109/32.21738

Abdelsalam, H. M., & El-Tagy, A. O. (2012). A simulation model for managing marketing multi-channel conflict. *International Journal of System Dynamics Applications, 1*(4), 59–76. doi:10.4018/ijsda.2012100103

Abdo, H., & Flaus, J. M. (2016). Uncertainty quantification in dynamic system risk assessment: A new approach with randomness and fuzzy theory. *International Journal of Production Research, 54*(19), 5862–5885. doi:10.1080/002075 43.2016.1184348

Abdullah, Z., Herawan, T., Noraziah, A., & Deris, M. M. (2014). A scalable algorithm for constructing Frequnt pattern Tree. *International Journal of Intelligent Information Technologies, 10*(1), 42–56. doi:10.4018/ijiit.2014010103

Aburomman, A. A., & Reaz, M. B. I. (2017). A novel weighted support vector machines multiclass classifier based on differential evolution for intrusion detection systems. *Information Sciences, 414*, 225–246. doi:10.1016/j.ins.2017.06.007

Aburomman, A., & Reaz, M. (2016). A novel svm-knn-pso ensemble method for intrusion detection system. *Applied Soft Computing, 38*, 360–372. doi:10.1016/j.asoc.2015.10.011

Acharya, S. G., Sheladiya, M. V., & Acharya, G. D. (2017). Process parameter optimization for sand inclusion defect in furan no-bake casting by grey relational analysis. *IUP Journal of Mechanical Engineering, 10*(4), 7–19.

Acharya, S. G., & Vadher, J. A. (2016). Parametric analyses on compressive strength of furan no bake mould system using ANN. *Archives of Foundry Engineering, 16*(4), 5–10. doi:10.1515/afe-2016-0074

Adachi, Y., Kuno, Y., Shimada, N., & Shirai, Y. (1998). Intelligent wheelchair using visual information on human faces. In *Intelligent Robots and Systems, Proceedings: IEEE/RSJ International Conference* (vol. 1, pp. 354–359). IEEE.

Adrian, A. M., Utamima, A., & Wang, K. J. (2015). A comparative study of GA, PSO and ACO for solving construction site layout optimization. *KSCE Journal of Civil Engineering, 19*(3), 520–527. doi:10.100712205-013-1467-6

Afrati, F. N., Koutris, P., Suciu, D., & Ullman, J. D. (2012). Parallel Skyline Queries. In *Proc. of ICDT '12* (pp. 274–284). New York: ACM. 10.1145/2274576.2274605

Agustina, F., Lukman, & Puspita, E. (2017, May 30). PMZ method for solving fuzzy transportation. In AIP Conference Proceedings. Melville, NY: American Institute of Physics (AIP) Publishing. doi:10.1063/1.4983945

Ahmed, M. M., Khan, A. R., Uddin, M. S., & Ahmed, F. (2016). A new approach to solve transportation problems. *Open Journal of Optimization*, 5(01), 22–30. doi:10.4236/ojop.2016.51003

Ahmed, N. U., Khan, A. R., & Uddin, M. S. (2015). Solution of mixed type transportation problem: A fuzzy approach. *Bul. Ins. Pol. Din Iasi, Romania. Secţia Automatica si Calculatoare*, 61(2), 19–32.

Akbar, A., Khan, A., Carrez, F., & Moessner, K. (2017). *Predictive Analytics for Complex IoT Data Streams*. IEEE Internet of Things.

Akpan, N. P., & Iwok, I. A. (2017). A minimum spanning tree approach of solving a transportation problem. *International Journal of Mathematics and Statistics Invention, 5*(3), 8-17.

Aladag, C. H. (2013). Using multiplicative neuron model to establish fuzzy logic relationships. *Expert Systems with Applications*, 40(3), 850–853. doi:10.1016/j.eswa.2012.05.039

Aladag, C. H., Yolcu, U., & Egrioglu, E. (2010). A high order fuzzy time series forecasting model based on adaptive expectation and artificial neural networks. *Mathematics and Computers in Simulation*, 81(4), 875–882. doi:10.1016/j.matcom.2010.09.011

Aladag, C. H., Yolcu, U., Egrioglu, E., & Bas, E. (2014). Fuzzy lagged variable selection in fuzzy time series with genetic algorithms. *Applied Soft Computing*, 22, 465–473. doi:10.1016/j.asoc.2014.03.028

Alguliyev, R., & Abdullayeva, F. (2015). Development of Fuzzy Risk Calculation Method for a Dynamic Federation of Clouds. *Intelligent Information Management*, 7(04), 230–241. doi:10.4236/iim.2015.74018

Ali, A. M., & Faraz, D. (2017). Solving fuzzy triangular transportation problem using fuzzy least cost method with ranking approach. *International Journal of Current Research in Science and Technology*, 3(7), 15–20.

Aliper, A., Plis, S., Artemov, A., Ulloa, A., Mamoshina, P., & Zhavoronkov, A. (2016). Deep Learning Applications for Predicting Pharmacological Properties of Drugs and Drug Repurposing Using Transcriptomic Data. *Molecular Pharmaceutics*, 13(7), 2524–2530. doi:10.1021/acs.molpharmaceut.6b00248 PMID:27200455

Aljanabi, K. B., & Jasim, A. N. (2015). An approach for solving transportation problem using modified Kruskal's algorithm. *International Journal of Science and Research*, 4(7), 2426–2429.

Allen, J. F. (1983). Maintaining knowledge about temporal intervals. *Communications of the ACM*, 26(11), 832–843. doi:10.1145/182.358434

Al-Masri, E., & Mahmoud, Q. H. (2008). Investigating Web services on the World Wide Web. *Proceeding of the 17th International Conference on the World Wide Web*, 795-804. 10.1145/1367497.1367605

Alves, V., Gheyi, R., Massoni, T., Kulesza, U., Borba, P., & Lucena, C. (2006). Refactoring product lines. In *Proceedings of the 5th international conference on Generative programming and component engineering* (pp. 201–210). ACM. doi:10.1109/ICSE.2009.5070568

Alyami, H., Yang, Z., Riahi, R., Bonsall, S., & Wang, J. (2016). Advanced uncertainty modelling for container port risk analysis. *Accident; Analysis and Prevention*. doi:10.1016/j.aap.2016.08.007 PMID:27530609

Ambler, S. W. (1998). *Process patterns: building large-scale systems using object technology*. Cambridge University Press.

Anacta, V. J. A., Schwering, A., Li, R., & Muenzer, S. (2016). Orientation information in wayfinding instructions: Evidences from human verbal and visual instructions. *GeoJournal*, 1–17.

Anbumani, K., & Nedunchezhian, R. (2006). Rapid Privacy preserving algorithms for large databases. *International Journal of Intelligent Information Technologies*, 2(1), 68–81. doi:10.4018/jiit.2006010104

Anderson, J. P. (1980). *Computer security threat monitoring and surveillance. Technical report*. Fort Washington, PA: James P Anderson Co.

Andrearczyk, V., & Whelan, P. F. (2016). Using filter banks in Convolutional Neural Networks for texture classification. *Pattern Recognition Letters, 84*, 63–69. doi:10.1016/j.patrec.2016.08.016

Andrysiak, T., Saganowski, Ł., Choraś, M., & Kozik, R. (2016). Proposal and comparison of network anomaly detection based on long-memory statistical models. *Logic Journal of the IGPL, 24*(6), 944–956. doi:10.1093/jigpal/jzw051

AnithaKumari, T., Venkateswarlu, B., & Murthy, A. S. (2017). Fuzzy transportation problems with new kind of ranking function. *International Journal of Engineering Science, 6*(11), 15–19.

Annoni, A., Bernard, L., Douglas, J., Greenwood, J., Laiz, I., Lloyd, M., ... Usländer, T. (2005). Orchestra: developing a unified open architecture for risk management applications. In *Geo-Information for Disaster Management* (pp. 1–17). Springer. doi:10.1007/3-540-27468-5_1

Anoop, M. B., Rao, K. B., & Lakshmanan, N. (2008). Safety assessment of austenitic steel nuclear power plant pipelines against stress corrosion cracking in the presence of hybrid uncertainties. *International Journal of Pressure Vessels and Piping, 85*(4), 238–247. doi:10.1016/j.ijpvp.2007.09.001

Anquetil, N., Kulesza, U., Mitschke, R., Moreira, A., Royer, J.-C., Rummler, A., & Sousa, A. (2010). A model-driven traceability framework for software product lines. *Software & Systems Modeling, 9*(4), 427–451. doi:10.100710270-009-0120-9

Anuradha, D., & Sobana, V. E. (2017, November). A survey on fuzzy transportation problems. In IOP Conference Series: Materials Science and Engineering (Vol. 263, No. 4, p. 042105). IOP Publishing. doi:10.1088/1757-899X/263/4/042105

Appa, G. M. (1973). The transportation problem and its variants. *The Journal of the Operational Research Society, 24*(1), 79–99. doi:10.1057/jors.1973.10

Arel, I., Rose, D. C., & Karnowski, T. P. (2010). Deep Machine Learning - A New Frontier in Artificial Intelligence Research. *IEEE Computational Intelligence Magazine, 5*(4), 13–18. doi:10.1109/MCI.2010.938364

Aridor, Y., & Lange, D. B. (1998, May). Agent design patterns: elements of agent application design. In *Proceedings of the second international conference on Autonomous agents* (pp. 108-115). ACM. 10.1145/280765.280784

Arsham, H., & Kahn, A. B. (1989). A simplex-type algorithm for general transportation problems: An alternative to stepping-stone. *The Journal of the Operational Research Society, 40*(6), 581–590. doi:10.1057/jors.1989.95

Arunraj, N. S., Mandal, S., & Maiti, J. (2013). Modeling uncertainty in risk assessment: An integrated approach with fuzzy set theory and Monte Carlo simulation. *Accident; Analysis and Prevention, 55*, 242–255. doi:10.1016/j.aap.2013.03.007 PMID:23567215

Ashrafi, M. Z., Taniar, D., & Smith, K. (2005). PPDAM: Privacy Preserving Distributed Association Rule - Mining Algorithm. *International Journal of Intelligent Information Technologies, 1*(1), 49–69. doi:10.4018/jiit.2005010104

Askari, S., & Montazerin, N. (2015). A high-order multi-variable fuzzy time series forecasting algorithm based on fuzzy clustering. *Expert Systems with Applications, 42*(4), 2121–2135. doi:10.1016/j.eswa.2014.09.036

Atanassov, K.T. (1983). Intuitionistic fuzzy sets. *Library of Bulg. Acad. of Sci., 1697*(84).

Axelsson, S. (2000). *Intrusion detection systems: A survey and taxonomy*. Department of Computer Engineering, Chalmers University of Technology, Tech Rep.

Babagholami-Mohamadabadi, B., Jourabloo, A., Zarghami, A., & Kasaei, S. (2014). A bayesian framework for sparse representation-based 3-d human pose estimation. *IEEE Signal Processing Letters*, *21*(3), 297–300. doi:10.1109/LSP.2014.2301726

Babcock, B., Babu, S., Datar, M., Motwani, R., & Widom, J. (2002). Models and Issues in Data Stream Systems. PODS '02, 1-16. doi:10.1145/543613.543615

Babu, S., Chandini, M., Lavanya, P., Ganapathy, K., & Vaidehi, V. (2013). Integrating Wireless Sensor Network with Sensor Web Enablement for Remote Health Care Decision Making in Cloud. *International Conference on Recent Trends in Information Technology, ICRTIT 2013*.

Babu, S., & Widom, J. (2001). Continuous Queries over Data Streams. *Proceedings of SIGMOD Rec., 30*(3), 109-120.

Bace, R., & Mell, P. (2001). *Nist special publication on intrusion detection systems*. National Institute of Standards and Technology, Tech Rep.

Bajestani, N. S., & Zare, A. (2011). Forecasting TAIEX using Improved Type-2 Fuzzy Time Series. *Expert Systems with Applications*, *38*(5), 5816–5821. doi:10.1016/j.eswa.2010.10.049

Bali, M. (2009). *Drools JBoss Rules 5.0 Developer's Guide*. Packt Publishing Ltd.

Balke, W.-T., Güntzer, U., & Zheng, J. X. (2004). Efficient Distributed Skylining for Web Information Systems. *EDBT '04: Proceedings of the 9th International Conference on Extending Database Technology*, 256–273. 10.1007/978-3-540-24741-8_16

Bamakan, S., Amiri, B., Mirzabagheri, M., & Shi, Y. (2015). A new intrusion detection approach using pso based multiple criteria linear programming. *Procedia Computer Science*, *55*, 231–237. doi:10.1016/j.procs.2015.07.040

Baraldi, P., & Zio, E. (2008). A combined Monte Carlo and possibilistic approach to uncertainty propagation in event tree analysis. *Risk Analysis*, *28*(5), 1309–1326. doi:10.1111/j.1539-6924.2008.01085.x PMID:18631304

Barea, R., Boquete, L., Mazo, M., López, E., & Bergasa, L. M. (2000). EOG guidance of a wheelchair using neural networks. In *Proceedings of the 15th International Conference on Pattern Recognition* (vol. 4, pp. 668–671). Academic Press. 10.1109/ICPR.2000.903006

Barea, R., Boquete, L., Bergasa, L. M., López, E., & Mazo, M. (2003). Electrooculography guidance of a wheelchair using eye movement's codification. *The International Journal of Robotics Research*, *22*(7-8), 641–652. doi:10.1177/02783649030227012

Bargaoui, H., Azzouz, F., Thibault, D., & Cailletaud, G. (2017). Thermomechanical behavior of resin bonded foundry sand cores during casting. *Journal of Materials Processing Technology*, *246*, 30–41. doi:10.1016/j.jmatprotec.2017.03.002

Barker, T. (2008). The economics of avoiding dangerous climate change. An Editorial Essay on *The Stern Review*. *Climatic Change*, *89*(3-4), 173–194. doi:10.100710584-008-9433-x

Barkowsky, T., Latecki, L., & Richter, K. (2000). Schematizing maps: Simplification of geographic shape by discrete curve evolution. In C. Freksa, C. Habel, W. Brauer, & K. F. Wender (Eds.), *Spatial Cognition II: Integrating Abstract Theories, Empirical Studies, Formal Methods, and Practical Applications* (Vol. 1849, pp. 41–53). Berlin: Springer. doi:10.1007/3-540-45460-8_4

Barlow, T. E. (1966). Precision green sand molding. *AFS Transactions*, *74*, 70–81.

Baron, G. (2010). Response suggestions and public participation the new norm in response management. *Crisis Comm*. Retrieved from: http://www.emergencymgmt.com/emergency-blogs/crisis-comm/Response-Suggestions-and-Public-111510.html

Barros, R. C., Basgalupp, M. P., De Carvalho, A. C. P. L. F., & Freitas, A. A. (2012). A survey of evolutionary algorithms for decision-tree induction. *Systems, Man, and Cybernetics, Part C: Applications and Reviews. IEEE Transactions on*, *42*(3), 291–312.

Bartolein, C., Wagner, A., Jipp, M., & Badreddin, E. (2008). Easing wheelchair control by gaze-based estimation of intended motion. In *Proceedings of the International Federation of Automatic Control World Congress* (*vol. 17*, pp. 9162–9167). Academic Press. 10.3182/20080706-5-KR-1001.01549

Bartolini, I., Ciaccia, P., & Patella, M. (2006). SaLSa: Computing the Skyline without Scanning the Whole Sky. In *Proceedings of CIKM '06* (pp. 405-414). New York, NY: ACM. 10.1145/1183614.1183674

Bas, E., Egrioglu, E., Aladag, C. H. & Yolcu, U. (2015). Fuzzy-time-series network used to forecast linear and nonlinear time series, *Applied Intelligence*, *43*, 343–355.

Bas, E., Uslu, V. R., Yolcu, U., & Egrioglu, E. (2014). A modified genetic algorithm for forecasting fuzzy time series. *Applied Intelligence*, *41*(2), 453–463. doi:10.100710489-014-0529-x

Basili, V. (1992). The experimental paradigm in software engineering. In *Experimental Software Engineering Issues: Critical Assessment and Future Directives*. Springer-Verlag.

Basirzadeh, H. (2011). An approach for solving fuzzy transportation problem. *Applied Mathematical Sciences*, *5*(32), 1549–1566.

Baudrit, C., & Dubois, D. (2006). Practical representations of incomplete probabilistic knowledge. *Computational Statistics & Data Analysis*, *51*(1), 86–108. doi:10.1016/j.csda.2006.02.009

Baudrit, C., Dubois, D., & Guyonnet, D. (2006). Joint propagation and exploitation of probabilistic and possibilistic information in risk assessment. *IEEE Transactions on Fuzzy Systems*, *14*(5), 593–608. doi:10.1109/TFUZZ.2006.876720

Baudrit, C., Dubois, D., & Perrot, N. (2008). Representing parametric probabilistic models tainted with imprecision. *Fuzzy Sets and Systems*, *159*(15), 1913–1928. doi:10.1016/j.fss.2008.02.013

Bauer, M. (1997). Approximation algorithms and decision making in the Dempster-Shafer theory of evidence—An empirical study. *International Journal of Approximate Reasoning*, *17*(2-3), 217–237. doi:10.1016/S0888-613X(97)00013-3

Baykasoğlu, A., & Subulan, K. (2017). Constrained fuzzy arithmetic approach to fuzzy transportation problems with fuzzy decision variables. *Expert Systems with Applications*, *81*, 193–222. doi:10.1016/j.eswa.2017.03.040

Beck, K., & Cunningham, W. (1987). Using Pattern Languages for Object-Oriented Programs. *Workshop on the Specification and Design for Object-Oriented Programming (OOPSLA'87)*.

Bellifemine, F. L., Caire, G., & Greenwood, D. (2007). *Developing multi-agent systems with JADE* (Vol. 7). John Wiley & Sons. doi:10.1002/9780470058411

Bellman, R. E., & Zadeh, L. A. (1970). Decision-making in a fuzzy environment. *Management Science*, *17*(4), B-141–B-164. doi:10.1287/mnsc.17.4.B141

Ben-Bassat, M. (1982). Pattern recognition and reduction of dimensionality, volume 1. Handbook of Statistics II. North-Holland.

Benguluri, S., Vundavilli, P. R., Bhat, R. P., & Parappagoudar, M. B. (2011). Forward and reverse mappings in metal casting—A step towards quality casting and automation (11-009). *AFS Transactions, 119*, 19.

Benlarabi, A., Khtira, A., & El Asri, B. (2015). A co-evolution analysis for software product lines: An approach based on evolutionary trees. *International Journal of Applied Evolutionary Computation, 6*(3), 9–32.

Berberoglu, T., & Kaya, M. (2008), Hiding Fuzzy Association Rules in Quantitative Data. *The 3rd International Conference on Grid and Pervasive Computing – Workshops,* 387-392.

Bergasa, L. M., Mazo, M., Gardel, A., Barea, R., & Boquete, L. (2000). Commands generation by face movements applied to the guidance of a wheelchair for handicapped people. In *Proceedings of the 15th International Conference on Pattern Recognition (vol. 4,* pp. 660–663). Academic Press. 10.1109/ICPR.2000.903004

Bertel, S., Dressel, T., Kohlberg, T., & von Jan, V. (2017). Spatial knowledge acquired from pedestrian urban navigation systems. In *Proceedings of the 19th International Conference on Human-Computer Interaction with Mobile Devices and Services* (p. 32). ACM. 10.1145/3098279.3098543

Beynon, M. (2002). DS/AHP method: A mathematical analysis, including an understanding of uncertainty. *European Journal of Operational Research, 140*(1), 148–164. doi:10.1016/S0377-2217(01)00230-2

Beynon, M. J. (2005). A method of aggregation in DS/AHP for group decision-making with the non-equivalent importance of individuals in the group. *Computers & Operations Research, 32*(7), 1881–1896. doi:10.1016/j.cor.2003.12.004

Beynon, M., Cosker, D., & Marshall, D. (2001). An expert system for multi-criteria decision making using Dempster Shafer theory. *Expert Systems with Applications, 20*(4), 357–367. doi:10.1016/S0957-4174(01)00020-3

Beynon, M., Curry, B., & Morgan, P. (2000). The Dempster–Shafer theory of evidence: An alternative approach to multicriteria decision modelling. *Omega, 28*(1), 37–50. doi:10.1016/S0305-0483(99)00033-X

Bezdek, J. C. (1981). *Pattern recognition with fuzzy objective function algorithms.* New York: Plenum Press. doi:10.1007/978-1-4757-0450-1

Bezdek, J. C. (1994). What is computational intelligence? In *Computational Intelligence Imitating Life.* New York: IEEE Press.

Bhargavi, R., Ravi Pathak, Vaidehi, V. (2013). Dynamic Complex Event Processing – Adaptive Rule Engine. *International Conference on Recent Trends in Information Technology, ICRTIT 2013.*

Bhargavi, R., & Vaidehi, V. (2013). Semantic intrusion detection with multisensor data fusion using complex event processing. *Sadhana, 38*(2), 169–185.

Bhushan, S. (2012). System dynamics integrative modeling and simulation for mobile telephony innovation diffusion: A study of emerging Indian telecom market. *International Journal of System Dynamics Applications, 2*(3), 84–121. doi:10.4018/ijsda.2012070103

Bhushan, S. (2013). Capturing structural complexity of innovation diffusion through system dynamics: A discussion on model development, calibration and simulation results. *International Journal of System Dynamics Applications, 2*(1), 59–96. doi:10.4018/ijsda.2013010104

Biermann, E., Cloete, E., & Venter, L. M. (2001). A comparison of intrusion detection systems. *Computers & Security, 20*(8), 676–683. doi:10.1016/S0167-4048(01)00806-9

Biswas, A., & Modak, N. (2012). Using fuzzy goal programming technique to solve multiobjective chance constrained programming problems in a fuzzy environment. *International Journal of Fuzzy System Applications*, 2(1), 71–80. doi:10.4018/ijfsa.2012010105

Black, L. J. (2013). When visuals are boundary objects in system dynamics work. *System Dynamics Review*, 29(2), 70–86. doi:10.1002dr.1496

Boehm, B., Rombach, H. D., & Zelkowitz, M. V. (Eds.). (2005). *Foundations of empirical software engineering: The legacy of Victor R. Basili*. Springer Science & Business Media. doi:10.1007/3-540-27662-9

Bøgh, K. S., Assent, I., & Magnani, M. (2013). Efficient GPU-based Skyline computation. In Proc. Of DaMoN '13 (5:1–5:6). New York, NY: ACM.

Bøgh, K. S., Chester, S., & Assent, I. (2015). Work-Efficient Skyline Computation for the GPU. *Proceedings of the Very Large Databases Endowment (PVLDB)*, 8(9), 962-973.

Bollegala, D., Matsuo, Y., & Ishizuka, M. (2007). Measuring Semantic Similarity between Words using Web Search Engines. *Proceeding of the 16th International World Wide Web Conference*, 757-766.

Bonam, J., Reddy, A. R., & Kalyani, G. (2014), Privacy Preserving in Association Rule Mining by Data Distortion Using PSO, ICT and Critical Infrastructure. In *Proceedings of the 48th Annual Convention of Computer Society of India*. Springer International Publishing.

Borland Together. (2007). Available at: http://www.borland.com/downloads/download_together.html

Börzsönyi, S., Kossmann, D., & Stocker, K. (2001). The Skyline Operator. In *Proc. of ICDE '01* (pp. 421–430). Washington, DC: IEEE.

Bosch, J. (1998). Design Patterns as Language Constructs. *Journal of Object-Oriented Programming*, 11(2), 18–32.

Bose, M., & Mali, K. (2016). High order time series forecasting using fuzzy discretization. *International Journal of Fuzzy System Applications*, 5(4), 147–164. doi:10.4018/IJFSA.2016100107

Bouhamed, H., Masmoudi, A., Lecroq, T., & Rebaï, A. (2012). A new approach for Bayesian classifier learning structure via K2 Algorithm. In *Emerging Intelligent Computing Technology and Applications* (pp. 387–393). Springer Berlin Heidelberg. doi:10.1007/978-3-642-31837-5_56

Bourke, A. K., & Lyons, G. M. (2008). A threshold-based fall-detection algorithm using a bi-axial gyroscope sensor. *Medical Engineering & Physics*, 30(1), 84–90. doi:10.1016/j.medengphy.2006.12.001 PMID:17222579

Boutilier, C., Brafman, R. I., Domshlak, C., Hoos, H. H., & Poole, D. (2004). CP-nets: A Tool for Representing and Reasoning with Conditional Ceteris Paribus Preference Statements. *Journal of Artificial Intelligence Research*, 21, 135–191.

Bouton, C., Shaikhouni, A., Annetta, N., Bockbrader, M., Friedenberg, D., Nielson, D., ... Deogaonkar, M. M. and A. Rezai, "Restoring cortical control of functional movement in a human with quadriplegia. *Nature*. doi:10.1038/nature17435

Brabazon, A., Neill, M. O., & McGarraghy, S. (2015). *Natural Computing Algorithms*. Springer Verlag. doi:10.1007/978-3-662-43631-8

Brach, J. S., Berlin, J. E., VanSwearingen, J. M., Newman, A. B., & Studenski, S. A. (2005). Too much or too little step width variability is associated with a fall history in older persons who walk at or near normal gait speed. *Journal of Neuroengineering and Rehabilitation*, 2(1), 1. doi:10.1186/1743-0003-2-21 PMID:16042812

Brown, D. J., Suckow, B., & Wang, T. (2001). *A survey of intrusion detection systems*. Academic Press.

Brown, W. J., Malveau, R. C., Hays, W., McCormick Iii, H., & Mowbray, T. J. (1998). *AntiPatterns: Refactoring Software, Architectures, and Projects in Crisis*. John Wiley & Sons.

Brunyé, T. T., Taylor, H. A., & Worboys, M. (2007). Levels of detail in descriptions and depictions of geographic space. *Spatial Cognition and Computation, 7*(3), 227–266. doi:10.1080/13875860701515472

Buchanan, S., Huang, J., & Triantafilis, J. (2017). Salinity risk assessment using fuzzy multiple criteria evaluation. *Soil Use and Management, 33*(2), 216–232. doi:10.1111um.12301

Bulldog Reporter. (2010). *Web users increasingly rely on social media to seek help in a disaster: New Red Cross survey shows that 74 percent expect response agencies to answer social media call for help within an hour*. Available at: https://www.bulldogreporter.com/web-users-increasingly-rely-social-media-seek-help-disaster-new-red-cross-survey-sh/

Burges, C. J. C. (1998). A tutorial on support vector machines for pattern recognition. *Data Mining and Knowledge Discovery, 2*(2), 121–167. doi:10.1023/A:1009715923555

Burke, R. (2007). Hybrid Web Recommender Systems. In P. Brusilovsky, A. Kobsa, & W. Nejdl (Eds.), *The Adaptive Web: Methods and Strategies of Web Personalization. In LNCS, 4321* (pp. 377–408). Heidelberg, Germany: Springer. doi:10.1007/978-3-540-72079-9_12

Buschmann, F., Meunier, R., Rohnert, H., Sommerlad, P., & Stal, M. (1996). *Pattern-Oriented Software Architecture - A System of Patterns*. John Wiley & Sons.

Buzsaki, G. (2002). Theta oscillations in the hippocampus. *Neuron, 33*(3), 325–340. doi:10.1016/S0896-6273(02)00586-X PMID:11832222

Cai, C. H., Fu, W. C., Cheng, C. H., & Kwong, W. W. (1998). Mining association rules with weighted items. *Proceedings of the International Database Engineering and Applications Symposium*, 68–77.

Cai, Q., Zhang, D., Wu, B., & Leung, S. C. H. (2013). A novel stock forecasting model based on fuzzy time series and genetic algorithm, The 13th International Conference on Computational Science (2013 ICCS). *Procedia Computer Science, 18*, 1155–1162. doi:10.1016/j.procs.2013.05.281

Cai, Q., Zhang, D., Wu, B., & Leung, S. C. H. (2015). A new fuzzy time series forecasting model combined with ant colony optimization and auto-regression. *Knowledge-Based Systems, 74*, 61–68. doi:10.1016/j.knosys.2014.11.003

Caire, J., & ... . (2002). Agent-oriented analysis using MESSAGE/UML. *Proceedings of the 2nd Int. Workshop on Agent-Oriented Software Engineering*, 119-135. 10.1007/3-540-70657-7_8

Canadian Institute for Cybersecurity. (n.d.). *NSL-KDD*. Retrieved from http://nsl.cs.unb.ca/NSL-KDD/

Cannady, J., & Harrell, J. (1996, May). A comparative analysis of current intrusion detection technologies. *Proceedings of the Fourth Technology for Information Security Conference*, 96.

Cao, L., Li, J., Ji, H., & Jiang, C. (2014). A hybrid brain computer interface system based on the neurophysiological protocol and brain-actuated switch for wheelchair control. *Journal of Neuroscience Methods, 229*, 33–43. doi:10.1016/j.jneumeth.2014.03.011 PMID:24713576

Carzaniga, A., Rosenblum, D. S., & Wolf, A. L. (2001). Design and evaluation of a wide-area event notification service. *ACM Transactions on Computer Systems, 19*(3), 332–383. doi:10.1145/380749.380767

Castro, J., Kolp, M., & Mylopoulos, J. (2002). Towards Requirements-Driven Information Systems Engineering: The Tropos Project. *Information Systems, 27*(6), 365–389. doi:10.1016/S0306-4379(02)00012-1

Caylak, I., & Mahnken, R. (2010). Thermo-mechanical characterization of a cold box sand including optical measurements. *International Journal of Cast Metals Research, 23*(3), 176–184. doi:10.1179/174313309X451261

CBS News. (2015). Ocean fish numbers on 'brink of collapse,' WWF reports. Science and Technology. *CBS News.* Retrieved on 1/23/2018 from: http://www.cbc.ca/news/technology/ocean-fish-wwf-1.3230157

Céline Bérard, C. (2005). Performance evaluation of management information systems in clinical trials: A system dynamics approach. In *Proceedings of the 2005 System Dynamics Conference.* The System Dynamics Society.

Chanas, S., Delgado, M., Verdegay, J. L., & Vila, M. A. (1993). Interval and fuzzy extensions of classical transportation problems. *Transportation Planning and Technology, 17*(2), 203–218. doi:10.1080/03081069308717511

Chanas, S., Kołodziejczyk, W., & Machaj, A. (1984). A fuzzy approach to the transportation problem. *Fuzzy Sets and Systems, 13*(3), 211–221. doi:10.1016/0165-0114(84)90057-5

Chanas, S., & Kuchta, D. (1996). A concept of the optimal solution of the transportation problem with fuzzy cost coefficients. *Fuzzy Sets and Systems, 82*(3), 299–305. doi:10.1016/0165-0114(95)00278-2

Chanas, S., & Kuchta, D. (1998). Fuzzy integer transportation problem. *Fuzzy Sets and Systems, 98*(3), 291–298. doi:10.1016/S0165-0114(96)00380-6

Chang, C. Y., Jagadish, H. V., Tan, K.-L., Tung, A. K. H., & Zhang, Z. (2006). On High Dimensional Skylines. In *EDBT '06: Proceedings of the 10th International Conference on Extending Database Technology (vol. 3896,* pp. 478–495). Springer.

Charnes, A., & Cooper, W. W. (1954). The stepping stone method of explaining linear programming calculations in transportation problems. *Management Science, 1*(1), 49–69. doi:10.1287/mnsc.1.1.49

Chate, G. R., Patel, G. C. M., Parappagoudar, M. B., & Deshpande, A. S. (2017). Modeling and optimization phenol formaldehyde resin sand mould system. *Archives of Foundry Engineering, 17*(2), 162–170. doi:10.1515/afe-2017-0069

Chattopadhyay, S., Davis, R. M., Menezes, D. D., Singh, G., Acharya, R. U., & Tamura, T. (2012). Application of Bayesian classifier for the diagnosis of dental pain. *Journal of Medical Systems, 36*(3), 1425–1439. doi:10.100710916-010-9604-y PMID:20945154

Chen, Y. (2005). Data Mining and Service Rating in Service-Oriented Architectures to Improve Information Sharing. 2005 IEEE Aerospace Conference, 1-11.

Chen, B., & Cheng, H. H. (2010). A review of the applications of agent technology in traffic and transportation systems. *IEEE Transactions on Intelligent Transportation Systems, 11*(2), 485–497. doi:10.1109/TITS.2010.2048313

Cheng, P., & Shyang, J. (2014), Completely Hide Sensitive Association Rules using EMO by Deleting Transactions. *Proceedings 2014 Annual Conference on Genetic and Evolutionary Computation,* 167-168.

Chen, G., Liu, H., Yu, L., Wei, Q., & Zhang, X. (2006). A new approach to classification based on association rule mining. *Decision Support Systems, 42*(2), 674–689. doi:10.1016/j.dss.2005.03.005

Cheng, C. H., Chen, T. L., & Wei, L. Y. (2010). A hybrid model based on rough sets theory and genetic algorithms for stock price forecasting. *Information Sciences, 180*(9), 1610–1629. doi:10.1016/j.ins.2010.01.014

Cheng, S.-H., Chen, S.-M., & Jian, W.-S. (2016). Fuzzy time series forecasting based on fuzzy logical relationships and similarity measures. *Information Sciences, 327,* 272–287. doi:10.1016/j.ins.2015.08.024

Chen, L., Yang, G., Zhang, Y., & Chen, Z. (2010). Web services clustering using SOM based on kernel cosine similarity measure. *Proceeding of the 2nd International Conference on Information Science and Engineering*, 846–850. 10.1109/ICISE.2010.5689254

Chen, M. Y., & Chen, B. T. (2014). Online fuzzy time series analysis based on entropy discretization and a fast fourier transform. *Applied Soft Computing*, *14*, 156–166. doi:10.1016/j.asoc.2013.07.024

Chen, M. Y., & Chen, B. T. (2015). A hybrid fuzzy time series model based on granular Computing for stock price forecasting. *Information Sciences*, *294*(2), 227–241. doi:10.1016/j.ins.2014.09.038

Chen, M., Ishii, H., & Wu, C. (2008). Transportation problems on a fuzzy network. *International Journal of Innovative Computing, Information, & Control*, *4*(5), 1105–1109.

Chen, S. H. (1985). Operations on fuzzy numbers with function principal. *Tamkang Journal of Management Sciences*, *6*(1), 13–25.

Chen, S. H. (1999). Ranking generalized fuzzy number with graded mean integration. *Proceeding 8th International Fuzzy Systems Association World Congress*, 2, 899-902.

Chen, S. H., & Hsieh, C. H. (1999). Graded mean integration representation of generalized fuzzy numbers. *Journal of the Chinese Fuzzy Systems Association*, *5*(2), 1–7.

Chen, S. M. (1996). Forecasting enrollments based on fuzzy time series. *Fuzzy Sets and Systems*, *81*(3), 311–319. doi:10.1016/0165-0114(95)00220-0

Chen, S. M. (2002). Forecasting enrollments based on high-order fuzzy time series. *Cybernetics and Systems: An International Journal*, *33*(1), 1–16. doi:10.1080/019697202753306479

Chen, S. M., & Hsu, C. C. (2004). A new method to forecast enrollments using fuzzy time series. *International Journal of Applied Sciences and Engineering*, *2*(3), 234–244.

Chen, S. M., & Kao, P. Y. (2013). TAIEX forecasting based on fuzzy time series, particle Swarm optimization techniques and support vector machines. *Information Sciences*, *247*, 62–71. doi:10.1016/j.ins.2013.06.005

Chen, S.-M., & Tanuwijaya, K. (2011). Fuzzy forecasting based on high-order fuzzy logical relationships and automatic clustering techniques. *Expert Systems with Applications*, *38*(12), 15425–15437. doi:10.1016/j.eswa.2011.06.019

Chen, T. H., Shang, W., Jiang, Z. M., Hassan, A. E., Nasser, M., & Flora, P. (2014). Detecting performance anti-patterns for applications developed using object-relational mapping. In *Proceedings of the 36th International Conference on Software Engineering* (pp. 1001-1012). ACM. 10.1145/2568225.2568259

Chentouf, Z. (2014). Cognitive software engineering: A research framework and roadmap. *Journal of Software Engineering and Applications*, *7*(6), 530–539. doi:10.4236/jsea.2014.76049

Chen, W., Paik, I., & Hung, P. C. K. (2014). Constructing a Global Social Service Network for Better Quality of Web Service Discovery. *IEEE Transactions on Services Computing*, *26*(5), 1466–1476.

Chen, X., Zhang, Y., Xu, J., Xing, C., & Chen, H. (2016). Deep learning based topic identification and categorization: Mining diabetes-related topics on Chinese health website. In Lecture Notes in Computer Science: Vol. 9642 (pp. 481–500). Springer Verlag. doi:10.1007/978-3-319-32025-0_30

Chen, Z., Zhao, L., & Lee, K. (2010). Environmental risk assessment of offshore produced water discharges using a hybrid fuzzy-stochastic modeling approach. *Environmental Modelling & Software*, *25*(6), 782–792. doi:10.1016/j.envsoft.2010.01.001

Chester, S., Sidlauskas, D., Assent, I., & Bøgh, K. S. (2015). Scalable Parallelization of Skyline Computation for Multi-Core Processors. *ICDE '15: 31st IEEE International Conference on Data Engineering, ICDE 2015*, 1083–1094. 10.1109/ICDE.2015.7113358

Cheung, A. K. Y., & Jacobsen, H. A. (2010). Load balancing content-based publish/subscribe systems. *ACM Transactions on Computer Systems*, 28(4), 9. doi:10.1145/1880018.1880020

Chiang, J. (2005). The optimal solution of the transportation problem with fuzzy demand and fuzzy product. *Journal of Information Science and Engineering*, 21(2), 439–451.

Chiappalone, M., Vato, A., Berdondini, L., Koudelka-Hep, M., & Martinoia, S. (2007). Network dynamics and synchronous activity in cultured cortical neurons. *International Journal of Neural Systems*, 17(02), 87–103. doi:10.1142/S0129065707000968 PMID:17565505

Chidamber, S.R., & Kemerer, C.F. (1994). A Metrics Suite for Object-Oriented Design. *IEEE Transactions on Software Engineering*, 20(6), 476-493.

Chifu, V. R., Pop, C. B., Salomie, I., Dinsoreanu, M., Acretoaie, V., & David, T. (2010). An ant-inspired approach for semantic web service clustering. *Proc. 9th Roedunet International Conference (RoEduNet)*, 145–150.

Chipofya, M., Schwering, A., Schultz, C., Harason, E., & Jan, S. (2015). Left-Right Relations for Qualitative Representation and Alignment of Planar Spatial Networks. In *Proceedings of the Mexican International Conference on Artificial Intelligence* (pp. 435-450). Springer. 10.1007/978-3-319-27101-9_33

Choi, J., Nazareth, D. L., & Jain, H. K. (2008). Information technology skill management: A systems dynamics approach. *Proceedings of the 41st Hawaii International Conference on System Sciences*. 10.1109/HICSS.2008.206

Chomicki, J., Ciaccia, P., & Meneghetti, N. (2013). Skyline Queries, Front and Back. *SIGMOD Rec., 42*(3), 6–18.

Chomicki, J., Godfrey, P., Gryz, J., & Liang, D. (2003). Skyline with Presorting. *ICDE '03: Proceedings of the 19th International Conference on Data Engineering*, 717–816.

Chomicki, J., Godfrey, P., Gryz, J., & Liang, D. (2003). Skyline with Presorting. *Proceedings of ICDE '03*, 717-816.

Christensen, H. V., & Garcia, J. C. (2005). Infrared non-contact head sensor for control of wheelchair movements. In A. Pruski & H. Knops (Eds.), *Assistive technology: from virtuality to reality* (pp. 336–340). IOS Press.

Christi, M. S. A., & Malini, D. (2016). An approach to solve transportation problems with octagonal fuzzy numbers using best candidates method and different ranking techniques. *International Journal of Computers and Applications*, 6(1), 71–85.

Clements, P. P., & Northrop, L. (2002). *Software product lines: Practices and patterns*. Academic Press.

Cochrane, K. L., & Garcia, S. M. (2009). *A fishery manager's guidebook* (2nd ed.). Wiley-Blackwell. doi:10.1002/9781444316315

Cockburn, A. (1996). The Interaction of Social Issues and Software Architecture. *Communications of the ACM*, 39(10), 40–49. doi:10.1145/236156.236165

CogAge project. (n.d.). *German government-funded project 2015-2018*. Retrieved from https://www.technik-zum-menschen-bringen.de/projekte/cogage

Conte, R., & Paolucci, M. (2014). On agent-based modeling and computational social science. *Frontiers in Psychology*, 5. PMID:25071642

Coplien, J., & Schmidt, D. (1995). *Pattern Languages of Program Design*. Addison-Wesley.

Coplien, O. (1991). *Advanced C++ Programming Styles and Idioms*. Addison-Wesley International.

Cosgaya-Lozano, A., Rau-Chaplin, A., & Zeh, N. (2007). Parallel Computation of Skyline Queries. *Proc. of HPCS '07*, 12.

Crisman, E. E., Loomis, A., Shaw, R., & Laszewski, Z. (1991). Using the eye wink control interface to control a powered wheelchair. In *Engineering in Medicine and Biology Society: Proceedings of the Annual International Conference of the IEEE* (vol. 13, pp.1821–1822). IEEE.

Crosbie, M., & Spafford, E. (1995). Applying genetic programming to intrusion detection. *Proceedings of AAAI Fall Symposium on Genetic Programming*, 1–8.

Dalton, R. C. (2003). The secret is to follow your nose: Route path selection and angularity. *Environment and Behavior*, *35*(1), 107–131. doi:10.1177/0013916502238867

Damousis, I. G., Satsios, K. J., Labridis, D. P., & Dokopoulos, P. S. (2002). Combined fuzzy logic and genetic algorithm techniques—application to an electromagnetic field problem. *Fuzzy Sets and Systems*, *129*(3), 371–386. doi:10.1016/S0165-0114(01)00137-3

Danane, Y., & Parvat, T. (2015, January). Intrusion detection system using fuzzy genetic algorithm. In *Pervasive Computing (ICPC), 2015 International Conference on* (pp. 1-5). IEEE. 10.1109/PERVASIVE.2015.7086963

Dang, J., Hedayati, A., Hampel, K., & Toklu, C. (2008). An ontological knowledge framework for adaptive medical workflow. *Journal of Biomedical Informatics*, *41*(5), 829–836. doi:10.1016/j.jbi.2008.05.012 PMID:18602872

Dasgupta, S., Bhat, S., & Lee, Y. (2011). Taxonomic clustering and query matching for efficient service discovery. *Proceeding of the 9th IEEE International Conference on Web Services*, 363–370. 10.1109/ICWS.2011.112

Dash, M., Choi, K., Scheuermann, P., & Liu, H. (2002). Feature selection for clusteringâŁ"a filter solution. *Proceedings of the Second International Conference on Data Mining*, 115-122.

Das, M., & Baruah, H. K. (2007). Solution of the transportation problem in fuzzified form. *Journal of Fuzzy Mathematics*, *15*(1), 79–95.

Dastanpour, A., Ibrahim, S., Mashinchi, R., & Selamat, A. (2014, October). Comparison of genetic algorithm optimization on artificial neural network and support vector machine in intrusion detection system. In *Open Systems (ICOS), 2014 IEEE Conference on* (pp. 72-77). IEEE. 10.1109/ICOS.2014.7042412

Davey, B. A., & Priestley, H. A. (2002). *Introduction to Lattices and Order* (2nd ed.). Cambridge, UK: Cambridge University Press. doi:10.1017/CBO9780511809088

de Oude, P., Pavlin, G., Quillinan, T., Jeraj, J., & Abouhafc, A. (2017). Cloud-Based Intelligence Aquisition and Processing for Crisis Management. In B. Akhgar, A. Staniforth, & D. Waddington (Eds.), *Application of Social Media in Crisis Management* (pp. 133–153). Springer. doi:10.1007/978-3-319-52419-1_9

Debar, H., Dacier, M., & Wespi, A. (1999). Towards a taxonomy of intrusion-detection systems. *Computer Networks*, *31*(8), 805–822. doi:10.1016/S1389-1286(98)00017-6

Dehkordi, M. N., Badie, K., & Zadeh, A. K. (2009). A Novel Method for Privacy Preserving in Association Rule Mining Based on Genetic Algorithms. *Journal of Software*, *4*(6), 555–562. doi:10.4304/jsw.4.6.555-562

del Águila, I. M., Palma, J., & Túnez, S. (2014). Milestones in software engineering and knowledge engineering history: A comparative review. *The Scientific World Journal*. PMID:24624046

DeMarse, T., Wagenaar, D., Blau, A., & Potter, S. (2001). The neutrally controlled animat: Biological brains acting with simulated bodies. *Autonomous Robots*, *11*(3), 305–310. doi:10.1023/A:1012407611130 PMID:18584059

Deng, X., & Jiang, W. (2017). Fuzzy risk evaluation in failure mode and effects analysis using a D numbers based multi-sensor information fusion method. *Sensors (Basel)*, *17*(9), 2086. doi:10.339017092086 PMID:28895905

Deng, Y., & Chan, F. T. S. (2011). A new fuzzy Dempster MCDM method and its application in supplier selection. *Expert Systems with Applications*, *38*(8), 9854–9861. doi:10.1016/j.eswa.2011.02.017

Denis, M. (1997). The description of routes: A cognitive approach to the production of spatial discourse. *Cahiers de Psychologie Cognitive*, *16*(4), 409–458.

Denning, D. (1987). An intrusion detection model. *IEEE Transactions on Software Engineering*, *13*(2), 222–232. doi:10.1109/TSE.1987.232894

De, P. K., & Yadav, B. (2010). Approach to defuzzify the trapezoidal fuzzy number in transportation problem. *International Journal of Computational Cognition*, *8*(4), 64–67.

Derringer & Suich. (1980). Simultaneous optimization of several response variables. *Journal of Quality Technology*, *12*, 214-219.

Deugo, D., Oppacher, F., Kuester, J., & Otte, I. V. (1999). Patterns as a Means for Intelligent Software Engineering. *Proceedings of the Int. Conf. on Artificial Intelligence*, 605-611.

Dhungana, D., Grünbacher, P., Rabiser, R., & Neumayer, T. (2010). Structuring the modeling space and supporting evolution in software product line engineering. *Journal of Systems and Software*, *83*(7), 1108–1122. doi:10.1016/j.jss.2010.02.018

Diao, Y., Li, B., Liu, A., Peng, L., Sutton, C., Tran, T., & Zink, M. (2009). *Capturing data uncertainty in high-volume stream processing*. arXiv preprint arXiv:0909.1777

Dickerson, J., & Dickerson, J. (2000). Fuzzy network profiling for intrusion detection. *19th International Conference of the North American Fuzzy Information Processing Society (NAFIPS)*, 301–306.

Dimarogonas, D. V., Frazzoli, E., & Johansson, K. H. (2012). Distributed event-triggered control for multi-agent systems. *IEEE Transactions on Automatic Control*, *57*(5), 1291–1297. doi:10.1109/TAC.2011.2174666

Dinagar, D. S., & Palanivel, K. (2009). The transportation problem in fuzzy environment. *International Journal of Algorithms. Computing and Mathematics*, *2*(3), 65–71.

Ding, G., Zhang, Q., & Zhou, Y. (1997). Strengthening of cold-setting resin sand by the additive method. *Journal of Materials Processing Technology*, *72*(2), 239–242. doi:10.1016/S0924-0136(97)00174-X

Dintzner, N. (2015). Safe evolution patterns for software product lines. In *Proceedings of the 37th International Conference on Software Engineering* (vol. 2, pp. 875–878). IEEE Press.

Domdouzis, K., Andrews, S., Akhgar, B. (2016). Application of a New Service-Oriented Architecture (SOA) Paradigm on the Design of a Crisis Management Distributed System. *International Journal of Distributed Systems and Technologies*.

Do, T. T., Faulkner, S., & Kolp, M. (2003). Organizational Multi-Agent Architectures for Information Systems. *Proceedings of the 5th International Conference on Enterprise Information Systems, ICEIS 2003*, 89-96.

Dote, Y., & Ovaska, S. J. (2001). Industrial applications of soft computing: A review. *Proceedings of the IEEE*, 1243–1265. 10.1109/5.949483

Dovzan, D., Logar, V., & Skrjanc, I. (2015). Implementation of an Evolving Fuzzy Model (eFuMo) in a Monitoring System for a Waste-Water Treatment Process. *IEEE Transactions on Fuzzy Systems*, *23*(5), 1761–1776. doi:10.1109/TFUZZ.2014.2379252

Downs, R. M., & Stea, D. (1973). Cognitive maps and spatial behavior: Process and products. In R. M. Downs & D. Stea (Eds.), *Image and Environment*. Chicago: Aldine.

Duda, R., Hart, P., & Stork, D. (2001). *Pattern Classification* (2nd ed.). John Wiley & Sons.

Duraiswamy, K., Manjula, D., & Maheswari, N. (2010). A New Approach to Sensitive Rule Hiding. *CCSENET Journal*, *1*(3), 107-111.

Durst, R., Champion, T., Witten, B., Miller, E., & Spagnuolo, L. (1999). Testing and evaluating computer intrusion detection systems. *Communications of the ACM*, *42*(7), 53–61. doi:10.1145/306549.306571

Dussauge, P., & Garrette, B. (1999). *Cooperative Strategy: Competing Successfully Through Strategic Alliances*. Wiley and Sons.

Dutta, P. (2011). Arithmetic operations of fuzzy focal elements in evidence theory. *International Journal of Latest Trends in Computing*, *2*(4).

Dutta, P. (2015). Uncertainty modeling in risk assessment based on Dempster–Shafer theory of evidence with generalized fuzzy focal elements. *Fuzzy Information and Engineering*, *7*(1), 15–30. doi:10.1016/j.fiae.2015.03.002

Dutta, P. (2016). Comparison of arithmetic operations of generalized fuzzy numbers: Case study in risk assessment. *Cybernetics and Systems*, *47*(4), 290–320. doi:10.1080/01969722.2016.1182354

Dutta, P. (2016). Dempster shafer structure-Fuzzy number based uncertainty modeling in human health risk assessment. *International Journal of Fuzzy System Applications*, *5*(2), 96–117. doi:10.4018/IJFSA.2016040107

Dutta, P. (2017). Modeling of variability and uncertainty in human health risk assessment. *MethodsX*, *4*, 76–85. doi:10.1016/j.mex.2017.01.005 PMID:28239562

Dutta, P., & Ali, T. (2011). Fuzzy focal elements in dempster-shafer theory of evidence: Case study in risk analysis. *International Journal of Computers and Applications*, *34*, 46–53.

Dutta, P., Boruah, H., & Ali, T. (2011a). Fuzzy arithmetic with and without using α-cut method: A comparative study. *International Journal of Latest Trends in Computing*, *2*(1), 99–108.

Dylla, F., & Moratz, R. (2005). Exploiting qualitative spatial neighborhoods in the situation calculus. *LNAI*, *3343*, 304–322.

Eberhart, R., & Kennedy, J. (1995). A new optimizer using particle swarm theory. *Sixth International Symposium on Micro Machine and Human Science*, 39–43. 10.1109/MHS.1995.494215

Eberhart, R., Simpson, P., & Dobbins, R. (1996). *Computational Intelligence PC Tools*. Boston: Academic Press.

Eberlein, R. L., & Thompson, J. P. (2013). Precise modeling of aging populations. *System Dynamics Review*, *29*(2), 87–101. doi:10.1002dr.1497

Ebrahimnejad, A. (2012). Cost efficiency measures with trapezoidal fuzzy numbers in data envelopment analysis based on ranking functions: Application in insurance organization and hospital. *International Journal of Fuzzy System Applications*, *2*(3), 51–68. doi:10.4018/ijfsa.2012070104

Ebrahimnejad, A. (2016a). Fuzzy linear programming approach for solving transportation problems with interval-valued trapezoidal fuzzy numbers. *Sadhana*, *41*(3), 299–316.

Ebrahimnejad, A. (2016b). New method for solving fuzzy transportation problems with LR flat fuzzy numbers. *Information Sciences*, *357*, 108–124. doi:10.1016/j.ins.2016.04.008

Egenhofer, M. J. (1997). Query processing in spatial-query-by-sketch. *Journal of Visual Languages and Computing*, *8*(4), 403–424. doi:10.1006/jvlc.1997.0054

Egrioglu, E., Aladag, C. H., Yolcu, U., Uslu, V. R., & Erilli, N. A. (2011). Fuzzy time series forecasting method based on Gustafson–Kessel fuzzy clustering. *Expert Systems with Applications*, *38*(8), 10355–10357. doi:10.1016/j.eswa.2011.02.052

Egrioglu, E., Aladag, C., Basaran, M., Yolcu, U., & Uslu, V. (2011). A new approach based on the optimization of the length of intervals in fuzzy time series. *Journal of Intelligent & Fuzzy Systems*, *22*(1), 15–19.

Egrioglu, E., Aladag, C., & Yolcu, U. (2013). Fuzzy time series forecasting with a novel hybrid approach combining fuzzy c-means and neural networks. *Expert Systems with Applications*, *40*(3), 854–857. doi:10.1016/j.eswa.2012.05.040

Ehrlich, P. R., & Raven, P. H. (1964). Butterflies and plants: A study in coevolution. *Evolution; International Journal of Organic Evolution*, *18*(4), 586–608. doi:10.1111/j.1558-5646.1964.tb01674.x

Eichenbaum, H. (2010). Hippocampus: Mapping or memory? *Current Biology*, *10*(21), 785–787. doi:10.1016/S0960-9822(00)00763-6 PMID:11084350

Eid, H. F., Azar, A. T., & Hassanien, A. E. (2013). Improved real-time discretize network intrusion detection system. *Seventh International Conference on Bio-Inspired Computing Theories and Applications (BIC-TA 2012) Advances in Intelligent Systems and Computing*, 99–109. 10.1007/978-81-322-1038-2_9

Eid, H. F., Darwish, A., Hassanien, A. E., & Abraham, A. (2010). Principle components analysisand support vector machine based intrusion detection system. *The 10th IEEE international conference in Intelligent Design and Application (ISDA2010).*

Eid, H. F., Darwish, A., Hassanien, A. E., & Hoon Kim, T. (2011). *Intelligent hybrid anomaly network intrusion detection system. In International Conference on Future Generation Communication and Networking.* CCIS/ LNCS series, Jeju Island, Korea.

Elgazzar, K., Hassan, A. E., & Martin, P. (2010). Clustering WSDL Documents to Bootstrap the Discovery of Web Services. *Proceeding of the 8th IEEE International Conference on Web Services*, 147-154. 10.1109/ICWS.2010.31

Elhag, S., Fernandez, A., Bawakid, A., Alshomrani, S., & Herrera, F. (2015). On the combination of genetic fuzzy systems and pairwise learning for improving detection rates on intrusion detection systems. *Expert Systems with Applications*, *42*(1), 193–202. doi:10.1016/j.eswa.2014.08.002

Elshazly, H. I., Azar, A. T., Hassanien, A. E., & Elkorany, A. M. (2013). Hybrid system based on rough sets and genetic algorithms for medical data classifications. *International Journal of Fuzzy System Applications*, *3*(4), 31–46. doi:10.4018/ijfsa.2013100103

Elvesæter, B. (2011). *Service Modelling Service Modelling with SoaML*. Available at: http://www.uio.no/studier/emner/matnat/ifi/INF5120/v11/div/SoaML_Tutorial.pdf

Emotiv SDK. (2010. *Software Development Kit User manual for release 1.0.0.4*. Author.

Endorf, C., Schultz, E., & J., M. (2004). *Intrusion Detection and Prevention*. McGraw-Hill.

Endrei, M., Ang, J., Arsanjani, A., Chua, S., Comte, P., Krogdahl, P., Luo, M., & Newling, T. (2004, April). Patterns: Service-Oriented Architecture and Web Services. *IBM Redbooks*.

Endres, M. & Kießling, W. (2015). Parallel Skyline Computation Exploiting the Lattice Structure. *JDM: Journal of Database Management, 26*(4).

Endres, M., & Kießling, W. (2014). High Parallel Skyline Computation over Low-Cardinality Domains. In *Proceedings of ADBIS '14* (pp. 97–111). Springer. 10.1007/978-3-319-10933-6_8

Endres, M., & Weichmann, F. (2017). Index Structures for Preference Database Queries. In *FQAS '17: Proceedings of the 12th International Conference on Flexible Query Answering Systems, Lecture Notes in Computer Science*. Springer-Verlag.

Endres, M., & Preisinger, T. (2017). Beyond Skylines: Explicit Preferences. In *DASFAA '17* (pp. 327–342). Cham: Springer International Publishing.

Endres, M., Roocks, P., & Kießling, W. (2015). Scalagon: An Efficient Skyline Algorithm for all Seasons. *Proceedings of DASFAA '15*. 10.1007/978-3-319-18123-3_18

Eskin, E., Arnold, A., Prerau, M., Portnoy, L., & Stolfo, S. (2002). A geometric framework for unsupervised anomaly detection: detecting intrusions in unlabeled data. In *Data Mining in Computer Security*. Kluwer. doi:10.1007/978-1-4615-0953-0_4

Esmael, B., Arnaout, A., Fruhwirth, R. K., & Thonhauser, G. (2012). *Improving time series classification using Hidden Markov Models* (pp. 502–507). HIS. doi:10.1109/HIS.2012.6421385

Esposito, C., Ficco, M., Palmieri, F., & Castiglione, A. (2014). A knowledge-based platform for Big Data analytics based on publish/subscribe services and stream processing. *Knowledge-Based Systems*.

Eto, F. (2001). Causes of Falls in the Elderly. *Japan Medical Association Journal: JMAJ, 44*(7), 299–305.

Euzenat, J., & Shvaiko, P. (2007). *Ontology matching*. Berlin: Springer-Verlag.

Evfimievski, A. (2002). Randomization in privacy preserving data mining. *ACM SIGKDD Explorations Newsletter, 4*(2), 43–48. doi:10.1145/772862.772869

Evfimievski, A., Srikant, R., Agrawal, R., & Gehrke, J. (2002). Privacy preserving mining of association rules. *8th ACM SIGKDD International Conference on Knowledge Discovery and Data Mining*, 217–228.

Faquir, S., Yahyaouy, A., Tairi, H., & Sabor, J. (2017). Implementing a fuzzy logic based algorithm to predict solar and wind energies in a hybrid renewable energy system. In Renewable and Alternative Energy: Concepts, Methodologies, Tools, and Applications (pp. 1220-1235). IGI Global. doi:10.4018/978-1-5225-1671-2.ch040

Farakos, S. M. S., Pouillot, R., Anderson, N., Johnson, R., Son, I., & Van Doren, J. (2016). Modeling the survival kinetics of Salmonella in tree nuts for use in risk assessment. *International Journal of Food Microbiology, 227*, 41–50. doi:10.1016/j.ijfoodmicro.2016.03.014 PMID:27062527

Farakos, S. S. M., Schaffner, D. W., & Frank, J. F. (2014). Predicting survival of Salmonella in low–water activity foods: An analysis of literature data. *Journal of Food Protection, 77*(9), 1448–1461. doi:10.4315/0362-028X.JFP-14-013 PMID:25198835

Farakos, S. S., Frank, J. F., & Schaffner, D. W. (2013). Modeling the influence of temperature, water activity and water mobility on the persistence of Salmonella in low-moisture foods. *International Journal of Food Microbiology, 166*(2), 280–293. doi:10.1016/j.ijfoodmicro.2013.07.007 PMID:23973840

Faria, E. R., Goncalves, I. J. C. R., de Carvalho, A. C. P. L. F., & Gama, J. (2016). Novelty Detection in Data Streams. *Artificial Intelligence Review, 45*(2), 235–269. doi:10.100710462-015-9444-8

Fathima, A. A., Vaidehi, V., & Selvaraj, K. (2014). Fall detection with part-based approach for Indoor Environment. *International Journal of Intelligent Information Technologies*, *10*(4), 51–69. doi:10.4018/ijiit.2014100104

Faulkner, S., Kolp, M., Wautelet, Y., & Achbany, Y. (2008). A formal description language for multi-agent architectures. *Agent-Oriented Information Systems*, *IV*, 143–163. doi:10.1007/978-3-540-77990-2_9

Felzer, T., & Freisleben, B. (2002). HaWCoS: the hands-free wheelchair control system. In *Proceedings of the fifth international ACM conference on assistive technologies* (pp. 127–134). ACM. 10.1145/638249.638273

Fernandez, E. B., & Pan, R. (2001). A Pattern Language for Security Models. *Proceedings of the 8th Conference on Pattern Language of Programs*.

Figueiredo, E., Cacho, N., Sant'Anna, C., Monteiro, M., Kulesza, U., Garcia, A., . . . Dantas, F. (2008). Evolving software product lines with aspects. In *2008 ACM/IEEE 30th International Conference on Software Engineering* (pp. 261–270). IEEE.

Fiksel, J. (2006). Sustainability and resilience: Toward a systems approach. *Sustainability: Science, Practice, & Policy, 2*(2).

FIPA. (2017). *The Foundation for Intelligent Physical Agent (FIPA)*. Retrieved from http://www.fipa.org/

Firoozabadi, S. M. P., Oskoei, M. A., & Hu, H. (2008). A human-computer Interface based on forehead multi-channel bio-signals to control a virtual wheelchair. In *Proceedings of the 14th Iranian Conference on Biomedical Engineering* (pp. 272–277). Academic Press.

Flage, R., Baraldi, P., Zio, E., & Aven, T. (2010, September). Possibility-probability transformation in comparing different approaches to the treatment of epistemic uncertainties in a fault tree analysis. In Reliability, Risk and Safety-Proceedings of the European Safety and Reliability (ESREL) 2010 Conference, Rhodes, Greece (pp. 5-9). Academic Press.

Flage, R., Baraldi, P., Zio, E., & Aven, T. (2013). Probabilistic and possibilistic treatment of epistemic uncertainties in fault tree analysis. *Risk Analysis*, *33*(1), 121–133. doi:10.1111/j.1539-6924.2012.01873.x PMID:22831561

Flottmann, M. (2014). *Population dynamics: A catastrophe model for fishing*. Retrieved on 01/23/2018 from: http://jaguar.biologie.hu-berlin.de/~wolfram/pages/seminar_theoretische_biologie_2007/ausarbeitungen/floettmann.pdf

Fondo Xavier Clavigero, S. J., Ferreira, F., Borba, P., Soares, G., & Gheyi, R. (2012). Making software product line evolution safer. In *Software Components Architectures and Reuse (SBCARS), 2012 Sixth Brazilian Symposium on* (pp. 21–30). IEEE.

Forbus, K., & Gentner, D. (1997). Qualitative mental models: Simulations or memories? *Proceedings of the 11th International Workshop on Qualitative Reasoning*.

Forbus, K., Usher, J., Lovett, A., Lockwood, K., & Wetzel, J. (2011). CogSketch: Sketch understanding for cognitive science research and for education. *Topics in Cognitive Science*, *3*(4), 648–666. doi:10.1111/j.1756-8765.2011.01149.x PMID:25164503

Forgy, C. L. (1982). Rete: A fast algorithm for the many pattern/many object pattern match problem. *Artificial Intelligence*, *19*(1), 17–37. doi:10.1016/0004-3702(82)90020-0

Fortino, G., & Trunfio, P. (Eds.). (2014). *Internet of things based on smart objects: Technology, middleware and applications*. Springer Science & Business Media. doi:10.1007/978-3-319-00491-4

Foster, K., & Jaeger, J. (2007). RFID inside. *IEEE Spectrum*, *44*(3), 24–29. doi:10.1109/MSPEC.2007.323430

Fowler, M. (1997). *Analysis Patterns: Reusable Object Models*. Addison-Wesley.

Frank, A., & Asuncion, A. (2010). *UCI Machine Learning Repository*. Irvine, CA: University of California, School of Information and Computer Science.

Fraser, G. D., Chan, A. D., Green, J. R., & MacIsaac, D. T. (2014). Automated biosignal quality analysis for electromyography using a one-class support vector machine. *IEEE Transactions on Instrumentation and Measurement, 63*(12), 2919–2930. doi:10.1109/TIM.2014.2317296

Fried, D. J., Graf, I., Haines, J. W., Kendall, K. R., Mcclung, D., Weber, D., . . . Zissman, M. A. (2000). Evaluating intrusion detection systems: The 1998 darpa off-line intrusion detection evaluation. *Proceedings of the DARPA Information Survivability Conference and Exposition*, 12-26.

Fuxman, A., Pistore, M., Mylopoulos, J., & Traverso, P. (2001). Model Checking Early Requirements Specifications in Tropos. *Proc. of the 5th IEEE Int. Symposium on Requirements Engineering*, 174-181.

Gaia, G. N., Ferreira, G. C. S., Figueiredo, E., & Maia, M. A. (2014). A quantitative and qualitative assessment of aspectual feature modules for evolving software product lines. *Science of Computer Programming, 96*, 230–253. doi:10.1016/j.scico.2014.03.006

GAITRite® gait analysis mat. (n.d.). Retrieved from http://www.gaitrite.com

Gajwani, P. S., & Chhabria, S. A. (2010). Eye motion tracking for wheelchair control. *International Journal of Information Technology, 2*(2), 185–187.

Gamma, E., Helm, R., Johnson, R., & Vlissides, J. (1995). *Design Patterns: Elements of Reusable Object-Oriented Software*. Addison-Wesley.

Ganapathy, Vaidehi, & Raghuraman. (2015). An Efficient Remote Healthcare using Parallel Genetic approach. *International Journal of Applied Engineering Research, 9*(21), 4961–4966.

Ganapathy, K., Priya, B., Dhivya, B. P., Prashanth, V., & Vaidehi, V. (2013). SOA Framework for Geriatric Remote Health Care Using Wireless Sensor Network. *Procedia Computer Science, 19*, 1012–1019. doi:10.1016/j.procs.2013.06.141

Gani, A. N., & Razak, K. A. (2006). Two stage fuzzy transportation problem. *The Journal of Physiological Sciences; JPS, 10*, 63–69.

Gani, A. N., Samuel, A. E., & Anuradha, D. (2011). Simplex type algorithm for solving fuzzy transportation problem. *Tamsui Oxford Journal of Information and Mathematical Sciences, 27*(1), 89–98.

Gardner, G. R. (1948). Physical properties of molding sands. *AFS Transactions, 55*, 331–335.

Garlapati, V. K., Vundavilli, P. R., & Banerjee, R. (2010). Evaluation of lipase production by genetic algorithm and particle swarm optimization and their comparative study. *Applied Biochemistry and Biotechnology, 162*(5), 1350–1361. doi:10.100712010-009-8895-2 PMID:20099046

Gascueña, J. M., Navarro, E., & Fernández-Caballero, A. (2012). Model-driven engineering techniques for the development of multi-agent systems. *Engineering Applications of Artificial Intelligence, 25*(1), 159–173. doi:10.1016/j.engappai.2011.08.008

Gasson, M., Hutt, B., Goodhew, I., Kyberd, P., & Warwick, K. (2005). Invasive neural prosthesis for neural signal detection and nerve stimulation. *International Journal of Adaptive Control and Signal Processing, 19*(Issue.5), 365–375.

Gatton, T. M., & Lee, M. (2010). Fuzzy logic decision making for an intelligent home healthcare system. In *Future Information Technology (FutureTech), 2010 5th International Conference on* (pp. 1-5). IEEE. 10.1109/FUTURETECH.2010.5482667

Gaynor, M., Moulton, S. L., Welsh, M., LaCombe, E., Rowan, A., & Wynne, J. (2004). Integrating wireless sensor networks with the grid. *IEEE Internet Computing, 8*(4), 32–39. doi:10.1109/MIC.2004.18

Geurts, K., Wets, G., Brijs, T., & Vanhoof, K. (2003). Profiling High Frequency Accident Locations Using Association Rules. *Electronic Proceedings of the 82ᵗʰ Annual Meeting of the Transportation Research Board, 18*.

Giannotti, F., Lakshmanan, L., Monreale, A., Pedreschi, D., & Wang, H. (2013). Privacy-preserving mining of association rules from outsourced transaction databases. *IEEE Systems Journal, 7*(3), 385–395. doi:10.1109/JSYST.2012.2221854

Godfrey, P., Shipley, R., & Gryz, J. (2005). Maximal Vector Computation in Large Data Sets. In *VLDB '05: Proceedings of the 31ˢᵗ International Conference on Very Large Data Bases* (pp. 229-240). VLDB Endowment.

Godfrey, P., Shipley, R., & Gryz, J. (2007). Algorithms and Analyses for Maximal Vector Computation. *The VLDB Journal, 16*(1), 5–28. doi:10.100700778-006-0029-7

Göktürk, E., & Akkok, N. (2004). Paradigm and software engineering. Proceedings of Impact of Software Process on Quality.

Golledge, R. G. (1999). Human wayfinding and cognitive maps. In R. G. Golledge (Ed.), *Wayfinding behavior: Cognitive mapping and other spatial processes* (pp. 5–45). The Johns Hopkins University Press.

Gong, F. (2003). *Deciphering detection techniques: Part ii anomaly-based intrusion detection*. Network Associates.

Goonatilake & Khebbal. (1993). *Genetic programming of Neural Networks: Theory and practice. Intelligent hybrid systems*. John Wiley & Sons.

Goyal, A., & Kumar, C. (2008). *A genetic algorithm based network intrusion detection system*. Academic Press.

Graafstra, A. (2007). Hands on. *IEEE Spectrum, 44*(3), 318–323. doi:10.1109/MSPEC.2007.323420

Guharaja, S., Noorul Haq, A., & Karuppannan, K. M. (2006). Optimization of green sand casting process parameters by using Taguchi's method. *International Journal of Advanced Manufacturing Technology, 30*(11-12), 1040–1048. doi:10.100700170-005-0146-2

Gulisano, Jimenez-Peris, Patino-Martinez, & Valduriez. (2010). Streamcloud: A large scale data streaming system. In *Distributed Computing Systems (ICDCS), 2010 IEEE 30th International Conference on*. IEEE.

Gündüz, G., Yaman, Ç., Peker, A. U., & Acarman, T. (2017, June). Driving pattern fusion using dempster-shafer theory for fuzzy driving risk level assessment. In *Intelligent Vehicles Symposium (IV)*, 2017 IEEE (pp. 595-599). IEEE. 10.1109/IVS.2017.7995783

Guo, Y. (2007). Reconstruction-Based Association Rule Hiding. *Proceedings of SIGMOD2007 Ph.D. Workshop on Innovative Database Research 2007*, 51-56.

Gupta, M., & Joshi, R. C. (2009). Privacy Preserving Fuzzy Association Rules in Quantitative Data. *International Journal of Computer Theory and Engineering, 1*(4), 382–388. doi:10.7763/IJCTE.2009.V1.60

Guyonnet, D., Bourgine, B., Dubois, D., & Fargier, H., Coₓ me, B., & Chilès, J. P. (2003). Hybrid approach for addressing uncertainty in risk assessments. *Journal of Environmental Engineering, 129*(1), 68–78. doi:10.1061/(ASCE)0733-9372(2003)129:1(68)

Guyonnet, D., Côme, B., Perrochet, P., & Parriaux, A. (1999). Comparing two methods for addressing uncertainty in risk assessments. *Journal of Environmental Engineering, 125*(7), 660–666. doi:10.1061/(ASCE)0733-9372(1999)125:7(660)

Hajihashemi, Z., & Popescu, M. (2016). A Multidimensional Time-Series Similarity Measure With Applications to Eldercare Monitoring. *IEEE Journal of Biomedical and Health Informatics*, *20*(3), 953–962. doi:10.1109/JBHI.2015.2424711 PMID:25910260

Hallam, T. G., Lassiter, R. R., & Henson, S. M. (2000). Modeling fish population dynamics. *Nonlinear Analysis*, *40*(1-8), 227–250. doi:10.1016/S0362-546X(00)85013-0

Han, J. S., Zenn Bien, Z., Kim, D. J., & Lee, H. E., & Kim. J.S. (2003). Human machine interface for wheelchair control with EMG and its evaluation. In *Engineering in Medicine and Biology Society: Proceedings of the 25th Annual International Conference of the IEEE* (*vol. 2*, pp.1602–1605). IEEE.

Han, J., & Fu, Y. (1995). Discovery of multiple-level association rules from large database. *Proceedings of the 21st International Conference on Very Large Data Bases*, 420–431.

Harington, J. (1965). The desirability function. *Industrial Quality Control*, *21*, 494–498.

Hartley, T., Lever, C., Burgess, N., & O'Keefe, J. (2014). Space in the brain: How the hippocampal formation supports spatial cognition. *Philosophical Transactions of the Royal Society of London. Series B, Biological Sciences*, *369*(1635), 20120510. doi:10.1098/rstb.2012.0510 PMID:24366125

Hasan, M. K. (2012). Direct methods for finding optimal solution of a transportation problem are not always reliable. *International Refereed Journal of Engineering and Science*, *1*(2), 46–52.

Hausdorff, J. M., Rios, D. A., & Edelberg, H. K. (2001). Gait variability and fall risk in community-living older adults: A 1-year prospective study. *Archives of Physical Medicine and Rehabilitation*, *82*(8), 1050–1056. doi:10.1053/apmr.2001.24893 PMID:11494184

Hayden, S., Carrick, C., & Yang, Q. (1999). Architectural Design Patterns for Multiagent Coordination. *Proceedings of the 3rd Int. Conf. on Agent Systems*.

Hayes, D., Jones, M., Lester, N., Chu, C., Doka, S., Netto, J., ... Collins, N. (2009). Linking fish population dynamics to habitat conditions: Insights from the application of a process-oriented approach to several Great Lakes species. *Reviews in Fish Biology and Fisheries*, *19*(3), 295–312. doi:10.100711160-009-9103-8

Heady, R., Luger, G., Maccabe, A., & Servilla, M. (1990). *The architecture of a network level intrusion detection system. Technical report*. Computer Science Department, University of New Mexico. doi:10.2172/425295

Heath, R. L. (1997). *Strategic Issues Management*. Thousand Oaks, CA: Sage.

Heath, R. L. (1998). New Communication Technologies: An Issues Management Point of View. *Public Relations Review*, *24*(3), 273–288. doi:10.1016/S0363-8111(99)80140-4

Hebb, D. (1949). *The organisation of behaviour*. New York: Wiley.

Heiss, J. E., Held, C. M., Estevez, P. A., Perez, C. A., Holzmann, C. A., & Perez, J. P. (2002). Classification of sleep stages in infants: A neuro fuzzy approach. *Engineering in Medicine and Biology Magazine, IEEE*, *21*(5), 147–151. doi:10.1109/MEMB.2002.1044185 PMID:12405069

Helton, J. C., Oberkampf, W. L., & Johnson, J. D. (2005). Competing failure risk analysis using evidence theory. *Risk Analysis*, *25*(4), 973–995. doi:10.1111/j.1539-6924.2005.00644.x PMID:16268945

Hemalatha, C. S., & Vaidehi, V. (2013). Associative Classification based Human Activity Recognition and Fall Detection using Accelerometer. *International Journal of Intelligent Information Technologies*, *9*(3), 20–37. doi:10.4018/jiit.2013070102

Herweg, A., Gutzeit, J., Kleih, S., & Kübler, A. (2016). Wheelchair control by elderly participants in a virtual environment with a brain-computer interface (BCI) and tactile stimulation. *Biological Psychology*, *121*(Pt A), 117-124.

He, S., Zhang, R., Wang, Q., Chen, Y., Yang, T., Feng, Z., & Li, Y. (2017). A P300-Based Threshold-Free Brain Switch and Its Application in Wheelchair Control. *IEEE Transactions on Neural Systems and Rehabilitation Engineering*, *25*(6), 715–725. doi:10.1109/TNSRE.2016.2591012 PMID:27416603

Hinton, G. (2010). Deep Belief Nets. Encyclopedia of Machine Learning, 267-269.

Hippisley, A., Cheng, D., & Ahmad, K. (2005). The head-modifier principle and multilingual term extraction. *Natural Language Engineering*, *11*(2), 129–157. doi:10.1017/S1351324904003535

Hirel, J., Gaussier, P., Quoy, M., Banquet, J. P., Save, E., & Pucet, B. (2013). The hippocampo-cortical loop: Spatio-temporal learning and goal-oriented planning in navigation. *Neural Networks*, *43*, 8–21. doi:10.1016/j.neunet.2013.01.023 PMID:23500496

Hitchcock, F. L. (1941). The distribution of a product from several sources to numerous localities. *Journal of Mathematics and Physics*, *20*(2), 224–230. doi:10.1002apm1941201224

Hochberg, L., Bacher, D., Jarosiewicz, B., Masse, N., Simeral, J., Vogel, J., ... Donoghue, J. (2012). Reach and grasp by people with tetraplegia using a neurally controlled robotic arm. *Nature*, *485*(7398), 372–375. doi:10.1038/nature11076 PMID:22596161

Hochberg, L., Serruya, M., Friehs, G., Mukand, J., Saleh, M., Caplan, A., ... Donoghue, J. (2006). Neuronal ensemble control of prosthetic devices by a human with tetraplegia. *Nature*, *442*(7099), 164–171. doi:10.1038/nature04970 PMID:16838014

Hoffmann, R., Lauterbach, C., Techmer, A., Conradt, J., & Steinhage, A. (2016). Recognising gait patterns of people in risk of falling with a multi-layer perceptron. In *Information Technologies in Medicine* (pp. 87–97). Springer. doi:10.1007/978-3-319-39904-1_8

Holland, J. (1975). *Adaptation in Natural and Artificial Systems*. University of Michigan Press.

Hong, T. P., Kuo, C. S., & Chi, S. C. (1999). Mining association rules from quantitative data. *Intelligent Data Analysis*, *3*(5), 363–376. doi:10.1016/S1088-467X(99)00028-1

Hose, K., & Vlachou, A. (2012). A Survey of Skyline Processing in Highly Distributed Environments. *The VLDB Journal*, *21*(3), 359–384. doi:10.100700778-011-0246-6

Hoßbach, B., & Seeger, B. (2013). Anomaly management using complex event processing: extending data base technology paper. In *Proceedings of the 16th International Conference on Extending Database Technology* (pp. 149-154). ACM.

Huang, Y. M., Hsieh, M. Y., Chao, H. C., Hung, S. H., & Park, J. H. (2009). Pervasive, secure access to a hierarchical sensor-based healthcare monitoring architecture in wireless heterogeneous networks. *Selected Areas in Communications. IEEE Journal on*, *27*(4), 400–411.

Huarng, K. (2001). Effective lengths of intervals to improve forecasting in fuzzy time series. *Fuzzy Sets and Systems*, *123*(3), 387–394. doi:10.1016/S0165-0114(00)00057-9

Huarng, K., & Yu, T. H. K. (2005). A Type-2 Time Series Model for Stock Index Forecasting. *Physica A*, *353*, 445–462. doi:10.1016/j.physa.2004.11.070

Huarng, K., & Yu, T. H. K. (2006). Ratio-based lengths of intervals to improve fuzzy time series forecasting. *IEEE Transactions on Systems, Man, and Cybernetics. Part B, Cybernetics, 36*(2), 328–340. doi:10.1109/TSMCB.2005.857093 PMID:16602593

Hunwisai, D., & Kumam, P. (2017). A method for solving a fuzzy transportation problem via Robust ranking technique and ATM. *Cogent Mathematics, 4*(1), 1283730. doi:10.1080/23311835.2017.1283730

Huo, X., & Ghovanloo, M. (2009). Using unconstrained tongue motion as an alternative control mechanism for wheeled mobility. *IEEE Transactions on Biomedical Engineering, 56*(6), 1719–1726. doi:10.1109/TBME.2009.2018632 PMID:19362901

Hussain, R. J., & Kumar, P. S. (2012a). The transportation problem with the aid of triangular intuitionistic fuzzy numbers. In *Proceedings in International Conference on Mathematical Modeling and Applied Soft Computing (MMASC-2012)*. Coimbatore Institute of Technology.

Hussain, R. J., & Kumar, P. S. (2012b). The transportation problem in an intuitionistic fuzzy environment. *International Journal of Mathematics Research, 4*(4), 411–420.

Hussain, R. J., & Kumar, P. S. (2012c). Algorithmic approach for solving intuitionistic fuzzy transportation problem. *Applied Mathematical Sciences, 6*(80), 3981–3989.

Hussain, R. J., & Kumar, P. S. (2013). An optimal more-for-less solution of mixed constraints intuitionistic fuzzy transportation problems. *International Journal of Contemporary Mathematical Sciences, 8*(12), 565–576. doi:10.12988/ijcms.2013.13056

Huynh, K. T., Quan, T. T., & Bui, T. H. (2017). A quality-controlled logic-based clustering approach for web service composition and verification. *International Journal of Web Information Systems, 13*(2), 173–198. doi:10.1108/IJWIS-12-2016-0068

IBM Rational Rose. (2007). Available at: http://www-306.ibm.com/software/rational

IEEE-BAN. (n.d.). Retrieved from http://www.ieee802.org/15/pub/TG6.html

Ilgun, K., Kemmerer, R. A., & Porras, P. A. (1995). State transition analysis: A rule-based intrusion detection approach. *IEEE Transactions on Software Engineering, 21*, 181–199.

ILOG JRules. (2002). ILOG, Inc. Retrieved from http://www.ilog.com/products/jrules/whitepapers/index.cfm?filename=WPJRules4.0.pdf

Innal, F., Chebila, M., & Dutuit, Y. (2016). Uncertainty handling in safety instrumented systems according to IEC 61508 and new proposal based on coupling Monte Carlo analysis and fuzzy sets. *Journal of Loss Prevention in the Process Industries, 44*, 503–514. doi:10.1016/j.jlp.2016.07.028

IPCC. (2012). Managing the risks of extreme events and disasters to advance climate change adaptation. In *The SREX Report*. Cambridge, UK: Cambridge University Press.

Ishikawa, T., Fujiwara, H, Imai, O., & Okabe, A. (2008). Wayfinding with a GPS-based mobile navigation system: A comparison with maps and direct experience. *Journal of Environmental Psychology, 28*(1), 74–82. doi:10.1016/j.jenvp.2007.09.002

Isoyama, K., Kobayashi, Y., Sato, T., Kida, K., Yoshida, M., & Tagato, H. (2012, July). A scalable complex event processing system and evaluations of its performance. In *Proceedings of the 6th ACM International Conference on Distributed Event-Based Systems* (pp. 123-126). ACM. 10.1145/2335484.2335498

Izakian, H., Pedrycz, W., & Jamal, I. (2015). Fuzzy clustering of time series data using dynamic time warping distance. *Engineering Applications of Artificial Intelligence*, *39*, 235–244. doi:10.1016/j.engappai.2014.12.015

JACK Intelligent Agents. (2006). Retrieved from http://www.agent-software.com

Jafari, H., Idris, M. H., Ourdjini, A., Karimian, M., & Payganeh, G. (2010). Influence of gating system, sand grain size, and mould coating on microstructure and mechanical properties of thin-wall ductile iron. *Journal of Iron and Steel Research International*, *17*(12), 38–45. doi:10.1016/S1006-706X(10)60195-1

Jakubski, J., Dobosz, M., & Major-Gabrys, K. (2012). The influence of changes in active binder content on the control system of the moulding sand quality. *Archives of Foundry Engineering*, *12*(4), 71–74. doi:10.2478/v10266-012-0109-7

Jammes, F., & Smit, H. (2005). Service-Oriented Paradigms in Industrial Automation. *IEEE Transactions on Industrial Informatics*, *1*(1), 62–70. doi:10.1109/TII.2005.844419

Jammoussi, H., Franchek, M., Grigoriadis, K., & Books, M. (2013). Closed-loop system identification based on data correlation. *Journal of Dynamic Systems, Measurement, and Control*, *136*(1), 014507. doi:10.1115/1.4025158

Jemili, F., Zaghdoud, M., & Ahmed, M. (2009). Intrusion detection based on hybrid propagation in Bayesian networks. Proceedings of the IEEE international conference on Intelligence and security informatics, 137–142.

Jennings, N. R., & Wooldridge, M. (2001). Agent-Oriented Software Engineering. In *Handbook of Agent Technology*. AAAI/ MIT Press.

Jiang, B., Ye, L., Wang, J., & Wang, Y. (2017). A Semantic-Based Approach to Service Clustering from Service Documents. *Services Computing (SCC), 2017 IEEE International Conference on*, 265-272.

Jiang, B., Ding, X., Ma, L., He, Y., Wang, T., & Xie, W. (2008). A hybrid feature selection algorithm:combination of symmetrical uncertainty and genetic algorithms. *The Second International Symposium on Optimization and Systems Biology OSB'08*, 152–157.

Jiang, C., Zheng, J., & Han, X. (2017). Probability-interval hybrid uncertainty analysis for structures with both aleatory and epistemic uncertainties: A review. *Structural and Multidisciplinary Optimization*, 1–18.

Jiang, L., Zhang, H., & Cai, Z. (2009). A novel Bayes model: Hidden naive Bayes. *IEEE Transactions on Knowledge and Data Engineering*, *2*(10), 1361–1371. doi:10.1109/TKDE.2008.234

Jia, P., Hu, H., Lu, T., & Yuan, K. (2007). Head gesture recognition for hands-free control of an intelligent wheelchair. *Industrial Robot: An International Journal*, *34*(1), 60–68. doi:10.1108/01439910710718469

Jie, Y., Wang, W., Bai, X., & Li, Y. (2016, October). Uncertainty analysis based on probability bounds in probabilistic risk assessment of high microgravity science experiment system. In *Reliability, Maintainability and Safety (ICRMS), 2016 11th International Conference on* (pp. 1-6). IEEE. 10.1109/ICRMS.2016.8050109

Jin, X., Xu, A., Bie, R., & Guo, P. (2006). Machine learning techniques and chi-square feature selection for cancer classification using sage gene expression profiles. Lecture Notes in Computer Science, 3916, 106-115. doi:10.1007/11691730_11

Ji, S., Xu, W., Yang, M., & Yu, K. (2013). 3D Convolutional Neural Networks for Human Action Recognition. *IEEE Transactions on Pattern Analysis and Machine Intelligence*, *35*(1), 221–231. doi:10.1109/TPAMI.2012.59 PMID:22392705

Jones, Q., Ravid, G., & Rafaeli, S. (2002). An empirical exploration of mass interaction system dynamics: Individual information overload and Usenet discourse. *Proceedings of the 35th Hawaii International Conference on System Sciences*. 10.1109/HICSS.2002.994061

Joshi, B.P. & Kumar, S.(2013) A Computational method for fuzzy time series forecasting based on difference parameters. *International Journal of Modeling, Simulation and Scientific Computing*, *4*(1), 1250023-11250023-12.

Jothi, G., Inbarani, H. H., & Azar, A. T. (2013). Hybrid Tolerance Rough Set: PSO Based Supervised Feature Selection for Digital Mammogram Images. *International Journal of Fuzzy System Applications*, *3*(4), 15–30. doi:10.4018/ijfsa.2013100102

Ju, J. S., Shin, Y., & Kim, E. Y. (2009). Intelligent wheelchair interface using face and mouth recognition. In *Proceedings of the 14th international conference on Intelligent user interfaces* (pp. 307–314). Academic Press.

Juang, C. F. (2002). A TSK-type recurrent fuzzy network for dynamic systems processing by neural network and genetic algorithms. *Fuzzy Systems. IEEE Transactions on*, *10*(2), 155–170.

Juziuk, J., Weyns, D., & Holvoet, T. (2014). Design patterns for multi-agent systems: a systematic literature Review. In *Agent-Oriented Software Engineering* (pp. 79–99). Springer Berlin Heidelberg. doi:10.1007/978-3-642-54432-3_5

Kaelbling, L. P., Littman, M. L., & Moore, A. W. (1996). Reinforcement Learning: A Survey. *Journal of Artificial Intelligence Research*, *4*, 237–285.

Kaiser, M. S., Chowdhury, Z. I., Al Mamun, S., Hussain, A., & Mahmud, M. (2016). A neuro-fuzzy control system based on feature extraction of surface electromyogram signal for solar-powered wheelchair. *Cognitive Computation*, *8*(5), 946–954. doi:10.100712559-016-9398-4

Kaisler, S.H. (2005). *Software Paradigms*. John Wiley & Son.

Kargupta, H., Datta, S., Wang, Q., & Sivakumar, K. (2003). On the privacy preserving properties of random data perturbation techniques. *3rd Int'l Conference on Data Mining*, 99–106. 10.1109/ICDM.2003.1250908

Karlen, W., Mattiussi, C., & Floreano, D. (2009). Sleep and wake classification with ECG and respiratory effort signals. *Biomedical Circuits and Systems. IEEE Transactions on*, *3*(2), 71–78. PMID:23853198

Kasabov, N. K., & Song, Q. (2002). DENFIS: Dynamic Evolving Neural-Fuzzy Inference System and its Application for Time-Series Prediction. *IEEE Transactions on Fuzzy Systems*, *10*(2), 144–154. doi:10.1109/91.995117

Kastner, J., Endres, M., & Kießling, W. (2017). A Pareto-Dominant Clustering Approach for Pareto-Frontiers. *19th International Workshop on Design, Optimization, Languages and Analytical Processing of Big Data (DOLAP)*.

Kastner, C., Thum, T., Saake, G., Feigenspan, J., Leich, T., Wielgorz, F., & Apel, S. (2009) Featureide: A tool framework for feature-oriented software development. In *Proceedings of the 31st International Conference on Software Engineering* (pp. 611–614). IEEE Computer Society.

Kaur, Sharma, & Vohra. (2015). An Ontology Based Text Analytics on Social Media. *International Journal of Database Theory and Application*, *8*(5), 233–240.

Kawamoto, K., & Lobach, D. F. (2007, March 1). Proposal for Fulfilling Strategic Objectives of the U.S. Roadmap for National Action on Decision Support through a Service-oriented Architecture Leveraging HL7 Services. *Journal of the American Medical Informatics Association*, *14*(2), 146–155. doi:10.1197/jamia.M2298 PMID:17213489

Kawashima, H., Kitagawa, H., & Li, X. (2010, November). Complex event processing over uncertain data streams. In *P2P, Parallel, Grid, Cloud and Internet Computing (3PGCIC), 2010 International Conference on* (pp. 521-526). IEEE. 10.1109/3PGCIC.2010.89

KDD99. (n.d.). Retrieved from http://kdd.ics.uci.edu/databases

Kennedy, J., & Eberhart, R. (1995). Particle Swarm Optimization. *Proceedings of IEEE Conference on Neural Networks*, *4*, 1942 – 1948.

Kentel, E., & Aral, M. M. (2004). Probabilistic-fuzzy health risk modeling. *Stochastic Environmental Research and Risk Assessment*, *18*(5), 324–338. doi:10.100700477-004-0187-3

Khakpour, N., Jalili, S., Talcott, C., Sirjani, M., & Mousavi, M. R. (2010). PobSAM: Policy-based managing of actors in self-adaptive systems. *Electronic Notes in Theoretical Computer Science*, *263*, 129–143. doi:10.1016/j.entcs.2010.05.008

Khan, A., Qureshi, M. S., & Hussain, A. (2014). Improved Genetic Algorithm Approach for Sensitive Association Rules Hiding. *World Applied Sciences Journal*, *31*(12), 2087–2092.

Khandelwal, H., & Ravi, B. (2016). Effect of molding parameters on chemically bonded sand mold properties. *Journal of Manufacturing Processes*, *22*, 127–133. doi:10.1016/j.jmapro.2016.03.007

Khan, M. (2011). Rule based network intrusion detection using genetic algorithm. *International Journal of Computers and Applications*, *18*(8), 26–29. doi:10.5120/2303-2914

Kharola, A. (2017). Design of a hybrid adaptive neuro fuzzy inference system (ANFIS) controller for position and angle control of inverted pendulum (IP) systems. *Fuzzy Systems: Concepts, Methodologies, Tools, and Applications: Concepts, Methodologies, Tools, and Applications*, 308.

Khatibi, V., & Montazer, G. A. (2009, October). Coronary heart disease risk assessment using dempster-shafer theory. In *Computer Conference, 2009. CSICC 2009. 14th International CSI* (pp. 361-366). IEEE. 10.1109/CSICC.2009.5349607

Kießling, W. (2002). Foundations of Preferences in Database Systems. In *Proceedings of the 28th international conference on Very Large Data Bases* (pp. 311-322). VLDB Endowment. 10.1016/B978-155860869-6/50035-4

Kießling, W. (2005). Preference Queries with SV-Semantics. In *Proceedings of COMAD '05* (pp. 15-26). Computer Society of India.

Kießling, W., Endres, M., & Wenzel, F. (2011). The Preference SQL System - An Overview. *Bulletin of the Technical Committee on Data Engineering*, *34*(2), 11–18.

Kikuchi, S. (2000). A method to defuzzify the fuzzy number: Transportation problem application. *Fuzzy Sets and Systems*, *116*(1), 3–9. doi:10.1016/S0165-0114(99)00033-0

Kim, Y., Street, W., & Menczer, F. (2000). Feature selection for unsupervised learning via evolutionary search. *Proceedings of the Sixth ACM SIGKDD International Conference on Knowledge Discovery and Data Mining*, 365-369. 10.1145/347090.347169

Kim, S., Shin, K. S., & Park, K. (2005a). An application of support vector machines for customer churn analysis: Credit card case. *Lecture Notes in Computer Science*, *3611*, 636–647. doi:10.1007/11539117_91

Kim, S., Yang, S., Seo, K. S., Ro, Y. M., Kim, J.-Y., & Seo, Y. S. (2005b). Home photo categorization based on photographic region templates. *Lecture Notes in Computer Science*, *3689*, 328–338. doi:10.1007/11562382_25

Kim, Y. O., & Penn, A. (2004). Linking the Spatial Syntax of Cognitive Maps to the Spatial Syntax of the Environment. *Environment and Behavior*, *36*(4), 483–504. doi:10.1177/0013916503261384

Kim, Y., & Moon, T. (2016). Human detection and activity classification based on micro-Doppler signatures using deep convolutional neural networks. *IEEE Geoscience and Remote Sensing Letters*, *13*(1), 8–12. doi:10.1109/LGRS.2015.2491329

Klippel, A., Lee, P. U., Fabrikant, S., Montello, D. R., & Bateman, J. (2005). The cognitive conceptual approach as a leitmotif for map design. In *Reasoning with Mental and External Diagrams: Computational Modeling and Spatial Assistance, Proceedings of the AAAI 2005 Spring Symposium* (pp. 21-23). Stanford, CA: AAAI Press.

Klusch, M., Fries, B., & Sycara, K. (2006). Automated semantic Web service discovery with OWLS-MX. *Proceeding of the 5th International Conference on Autonomous Agents and Multi-Agent Systems*, 915-922. 10.1145/1160633.1160796

Knight, W. (2017). 5 Big Predictions for Artificial Intelligence in 2017. *MIT Technology Review*. Available at: https://www.technologyreview.com/s/603216/5-big-predictions-for-artificial-intelligence-in-2017/

Koc, L., & Carswell, A. D. (2015). Network intrusion detection using a hnb binary classifier. In *17th UKSIM-AMSS International Conference on Modelling and Simulation* (pp. 81–85). IEEE. 10.1109/UKSim.2015.37

Kohavi, R., & John, G. H. (1997). Wrappers for feature subset selection. *Artificial Intelligence, 97*(1-2), 273–324. doi:10.1016/S0004-3702(97)00043-X

Köhler, H., Yang, J., & Zhou, X. (2011). Efficient Parallel Skyline Processing Using Hyperplane Projections. *Proceedings of the 2011 ACM SIGMOD International Conference on Management of Data (SIGMOD '11)*, 85-96. 10.1145/1989323.1989333

Koller, D., & Sahami, M. (1996). Toward optimal feature selection. *Proceedings of the Thirteenth International Conference on Machine Learning*, 284-292.

Kolp, M., Giorgini, P., & Mylopoulos, J. (2002). Information Systems Development through Social Structures. *Proceedings of the 14th Int. Conference on Software Engineering and Knowledge Engineering*, 183-190.

Kolp, M., & Wautelet, Y. (2015). Human organizational patterns applied to collaborative learning software systems. *Computers in Human Behavior, 51*, 742–751. doi:10.1016/j.chb.2014.11.094

Kolp, M., Wautelet, Y., & Faulkner, S. (2011). Social-Centric Design of Multi-Agent Architectures. In E. Yu, P. Giorgini, N. Maiden, & J. Mylopoulos (Eds.), *Social Modeling for Requirements Engineering*. MIT Press.

Kontaki, M., Papadopoulos, A. N., & Manolopoulos, Y. (2010). Continuous Processing of Preference Queries in Data Streams. In SOFSEM '10 (pp. 47-60). Springer. doi:10.1007/978-3-642-11266-9_4

Kotekar, S., & Kamath, S. S. (2018). Enhancing Web Service Discovery Using Meta-heuristic CSO and PCA Based Clustering. *Progress in Intelligent Computing Techniques: Theory, Practice, and Applications*, 393-403.

Kotsiantis, S., & Kanellopoulos, D. (2006). Discretization techniques: A recent survey. *GESTS International Transactions on Computer Science and Engineering, 32*, 47–58.

Krempl, G., Zliobaite, I., Brzezinski, D., Hüllermeier, E., Last, M., Lemaire, V., … Stefanowski, J. (2014). Open Challenges for Data Stream Mining Research. SIGKDD '14, Explor. Newsl., 16(1).

Krishnamoorthy, S., Sadasivam, S., Rajalakshmi, M., Kowsalyaa, K., & Dhivya, M. (2017). Privacy Preserving Fuzzy Association Rule Mining in Data Clusters Using Particle Swarm Optimization. *International Journal of Intelligent Information Technologies, 13*(2), 1–20. doi:10.4018/IJIIT.2017040101

Krishnan, S., Strasburg, C., Lutz, R. R., Goseva-Popstojanova, K., & Dorman, K. S. (2013). Predicting failure-proneness in an evolving software product line. *Information and Software Technology, 55*(8), 1479–1495. doi:10.1016/j.infsof.2012.11.008

Kronprasert, N., & Thipnee, N. (2016, September). Use of Evidence Theory in Fault Tree Analysis for Road Safety Inspection. In *International Conference on Belief Functions* (pp. 84-93). Springer International Publishing. 10.1007/978-3-319-45559-4_9

Krüger, A., Aslan, I., & Zimmer, H. (2004). *The effects of mobile pedestrian navigation systems on the concurrent acquisition of route and survey knowledge. In Mobile Human-Computer Interaction-MobileHCI 2004* (pp. 446–450). Springer. doi:10.1007/978-3-540-28637-0_54

Kuanga, F., Xu, W., & Zhang, S. (2014). A novel hybrid kpca and svm with ga model for intrusion detection. *Applied Soft Computing*, *18*, 178–184. doi:10.1016/j.asoc.2014.01.028

Kuchta, D., & Ptaszyńska, E. (2017, July). Fuzzy based risk register for construction project risk assessment. In AIP Conference Proceedings: Vol. 1863. *No. 1* (p. 230006). AIP Publishing. doi:10.1063/1.4992391

Kuhn, T. (1996). *The structure of scientific revolutions* (3rd ed.). University of Chicago Press. doi:10.7208/chicago/9780226458106.001.0001

Kuipers, B. (1978). Modeling spatial knowledge. *Cognitive Science*, *2*(2), 129–153. doi:10.120715516709cog0202_3

Kumar, G. S., Sirisha, C. V. K., Durga, R, K., & Devi, A. (2012). Robust preprocessing and random forests technique for network probe anomaly detection. *International Journal of Soft Computing and Engineering, 6.*

Kumar, P. S. (2017a). PSK method for solving type-1 and type-3 fuzzy transportation problems. In I. Management Association (Ed.), Fuzzy Systems: Concepts, Methodologies, Tools, and Applications (pp. 367-392). Hershey, PA: IGI Global. doi:10.4018/978-1-5225-1908-9.ch017

Kumar, P. S. (2017b). *Algorithmic approach for solving allocation problems under intuitionistic fuzzy environment* (Unpublished doctoral dissertation). Jamal Mohamed College (Autonomous), Tiruchirappalli, India.

Kumar, P. S., & Hussain, R. J. (2014c) A method for finding an optimal solution of an assignment problem under mixed intuitionistic fuzzy environment. In *Proceedings in International Conference on Mathematical Sciences (ICMS-2014)*. Elsevier.

Kumara, B. T. G. S., Paik, I., & Koswatte, K. R. C. (2016). Cluster-Based Web Service Recommendation. *Proceedings on IEEE International Conference on Service Computing*. 10.1109/SCC.2016.52

Kumara, B. T. G. S., Paik, I., Siriweera, T. H. A. S., & Koswatte, K. R. C. (2017) QoS Aware Service Clustering to Bootstrap the Web Service Selection. *Proceedings on IEEE International Conference on Service Computing*. 10.1109/SCC.2017.37

Kumar, A., & Kaur, A. (2013). Methods for solving fully fuzzy transportation problems based on classical transportation methods. In J. Wang (Ed.), *Optimizing, Innovating, and Capitalizing on Information Systems for Operations* (pp. 328–347). Hershey, PA: IGI Global. doi:10.4018/978-1-4666-2925-7.ch017

Kumar, A., Kaur, A., & Gupta, A. (2011). Fuzzy linear programming approach for solving fuzzy transportation problems with transhipment. *Journal of Mathematical Modelling and Algorithms*, *10*(2), 163–180. doi:10.100710852-010-9147-8

Kumara, B. T. G. S., Paik, I., Chen, W., & Ryu, K. (2014). Web Service Clustering using a Hybrid Term-Similarity Measure with Ontology Learning. *International Journal of Web Services Research*, *11*(2), 24–45. doi:10.4018/ijwsr.2014040102

Kumara, B. T. G. S., Paik, I., Ohashi, H., Yaguchi, Y., & Chen, W. (2014). (accepted). Context Aware Filtering and Visualization of Web Service Clusters. *International Journal of Web Services Research*.

Kumaravadivel, A., & Natarajan, U. (2013). Application of six-sigma DMAIC methodology to sand-casting process with response surface methodology. *International Journal of Advanced Manufacturing Technology, 69*(5-8), 1403–1420. doi:10.100700170-013-5119-2

Kumar, P. S. (2016a). PSK method for solving type-1 and type-3 fuzzy transportation problems. *International Journal of Fuzzy System Applications, 5*(4), 121–146. doi:10.4018/IJFSA.2016100106

Kumar, P. S. (2016b). A simple method for solving type-2 and type-4 fuzzy transportation problems. *International Journal of Fuzzy Logic and Intelligent Systems, 16*(4), 225–237. doi:10.5391/IJFIS.2016.16.4.225

Kumar, P. S. (2018a). A note on 'a new approach for solving intuitionistic fuzzy transportation problem of type-2'. *International Journal of Logistics Systems and Management, 29*(1), 102–129. doi:10.1504/IJLSM.2018.088586

Kumar, P. S. (2018b). Linear programming approach for solving balanced and unbalanced intuitionistic fuzzy transportation problems. *International Journal of Operations Research and Information Systems, 9*(2), 73–100. doi:10.4018/IJORIS.2018040104

Kumar, P. S. (2018c). Intuitionistic fuzzy zero point method for solving type-2 intuitionistic fuzzy transportation problem. *International Journal of Operational Research.*

Kumar, P. S. (2018d). PSK method for solving intuitionistic fuzzy solid transportation problems. *International Journal of Fuzzy System Applications.*

Kumar, P. S. (2018e). A simple and efficient algorithm for solving type-1 intuitionistic fuzzy solid transportation problems *International Journal of Operations Research and Information Systems.*

Kumar, P. S., & Hussain, R. J. (2014a). *New algorithm for solving mixed intuitionistic fuzzy assignment problem. In Elixir Applied Mathematics* (pp. 25971–25977). Salem, Tamilnadu, India: Elixir Publishers.

Kumar, P. S., & Hussain, R. J. (2014b). A systematic approach for solving mixed intuitionistic fuzzy transportation problems. *International Journal of Pure and Applied Mathematics, 92*(2), 181–190. doi:10.12732/ijpam.v92i2.4

Kumar, P. S., & Hussain, R. J. (2015). A method for solving unbalanced intuitionistic fuzzy transportation problems. *Notes on Intuitionistic Fuzzy Sets, 21*(3), 54–65.

Kumar, P. S., & Hussain, R. J. (2016a). An algorithm for solving unbalanced intuitionistic fuzzy assignment problem using triangular intuitionistic fuzzy number. *The Journal of Fuzzy Mathematics, 24*(2), 289–302.

Kumar, P. S., & Hussain, R. J. (2016b). Computationally simple approach for solving fully intuitionistic fuzzy real life transportation problems. *International Journal of System Assurance Engineering and Management, 7*(1), 90–101. doi:10.100713198-014-0334-2

Kumar, P. S., & Hussain, R. J. (2016c). A simple method for solving fully intuitionistic fuzzy real life assignment problem. *International Journal of Operations Research and Information Systems, 7*(2), 39–61. doi:10.4018/IJORIS.2016040103

Kumar, S., & Gangwar, S. S. (2012). Partitions based computational method for high-order Fuzzy time series forecasting. *Expert Systems with Applications, 39*(15), 12158–12164. doi:10.1016/j.eswa.2012.04.039

Kumar, S., Satsangi, P. S., & Prajapati, D. R. (2011). Optimization of green sand casting process parameters of a foundry by using Taguchi's method. *International Journal of Advanced Manufacturing Technology, 55*(1-4), 23–34. doi:10.100700170-010-3029-0

Kunsmann, H. G. F. (1971). Hot strength and collapsibility of CO_2 sand. *AFS Transactions, 79*, 488–492.

Kuo, C. H., Chan, Y. C., Chou, H. C., & Siao, J. W. (2009). Eyeglasses based electro-oculography human-wheelchair interface. In *Systems* (pp. 4746–4751). Man and Cybernetics.

Laguna, M., & Markland, J. (2005). *Business process modeling, simulation, and Design*. Upper Saddle River, NJ: Pearson Education, Inc.

Lakshmanan, Rabinovich, & Etzion. (2009). A stratified approach for supporting high throughput event processing 99 applications. In *Proceedings of the Third ACM International Conference on Distributed Event-Based Systems*. ACM.

Laskov, P., Dussel, P., Schafer, C., & K., R. (2005). Learning intrusion detection: supervised or unsupervised? *Image Analysis and Processings ICIAP*, 50–57.

Lauterbach, C., & Steinhage, A. (2009). Large-area smart textiles. In Technical Textiles 4/09. IBP International Business Press Publisher.

Lauterbach, C., & Steinhage, A. (2012). A large-area sensor system for Ambient Assisted Living. *Toward Optimal Healing Environments: Proc. of Symposium on Assistive Systems for Social, Personal, and Health Interaction 2010/2011*, 59-63.

Lauterbach, C., Glaser, R., Savio, D., Schnell, M., Weber, W., Kornely, S., & Stöhr, A. (2005). A self-organizing and fault-tolerant wired peer-to-peer sensor network for textile applications. In *Engineering self-organizing applications* (pp. 256-266). Springer-Verlag Berlin Heidelberg.

Lauterbach, C., Steinhage, A., & Techmer, A. (2013). A large-area sensor system underneath the floor for Ambient Assisted Living applications. In Pervasive and Mobile Sensing and Computing for Healthcare (pp. 69-87). Springer Verlag. doi:10.1007/978-3-642-32538-0_3

Lauterbach, C., Steinhage, A., Techmer, A., Jakob, M. M., Nowakowski, C., & Pessenhofer, W. (2010). Large-area smart textiles. Word Journal of Engineering, 7(2), 266-271.

Lauterbach, C., Steinhage, A., & Techmer, A. (2012). *Large-area wireless sensor system based on smart textiles. In Proc. of the 9th International Multi-Conference on Systems, Signals & Devices, SSD'12*. Chemnitz, Germany: IEEE publications.

Lauterbach, C., Steinhage, A., & Techmer, A. (2014). Ambient Assisted Living Concept Based on a Sensitive Floor. *Proc. of the 9th IEEE Int. Symposium on Medical Measurements and Applications MeMeA*.

Law, C. K. H., Leung, M. Y. Y., Xu, Y., & Tso, S. K. (2002). A cap as interface for wheelchair control. In Intelligent Robots and Systems (vol. 2, pp. 1439–1444). Academic Press.

Lee, K., Zheng, B., Li, H., & Lee, W.-C. (2007). Approaching the Skyline in Z Order. In *VLDB '07: Proceedings of the 33rd international conference on Very large data bases* (pp. 279–290). VLDB Endowment.

Lee, S. X., & McLachlan, G. J. (2013). *Modelling asset return using multivariate asymmetric mixture models with applications to estimation of Value-at-Risk*. Academic Press.

Leea, T. S., Mumfordb, D., Romeroa, R., & Lammec, A. F. V. (1998). The role of the primary visual cortex in higher level vision. *Vision Research*, 38(15-16), 2429–2454. doi:10.1016/S0042-6989(97)00464-1 PMID:9798008

Lee, J., & Hwang, S.-W. (2010). BSkyTree: Scalable Skyline Computation Using a Balanced Pivot Selection. *EDBT '10: Proceedings of the 13th International Conference on Extending Database Technology*, 195-206. 10.1145/1739041.1739067

Lee, K. H., Kung, S. Y., & Verma, N. (2012). Low-energy formulations of support vector machine kernel functions for biomedical sensor applications. *Journal of Signal Processing Systems for Signal, Image, and Video Technology*, 69(3), 339–349. doi:10.100711265-012-0672-8

Lee, L. W., Wang, L. H., Chen, S. M., & Leu, Y. H. (2006b). Handling forecasting problems based on two-factors high-order fuzzy time series. *IEEE Transactions on Fuzzy Systems*, *14*(3), 468–477. doi:10.1109/TFUZZ.2006.876367

Lee, O. J., & Jung, J. E. (2017). Sequence clustering-based automated rule generation for adaptive complex event processing. *Future Generation Computer Systems*, *66*, 100–109. doi:10.1016/j.future.2016.02.011

Lee, T., & Mumford, D. (2003). Hierarchical Bayesian inference in the visual cortex. *Journal of the Optical Society of America*, *20*(7), 1434–1448. doi:10.1364/JOSAA.20.001434 PMID:12868647

Lee, Y. W., Lee, K. Y., & Kim, M. H. (2013). Efficient Processing of Multiple Continuous Skyline Queries over a Data Stream. *Information Science*, *221*, 316–337. doi:10.1016/j.ins.2012.09.040

Leite, R. M. C., Sizilio, G. R. M. A., Ribeiro, A. G. C. D., Valentim, R., Pedro, F. R., & Ana Guerreiro, M. G. (2012). *Mobile Technologies Applied to Hospital Automation, Advances and Applications in Mobile Computing*. Retrieved from http://www.intechopen.com/books/advances-and-applications-in-mobilecomputing/mobile-technologies-applied-to-hospital-automation

Leung, K., & Leckie, C. (2005). Unsupervised anomaly detection in network intrusion detection using clusters. *Proceedings of the Twenty-eighth Australasian conference on Computer Science*, 333–342.

Leung, Y., Li, R., & Ji, N. (2017). Application of extended Dempster–Shafer theory of evidence in accident probability estimation for dangerous goods transportation. *Journal of Geographical Systems*, 1–23.

Levhari, D., & Mirman, L. J. (1980). The Great Fish War: An example using a dynamic Cournot-Nash solution. *The Bell Journal of Economics*, *11*(1), 322–334. doi:10.2307/3003416

Li, L., Huang, Z., Da, Q., & Hu, J. (2008, May). A new method based on goal programming for solving transportation problem with fuzzy cost. In Information Processing (ISIP), 2008 International Symposiums on (pp. 3-8). IEEE. doi:10.1109/ISIP.2008.9

Li, S. T., & Chen, Y. P. (2004). Natural partition-based forecasting model for fuzzy time series. *IEEE International Conference on Fuzzy Systems*, 25–29.

Liao, X. (2015). Decision method of optimal investment enterprise selection under uncertain information environment. *International Journal of Fuzzy System Applications*, *4*(1), 33–42. doi:10.4018/IJFSA.2015010102

Liknes, S., Vlachou, A., Doulkeridis, C., & Nørvåg, K. (2014). APSkyline: Improved Skyline Computation for Multicore Architectures. *Proc. of DASFAA '14*. 10.1007/978-3-319-05810-8_21

Limbourg, P., & De Rocquigny, E. (2010). Uncertainty analysis using evidence theory–confronting level-1 and level-2 approaches with data availability and computational constraints. *Reliability Engineering & System Safety*, *95*(5), 550–564. doi:10.1016/j.ress.2010.01.005

Lin, F. T. (2009, August). Solving the transportation problem with fuzzy coefficients using genetic algorithms. In *Fuzzy Systems, 2009. FUZZ-IEEE 2009. IEEE International Conference on* (pp. 1468-1473). IEEE. 10.1109/FUZZY.2009.5277202

Lincoln Laboratory, Massachusetts Institute of Technology. (2017a). *1998 DARPA Intrusion Detection Evaluation Data Set*. Retrieved from http://www.ll.mit.edu/mission/communications/cyber/CSTcorpora/ideval/data/1998data.html

Lincoln Laboratory, Massachusetts Institute of Technology. (2017b). *1999 DARPA Intrusion Detection Evaluation Data Set*. Retrieved from http://www.ll.mit.edu/mission/communications/cyber/CSTcorpora/ideval/data/1999data.html

Lindenmayer, D. B., Lacy, R. C., & Pope, M. L. (2000). Testing a simulation model for population variability analysis. *Ecological Applications*, *10*(2), 580–597. doi:10.1890/1051-0761(2000)010[0580:TASMFP]2.0.CO;2

Liou, T. S., & Wang, M. J. J. (1992). Ranking fuzzy numbers with integral value. *Fuzzy Sets and Systems*, *50*(3), 247–255. doi:10.1016/0165-0114(92)90223-Q

Li, Q., & Clifford, G. D. (2012). Dynamic time warping and machine learning for signal quality assessment of pulsatile signals. *Physiological Measurement*, *33*(9), 1491–1501. doi:10.1088/0967-3334/33/9/1491 PMID:22902950

Li, S. (1998). Hayashi, a.robot navigation in outdoor environments by using GPS information and panoramic views. *Proc. of International Conference on Intelligent Robots and Systems*, 1, 570-575.

Liu, D., Deters, R., & Zhang, W. J. (2010). Architectural design for resilience. *Enterprise Information Systems*, *4*(2), 137–152. doi:10.1080/17517570903067751

Liu, H., Deng, X., & Jiang, W. (2017). Risk Evaluation in Failure Mode and Effects Analysis Using Fuzzy Measure and Fuzzy Integral. *Symmetry*, *9*(8), 162. doi:10.3390ym9080162

Liu, J., Li, Y., Huang, G., Fu, H., Zhang, J., & Cheng, G. (2017). Identification of water quality management policy of watershed system with multiple uncertain interactions using a multi-level-factorial risk-inference-based possibilistic-probabilistic programming approach. *Environmental Science and Pollution Research International*, 1–21. doi:10.100711356-017-9106-2 PMID:28488149

Liu, W., Li, Y., Qu, X., & Liu, X. (2008). Study on binder system of CO2 cured phenol formaldehyde resin used in foundry. *68th World Foundry Congress*, 313-317.

Liu, W., & Wong, W. (2009). Web service clustering using text mining techniques, International Journal of Agent-*oriented. Software Engineering*, *3*(1), 6–26.

Liu, Y., Yi, T. H., & Wang, C. Q. (2012). Investment Decision Support for Engineering Projects Based on Risk Correlation Analysis. *Mathematical Problems in Engineering*.

Livingood, S. (2011). Issues in software product line evolution: complex changes in variability. *PLEASE '11 Proceedings of the 2nd International Workshop on Product Line Approaches in Software Engineering*.

Li, Y., Fang, B., Guo, L., & Chen, Y. (2007). Network anomaly detection based on tcmknn algorithm. In *Proceedings of the 2nd ACM symposium on Information computer and communications security*. ACM.

Lo, E., Yip, K. Y., Lin, K.-I., & Cheung, D. W. (2006). Progressive Skylining over Web-accessible Databases. *IEEE TKDE*, *57*(2), 122–147.

Loebbecke, C. (1997). A system dynamics approach to modeling a nationwide mobile communication market. *IFAC, Symposium Automated Systems Based on Human Skill - Joint Design of Technology and Organization*, 27-42.

Love, T. (1997). *Object Lessons*. Cambridge University Press.

LoweC. (2013). Retrieved from http://telecareaware.com/smart-flooring-that-can-simplify-alerting/

Löwe, P., Wächter, J., Hammitzsch, M., Lendholt, M., & Häner, R. (2013). The Evolution of Disaster Early Warning Systems in the TRIDEC Project. *Proceedings of the Twenty-third (2013) International Offshore and Polar Engineering*, 48-52.

Lundin, E., & Jonsson, E. (2002). Anomaly-based intrusion detection: Privacy concerns and other problems. *Computer Networks*, *34*(4), 623–640. doi:10.1016/S1389-1286(00)00134-1

Lu, W., Chen, X., Pedrycz, W., Liu, X., & Yang, J. (2015). Using interval information granules to improve forecasting in fuzzy time series. *International Journal of Approximate Reasoning*, *57*, 1–18. doi:10.1016/j.ijar.2014.11.002

Lu, W., Pedrycz, W., Liu, X., Yang, J., & Li, P. (2014). The modeling of time series based on fuzzy information granules. *Expert Systems with Applications*, *41*(8), 3799–3808. doi:10.1016/j.eswa.2013.12.005

Lu, Y., Wang, H., Luo, A. A., & Ripplinger, K. (2017). Process simulation and experimental validation of resin-bonded silica sand mold casting. *AFS Transactions*, *125*, 215–220.

Lynch, K. (1960). *The Image of the City*. Cambridge, MA: MIT Press.

Ma, H., King, I., & Lyu, M. R. (2007). Effective missing data prediction for collaborative filtering. *SIGIR*, 39–46.

Ma, J., Zhang, Y., & He, J. (2008). Efficiently finding Web services using a clustering semantic approach. *Proceeding of the International Workshop on Context-enabled Source and Service Selection, Integration and Adaptation, organized with the 17th International World Wide Web Conference*, 1–8. 10.1145/1361482.1361487

MacEachren, A. M. (1991). The role of maps in spatial knowledge acquisition. *The Cartographic Journal*, *28*(2), 152–162. doi:10.1179/caj.1991.28.2.152

Mahapatra, S. S., & Patnaik, A. (2007). Optimization of wire electrical discharge machining (WEDM) process parameters using Taguchi method. *International Journal of Advanced Manufacturing Technology*, *34*(9-10), 911–925. doi:10.100700170-006-0672-6

Mahoney, M. V., & Chan, P. K. (2003). An analysis of the 1999 darpa/lincoln laboratory evaluation data for network anomaly detection. In *Sixth International Symposium on Recent Advances in Intrusion Detection* (pp. 220-237). Springer-Verlag.

Maity, G., & Roy, S. K. (2017). Multiobjective transportation problem using fuzzy decision variable through multi-choice programming. *International Journal of Operations Research and Information Systems*, *8*(3), 82–96. doi:10.4018/IJORIS.2017070105

Maliska, M., Simo, B., Ciglan, M., Slizik, P., & Hluchy, L. (2006). Lecture Notes in Computer Science: Vol. 3911. *Service oriented architecture for risk assessment of natural disasters*. Berlin: Springer. doi:10.1007/11752578_43

Mandal, A. (2014). *Hippocampus Functions*. News Medical Life Sciences. Available at: https://www.news-medical.net/health/Hippocampus-Functions.aspx

Mandl, S., Kozachuk, O., Endres, M., & Kießling, W. (2015). Preference Analytics in EXASolution. *BTW , 15, the 16*[th] *Conference on Database Systems for Business, Technology, and Web*.

Mannini, A., & Sabatini, A. M. (2011). Accelerometry-based classification of human activities using markov modeling. *Computational Intelligence and Neuroscience*, *2011*, 4. doi:10.1155/2011/647858 PMID:21904542

Marchette, D. (1999). A statistical method for profiling network traffic. *Proceedings of the First USENIX Workshop on Intrusion Detection and Network Monitoring*, 119–128.

Marler, R. T., & Arora, J. S. (2004). Survey of multi-objective optimization methods for engineering. *Structural and Multidisciplinary Optimization*, *26*(6), 369–395. doi:10.100700158-003-0368-6

Marler, R. T., & Arora, J. S. (2010). The weighted sum method for multi-objective optimization: New insights *Structural and Multidisciplinary Optimization*, *41*(6), 853–862. doi:10.100700158-009-0460-7

Martinez-Moyano, I. J., & Richardson, G. P. (2013). Best practices in system dynamics modeling. *System Dynamics Review*, *29*(2), 102–123. doi:10.1002dr.1495

Masterman, M. (1970). The nature of paradigm. In I. Lakatos & A. Musgrave (Eds.), *Criticism and the Growth of Knowledge*. Cambridge University Press. doi:10.1017/CBO9781139171434.008

Mathur, N., Srivastava, P. K., & Paul, A. (2016). Trapezoidal fuzzy model to optimize transportation problem. *International Journal of Modeling, Simulation, and Scientific Computing, 7*(3). DOI: 10.1142/S1793962316500288

Ma, X., Wang, Y., Qiu, Q., Sun, W., & Pei, X. (2014). Scalable and elastic event matching for attribute-based publish/subscribe systems. *Future Generation Computer Systems, 36*, 102–119. doi:10.1016/j.future.2013.09.019

McCallum, A. K. (1996). *Reinforcement Learning with Selective Perception and Hidden State (PhD Thesis)*. Rochester, NY: University of Rochester.

McCarthy, M. W., James, D. A., Lee, J. B., & Rowlands, D. D. (2015). Decision-tree-based human activity classification algorithm using single-channel foot-mounted gyroscope. *Electronics Letters, 51*(9), 675–676. doi:10.1049/el.2015.0436

McHugh, J. (2000). Testing intrusion detection systems: A critique of the 1998 and 1999 darpa intrusion detection system evaluations as performed by lincoln laboratory. *ACM Transactions on Information and System Security, 3*(4), 262–294. doi:10.1145/382912.382923

Meadows, D., Randers, J., & Meadows, D. (2004). *Limits to growth: The 30-Year Update*. Chelsea Green.

Mercier, D., Cron, G., Denoeux, T., & Masson, M. H. (2007). Postal decision fusion based on the transferable belief model. *Traitement Du Signal, 24*(2), 133–151.

Mezaal, M. R., Pradhan, B., Shafri, H. Z. M., & Yusoff, Z. M. (2017). Automatic landslide detection using Dempster–Shafer theory from LiDAR-derived data and orthophotos. *Geomatics, Natural Hazards & Risk, 8*(2), 1935–1954. doi:10.1080/19475705.2017.1401013

Michalik, B., & Weyns, D. (2011). Towards a solution for change impact analysis of software product line products. In *Software Architecture (WICSA), 2011 9th Working IEEE/IFIP Conference on* (pp. 290–293). IEEE. 10.1109/WICSA.2011.45

Miller, T., Lu, B., Sterling, L., Beydoun, G., & Taveter, K. (2014). Requirements elicitation and specification using the agent paradigm: The case study of an aircraft turnaround simulator. *IEEE Transactions on Software Engineering, 40*(10), 1007–1024. doi:10.1109/TSE.2014.2339827

Mintzberg, H. (1992). *Structure in fives: designing effective organizations*. Prentice-Hall.

Mishra, S., Norton, J. J., Lee, Y., Lee, D. S., Agee, N., Chen, Y., ... Yeo, W. H. (2017). Soft, conformal bioelectronics for a wireless human-wheelchair interface. *Biosensors & Bioelectronics, 91*, 796–803. doi:10.1016/j.bios.2017.01.044 PMID:28152485

Mizianty, M., Kurgan, L., & Ogiela, M. (2010). Discretization as the enabling technique for the naïve Bayes and semi-naïve Bayes-based classification. *The Knowledge Engineering Review, 25*, 421–449.

Mnih, V., Kavukcuoglu, K., Silver, D., Rusu, A. A., Veness, J., Bellemare, M. G., ... Hassabis, D. (2015). Human-level control through deep reinforcement learning. *Nature, 518*(7540), 529–533. doi:10.1038/nature14236 PMID:25719670

Mofarrah, A., & Hussain, T. (2010). Modeling for uncertainty assessment in human health risk quantification: A fuzzy based approach. *International congress on environmental modeling and soft modeling for environment's sake*.

Mohamed, A.-r., Yu, D., & Deng, L. (2010). Investigation of Full-Sequence Training of Deep Belief Networks for Speech Recognition. *Interspeech 2010*, 2846-2849.

Mohideen, S. I., & Kumar, P. S. (2010). *A comparative study on transportation problem in fuzzy environment* (Unpublished master's thesis). Jamal Mohamed College (Autonomous), Tiruchirappalli, India.

Mohideen, S. I., & Kumar, P. S. (2010). A comparative study on transportation problem in fuzzy environment. *International Journal of Mathematics Research, 2*(1), 151–158.

Molchanov, P., Gupta, S., & Kim, K. (2015a). Hand gesture recognition with 3D convolutional neural networks. *IEEE Conference on Computer Vision and Pattern Recognition Workshops (CVPRW)*. 10.1109/CVPRW.2015.7301342

Molchanov, P., Gupta, S., Kim, K., & Pulli, K. (2015b). Multi-sensor System for Driver's Hand-Gesture Recognition. *11th IEEE International Conference and Workshops on Automatic Face and Gesture Recognition (FG)*, 1.

Möller, B., Roocks, P., & Endres, M. (2012). An Algebraic Calculus of Database Preferences. *MPC '12, the International Conference on Mathematics of Program Construction*, 241-262. 10.1007/978-3-642-31113-0_13

Moller, S., Engelbrecht, K. P., Kuhnel, C., Wechsung, I., & Weiss, B. (2009, July). A taxonomy of quality of service and quality of experience of multimodal human-machine interaction. In *Quality of Multimedia Experience, 2009. QoMEx 2009. International Workshop on* (pp. 7-12). IEEE. 10.1109/QOMEX.2009.5246986

Montello, D. R. (1993). Scale and multiple psychologies of space. In A. U. Frank & I. Campari (Eds.), *Spatial information theory: A theoretical basis for GIS* (pp. 312–321). Berlin: Springer-Verlag. doi:10.1007/3-540-57207-4_21

Montello, D. R. (2001). Spatial Cognition. In N. J. Smelser & P. B. Baltes (Eds.), *International Encyclopedia of the Social and Behavioral Science* (pp. 14771–14775). Oxford, UK: Pergamon Press. doi:10.1016/B0-08-043076-7/02492-X

Montello, D. R. (2005). Navigation. In P. Shah & A. Miyake (Eds.), *Cambridge handbook of visuospatial thinking* (pp. 257–294). Cambridge, UK: Cambridge University Press. doi:10.1017/CBO9780511610448.008

Montgomery, D. C. (2004). *Design and analysis of experiments* (5th ed.). New York: John Wiley & Sons.

Moon, I., Lee, M., Chu, J., & Mun, M. (2005). Wearable EMG-based HCI for electric-powered wheelchair users with motor disabilities. In *Proceedings of the IEEE International Conference on Robotics and Automation* (pp. 2649–2654). IEEE.

Morabito, J., Sack, I., & Bhate, A. (1999). *Organization modeling: innovative architectures for the 21st century*. Prentice Hall.

Morrison, J. B. (2012). Process improvement dynamics under constrained resources: Managing the work harder versus work smarter balance. *System Dynamics Review*, *28*(4), 329–350. doi:10.1002dr.1485

Morrison, J. B., Rudolphb, J. W., & Carrollc, J. S. (2013). Dynamic modeling as a multidiscipline collaborative journey. *System Dynamics Review*, *29*(1), 4–25. doi:10.1002dr.1492

Morse, M., Patel, J. M., & Jagadish, H. V. (2007). Efficient Skyline Computation over Low-Cardinality Domains. In *Proc. of VLDB '07* (pp. 267–278). VLDB.

Moser, E. I., Kropff, E., & Moser, M. B. (2008). Place Cells, Grid Cells, and the Brain's Spatial Representation System. *Annual Review of Neuroscience*, *31*(1), 69–89. doi:10.1146/annurev.neuro.31.061307.090723 PMID:18284371

Mouratidis, H., Giorgini, P., & Manson, G. (2003). Modelling Secure Multiagent Systems. *Proceedings of the 2nd International Joint Conference on Autonomous Agents and Multiagent Systems*, 859-866.

Mousheimish, R., Taher, Y., & Zeitouni, K. (2016, June). Automatic learning of predictive rules for complex event processing: doctoral symposium. In *Proceedings of the 10th ACM International Conference on Distributed and Event-based Systems* (pp. 414-417). ACM. 10.1145/2933267.2933430

Mukkamala, S., Janoski, G., & Sung, A. (2002). Intrusion detection: support vector machines and neural networks. *Proceedings of the IEEE International Joint Conference on Neural Networks (ANNIE)*, 1702–1707. 10.1109/IJCNN.2002.1007774

Nadiri, A. A., Gharekhani, M., Khatibi, R., & Moghaddam, A. A. (2017). Assessment of groundwater vulnerability using supervised committee to combine fuzzy logic models. *Environmental Science and Pollution Research International*, *24*(9), 8562–8577. doi:10.100711356-017-8489-4 PMID:28194673

Narmadha, S., & Vijayarani, S. (2011). Protecting sensitive association rules in privacy preserving data mining using genetic algorithms. *International Journal of Computers and Applications*, *33*(7), 37–34.

Nasseri, S. H., & Ebrahimnejad, A. (2011). Sensitivity analysis on linear programming problems with trapezoidal fuzzy variables. *International Journal of Operations Research and Information Systems*, *2*(2), 22–39. doi:10.4018/joris.2011040102

National Radiation Laboratory. (n.d.). *Radiation in the environment*. Retrieved from www.nrlmoh.govtnz/fq/radiation-intheenvironment.asp.

Nayak, R., & Lee, B. (2007). Web service discovery with additional semantics and clustering. *Proc. IEEE/WIC/ACM International Conference on Web Intelligence*, 555–558. 10.1109/WI.2007.82

Nazmy, T. M., El-Messiry, H., & Al-Bokhity, B. (2010, March). Adaptive neuro-fuzzy inference system for classification of ECG signals. In *Informatics and Systems (INFOS), 2010 The 7th International Conference on* (pp. 1-6). IEEE.

Neumeyer, Robbins, Nair, & Kesari. (2010). S4: Distributed stream computing platform. In *Data Mining Workshops (ICDMW), 2010 IEEE International Conference*. IEEE.

Newcombe, N. S., & Huttenlocher, J. (2000). *Making space: The development of spatial representation and reasoning*. Cambridge, MA: MIT Press.

Ng, P. S., & Zhang, F. (2016). An Improved Hybrid Model for Order Quantity Allocation and Supplier Risk Exposure. *International Journal of Fuzzy System Applications*, *5*(3), 120–147. doi:10.4018/IJFSA.2016070107

Ng, T. S., Sy, C. L., & Loo Hay Lee, L. H. (2012). Robust parameter design for system dynamics models: A Formal approach based on goal-seeking behavior. *System Dynamics Review*, *28*(3), 230–254. doi:10.1002dr.1475

Nguyen, Q. X., & Jo, S. (2012). Electric wheelchair control using head pose free eye-gaze tracker. *Electronics Letters*, *48*(13), 750–752. doi:10.1049/el.2012.1530

Nielsen, M., Andersen, P., Ravensbeck, L., Laugesen, F., Kristofersson, D. M., & Ellefsen, H. (2017). Fisheries management and the value chain: The Northeast Atlantic pelagic fisheries case. *Fisheries Research*, *186*, 36–47. doi:10.1016/j.fishres.2016.08.004

NOAA Fisheries. (2015). *Fish population dynamics and modeling*. Southwest Fisheries Science Center, NOOA Fisheries. Retrieved on 1/23/2018 from: https://swfsc.noaa.gov/textblock.aspx?Division=FRD&id=1111

Nonin-Pulse oximeter. (n.d.). Retrieved from http://www.nonin.com/pulseoximetry/fingertip/onyx9550

Nyan, M. N., Tay, F. E., Tan, A. W. Y., & Seah, K. H. W. (2006). Distinguishing fall activities from normal activities by angular rate characteristics and high-speed camera characterization. *Medical Engineering & Physics*, *28*(8), 842–849. doi:10.1016/j.medengphy.2005.11.008 PMID:16406739

O'Keefe, J., & Burgess, N. (2005). Dual phase and rate coding in hippocampal place cells: Theoretical significance and relationship to entorhinal grid cells. *Hippocampus*, *15*(7), 853–866. doi:10.1002/hipo.20115 PMID:16145693

O'Keefe, J., & Dostrovsky, J. (1971). The hippocampus as a spatial map. Preliminary evidence from unit activity in the freely-moving rat. *Brain Research*, *34*(1), 171–175. doi:10.1016/0006-8993(71)90358-1 PMID:5124915

O'Keefe, J., & Recce, M. L. (1993). Phase relationship between hippocampal place units and the EEG theta rhythm. *Hippocampus*, *3*(3), 317–330. doi:10.1002/hipo.450030307 PMID:8353611

Object Management Group (OMG). (2017). *Business Architecture Overview*. Available at: http://bawg.omg.org/business_architecture_overview.htm

Occhiuzzi, C., & Marrocco, G. (2010). The RFID technology for neurosciences: Feasibility of limbs' monitoring in sleep diseases. *Information Technology in Biomedicine. IEEE Transactions on, 14*(1), 37–43. PMID:19726273

Oheigeartaigh, M. (1982). A fuzzy transportation algorithm. *Fuzzy Sets and Systems, 8*(3), 235–243. doi:10.1016/S0165-0114(82)80002-X

Ohn-Bar, E., & Trivedi, M. (2014). Hand gesture recognition in real time for automotive interfaces: A multimodal vision-based approach and evaluations. *IEEE Transactions on Intelligent Transportation Systems, 15*(6), 1–10. doi:10.1109/TITS.2014.2337331

Olawoyin, R. (2017). Risk and reliability evaluation of gas connector systems using fuzzy theory and expert elicitation. *Cogent Engineering, 4*(1), 1372731. doi:10.1080/23311916.2017.1372731

OMG. (2005). *The Software Process Engineering Metamodel Specification*. Version 1.1. OMG.

Onggo, S. (2012). Adult social care workforce analysis in England: A system dynamics approach. *International Journal of System Dynamics Applications, 1*(4), 1–20. doi:10.4018/ijsda.2012100101

Ordonez, F. J., Englebienne, G., De Toledo, P., Van Kasteren, T., Sanchis, A., & Krose, B. (2014). In-home activity recognition: Bayesian inference for hidden Markov models. *IEEE Pervasive Computing, 13*(3), 67–75. doi:10.1109/MPRV.2014.52

Orfila, A., Carbo, J., & Ribagorda, A. (2003). Fuzzy logic on decision model for intrusion detection systems. *Proceedings of the 2003 IEEE International Conference on Fuzzy Systems*, 1237–1242. 10.1109/FUZZ.2003.1206608

Paik, I., Chen, W., & Huhns, M. N. (2014). A scalable architecture for automatic service composition. *IEEE Transactions on Services Computing, 7*(1), 82–95. doi:10.1109/TSC.2012.33

Palankar, M., De Laurentis, K. J., Alqasemi, R., Veras, E., Dubey, R., Arbel, Y., & Donchin, E. (2008). Control of a 9-DoF wheelchair-mounted robotic arm system using a P300 brain computer interface: Initial experiments. In Robotics and Biomimetics (pp. 348–353). Academic Press.

Pamučar, D. S., Božanić, D., & Komazec, N. (2017). Risk assessment of natural disasters using fuzzy logic system of type 2. *Management: Journal of Sustainable Business and Management Solutions in Emerging Economies, 21*(80), 23–34.

Pandian, P., & Natarajan, G. (2010). A new algorithm for finding a fuzzy optimal solution for fuzzy transportation problems. *Applied Mathematical Sciences, 4*(2), 79–90.

Pannell, D. J. (1997b). *Sensitivity analysis: strategies, methods, concepts, examples*. Retrieved on 01/23/2018 from: http://dpannell.fnas.uwa.edu.au/dpap971f.htm

Pannell, D. J. (1997a). Sensitivity Analysis of Normative Economic Models: Theoretical Framework and Practical Strategies. *Agricultural Economics, 16*(2), 139–152. doi:10.1016/S0169-5150(96)01217-0

Pantelopoulos, A., & Bourbakis, N. G. (2010). A survey on wearable sensor-based systems for health monitoring and prognosis. *Systems, Man, and Cybernetics, Part C: Applications and Reviews. IEEE Transactions on, 40*(1), 1–12.

Papadias, D., Tao, Y., Fu, G., & Seeger, B. (2003). An Optimal and Progressive Algorithm for Skyline Queries. In *SIGMOD '03: Proceedings of the 2003 ACM SIGMOD international conference on Management of data* (pp. 467–478). New York, NY: ACM. 10.1145/872757.872814

Papazoglou & Heuvel. (2007). Service oriented architectures: approaches, technologies and research issues. *The VLDB Journal - The International Journal on Very Large Data Bases, 16*(3), 389-415.

Parappagoudar, M. B., Pratihar, D. K., & Datta, G. L. (2005). Green sand mould system modelling through design of experiments. *Indian Foundry Journal, 51*, 40–51.

Parappagoudar, M. B., Pratihar, D. K., & Datta, G. L. (2007). Non-linear modelling using central composite design to predict green sand mould properties. *Proceedings of the Institution of Mechanical Engineers. Part B, Journal of Engineering Manufacture, 221*(5), 881–895. doi:10.1243/09544054JEM696

Parappagoudar, M. B., Pratihar, D. K., & Datta, G. L. (2008). Linear and non-linear modeling of cement-bonded moulding sand system using conventional statistical regression analysis. *Journal of Materials Engineering and Performance, 17*(4), 472–481. doi:10.100711665-007-9172-6

Parappagoudar, M. B., Pratihar, D. K., & Datta, G. L. (2011). Modeling and analysis of sodium silicate-bonded moulding sand system using design of experiments and response surface methodology. *Journal for Manufacturing Science & Production, 11*(1-3), 1–14. doi:10.1515/jmsp.2011.011

Park, S., Kim, T., Park, J., Kim, J., & Im, H. (2009). Parallel Skyline Computation on Multicore Architectures. *Proc. of ICDE '09*, 760–771.

Park, Y., Min, J.-K., & Shim, K. (2013). Parallel Computation of Skyline and Reverse Skyline Queries Using MapReduce. *PVLDB, 6*(14), 2002–2013.

Parush, A., Ahuvia, S., & Erev, I. (2007). Degradation in spatial knowledge acquisition when using automatic navigation systems. In S. Winter (Ed.), COSIT 2007, LNCS 4736 (pp. 238-254). Springer. doi:10.1007/978-3-540-74788-8_15

Paschke, A., Kozlenkov, A., & Boley, H. (2007). *A homogeneous reaction rule language for complex event processing*. Academic Press.

Pastoor, T. P., Bachman, A. N., Bell, D. R., Cohen, S. M., Dellarco, M., Dewhurst, I. C., ... Moretto, A. (2014). A 21st century roadmap for human health risk assessment. *Critical Reviews in Toxicology, 44*(sup3), 1-5.

Patel, G. C. M., Krishna, P., Parappagoudar, M. B., & Vundavilli, P. R. (2016b). Multi-objective optimization of squeeze casting process using evolutionary algorithms. *International Journal of Swarm Intelligence Research, 7*(1), 55–74. doi:10.4018/IJSIR.2016010103

Patel, G. C. M., Krishna, P., Vundavilli, P. R., & Parappagoudar, M. B. (2016a). Multi-objective optimization of squeeze casting process using genetic algorithm and particle swarm optimization. *Archives of Foundry Engineering, 16*(3), 172–186. doi:10.1515/afe-2016-0073

Patel, S., Park, H., Bonato, P., Chan, L., & Rodgers, M. (2012). A review of wearable sensors and systems with application in rehabilitation. *Journal of Neuroengineering and Rehabilitation, 9*(1), 21. doi:10.1186/1743-0003-9-21 PMID:22520559

Pathak, R., & Vaidehi, V. (2014). Event Refinement Model Augmented Complex Event Processing for efficient decision making. In *International Conference on Intelligent Information Technology, ICIIT 2014*. Anna University.

Pathak, R., & Vaidehi, V. (2015). An efficient rule balancing for scalable complex event processing. *Electrical and Computer Engineering (CCECE), 2015 IEEE 28th Canadian Conference on*, 190-195. 10.1109/CCECE.2015.7129184

Pattnaik, M. (2015). Decision making approach to fuzzy linear programming (FLP) problems with post optimal analysis. *International Journal of Operations Research and Information Systems, 6*(4), 75–90. doi:10.4018/IJORIS.2015100105

Pazzani, M. J, Billsus, D., (2007). Content-based recommendation systems. *The Adaptive Web*, 325–341.

Pedroni, N., Zio, E., Ferrario, E., Pasanisi, A., & Couplet, M. (2012, June). Propagation of aleatory and epistemic uncertainties in the model for the design of a flood protection dike. In PSAM 11 & ESREL 2012 (pp. 1-10). Academic Press.

Pedroni, N., Zio, E., Ferrario, E., Pasanisi, A., & Couplet, M. (2013). Hierarchical propagation of probabilistic and non-probabilistic uncertainty in the parameters of a risk model. *Computers & Structures, 126*, 199–213. doi:10.1016/j.compstruc.2013.02.003

Pedrycz, W. (1998). Shadowed sets: Representing and processing fuzzy sets. *IEEE Transactions on Systems, Man, and Cybernetics. Part B, Cybernetics, 28*(1), 103–109. doi:10.1109/3477.658584 PMID:18255928

Peng, H., Long, F., & Ding, C. (2005). Feature selection based on mutual information criteria of max-dependency, max-relevance, and min redundancy. *IEEE Transactions on Pattern Analysis and Machine Intelligence, 1226*, 12–38. PMID:16119262

Pereira, H. E. (2009). Conversion methods for symbolic features: A comparison applied to an intrusion detection problem. *Expert Systems with Applications, 36*(7), 10612–10617. doi:10.1016/j.eswa.2009.02.054

Phillips, D. R. (1970). Sand control by independent variables. *AFS Transactions, 78*, 251–258.

Pierson, K., & Sterman, J. D. (2013). Cyclical dynamics of airline industry earnings. *System Dynamics Review, 29*(3), 129–156. doi:10.1002dr.1501

Ping, J. I., & Chu, K. F. (2002). A dual-matrix approach to the transportation problem. *Asia-Pacific Journal of Operational Research, 19*(1), 35–45.

Platzer, C., Rosenberg, F., & Dustdar, S. (2009). Web service clustering using multidimensional angles as proximity measures. *ACM Transactions on Internet Technology, 9*(3), 1–26. doi:10.1145/1552291.1552294

Pohl, K., Bockle, G., & Van der Linden, F. J. (2005). *Software product line engineering: foundations, principles and techniques*. Springer. doi:10.1007/3-540-28901-1

Poole, D., Mackworth, A., & Goebel, R. (1998). *Computational Intelligence: A Logical Approach*. Oxford, UK: Oxford University Press.

Portnoy, L., Eskin, E., & Stolfo, S. (2001). Intrusion detection with unlabeled data using clustering. *Proc. ACM CSS Workshop on Data Mining Applied to Security*.

Poslad, S., Middleton, S. E., Chaves, F., Tao, R., Necmioglu, O., & Bugel, U. (2015). A Semantic IoT Early Warning System for Natural Environment Crisis Management. *IEEE Transactions on Emerging Topics in Computing, 3*(2), 246–257. doi:10.1109/TETC.2015.2432742

Pree, W. (1994). *Design Patterns for Object Oriented Development*. Addison Wesley.

Preisinger, T. (2009). *Graph-based Algorithms for Pareto Preference Query*. Books on Demand.

Preisinger, T., & Kießling, W. (2007). The Hexagon Algorithm for Evaluating Pareto Preference Queries. *Proc. of MPref '07*.

Preisinger, T., Kießling, W., & Endres, M. (2006). The BNL++ Algorithm for Evaluating Pareto Preference Queries. *Proc. of MPref '06*.

Pruyt, E. (2006a). System dynamics and decision-making in the context of dynamically complex multi-dimensional societal issues. *Proceedings of the 2006 Conference of the System Dynamics Society*.

Pruyt, E. (2006b). What is system dynamics? A paradigmatic inquiry. *Proceedings of the 2006 Conference of the System Dynamics Society*.

Purushothkumar, M.K., & Ananathanarayanan, M. (2017). Fuzzy transportation problem of trapezoidal fuzzy numbers with new ranking technique. *IOSR Journal of Mathematics, 13*(6), 6-12.

Qayyum, A., Islam, M. H., & Jamil, M. (2005, September). Taxonomy of statistical based anomaly detection techniques for intrusion detection. In *Emerging Technologies, 2005. Proceedings of the IEEE Symposium on* (pp. 270-276). IEEE. 10.1109/ICET.2005.1558893

Qin, Y., Nakatani, N., & Tsukahara, Y. (2016). Study on the formulation of fish population dynamics model using statistical data. *Proceedings of the Techno-Ocean (Techno-Ocean) Conference.* 10.1109/Techno-Ocean.2016.7890654

Qi, X., & Cheng, Q. (2017). Imprecise reliability assessment of generating systems involving interval probability. *IET Generation, Transmission & Distribution, 11*(17), 4332–4337. doi:10.1049/iet-gtd.2017.0874

Qu, X., Sun, H., Li, X., Liu, X., & Lin, W. (2009). WSSM: A WordNet-Based Web Services Similarity Mining Mechanism. *Proceeding of the Future Computing, Service Computation, Cognitive, Adaptive, Content, Patterns,* 339–345. 10.1109/ComputationWorld.2009.96

Quinlan, J. R. (1986). Induction of decision trees. *Machine Learning, 1*(1), 81–106. doi:10.1007/BF00116251

Rahman, N. (2018b). Environmental sustainability in the computer industry for competitive advantage. In Green Computing Strategies for Competitive Advantage and Business Sustainability. IGI Global. Doi:10.4018/978-1-5225-5017-4.ch006

Rahman, N. (2014). A system dynamics model for a sustainable fish population. *International Journal of Technology Diffusion, 5*(2), 39–53. doi:10.4018/ijtd.2014040104

Rahman, N. (2016). Toward achieving environmental sustainability in the computer industry. *International Journal of Green Computing, 7*(1), 37–54. doi:10.4018/IJGC.2016010103

Rahman, N. (2018a). A simulation model for application development in data warehouses. *International Journal of Operations Research and Information Systems, 9*(1), 66–80. doi:10.4018/IJORIS.2018010104

Rahman, N., & Akhter, S. (2010). Incorporating sustainability into information technology management. *International Journal of Technology Management & Sustainable Development, 9*(2), 95–111. doi:10.1386/tmsd.9.2.95_1

Rajalakshmi, M., Purusothaman, T., & Pratheeba, S. (2010). Collusion free privacy preserving Data Mining. *International Journal of Intelligent Information Technologies, 6*(4), 30–45. doi:10.4018/jiit.2010100103

Rajarajeswari, P. & Sangeetha, M. (2016). New similarity performance measures of fuzzy transportation and its application. *International Journal of Innovative Research in Computer and Communication Engineering, 4*(4), 6353-6360. DOI: .040400910.15680/IJIRCCE.2016

Raman, M. R. G., Somu, N., Kirthivasan, K., Liscano, R., & Sriram, V. S. S. (2017). *An efficient intrusion detection system based on hypergraph -genetic algorithm for parameter optimization and feature selection in support vector machine.* Knowledge-Based System.

Rani, D., Gulati, T. R., & Kumar, A. (2014). A method for unbalanced transportation problems in fuzzy environment. *Indian Academy of Sciences Sadhana, 39*(3), 573–581. doi:10.100712046-014-0243-8

Rao, K. R., Mudaliar, R. K., Hasan, M. K., & Alam, M. K. (2016, December). A perfect mathematical formulation of fuzzy transportation problem provides an optimal solution speedily. In *Computer Science and Engineering (APWC on CSE), 2016 3rd Asia-Pacific World Congress on* (pp. 271-278). IEEE. 10.1109/APWC-on-CSE.2016.051

Rębiasz, B., Gaweł, B., & Skalna, I. (2017). Joint Treatment of Imprecision and Randomness in the Appraisal of the Effectiveness and Risk of Investment Projects. In *Information Systems Architecture and Technology: Proceedings of 37th International Conference on Information Systems Architecture and Technology–ISAT 2016–Part IV* (pp. 21-31). Springer International Publishing. 10.1007/978-3-319-46592-0_2

Rebsamen, B., Burdet, E., Guan, C., Teo, C. L., Zeng, Q., Ang, M., & Laugier, C. (2007). Controlling a wheelchair using a BCI with low information transfer rate. In Rehabilitation Robotics (pp. 1003–1008). Academic Press.

Rechy-Ramirez, E. J., Marin-Hernandez, A., & Rios-Figueroa, H. V. (2017). Impact of commercial sensors in human computer interaction: a review. Journal of Ambient Intelligent Human Computing. doi:10.100712652-017-0568-3

Rechy-Ramirez, E. J., Hu, H., & McDonald-Maier, K. (2012). Head movements based control of an intelligent wheelchair in an indoor environment. In *Proceedings of IEEE International Conference on Robotics and Biomimetics (ROBIO)* (pp. 1464-1469). IEEE. 10.1109/ROBIO.2012.6491175

Reddy, M. R., Raman, P. V., & Kumar, M. V. (2016). Unclear carrying problem of triangular numbers with α–slash and position method. *International Journal of Mathematical Archive, 7*(10), 66–68.

Renjit, K., & Shunmuganathan, K. (2010). Mining the data from distributed database using an improved mining algorithm. *International Journal of Computer Science and Information Security, 7*(3), 116–121.

Ribeiro, M. R., Barioni, M. C. N., de Amo, S., Roncancio, C., & Labbe, C. (2017). Reasoning with Temporal Preferences over Data Streams. *Proceedings of the Florida Artificial Intelligence Research Society Conference (FLAIRS).*

Richardson, J. (2013). The past is prologue: Reflections on forty-plus years of system dynamics modeling practice. *System Dynamics Review, 29*(3), 172–187. doi:10.1002dr.1503

Richardson, R., Paradiso, J., Leydon, K., & Fernstrom, M. (2004). Z-tiles: Building blocks for modular pressure-sensing. *Proc of Conf. on Human Factors in Computing Systems Chi04*, 1529-1532.

Riehle, D., & Züllighoven, H. (1996). Understanding and Using Patterns in Software Development. Theory and Practice of Object Systems, 2(1), 3-13. doi:10.1002/(SICI)1096-9942(1996)2:1<3::AID-TAPO1>3.0.CO;2-#

Rinaldi, S. M., Peerenboom, J. P., & Kelly, T. K. (2001). Identifying, understanding, and analyzing critical infrastructure interdependencies. *IEEE Control Systems, 21*(6), 11–25. doi:10.1109/37.969131

Rocha-Junior, J., Vlachou, A., Doulkeridis, C., & Nørvåg, K. (2009). AGiDS: A Grid-based Strategy for Distributed Skyline Query Processing. Data Management in Grid and Peer-to-Peer Systems, 12-23. doi:10.1007/978-3-642-03715-3_2

Rose, K. A., Cowan, J. H. Jr, Winemiller, K. O., Myers, R. A., & Hilborn, R. (2001). Compensatory density dependence in fish populations: Importance, controversy, understanding and prognosis. *Fish and Fisheries, 2*(4), 293–327. doi:10.1046/j.1467-2960.2001.00056.x

Rosenberg, R. S. (1967). *Simulation of genetic populations with biochemical properties* (Ph.D. Thesis). University of Michigan, Ann Arbor, MI.

Roy, A., & Pal, S. K. (2003). Fuzzy discretization of feature space for a rough set classifier. *Pattern Recognition Letters, 24*(6), 895–902. doi:10.1016/S0167-8655(02)00201-5

Rozenberg, G., Back, T., & Kok, J. (2011). *Handbook of Natural Computing.* Springer Verlag.

Rudenko, L., & Endres, M. (2017). Personalized Stream Analysis with PreferenceSQL. *PPI Workshop of BTW '17*, 181–184.

Rudenko, L., Endres, M., Roocks, P., & Kießling, W. (2016). A Preference-based Stream Analyzer. *STREAMVOLV Workshop of ECML PKKD'16.*

Rupasingha, R. A., Paik, I., & Kumara, B. T. (2017). Improving Web Service Clustering through a Novel Ontology Generation Method by Domain Specificity. *Web Services (ICWS), 2017 IEEE International Conference on*, 744-751.

Saad, O. M., & Abass, S. A. (2003). A parametric study on transportation problem under fuzzy environment. *Journal of Fuzzy Mathematics*, *11*(1), 115–124.

Saati, S., Hatami-Marbini, A., Tavana, M., & Hajiahkondi, E. (2012). A two-fold linear programming model with fuzzy data. *International Journal of Fuzzy System Applications*, *2*(3), 1–12. doi:10.4018/ijfsa.2012070101

Sabouri, H., & Khosravi, R. (2011). Efficient verification of evolving software product lines. In *International Conference on Fundamentals of Software Engineering* (pp. 351–358). Springer.

Sahib, J., Schwering, A., Schultz, C., & Chipofya, M. C. (2017). Cognitively plausible representations for the alignment of sketch and geo-referenced maps. *Journal of Spatial Information Science*, *2017*(14), 31-59.

Sahib, J., Schultz, C., Schwering, A., & Chipofya, M. (2015). Spatial Rules for Capturing Qualitatively Equivalent Configurations in Sketch Maps. *Annals of Computer Science and Information Systems*, *7*, 13–20. doi:10.15439/2015F372

Sahoo, P. K., Behera, S. K., & Nayak, J. R. (2016). Solution of fuzzy transportation problem by using ranking function. *Advanced Science Letters*, *22*(2), 564–566. doi:10.1166/asl.2016.6864

Sahu, A. K., Sahu, N. K., & Sahu, A. K. (2015). Benchmarking CNC Machine Tool Using Hybrid-Fuzzy Methodology: A Multi-Indices Decision Making (MCDM) Approach. *International Journal of Fuzzy System Applications*, *4*(2), 28–46. doi:10.4018/IJFSA.2015040103

Saikaew, C., & Wiengwiset, S. (2012). Optimization of molding sand composition for quality improvement of iron castings. *Applied Clay Science*, *67*, 26–31. doi:10.1016/j.clay.2012.07.005

Samuel, A. E., & Raja, P. (2017a). Algorithmic approach to unbalanced fuzzy transportation problem. *International Journal of Pure and Applied Mathematics*, *113*(5), 553–561.

Samuel, A. E., & Raja, P. (2017b). Advanced approximation method for finding an optimal solution of unbalanced fuzzy transportation problems. *Global Journal of Pure and Applied Mathematics*, *13*(9), 5307–5315.

Sankey, H. (1994). *The Incommensurability Thesis*. Ashgate.

Sanz, J., Fernández, A., Bustince, H., & Herrera, F. (2011). A genetic tuning to improve the performance of fuzzy rule-based classification systems with interval-valued fuzzy sets: Degree of ignorance and lateral position. *International Journal of Approximate Reasoning*, *52*(6), 751–766. doi:10.1016/j.ijar.2011.01.011

Sasaki, T., Yaguchi, Y., Watanobe, Y., & Oka, R. (2012). Extracting a Spatial Ontology from a Large Flickr Tag Dataset. *IEEE on 4th International Conference on Awareness Science and Technology (iCAST)*.

Sathiyapriya, K., Sudha, G., & Karthikeyan, V.B. (2012). A New Method for Preserving Privacy in Quantitative Association Rules using Genetic Algorithm. *International Journal of Computer Applications, 60*(12), 12-19.

Sathiyapriya, K., Sudhasadasivam, G., & Celin, N. (2011). A New Method for preserving privacy in Quantitative Association Rules Using DSR Approach with Automated Generation of Membership Function. *Proceedings of World Congress on Information and Communication Technologies*, 48-153.

Sathiyapriya, K., & Sudha Sadasivam, G. (2016). Hybrid Evolutionary Algorithm for Preserving Privacy of sensitive data in Quantitative Databases. *Journal of Scientific and Industrial Research*, *75*(7), 399–403.

Sathiyapriya, K., Sudhasadasivam, G., & Suganya, C.J.P. (2014). Hiding Sensitive Fuzzy Association rules Using Weighted Item Grouping and Rank Based Correlated Rule Hiding Algorithm. *WSEAS Transactions on Computers*, *13*, 78–89.

Satzger, B., Endres, M., & Kießling, W. (2006). A Preference-based Recommender Systems. *Proceedings of EC-Web '06, the 7ᵗʰ International Conference on Electronic Commerce and Web Technologies*. 10.1007/11823865_4

Saygin, Y., Verykios, V., & Clifton, C. (2001). Using Unknowns to Prevent Discovery of Association Rules. *SIGMOD Record*, *30*(4), 45–54. doi:10.1145/604264.604271

Schaffer, J. D. (1985). Multiple objective optimization with vector evaluated genetic algorithm. *Proceedings of 1st International Conference on Genetic Algorithms*, 93–100.

Schilling, B., Koldehofe, B., Pletat, U., & Rothermel, K. (2012). Distributed heterogeneous event processing. In Computer-based medical consultations: MYCIN. Elsevier.

Schlieder, C. (1995). Reasoning about ordering. *Proceedings of Spatial Information Theory (COSIT '95): A Theoretical Basis for GIS*, *988*, 341-349.

Schoenharl, T., Bravo, R., & Madey, G. (2006). WIPER: Leveraging the Cell Phone Network for Emergency Response. *International Journal of Intelligent Control and Systems*, *11*(4), 206–216.

Schubanz, M., Pleuss, A., Pradhan, L., Botterweck, G., & Thurimella, A. K. (2013). Model-driven planning and monitoring of long-term software product line evolution. In *Proceedings of the Seventh International Workshop on Variability Modelling of Softwareintensive Systems* (p. 18). ACM. 10.1145/2430502.2430527

Schwering, A., Li, R., & Anacta, V. J. A. (2013). Orientation information in different forms of route instructions. *Short Paper Proceedings of the 16th AGILE Conference on Geographic Information Science*.

Schwering, A., Wang, J., Chipofya, M., Jan, S., Li, R., & Broelemann, K. (2014). SketchMapia: Qualitative representations for the alignment of sketch and metric maps. *Spatial Cognition and Computation*, *14*(3), 220–254. doi:10.1080/13875868.2014.917378

Scivos, A., & Nebel, B. (2004). The finest of its class: The natural, point-based ternary calculus LR for qualitative spatial reasoning. *Spatial Cognition IV. Reasoning, Action, Interaction*, *3343*, 283–303.

Scott, W. R. (1998). *Organizations: Rational, natural, and open systems*. Prentice Hall.

Searle, J. (1990). *The mystery of consciousness*. New York: The New York Review of Books.

Segil, L. (1996). *Intelligent business alliances: how to profit using today's most important strategic tool*. Times Business.

Selke, J., Lofi, C., & Balke, W.-T. (2010). Highly Scalable Multiprocessing Algorithms for Preference-Based Database Retrieval. *Proc. of DASFAA '10*. 10.1007/978-3-642-12098-5_19

Senthil, P., & Amirthagadeswaran, K. (2014). Experimental study and squeeze casting process optimization for high quality AC2A aluminium alloy castings. *Arabian Journal for Science and Engineering*, *39*(3), 2215–2225. doi:10.100713369-013-0752-5

Shafer, G. (1976). *A Mathematical Theory of Evidence*. Princeton University Press.

Shah, R. A., & Asghar, S. (2014). Privacy preserving in association rules using genetic algorithm. *Turkish Journal of Electrical Engineering and Computer Sciences*, *22*(2), 434–450. doi:10.3906/elk-1206-66

Shang, C., & Shen, Q. (2006). Aiding classi cation of gene expression data with feature selection: A comparative study. *Computational Intelligence Research*, *1*, 68–76.

Shang, H., & Kitsuregawa, M. (2013). Skyline Operator on Anti-correlated Distributions. *Proc. of VLDB '13*.

Shankar, N. R., Saradhi, B. P., & Babu, S. S. (2013). Fuzzy critical path method based on a new approach of ranking fuzzy numbers using centroid of centroids. *International Journal of Fuzzy System Applications*, *3*(2), 16–31. doi:10.4018/ijfsa.2013040102

Shanmugavadivu, R., & Nagarajan, N. (2012). Learning of intrusion detector in conceptual approach of fuzzy towards intrusion methodology. *Int. J. of Advanced Research in Computer Science and Software Engineering, 2*.

Sharlach, M., & Vence, T. (2014). Brain's "Inner GPS" Wins Nobel. *TheScientist*. Available at: http://www.the-scientist.com/?articles.view/articleNo/41155/title/Brain-s--Inner-GPS--Wins-Nobel/

Shelton, A. O., & Mangel, M. (2011). Fluctuations of fish populations and the magnifying effects of fishing. *Proceedings of the National Academy of Sciences of the United States of America, 108*(17), 7075–7080. doi:10.1073/pnas.1100334108 PMID:21482785

Shin, H.-C., Orton, M. R., Collins, D. J., Doran, S. J., & Leach, M. O. (2013). Stacked Autoencoders for Unsupervised Feature Learning and Multiple Organ Detection in a Pilot Study Using 4D Patient Data. *IEEE Transactions on Pattern Analysis and Machine Intelligence, 35*(8), 1930–1943. doi:10.1109/TPAMI.2012.277 PMID:23787345

Shon, T., & Moon, J. S. (2007). A hybrid machine learning approach to network anomaly detection. *Information Sciences, 177*(18), 3799–3821. doi:10.1016/j.ins.2007.03.025

Silva, A. V., Neto, S. A. D., & de Sousa Filho, F. D. A. (2016). A Simplified Method for Risk Assessment in Slope Stability Analysis of Earth Dams Using Fuzzy Numbers. *The Electronic Journal of Geotechnical Engineering, 21*(10), 3607–3624.

Singh, P. (2015). A brief review of modeling approaches based on fuzzy time series. *International Journal of Machine Learning and Cybernetics*, 1–24.

Singh, P. (2016a). High-order fuzzy-neuro-entropy integration-based expert system for time series forecasting. *Neural Computing & Applications*, 1–18.

Singh, P. (2016b). Rainfall and financial forecasting using fuzzy time series and neural networks based model. *International Journal of Machine Learning and Cybernetics*. doi:10.100713042-016-0548-5

Singh, P., & Borah, B. (2013a). An efficient time series forecasting model based on fuzzy time series. *Engineering Applications of Artificial Intelligence, 26*(10), 2443–2457. doi:10.1016/j.engappai.2013.07.012

Singh, P., & Borah, B. (2013b). High-order fuzzy-neuro expert system for time series forecasting. *Knowledge-Based Systems, 46*, 12–21. doi:10.1016/j.knosys.2013.01.030

Singh, P., & Borah, B. (2014a). An effective neural network and fuzzy time series-based hybridized model to handle forecasting problems of two factors. *Knowledge and Information Systems, 38*(3), 669–690. doi:10.100710115-012-0603-9

Singh, P., & Borah, B. (2014b). Forecasting stock index price based on m-factors fuzzy time series and particle swarm optimization. *International Journal of Approximate Reasoning, 55*(3), 812–833. doi:10.1016/j.ijar.2013.09.014

Singh, R. R., Conjeti, S., & Banerjee, R. (2013). A comparative evaluation of neural network classifiers for stress level analysis of automotive drivers using physiological signals. *Biomedical Signal Processing and Control, 8*(6), 740–754. doi:10.1016/j.bspc.2013.06.014

Singh, R., & Saxena, V. (2017). A new data transfer approach through fuzzy Vogel's approximation method. *International Journal of Advanced Research in Computer Science, 8*(3), 515–519.

Singh, S. R. (2009). A computational method of forecasting based on high-order fuzzy time series. *Expert Systems with Applications, 36*(7), 10551–10559. doi:10.1016/j.eswa.2009.02.061

SIRENA. (2017). *Service Infrastructure for Real-time Embedded Networked Applications*. Available at: https://itea3.org/project/sirena.html

Sivertson, S. (2018). A system dynamics model of fish populations in Western Lake Superior. *Semantics Scholar*. Retrieved on 1/23/2018 from: https://pdfs.semanticscholar.org/2385/9916484ba4c2a318720ee4e092c368a91276.pdf

Smith, B., Malytua, T., Rudnick, R., Mandrick, W., Salmen, D., ...Parent, K. (2013). IAO-Intel: an ontology of information artifacts in the intelligence domain. In *Proceedings of the 8th Conference on semantic technologies for intelligence, defense, and security*, 12-15 November 2013, Fairfax, VA, USA: CEUR, 33–40.

Solaiappan, S., & Jeyaraman, K. (2014). A new optimal solution method for trapezoidal fuzzy transportation problem. *International Journal of Advanced Research*, 2(1), 933–942.

SolSEns. (2017). *Sol Sensitif pour Analyse Cognitive et Actimétrique*. Brest, France: IMT Atlantique.

Sommers, J., Yegneswaran, V., & Barford, P. (2004). A framework for malicious workload generation. In *4th ACM SIGCOMM conference on Internet measurement* (pp. 82-87). ACM.

Song, Q., & Chissom, B. S. (1993a). Fuzzy time series and its models. *Fuzzy Sets and Systems*, 54(3), 269–277. doi:10.1016/0165-0114(93)90372-O

Song, Q., & Chissom, B. S. (1993b). Forecasting enrollments with fuzzy time series – part I. *Fuzzy Sets and Systems*, 54(1), 1–9. doi:10.1016/0165-0114(93)90355-L

Song, Q., & Chissom, B. S. (1994). Forecasting enrollments with fuzzy time series – part II. *Fuzzy Sets and Systems*, 62(1), 1–8. doi:10.1016/0165-0114(94)90067-1

Soule, A., Salamatian, K., & Taft, N. (2005, October). Combining filtering and statistical methods for anomaly detection. In *Proceedings of the 5th ACM SIGCOMM conference on Internet Measurement* (pp. 31-31). USENIX Association. 10.1145/1330107.1330147

Sriganesh, K., Seshradri, M., & Ramachandran, A. (1966). On the compaction of bonded grains. *AFS Transactions, 74*, 27–36.

Srikant, R., & Agrawal, R. (1995). Mining generalized association rules. *Proceedings of the 21st International Conference on Very Large Data Bases*, 407–419.

Srikant, R., & Agrawal, R. (1996). Mining Quantitative Association Rules in Large Relational Tables. *Proceedings of the ACM SIGMOD International Conference on Management of Data*, 1-12. 10.1145/233269.233311

Srinoy, S. (2007). Intrusion detection model based on particle swarm optimization and support vector machine. Proceeding of Computational Intelligence in Security and Defense Applications. doi:10.1109/CISDA.2007.368152

Srivastava, R. P., & Liu, L. (2003). Applications of belief functions in business decisions: A review. *Information Systems Frontiers*, 5(4), 359–378. doi:10.1023/B:ISFI.0000005651.93751.4b

Stallings, W. (2006). *Cryptography and network security principles and practices*. Prentice Hall.

Steelman, T. A., & McCaffrey, S. (2013). Best practices in risk and crisis communication: Implications for natural hazards management. *Natural Hazards*, 65(1), 683–705. doi:10.100711069-012-0386-z

Stein, G., & Chen, B. W., & K, H. (2005). decision tree classifier for network intrusion detection with ga-based feature selection. *Proceedings of 43rd annual Southeast regional conference*, 136–141. 10.1145/1167253.1167288

Steinhage, A., & Lauterbach, C. (2011). SensFloor® and NaviFloor®: Large-area sensor systems beneath Your Feet. In Ambient Intelligence and Smart Environments, Trends and Perspectives. IGI Global.

Steinhage, A., Lauterbach, C., Schmitmeier, H., & Plischke, H. (2014). Erste Seniorenresidenz mit ganzheitlichem AAL Konzept. *Proc. of the 7. Deutscher AAL-Kongress 2014*. Retrieved from http://www.tekscan.com

Steinhage, A., & Lauterbach, C. (2008). Monitoring movement behaviour by means of a large-area proximity sensor array in the floor. *Proc. of the 2nd Workshop on Behaviour Monitoring and Interpretation (BMI 2008). 31st German Conference on Artificial Intelligence (KI2008)*, 15-27.

Sterman, J. D. (2000). *Business dynamics: Systems thinking and modeling for a complex world*. McGraw-Hill Higher Education.

Stevens, L. (2017). *Sporty cyborgs: Microchips in humans to prevent doping in athletes, suggests Olympians chief*. Retrieved from http://home.bt.com/tech-gadgets/future-tech/microchips-in-humans-to-prevent-doping-11364220161232

Straszecka, E. (2006a). A Model of a Diagnostic Rule in the Dempster-Shafer Theory. *ICAISC, 8th international conference on Artificial intelligence and soft computing*.

Straszecka, E. (2003). An interpretation of focal elements as fuzzy sets. *International Journal of Intelligent Systems*, *18*(7), 821–835. doi:10.1002/int.10118

Straszecka, E. (2006b). Combining uncertainty and imprecision in models of medical diagnosis. *Information Sciences*, *176*(20), 3026–3059. doi:10.1016/j.ins.2005.12.006

Subramanian, T., & Savarimuthu, N. (2016). Cloud Service Evaluation and Selection Using Fuzzy Hybrid MCDM Approach in Marketplace. *International Journal of Fuzzy System Applications*, *5*(2), 118–153. doi:10.4018/IJFSA.2016040108

Sudha, G., Sangeetha, S., & Sathiyapriya, K., (2012). Privacy Preservation with Attribute Reduction in Quantitative Association Rules using PSO and DSR. *International Journal of Computer Applications*, 19-30.

Sudhakar, V. J., & Kumar, V. N. (2011). A different approach for solving two stage fuzzy transportation problems. *International Journal of Contemporary Mathematical Sciences*, *6*(11), 517–526.

Suk, H.-I., Lee, S.-W., & Shen, D. (2015). Latent Feature Representation with Stacked Auto-Encoder for AD/MCI Diagnosis. *Brain Structure & Function*, *220*(2), 841–859. doi:10.100700429-013-0687-3 PMID:24363140

Suknovic, M., Delibasic, B., Jovanovic, M., Vukicevic, M., Becejski-Vujaklija, D., & Obradovic, Z. (2012). Reusable components in decision tree induction algorithms. *Computational Statistics*, *27*(1), 127–148. doi:10.100700180-011-0242-8

Sun, P. (2010). Service Clustering Based on Profile and Process Similarity. *Proceeding of the International Symposium on Information Science and Engineering*, 535–539. 10.1109/ISISE.2010.151

Sun, B., Guo, H., Karimi, H. R., Ge, Y., & Xiong, S. (2015). Prediction of stock index futures prices based on fuzzy sets and multivariate fuzzy time series. *Neurocomputing*, *151*, 1528–1536. doi:10.1016/j.neucom.2014.09.018

Sung, A., & Mukkamala, S. (2003). Identifying important features for intrusion detection using support vector machines and neural networks. *Proceedings of the 2003 Symposium on Applications and the Internet*, 209–216. 10.1109/SAINT.2003.1183050

Surekha, B., Hanumanth, R. D., & Krishnamohan, R. G. (2013). Application of response surface methodology for modeling the properties of chromite-based resin bonded sand cores. *International Journal of Mechanics*, *7*(4), 443–458.

Surianarayanan, C., & Ganapathy, G. (2016). An Approach to Computation of Similarity Inter-Cluster Distance and Selection of Threshold for Service Discovery using Clusters. *IEEE Transactions on Services Computing*, *9*(4), 524–536. doi:10.1109/TSC.2015.2399301

Sutton, R. S., & Barto, A. G. (1998). *Reinforcement Learning - An Introduction*. Cambridge, MA: The MIT Press.

Taha, H. A. (2008). *Operations Research: An Introduction* (8th ed.). Pearson Education.

Taher, F. B., Amor, N. B., & Jallouli, M. (2015). A multimodal wheelchair control system based on EEG signals and Eye tracking fusion. In *Innovations in Intelligent SysTems and Applications (INISTA), 2015 International Symposium on* (pp. 1-8). Academic Press.

Talmy, L. (1983). How language structures space. In Spatial Orientation (pp. 225-282). Springer US. doi:10.1007/978-1-4615-9325-6_11

Tamura, H., Manabe, T., Goto, T., Yamashita, Y., & Tanno, K. (2010). A study of the electric wheelchair hands-free safety control system using the surface-electromygram of facial muscles. *Intelligent Robotics and Applications LNCS*, *6425*, 97–104. doi:10.1007/978-3-642-16587-0_10

Tan, K.-L., Eng, P.-K., & Ooi, B. C. (2001). Efficient Progressive Skyline Computation. In *VLDB '01: Proceedings of the 27th International Conference on Very Large Data Bases* (pp. 301–310). San Francisco, CA: Morgan Kaufmann Publishers Inc.

Tapia, D. I., Rodríguez, S., Bajo, J., & Corchado, J. M. (2008). FUSION@, A SOA-Based Multi-agent Architecture. *International Symposium on Distributed Computing and Artificial Intelligence 2008 (DCAI 2008)*, 99-107.

Tarkett Floor in Motion. (2018). Retrieved from http://www.floorinmotion.com/en

Tartarisco, G., Carbonaro, N., Tonacci, A., Bernava, G. M., Arnao, A., Crifaci, G., ... Tognetti, A. (2015). Neuro-fuzzy physiological computing to assess stress levels in virtual reality therapy. *Interacting with Computers*, *27*(5), 521–533. doi:10.1093/iwc/iwv010

Tavallaee, M., Bagheri, E., Lu, W., & Ghorbani, A. A. (2009). A detailed analysis of the kdd cup 99 data set. *Proceeding of the 2009 IEEE symposium on computational Intelligence in security and defense application (CISDA)*. 10.1109/CISDA.2009.5356528

Taylor, H. A., & Tversky, B. (1992). Spatial mental models derived from survey and route descriptions. *Journal of Memory and Language*, *31*(2), 261–292. doi:10.1016/0749-596X(92)90014-O

Ter Beek, M. H., Muccini, H., & Pelliccione, P. (2011). Guaranteeing correct evolution of software product lines: setting up the problem. In *International Workshop on Software Engineering for Resilient Systems* (pp. 100–105). Springer. 10.1007/978-3-642-24124-6_9

Teyler, T. J., & DiScenna, P. (1985). The role of hippocampus in memory: A hypothesis. *Neuroscience and Biobehavioral Reviews*, *9*(3), 377–389. doi:10.1016/0149-7634(85)90016-8 PMID:2999655

Thakker, B., & Vyas, A. L. (2011). Support vector machine for abnormal pulse classification. *International Journal of Computers and Applications*, *22*(7), 13–19. doi:10.5120/2597-3610

Thakker, R., Eveleigh, T., Holzer, T., & Sarkani, S. (2013). A system dynamics approach to quantitatively analyze the effects of mobile broadband ecosystem's variables on demands and allocation of wireless spectrum for the cellular industry. *International Journal of System Dynamics Applications*, *2*(3), 73–93. doi:10.4018/ijsda.2013070105

Thomsen, S. R. (1995). Using Online Databases in Corporate Issues Management. *Public Relations Review*, *21*(2), 103–122. doi:10.1016/0363-8111(95)90002-0

Thorp, E. B., Abdollahi, F., Chen, D., Farshchiansadegh, A., Lee, M. H., Pedersen, J. P., ... Mussa-Ivaldi, F. A. (2016). Upper body-based power wheelchair control interface for individuals with tetraplegia. *IEEE Transactions on Neural Systems and Rehabilitation Engineering*, *24*(2), 249–260. doi:10.1109/TNSRE.2015.2439240 PMID:26054071

Thulasidas, M., Guan, C., & Wu, J. (2006). Robust classification of EEG signal for brain-computer interface. *IEEE Transactions on Neural Systems and Rehabilitation Engineering*, *14*(1), 24–29. doi:10.1109/TNSRE.2005.862695 PMID:16562628

Tiwari, S. K., Singh, R. K., & Srivastava, S. C. (2016). Optimisation of green sand casting process parameters for enhancing quality of mild steel castings. *International Journal of Productivity and Quality Management*, *17*(2), 127–141. doi:10.1504/IJPQM.2016.074446

Toreyin, B. U., Soyer, E. B., Onaran, I., & Cetin, A. E. (2008). Falling person detection using multisensor signal processing. *EURASIP Journal on Advances in Signal Processing*, *2008*, 29.

Trinowski, D. M. (1999). New cold box binder system for improved productivity. *AFS Transactions*, *107*, 51–57.

Tsang, C., Kwong, S., & Wang, H. (2007). Genetic-fuzzy rule mining approach and evaluation of feature selection techniques for anomaly intrusion detection. *Pattern Recognition*, *40*(9), 2373–2391. doi:10.1016/j.patcog.2006.12.009

Tsaur, R.-C. (2012). A fuzzy time series-markov chain model with an Application to forecast the exchange rate between the Taiwan and us dollar. *International Journal of Innovative Computing, Information, & Control*, *8*(7B), 4931–4942.

Tsui, C. S. L., Jia, P., Gan, J. Q., Hu, H., & Yuan, K. (2007). EMG-based hands-free wheelchair control with EOG attention shift detection. In *IEEE International Conference on Robotics and Biomimetics* (pp. 1266–1271). IEEE.

Turchin, Y., Gal, A., & Wasserkrug, S. (2009, July). Tuning complex event processing rules using the prediction-correction paradigm. In *Proceedings of the Third ACM International Conference on Distributed Event-Based Systems* (p. 10). ACM. 10.1145/1619258.1619272

Tversky, B. (2000). Levels and structure of spatial knowledge. *Cognitive mapping: past, present and future*, 24–43.

Tversky, B. (2003). Structure of mental spaces: How people think about space. *Environment and Behavior*, *35*(1), 66–80. doi:10.1177/0013916502238865

Tversky, B. (2005). How to get around by mind and body - Spatial thought, spatial action. In A. Zilhao (Ed.), *Evolution, Rationality and Cognition: A Cognitive Science for the Twenty-first Century* (pp. 135–147). Routledge.

UKARI project. (2013). Retrieved from http://open-ukari.nict.go.jp/Ukari-Project-e.html

UNCAP. (n.d.). *EU Horizon 2020 project 2014-2017*. Retrieved from http://www.uncap.eu/

Up2Europe. (2017). *Collaborative, Complex and Critical Decision-Support in Evolving Crises (TRIDEC)*. Available at: https://www.up2europe.eu/european/projects/collaborative-complex-and-critical-decision-support-in-evolving-crises_9985.html

Vaidehi, V., Bhargavi, R., Ganapathy, K., & Sweetlin Hemalatha, C. (2012). Multi-sensor based in-home health monitoring using Complex Event Processing. In *Proceedings of IEEE International Conference on Recent Trends in Information Technology (ICRTIT 2012)*. MIT, Anna University.

Valdes, A., & Skinner, K. (2000). Adaptive model-based monitoring for cyber attack detection. Recent Advances in Intrusion Detection, 80–92. doi:10.1007/3-540-39945-3_6

Valkeapaa, O., Alm, O., & Hyvonen, E. (2007). An adaptable framework for ontology-based content creation on the semantic web. *J. UCS*, *13*(12), 1825–1853.

Vapnik, V. (1998). *Statistical learning theory*. New York: Wiley.

Varelas, G., Voutsakis, E., Raftopoulou, P., Petrakis, E. G., & Milios, E. E. (2005). Semantic similarity methods in wordnet and their application to information retrieval on the web. *Proceedings of the 7th annual ACM International Workshop on Web Information and Data Management*, 10-16. 10.1145/1097047.1097051

Vasnjik, F. (2014). *Breaking the Surface – Responsive 'ocean' of acrylic actuators*. Retrieved from http://www.creative-applications.net/openframeworks/breaking-the-surface/

Veil, S. R., Buehner, T., & Palenchar, M. J. (2011). A Work-In-Process Literature Review: Incorporating Social Media in Risk and Crisis Communication. *Journal of Contingencies and Crisis Management*, *19*(2), 110–122. doi:10.1111/j.1468-5973.2011.00639.x

Ventana Systems, Inc. (2011). *Vensim® from Ventana Systems, Inc*. Retrieved on 1/30/2018: http://www.vensim.com/

Venter, G., & Sobieski, J. S. (2003). Particle swarm optimization. *AIAA Journal*, *41*(8), 1583–1589. doi:10.2514/2.2111

Verghese, J., Holtzer, R., Lipton, R. B., & Wang, C. (2009). Quantitative gait markers and incident fall risk in older adults. *The Journals of Gerontology. Series A, Biological Sciences and Medical Sciences*, *64*(8), 896–901. doi:10.1093/gerona/glp033 PMID:19349593

Verwoerd, T., & Hunt, R. (2002). Intrusion detection techniques and approaches. *Computer Communications*, *25*(15), 1356–1365. doi:10.1016/S0140-3664(02)00037-3

Verykios, V., Elmagarmid, A. K., Bertino, E., Saygin, Y., & Dasseni, E. (2004). Hiding Sensitive Association Rule using Heuristic Approach. *IEEE Transactions on Knowledge and Data Engineering*, *16*(4), 434–447. doi:10.1109/TKDE.2004.1269668

Vescoukis, V., Doulamis, N., & Karagiorgou, S. (2012). A service oriented architecture for decision support systems in environmental crisis management. *Future Generation Computer Systems*, *28*(3), 593–604. doi:10.1016/j.future.2011.03.010

Vijian, P., & Arunachalam, V. P. (2007). Modelling and multi objective optimization of LM24 aluminium alloy squeeze cast process parameters using genetic algorithm. *Journal of Materials Processing Technology*, *186*(1), 82–86. doi:10.1016/j.jmatprotec.2006.12.019

Vimala, S., & Prabha, S. K. (2016). Fuzzy transportation problem through monalisha's approximation method. *British Journal of Mathematics & Computer Science*, *17*(2), 1–11. doi:10.9734/BJMCS/2016/26097

Vlachou, A., Doulkeridis, C., & Kotidis, Y. (2008). Angle-based Space Partitioning for Efficient Parallel Skyline Computation. *Proceedings of the 2008 ACM SIGMOD International Conference on management of Data (SIGMOD '08)*, 227-238. 10.1145/1376616.1376642

Vundavilli, P. R., Kumar, J. P., & Parappagoudar, M. B. (2013). Weighted average-based multi-objective optimization of tube spinning process using non-traditional optimization techniques. *International Journal of Swarm Intelligence Research*, *4*(3), 42–57. doi:10.4018/ijsir.2013070103

Wagner, F., Ishikawa, F., & Honiden, S. (2011). QoS-aware Automatic Service Composition by Applying Functional Clustering. *Proceeding of the 9th IEEE International Conference on Web Services*, 89–96. 10.1109/ICWS.2011.32

Wakeland, W., Cangur, O., Rueda, G., & Scholz, A. (2003). A system dynamics model of the pacific coast rockfish fishery. *Proceedings of the 21st International Conference of the System Dynamics Society*.

Walrave, B. (2016). Determining intervention thresholds that change output behavior patterns. *System Dynamics Review*, *32*(3-4), 261–278. doi:10.1002dr.1564

Walter, K., & Nash, E. (2009, June). Coupling wireless sensor networks and the Sensor Observation Service—bridging the interoperability gap. *Proceedings of 12th AGILE International Conference on Geographic Information Science 2009*.

Walzer, K., Breddin, T., & Groch, M. (2008, July). Relative temporal constraints in the Rete algorithm for complex event detection. In *Proceedings of the second international conference on Distributed event-based systems* (pp. 147-155). ACM. 10.1145/1385989.1386008

Wang, J. (2014). *Qualitative sketch aspects for sketch map alignment* (PhD thesis). University of Münster.

Wang, J., & Schwering, A. (2015). Invariant spatial information in sketch maps—a study of survey sketch maps of urban areas. *Journal of Spatial Information Science*, *2015*(11), 31-52.

Wang, J., & Worboys, M. (2016). Pedestrian navigation aids, spatial knowledge and walkability. In *Short Paper Proceedings of the 9th International Conference on GIScience* (Vol. 1, No. 1). Montreal, Canada: Academic Press. 10.21433/B3114B58K9TP

Wang, Y., & Yang, S. (2010, July). High-performance complex event processing for large-scale RFID applications. In *Signal Processing Systems (ICSPS), 2010 2nd International Conference on* (Vol. 1, pp. V1-127). IEEE. 10.1109/ICSPS.2010.5555586

Wang, H. T., Li, Y. Q., & Yu, T. Y. (2014b). Coordinated control of an intelligent wheelchair based on a brain-computer interface and speech recognition. *Journal of Zhejiang University-SCIENCE C*, *15*(10), 832–838. doi:10.1631/jzus.C1400150

Wang, H., Li, Y., Long, J., Yu, T., & Gu, Z. (2014a). An asynchronous wheelchair control by hybrid EEG–EOG brain–computer interface. *Cognitive Neurodynamics*, *8*(5), 399–409. doi:10.100711571-014-9296-y PMID:25206933

Wang, J., Hong, X., Ren, R., & Li, T. (2009). A real-time intrusion detection system based on pso-svm. *Proceeding of the 2009 International Workshop on Information Security and Application*, 319–321.

Wang, J., & Li, R. (2013). An empirical study on pertinent aspects of sketch maps for navigation. *International Journal of Cognitive Informatics and Natural Intelligence*, *7*(4), 26–43. doi:10.4018/ijcini.2013100102

Wang, J., & Worboys, M. (2017). Ontologies and representation spaces for sketch map interpretation. *International Journal of Geographical Information Science*, 1–25.

Wang, L., Liu, X., & Pedrycz, W. (2013). Effective intervals determined by information granules to improve forecasting in fuzzy time series. *Expert Systems with Applications*, *40*(14), 5673–5679. doi:10.1016/j.eswa.2013.04.026

Wang, L., Liu, X., Pedrycz, W., & Shao, Y. (2014). Determination of temporal information granules to improve forecasting in fuzzy time series. *Expert Systems with Applications*, *41*(6), 3134–3142. doi:10.1016/j.eswa.2013.10.046

Wang, S. L., & Jafari, A. (2005). Using unknowns for hiding sensitive predictive association rules. *Proceedings of the 2005 IEEE International Conference on Information Reuse and Integration (IRI 2005)*, 223–228. 10.1109/IRI-05.2005.1506477

Wang, S. L., Parikh, B., & Jafari, A. (2007, August). Hiding Sensitive Association Rules without Altering the Support of Sensitive Item. *Expert Systems with Applications*, *33*(2), 316–323. doi:10.1016/j.eswa.2006.05.022

Wang, W., Pedrycz, W., & Liu, X. (2015). Time series long-term forecasting model based on information granules and fuzzy clustering. *Engineering Applications of Artificial Intelligence*, 4117–4124.

Wang, Y. H., Cao, K., & Zhang, X. M. (2013). Complex event processing over distributed probabilistic event streams. *Computers & Mathematics with Applications (Oxford, England)*, *66*(10), 1808–1821. doi:10.1016/j.camwa.2013.06.032

Wang, Y., & Hu, X. (2013). Fuzzy reasoning of accident provenance in pervasive healthcare monitoring systems. *IEEE Journal of Biomedical and Health Informatics*, *17*(6), 1015–1022. doi:10.1109/JBHI.2013.2274518 PMID:24240719

Warwick, K. (2010). Implications and consequences of robots with biological brains. *Ethics and Information Technology, 12*(3), 223–234. doi:10.100710676-010-9218-6

Warwick, K. (2013a). Cyborgs—the neuro-tech version. In E. Katz (Ed.), *Implantable bioelectronics—devices, materials and applications*. New York: Wiley–VCH.

Warwick, K. (2013b). Cyborgs. In *Encyclopaedia of Sciences and Religions* (pp. 570–576). Springer, Netherlands. doi:10.1007/978-1-4020-8265-8_1210

Warwick, K., Gasson, M., Hutt, B., Goodhew, I., Kyberd, P., Andrews, B., ... Shad, A. (2003). The application of implant technology for cybernetic systems. *Archives of Neurology, 60*(10), pp1369–pp1373. doi:10.1001/archneur.60.10.1369 PMID:14568806

Warwick, K., Gasson, M., Hutt, B., Goodhew, I., Kyberd, P., Schulzrinne, H., & Wu, X. (2004). Thought communication and control: A first step using radiotelegraphy. *IEE Proceedings. Communications, 151*(3), 185–189. doi:10.1049/ip-com:20040409

Warwick, K., & Harrison, I. (2014). Feelings of a Cyborg. *International Journal of Synthetic Emotions, 5*(2), 1–6. doi:10.4018/ijse.2014070101

Warwick, K., Xydas, D., Nasuto, S., Becerra, V., Hammond, M., Marshall, S., & Whalley, B. (2010). Controlling a mobile robot with a biological brain. *Defence Science Journal, 60*(1), 5–14. doi:10.14429/dsj.60.11

Wasserkrug, S., Gal, A., Etzion, O., & Turchin, Y. (2008, July). Complex event processing over uncertain data. In *Proceedings of the second international conference on Distributed event-based systems* (pp. 253-264). ACM. 10.1145/1385989.1386022

Wasserkrug, S., Gal, A., Etzion, O., & Turchin, Y. (2012b). Efficient processing of uncertain events in rule-based systems. *Knowledge and Data Engineering. IEEE Transactions on, 24*(1), 45–58.

Wautelet, Y. (2008). *A goal-driven project management framework for multi-agent software development: The case of i-tropos* (PhD Thesis). Université Catholique de Louvain, Belgium.

Wautelet, Y., Heng, S., Kolp, M., Penserini, L., & Poelmans, S. (2016a). Designing an MOOC as an agent-platform aggregating heterogeneous virtual learning environments. *Behaviour & Information Technology, 35*(11), 980–997. doi:10.1080/0144929X.2016.1212095

Wautelet, Y., & Kolp, M. (2016b). Business and model-driven development of BDI multi-agent systems. *Neurocomputing, 182*, 304–321. doi:10.1016/j.neucom.2015.12.022

Wautelet, Y., & Poelmans, S. (2017). An Integrated Enterprise Modeling Framework Using the RUP/UML Business Use-Case Model and BPMN. In *IFIP Working Conference on The Practice of Enterprise Modeling* (pp. 299-315). Springer. 10.1007/978-3-319-70241-4_20

Wayne, P. M., & David, R. M. (2001). *Mesquite: a modular system for evolutionary analysis*. Retrieved from: http://www.cs.mcgill.ca/~birch/doc/mesquite/doc/MesquiteManual.pdf

Webster, B. F. (1995). *Pitfalls of Object Oriented Development*. John Wiley & Sons Inc.

Wei, L., & Hu, H. (2010). EMG and visual based HMI for hands-free control of an intelligent wheelchair. In *8th World Congress on Intelligent Control and Automation* (pp. 1027–1032). Academic Press. 10.1109/WCICA.2010.5554766

Wei, L. Y., Cheng, C. H., & Wu, H. H. (2014). A hybrid ANFIS based on n-period moving Average model to forecast TAIEX stock. *Applied Soft Computing, 19*, 86–92. doi:10.1016/j.asoc.2014.01.022

Wen, T., Sheng, G., Li, Y., & Guo, Q. (2011). Research on Web service discovery with semantics and clustering. *Proceeding of the 6th IEEE Joint International Information Technology and Artificial Intelligence Conference*, 62–67. 10.1109/ITAIC.2011.6030151

Weng, C. C., Chen, S. T., & Chang, Y. C. (2007). A Novel Algorithm for Completely Hiding Sensitive Frequent Itemset. *Proceedings of the eighth International Symposium on Advanced Intelligent Systems*, 753-757.

Weng, C. C., Chen, S. T., & Lo, H. C. (2008). A Novel Algorithm for Completely Hiding Sensitive Association Rules. *Eighth International Conference on Intelligent Systems Design and Applications*, 3, 202-208. 10.1109/ISDA.2008.180

Wessiani, N. A., & Sarwoko, S. O. (2015). Risk analysis of poultry feed production using fuzzy FMEA. *Procedia Manufacturing*, 4, 270–281. doi:10.1016/j.promfg.2015.11.041

White, S. A. (2004). Introduction to BPMN. *BPTrends*. Available at: http://yoann.nogues.free.fr/IMG/pdf/07-04_WP_Intro_to_BPMN_-_White-2.pdf

Widom, J. (1995). Research Problems in Data Warehousing. *Proceedings of the Fourth Int. Conf. on Information and Knowledge Management*, 25-30.

Willis, K. S., Hölscher, C., Wilbertz, G., & Li, C. (2009). A comparison of spatial knowledge acquisition with maps and mobile maps. *Computers, Environment and Urban Systems*, 33(2), 100–110. doi:10.1016/j.compenvurbsys.2009.01.004

Wood, M., DeLoach, S. A., & Sparkman, C. (2001). Multi-Agent System Engineering. *International Journal of Software Engineering and Knowledge Engineering*, 11(3), 231–258. doi:10.1142/S0218194001000542

Woodridge, M., & Jennings, N. R. (1995). Intelligent agents: Theory and practice. *The Knowledge Engineering Review*, 10(2), 115–152. doi:10.1017/S0269888900008122

Woodridge, M., Jennings, N. R., & Kinny, D. (2000). The Gaia Methodology for Agent-Oriented Analysis and Design. *Autonomous Agents and Multi-Agent Systems*, 3(3), 285–312. doi:10.1023/A:1010071910869

Woods, L., Alonso, G., & Teubner, J. (2013). Parallel Computation of Skyline Queries. In *Proc. of the FCCM* (pp. 1–8). Washington, DC: IEEE.

Wu, F., Zhao, H., Zhao, Y., & Zhong, H. (2015). Development of a Wearable-Sensor-Based Fall Detection System. *Int. Journal of Telemedicine and Applications*.

Wu, D. D. (2009). Supplier selection in a fuzzy group setting: A method using grey related analysis and Dempster–Shafer theory. *Expert Systems with Applications*, 36(5), 8892–8899. doi:10.1016/j.eswa.2008.11.010

Wu, P., Zhang, C., Feng, Y., Zhao, B. Y., Agrawal, D., & Abbadi, A. E. (2006). Parallelizing Skyline Queries for Scalable Distribution. *Proc. of EDBT '06*.

Wu, S., & Banzhaf, W. (2010). The use of computational intelligence in intrusion detection systems: A review. *Applied Soft Computing*, 10(1), 1–35. doi:10.1016/j.asoc.2009.06.019

Wu, Y. H., Chiang, C. M., & Chen, A. L. P. (2007). Hiding Sensitive Association Rules with Limited Side Effects. *IEEE Transactions on Knowledge and Data Engineering*, 19(1), 29–42. doi:10.1109/TKDE.2007.250583

Wyburn, J., & Roach, P. A. (2013). A system dynamics model of the American collectable comic book market. *International Journal of System Dynamics Applications*, 2(1), 37–58. doi:10.4018/ijsda.2013010103

Xie, L., Chen, F., & Kou, J. (2011). Ontology-based semantic Web services clustering. *Proceeding of the 18th IEEE International Conference on Industrial Engineering and Engineering Management*, 2075–2079.

Xu, P., Deng, Y., Xu, J., & Su, X. (2010, June). Risk analysis of system security based on evidence theory. In *Computer Design and Applications (ICCDA), 2010 International Conference on* (Vol. 5, pp. V5-610). IEEE.

Xu, X. D., Zhang, Y., Luo, Y., & Chen, D. Y. (2013). Robust Bio-Signal based Control of an Intelligent Wheelchair. *Robotics*, *2*(4), 187–197. doi:10.3390/robotics2040187

Yager, R. R. (2008). A knowledge-based approach to adversarial decision making. *International Journal of Intelligent Systems*, *23*(1), 1–21. doi:10.1002/int.20254

Yan, Yin, Zhang, Yang, & Hao. (2016). Semantic indexing with deep learning: A case study. *Big Data Analytics, 1*(7).

Yang, C. S., & Chang, P. C. (2015). Mining Social Media for Enhancing Personalized Document Clustering. In F. Fui-Hoon Nah & C. H. Tan (Eds.), Lecture Notes in Computer Science: Vol. 9191. *HCI in Business. HCIB 2015*. Cham: Springer. doi:10.1007/978-3-319-20895-4_18

Yang, J. B., & Sen, P. (1997). Multiple attribute design evaluation of complex engineering products using the evidential reasoning approach. *Journal of Engineering Design*, *8*(3), 211–230. doi:10.1080/09544829708907962

Yang, J. B., & Xu, D. L. (2002). On the evidential reasoning algorithm for multiple attribute decision analysis under uncertainty. *IEEE Transactions on Systems, Man, and Cybernetics. Part A, Systems and Humans*, *32*(3), 289–304. doi:10.1109/TSMCA.2002.802746

Yang, J., Huang, H. Z., He, L. P., Zhu, S. P., & Wen, D. (2011). Risk evaluation in failure mode and effects analysis of aircraft turbine rotor blades using Dempster–Shafer evidence theory under uncertainty. *Engineering Failure Analysis*, *18*(8), 2084–2092. doi:10.1016/j.engfailanal.2011.06.014

Yang, Z., Zhong, S., & Wright, R. N. (2005). Privacy-Preserving Classification of Customer Data without Loss of Accuracy. *Proceedings of the Fifth SIAM International Conference on Data Mining*, 92-102. 10.1137/1.9781611972757.9

Yan, Yin, & Li, Yang, & Hao. (2015). Learning Document Semantic Representation with Hybrid Deep Belief Network. *Computational Intelligence and Neuroscience*, 9.

Yao, A. C. (1986). How to generate and exchange secrets. *27th IEEE Symposium on Foundations of Computer Science*, 162–167.

Yao, J., Zhao, S., & Fan, L. (2006). An enhanced support vector machine model for intrusion detection. *Proceedings of the First international conference on Rough Sets and Knowledge Technology*, 538–543. 10.1007/11795131_78

Yazdanshenas, A. R., & Moonen, L. (2012). Fine-grained change impact analysis for component-based product families. In *Software Maintenance (ICSM), 2012 28th IEEE International Conference on* (pp. 119–128). IEEE. 10.1109/ICSM.2012.6405262

Ye, N., Emran, S. M., Chen, Q., & Vilbert, S. (2002). Multivariate statistical analysis of audit trails for host-based intrusion detection. *Computers. IEEE Transactions on*, *51*(7), 810–820.

Yeung, D., & Chow, C. (2002). Parzen-window network intrusion detectors. *International Conference on pattern recognition*, 385–388. 10.1109/ICPR.2002.1047476

Ye, X. W., Ran, L., Yi, T. H., & Dong, X. B. (2012). Intelligent risk assessment for dewatering of metro-tunnel deep excavations. *Mathematical Problems in Engineering*.

Yi, J., Zhang, Y., Zhao, X., & Wan, J. (2017). A Novel Text Clustering Approach Using Deep-Learning Vocabulary Network. *Mathematical Problems in Engineering*, 13.

Yi, X., & Zhang, Y. (2007). Privacy-preserving distributed association rule mining via semi-trusted mixer. *Data & Knowledge Engineering, 63*(2), 550–567. doi:10.1016/j.datak.2007.04.001

Yokota, S., Hashimoto, H., Ohyama, Y., & She, J. H. (2009). Electric wheelchair controlled by human body motion interface. *IEEJ Transactions on Electronics Information Systems, 129*(10), 1874–1880.

Yoshino, M. Y., & Srinivasa Rangan, U. (1995). *Strategic alliances: an entrepreneurial approach to globalization.* Harvard Business School Press.

Yu, H. C. J., Lee, Z. H., Ye, C. F., Chung, L. K., & Fang, Y. M. (2009). *SWE Application for Debris Flow Monitoring System in Taiwan.* OGC 09-082 Version: 0.3.0, OGC® Discussion Paper.

Yu, L., & Liu, H. (2003). Feature selection for high-dimensional data: a fast correlation-based filter solution. *Proceedings of the twentieth International Conference on Machine Learning*, 856-863.

Yu, E., Giorgini, P., Maiden, N., & Mylopoulos, J. (2011). *Social modeling for requirements engineeing.* MIT Press.

Yu, E., Giorgini, P., Maiden, N., & Mylopoulos, J. (2011). *Social Modeling for Requirements Engineering.* MIT Press.

Yu, T. H. K., & Huarng, K. H. (2008). A bivariate fuzzy time series model to forecast the TAIEX. *Expert Systems with Applications, 34*(4), 2945–2952. doi:10.1016/j.eswa.2007.05.016

Yu, T. H. K., & Huarng, K. H. (2010). A neural network- based fuzzy time series model to improve forecasting. *Expert Systems with Applications, 37*(4), 3366–3372. doi:10.1016/j.eswa.2009.10.013

Zadeh, L. (1965). Fuzzy sets. *Information and Control, 8*, 338-352.

Zadeh, L. A. (1965). Information and control. *Fuzzy Sets, 8*(3), 338-353.

Zadeh, L. (1975). Fuzzy logic and approximate reasoning. *Synthese, 30*(3), 407–428. doi:10.1007/BF00485052

Zadeh, L. A. (1965). Fuzzy Sets. *Information and Control, 8*(3), 338–353. doi:10.1016/S0019-9958(65)90241-X

Zadeh, L. A. (1975). The concept of a linguistic variable and its application to approximate reasoning. – Part I. *Information Sciences, 8*(3), 199–249. doi:10.1016/0020-0255(75)90036-5

Zadeh, L. A. (1978). Fuzzy sets as a basis for a theory of possibility. *Fuzzy Sets and Systems, 1*(1), 3–28. doi:10.1016/0165-0114(78)90029-5

Zambonelli, F., Jennings, N. R., Omicini, A., & Wooldridge, M. (2000). Agent-Oriented Software Engineering for Internet Applications. In *Coordination of Internet Agents: Models, Technologies and Applications* (pp. 326–346). Springer Verlag.

Zambonelli, F., Jennings, N. R., & Wooldridge, M. (2000). Organizational abstractions for the analysis and design of multi-agent systems. *Proceedings of the 1st International Workshop on Agent-Oriented Software Engineering*, 243-252.

Zararsız, Z. (2015). Similarity measures of sequence of fuzzy numbers and fuzzy risk analysis. *Advances in Mathematical Physics.* http://dx.doi.org/10.1155/2015/724647.

Zeigler, B. P. (2014). *Object-oriented simulation with hierarchical, modular models: intelligent agents and endomorphic systems.* Academic Press.

Zephyr-Bioharness. (n.d.). Retrieved from http://www.zephyr-technology.com/, http://www.zephyranywhere.com/healthcare/zephyrlife/

Zephyr-Pressure Monitor. (n.d.). Retrieved from http://www.zephyranywherestore.com/Automatic-Bluetooth-Pressure-Monitor-HPL-108/dp/B009ZUG2Z8

Zhang, D., Han, J., Song, J., & Yuan, L. (2016, October). A risk assessment approach based on fuzzy 3D risk matrix for network device. In *Computer and Communications (ICCC), 2016 2nd IEEE International Conference on* (pp. 1106-1110). IEEE.

Zhang, X., Jing, L., Hu, X., Ng, M., & Zhou, X. (2007). A comparative study of ontology based term similarity measures on PubMed document clustering. *Proceeding of the 12th International Conference on Database Systems for Advanced Applications*, 115-126. 10.1007/978-3-540-71703-4_12

Zhang, N., Li, M., & Lou, W. (2011). Distributed data mining with differential privacy. *Proceedings of the IEEE International Conference on Communications (ICC)*, 1.

Zhang, Q., Zhou, C., Tian, Y. C., Xiong, N., Qin, Y., & Hu, B. (2017). A Fuzzy Probability Bayesian Network Approach for Dynamic Cybersecurity Risk Assessment in Industrial Control Systems. *IEEE Transactions on Industrial Informatics*.

Zhang, R., Li, Y., Yan, Y., Zhang, H., Wu, S., Yu, T., & Gu, Z. (2016). Control of a Wheelchair in an Indoor Environment Based on a Brain–Computer Interface and Automated Navigation. *IEEE Transactions on Neural Systems and Rehabilitation Engineering*, *24*(1), 128–139. doi:10.1109/TNSRE.2015.2439298 PMID:26054072

Zhang, W., Li, R., Deng, H., Wang, L., Lin, W., Ji, S., & Shen, D. (2015). Deep comvolutional neural networks for multi-modality isointense infant brain image segmentation. *NeuroImage*, *108*, 214–224. doi:10.1016/j.neuroimage.2014.12.061 PMID:25562829

Zhang, X., Sun, M., Wang, N., Huo, Z., & Huang, G. (2016). Risk assessment of shallow groundwater contamination under irrigation and fertilization conditions. *Environmental Earth Sciences*, *75*(7), 603. doi:10.100712665-016-5379-x

Zhengbing, H., Zhitang, L., & Junqi, W. (2008). A novel network intrusion detection system (nids) based on signatures search of data mining. In *1st international conference on Forensic applications and techniques in telecommunications information, and multimedia* (pp. 1-7). ICST.

Zhou, D., Tang, Y., & Jiang, W. (2017). An improved belief entropy and its application in decision-making. *Complexity*.

Zhou, P., & El-Gohary, N. (2015). Domain-specific hierarchical text classification for supporting automated environmental compliance checking. *Journal of Computing in Civil Engineering*. doi:10.1061/(ASCE)CP.1943-5487

Zwietering, M. H. (2015). Risk assessment and risk management for safe foods: Assessment needs inclusion of variability and uncertainty, management needs discrete decisions. *International Journal of Food Microbiology*, *213*, 118–123. doi:10.1016/j.ijfoodmicro.2015.03.032 PMID:25890788

About the Contributors

Anissa Benlarabi has a Phd in Software product line evolution issues. I worked with the IMS Team, SIME Laboratory ENSIAS, Mohamed V University, Rabat on many challenges related to software product lines.

P. T. V. Bhuvaneswari received her B.E. degree of Electrical and Electronics Engineering in 1997 and her M.E. degree of Applied Electronics in 2000. She obtained her Ph.D. degree in Electronics and Communication Engineering from Anna University in 2011. From June 2000 to July 2004, she worked as lecturer in Sathayabama Institute of Technology, Anna University. And from July 2004 to till date, she is working as a Professor in the Department of Electronics Engineering, MIT Campus, Anna University. She has completed five sponsored research projects. She is the author/co-author of about seven six publication in Conferences and Journals. She has also served as Chair and Member of Technical Program Committees for several National and International conferences. Her research focus includes Wireless Sensor Network, Computer Networks, Wireless Network, Wireless Communication, and Internet of Things

Mahua Bose received postgraduate degree in computer Applications from the School of Computer and Information Sciences, Indira Gandhi National Open University, New Delhi, India in the year 2003. Currrently, she is a Research Scholar, in the Deptt. of Computer Science & Engineering, Kalyani University, West Bengal, India. Her current research interests include Time Series Analysis, Data Mining, and Pattern Recognition.

Ganesh Chate is a Faculty in the Department of Industrial Production and Engineering and pursuing his PhD at KLS Gogte Institute of Technology, Belagavi, Karnataka State, India. He holds a Master's degree in Production Management from KLS Gogte Institute of Technology, Belagavi. He has published many papers in national and international conferences and journals. His research areas include manufacturing process, 3D printing, CAD and automation.

Anand S. Deshpande is a Professor in Mechanical Engineering Department and the Principal of KLS Gogte Institute of Technology, Belagavi, Karnataka State, India. He has published more than 50 papers in various international journals and conferences and has many research grants to his credit. His experience in the field of academics and industry extends over a period of 29 years. His areas of interest include manufacturing, CAD, and process planning.

Konstantinos (or Kostas) Domdouzis is a Computer Scientist with a BSc (Hons) in Computer Science from the University of Luton (currently renamed to University of Bedfordshire) and an MSc in Computer Networks & Communications from the University of Westminster. Kostas has realized his PhD at the Department of Civil & Building Engineering of Loughborough University focusing on the applications of Wireless Sensor Technologies in the Construction Industry. He undertook postdoctoral research at the Department of Agricultural & Biological Engineering at the University of Illinois at Urbana-Champaign, United States, focusing on Systems Informatics for Biomass Feedstock Production. Since then, Kostas joined the Hellenic Army in order to realize his compulsory service and also worked as a KTP Associate/Software & Systems Developer at Whole Systems Partnership, a healthcare modelling consultancy, in collaboration with Brunel University. Kostas was a researcher within the Centre of Excellence in Terrorism, Resilience, Intelligence and Organised Crime Research (CENTRIC) at Sheffield Hallam University, and his work was focused on the EU-FP7-funded project ATHENA; his main role in the project was the development of computational tools for crisis management. Currently, he is a lecturer in Databases at the Department of Computing at Sheffield Hallam University.

Palash Dutta received his M. Sc. Degree in Mathematics from Dibrugarh University, Dibrugarh, India, in 2006, and his M. Phil. and Ph. D. degree in Mathematics from the same University in 2009 and 2012 respectively. He is an Assistant Professor in the Department of Mathematics, Dibrugarh University, since 2013. His research interests are uncertainty modelling using possibility approaches and decision making under the situations of uncertainty.

Heba Fathy Eid received her B.Sc. with honors in 2005 at Pure Mathematics and Computer Science, from Faculty of Science, Al-Azhar University. She received her MSc degree 2009 in Distributed database systems and her doctoral degree 2013 in Network security, both from Faculty of Science, Al-Azhar University, Egypt. She is currently Assistant Professor at Al-Azhar University. Her main research interests are in the areas of machine learning, network security, intrusion detection, computer vision and Bio-Inspired.

Markus Endres is an associate professor at the Department of Computer Science at the University of Augsburg (Germany). His research interests are preference based database systems and regard several aspects of parallel preference query evaluation on modern multi-core systems, e.g., Pareto (Skyline) computation, preference query optimization, and preference recommender systems. He is the author of several publications, including journals and papers in proceedings of international conferences and workshops, and a book on Semi-Skyline query computation.

Annis Fathima obtained BE (ECE) from Madras University, ME (VLSI Design) and Ph.D. in Image processing and pattern recognition from Anna University, Chennai. Currently working as Associate Professor, School of Electronics Engineering at VIT Chennai. The area of interest includes Computer Vision, Video Analytics, Pattern Recognition, Biometrics.

Xavier N. Fernando is a Professor and Director of Ryerson Communications Lab. He was an IEEE Distinguished Lecturer and delivered over 40 invited lectures worldwide. He earned his PhD from the University of Calgary, Alberta in 2001 in affiliation with TRLabs. His PhD work won the Canadian best paper award and a US patent. He joined Ryerson University in 2001, received early tenure and established Ryerson Communications Lab. He has (co-)authored over 150 research articles and holds three patents. He has monographed a widely selling book on Radio over Fiber systems, which is translated in Mandarin. He was a member in the IEEE COMSOC Education Board Working Group on Wireless Communications, 2010-2012. He was a member of Ryerson Board of Governors during 2010-2011. He is a program evaluator for ABET and has visited American Universities for accreditation. He was a finalist for the Top 25 Immigrant Award of Canada in 2012. He has served as Chair, General Chair for several IEEE conferences. He has received over $680,000 in research grants received just in 2016 (and another $380,000 in 2017) from the industry and government. He and his students have won several awards and prizes including; the First prize at the Humanitarian Initiatives Workshop of CCECE 2014; Second Prize at the 2014 IHTC Conference in Montreal; Best Paper Award at the International Conference of Smart Grid Engineering (SEGE 2014), UOIT, Canada, 2014; IEEE Microwave Theory and Techniques Society Prize in 2010, Sarnoff Symposium prize in 2009, Opto-Canada best poster prize in 2003 and CCECE best paper prize in 2001.

Kirupa Ganapathy working as Associate Professor in department of Electronics and Communication Engineering at Saveetha School of Engineering. Pursued BE in Electronics and Communication Engineering and ME in Applied Electronics. Awarded with a Ph.D. degree for specialization in Soft Computing and Wireless Sensor Networks. Worked for various funded projects in Healthcare Applications and Surveillance Applications. She has published papers in various international and national journals with high impact factor. Areas of interest include sensor network, machine learning, artificial intelligence, image processing, network security and IoT. Guided many of the B.E and M.E. students in various domains.

C. Sweetlin Hemalatha received her BE degree in Computer Science and Engineering from Sethu Institute of Technology, Kariapatti, Tamilnadu, India in 2000, ME degree in Computer Science and Engineering from Mepco Schlenk Engineering college, Sivakasi, Tamilnadu, India in 2005 and Ph.D. in Information and Communication Engineering from Madras Institute of Technology, Anna University, Chennai, India. She is currently working as Assistant Professor in Vellore Institute of Technology (VIT) University, Chennai. She has 8+ years of teaching experience and 4 years of research experience. Her research interest includes machine learning and data mining, especially classification and clustering problems. She has worked on mining interesting patterns from sensor observation using pattern mining algorithms and its application in health care.

Samedi Heng is a postdoctoral research assistant at the Louvain Research Institute in Management and Organization attached to the Center in Management Information Systems at the Universitécatholique de Louvain. He was previously a lecturer in Computer Science at the Institute of Technology of Cambodia (ITC) from 2007 to 2010. He got a Ph.D. degree in Information Systems from the Université catholique de Louvain in 2017 with a PhD untitled "Impact of Unified User-Story-Based Modeling on Agile Methods: Aspects on Requirements, Design and Life Cycle Management." He also obtained a Master's degree in Networking and Telecommunication from the Institut National Politechnique de Toulouse, France in 2007 supported by the French Government Scholarships and an engineering degree in Computer Science from ITC in 2006. His research interests include Software Engineering, Agile Methods, Requirements Engineering, Multi-Agent Systems, Business Intelligence and Business (Re)engineering.

Huosheng Hu is a Professor in the School of Computer Science & Electronic Engineering at the University of Essex, U.K., leading the Robotics Research Group. His research interests include behaviour-based robotics, human-robot interaction, embedded systems, data fusion, machine learning algorithms, mechatronics, and pervasive computing. He has published over 500 papers in journals, books and conferences in these areas, and received a number of best paper awards. Prof. Hu is Fellow of the Institution of Engineering and Technology, and Fellow of the Institute of Measurement and Control. He has been a Program Chair or a member of Advisory Committee of many IEEE international conferences, such as the IEEE ICRA, IROS, ICMA, ROBIO, ICIA, ICAL, etc. He currently serves as the Editor-in-Chief of the International Journal of Automation and Computing, the Editor-in-Chief for MDPI Robotics Journal, and the Executive Editor of the International Journal of Mechatronics and Automation.

Amal Khtira received a degree in software engineering from National High School of Computer Science and Systems Analysis (ENSIAS) in 2008. She is currently a PhD student in the IMS (Models and Systems Engineering) Team of ADMIR Laboratory at ENSIAS. Her research interests include Software Product Line Engineering, Requirements Engineering, Feature Modeling and Software Evolution.

Manuel Kolp is Full Professor in IT Management and Information Systems at UCLouvain where he heads the Center in Management Information Systems. He was previously Adjunct Professor at the Faculty of Information and Senior Research Associate at the Department of Computer Science at the University of Toronto, Canada. He is or has been appointed invited professor at KU Leuven, the University of Brussels, the University of Namur and the University Saint-Louis-Brussels. Manuel Kolp has about 150 publications in international journals, books and scientific conferences and has supervised a dozen of Ph.D. theses. He acts regularly as an expert for the European Commission and foreign and national research agencies on projects focusing on IT and software engineering. He will be co-general chair of RCIS 2019, the IEEE 13th International Conference on Research Challenges in Information Science. His main expertise is related to Information Systems Analysis and Design, Data and Information Management, Software Project Management, Business Process and Requirements Modeling and Agent-Oriented/Knowledge Systems, fields for which he also serves regularly as an expert, consultant and executive educator for (IT) companies and managers. He did a PostDoc in Computer Science (Requirements Engineering and Multi-Agent Systems) at the University of Toronto, Canada and got a Ph.D. degree in Information Sciences (Information Systems) from the University of Brussels supported by the Belgian National Fund for Scientific Research (FNRS). He also holds an MIS and an M.A. degrees from the same university.

Koswatte R. C. Koswatte received the bachelor's degree in 2006 from Sri Lanka Institute of Information Technology, Sri Lanka. She completed master degree in Information Management in 2010 from Sri Lanka Institute of Information Technology, Sri Lanka and master degree in computer science and Engineering in 2015 from School of Computer Science and Engineering, University of Aizu, Japan. Her research interests include Semantic Web, Ontology Learning and ICT Education.

Sathiyapriya Krishnamoorthy is working as an Assistant Professor(Selection Grade) in Department of Computer Science & Engineering in PSG College of Technology, Coimbatore, India. Her research area is Privacy Preserving Data Mining. She published around 13 International Journal and Conference papers. Her area of interest includes Data mining, Software Engineering and Data Structures. She has around 12 years of teaching experience.

P. Senthil Kumar is an Assistant Professor in PG and Research Department of Mathematics at Jamal Mohamed College (Autonomous), Tiruchirappalli, Tamil Nadu, India. He has seven years (approximately) of teaching experience. He received his BSc, MSc and MPhil from Jamal Mohamed College, Tiruchirappalli in 2006, 2008, 2010 respectively. He completed his BEd in Jamal Mohamed College of Teacher Education in 2009. He completed PGDCA in 2011 in the Bharathidasan University and PGDAOR in 2012 in the Annamalai University, Tamil Nadu, India. He has done his Ph.D titled "Algorithmic approach for solving allocation problems under intuitionistic fuzzy environment" at Jamal Mohamed College in 2017. He has published many research papers in referred national and international journals like Springer, IGI Global, Inderscience, etc. He also presented his research paper in Elsevier Conference Proceedings (ICMS-2014), MMASC-2012, etc. His areas of research interest include operations research, fuzzy optimization, intuitionistic fuzzy optimization, numerical analysis and graph theory, etc.

Banage T. G. S. Kumara received the bachelor's degree in 2006 from Sabaragamuwa University of Sri Lanka. He received the master's degree in 2010 from University of Peradeniya and Ph.D degree in 2015 from School of Computer Science and Engineering, University of Aizu, Japan. His research interests include Semantic Web, Web Data Mining, Web Service Discovery and Composition.

Christl Lauterbach is founder and Managing Director of Future-Shape GmbH since 2005; for 6 years Infineon Research, Senior staff Engineer for Emerging Technologies, Project Manager Smart Textiles; 22 years at Siemens AG, Corporate Research and Technology Group, developer semiconductor technology and circuit design; more than 200 patents and patent pendings, & some 120 scientific publications.

Rui Li is currently an assistant professor at the Department of Geography and Planning at University at Albany, State University of New York. His research interests address various aspects of Geographic Information Science with a special focus on spatial cognition such as wayfinding behaviors and navigation systems. Rui is also an affiliated member of the Arts and Design Academy at Sichuan Fine Arts Institute in China. Dr. Rui Li received his Phd in Geography from the Pennsylvania State University.

Kalyani Mali received B. Tech and M. Tech Degree in 1987 and 1989 from university of Calcutta, India and Ph.D Degree in Computer Science and Engineering from Jadavpur University, Kolkata, India in 2005. She joined faculty of Deptt. of Computer Science and and Engineering, University of Kalyani, India in 1992. She currently holds the rank of Professor. Her current research interests include Pattern Recognition, Image Processing, Data Mining and Soft Computing. She has published 50 journal papers.

Rajalakshmi Nedunchezhian is currently working as an Associate Professor at Coimbatore Institute of Technology, Coimbatore in the Department of Computer Science Engineering & Information Technology. Her area of interests includes Data Structures, Data Mining and Distributed Systems. Her research area is Distributed data mining and privacy preserving data mining. She has 20 years of teaching experience and published twenty papers in international journals and international conferences.

Incheon Paik received the M.E. and Ph.D. degrees in Electronics Engineering from Korea University in 1987 and 1992, respectively. During 1993-2000, he worked as an associate professor in Soonchunhyang university, Korea. From 1996 to 1998, he was a visiting researcher of State Key Laboratory, Beihang University, Beijing, China. He moved to the University of Aizu in Japan in 2001, and is a professor in the university. Research interests include Semantic Web, Web Services and Their Composition, Web Data Mining, Big Data Infrastructure and Analytics, Deep Learning, Awareness Computing, Security for e-Business, and Agents on Semantic Web. He has organized numerous international conferences, and has served as a reviewer or editor of journals of JIPS, IEICE, Hindawi, and IEEE. He is a member of IEEE, IEICE, IEIE, and IPSJ. Also, he is serving as a chair of IEICE Service Computing Technical Committee, and a director of IEIE Japan Branch.

Mahesh B. Parappagoudar did his engineering graduation in industrial & production engineering from B.V. Bhoomaraddi College of Engineering and Technology, Hubli, affiliated to Karnataka University, Dharwad. He obtained his master of engineering degree in production management from Gogte Institute of Technology, affiliated to Karnataka University, Dharwad, India, in 1996. He joined Indian Institute of Technology, Kharagpur in 2004 as a research scholar, in the mechanical engineering department under the quality improvement program funded by MHRD, Govt. of India. Further, he obtained Ph.D. degree in mechanical engineering from Indian Institute of Technology, Kharagpur - 721302, India during 2008. Presently he is working as the principal and professor in Padre Conceicao College of Engineering, Verna, Goa 403722, India. His total experience (Industry, Teaching, Research, Administration) extends over a period of 27 years. His Biography (distinguished personality) is published in 30th edition of Marquis Who's Who in the world 2013. His research interests include application of statistical and soft computing tools in manufacturing and industrial engineering.

G. C. Manjunath Patel received his Bachelor Degree in Mechanical Engineering from Jawaharlal Nehru National College of Engineering, Shimoga, and M. Tech in Production Management from Gogte Institute of Technology, Belgaum, affiliated to Visvesvaraya Technological University, Belgaum, India in 2009 and 2011, respectively. He completed Ph. D in Mechanical Engineering, National Institute of Technology Karnataka, Surathkal, India in 2015. Presently working in Sahyadri College of Engineering and Management, India. His area of interests includes Casting and Solidification, Modelling and Optimization of Manufacturing Processes. He has published 35 publications in various International Journals and Conferences.

Ravi Pathak is Software Developer at Global Biodiversity Information Facility Secretariat Copenhagen. Most of his career is involved in field of Distributed Systems and Data management. He has worked closely with Stream Processing Platforms, mostly involved in designing and developing third party Connectors, Fault tolerance and Load Balancing. His interests are in Distributed systems, Data mining and Sensor network related applications. Ravi holds a master's degree in information and communication from Anna University. In his spare time he enjoys hiking and traveling

Bhargavi R. is an Associate professor in VIT in the school of computing science and engineering.

Nayem Rahman is an Information Technology (IT) Professional. He holds an M.S. in Systems Science (Computer Modeling & Simulation) from Portland State University, Oregon, USA and an MBA in Management Information Systems (MIS), Project Management, and Marketing from Wright State University, Ohio, USA. He holds many professional credentials, including Teradata Certified Master, and Oracle Certified Developer and Oracle Certified DBA. His most recent publications appeared in Proceedings of the IEEE 26th Canadian Conference of Electrical and Computer Engineering (CCECE 2013) and the International Journal of Computer and Information Technology (IJCIT). His principal research interests include Active Data Warehousing, Data Mining for Business Intelligence, Big Data Analytics, Intelligent Data Understanding using Simulation, and Simulation-based Decision Support System (DSS).

Ericka Janet Rechy-Ramirez is a full time researcher in the Research Center for Artificial Intelligence at Universidad Veracruzana (Mexico). She holds a PhD in Computer Science from the University of Essex (United Kingdom). She received a MPhil in Computer Science from the National Laboratory for Advanced Informatics (Mexico) and BSc degree in Administrative Computer Systems from the Universidad Veracruzana (Mexico). Her research interests include human computer interaction, serious games, and assistive technology.

Bhargavi Rentachintala is presently working as Associate Professor in the School of Computing Science and Engineering, VIT University, Chennai Campus, India. She has more than 20 years of Industry, Academic and Research experience She received her M.Tech and Ph.D degrees from IIT Madras and Anna University respectively. Her research interests include Complex Event Processing, Machine learning, in Healthcare and Data Science. She has authored and published several research papers in IEEE/ACM/Springer international conferences and refereed Journals. She also authored chapters in highly reputed research reference books.

Lena Rudenko is a doctoral researcher at the Department of Computer Science at the University of Augsburg (Germany). Her research interests are preference-based information systems, which incorporates the analysis of data streams w.r.t. the extraction of personalized and customized information from large time-oriented data. This also includes the development of efficient algorithms for preference-based evaluation of streams. She is the author of several publications in proceedings of international conferences and workshops.

Sibi Chakkaravarthy S. holds an M. Tech degree in computer science and engineering, and is currently pursuing PhD at Anna University. He is with the department of electronics engineering, MIT, Chennai, and can be reached at sb.sibi@gmail.com. His research interest includes network security, malware analysis, sensor networks, cloud security etc.

G. Sudha Sadasivam is working as professor in the department of Computer Science and Engineering for the past 15 years. She has completed many research projects for DRDO, UGC, Nokia, Yahoo, Xurmo in the areas of Grid and Cloud Computing, Big Data Analytics, Distributed Systems and Data Mining. She had published around 25 international journal papers, 6 national journal papers and 50 papers in various international conferences. She had authored 5 books. She is a member of ACM, ACCS and ISTE.

Axel Steinhage is Director R&D at Future-Shape GmbH since 2006. From 2001 to 2005 he was manager of the Man-Machine-Interaction group at Infineon Technologies in Germany. 1998 to 2000, he led the Anthropomorphic Robotics Group and the Behavioural Dynamics Group at the Institute for Neuroinformatics in Bochum, Germany. 1998 he received his PhD in theoretical physics at the Ruhr-University of Bochum, Germany. The research topics of Dr. Steinhage cover the areas Robotics, Neuroinformatics, Artificial Intelligence, Sensor Fusion and Nonlinear Dynamical Systems. He has over 100 peer reviewed publications and is reviewer for IEEE journals.

Mahmud Ullah is an Associate Professor of Marketing at the Faculty of Business Studies, University of Dhaka, Bangladesh. He teaches Behavioral and Quantitative courses in Business, e.g. Psychology, Organizational Behavior, Consumer Behavior, Business Mathematics, Business Statistics, Quantitative Analyses in Business etc., in addition to the Basic and Specialized Marketing courses like Marketing Management, Non-Profit Marketing, E-Marketing etc. He also taught Basic & Advanced English, and IELTS in a couple of English language Schools in New Zealand during his stay over there between 2002 and 2006. He has conducted a number of research projects sponsored by different international and national organizations like the World Bank (RMB), UNICEF, UNFPA, USAID, JAICA, AUSAID, IPPF, PPD, Die Licht Brucke, Andheri Hilfe, BNSB, FPAB etc. He did most of his research in the field of Health, Education, and Environment. His research interests include ethical aspects of human behavior in all these relevant fields, specifically in the continuously evolving and changing field of Digital Business and Marketing.

V. Vaidehi is a Senior Professor and Dean at VIT University, Chennai Campus. She is a Senior Member IEEE. Previously she was with Department of Electronics Engineering, MIT, Anna University, Chennai. She obtained her BE from College of Engineering, Guindy, M.E and Ph.D. from Madras Institute of Technology, Anna University, Chennai. She was a task team member in Micro Satellite (ANUSAT) and executed several funded projects in the area of Tracking, Multi-Sensor Fusion, Semantic intrusion detection, GPS, Video analytics and Healthcare. Her research interest includes Networking, Parallel and Distributed Processing, Adaptive Digital Signal Processing, Wireless Sensor Networks, Video and Image Processing, Network and Information Security

Jia Wang is a researcher from the Department of Computing & Information Systems at the University of Greenwich (UK). Her current work focuses on spatial knowledge acquisition, cognitive maps and sketch maps, and pedestrian walkability and movement in urban spaces with development of formal models. Applications of her work include volunteered geographic information systems, smart pedestrian navigation aids, and walkable cities. Jia has a PhD in Geoinformatics from the University of Münster in Germany.

Kevin Warwick is Emeritus Professor at Reading and Coventry Universities. His research areas are artificial intelligence, biomedical systems, robotics and cyborgs. Kevin is a Chartered Engineer and a Fellow of the IET who has published over 600 research papers. His experiments into implant technology led to him being the cover story on the US magazine, 'Wired'. He achieved the world's first direct electronic communication between two human nervous systems, the basis for thought communication. He has been awarded higher doctorates (DSc) by Imperial College and the Czech Academy of Sciences. He received the IET Mountbatten Medal, the Ellison-Cliffe Medal from the Royal Society of Medicine and presented the Royal Institution Christmas Lectures.

Yves Wautelet is an Assistant Professor in Information Systems at KU Leuven and invited professor at UNamur. He formerly has been an IT project manager and a Postdoc Fellow at Université catholique de Louvain, Belgium. He completed a Ph.D. thesis focusing on project and risk management issues in large enterprise software design. Yves also holds a Master of Management Sciences as well as a Master of Information Systems. His research interests include various aspects of software engineering and enterprise information systems such as life-cycle management, requirements engineering, agent-oriented development and e-learning. He also focuses on the application of his research into industrial environments.

Index

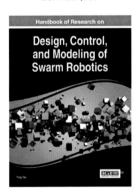
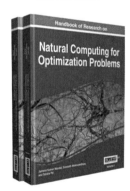

Stay Current on the Latest Emerging Research Developments

Become an IGI Global Reviewer for Authored Book Projects

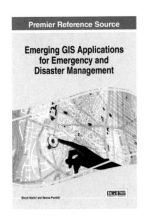

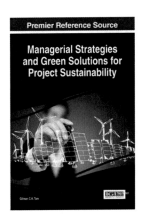

The overall success of an authored book project is dependent on quality and timely reviews.

In this competitive age of scholarly publishing, constructive and timely feedback significantly decreases the turnaround time of manuscripts from submission to acceptance, allowing the publication and discovery of progressive research at a much more expeditious rate. Several IGI Global authored book projects are currently seeking highly qualified experts in the field to fill vacancies on their respective editorial review boards:

Applications may be sent to:
development@igi-global.com

Applicants must have a doctorate (or an equivalent degree) as well as publishing and reviewing experience. Reviewers are asked to write reviews in a timely, collegial, and constructive manner. All reviewers will begin their role on an ad-hoc basis for a period of one year, and upon successful completion of this term can be considered for full editorial review board status, with the potential for a subsequent promotion to Associate Editor.

If you have a colleague that may be interested in this opportunity, we encourage you to share this information with them.

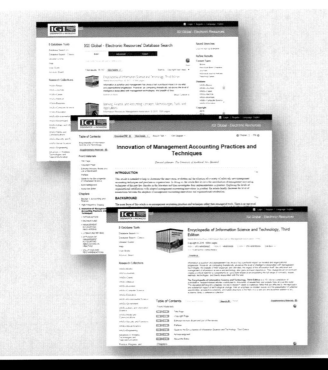

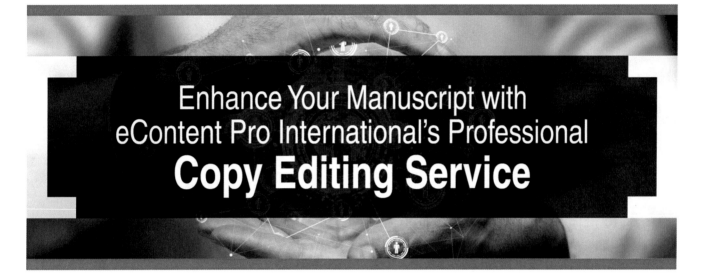

Printed in the United States
By Bookmasters